CANADA
A NORTH AMERICAN NATION
SECOND EDITION

CANADA

A NORTH AMERICAN NATION

SECOND EDITION

SENIOR AUTHOR AND EDITOR
Paul W. Bennett
Upper Canada College

CO-AUTHORS
Cornelius J. Jaenen
University of Ottawa

Nick Brune
M.M. Robinson High School

CONTRIBUTING AUTHOR
Cecilia Morgan

McGraw-Hill Ryerson Limited

Toronto   New York   Auckland   Bogotá   Caracas
Lisbon   London   Madrid   Mexico   Milan   New Delhi
San Juan   Singapore   Sydney   Tokyo

Canada: A North American Nation, Second Edition

Copyright © McGraw-Hill Ryerson Limited, 1995, 1989. All rights reserved. No part of this publication may be reproduced or transmitted in any form or by any means, or stored in a data base or retrieval system, without the prior written permission of McGraw-Hill Ryerson Limited.

ISBN 0-07-551732-9

1 2 3 4 5 6 7 8 9 10 BBM 4 3 2 1 0 9 8 7 6 5

Printed and bound in Canada

Care has been taken to trace ownership of copyright material contained in this text. The publishers will gladly accept any information that will enable them to rectify any reference or credit in subsequent editions.

Canadian Cataloguing in Publication Data

Main entry under title:

Canada, a North American nation

2nd ed.
Includes bibliographical references and index.
ISBN 0-07-551732-9

1. Canada—History. 2. United States—History.
I. Bennett, Paul W., date.

FC170.C35 1995   971   C95-931138-6
F1026.C35 1995

PUBLISHERS: Janice Matthews and Anne Louise Currie
ASSOCIATE EDITOR: Denise Shortt
SENIOR SUPERVISING EDITOR: Carol Altilia
PERMISSIONS EDITOR: Jacqueline Donovan
COPY EDITOR: John Eerkes
PRODUCTION CO-ORDINATOR: Yolanda Pigden
COVER AND INTERIOR DESIGN: Sylvia Vander Schee/ArtPlus Limited

This book was manufactured in Canada using acid-free and recycled paper.

Note: The endnotes for Parts I, II, III, and IV can be found in the Notes section of the *Teacher's Resource to accompany Canada: A North American Nation*, Second Edition.

CONTENTS

PREFACE AND ACKNOWLEDGEMENTS

Since its publication six years ago, *Canada: A North American Nation* has emerged as one of the most popular textbooks in academic high schools across Canada. Those six years have produced remarkable changes. Since 1989, the Soviet Union has dissolved and the Cold War has come to an end. Canada and the United States have entered into a free-trade agreement and fully embraced "globalization" within a new international economic order. In this changing global context, Canada was described as a postmodern, borderless state where "global culture" seemed to be transcending traditional national loyalties. Questions were raised whether Canada would survive—with or without Quebec—as North America approached the new millennium.

In revising the text, the authors attempted to consolidate the content while updating the shorter volume with material covering North American developments since the mid-1980s. They have also revised the book with the intent of incorporating valuable social history into every chapter of the unfolding story. A new *Teacher's Resource* has been developed as well, to provide more ideas, resources, and activities to stimulate classroom discussion.

The original author team has changed slightly for the second edition. Dr. Paul W. Bennett served as senior author and editor, as well as principal author of Parts III and IV. Part I was originally written and later revised by Dr. Cornelius Jaenen, one of Canada's leading historians specializing in Amerindian–European relations and New France. Nick Brune, a Halton Board of Education history teacher, rewrote Part II for the new edition. As the *CBC-TV News in Review* educational consultant, he also contributed topical material on contemporary Canadian and world affairs. The author team was rounded out by a new member, Dr. Cecilia Morgan, a specialist in women's history who was recently awarded a postdoctoral fellowship at Queen's University, Kingston.

The second edition would not have come to fruition without the efforts of a fine publishing team at McGraw-Hill Ryerson. Janice Matthews, Editorial Director, encouraged us to embark on the major text revision, and showed remarkable patience throughout the arduous process. Our editor, Denise Shortt, demonstrated high standards of professionalism, combined with remarkable tolerance and a delightful sunny disposition. We would also like to thank Jacqueline Donovan, Permissions Editor, Carol Altilia, Senior Supervising Editor, and John Eerkes, copy editor, for their important contributions to the final published volume. Special mention should also be made of Mary McGuinness, who provided valuable input as a consultant and reviewer, and Tessa Wassyng, who provided dedicated word processing assistance. McGraw-Hill Ryerson and the authors would also like to thank reviewers Ludi Habs and Ian Andrews for their helpful contributions.

Canada: A North American Nation, Second Edition, is dedicated, first and foremost, to our spouses and families, who have spared us the time to complete such a major project. It is their book as much as ours.

May small differences continue to really matter, especially when it comes to Canada and the United States.

Paul W. Bennett, Senior Author

THE CANADIAN EXPERIENCE IN NORTH AMERICA

CANADA AND THE UNITED STATES share both a continent and a history of common experiences. Since their formation, the two North American societies have responded in markedly similar ways to challenges such as early contact with Native peoples, the Industrial Revolution, nation-building, world wars, depression, and trade relations. Yet the American republic was born in revolution, while Canada followed a different, negotiated path to political maturity. Differing colonial origins, frontier experiences, political institutions, and social-security arrangements have reinforced the continental differences between the two nations and peoples. As American political sociologist Seymour Martin Lipset amply demonstrated in his book *Continental Divide*, a landmark 1989 study, the two North American societies exhibit small differences, but nonetheless differences that matter. "Like two trains that have moved thousands of miles along parallel railway tracks," he contended, Canada and the United States "are far removed from where they started, but they are still separated."

OVERVIEW: HOW SIMILAR? HOW DIFFERENT?

THE TWO NORTH AMERICAN NATIONS AND PEOPLES bear more than a passing resemblance to one another. Both nations in the 1990s have become largely urbanized, heavily industrialized, and politically stabilized. As occupiers of the North American continent, they share many geographic and environmental conditions, a common mass culture, comparable levels of economic development, and reasonably similar socio-economic systems. To a large extent, Canadians and Americans share the same liberal–democratic and even capitalist values, but in Canada these values seem to be held more tentatively. Both are "new" peoples and newly formed states by European standards, yet Canada's historic relationship with Britain helped to preserve in a North American nation remnants of a certain conservative, Old World character. In a 1988 feature article lampooning the bland conservatism of Canadians, the American satire magazine *Spy* put it this way: "America had people before it had laws; Canada had laws before it had people. Order in Canada has a higher value than freedom. Obedience is in Canadians' blood; every Canadian knows the thrill of being a follower, the deep, abiding pleasure of conforming."

Canada and the United States may resemble each other more than any other two nations on earth. Yet commentators throughout the nineteenth and twentieth centuries have identified consistent patterns of difference between the two North American nations. In *Letters to Americans* the German radical Friedrich Engels observed that in coming to Canada from the United States he imagined he was "in Europe again." James Bryce, writing in *Modern Democracies* (1921), noted that in spite of "external resemblances" to the political culture of the United States, the Canadian political tradition, rooted in the British monarchy, had imparted differences in national character and

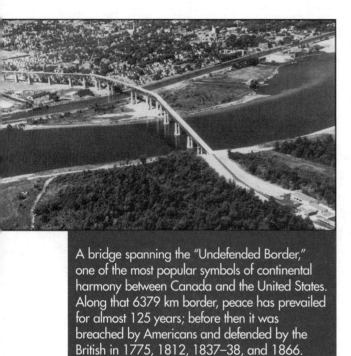

A bridge spanning the "Undefended Border," one of the most popular symbols of continental harmony between Canada and the United States. Along that 6379 km border, peace has prevailed for almost 125 years; before then it was breached by Americans and defended by the British in 1775, 1812, 1837–38, and 1866.

habits. More recent analyses have echoed the influential assessment offered in the mid-1960s by Lipset. Compared with the United States, we are told, "Canada has been a more conservative, traditional, law-abiding, statist, and elitist society." The marked differences in the prevailing values of English-speaking Canada, according to Lipset, "stem from a counter-revolutionary past, a continuing need to differentiate itself from the United States, the influence of monarchical institutions, a dominant Anglican religious tradition, and a less individualistic and more governmentally controlled frontier expansion than was present on the American frontier."[1]

The two North American nations share a British legacy, frontier areas of settlement, immigrants of comparable origin, and the same continent. Yet a close analysis of Canada and the United States and of their interconnected histories reveals a consistent pattern of differences. Exploring the nature and sources of these national differences is one of the more intriguing and difficult challenges facing students of the Canadian experience in North America.

HISTORICAL TRADITIONS

Comparing Canada and the United States in historical perspective has generated a huge volume of research and writing in recent decades. A brief sampling underlines some of the prevailing points of view on the question of Canadian–American differences and provides a stimulating starting point for debate and discussion.

Many commentators see the differences stemming in large part from the countries' formative events — the revolutionary origins of America and the counter-revolutionary response of Canada — the two "disparate founding ethos," according to Lipset. The American Revolution gave ascendancy to democratic values and undermined the prestige of colonial élites; Canada rejected the American Revolution and received a migration of Loyalists, many of whom clung to British aristocratic values as a means of preserving social order. As W.L. Morton wrote in *The Canadian Identity* (1961), Canada "arrived at freedom through evolution in allegiance and not by revolutionary compact." Thus, its "final governing force…is tradition and convention."

THE U.S. AND US: WHAT'S THE DIFFERENCE?

DISTINGUISHING CANADA FROM THE UNITED STATES and Canadians from Americans has long been a subject of fascination on both sides of the border. Following is a selection of contending viewpoints expressed by prominent Canadian and American historians and commentators.

> Canadian history is not a parody of American, as Canada is not a second-rate United States, still less a United States that failed. Canadian history is rather an important chapter in a distinct and even a unique human endeavour, the civilization of the northern and arctic lands. From its deepest origins and remotest beginnings, Canadian history has been separate and distinct in America. The existence of large areas of common experience and territorial overlap no one would deny. History is neither neat nor categorical; it defines by what is central, not by what is peripheral. And because of this separate origin in the northern frontier, economy, and approach, Canadian life to this day is marked by a northern quality.... The line which marks off the frontier from the farmstead, the wilderness from the baseland, the hinterland from the metropolis, runs through every Canadian psyche.

W.L. Morton, *The Canadian Identity* (Madison, WI: University of Wisconsin Press, 1961), p. 93. Reprinted by permission of the University of Wisconsin Press.

> *E pluribus unum.* The United States had a brilliant solution for the inherent fragility of a multiethnic society: the creation of a brand-new national identity, carried forward by individuals who, in forsaking old loyalties and joining to make new lives, melted away ethnic differences. Those intrepid Europeans who had torn up their roots to brave the wild Atlantic *wanted* to forget a horrid past and to embrace a hopeful future. They *expected* to become Americans. Their goals were escape, deliverance, assimilation. They saw America as a transforming nation, banishing dismal memories and developing a unique national character based on common political ideals and shared experiences. The point of America was not to preserve old cultures, but to forge a new *American* culture.
>
> One reason why Canada, despite all its advantages, is so vulnerable to schism is that, as Canadians freely admit, their country lacks such a unique national identity. Attracted variously to Britain, France, and the United States, inclined for generous reasons to a policy of official multiculturalism, Canadians have never developed a strong sense of what it is to be a Canadian. As Sir John Macdonald, their first prime minister, put it, Canada has "too much geography and too little history."

Reprinted from *The Disuniting of America*, by Arthur M. Schlesinger, Jr., which was first published by Whittle Books as part of the Larger Agenda Series. Reprinted by arrangement with Whittle Communications Ltd.

The advanced industrial world may be a world of transnational relations, but so far the transnational world of North America is not a postnationalist world. The eagle may soar; beavers build dams.

Joseph S. Nye, Jr., "Transnational Relations and Interstate Conflicts," in Annette Baker Fox et al., eds., *Canada and the United States* (New York, 1976), p. 402.

Canadians are no longer "not Americans." Here...truly lies *The 49th Paradox*. We have evolved into a people who are as fully North American as are Americans, and yet who, because of our political culture, are now a quite distinct kind of North American.

Richard Gwyn, *The 49th Paradox: Canada in North America* (Toronto: McClelland and Stewart, 1985), p. 11.

Throughout its history Canada, what President Ulysses S. Grant once called "this semi-independent and irresponsible agency," has been many things to Americans, including a puzzlement. It has been friendly neighbor, ally, vacation playground, enemy, investment paradise, provider of raw materials, electricity, and numerous inventions, refugee haven, guerrilla base camp, rumrunner, military buffer, hostage rescuer, prime trading partner, practice bombing range, and recalcitrant cousin. It has also been taken for granted. But one thing Canada has never been to Americans is understood.

Andrew H. Malcolm, *The Canadians* (Toronto and New York: Fitzhenry & Whiteside Ltd., 1985), pp. xiii–xiv. Reprinted by permission of the publisher.

Another popular but contentious interpretation is the "founding fragments" theory, advanced by American political theorist Louis Hartz. The Hartzian theory contends that the two North American democracies are New World liberal societies with few real variations. Both the United States and Canada are described as "fragment societies" that "broke off" from Europe and left behind in the Old World those classes and values identified with "feudal" or "Tory" class relations and institutions. English-speaking Canada is considered almost as liberal and democratic as America; French Canada is a kind of "feudal fragment" because it was founded before the revolution. British North America, in the Hartzian approach, is a new American liberal society much like its neighbour, albeit one evolving in a slightly slower fashion. Yet even Hartz concedes that English Canada has a certain "Tory touch," that it is "etched with a Tory streak coming out of the American revolution."[2]

For the most part Canadian historians have looked upon these theories with some scepticism. From the mid-1930s until the late 1960s, one dominant doctrine held sway: the Laurentian thesis. First proposed by Harold Innis and popularized by Donald G. Creighton, the Laurentian thesis held that Canada, as distinct from the United States, emerged as an outgrowth of the St. Lawrence waterway system and expanded from the Atlantic coast along an east–west axis across the northern half of the continent. The St. Lawrence system, according to Creighton, "inspired generations of Canadians to build a great territorial empire, both commercial and political, in the western interior of the continent," and later formed the basis for a Canadian confederation separate and distinct from the American republic. In the second stage of the Laurentian thesis, the Canadian nation was the political embodiment of "economic nationalism" — protective tariffs, railways, and commercial links to Britain — inspired by John A. Macdonald.

The old Laurentian thesis was superseded in the 1970s and 1980s by what J.M.S. Careless termed the "limited identities" interpretation of Canada's past. Much of the "distinctive Canadian experience," in Careless's words, "lies in the 'limited identities' of region, culture, and class," and in the articulation of those identities since 1867 within a diverse transcontinental nation-state. In comparison with the United States, Canada was depicted as a collection of diverse communities characterized by regional distinctiveness, ethnic multiplicity, and relatively weak nationalizing forces. In place of pan-Canadian visions, historians explored multiple identities of region, class, gender, and ethnicity and, according to historian Michael Bliss, failed to explain the links that bound Canadians to one another. "The sundering of a sense of Canadian history," he wrote in 1991, "became part and parcel of the sundering of Canadians' consciousness of themselves as a people."[3]

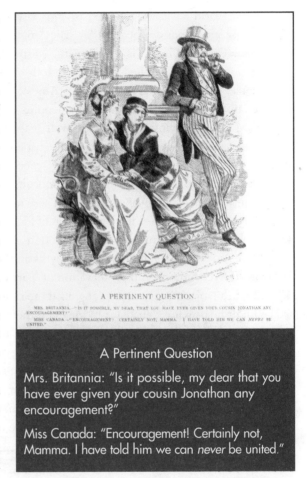

A PERTINENT QUESTION.

MRS. BRITANNIA.—"IS IT POSSIBLE, MY DEAR, THAT YOU HAVE EVER GIVEN YOUR COUSIN JONATHAN ANY ENCOURAGEMENT?"
MISS CANADA.—"ENCOURAGEMENT! CERTAINLY NOT, MAMMA. I HAVE TOLD HIM WE CAN NEVER BE UNITED."

A Pertinent Question

Mrs. Britannia: "Is it possible, my dear that you have ever given your cousin Jonathan any encouragement?"

Miss Canada: "Encouragement! Certainly not, Mamma. I have told him we can *never* be united."

MYTHS, SYMBOLS, AND VALUE DIFFERENCES

SINCE THE EARLIEST FOUNDING OF THE UNITED STATES, generations of Americans have celebrated the American experiment in a widely accepted national mythology. The "City Upon a Hill" founded by John Winthrop and the Puritans in the 1630s has served as an enduring symbol of the "American mission" to build a colony based upon "liberty" and "freedom" as an example to the world. The American people have also drawn strength from the idealized views of their New World society expressed by two visiting French noblemen, Hector St. John de Crevecoeur and Alexis de Tocqueville. "The American," Crevecoeur proclaimed in *Letters from an American Farmer* (1782), "is a new man.... From involuntary idleness, servile dependence, poverty, and useless labor, he has passed to toils of a very different nature, rewarded by ample subsistence. This is an American." Touring America in 1848, de Tocqueville was struck by "the general equality of condition among the people," which he saw influencing "the whole course of society," the governing authorities as well as the governed.

These national myths contributed to the shaping of a predominant American belief in a universal set of social values. Through time, the American commitment to liberty, equality, material progress, and the "melting" of diverse ethnocultural groups into one culturally unified whole has not only persisted, but gained strength. These universal national values were expressed in the nation's founding principles, the Declaration of Independence (1776), and hardened into what is known as the "American mission" and the notion of American exceptionalism.[4]

While Americans celebrate national myths and universalist values, Canadians have tended to favour the recognition and preservation of "particularist" loyalties. Since the Quebec Act of 1774, British North America has recognized the right of the French-speaking *Canadiens* as well as the English-speaking Canadians to maintain their cultural and linguistic distinctiveness. The *Canadiens* and their clerical leaders remained loyal to British monarchical rule as a protection against the threatening forces of democratic revolution and Puritanism brewing in the Thirteen Colonies. Because of the size and relative influence of the French-speaking community in British North America, the federal state created at Confederation incorporated protections for minority-language groups, and the Canadian provinces were granted considerable power to manage their own cultural and economic matters.

Land rush at Hollister, Idaho. "[Frederick Jackson] Turner's frontier was a process, not a place. When "civilization" had conquered "savagery" at any one location, the process— and the historian's attention—moved on. In rethinking Western history, we gain the freedom to think of the West as a place—as many complicated environments occupied by natives who considered their homelands to be the center, not the edge."

REVOLUTION AND COUNTERREVOLUTION: THE LIPSET THESIS

THE BEST-KNOWN THESIS pertaining to the Canadian and American historical experience was first put forward in the mid-1960s by American political sociologist Seymour Martin Lipset. According to Lipset, the two North American societies display clear value differences rooted in their "formative events." Here is how Dr. Lipset set out the case in *Continental Divide* (1989):

> Societies vary in their organizing principles, in their basic beliefs about the sources of authority and values, and in their conceptions about the nature of their societies. The two nations once part of British North America were separated by the outcome of the American Revolution. One, the country of the Revolution, elaborated on the populist and meritocratic themes subsumed in stating the objectives of the good society as "life, liberty, and the pursuit of happiness." The founding fathers of the counterrevolutionary nation defined their rationale as "peace, order, and good government" when they put together the new Dominion of Canada in 1867. The source of authority for one, as stated in the preamble to its Constitution, was "the people," and the document was submitted for ratification by the state legislatures. The other saw its new government as a continuation of the ancient English monarchy and sent its constitution to London to be enacted by the British Parliament and proclaimed by the Queen. The revolutionary Republic was suspicious of state authority and adopted a power-constraining bill of rights, which produced a strong emphasis on due process, judicial power, and litigiousness. The counterrevolutionary dominion followed the Westminster model, with power centered in a cabinet based on a parliamentary majority and with no limits on the authority of the state other than those derived from a division jurisdictions between national and provincial governments. The American Constitution rejected church establishment; the Canadian did not....
>
> The very organizing principles that framed these nations, the central cores around which institutions and events were to accommodate, were different. One was Whig and classically liberal or libertarian — doctrines that emphasize distrust of the state, egalitarianism, and populism — reinforced by a voluntaristic and congregational religious tradition. The other was Tory and conservative in the British and European sense — accepting of the need for a strong state, for respect for authority, for deference — and endorsed by hierarchically organized religions that supported and were supported by the state.*

Lipset's comparative approach and his thesis have drawn much critical fire. Some Canadian historians took great exception to Lipset's regular tendency to downplay, if not

*Excerpted from Seymour Martin Lipset, *Continental Divide: The Values and Institutions of the United States and Canada* (Toronto: C.D. Howe Institute, 1989), pp. xiii and 2. Reprinted by permission of Routledge, Chapman & Hall.

muddy, the distinctions between English-speaking and French-speaking Canada in making his historical comparisons. His analysis of data measuring national behaviour — crime and divorce rates, for example — simply lumped together anglophone and francophone Canadians as if their experiences were the same.

One leading critic, Fred Matthews, a professor of American history at York University, questioned the validity of Lipset's focus on real or imagined "national values." Matthews asked: What really are values, and whose values is Lipset discussing? Is the description of American values meant to describe every single American, the statistically "average American," or only American institutions? Lipset, in his view, is not explicit on this fundamental point.

A more recent critique of Lipset's grand thesis pointed out that it was functionalist (i.e., a mostly descriptive analysis of societal functions) and almost frozen in historical time. "Functionalism," historian J.F. Conway argued, "fails to tell us how we got here and how, having learned that, we can go somewhere else we may want to go." Professor Conway offered a starkly different perspective on Canadian–American differences. "With the benefit of hindsight, given Canada's much later development, Canadians have been able to embrace the good things about the 'American Way' while avoiding, more or less successfully for now, some of the bad things." [†]

[†] Fred Matthews, "The 'Myth' and 'Value' Approaches to American Studies," *Canadian Review of American Studies* 3(2) (Fall 1972); and J.F. Conway, "Canada and the U.S.: What Makes Us Different?" *Labour/Le Travail* 28 (Fall 1991): 311–321.

RELIGION AND VALUES

Religious institutions have had an impact on popular attitudes and values and the differences between the two North American nations. Commentators have emphasized the distinctly different pattern of church–state relations in the two societies. Lipset has argued that American tradition and law, since their colonial origins, have placed much more emphasis on the separation of church and state than have Canadian tradition and law. A large majority of Americans have adhered to Protestant sects, which had opposed the established state church in England. These have a communal congregational structure and foster the idea of a person's individual relationship with God. Most Canadians belong to either the Roman Catholic or the Anglican churches, which are hierarchically organized state religions, or to the more liberal-oriented United Church, with its Methodist and Presbyterian roots. Although efforts to sustain church establishment ultimately failed in Canada, state support of religious institutions, particularly Roman Catholic schools, has continued into the present.

These differences in religious development have had important consequences. While in Canada religion served mainly to reinforce and perpetuate the established churches, in the United States it tended to encourage "anti-élitist" and "individualist" beliefs, most strongly reflected in American evangelical and Protestant sects. A 1984 U.S. Gallup poll found that 38 percent of Americans held a strict fundamentalist view of the Bible and that 22 percent were identified as evangelicals, or believers in spreading the gospel of Jesus Christ.

WHO IS THE AMERICAN? HECTOR ST. JOHN DE CREVECOEUR'S CLASSIC VISION OF AMERICA

A FRENCH-BORN FARMER AND NATURALIST, J. Hector St. John de Crevecoeur, published an influential collection of essays entitled *Letters from an American Farmer* in 1782. This book won him fame in France and Europe and helped shape public perceptions about the fledgling American republic. For many years, Crevecoeur's graphic and sympathetic descriptions of the new country made him the most widely read commentator on America. In this passage from his *Letters*, he introduced the now-popular concept of America as a melting pot for the people of many nations. Which other elements of the American national mythology occur in the excerpt?

What then is the American, this new man? He is either an European, or the descendant of an European, hence that strange mixture of blood, which you will find in no other country. I could point out to you a family whose grandfather was an Englishman, whose wife was Dutch, whose son married a French woman, and whose present four sons have now four wives of different nations. *He* is an American, who, leaving behind him all his ancient prejudices and manners, receives new ones from the new mode of life he has embraced, the new government he obeys, and the new rank he holds. He becomes an American by being received in the broad lap of our great *Alma Mater*. Here individuals of all nations are melted into a new race of men, whose labours and posterity will one day cause great changes in the world.... Here the rewards of his industry follow with equal steps the progress of his labour; his labour is founded on the basis of nature, *self-interest*; can it want a stronger allurement? Wives and children, who before in vain demanded of him a morsel of bread, now, fat and frolicsome, gladly help their father to clear those fields whence exuberant crops are to arise to feed and to clothe them all; without any part being claimed, either by a despotic prince, a rich abbot, or a mighty lord. Here religion demands but little of him; a small voluntary salary to the minister, and gratitude to God; can he refuse these? The American is a new man, who acts upon new principles; he must therefore entertain new ideas, and form new opinions. From involuntary idleness, servile dependence, penury, and useless labour, he has passed to toils of a very different nature, rewarded by ample subsistence. —This is an American.

LAW AND PUBLIC AUTHORITY

Many analysts of Canada and the United States have identified differences in the role of law and in respect for public authority. The apparent variations in American and Canadian attitudes toward individual rights and community obligations are often traced back to each country's founding principles. Under the "Peace, Order and Good Government" clause of the British North America Act (1867), the Fathers of Canadian Confederation expressed their firm commitment to an "ordered" society and collective responsibilities. In stark contrast, the American Declaration of Independence (1776) stressed "Life, Liberty and the Pursuit of Happiness," clearly asserting the inalienable rights of the individual. It has been argued that this overriding concern for individual rights, whether the rights of political dissidents, accused criminals, or ordinary citizens bearing arms, continues to mark much of American life.

Canada's adoption in 1982 of the Canada Act, with its entrenched Canadian Charter of Rights and Freedoms, did represent a step in the direction of "Americanization." However, despite similarities to the U.S. Bill of Rights, it stopped short of extending American-style individual rights. The Charter protected traditional language and minority educational rights, permitted Parliament or provincial legislatures to "opt out" of constitutional provisions, and entrenched protections for affirmative-action programs. Unlike the U.S. Bill of Rights, it did not expressly protect private property rights.[5]

Canadians are often thought to be more law-abiding than their North American neighbours. This popular assumption found powerful support in the studies of both S.M. Lipset and the American-born sociologist Edgar Z. Friedenberg. Canadian–American statistical comparisons since 1960 indicate that Canadians exhibit greater respect for the law. Americans are much more prone to commit murder and violent crimes and to engage in political protests. Rates of crime and violence are lower in Canada. Canadians have a greater respect for police, they provide more public support for longer criminal sentences, and they have a stronger commitment to gun-control legislation. The idealized "heroic" image of the Royal Canadian Mounted Police and the overwhelming public approval of Prime Minister Pierre Trudeau's imposition of the War Measures Act during the 1970 Quebec crisis are only two examples of Canadians' deeply ingrained, perhaps inordinate, respect for public authority.

THE ECONOMIC CULTURE

A Canadian attachment to community obligations rather than individualism has also been identified in the economic sphere. Historically, the American "free enterprise" ideology — though accepted in Canada — has been less pronounced and has served less as a source of intense political conflict. The extreme economic individualism expressed by such slogans as "the best government is the one that governs least" has never been as prevalent in Canada as south of the

What do you think this cartoon tells us about the differences in popular culture, economy, and society between Canada and the United States? Do you think this is an accurate view?

border. The weakness of this sort of rugged individualism has had a variety of effects. The American model of "rags to riches" economic success, popularized by the late-nineteenth-century Horatio Alger "dime novels," never took hold in Canadian society. A certain undercurrent of resistance to economic aggressiveness, social informality, and unabashed materialism was reflected in the prevailing Canadian attitude toward business life. As Canadian historian Arthur M. Lower aptly put it long ago: "Henry Ford was a figure who could hardly have been other than American. Canada did not provide a stage for such as he."

Since 1867 and perhaps earlier, Canadian governments have been willing to use the state as a constructive partner in national development. Federal tariffs, government-supported railways and banking policies, public ownership of major enterprises, state-run medicare, and social-security measures have all engendered much less opposition north of the border than south of it. Some commentators contend that Canada has spawned a vibrant Tory-statist or "Red Tory" tradition, in which Canadian conservatives are inclined to support state intervention and social-democratic movements like the Co-operative Commonwealth Federation (CCF), now the New Democratic Party (NDP), enjoy significant popular support. In his remarkably original work, *A Nation Unaware* (1974), Herschel Hardin went so far as to claim that "Canada, in its essentials, is a public enterprise country," while the United States remains a "private enterprise culture."

ELITISM AND EQUALITY

Since the publication of Lipset's 1965 essay "Revolution and Counterrevolution" it has become commonplace to assert that Canada has been historically more elitist, stratified, and status-oriented than the United States. Status distinctions were firmly implanted in the early French- and British-Canadian societies and were strengthened by the Loyalist migrations after the American Revolution. Throughout the nineteenth and early twentieth centuries, "élitist tendencies" were strongly reflected in Canadian educational as well as political institutions. In sharp contrast to the United States, the Canadian school system in various provinces was primarily based on the British and French model, which was aimed at training a political and ecclesiastical elite. Unlike the United States, with its strong tradition of accessible higher education, Canadian university education until the 1960s remained geared to training a limited few. Clearly, preparing those few for positions of social and political leadership received much more emphasis than did the extension of educational opportunities for the many, as was favoured in the United States.

Studies of wealth, class, and power corroborate the contention that Canada has been, and remains, more élitist than the United States. The predominant influence of the Canadian economic élite and the concentration of economic power in their hands in Canada has been recognized since the publication of John Porter's classic study, *The Vertical Mosaic*, in 1965. Porter documented the existence of a socially homogeneous élite group recruited from narrow circles of private schools and clubs, family links, business associations, and philanthropic

A symbol of North American mass culture. The first McDonald's was opened by founder Ray Kroc in a Chicago suburb in 1955. In the late 1960s the fast food chain entered Canada. By 1995 there were more than 700 McDonald's outlets in Canada and more than 14 000 world-wide.

organizations. Later studies by sociologist Wallace Clement and business journalist Diane Francis seem to confirm that Canadian business élites not only have less specialized education than do their American counterparts, but also are more likely to be drawn from favoured social backgrounds. "Entrance to the economic élite," Clement claimed in *Continental Corporate Power* (1977), "is easier for persons from outside the upper class in the United States than in Canada....The U.S. elite is more open, recruiting from a much broader class base than is the case in Canada."

MOSAIC OR MELTING POT?

In recent years it has become fashionable to contrast the "particularistic" nature of Canadian society with a seemingly more "universalistic" and nationalist-oriented United States. This consistent pattern of differences is most often associated with, or attributed to, the Canadian conception of the "cultural mosaic," as compared with the American notion of the "melting pot." It is also often linked to the greater incidence and vitality of regionally based third parties in Canada than in the United States, and to the relative strength of provinces and provincial rights in the Canadian federal system, compared with the powerful nationalizing forces and apparent weakness of the states in the American union.

The strength and persistence of ethnic and regional diversity in Canada has been widely heralded as a unique characteristic of the society. While the "melting pot" philosophy has thrived in the United States since at least the late nineteenth century, there has been much less pressure placed on immigrants in Canada to assimilate into the majority white, Anglo-Canadian culture. From the 1960s onward, the United States, Canada, and other western countries experienced a wave of "ethnic revival." But in Canada, with its firmer tradition of accepting ethnic differences, the revival yielded more enduring results: the various ethno-cultural minorities, in addition to francophone Canadians, received a much stronger inducement to sustain their own cultural identities than did comparable groups in the United States. With the official acceptance of "multiculturalism" as federal policy in 1971, Canada's ethno-cultural groups enjoyed a more protective and supportive environment than did their American counterparts.

The pursuit of multicultural pluralism in Canada since the 1970s may well have produced what University of Lethbridge sociologist Reginald Bibby called "the unassembled mosaic." Providing individuals, ethno-cultural groups, and social institutions with unprecedented freedom and tolerance of differences did not lead to cultural integration. By the early 1990s, Bibby saw Canadian society as an array of isolated mosaic tiles, a fragmented society in which individual and group rights were valued over the collective good, where mere coexistence was elevated to a national goal.[6] Dwindling support for established Canadian churches, regionalized political loyalties, and the rejection of the 1992 Charlottetown Accord all seemed to support Bibby's analysis of contemporary social trends.

LAMENT FOR A NATION: GEORGE GRANT'S PROPHECY FOR CANADA

ONE OF CANADA'S MOST INFLUENTIAL CONSERVATIVE nationalist intellectuals, George Grant, spent most of his life pondering the fate of Canada in a twentieth-century world rushing headlong into the age of material and technological progress. His classic work, *Lament for a Nation* (1965), saw the defeat of John Diefenbaker's nationalist government as the precursor of "the end of Canada as a sovereign state." The little book raised fundamental questions about Canada's long-term viability in an age of progress dominated by what he termed "the homogenized culture of the American Empire." Will George Grant's dire prophecy come to pass — or has it already arrived?

To lament is to cry out at the death or at the dying of something loved. This lament mourns the end of Canada as a sovereign state. Political laments are not usual in the age of progress, because most people think that society always moves forward to better things. Lamentation is not an indulgence in despair or cynicism. In a lament for a child's death, there is not only pain and regret, but also celebration of passed good....

I have implied that the existence of a sovereign Canada served the good. But can the disappearance of an unimportant nation be worthy of serious grief? For some older Canadians it can. Our country is the only political entity to which we have been trained to pay allegiance. Growing up in Ontario, the generation of the 1920s took it for granted that they belonged to a nation. The character of the country was self-evident. To say it was British was not to

George Grant's *Lament for a Nation* (1965) attracted wide attention for its sombre conclusion that Canada was doomed to disappear in the American empire of modern liberalism.

deny it was North American. To be a Canadian was to be a unique species of North American. Such alternatives as F.H. Underhill's — "Stop being British if you want to be a nationalist" — seemed obviously ridiculous. We were grounded in the wisdom of Sir John A. Macdonald, who saw plainly more than a hundred years ago that the only threat to nationalism was from the South, not from across the sea. To be a Canadian was to build, along with the French, a more ordered and stable society than the liberal experiment in the United States. Now that this hope has been extinguished, we are too old to be retrained by a new master. We find ourselves like fish left on the shores of a drying lake. The element necessary to our existence has passed away. As some form of political loyalty is part of the good life, and as we are not flexible enough to kneel to the rising sun, we must be allowed to lament the passing of what had claimed our allegiance. Even on a continent too dynamic to have memory, it may still be salutary to celebrate memory. The history of the race is strewn with gasping political fish....

The Americans who call themselves "Conservatives" have the right to the title only in a particular sense. In fact, they are old-fashioned liberals. They stand for the freedom of the individual to use his property as he wishes, and for a limited government which must keep out of the marketplace. Their concentration on freedom from governmental interference has more to do with nineteenth-century liberalism than with traditional conservatism, which asserts the right of the community to restrain freedom in the name of the common good....

The impossibility of conservatism in our era is the impossibility of Canada. As Canadians we attempted a ridiculous task in trying to build a conservative nation in the age of progress, on a continent we share with the most dynamic nation on earth. The current of modern history was against us.

George Grant, *Lament for A Nation: The Defeat of Canadian Nationalism*. Reprinted by permission of Carleton University Press.

THE MULRONEY LEGACY: A RECENT POSTSCRIPT

The continentalist policies of Brian Mulroney's government (1984–93) seemed to confirm, in the view of Canadian nationalists, the dire predictions of Grant's *Lament for a Nation*. One popular journalistic analysis, Lawrence Martin's *Pledge of Allegiance*, put it this way:

Through Canadian history, the march of integration and continentalism had never been reversed. It had been contained, checked, but only until the next irresistible rush forward. The rushes had taken Canada to an 80 percent economic dependency on the United States and a cultural engulfment of equally egregious magnitude. Among the side effects of this had been the breeding of border-boy politicians whose mind-sets were but American attenuations, and who, in the years from 1984 to 1992, closed down the Canadian dream of building something unique and better. They were the years when, instead of attempting to contain the American influence, Canada avidly sought out that influence. They were the years when national policy was abandoned, when the goal of the Just Society was forsaken in favour of that of the American Society.

From *Pledge of Allegiance*, by Lawrence Martin. Used by permission of the Canadian Publishers, McClelland & Stewart, Toronto.

CENTRE VERSUS PERIPHERY

Although regional differences have declined in the United States over the past century, provincialism and regionalism have flourished in the Canadian federal union. Since 1867, Canadian provinces have shown far more of a tendency than have American states to challenge the power of federal authorities. Movements advocating provincial autonomy and outright secession — rare in the United States since the Civil War — have recurred north of the border in Nova Scotia, the prairie West, and British Columbia as well as in Quebec. The two federal states have evolved in opposite directions from their founders' intentions. Simply put, Canada in the late twentieth century has strong provinces and a relatively weak central authority, while the United States has weak states and a strong centre.

Tensions between the centre and the periphery, between Ottawa and the provinces, have been more than just conflicts among politicians over the distribution of power. Public sentiment in Canada, according to Alberta political scientist Roger Gibbins, remains "much more territorial" than in the United States, reflecting more distinct regional and provincial interests and values, ranging from *la survivance* in Quebec to the rights to resources in Alberta and the Maritimes. "The *Québécois*," according to Gibbins, "have used the Quebec provincial government as an instrument of cultural survival and, because the stakes are so high, provincial rights have been guarded with a vigor unknown in the United States." Provinces in the West and in Atlantic Canada, it might be added, have also been able to assert their autonomy because Quebec has always been in the vanguard of the struggle.

SOCIAL SECURITY AND HEALTH CARE

Since the 1930s, Canada and the United States have exhibited differing approaches toward social security and health care. The Great Depression gave a strong impetus to the emergence of the modern welfare state, as both governments assumed a more activist role in the provision of income payments and services to the old, the poor, and the unemployed. Canadian governments, spurred by Canadian social-democratic parties since the 1930s, spend more proportionately on social security through a vast array of programs, including the Canada Pension Plan, family allowances, and national unemployment insurance. For many Canadians, Canada's compassionate attitude reflects deeply held values, and its universal social programs amount to what a former prime minister, Brian Mulroney, once termed "a sacred trust." Somewhat paradoxically, however, Canadian citizens and corporate firms donate much less to charitable causes than do Americans.[7]

Canada's health-care system is often cited when Canadians are asked to differentiate themselves from Americans. Canadian state health-insurance programs not only originated earlier, but remain more extensive in coverage and benefits. All Canadian residents are fully covered for all "medically necessary" hospital and physicians' services, which are paid by provincial governments out of general tax revenues. In Ontario, universal health care was safeguarded in the mid-1980s, when the provincial government passed legislation preventing "extra-billing" by doctors and hospital user fees. Unlike Canada's system, the American system consists of privately paid health insurance, medicare for seniors, and medicaid for low-income earners. Some 62 percent of Americans in the early 1990s relied primarily on private coverage, but this paid only 32 percent of all health costs and an estimated 37 million citizens had no health-insurance coverage whatsoever.[8] In stark contrast to the U.S. system, universal health care is widely seen in Canada as a symbol of community values, a vital component of the much-prized "social safety net."

UNANSWERED QUESTIONS

CANADA IS, FOR BETTER OR WORSE, a North American nation. To the degree that Canada and the United States differ in the 1990s, it is because their historical experience has not only been different but — at times — divergent. Critics of comparative studies of the two North American nations contend that analyses of observed "value differences" are speculative and at best problematic. A few sceptics have argued that Canadian–American differences can be explained by a "cultural lag" between the two societies. According to this theory, Canada is much like the United States, but historically lags behind the American republic in its economic and cultural development by two, three, or four decades.[9]

Examining Canada and the United States in comparative perspective raises many intriguing — and unanswered — questions. Is Canada distinctly different from the United States in its historical origins and founding myths? What is the "American mission" or "creed," and is there a Canadian counterpart? Does the Canadian community "lag" behind American society in its historical pattern of economic and cultural development? Why has Canada, in defiance of persistent and varied north–south pressures, grown and survived as a distinct sovereign nation on the northern half of the continent? To what extent is Canada a more "conservative, traditional, law-abiding, statist, and elitist society" than the United States? And where are we heading as North America approaches the new millenium? These are just some of the fundamental questions explored in *Canada: A North American Nation*.

ACTIVITIES

KEY TERMS AND CONCEPTS

Identify and explain the historical significance of each of the following terms and concepts:

- Founding ethos
- Revolution–counterrevolution thesis
- Hartzian fragment theory
- "Tory touch"
- Laurentian thesis
- Limited identities
- "Peace, order and good government"
- "Life, liberty and the pursuit of happiness"
- Deference to authority
- Horatio Alger myth
- Red Toryism
- Public-enterprise culture
- Mosaic (particularist) society
- Melting-pot (universalist) society
- The American mission
- Social-safety net
- Mosaic madness
- Cultural-lag theory

ANALYZING INTERPRETATIONS

For each of the following statements of interpretation, identify the thesis or central argument and assess the validity of the explanation. Use historical examples to *support* or *refute* the thesis.

1. "The American Revolution produced not one country but two: a nation and a non-nation. By virtue of the Revolution, the nation (the United States) acquired a set of national symbols, a gallery of heroes, and a national identity....

   "Like all 'internal wars,' the Revolution had losers as well as victors. The Loyalists, as the losers were called...were expelled. Most of them migrated north and became the founders of the English-speaking component of the non-nation — modern Canada. With them they brought broken dreams, a distorted image of their experience, and a profound sense of indignation bordering on rage."

   — David V.J. Bell, "The Loyalist Tradition in Canada," *Journal of Canadian Studies* 5 (May 1970). Reprinted with the permission of the *Journal of Canadian Studies/Revue l'études Canadiennes.*

2. "What is un-American about English Canada can be summed up in one word: British. The American society was the product of a 'liberal revolution,' and it has remained monolithically liberal until the present day. English Canada's dominant ideology has always been a liberalism quite similar to the American, but there has always been a Britishness about English Canada which has expressed itself in two ideologies, each of which is 'alien,' beyond the pale of legitimacy, in the United States. These two ideologies are 'conservatism' [Toryism] and 'socialism.'"

   — Gad Horowitz, "Tories, Socialists and the Demise of Canada," *Canadian Dimension* (May 1965). Reprinted with permission from *Canadian Dimension Magazine* (CD), 228 Notre Dame Ave., Rm. 707, Winnipeg, MB, R3B 1N7.

3. "[In Canadian history] one anticipates the re-enactment of the American success story and, when it does not come, particularly blames the presence of the huge American neighbour itself.... Obviously, a transcontinental Canadian union has been established and has been constantly subjected to powerful American influences. But it still can be contended that the nation-building approach to Canadian history...may tell us less about the Canada that now *is* than the Canada that *should* have been — but has not come to pass....

   "...[I]f the Canadian people have fallen short of the Canadian dream...it could be because their interests lay elsewhere — and that they nevertheless shared in a viable Canada, if not that laid up in heaven for them....

"How, then, is Canadian experience to be discerned and defined? Some of it is doubtless common to all as citizens in one political sovereignty, with many economic and social interconnections besides. But much of it surely lies in the 'limited identities' of region, culture and class...."

— J.M.S. Careless, "Limited Identities in Canada," *Canadian Historical Review* 50 (March 1969). Reprinted with permission of the University of Toronto Press, Inc.

4. "Canada and the United States continue to differ considerably. America reflects the influence of its classically liberal, Whig, individualistic, antistatist, populist, ideological origins. Canada...can still be seen as Tory-mercantilist, group-oriented, statist, deferential to authority — a 'socialist monarch,' to use Robertson Davies' phrase.... To reiterate an analogy, the two are like trains that have moved thousands of miles along parallel railway tracks. They are far from where they started, but they are still separated."

— Seymour Martin Lipset, *Continental Divide: The Values and Institutions of the United States and Canada* (Toronto: C.D. Howe Institute, 1989), p. 212. Reprinted by permission of Routledge, Chapman & Hall.

ENDNOTES

1. See Seymour Martin Lipset, *Continental Divide: The Values and Institutions of the United States and Canada* (Toronto: C.D. Howe Institute, 1989); and his earlier work, *Revolution and Counter-Revolution* (New York: Basic Books, 1968).

2. See Louis Hartz, *The Founding of New Societies* (New York: Harcourt, Brace, 1964), pp. 1–3, 25, 34, and 71–72; and Gad Horowitz, "Conservatism, Liberalism and Socialism in Canada: An Interpretation," *Canadian Journal of Economics and Political Science* 22 (May 1966):144–171.

3. J.M.S. Careless, "Limited Identities in Canada," *Canadian Historical Review* 50 (March 1969): 1–10, sets out the multiple identities perspective. For the recent debate, see Michael Bliss, "Privatizing the Mind: The Sundering of Canada," *Journal of Canadian Studies* 26 (Winter 1991–92); and the responses in vol. 27 (Summer 1992), pp. 123–135.

4. See Byron Shafer, ed., *Is America Different?: A New Look at American Exceptionalism* (New York: Oxford University Press, 1991), especially chapters 1 and 8.

5. Christopher P. Manfredi, *Judicial Power and the Charter: Canada and the Paradox of Liberal Constitutionalism*. (Toronto: McClelland and Stewart, 1993). See also W.R. McKercher, ed., *The U.S. Bill of Rights and the Canadian Charter* (Toronto: Ontario Economic Council, 1983).

6. See Reginald W. Bibby, *Mosaic Madness: The Poverty and Potential of Life in Canada* (Toronto: Stoddart Publishing, 1990), especially pp. 92–95, 103–105, and 206–207.

7. For a recent analysis see David Card and Richard Freeman, eds., *Small Differences that Matter: Labor Markets and Income Maintenance in Canada and the United States* (Chicago: University of Chicago Press, 1993); and Lipset, *Continental Divide*, chapter 8.

8. A thoughtful review of North American health-care systems is found in Robert G. Evans, "Less Is More: Contrasting Styles in Health Care," in David Thomas, ed., *Canada and the United States: Differences That Count* (Peterborough: Broadview Press, 1993), pp. 21–41.

9. For an exposition of the "cultural-lag" theory see I.L. Horowitz, "The Hemispheric Connection," *Queen's Quarterly* 80 (Autumn 1973): 327–359.

PART I

THE FOUNDING SOCIETIES

ORIGINS TO 1763

It is now widely believed that North America was first inhabited between 20 000 and 40 000 years ago by people who migrated from northeastern Asia. Their descendants evolved a rich diversity of cultures, including unique legends and myths, and developed systems of agriculture, complex political and social structures, and various languages. About 500 years ago, another people — the Europeans — settled in North America, a land they called the "New World." In the following centuries, successive waves of immigrants explored and exploited the continent.

Overseas expansion in the sixteenth and seventeenth centuries led to the establishment of European colonies in North America. From the earliest period of contact with Native peoples to the end of the eighteenth century, the European newcomers engaged in a contest of cultures — Amerindian, French, and English — and gradually adjusted their attitudes and values to meet North American conditions. Part I explores Native–European relations, French and English experiments in building New World societies, and the imperial contest for control of North America. It concludes with the British conquest and unification of North America as a prelude to the American War of Independence.

MAKING CONNECTIONS TIMELINE

	CANADA	NORTH AMERICA	UNITED STATES
B.C.			
30 000	•	First North Americans cross Bering Strait into North America	
8000	•	End of last Ice Age	•
7000	•	Development of agriculture	•
A.D.			
50	•	First Mayan writing in Central America	•
250	•	•	Mound builders settle in Mississippi valley
900	Early Inuit Thule culture moves east to hunt whales	•	•
1000	Vikings reach Labrador coast and Newfoundland	•	•
1400	•	Iroquois Five Nations formed	•
1492	•	First voyage of Columbus to the New World	•
1534	Jacques Cartier discovers the St. Lawrence waterway	•	•
1607	•	•	Founding of Jamestown, Virginia
1608	Founding of Quebec by Samuel de Champlain	•	•
1619	•	•	First shipload of slaves and House of Burgesses appear in Virginia
1620	•	•	Founding of New England by Pilgrims
1625	First Jesuit missionaries arrive in New France	•	•

Year			
1639	Marie de l'Incarnation and Ursulines found first Canadian convent	•	•
1663	Royal Government established in New France	•	•
1670	Founding of the Hudson's Bay Company	•	•
1676	•	•	Bacon's Rebellion in Virginia
1692	•	•	Witchcraft trials at Salem
1713	France cedes Acadia, Newfoundland, and Hudson Bay to Britain	•	•
1739 –41	•	•	The Great Awakening among American Protestants
1745	British capture Fortress Louisbourg	•	•
1754	•	Beginning of the Inter-colonial War in Ohio Valley	English under George Washington driven from Fort Necessity in Ohio country
1755	Expulsion of the Acadians	•	•
1759	British defeat French at Quebec on the Plains of Abraham	•	•
1760	Capitulation of Montreal and fall of New France	•	•
1763	•	End of the Seven Years' War in Europe	•

CHAPTER I

FROM TIME IMMEMORIAL

IMAGINE WHAT it would be like to enter a vast new continent, uninhabited by other humans. The first North Americans — the ancestors of the Native peoples — entered such a land 25 000 to 40 000 years ago from northern Asia. They spent most of their time searching for food and stalking animals with weapons made of wood, bone, and stone. In the centuries that followed, these earliest North Americans survived the Ice Age, adapted to a host of new environments, and by about 5000 years ago had established many diverse and thriving cultures.

ORIGINS AND ARRIVAL OF THE FIRST PEOPLES

THERE IS STILL NO ABSOLUTE AGREEMENT about the origins of the Native peoples or the dates to be assigned to the earliest known inhabited sites.[1] Only a careful examination of the artifacts and fossils left by early peoples, using modern dating techniques, as well as studies of Native oral traditions, will enable a clearer picture of these early American cultures to emerge.

There are two main theories about the origins of North America's first inhabitants. The Amerindians,* or First Nations, generally have assumed that they originated on this continent, as their various creation myths asserted, and that they are therefore an indigenous people and not just the first of several waves of immigrants. The first European colonizers thought of them as having originated somewhere in the Old World and came to assign an Asian homeland to them. Archaeological evidence, supported by modern physiological and medical evidence, points to a Mongoloid racial origin and a migration from northeastern Asia in prehistoric times.[2]

The question of the time when the first migrations occurred has been more difficult to resolve. Until recently it was believed that people had lived in North America for only a few thousand years, but archaeological digs at sites ranging from Mexico to the Yukon and increasingly sophisticated dating procedures point to human occupation as early as 30 000 years ago. Thus, people have lived in North America through at least one ice age.

MIGRATION THEORIES

It is widely believed that the earliest North Americans entered the continent from northeastern Asia by crossing at the Bering Strait. Depending on the time of entry, estimated at between 25 000 and 40 000 years ago, these early people may have crossed on a land bridge, by boat,

---

* "Amerindian" is a comprehensive term comparable to European, Asiatic, or African; it designates a wide range of cultures, languages, and traditions that historically shared a continent and were perceived by "outsiders" as sharing certain broad social, political, and intellectual attributes. "Indian" is a misnomer attributed to Christopher Columbus.

or over the ice to Beringia — present-day Alaska. During the last or Wisconsin Ice Age, much of the earth's moisture was locked up in glaciers and ice fields that lowered ocean levels. This may have created a land passage that allowed animals and humans to pass over into North America. But since the Bering Strait is only about 50 km wide at its narrowest point, crossings by ice bridge or open water are also distinct possibilities.

Three competing theories have been proposed to explain the time of arrival of North America's first inhabitants. The "early arrival" theory postulates human habitation south of the ice sheets about 40 000 years ago. This theory suggests that *Homo erectus*, humanity's earliest known ancestor, may have appeared on this continent. Amerindian creation myths point in the same direction. The "middle entry" theory is that the first migrants derived from earlier nomadic cultures in Siberia and spread northeastward into Alaska about 30 000 years ago. Proponents of this view point to scraping and fleshing tools found at Old Crow in the Yukon as evidence of this movement of people and animals. Finally, there is the "late arrival" theory, which asserts that people arrived only about 12 000 years ago and fanned out over the ice-free Mackenzie valley down onto the Great Plains.

Recently, geologists and archaeologists have collaborated in proposing an intriguing alternative migration route. Ice-free tundra-like plains, evidence of which now rests on the ocean bed, existed along the British Columbia coast about 14 000 years ago. This would have been a much more direct and hospitable route for humans and animals than was the icy corridor between the glaciers in Alberta. Also, there may have been occasional direct contacts from East Asia and Polynesia across the Pacific Ocean, evidence for which exists in South and Central America.[3]

PREHISTORIC NATIVE CULTURES

THE EARLIEST INHABITANTS OF NORTH AMERICA lived in the Paleolithic Age, when stone was widely used for tools, utensils, and weapons. These early stone age people had to make a number of adaptations to widely varying environments from the Arctic coast of Beringia to the tropical areas of Central and South America.

The oldest human remains in North America are often found with the bones of now-extinct horses, camels, mammoths, giant sloths, bison, wolves, sabre-toothed tigers, and giant panthers. Some of these animals were valuable sources of food, clothing, and materials for making shelters. Archaeological information indicates that early North Americans lived in bands, were probably semi-nomadic, and relied heavily on big game and fish for sustenance. On the vast prairie lands they organized drives to stampede herds of bison or mammoths over cliffs and into ravines. These kill sites, or "jumps," date from about 10 000 years ago. The Amerindian world view that there was a time when animals ruled the world and that early hunters enjoyed an interdependent relationship with them seems to refer to this

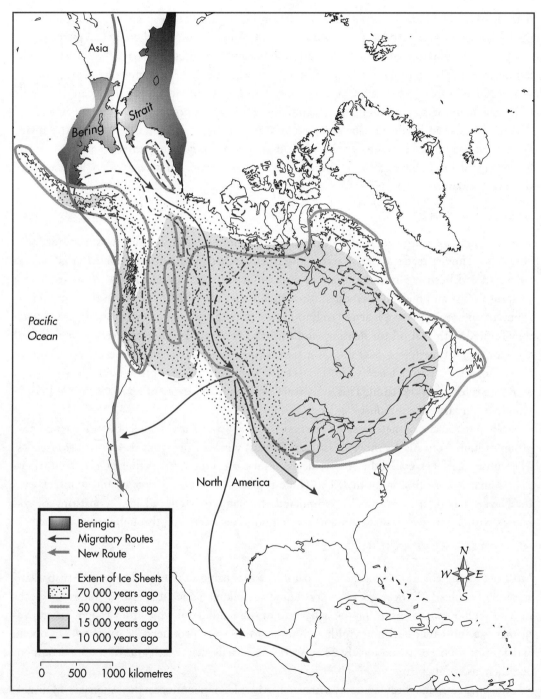

Early migration to North America from Siberia.

period. Men, as hunters, established a relationship of mutual respect with wild animals, while women appear to have pioneered the use of plants for food and medicinal purposes.[4]

Between 8000 and 5000 B.C., the climate became warmer and drier. As human populations increased and techniques for killing game were perfected, numerous animal species were reduced through overhunting and about 100 species of large animals became extinct. Fish, sea mammals, and shellfish became increasingly important along the Pacific and Atlantic coasts, and wild rice became a staple in the Great Lakes area. Among the lower Great Lakes and St. Lawrence valley cultures, people began to cultivate plants — the beginning of horticulture. Since these people raised crops, they began to lead a more sedentary existence.[5]

INUIT PREHISTORY

The oldest camps of the ancestors of the Inuit first appeared in western Alaska about 5000 years ago. They spread eastward across the Arctic shores and into the northern islands as far north as Ellesmere Island and as far east as Greenland. They had small flint tools and weapon points and hunted caribou and sea mammals. They had to adapt to the harsh environment and seem to have learned to build snow houses, to fashion soapstone lamps, which they fuelled with seal oil for heating, and to make ivory tools. This culture has been called the Dorset culture (circa 500 B.C. – A.D. 1500) because its remains were first found at Cape Dorset on Baffin Island. The Dorset are probably the people whom the Inuit oral accounts refer to as the Tunit. The Tunit were described as strong and rather simple people who lived in large stone houses.

When the Arctic climate became warmer for a few centuries about 1000 years ago, a new group of Inuit from Alaska moved eastward to hunt whales from umiaks, or open skin-boats. This culture has been called the Thule culture, after a settlement in northern Greenland where their remains were first identified. The Thule replaced the Tunit and came into contact with the Norse, whom they eventually assimilated. Remains of Thule villages, consisting of sod houses with a framework of stones and whale bones, are scattered throughout the Arctic.[6]

NORTHERN HUNTING BANDS

Most of North America above the 55th parallel was inhabited by Algonkian- and Athapaskan-speaking peoples.[7] All these people were skilled at stalking game, at preparing hides for clothing and shelter, and at observing the behaviour of the wildlife on which they relied. Theirs was primarily a subsistence economy, although some goods were produced for exchange, to obtain articles not found or made locally. They were necessarily very conscious of the environment and their use of its resources.

Europeans made first contact with such Algonkian peoples as the Abenaki, Maliseet, Micmac, Beothuk, Montagnais, and Algonkins.[8] The Montagnais, who lived in small bands of three to five related families, hunted moose in winter. In the spring they moved down the rivers as far south as the Gulf of St. Lawrence to spear salmon and eels and to harpoon seals. After the introduction of the fur trade by Europeans and the resulting overhunting and competitiveness, the groups became larger and the hunting regions were divided into family hunting territories.

The Maliseet of present-day New Brunswick and the Micmac of Nova Scotia and Prince Edward Island were skilled sailors, fishers, hunters, and food gatherers. During the winter they used snowshoes to stalk moose and caribou, killing the big game with spears or arrows. In the spring they moved to the seashore to gather shellfish, to fish at the mouths of rivers, and to venture out to sea to hunt seals and porpoises. The Micmac were known for their fine handicrafts — basketry, leatherwork, and beadwork — and traded actively with the French explorers.

The Cree also lived in small bands made up of related families in the northern plateau lands of what is now northern Quebec and Ontario. They were known for their soapstone pots, woven hare-skin fur coats and blankets, and beadwork. Those who maintained the traditional culture are identified as Woodland Cree, while those who moved onto the plains and adopted many of the characteristics of other bands and tribes came to be known as Plains Cree. Bison (commonly but inaccurately called buffalo) formed the basis of the Plains Cree way of life, supplying food, hides for lodge coverings, clothing, and bone for tools. On the northern shores of Lakes Huron and Superior were the Ojibwa bands, which included the Ottawa, Saulteux, and Mississauga.

The Blackfoot, a loose confederacy of three southwestern Prairie peoples — the Siksika or Blackfoot proper, the Peigan, and the Blood — shared a tradition of common origin, similar customs, and a common language. Their economy revolved about the bison, whose meat was sun-dried (jerked) or pounded fine and mixed with fat and dried berries to form the highly nutritious pemmican. Nothing was wasted: bison horns were carved into cups; bones were fashioned into knives, projectile points, and awls; scraped skins made bags and shields; sinews were woven into lines and ropes; hides served as cloaks and bed coverings. The great summer "buffalo hunt" involved the co-operation of many people and was the occasion for various social activities and religious ceremonies. During the winter the Blackfoot separated into small bands to take shelter in coulees and river valleys.

IROQUOIAN AGRICULTURAL SOCIETIES

The most populous groups inhabiting the northeast woodlands area were the Iroquoians, who lived in the St. Lawrence valley and around the lower Great Lakes in what is now New York state and southern Ontario. The Laurentian Iroquois, to which the Stadaconans (Quebec) and Hochelagans (Montreal) belonged, disappeared some time after 1543. They were probably absorbed into neighbouring groups. All Iroquoian peoples raised crops and lived in large villages of "longhouses" containing 300 to 400 families.[9] Within the Iroquoian language group, two competing alliances formed. A League of Five Nations was established around A.D. 1400, uniting a confederacy of Mohawks, Cayuga, Onondaga, Oneida, and Seneca. To counter that alliance, the Hurons formed a league of four tribes in alliance with the Neutral, Erie, and Tobacco nations.

Although the Iroquoians were primarily subsistence farmers, there was considerable trade among the tribes, as well as with neighbouring groups such as the Algonkians. The Hurons traded corn, wampum, and gill nets with the Algonkians in return for meat, beaver skins, and birch-bark canoes.

THE NORTHWEST COAST SOCIETIES

Amerindian societies that were relatively densely populated and culturally sophisticated arose in the hospitable natural environments of the Pacific coast of British Columbia and its adjoining islands.

Each nation developed its own language, a sophisticated political and social structure, and an economy based on the sea. The societies were organized into castes, with slaves constituting the lowest rung of the social ladder. Their settled way of life permitted substantial buildings and the accumulation of goods. The presence of huge cedar trees enabled them to make elaborate plank houses, majestic totem poles, finely carved storage boxes, cedar-bark clothing, and swift-moving seagoing vessels. The northern tribes hunted sea otters, the Nootka engaged in whaling, and all caught salmon, oolachan (prized for its oil), shellfish, and waterfowl. Mounds of discarded shells today mark ancient village sites that date back at least 5000 years.[10]

MANY CULTURES, MANY LANGUAGES

OVER A PERIOD OF SEVERAL THOUSAND YEARS, a great diversity of cultures and complex societies emerged in North America. By A.D. 1500, Amerindians inhabited almost every environment in the Americas. Estimates of their population north of Mexico vary from 3.5 million to over 10 million. More than 500 language dialects had developed, and seven major "culture areas," or geographic adaptations, have been identified throughout the continent. The Native cultures varied from the Algonkian hunting bands to the hierarchical Pacific Northwest societies to the southwestern cliff dwellers. To the south, the Aztecs of the Mexican highlands, the Mayans of the Yucatan peninsula and Guatemala, and the Incas of Peru developed cultures as advanced as the greatest civilizations of Europe, Asia, and Africa at that time.

LANGUAGE GROUPS

The Amerindian peoples were as diverse as Europeans; Mohawks were as different from Athapaskans as Portuguese were from Russians. Yet, just as all Europeans share some common

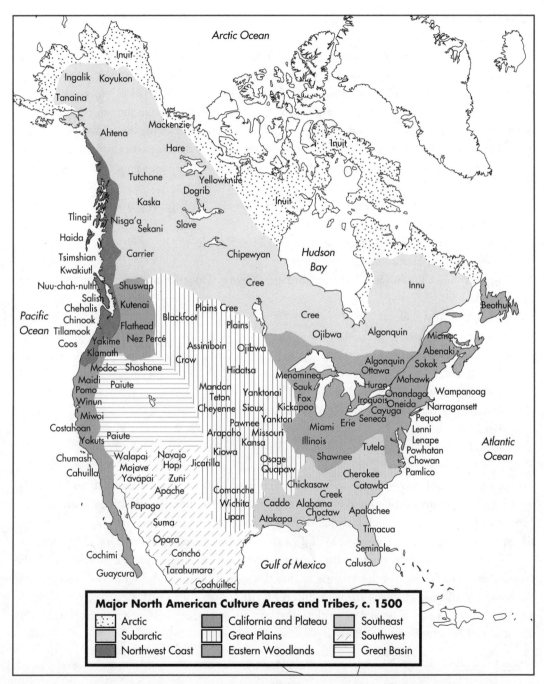

Major North American culture areas and tribes, 1500. How much do the geographical and environmental features of the land determine the cultural areas and lifestyles of the Amerindians?

cultural elements, so do all aboriginal groups in North America share some common cultural values and concepts.

Linguists have classified the aboriginal languages of Canada into eleven families. Six of these languages are found in the comparatively small area west of the Rocky Mountains, three are on the Prairies, only two families occur east of Lake Winnipeg, and one exists in the Arctic. In prehistoric times, many more languages were spoken. Languages classified in the same "family" have descended from a common ancestral language. The fact that seven of the eleven indigenous language families are found in British Columbia suggests that it is the linguistically "old" area.[11]

The major linguistic families within Canada and the Native languages comprehended in each are:

- *Algonkian*: Micmac, Maliseet, Abenaki, Montagnais, Naskapi, Algonkin, Cree, Ottawa, Ojibwa, Blackfoot
- *Iroquoian:* Huron, Petun, Neutral, Iroquois Five Nations
- *Siouan:* Sioux, Assiniboine
- *Athapaskan:* Chipewyan, Carrier, Beaver, Slavey, Dogrib, Tahltan, Tutchone, Hare, Kutchin
- *Inuit:* Inuktitut dialects
- *Kutenai:* Kutenai
- *Salishan:* Bella Coola, Comox, Sechelt, Squamish, Halkomelem, Straits, Lillooet, Thompson, Okanagan, Shuswap
- *Wakashan:* Kwakiutl, Nuu-chah-nulth
- *Tsimshian:* Coast Tsimshian, Nisga'a, Gitskan
- *Haida:* Haida
- *Tlingit:* Tlingit

As the fur trade moved from the eastern seaboard to the Great Lakes basin and onto the western plains, many French-speaking men established stable unions with Amerindian women. From these kinship ties, which facilitated the fur trade and military alliances, a "new people," the Métis, emerged. Their language, Michif, was originally a mixture of French and Algonkian.[12]

There is no absolute relationship between language and culture. The Blackfoot of the Prairies and the Micmacs of the Atlantic region, for example, are both Algonkian speakers, but their ways of life and cultures are very different. All Native cultures in what are now Canada and the United States were oral or preliterate, but the Micmacs, and later the Cree and Inuit, adopted syllabics to write their language.

CULTURAL AREAS

Nine major North American Native "culture areas" have been identified, six of which extend into present-day Canada. Tribes and bands occupying each geographical area show great cultural similarities to each other, even though they may speak widely different languages. In Canada, the six culture areas are:

- *Arctic:* a region of treeless tundra where widely dispersed bands of Inuit move in seasonal pursuit of sea animals and caribou.
- *Subarctic:* a region of Precambrian Shield, forests, lakes, and muskeg where food resources are more dependable but where hunting bands follow a seasonal cycle.
- *Northeast (Eastern Woodlands):* the Maritime coast to the St. Lawrence–Great Lakes region of forests, lakes, and rivers, and suitable for growing corn, beans, and squash.
- *Great Plains:* a prairie region where nomadic tipi dwellers hunted buffalo over large areas after the introduction of the horse in the 1500s.
- *Interior Plateau:* an intermountain region between the Rocky Mountains and the Coastal Range marked by geographic extremes, from arid semi-desert to moist coniferous forests.
- *Northwest Coast:* a region of rugged mountainous slopes supporting maritime fishing cultures, dense population concentrations, and complex social institutions.

CHANGE AND STABILITY

Language and culture groupings can delineate various societies, but they convey the impression that the Amerindian experience was static. Although the pace of social change was slower before A.D. 1600 than it was afterward, Amerindian societies were always changing and evolving. As contact among tribal groups developed, items were traded over great distances, and nomadic bands spread new ideas and tools. Many Amerindian stories, legends, and practices originating in one tribal group appeared elsewhere in slightly different versions.

Native people hunting on snowshoes; from an engraving of 1575.

NATIVE SOCIETIES, CUSTOMS, AND BELIEFS

AT THE TIME OF THE FIRST Native–white contact, the incredible diversity of Amerindian societies extended to their social structures, customs and rituals, and religious beliefs. Although current knowledge of the various groups is limited, the picture that emerges of Amerindian cultural practices is varied and complex. Amerindian cultures were organized into political and social systems that took three distinct forms: *bands*, consisting of several families or clans; *tribes*, larger groups who shared common languages, customs, and beliefs; and *chiefdoms*, hierarchical, class-structured societies based on hereditary privileges and, sometimes, slave-holding.[13]

SOCIAL AND POLITICAL ORGANIZATION

At the band level of organization were the Algonkians and the Athapaskans of the Subarctic. They were more concerned with environmental adaptation and survival than with sophisticated social or religious organization.

Micmacs, for example, had a system of district chiefs and local chiefs. The district chiefs planned the seasonal movement of the people, assigned the hunting territories, and were responsible for seeing that hunting parties and war parties were properly provisioned. The local chiefs met at a general council regularly to discuss matters of peace and war. They practised polygamy in order to have many children, a sign of power and authority. Their war chiefs were men of special ability in tactics and leadership.

The Montagnais, in contrast, had no strong leaders and their chiefs had little or no authority. In times of war, a council of warriors made the plans. In general, these cultures were patrilineal and polygamous. There was a clearly defined division of labour along gender lines — men did the hunting and fishing, while women dressed the carcasses, tanned the hides, looked after domestic chores and the children, made and broke camp, and carried the heavy loads when travelling. Band societies did not recognize the principle of authority and did not exercise coercive power over their members. Decisions were arrived at by consensus, and the children were raised permissively and not subject to severe discipline.

The Iroquoian peoples were at the "tribal level" of social and political organization. Their system was basically democratic (see the feature study "The Iroquois Confederacy"), and both the Huron and the Five Nations Iroquois developed a super-tribal or proto-federal system of confederacy. The various Algonkian peoples who were allied with the French also developed a loosely organized confederacy, the Three Council Fires, in the eighteenth century. Each tribe had its own council and was represented at the confederacy council as well.

THE IROQUOIS CONFEDERACY: A PRECURSOR OF AMERICAN DEMOCRACY?

MANY NORTH AMERICAN HISTORIANS and political scientists have noted the striking similarities between the constitution of the Iroquois Confederacy (circa 1500) and the founding principles of the United States, enshrined in the Declaration of Independence (1776) and the American Constitution (1789). A few have even suggested that "the League of the Iroquois may have been the basis on which the United States government was organized."

Although the Iroquois Confederacy was founded probably after A.D. 1400, the constitution of the Five Nations (later Six Nations, when the Tuscoraras were admitted) was not put into writing until around the 1850s. Sections of the constitution, as inscribed by Seth Newhouse of the Seneca tribe in 1880, do bear a resemblance to the first principles of the American republic. Is there a connection? Compare the excerpts below with the Declaration of Independence.

CONSTITUTION OF THE FIVE NATIONS IROQUOIS CONFEDERACY

This is wisdom and justice on the part of the Great Spirit to create and raise chiefs, give and establish unchangeable laws, rules and customs between the Five Nation Indians, viz. the Mohawks, Oneidas, Onondagas, Cayugas and Senecas and the other nations of Indians here in North America. The object of these laws is to establish peace between the numerous nations of Indians, hostility will be done away with, for the preservation and protection of life, property and liberty.

Laws, rules and customs as follows:

1. And the number of chiefs in this confederation of the Five Nation Indians are fifty in number, no more and no less. They are the ones to arrange, to legislate and to look after the affairs of their people....

10. And the business of the council of the Five Nation Indians is transacted by two combinations of chiefs; viz. first the Mohawks and Senecas, and second the Oneidas and Cayugas.*

11. And when a case or proposition is introduced in the council of the Five Nations, the Mohawk chiefs with the Senecas shall first consider the matter, and whatever the decision may be; then the speaker will refer the matter to the other side of the council fire; to the

*Among the Five Nations, the central council fire was held at the Onondaga central village; the Senecas were responsible for guarding the western door and the Mohawks for guarding the eastern door. The Great White Pine, with four Roots of Peace and topped by the Great Eagle, was adopted as the symbol of the confederacy: Daniel K. Richter, *The Ordeal of the Longhouse: The Peoples of the Iroquois League in the Era of European Colonization* (Chapel Hill: University of North Carolina Press, 1992).

second combination chiefs, the Oneidas and Cayugas, for their consideration, and if they all agree unanimously then the speaker of the council shall refer the matter to the fire keepers; and it is then their duty to sanction it; and their speaker will then pronounce the case as passed in council....

14. And when there is a case, proposition, or any subject before the council of the Five Nation Indians, no chief or chiefs has any right to stand up to speak without permission from the council, and if he has anything to say by way of explanation, he can do so in a low tone to the combined chiefs whereof he is a member.

15. And when anything is under the consideration of the council, they must agree unanimously if possible before it is referred to the other side of the council fire, to the second combination chiefs; otherwise it would be illegal so to do by one or more chiefs, unless sanction[ed] by the rest of the combined chiefs of which he or they is a member....

30. And there [are] five arrows bound together. This is the symbol of Union, Power, Honour, and Dominion of the Five Nation Indians confederation, and if one of the five arrows was to be taken out then the remainder is easily broken asunder. This signifies if one of the Five Nations were to emigrate to a distant country of course they had withdrawn from the Confederation therefore the Power of the Five Nation confederation is decreased....

40. The Great Spirit the Supreme Being has chosen the Mohawk Nation as head in this confederation, for it is with them that the confederation originated. Therefore if the Mohawk chiefs disallow anything, or protest any case or proposition that is brought before the council it shall not be lawful for the council to pass it, for he hath chosen them to be the leader of this confederation government, and all the affairs of the Five Nation Indians, and others that are united with them are in their hands; and he hath given the Mohawk chiefs calm and tender hearts towards their people, and if any difficulty arise amongst them, the people, the chiefs in council will settle it for them.

THE AMERICAN DECLARATION OF INDEPENDENCE

When in the course of human events it becomes necessary for one people to dissolve the political bands which have connected them with another and to assume, among the powers of the earth, the separate and equal station to which the laws of nature and of nature's God entitle them, a decent respect to the opinions of mankind requires that they should declare the causes which impel them to the separation.

We hold these truths to be self-evident, that all men are created equal; that they are endowed by their Creator with certain unalienable rights; that among these are life, liberty, and the pursuit of happiness. That, to secure these rights, governments are instituted among men, deriving their just powers from the consent of the governed; that, whenever any form of government becomes destructive of these ends, it is the right of the people to alter or to abolish it, and to institute a new government, laying its foundation on such principles, and organizing its powers in such form, as to them shall seem most likely to effect their safety and happiness. Prudence, indeed, will dictate that governments long established should not be changed for light and transient causes; and, accordingly, all experience hath shown that mankind are more disposed to suffer, while evils are sufferable, than to right themselves by abolishing the forms to which they are accustomed. But when a long train of abuses and usurpations, pursuing invariably the same object, evinces a design to reduce them under absolute despotism, it is their right, it is their duty, to throw off such government and to provide new guards for their future security. Such has been the patient sufferance of these colonies, and such is now the necessity which constrains them to alter their former systems of government....

We, therefore, the representatives of the United States of America, in general Congress assembled, appealing to the Supreme Judge of the world for the rectitude of our intentions, do, in the name and by the authority of the good people of these colonies, solemnly publish and declare, that these united colonies are, and of right ought to be, free and independent states: that they are absolved from all allegiance to the British Crown, and that all political connection between them and the state of Great Britain is, and ought to be, totally dissolved; and that, as free and independent states, they have full power to levy war, conclude peace, contract alliances, establish commerce, and to do all other acts and things which independent states may of right do. And, for the support of this declaration, with a firm reliance on the protection of Divine Providence, we mutually pledge to each other our lives, our fortunes, and our sacred honor.

From *The Declaration of Independence, 1776, A Declaration of Congress*, July 4, 1776.

The Huron and Iroquois were agricultural peoples who lived in large villages surrounded by their cornfields. Each longhouse sheltered a number of families related to the clan matron. Iroquoian society was matrilineal, and the women, through their control of the food supply, exercised great influence over the councillors. The Iroquoian slash-and-burn method of farming resulted in a rapid depletion of soil fertility, so the villages were moved every decade or so to be near newly cleared fields. Their sedentary mode of life enabled them to organize elaborate ceremonial and religious observances.

A third socio-political system was restricted to the Pacific coast cultures. These peoples had a highly evolved system of chiefdoms or Native kingships, with a distinctive class structure and hereditary powers and privileges, and even practised slavery, as did many European civilizations at the time of contact. In these societies, status came from the disposal of wealth and the exercise of hospitality and generosity, not from the accumulation of material goods. Clan or lineage chiefs distributed their wealth at a great feast called a *potlatch*, from the Chinook trade jargon meaning "giving away." A group wishing to uphold the prestige and renown of its chief spent much time and effort in the collection of gifts and food for the feast. Potlatches were given for a number of reasons — to provide relief to a village struck by misfortune, to honour a dead chief, to regain lost prestige, or to celebrate the completion of a new house or the raising of a totem pole.[14]

Majestic, finely carved, and brightly painted totem poles were erected to impress all with the wealth, status, and ancestry of their owners. The clan crests represented elements of family history. Some were memorial poles, some were funerary poles, and others were house-portal poles. Hundreds, even thousands, of people attended the raising of a pole. All participants were paid for their help in raising the huge monuments, and all guests who witnessed the event were given presents.

CONCEPTS OF LAW, LAND, NATURE, AND TIME

All Amerindian societies shunned coercive law enforcement. They had no codified laws, no courts, and no prisons, but they did have a highly developed sense of justice and social responsibility. What European cultures considered crimes were seen by Native societies as disruptions of community peace and harmony. More emphasis was placed on compensation for victims of crime than on the punishment of the offender. The family, and sometimes the entire band, assumed responsibility for an aggressive act committed by one of its members. It made suitable retribution, on the advice of the council of elders and in consultation with all parties concerned, to restore harmony between families, bands, or entire nations.

The European concept of private property — property belonging to an individual to the exclusion of all others — was quite foreign to Amerindians. Land was no more viewed as personal property than were the waters of the lakes or the air — all were gifts of the Great Spirit for the benefit of all creatures, including animals, birds, and plants. Yet there were well-known boundaries between the ancestral territories of various groups. Hospitality was so highly prized that the sharing of goods was widely practised. Europeans, however, viewed some of these practices as theft.

Interpersonal, family, and band relations were all regulated by long-established traditions. Educating young people in the culture of the group and in the skills and knowledge required for filling a useful place in society was achieved through role playing and emulating the adults. Learning by seeing and doing was reinforced on ceremonial and religious occasions through reciting the history and customs of the people.

All Amerindians based their months on the phases of the moon. The months were usually named after some natural event, such as the salmon run, the corn harvest, or the departure of the migratory birds. Iroquoians divided their year into the seasons of planting, cultivating, harvesting, and resting. They had a Midwinter Festival, a Thanks-to-the-Maple Festival, a Corn Planting Ceremony, a Green Corn Festival, and a Harvest Festival. The Micmacs, like many other groups, held the sun in special reverence. The summer and winter solstices were usually marked by ceremonies throughout North America. The presence of "medicine-wheels" across the continent attests to a special interest in the night sky. Some groups counted time by the movement of the group of seven stars known as the Pleiades.[15]

RELIGIOUS BELIEFS

Amerindians were very spiritual people; even planting crops and hunting animals had a deep religious meaning and required the observance of certain reverent attitudes and practices. Although beliefs and practices varied from group to group, there were enough common elements to enable one to identify a traditional religion. It was commonly believed that a person had two souls: one gave life to the body and was centred in the heart; the other, a free soul, resided in the mind and was able to journey during sleep. The concept of spiritual life residing in the heart and mind appears to be as old as humanity itself.[16]

Moreover, the universe was animate; not only did animals and plants possess souls, but so did rocks, waterfalls, and clouds, inasmuch as they possessed some power. To live in peace with all creatures, therefore, required respect for all of nature. Equality between human beings and other living "persons" (all creation consisted of "relatives") was thought to continue beyond death.

Death represented separation from the earthly body, and in the afterworld — usually thought to be located in the west, where most of the dead went — there was neither reward nor punishment for one's manner of life on earth. The real test was the soul's four-day journey through many hazards to this blissful afterworld. It was also widely believed that the world was inhabited by many powerful spiritual beings, the *manitos*, some revered for their help in hunting and others feared for their ability to produce storms. Each species of animal had its own keeper, whose aid was essential for a successful hunt and an assured food supply. The hunters treated the animals they killed with respect to ensure that their future hunts would be successful. Each individual related to a personal guardian *manito*. After contact with Christian missionaries a concept of a supreme being, *Kitchi Manito*, or Master of Life, took on new importance.

The Native concept of creation, the origin of evil, and the causes of disease were very different from Christian beliefs. Good hunting and good health were the signs of a successful relationship with the spiritual universe. The maintenance of good health and the curing of disease were important aspects of Native religion. Cleanliness was considered essential to health. Campsites and villages were kept clean, refuse was burned, and cooking and eating utensils were washed. Frequent bathing, resort to sweat lodges, and the use of medicinal herbs and roots to sweeten the air were considered important.

Disease was viewed as abnormal, and it was attributed to a variety of causes. It might result from an improper relationship with the animals or *manitos*, from witchcraft, or from the intrusion of a foreign object into the body. After contact with Europeans, the intruders (especially the missionaries) and their goods were sometimes viewed as the cause of the new diseases.

The chief source of medicines were plants, which were used in accordance with traditional recipes and in conjunction with time-honoured rituals. Men and women who were believed to possess exceptional powers in dealing with illness were called shamans. They were called upon to divine the cause of illness and to heal. Curing rituals, such as the shaking-tent ceremony or the sundance, were an important part of religious life. The Iroquois had a number of "false face curing societies." Members of a curing society would put on painted grimacing wooden masks, both for private curing sessions with the sick and at public ceremonies such as the midwinter festival.

The Iroquois and Algonkians also held solemn feasts of the dead at least every decade in commemoration of departed relatives. The bones of the departed were gathered, scraped, and lovingly washed. They were then bundled in rich furs and buried in a large common grave to symbolize the fellowship they enjoyed together in the afterlife.

The *Midewiwin* or Grand Medicine Society of the Ojibwa is rooted in traditional religious belief, although it has taken on a number of foreign beliefs and symbolic acts. At every major ceremony the traditional creation story was recited, tobacco offerings and dog sacrifices were made, ceremonial sweat baths were taken, and feasting and ritual dancing followed. Members of the society had as their objective the intercession of spiritual beings for health, help, and blessing on their people. The society devoted much attention to gaining a knowledge of medicinal herbs and of power over sickness.

THE DEMOGRAPHIC TRAGEDY

THE AMERICAS were more densely populated at the time of European contact than is commonly supposed. Recent estimates place the population at perhaps 25 million north of Mexico in the year 1490, of whom about 1 million lived in what is now Canada. The highly developed civilizations of Mexico had a population of about 30 million. Such a high density was made possible by the cultivation of high-yielding cereals and tubers and a relatively disease-free environment.

A Huron village within a palisade.

AN AMERINDIAN MESSAGE TO HISTORY BOOK WRITERS

SINCE THE LATE 1960S the Native peoples have drawn attention to their proud traditions and have fought the distorted images presented in history books and popular culture. Among the most eloquent pleas for social justice was this sardonic verse attributed to the League of the Six Nations in New York state.

FOURTEEN STRINGS OF PURPLE WAMPUM TO WRITERS ABOUT INDIANS

We hold in our hand fourteen strings of purple wampum. These we hand, one by one, to you — authors of many American history books; writers of cheap, inaccurate, unauthentic, sensational novels; and other writers of fiction who have poisoned the minds of young Americans concerning our people, the Red Race of America; to the producers of many western cowboy and Indian television programs and moving picture shows; to those Treaty-breakers who delight in dispossessing Indian Peoples by constructing dams on Indian lands in violation of sacred treaties; and to those of this, our country, who are prone to build up the glory of their ancestors on the bonds and life-blood of our Old People:

—With this first string of wampum, we take away the fog that surrounds your eyes and obstructs your view, that you may see the truth concerning our people!

—With this second string of wampum, we pull away from your imprisoned minds the cobwebs, the net that prevents you from dealing justice to our people!

—With this third piece of wampum, we cleanse your hearts of revenge, selfishness, and injustice, that you may create love instead of hate!

— With this fourth string of wampum, we wash the blood of our people from your hands, that you may know the clasp of true friendship and sincerity!

—With this fifth string of wampum, we shrink your heads down to that of normal man, we cleanse your minds of the abnormal conceit and love of self that has caused you to walk blindly among the dark people of the world.

— With this sixth string of wampum, we remove your garments of gold, silver, and greed, that you may don the apparel of generosity, hospitality, and humanity!

— With this seventh string of wampum, we remove the dirt that fills your ears so you may hear the story and truth of our people!

—With this eighth string of wampum, we straighten your tongues of crookedness, that in the future you may speak the truth concerning Indian People!

— With this ninth string of wampum, we take away the dark clouds from the face of the sun, that its rays may purify your thoughts, that you may look forward and see America, instead of backward toward Europe!

—With this tenth string of wampum, we brush away the rough stones and sticks from your path, that you may walk erect as the first American whose name you have defamed and whose country you now occupy!

—With this eleventh string of wampum, we take away from your hands your implements of destruction — guns, bombs, firewater, diseases — and place in them instead the Pipe of Friendship and Peace, that you may sow brotherly love rather than bitter hate and injustice!

—With this twelfth string of wampum, we build you a new house with many windows and no mirrors, that you may look out and see the life and purpose of your nearest neighbor, the American Indian!

—With this thirteenth string of wampum, we tear down the wall of steel and stone you have built around the TREE OF PEACE, that you may shelter beneath its branches!

—With this fourteenth string of wampum, we take from the hen-coop the eagle that you have imprisoned, that this noble bird may once again fly in the sky over America!

I, Te-ha-ne-to-rens, say this!

From *Six Nations Pamphlet*, Akwesane Counselor Organization, *The People*, Vol. 1, No. 2, Aug. 1968, Hogansburg, New York.

THE IMPACT OF EPIDEMIC DISEASES

The Native peoples' contact with Europeans resulted in rapid depopulation, as new diseases and infections to which they had little or no natural immunity were introduced and quickly reached epidemic proportions. Smallpox was the greatest killer, followed closely by a variety of respiratory infections, contagious diseases associated in Europe with childhood, typhus, and the plague. The few statistical estimates made at the time of first contact indicate that over one-third, and perhaps as much as 50 or 60 percent, of the Native population perished in the first waves of epidemics that swept inland from the Atlantic coast.[17]

The depopulation and resulting demoralization of the Amerindians were further intensified by colonial warfare, by the increasing Native dependence on European supplies and even foodstuffs as the fur trade took up time and interest, and by the introduction of alcoholic beverages into Native societies. Later, the disappearance of the great bison herds on the western prairies in the 1880s resulted in mass starvation. The devastating epidemics associated with colonial times struck the isolated northern Inuit communities again in the 1920s and 1930s, when communications with southern Canada were accelerated.

LASTING CONTRIBUTIONS

THE AMERINDIAN CONTRIBUTIONS to Western civilization were much greater than the European invaders realized. Early French, English, and Dutch settlers relied heavily on the original inhabitants for their survival and well-being in what often seemed to be a harsh, inhospitable environment. It was the Native peoples who guided the explorers along forest trails and connecting waterways, who taught the missionaries new languages, who showed the soldiers the fine points of guerrilla warfare. They taught the European colonists about certain techniques of food collecting and preservation, building to withstand the extremes of temperature, sensible dress in a new environment, and woodcraft. Even in recent times, the Inuit taught Canada's armed forces techniques of survival under rigorous Arctic conditions. Canadians are especially aware of the value of the birch-bark canoe, toboggans, parkas, snowshoes, and dogsleds.[18]

European agriculture benefited greatly from contact with Amerindian cultures. Among the domesticated animals introduced to Europeans were the llama, guinea pig, and turkey. The Native peoples of the western hemisphere introduced Europeans to many new plants and taught them how to plant, cultivate, harvest, and use them. Corn, potatoes, tomatoes, cacao, various beans, squash, pumpkins, peanuts, sweet potatoes, chili peppers, and cassava or manioc are some of the staple foods that originated in the Americas. The world's food supply today depends in good measure on these plants. In addition, non-food products such as rubber, sisal, and cotton were important items.

Tobacco was introduced into Europe first as a medicine and then became popularized through the introduction of smoking and snuffing. Over 50 drugs used in modern medicine were known and used by Amerindians. The most notable are inchona bark, from which quinine was derived to treat malaria; cascara sagrada, used as a laxative; curare, used as a muscle relaxant and anaesthetic; coca, the source of cocaine and novocaine; witch hazel, used for muscular aches and pains; datura, a pain reliever; and ephedra, used to clear nasal passages and sinuses.

These are only a few examples of common elements in Native cultures that Europeans found useful to their survival and prosperity in the New World. During their many centuries of occupation and exploitation of the western hemisphere, the Native peoples had come to terms with the many challenges offered by their environment. The European newcomers quickly became the beneficiaries of this wisdom, accumulated over the millennia of habitation by the original peoples.

ACTIVITIES

KEY TERMS AND CONCEPTS

Identify and briefly explain the historical significance of the following terms and concepts:

- First Nations
- Prehistory
- Land bridge theory
- Inuit
- First contact
- Bison hunt
- League of Five Nations
- Social ladder
- Linguistic families
- Culture areas
- Chiefdoms
- Matrilineal society
- *Kitchi Manito*
- Shaman
- Demographic tragedy

QUESTIONS FOR DISCUSSION

1. When did Canadian and North American "history" begin — with the arrival of the first Europeans, or much earlier?
2. The ancestors of the Native peoples have lived in North America for about 30 000 years, yet most history books skim over their experiences and concentrate almost solely on the 500 years since European contact. Is this historical approach justifiable?
3. To what extent do the major "culture areas" defined and classified by historians and anthropologists tend to stereotype or distort Amerindian experiences? Do they "pigeon-hole" Native groups?

4. The societies of the northern Pacific Coast developed political and social structures similar to those found in Europe at the time of contact. In what ways were the Pacific Northwest and French forms of political and social organization alike? How did they differ?
5. Certain distinct values and beliefs characterized Amerindian culture in pre-contact North America. What were they, and what made them unique at the time?
6. Were the first North Americans more "advanced" than their supposed European civilizers? Argue your case with historical examples from the pre-contact period.
7. The First Nations have a reputation for being conservationists. Were the Native peoples always so inclined? What role, for example, did Amerindians play in the disappearance of the beaver in the hinterland of New France, of the large moose herds in Nova Scotia, and of the bison on the Prairies?

ANALYZING THE EVIDENCE

Amerindian rock art has served as an important source for anthropologists and historians exploring the cultures of the Native peoples. The accompanying photos of two sets of rock paintings are taken from different culture areas. Examine these rock paintings carefully and develop some hypotheses about their significance. What, for example, do the figures suggest about the lives, cultural practices, and traditions of the two tribal groups?

Culture A

Culture B

DEBATE AND DISCUSS

Analyze and take a stand on the issue raised in this statement:

"The study of Native people prior to the arrival of the Europeans is still viewed, not as part of Canadian history, but as the domain of prehistoric archaeology...."

— Bruce G. Trigger, *Natives and Newcomers* (Montreal: McGill–Queen's University Press, 1985).

CHAPTER 2

THE MEETING OF FRIENDS AND FOES

T HE OLD WORLD was once presumed to be the entire world. It consisted of Europe, Asia, and Africa — continents whose inhabitants were believed to represent the three distinct races of humanity. The Amerindians, coming from Asia, were the first people to discover and settle North America, and it is possible that other, later visitors came from Asia. The Europeans were the next Old World peoples to make contact with the Americas, which they called the "New World" because, in spite of scholarly speculations and fabulous sailors' tales, its existence came as quite a surprise. The term "European discovery" now seems strange because we know that North America had been inhabited for thousands of years before the arrival of the Norse *knörrs* and European fishing vessels.

THE EUROCENTRIC VIEW OF THE WORLD

E UROPEANS IN THE "AGE OF DISCOVERY" after A.D. 1000 approached the New World confident in the superiority of their civilization. From the earliest contacts of the Vikings to the later sixteenth-century attempts at exploration and settlement, the Old World intruders shared a deeply ingrained Eurocentric "world view" that influenced their attitudes toward and perceptions of the New World and its possessors, the Amerindians. To the Europeans, exploring this New World was a matter of expanding the limits of human civilization into a "savage," untamed world beyond.[1]

Profound economic, political, social, and cultural changes swept through Europe between the years 1200 and 1500. These changes created both the impetus and the means to explore the seas that lay beyond Europe. Trade between the Mediterranean world and the lands to the east — China, India, and the "Spice Islands" — gradually increased, as did the European demand for spices and luxury goods. Since the control of Mediterranean trade rested with the Italian merchants of Venice and Genoa, western Europeans began seeking new routes to "Cathay" that would bypass the Italian monopoly as well as the Muslims who controlled Middle Eastern trade. Stories of the great riches of China, sparked by Marco Polo's book about his late-thirteenth-century explorations, further heightened interest in Asia. Technological advances associated with the Renaissance — improved navigational methods, maps, and ship construction — all provided new inducements to venture onto the uncharted seas.

THE VIKING DISCOVERIES

T HE FIRST DOCUMENTED EUROPEAN SETTLEMENTS in North America were those of the Norse voyagers known as Vikings. Beginning in the ninth century, Vikings from Scandinavia embarked on campaigns of territorial expansion in continental Europe and beyond. A desire

Johann Froschauer's view of Amerindians, 1505.

to escape political turmoil and chaos in their homeland and pressure on farmlands and fishing grounds drove them to occupy and colonize a chain of islands in the North Atlantic, including the Orkneys, the Shetlands, the Faeroes, and Iceland. These islands would be the Norse stepping stones to Greenland and North America.[2]

Geographically, the Norse were well placed to undertake ocean crossings. A good sailor from Norway, using the prevailing winds from spring to autumn, would likely land in the northern islands, Greenland, or mainland America. Moreover, the Norse knew how to steer their long, shallow, double-ended and square-sailed vessels before a following gale, which could also result in far western landfalls. They sailed by taking sightings on the North Star and by dead-reckoning, estimating their progress on the basis of the velocity of the winds. Like other sailors at the time, they had no way of determining longitude, but they could find the latitude of their destination and with a favourable wind run it down. They observed the changing character and movements of marine life, the run and colour of the sea, the tides, the flights of birds, and the movements of sea ice as well. Thus Europe "discovered" the New World.

THE NORSE SAGAS

From their base in Iceland, the Norse under Eric Rauda (the Red) moved into Greenland in A.D. 986. By this time they had converted to western (Roman Catholic) Christianity. Two settlements were formed on the largely ice-free west coast of the island facing North America. Our chief source of information about their exploits is the sagas, oral epic accounts that were eventually committed to writing in the thirteenth century by Icelandic monks. Other sources of information are royal chronicles, Vatican correspondence, medieval geographical and historical treatises, maps, and recent archaeological digs.[3]

The first recorded voyage to the mainland of North America by a Viking was that of Bjarni Herjulfsson in A.D. 986. Sailing from Norway to Iceland, he was blown off course and landed on the Labrador coast. Soon Greenlanders began visiting the area to pick up cargoes of timber.

Three years later his neighbour, Leif Ericsson, using Bjarni's boat and possibly some of his crew, visited the same regions. First he landed in barren lands covered with flat stones, possibly Baffin Island, which he called Helluland; then he touched a wooded area, possibly Labrador, which he called Markland; finally, he landed in a beautiful bay with abundant meadowlands, which he called Vinland. Here Eric the Red's eldest son set up "booths," or temporary dwellings.

Not earlier than A.D. 1003, Leif's brother, Thorvald Ericsson, set out for Leif's booths and wintered there, living largely on fish. There is reason to suspect that this settlement was at the present archaeological site of Anse-aux-Meadows, Newfoundland, which Dr. Helge Ingstad started excavating in 1960.[4]

FIRST CONTACT WITH "SKRAELINGS"

During the second winter at Leif's booths, Thorvald's men had an encounter with some unidentified Native people whom they called Skraelings, who travelled in kayaks. The Vikings killed eight Skraelings in an unprovoked attack and were subsequently attacked by a large force of Native people. The Vikings' iron weapons were not greatly superior to the Skraelings' bows and arrows, lances, and clubs, and Thorvald was among those killed.

The Icelandic sagas tell us of several ill-fated expeditions. In the spring of 1008 the Icelandic sea captain Thorfinn Karlsefni, accompanied by about 250 men and women, left Greenland to found a farming community at Leif's booths in Vinland. The group found the old settlement site and began building a more permanent settlement, called Straumfjord. The winter was extremely hard, so in the spring Karlsefni and his group sailed south in search of a better site. They settled on a small, land-locked bay that offered good pastures and plenty of fish. At this settlement, called Hop, they were visited by more Skraelings, possibly Montagnais or Beothuks. There was some bartering, and friendly relations were established with these people.

After conflicts arose with the Skraelings over trade and quarrels broke out among the Norse over women, Karlsefni decided to abandon Hop. The little colony moved back up to Straumfjord, where it spent another disconcerting winter. The colonizing scheme collapsed, and all the settlers returned to Greenland. Freydis Ericsdotter organized a final colonization attempt, and then the sagas fall silent on the exploits of the family of Eric the Red. One may wonder if they were the only prominent family involved in colonization schemes, or if the Icelandic monks recorded their exploits and not those of others because they were influential supporters of the Roman Catholic church.

THE VIKING LEGACY

It is uncertain where the colony of Vinland was located, how extensive its settlements were, and precisely when it was abandoned. We do know from one source, however, that in 1121 "Eirik, Bishop of Greenland, went in search of Vinland." It seems reasonable to suppose that a churchman would not have sailed off to a strange and forbidding land unless a group of Vikings to whose needs he could minister were living there. As late as 1347 a ship loaded with lumber from Markland arrived in Norway. By 1397, however, no more than two ships reached Iceland, and none went beyond.

The Vikings were the first European colonizers in northeastern America. Their relations with the Native peoples were not always friendly, as several bloody encounters with Skraelings indicate. They did initiate some barter, in spite of these sometimes tense relations, but were unable either to convert the Native peoples to Christianity (if they tried) or to assimilate them. The Greenland colonies, which provided the springboard for activities in continental Markland and Vinland, managed to survive for five centuries, but their Christianity eventually gave way to Native religions and their people were assimilated by the Inuit.

EARLY MARITIME CONTACTS

THE LINK BETWEEN THE NORSE VOYAGES and the European Renaissance "discovery" of North America was the fishery. The Norse traders began exporting *skreid*, or dried cod, from Iceland in the tenth century. English fishers from Bristol were active off Iceland from about 1412 onward but were expelled from these waters in 1478. They began looking for new fishing grounds and commercial outlets.

THE COD FISHERY

With interest stirring in maritime exploration, Giovanni Caboto (John Cabot) arrived in Bristol from Spain in 1496, carrying word of Christopher Columbus's recent discoveries. He was quickly naturalized, given royal letters-patent, and provided with a small ship equipped by local merchants to go to the "new found land" and exploit its riches. The report of his 1497 voyage confirmed only "that they will fetch so many fish that this kingdom will have no more need of Iceland, from which country there comes a very great store of fish which are called stockfish." Cabot had hoped to find the riches of the Orient, not just this "sea silver."

Fishers from the Atlantic ports of England, Portugal, France, and Spain ventured farther and farther abroad as they harvested the seas. Newfoundland cod entered the markets of western Europe, where there was a great demand for fish because of Catholic dietary practices, at the end of the fifteenth century. In 1510, the cod market at Rouen, France, was organized to become the chief market in western Europe for Newfoundland cod.[5]

The hundreds of vessels that came to the Grand Banks off Newfoundland each season brought their catches green-salted to Europe. This "wet fishery" involved packing the cod with salt in the holds of the ships; it was the method favoured by the French (Bretons and Normans) and Basques. The English, who had less access to salt, anchored their ships in a bay and fished closer to shore from small boats. Their catches were brought on shore, where the fish were headed, gutted, and placed on stages, or flakes, for drying. This inshore fishery was called the "dry fishery."

The dry fishery favoured by the English in Newfoundland required the building of stages, storehouses, and boathouses. Some fishers took up temporary residence in makeshift shelters. Their arrival marked the beginning of bad relations with the Beothuks, who had already had unfortunate encounters with European intruders and were wary of attempts to engage in trade. They were, however, anxious to obtain metal goods and other artifacts, so sometimes plundered the English fishing stations. This inevitably led to retaliatory raids, and the Beothuks retreated into the interior as the English settlements became more numerous and permanent. The confrontations eventually led to the extinction of the Beothuks.[6]

The Micmacs along the shores of the Gulf of St. Lawrence were more anxious and willing to trade. Their contact was most often with the French, Spanish, and Portuguese, who established more amicable relations than the English.

IMAGINARY MEDALLION PORTRAIT OF JOHN CABOT.

By Carlo Barrera Pezzi. From a memoir published in Venice in 1881.

Imaginary medallion portrait of John Cabot.

THE BASQUE WHALERS

In the early 1500s, Spanish Basque fishers started whaling off the coasts of Newfoundland. By the middle of the century, at least nine whaling stations had been established in Labrador. The station at Red Bay had a summer population of at least 900 persons. The Basques hunted two species in particular — Arctic bowhead and white whales — because they had especially thick layers of oil-bearing blubber and long plates of baleen. Whale oil was the chief fuel used in sixteenth-century oil lamps, and baleen was used in dressmaking.

At its height, the Basque whaling operation in Labrador employed at least 2000 people each summer, but the operation seems to have collapsed by the early 1600s. Probably the two species of whales that had been so greatly prized were hunted into near extinction. Also, many whaling ships were pressed into naval service by the Spaniards in the European wars.[7]

Whaling spread from the Spanish Basques to seafarers of other nations. In the latter half of the sixteenth century the French engaged in whaling expeditions in the Gulf of St. Lawrence, and the English were active off the west coast of Newfoundland and the island of Anticosti.[8]

THE WALRUS HUNT

Another attraction for Europeans was the large colonies of walrus, much in demand for their prized ivory tusks, tough hides, and fat oils with sealant properties. The Portuguese began engaging in this trade at Sable Island around 1500 and competed with the French, who established a thriving trade in the early 1600s. Basques were the first Europeans to exploit the rookeries in the Gulf of St. Lawrence. Operating under chartered companies the Portuguese from the 1520s onward, and the French after 1570, joined in the slaughter of the "beast of the great teeth" each year.

An attempt by a company of London merchants to forcibly take over the Magdalen Island operations in 1597 was foiled by a peculiar alliance of Bretons, Basques, and Micmacs. The greed of the Europeans eventually resulted in the extinction of the walrus: the Gulf of St. Lawrence herds were gone by 1680, those of the gulf's north shore by 1704, and those of Sable Island by 1710.[9]

THE AGE OF EUROPEAN EXPLORATION

HISTORIANS HAVE TRADITIONALLY called the period between 1420 and 1620 the "Age of Discovery." It has long been viewed as the beginning of a "heroic age," during which European explorers, and later missionaries and settlers, performed noble deeds. Yet the European intrusion into North America was not always heroic and noble.[10]

PORTUGUESE ACTIVITIES

The Portuguese were masters of navigation and ship construction. Their technical skills gave them the edge over other Europeans in the scramble for trade and resources. They colonized islands off the west coast of Africa and by 1488 had opened a sea route around southern Africa to India. The Treaty of Tordesillas in 1494 divided the New World into two domains — Portuguese and Spanish — whose spheres lay east and west, respectively, of a meridian 1920 kilometres west of the Cape Verde islands. As a result, Portugal claimed Brazil and Spain got "the lion's share," South and Central America.

In 1500 the Portuguese mariner Pedro Alvarez Cabral landed in Brazil, an abundant source of brazilwood and its red dye, which was in great demand by Europe's textile industry. In the lush jungles the Portuguese met the Tupi-Guarani hunters, who had little to offer in trade and who, unlike Africans, were difficult to enslave. It was their nudity, their polygamy, their head hunting, their habit of washing, and their custom of painting their bodies and decorating themselves with bright feathers that established the European stereotype of wild immoral savages.[11]

In 1501 an Azorean, Gaspar Corte-Real, sailed for the "new found lands"; his brother Miguel went to search for him the following year. As a result of the Corte-Real expeditions Europeans concluded that Newfoundland, Labrador, and Greenland were distinct regions. The Portuguese also kidnapped about 50 men and women, probably Beothuks, from the southern regions of Newfoundland to use as slaves. They may have been planning extensive slaving expeditions, similar to those carried out in West Africa. Their captives, however, would not cooperate and discouraged the scheme.

An attempt at permanent settlement was made on Cape Breton Island in 1520–25 by John Alvarez Fagundes. The location of this Portuguese colony is still in doubt, but a French travel book of 1559 claimed that "the natives of the country put an end to the attempt and killed all of those who came there." The Portuguese thereafter restricted their activities in North America to annual fishing voyages. Their maps were the first to represent correctly the Nova Scotian region. However, although Portugal was the first European power to establish an offshore empire, it was not centred on North America.[12]

SPANISH EXPLORATIONS

The Spaniards opened the southern approaches to the Americas. In 1492, Christopher Columbus, with 90 sailors in three small ships, landed in the Bahamas. A small colony was left in Haiti. On his return in February 1493, the news quickly spread in Europe (now apparently ignorant of Viking activities) that Columbus had "found that way never before known to the east" by sailing west. In all, Columbus made four voyages to the New World.

THE SPANISH CONTRACT WITH COLUMBUS, 1492

CHRISTOPHER COLUMBUS'S voyage of 1492 is closely associated in the public mind with the "discovery of the New World." Columbus has been presented as the quintessential fifteenth- or sixteenth-century bold mariner setting out to perform noble deeds for the Spanish crown. However, a closer examination of Columbus's "contract" with King Ferdinand and Queen Isabella and his possible motives may shed a different light on his activities.

Columbus's vision. A detail from a sixteenth-century engraving.

The Genoese mariner drove a hard bargain with the Spanish royalty. Under the terms of the contract, Ferdinand and Isabella financed all but a small portion (one-eighth) of the cost of the expedition. Columbus obtained the small portion from some wealthy friends. The king and queen also agreed to terms that would make the mariner rich and powerful. Although Ferdinand and Isabella later broke their contract with Columbus, its actual terms reveal much about the voyage's objectives:

> First, that your Highnesses as Lords that are of the said oceans make from this time the said Don Christopher Columbus your Admiral in all those islands and mainlands which by his hand and industry shall be discovered or acquired in the said oceans during his life and after his death, his heirs and successors from one to another perpetually.

> Likewise that your Highness make the said Don Christopher your Viceroy and Governor General in all the said islands and mainlands.

> Item that all and whatever merchandise whether it be pearls, precious stones, gold, silver, spices, and other things whatsoever, and merchandise of whatever kind name and manner it may be, which may be bought, bartered, discovered, acquired, or obtained within the limits of the said Admiralty, your Highnesses grant henceforth to the said Don Christopher, and will that he may have and take for himself the tenth part of all of them, deducting all the expenses which may be incurred therein.

Columbus was not the only European who was once thought to be the discoverer of America. In 1499 the Florentine navigator, Amerigo Vespucci, sailed along the southern coasts of South America and began to doubt that the region was part of Asia. He said that it "may be called a new world, since our ancestors had no knowledge of it," but it seemed to him to be "a fourth part of the world." A cosmography published in 1507 mistakenly attributed the first discovery to Amerigo; the "fourth part" became known as America as a result of this mistake.

After Columbus's discoveries and claims, Hispaniola, Puerto Rico, and Cuba became bases for further Spanish penetration in the Caribbean and the Gulf of Mexico region. Juan Ponce de Leon attempted to colonize the Florida mainland between 1513 and 1521. Expeditions were also conducted to northern South America, the Isthmus of Panama, and the Yucatan Peninsula. In 1513, Vasco Nunez de Balboa crossed the Isthmus of Panama and is said to have waded in full armour into the Pacific Ocean, claiming for Spain all lands that touched its waters. Six years later, a Portuguese sailor flying the Spanish flag, Ferdinand Magellan, embarked on an ambitious voyage that took his battered crew around the southern tip of South America, across the Pacific Ocean and, some three years later, limping back to Spain.

THE "BLACK LEGEND" OF THE CONQUISTADORS

The Spaniards waged cruel warfare on the Native peoples and earned a bad reputation: the "Black Legend" of the genocide, or extermination, of Native peoples and cultures. In matters of religion, the conquerors, or conquistadors, offered the Amerindians a choice: submission to Roman Catholic authority or enslavement. They were brutal in their pursuit of tribute, and thousands of Amerindians died working as slaves in mines. Such treatment became so legendary that American historian Francis Parkman wrote in 1867 that "Spanish civilization crushed the Indian."[13]

Hernan Cortés conquered the Aztecs and took control of the entire Valley of Mexico between 1518 and 1521; a decade later Francisco Pizzaro subdued the Incas of Peru. By the 1540s the Spanish had pushed northward into Bolivia and Colombia and organized expeditions to southern North America to search for the fabled, but imaginary, cities of gold — the Seven Cities of Cibola. Although the conquistadors never found the expected treasures of gold in North America, they did explore large portions of the continent from Florida to the Colorado River and earned the hostility of the Amerindians. The Spaniards also introduced the horse, which by 1700 had spread to every Amerindian tribe on the Great Plains.[14]

ENGLISH AND FRENCH RECONNAISSANCE

THE SEARCH FOR A NORTHERN PASSAGE

THE ENGLISH TURNED THEIR ATTENTION to finding a northern passage to the riches of the Orient. The first to test the possibility was John Cabot's son, Sebastian, who set out in 1508 for the Arctic. Sebastian Cabot's expedition reached perhaps as far as the mouth of Hudson Bay before a mutinous crew forced him to turn back.[15]

Between 1553 and 1580, the Muscovy Company failed in its repeated attempts to reach the Orient in the other direction, by a northeast passage over Asia. Its failure apparently convinced English merchants and traders that a northwest passage, rather than an eastern one, was "more commodious for our traffic." In 1576 Martin Frobisher led an expedition to the shores of Baffin Island in search of the elusive passage, but his attention was taken up with loading a dark ore that, when rubbed, appeared to be gold. Two more expeditions were organized to establish working gold mines. The ore, however, turned out to be "fool's gold," and the Cathay Company, of which Frobisher was a partner, was ruined.

Frobisher was the first English explorer to provide Europe with detailed information about the Inuit. On his second journey, an attempt to capture a person who could be trained as an interpreter led to a skirmish in which the English had to retreat to their ships and Frobisher himself was slightly wounded. When Frobisher sailed for home with a couple of tons of "ore," he also brought along a captive man, woman, and child for public exhibition, as proof of having found "Asiatics."

The search for a northwest passage continued, and each successive English effort pushed farther into the northern reaches of the continent. In 1585 John Davis made three journeys northward into a strait that now bears his name. The best-known northern mariner, Henry Hudson, ventured into Hudson Strait in 1610 and sailed southward into a wide expanse of water that he supposed to be the northwest passage to the Orient. However, when the waterway proved to be an inland sea (Hudson Bay), the crew mutinied and the captain and his close associates were set adrift in the ship's boat. Four mutineers survived to tell the tale in England, but Hudson's party was never heard of again.

ABORTIVE ENGLISH SETTLEMENTS

During the reign of Elizabeth I (1558–1603), the English also attempted to counter Spain's imperial activities by reasserting England's supremacy on the seas and establishing colonies in America. The famous English "sea dog" Francis Drake and his fleet circumnavigated the globe in 1578–80, and in the process laid claim to the Pacific coast of the northern part of North America. In 1583, Humphrey Gilbert attempted to establish a colony in Newfoundland, but it collapsed within a year. In 1584, Walter Raleigh explored the Atlantic coast from Virginia to

Henry Hudson, with his loyal crew members and son, cast adrift in Hudson Bay in 1611. Hudson's ill-fated journey renewed interest in finding the Northwest Passage.

the Carolinas and Spanish Florida. He organized two colonizing ventures on Roanoke Island, Virginia, in 1585 and 1587. The Roanoke settlers disappeared; their fate remains a mystery to the present day.[16]

FRENCH EXPLORATIONS

The first recorded North American Native peoples to come to France were the captives of Thomas Aubert of Rouen. They were brought to Dieppe, along with their arms and canoes, in 1508 for public exhibition and baptism. Their presence aroused intellectual speculation as well as religious and commercial interest.[17]

The Florentine Giovanni de Verrazzano was sent by King Francis I in 1524 to survey the coastline between Spanish Florida and Newfoundland. He journeyed along the eastern coast as far north as the Bay of Fundy in search of "some strait to penetrate to the Eastern Ocean." He discovered an unexpected "obstacle of new land" on the route to Asia and established a French claim to the continent on the legal basis of "right of discovery." The fact that Verrazzano was killed and eaten by Caribs in a subsequent journey to the Antilles did little to reassure the French people about the New World and its inhabitants.[18]

THE "LOST COLONY" OF ROANOKE

IN JULY 1587, John White led a group of 119 colonists in a second major attempt to plant an English colony on Roanoke Island, a small island off the coast of present-day North Carolina. Governor White and the colonists christened the settlement Ralegh. Although it was spelled differently, the village was named after Walter Raleigh, the wealthy English noble who most actively promoted the establishment of colonies in America.

After only a few weeks on Roanoke Island, the English colonists realized that their supplies were inadequate and the settlement's survival was threatened. Governor White became so concerned that he returned to England to secure the needed supplies and promised to return to Roanoke — and to his wife and children — within six months. In the next two years White made several attempts to sail back to Roanoke on supply ships, but found the route blocked by the warships of the Spanish Armada.

In August 1590, three years after leaving Roanoke, White returned to the settlement to find smoke rising from some burning grass and tree stumps, but no sign of the colonists. The entire colony had disappeared. A search of the island turned up two possible clues to their whereabouts: the word "CROATOAN" was discovered carved into a tree near the settlers' palisades, and the letters "CRO" were carved into another tree nearby. "CROATOAN" had two possible meanings: it might refer to a nearby tribe of Amerindians or an island of that name just south of Roanoke, near Cape Hatteras. Five search parties were sent out to Roanoke between 1590 and 1602, but all attempts to find the "lost colonists" were in vain.

What happened to the Roanoke colonists? The mystery became a popular topic of conversation in England in the early 1600s, and several theories were proposed to explain their disappearance. Some people believed that since Spain and England were at war, the colonists were probably captured and killed by Spaniards. A second theory held that the Roanoke colonists — believing that Governor White would not return — built small boats and met their end trying to sail back to England through the so-called "graveyard of the Atlantic." In the early 1600s, many English people believed that the colonists had been captured and possibly enslaved by Amerindians. One final theory is that the Roanoke settlers went off to live with the Croatoan Indians, as indicated by the tree carvings. The notion that they were assimilated by the Amerindians gained some credence in 1719, when a tribe of English-speaking, light-skinned Amerindians was discovered in Robeson County, North Carolina — about 320 kilometres from the abandoned Roanoke site. To this day, the disappearance of the colony remains a mystery.

But tales of Spanish treasure motivated the French king in 1534 to commission Jacques Cartier, a navigator from St. Malo, to undertake a voyage to the "newly found land to discover certain isles and countries" believed to have "great quantities of gold and other riches." Cartier sailed directly to the Strait of Belle Isle and into the Gulf of St. Lawrence, following the route of the fishers. He met some Micmacs who were anxious to trade. They were, however, no longer satisfied with receiving trinkets and baubles. They wanted more substantial manufactured goods such as knives and iron goods, while the French were interested in acquiring the cloaks of beaver pelts that the Micmacs had worn for a season or two so that the long guard hairs had been rubbed out and the fur rendered smooth and glossy through the effects of the movement and body heat of the wearers. This prime-quality fur, or "greasy beaver" (*castor gras*), was eagerly sought by Parisian hatmakers, especially when it became stylish to wear broad-brimmed felt hats.

Some days later, Cartier encountered a party of Laurentian Iroquois who had come up with their headman, Donnacona, to fish along the Gaspé coast. After setting up a large cross at Gaspé to serve as a "landmark and navigational aid" and not, as the chief suspected, to claim the territory for France, Cartier's crew kidnapped the chief's two sons and took them to France with the intention of having them learn French so that they might serve as guides and interpreters on a later voyage.

SEEKING THE "KINGDOM OF THE SAGUENAY"

Since Cartier's 1534 voyage had found a possible route to the Orient, King Francis I sent the explorer with three ships to continue the search the following year. In late September 1535, Cartier set up a base camp just below the Iroquoian village of Stadacona, near the present site of Quebec City, which then was a cluster of unprotected lodges. The inhabitants were happy to see Donnacona's two sons again, but they became hostile when Cartier indicated that he wanted to press upstream and make contact with more westerly villages.

Nonetheless, Cartier decided to proceed, reaching Hochelaga on the island of Montreal in early October. Here he found "large fields covered with corn" and a mountain of fertile and cultivated slopes, which he named Mount Royal. The settlement near the mountain was a typical

Jacques Cartier.

Iroquoian village surrounded by three palisades for defence and cultivated fields of corn, beans, and pumpkins. From the top of the mountain, Cartier saw the widening of the Ottawa River where it joins the St. Lawrence. He was also regaled with tales of a not-too-distant "kingdom of the Saguenay," supposedly blessed with "immense quantities of gold, rubies, and other rich things."

Cartier and his men barely survived their first winter in "Canada," the name applied by the Stadacona Iroquoians to the immediate region. Because relations with the Amerindians had become strained and uneasy, Cartier and his crew built a fort near their anchored vessels. But the real enemy proved to be a dread disease, scurvy, which killed 25 of his party and incapacitated all but the captain and a handful of others. Just as Cartier's men were beginning to give up hope, one of Donnacona's sons, Domagaya, showed them the curative secret — a drink and a poultice made by boiling the bark and needles of the *annedda*, or white cedar.

When Cartier sailed for France in April 1536, he returned with a wealth of information about the new land, which soon found its way into sixteenth-century maps; ten Iroquoian hostages, including the chief, Donnacona; and some rocks Cartier believed contained gold. This voyage was judged sufficiently successful to convince the French king to confirm France's claims to this northern land by establishing a small settlement there. When Cartier returned to Stadacona five years later without the Amerindian captives, he told the Stadaconians that Donnacona had died but that the others lived in France as "great lords." In fact, nine of the ten had perished in the Old World.[19]

AN ILL-FATED FRENCH SETTLEMENT

In 1541 Cartier was commissioned to undertake a third voyage to "enter deeper into these lands, to converse with the peoples found there and live among them, if need be." This time he chose a new location upstream from Stadacona, at the western end of Cape Diamond, where he built a fort on shore and a second fort at the top of the promontory. Soon he was back on the island of Montreal, at a village called Tutonaguy, intent on exploring the rapids, which he had been told hampered navigation into the upper country. He wintered at his forts near Stadacona, awaiting the arrival of a contingent of settlers who were being sent out under the command of a French Protestant nobleman, Sieur de Roberval.

With no sign of Roberval, Cartier broke up camp in June 1542, loaded a cargo of what was believed to be gold, silver, pearls, and precious stones, and headed for France. In the natural harbour of St. John's, Newfoundland, on his homeward journey, he met the Roberval contingent, outbound with its settlers, cattle, and supplies. Cartier slipped away, leaving Roberval's group to face the Canadian winter and Native hostility before it, too, abandoned the settlement scheme.

FUR TRADE BEACHHEADS

THE FRENCH FUR TRADE had been initiated as early as 1504 by fishers as a sideline to the cod fisheries, but soon groups of merchants formed associations to send vessels to the New World specifically for furs. Fur became the chief source of revenue for French merchants; it also developed into the staple by which the Native peoples could obtain coveted European manufactured goods. The French penetration of North America began with the establishment of beachheads on the north Atlantic coast and the St. Lawrence River entrance to the continent. The initial phase was the ship-to-shore trade carried on from 1580 onward at the Montagnais village of Tadoussac, at the mouth of the Saguenay River. The Montagnais and other Algonkian bands came regularly to Tadoussac to trade their worn beaver cloaks for the most desired European goods — trinkets, beads, mirrors, ribbons, and small bells. Later the Native producers demanded more durable and practical goods, such as needles, knives, kettles, blankets, and firearms.[20]

Competition between French merchant associations became so keen that the crown granted exclusive trading rights, or monopolies, to certain individuals or groups for specific regions and limited periods. Thus, Pierre Du Gua de Monts obtained a monopoly in 1603 for the North American beaver trade on condition that he establish 60 settlers a year in Acadia and support Catholic missionaries among the Micmacs. He recruited Samuel de Champlain to carry out explorations to identify economic prospects, search for mines, and seek out a route to the wealth of Asia.

Under Champlain's direction, the first French beachheads were established at Port Royal in 1605 and Quebec in 1608. It marked the beginning of limited colonization in what became known as New France. Further French trading and fishing bases were established at La Hève and Canceau in Acadia and in Cape Breton.

Agricultural settlers along the salty marshlands of the Bay of Fundy exploited the coastal fisheries and pursued trade with the Micmacs. Miscou and Restigouche, on the Gulf of St. Lawrence, became important fishing centres, Recollet mission stations, and meeting places with the Maliseets, Abenakis, and Micmacs. In the valley of the St. Lawrence, three bridgeheads that would become the chief towns of the French colony — Quebec (1608), Trois-Rivières (1634), and Ville-Marie (1642) — became centres of French settlement and attracted Iroquoian and Algonkian parties.

Vital to French relations with the various bands was the fact that none of these strategic bases was established on lands inhabited by the Native peoples. There was from the outset no displacement of original inhabitants and no question of purchase, cession, or conquest of territories in order to establish New France. The Laurentian Iroquois who had received Jacques Cartier in the sixteenth century had all disappeared, and their territories had become a no-man's-land open to unchallenged European occupation. The first settlements in Newfoundland, English as well as French, were also begun in areas little frequented by the native Beothuks, such as St. Pierre (1604), Placentia (1638), and the southeasterly Avalon peninsula.

CHARTER COMPANY RULE

New France, like Virginia, was founded by monopolists associated with chartered trading companies. From 1603 to 1608, de Monts and his lieutenant, Champlain, enjoyed a monopoly on trade in the St. Lawrence valley but faced stiff competition from Norman and Breton merchants trading illegally. After de Monts's monopoly was cancelled at the end of 1608, his traders succeeded in forming new alliances with the Hurons and Ottawa Valley Algonkins and outflanked their French competitors by arranging to trade with these groups farther up the St. Lawrence River. But, because of heavy competition, de Monts's costs rose and profits fell.

Late in 1613, merchants from Saint Malo and Rouen formed the *Compagnie du Canada* and obtained a monopoly for 11 years in return for presenting the viceroy with a horse annually, paying Champlain's salary and expenses, and establishing a handful of settlers at Quebec. Like most trading companies, however, the *Compagnie du Canada* was in the business of trading for furs and loath to carry out even modest colonization. By 1627, after 20 years of promoting "growth," Champlain's colony numbered only 65 colonists.

In 1627 King Louis XIII's first minister, Cardinal Richelieu, organized a group of wealthy noblemen into a royal charter company, the *Compagnie de la Nouvelle-France* (One Hundred Associates), and gave them the property, trade monopoly, and administrative jurisdiction over the Laurentian colony in return for bringing out 200 settlers a year for 15 years, maintaining the number of clergy needed, and paying the soldiers required to defend the colonies against Iroquois threats. Since Champlain in 1609 had openly supported the Algonkians and Hurons in their wars against the Iroquois Five Nations, the latter had intermittently attacked the French outpost at Quebec in an effort to dominate the northern fur trade. In 1645, following the establishment of settlements at Trois-Rivières and on the island of Montreal, the Company of One Hundred Associates surrendered its monopoly of the fur trade to the leading colonists, organized as the Community of Habitants, with the obligation to pay all public expenses.

For the next 18 years the trade was directed by colonial entrepreneurs rather than metropolitan merchants, but it remained an export enterprise dependent on the demands of a European market. In 1664 another monopoly company, the *Compagnie des Indes occidentales*, obtained the monopoly of the fur trade and colonial commerce. The colonists, or *habitants*, as they preferred to be called, were given the right to trade freely, but all furs exported had to be delivered to the company warehouse in Quebec. Fur circulated as a currency in the colony, with even the clergy dealing in furs.[21]

Critics of the French fur trade, including Champlain and prominent Jesuit missionaries, argued that French policy should place more emphasis on agriculture and manufactures by artisans than on the exploitation of furs. But the Native peoples had developed a degree of dependency on European goods. If the French had suppressed their trade the Native peoples would turn to the English to the south and on Hudson Bay, become hostile, and force the closure of posts that had been established at Fort Frontenac and Niagara on Lake Ontario and at

Michilimackinac at the junction of the three westernmost Great Lakes, as well as of the Jesuit missions in the "upper country." The colony had also become dependent on the Native peoples. France could not extricate itself from its relationship with the Amerindians unless it withdrew completely from America.

HINTERLAND TRADE WITH THE AMERINDIANS

On arrival in the St. Lawrence valley, the French had been drawn into on ongoing war between the Algonkians and Hurons on the one hand, and the Five Nations Iroquois on the other. As this war developed in the years after 1612, the fur brigades to the Huron territory on Georgian Bay found it difficult to bring their furs via the Ottawa River route to the colony on the St. Lawrence. More and more, the local merchant middlemen sent voyageurs with supplies to the interior, especially up the Ottawa and Mattawa rivers to Lake Nipissing and by way of the French River to Lake Huron — the northern canoe route, as it came to be known. They also had the task of bringing down the furs. Young men in large numbers went off each year to the upper country of Canada to live and trade with the Amerindians. State and church officials were alarmed that such an exodus would slow the development of agriculture along the St. Lawrence, retard the founding of families, and set a poor example of conduct for the Native peoples, whom the missionaries were trying with limited success to convert to Roman Catholicism.

The English also became involved in the hinterland trade. In 1670, a royal charter was granted to the London-based Hudson's Bay Company, which had begun trading operations on the southern shores of the bay, explored by Henry Hudson in 1610. The wealth of furs to be obtained there had been brought to the attention of the London "merchant adventurers" by two Canadian free-traders, Pierre Esprit Radisson and Médard Chouart des Groseilliers. In 1682, the company built York Fort, as well as several smaller posts where small garrisons were left in charge. These posts were visited each summer by the Cree of the interior, who came with canoes loaded with furs, and by the annual supply ships from England as soon as the ice cleared. The unit of comparison for English traders was the pelt of a male or buck beaver; hence a dollar is commonly called a "buck" today.[22]

In response to the English activity on Hudson Bay, French traders led by La Chesnaye formed the *Compagnie du Nord* in 1682. Daniel Duluth built a French trading post on Lake Nipigon and succeeded in diverting more than 1500 Native traders away from the bay. In 1682, the French attacked the Hudson's Bay Company posts and held the region's trade until 1714. Numerous attempts by French officials to regulate the interior trade proved futile. In the upper country of Canada a system of *congés*, or annual official leaves from the governor and intendant at Quebec, was instituted whereby only licensed traders could take up supplies and bring down furs.

Despite the *congés*, unlicensed traders, known as *coureurs de bois*, continued to go up-country; some remained for a number of years among the Native peoples, acting as intermediaries for the licensed traders or covertly for merchants in Montreal. It is possible that holders of *congés* also engaged in illicit trade. Some *coureurs de bois* established families in the upper country and a new cultural group, the *Métis*, emerged in the Great Lakes basin. The system of *congés* was temporarily abandoned in 1696 when an overabundance of furs occurred in France.

In 1716, with the reintroduction of the *congés* system, the fur trade resumed its importance. A new role was assigned to post commanders; these officers of the small detachments of marine troops at the scattered military posts in the upper country were given control of the local trade. Posts were sometimes leased or farmed out, and beginning in 1742 they were even auctioned. Three strategic posts were used to keep out English traders: Frontenac (Kingston), Rouillé (Toronto), and Niagara.

THE CONSEQUENCES OF FUR TRADING

The movement of the fur trade to the interior had a dramatic impact on the Amerindian relationship with the land and wildlife. Traditionally, the Native Peoples had believed that the game animals each had a keeper and that hunters who showed respect to their prey were assured of success. As the Amerindian hunting bands began to produce pelts for the European market, both their traditional subsistence culture and their spiritual "conservationist" attitudes toward nature were slowly eroded. A greater demand arose for European goods such as kettles, knives, cloth, and even food items in order to lighten domestic chores and to allow the women extra time to prepare pelts and hides.

European officials and missionaries hoped to make Amerindians settled agriculturists. But the fur trade, and the resulting Native dependence on European goods, promoted a relentless pursuit of game. The Amerindian hunters concluded that because of the unprecedented spread of epidemic diseases the animals had broken their ancient compact with the Native peoples, so the hunters were justified in killing large numbers of fur-bearers over wider territories.[23] By the late seventeenth century, moose had all but disappeared in Micmac territories and beaver were extremely scarce in the regions bordering the St. Lawrence lowlands. For this reason, the French traders began to venture farther into the upper country, beginning at Fort Frontenac in 1673 and going as far west as Sioux country by 1680, in pursuit of new sources and new trading partners.

Métissage, or the intermarriage of French and Amerindians,

An Amerindian family bartering furs in exchange for guns, trinkets, and blankets from a European trader.

was promoted in New France in the early seventeenth century to overcome a shortage of French women in the colony and to establish kinship ties that would benefit the fur trade and military alliances. Although the Roman Catholic church forbade marriage with non-Christians, a significant Métis population emerged in the interior country, where the *coureurs de bois*, the *voyageurs*, and the garrison troops (including officers) took Native companions "according to the custom of the country." Some of these unions were dissolved when the trader or soldier returned to the Laurentian colony; others were permanent if the French partner remained in the upper country. After 1735, the French state no longer approved of inter-racial unions and discouraged them. But military reports claimed that *métissage* was "a circumstance that draws the ties of alliance closer" and missionaries in the upper country continued to perform mixed marriages to "avoid scandal intolerable to all."[24]

The association of brandy with trading customs was one of the most unfortunate aspects of Native–white contact. Alcoholic beverages were unknown to the first inhabitants, and the Amerindians had considerable difficulty in adjusting to its effects. The church tried repeatedly to stop the traffic in intoxicants, but to no avail. French monarchs and governors generally deplored the evil effects of the trade. Yet officials recognized also that the imported liquors brought the state an attractive revenue, that brandy was essential in keeping the Amerindians attached to French trade and military alliances, and that any attempt to enforce French laws on Native nations would result in confrontation. Competition with the English who supplied their trading partners with rum further encouraged brandy trafficking. Alcohol abuse contributed to violence in Native communities, to social disorganization, and to the physical deterioration of an originally healthy Amerindian population.[25]

FRENCH–AMERINDIAN RELATIONS

The French enjoyed a better relationship with Amerindians in Canada and Acadia than they did in their southern colonies, and much better than did the English colonists. There were a number of reasons for this. First, a consistent and centralized approach to Amerindian peoples helped to stabilize relations. The French were interested in trade, in establishing military posts and mission stations in regions occupied almost exclusively by various bands and tribes. Every year the governor-general of New France left the capital city of Quebec to spend the summer in Montreal and meet with Amerindian chiefs and delegates and the commanders of western posts. Annual gifts, the "king's presents," were distributed to leaders of allied nations. These important meetings were solemn occasions, in which the vocabulary and rituals of Native councils were observed. After 1720, a similar meeting was held each year at Port Toulouse on Île Royale (Cape Breton) with the Micmac chiefs.[26]

Second, although the French claimed sovereignty over large areas of North America, they did so through recognition of the independence and self-government of the Amerindian nations. The French avoided imposing three common characteristics of sovereignty: laws, taxes, and military service. Native nations were governed by their own customs, not French laws. They paid no taxes, but instead were paid for services rendered, for sharing lands on which the French erected forts and mission stations, and for French incursions into their territories. As for military service, they were allies of the French, not subjects, so they had their own military objectives, strategy, and rules of war. In joint expeditions the war chiefs and French officers consulted together to co-ordinate their efforts.[27]

Third, the French restricted their settlements to relatively small regions such as the lower St. Lawrence valley and the Acadian coastline, leaving most of the area of New France to its original inhabitants. There was no displacement or removal of Amerindians to make way for European settlers, as occurred in the English colonies. New France signed no treaties of land surrender with Native peoples and waged no wars to take territory from them. Orders sent to the colony in 1755, for example, were quite explicit: "The Natives are jealous of their liberty, and one could not without committing an injustice take away from them the primitive right of property to the lands on which Providence has given them birth and located them."

Fourth, the French pursued commerce with the Amerindians as part of their political and military interests, not just for economic profit. The French felt obliged to accept all the furs and hides the Amerindians wished to barter, and to do so at exchange rates acceptable to them and in return for goods that met their specifications. As one commentator wrote in 1717, "There is no middle course; one must have the Native either as friend or foe, and whoever wants him as a friend, must furnish him with his necessities at conditions which allow him to procure them." The Amerindian peoples were shrewd traders and could defend their interests, in this case from a position of strength, as the French depended on them in trade and war. It would be incorrect to view Native peoples at this time as victims of exploitation, pawns in imperial wars, and passive subjects of external authority.

Finally, the French system of *réductions* (reserves) differed radically in objective from the reserves of the English colonies. The Anglo-Americans began buying or seizing lands for settlement and left the Native peoples with only small reserves. In New France, the movement was the opposite: Amerindians voluntarily took up residence on specified seigneuries within the area of French colonization under missionary tutelage.[28] It was hoped these "domiciled" people would take up the French language, customs, and occupations. They did adopt Catholicism, but for the most part clung to their ancestral languages, customs, and beliefs. They eventually banded together, as allies of the French crown, under the title of the Seven Nations of Canada. These were originally the Hurons of Lorette, near Quebec; the Iroquois of Kahnawake, the Iroquois of Kanesatake, the Algonkians (Algonkins and Nipissings) of Kanesatake, near Montreal; the Abenakis of Wolinak, the Abenakis of Odanak, near Trois Rivières; and the Iroquois of Akwesasne, near Cornwall.

WOMEN IN AMERINDIAN SOCIETIES

ONE OF THE MANY ASPECTS OF AMERINDIAN SOCIETIES that puzzled and often distressed European Christians was that of women's status and role. To missionaries and colonial officials, Amerindian women were either degraded and enslaved or enjoyed far too much freedom and power vis-à-vis their male counterparts. Whatever the case, Europeans generally agreed that Amerindian women did not conform to their expectations of feminine behaviour. Consequently, European strategies for colonization frequently included attempts to change gender relations in Amerindian societies, particularly the division of labour within families, to conform to western European models.

Historians and anthropologists have found, however, that a gendered division of labour was common among many Amerindian groups. Certain tasks and responsibilities were assigned to women, and other duties were considered to be male prerogatives. Women usually were responsible for the care of infants and small children, and their daily work revolved around the demands of child care. Most of their duties did not take women too far away from their communities, nor did they place children in danger.

A common theme in many Amerindian communities was women's role in producing and distributing food. In agricultural societies, such as those of the Iroquois and Huron of the Great Lakes and St. Lawrence lowlands, men helped clear the land but generally women grew corn, beans, and squash, and thus provided the main food

Amerindian woman painting a hat.

supply. Women also participated in fishing, which contributed much to the diet. They also collected firewood and spun hemp into twine for fishing nets. In nomadic societies, such as those of the Ojibwa, Montagnais, Algonkins, and Cree, that relied more on game and gathered foodstuffs for their survival, men hunted large game, such as caribou, moose, elk, and deer. Women trapped the smaller animals, gathered wild rice, picked berries, found shellfish, prepared food, made clothing, looked after children, and often performed the heavy physical labour of breaking and moving campsites.

In the Amerindian societies of the Pacific coast, which were organized according to hierarchies of wealth and class (with chiefs, nobles, and commoners) and largely depended on the sea for survival, men were the fishers, hunters, and warriors. Like the women of eastern North America, Pacific coast Native women looked after the children, processed fish, collected, prepared, and distributed food, and performed such essential tasks as steering, packing, and carrying when accompanying the men on hunting and fishing expeditions.

The existence of separate tasks for men and women does not necessarily mean that the same kinds of economic, political, and social inequalities that existed between the sexes in western Europe were found in Amerindian societies. Given some of the important differences among Amerindian groups, one should be wary of making sweeping generalizations. It does, however, seem that few women engaged directly in warfare, and (apart from northwestern women) they rarely negotiated with European traders. Yet women often controlled the production and distribution of their communities' food supplies, a role that gave them both economic influence and, in the case of the Iroquois and Huron, political power.

As clan matrons, some women could play a pivotal role in shaping decisions concerning warfare and the fate of captives taken in battle. As the Jesuit missionaries discovered, Huron and Montagnais women could not be easily coerced by men into religious conversion, nor could they count on women's submission to the men on other issues, such as sexual monogamy or male authority over children. In the case of the northwestern nations, those women who belonged to powerful and influential families might, as members of these groups, exercise power and respect as chiefs and counsellors — at a time when European women were officially excluded from much of the formal political sphere.

ENGLISH COLONIZATION

THE FIFTEEN ANGLO-AMERICAN COLONIES

ENGLAND'S EFFORTS TO PLANT COLONIES in America in the early 1600s were inspired largely by English traders and commercial interests. In promoting colonial ventures, they argued that English expansion to the New World would meet imperial competition from Spain and France, improve the nation's foreign trade, and relieve England of its surplus population of urban labourers after the enclosure movement on farmlands. These arguments were used to bolster the campaign of a few English nobles to obtain charters or licences from the crown to establish Anglo-American colonies. Although the English crown was generally unwilling to

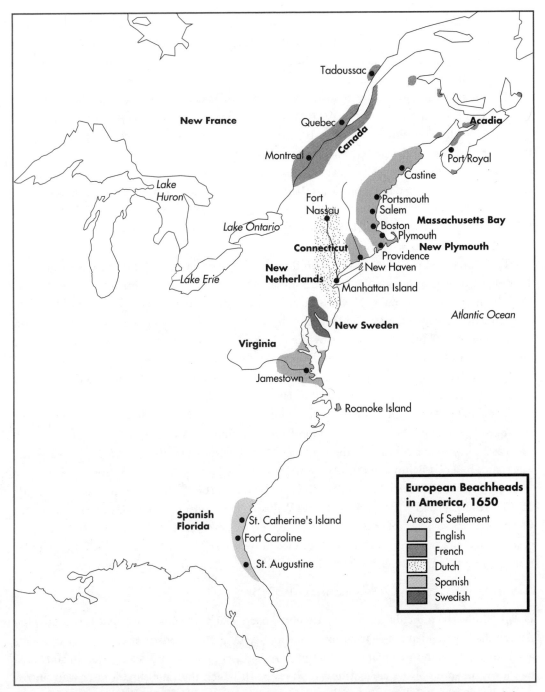

European nations staked out claims in the Americas and then sent colonists to inhabit and thus consolidate their claims to the New World.

organize or finance colonization, it did authorize two types of commercial agencies to plant colonies: the chartered trading company and the proprietorship. For most colonizing groups the enterprise was a profit-making venture, but a few communities of Protestant dissenters made the trans-Atlantic crossing in the hope of finding religious freedom.[29]

The first beachhead in the English invasion of the Atlantic coast was established by the Virginia Company at Jamestown, in 1607. The 104 settlers barely survived food shortages, disease, and the difficult winter of 1609–10. In 1620 the Pilgrims, a colony of separatists from the Church of England, arrived and settled in Plymouth, Massachusetts. Their colony was organized according to the Mayflower Compact, an agreement that established rudimentary self-government. A Puritan colony was planted at Massachusetts Bay under a chartered company in 1630, and in 1691 it assumed governorship of the nearby Plymouth settlement. Connecticut (1662) and Rhode Island (1663) were splinter colonies, originally settled by dissident Protestant sects from Massachusetts.

The Dutch and the Swedes also shared in the founding of the Anglo-American colonies. Two of the fifteen original colonies were initiated — and maintained for a time — by non-English chartered companies: New Netherland, later the colony of New York, by the Dutch West India Company in 1623, and Delaware by a Swedish company in 1638. New Amsterdam (later New York City) was captured by the English in 1664 and became a royal province in 1685. The Swedish colony at Delaware eventually fell under the control of William Penn and the Quakers as a proprietary province. Nova Scotia was acquired by conquest and was ceded to Great Britain by France by the Treaty of Utrecht in 1713.

Most Anglo-American colonies were established as proprietary grants rather than corporate or self-governing colonies. Newfoundland was first settled in the Avalon peninsula in 1610 as a proprietary colony. Of the original fifteen colonies, seven began as proprietorships: Maryland, by Lord Baltimore (1632); New Hampshire, by Captain John Mason (1635); New Jersey, by Sir William Berkeley and Sir George Carteret (1663); the two Carolinas, by friends of Charles II (1663); Pennsylvania, by William Penn (1682); and Georgia, by James Oglethorpe and a board of trustees (1732). In fact, seven-eighths of the Atlantic seaboard was granted to court favourites of the Stuart kings between 1632 and 1682. By 1732 the population of English America was 630 000, far exceeding the 35 000 people in New France.

ANGLO–AMERINDIAN RELATIONS

During the early, difficult years of settlement, particularly at Jamestown and Plymouth, the Amerindians extended some traditional hospitality by giving food to near-starving colonists and showing them how to plant and fertilize crops. Corn, pumpkins, beans, squash, and cranberries were some of the agricultural food crops to which the English colonists were introduced by the Amerindians. In exploring interior woodlands, the settlers also used Native trails. The friendly reception given to the Europeans owed much to the Amerindian belief that the settlers were spiritually powerful beings, or gods like the Native shamans and conjurers. When the first Roanoke settlers in the 1580s carried deadly diseases into the North Carolina coastal region, for example, they were feared by their Amerindian hosts for their spiritual power to kill people at a distance while remaining untouched by sickness.

As the English colonies expanded, Native–white conflicts reached a level and ferocity rarely seen in French America. The clash of cultures in the American colonies stemmed from two main sources of friction: English encroachment on Amerindian ancestral lands, and their relentless "violations" of nature and wildlife. When Amerindian chiefs signed land treaties with the colonists, they believed that such agreements conceded access, but not title, to the land. Most English colonists saw the Native peoples as inferiors, or perhaps "noble savages" at best. English settlers tended to value industry and material gain, believing that success in the New World meant exploiting its resources and remaking the environment. Thus, in ever-increasing numbers, they cut and burned stands of trees, planted fields, and built settlements where Amerindians had once hunted and fished. The eastern woodland tribes, who asserted their rights of possession, refused to accept such encroachments and violations of Mother Earth. They began to resist.

Within three years of the founding of Jamestown, conflict erupted between the Virginia colonists and the Powhatan tribe. The white settlement had been established in Powhatan territory, on ancestral lands. Chief Powhatan, watching the English settle on his people's land, warned the colonists that ignoring Native claims could only lead to enmity and eventual bloodshed. In the hostilities that erupted in 1622, hundreds of Powhatans were either killed or enslaved.

When the Puritans planted their colony in New England, they also encroached on territory inhabited by the Pequot tribe, occupying present-day southern Connecticut and Rhode Island. The growth of settlements aroused the anxiety of the Pequots, and the murder of a much-hated English trader and kidnapper of Amerindians sparked war in 1636. Punitive expeditions were launched from Massachusetts Bay against the Narragansetts and Pequots along the coast. Then, in 1637,

Captain John Mason of the Puritan colony launched a surprise attack in which some 500 Pequot men, women, and children died. Those who survived were sold into slavery. After this attack, the Pequots were dispersed and eventually ceased to exist as a nation.

Puritan missionary preaching Christian salvation to Amerindians.

Forty years after the Pequot War, the Puritans and the Amerindians clashed again. This time the conflict erupted with the Wampanoags, a tribe occupying the south shore of Massachusetts Bay, which was found to be trading land to white "outsiders," or non-members of the bay colony. The Amerindians, angry over territorial encroachments, the seizure of their property and lands, and unfair trade practices, attacked the Plymouth colony and other New England settlements. War raged along the frontier for more than a year. When the warfare ended in 1676, 3000 Amerindians and 600 colonists were dead, and the English emerged triumphant.

The unsettling effect of Amerindian discontent in the western frontier of Virginia sparked a colonial rebellion in 1676. It originated in the back country, where a class of poor white settlers felt threatened. After an escalating series of English atrocities and Amerindian reprisals, the Virginia frontier people, led by the poor back-country farmer Nathaniel Bacon, demanded that Governor Berkeley and the Jamestown élite take action to crush the Doeg and Susquehanna tribes. When Berkeley and the House of the Burgesses (the colonial assembly) attempted to restrain violence on the western frontier, Bacon and his followers launched their own punitive attacks and marched into

St. Regis Church, on Lake Ontario, 1760. A Jesuit priest, Anthony Gordon, joined an Amerindian colony and erected this church, in which he conducted services in the Mohawk language.

Jamestown, forced the governor to flee, and burned the town. Order was finally restored when Bacon died of a fever and an English force of 1000 soldiers subdued the rebel garrisons.[30]

Wars of conquest in the English colonies were accompanied by an equally devastating menace — infectious diseases. The English, as well as the Dutch, French, and Spanish, were aided in establishing a beachhead in America by the diseases they unwittingly introduced. A Dutch traveller in New Netherland reported in 1656 that since the arrival of "the Christians" the Amerindian tribes had been decimated by smallpox epidemics. Similarly, Jesuit missionaries in New France reported dramatic declines in the Huron population. Probably more than half the inhabitants of northeastern North America were carried off by the "invisible armies" of microbes.

ACTIVITIES

KEY TERMS AND CONCEPTS

Identify and briefly explain the historical significance of the following terms and concepts:

- Eurocentric world view
- Cathay
- Norse sagas
- Skraelings
- "Sea silver"
- Dry and wet fishery
- "Heroic age"
- The Black Legend
- English "sea dogs"
- Mount Royal
- Fur trade beachheads
- Charter company rule
- Buck beaver
- *Coureurs de bois*
- *Métissage*
- "King's presents"
- Jamestown
- Mayflower Compact (1620)
- Pequot War
- New England praying towns
- "Invisible armies"

QUESTIONS FOR DISCUSSION

1. The "Eurocentric" world view shaped the thinking of Europeans throughout the "Age of Discovery" after A.D. 1000. How did European monarchs, merchants, navigators, and mapmakers view the New World and its inhabitants?

2. Did the French, English, and Spanish differ significantly in their attitudes toward the New World and the exploitation of its resources?

3. During the period of first contact before 1600, how did the Europeans and the Amerindians view each other? Give some concrete historical examples.

4. Was the coming of the Europeans to the Americas an "invasion" of Amerindian territories in the New World? Do the orthodox interpretations that emphasize European "colonization" and "civilizing the Native peoples" still have some validity?

5. The French, the English, and the Spanish demonstrated different attitudes and earned

different reputations in their relations with the Amerindians. Did their actual treatment of the Native peoples reflect their reputations?

6. The period of Amerindian–European contact is usually interpreted as a time of defeat and subjugation for the Native peoples. How accurate is that portrayal in the case of New France, the Anglo-American colonies, and New Spain?

7. The contact period in colonial North America was largely a time of accommodation and adjustment for both the Europeans and the Amerindians. How did the two peoples affect each other?

ASSESSING HISTORICAL

Interpretations

Examine the following conflicting historical interpretations of three critical issues in Amerindian–European relations. Assess the validity of the various interpretations. Support or refute the argument by using specific historical evidence.

1. The Motives for European Exploration
"Economic motives predominated in the northern approaches during the fifteenth century and colonization lagged far behind the exploitation of primary resources. The religious motive was scarcely invoked except to justify the carving up on non-Christian lands among Christian princes. The great missionary impetus was yet to come."

— Cornelius J. Jaenen, *Friend and Foe* (Toronto: McClelland and Stewart, 1976).

"By 1540...an 'ostentatious show of missionary zeal' began to color royal colonial commissions in an effort to 'clothe the extra-territorial activities of the kings of France in apostolic respectability.' The monarch's worldly and even papal counterparts were not to be taken in by these semantical tactics, nor should we be...."

"The official French faith in malefactors and murders [the explorers and their crews] as missionaries to the Indians must be seen as either a severe case of noble dementia or, more plausible, strong evidence that until the French could plant themselves securely in a New France, all talk of religious conversion was premature and disingenuous."

— James Axtell, *The Invasion Within: The Contest of Cultures in Colonial North America* (New York: Oxford University Press, 1985), pp. 23, 32.

2. The European Treatment of the Amerindians
"Spanish civilization crushed the Indian; English civilization scorned and neglected him; French civilization embraced and cherished him."

— Francis Parkman, *The Jesuits in North America in the Seventeenth Century*, vol. 1 (Toronto, 1899), p. 131.

"The Spanish came as conquerors, but worried whether their actions were justified on moral or legal grounds.... Both the Portuguese and the French came as traders and stayed...in Brazil, in the West Indies, and in Louisiana to develop plantation economies based upon slavery, but in New France the French founded their hegemony on a system of alliances, which made concessions... such as on territorial rights.... The English came to farm, but found they had to conquer in order to stay...."

— Olive P. Dickason, "Europeans and Amerindians: Some Comparative Aspects of Early Contact," *CHA Historical Papers 1979*, p. 200.

3. The Legacy of Contact
"[The] larger societies, French, English, and Indian, waged war with each other on a number of fronts — over trading counters, in courts and councils, in plowed fields and on battlefields, as well as in classrooms and in church pews. Eventually, and with very few exceptions, the Indians lost badly, if not to deadly diseases alone. Sooner or later, in different ways and degrees, Indian communities were deprived of sovereignty,

land, economic independence, mobility, dignity, and living members."

— James Axtell, *The Invasion Within* (New York: Oxford University Press, 1985), p. 331.

"Acculturation is a two-way process. The French were affected by contact too. When any culture is transplanted it changes and varies, but such adaptations are more marked when the society comes into contact and into conflict with other cultures. There follows an exchange and interaction of cultures which can...enrich or impoverish both. Cultural métissage results, out of which a new culture can emerge. In a limited way this is what began to occur in New France in the seventeenth century."

— Cornelius J. Jaenen, *Friend and Foe* (Toronto: McClelland and Stewart, 1976), p. 196.

CHAPTER 3

VISIONS OF THE PERFECTIBLE SOCIETY

W HEN GIOVANNI DA VERRAZZANO in 1524 gave the northern continent the name *Nova Gallia*, he envisaged the extension of French rule over all the vast lands north of Spanish Florida. France, like its European rivals, dreamed not only of incorporating the Native peoples of America into its empire but also of planting colonies under its control. The dreams of the pioneering Europeans must be examined. The invasion of America — for so it was in the eyes of the Native peoples who had occupied it since time immemorial — has been described as motivated by the European search for "gold, glory, and God," and as a struggle for "fish, furs, and farmlands."

The French, like the English and the Spanish, became involved in the New World for many reasons. New France was a term that implied optimism, that conjured up visions of a powerful and prosperous overseas extension of the greatest power in western Europe. This vision included the finding of treasures and the possibility of pursuing profitable ventures.

EARLY VISIONS OF GOLD, GLORY, AND GOD

THE HOPE OF A NORTHERN PERU

F ROM THEIR FIRST SIGHTING OF THE NEW WORLD, the French hoped to find the equivalent of the fabulous treasures of New Spain, a "northern Peru" with productive mines. All the merchant associations and commercial companies that obtained royal charters for the exploitation of the New World hoped to reap rapid returns on their investments. Samuel de Champlain, however, was as disappointed as Cartier had been three-quarters of a century earlier. The gold, silver, and diamonds sent from Canada to France proved to be inferior and infinitely less valuable minerals. Champlain explored the deposits of copper, lead, and silver in Acadia and noted the seams of coal in Cape Breton. Since these were not the precious metals hoped for and since the fabulous kingdom of the Saguenay described to Cartier remained elusive, France's attention shifted to exploring the interior for a water route to the Orient.[1]

Explorers, missionaries, and traders who journeyed into the hinterland of Canada always hoped to find precious metals and exotic products. A reconnaissance mission sent into the Great Lakes basin in 1671 investigated the copper seams of the north shore of Lake Superior and the lead deposits of the Illinois country, long known to the Native peoples, but they offered few rewards. New France's economy would not be based on fabulous treasures plundered from Amerindians or taken from mines as rich as those of Peru and Mexico. France had to be content with the "sea silver," or cod, which was four times more valuable than the second staple product of the colony — furs.

LESCARBOT'S VISION OF ACADIA

Many Europeans saw colonization as an opportunity to create a purified society, a truly new and better version of the Old World, a place where the oppressed, unfortunate, disadvantaged, and persecuted could have new opportunities. Some saw colonies as a place where lost fortunes might be recouped and new ones gained, where careers might be advanced, or simply where life would be simpler and less restricted by tradition and convention.

In 1606 a Parisian lawyer, Marc Lescarbot, arrived in Port Royal to spend a year in the colony of Acadia (now Nova Scotia). He recorded his impressions in the first history of the colony, *Histoire de la Nouvelle-France*, published in Paris in 1609. He said that France's lower classes "gain nothing without incredible pains and labour" while the Amerindians "have abundance in every necessary of life." Therefore, poor French people should leave the "salt sea" of Old France and "go drink of the fresh waters of Port Royal in la Nouvelle-France." This is the first expression of a humanist vision of a better world, a New World colony where the downtrodden and oppressed of Europe would find new hope and an opportunity to build a better life and better society.[2]

Lescarbot was also remarkable for his tolerant attitude toward Protestants and Jews. However, the French authorities forbade the settlement of non–Roman Catholics in Acadia in 1659. In contrast, flight from religious persecution lay at the foundation of several English colonies — notably for the Pilgrims in Massachusetts, the Catholics in Maryland, and the Quakers in Pennsylvania.

Acadia was conceived with great hope, but it soon fell short of French expectations. Port Royal barely survived because it was not essential to the French fishery. The French settlers chose to establish their homes along the rich tidal marshlands of the eastern shore of the Bay of Fundy; thus they did not displace the Micmacs, who inhabited the inland portions of the peninsula, but rather maintained good relations with them. Agriculture prospered, a few schools and mills were built, and Capuchin friars came to assume pastoral and missionary duties. Yet there was little communication with either France or Canada.

Acadia soon began to show signs of being a marginal colony in the French world. The region was not organized along traditional institutional lines. There were no *seigneuries*; instead, the settlers held their lands directly from the crown. There were no militia districts organized for colonial defence; and the missions were not organized into parishes, with resident priests supported by tithes. The Acadians were much attached to their land, self-reliant, independent, and probably distinguished by their attachment to the patriarchal family. The fact that in a century they experienced fourteen changes of allegiance made them turn even more inward on themselves. By 1670 they numbered less than a thousand.[3]

CHAMPLAIN'S DREAM FOR CANADA

Father Louis Hennepin's sketch of Niagara Falls.

In 1618 Champlain proposed a colonization scheme, centred on a showpiece city to be called *Ludovica*, at the site of Quebec. It was to be a free port and major commercial *entrepôt* for the France–China trade. At this time he was still convinced he would find a water route through the American continent to the Orient, and he asserted that from Ludovica one could "easily reach the Kingdom of China and the East Indies from which we would derive great riches." Nothing came of Champlain's grandiose scheme. With no obvious route to the Orient, no evidence of gold or riches, and no willing French investors, the incentive in France for building a Laurentian duty-free port evaporated.

The more practical elements of Champlain's vision were retained. The maintenance of a commercial centre with a small agricultural support base, which did not neglect either the pursuit of the fur trade or the evangelization of the Native peoples, appeared to be in line with the views of the French court and the Roman Catholic church. However, the financial backers were merchants especially interested in the fur trade. They were not interested in active colonization, which might detract from an activity that did not require a large European labour force.[4]

"REDUCING AMERINDIANS TO HOSTILITY": THE ENGLISH PROTESTANT MISSIONS*

WHILE THE JESUITS AND RECOLLETS were carrying on their missionary work in New France, English Protestant missionaries were also at work in the eastern North American colonies. The French Roman Catholics enjoyed early success in the struggle for Amerindian souls, but most English Protestants believed that, once the Native peoples recognized and grew to appreciate the benefits of British material prosperity, conversions to their faith would follow. So confident were the English colonizers of their cultural superiority that they could envision the Amerindians calling, "Come over and help us," a message emblazoned on the official 1629 seal of the Massachusetts Bay Colony.

Protestant missionaries in English America from the early seventeenth century onward pursued a unique Christianizing mission. Up until the 1760s, the vast majority of Protestant missionaries believed that "in order to make them Christians, they must first be made [civilized] men." To the leaders of colonial Massachusetts, New Plymouth, and other colonies, wholesome laws and English schools for the Native peoples were the chosen ways to "reduce them to Civillitie and the knowledge of God."

NEW ENGLAND "PRAYING TOWNS"

Perhaps the most important agency of Protestant conversion was the so-called "New England praying town." The first such experiment in "reducing Amerindian disorder" was established in 1651 at Natick under the watchful supervision of John Eliot (1604–90), minister of First Church in Roxbury, Massachusetts. The purpose of the resettlement project, according to the founding committee's 1646 instructions, was to set aside land "for the incuragement [sic] of the Indians to live in an orderly way amongst us." Like the reserves established by the Roman Catholics in New France, the "praying town" was set up in the hope of segregating Christian converts from the poor example of the backwoods farmer or trapper and the lure of the Amerindian's "pagan ways." It was also aimed at breaking the Amerindians of their migratory or wandering habits by settling them in English-style towns with colonial houses and the latest English technology.

The Massachusetts authorities insisted that Amerindians who chose to adopt the Christian faith and resettle in "praying towns" did so freely and of their own volition. But

* A synopsis of James Axtell, *The Invasion Within* (New York: Oxford University Press, 1985), chapters 7 and 11.

for Native peoples deprived of their ancestral lands and struggling to survive, the New England praying town was one of the few alternatives conquest had left them. Like colonial institutions of confinement, the praying towns sought — in John Eliot's words — to "convince, bridle, restrain, and civilize" the Amerindians and also to "humble them." For the Amerindian, becoming a Christian meant assuming the demeanour of tame cattle — docile, obedient, and submissive.

THE RECORD OF THE MISSIONS

The English Protestant missions, which were all based on the "civilize first" philosophy, had only limited evangelical success. Unlike the Roman Catholic missions of New France, they were confined almost exclusively throughout the seventeenth century to a small area, specifically southern New England. Fourteen praying towns were created before the "Indian war" of 1676 upset mission activities, but none ever approached the scale or effectiveness of Natick. At the height of the movement, around 1674, about 2300 Amerindians had sought refuge in the praying towns, fleeing disease-ravaged tribes and English military actions, and having been dispossessed of their lands. By 1776, there had been at various times in New England 22 Amerindian churches, 90 praying towns or reserves, and about 130 Native preachers. Although most surviving Amerindians spoke English and had adopted white ways, only perhaps 500 ever became Anglicized Christians.

RICHELIEU'S COMMERCIAL OUTPOST

Cardinal Richelieu, who had become the king's chief minister in 1624, organized the Company of One Hundred Associates in 1627 to administer, settle, and develop New France. Under the charter, the company had an obligation to bring out 4000 settlers over a 15-year period, providing them with employment and their basic needs for the first three years. Three priests were to be maintained in each settlement at company expense as well. Settlers had to be "natural-born French Catholics," which meant that naturalized foreigners and Protestants could not become permanent residents. Settlers were allowed to hunt and trade for furs, but only the company could export furs from the colony.

In exchange for a monopoly on trade in all lands between Florida and the Arctic Circle, Cardinal Richelieu had managed to extract a commitment from the French investors to undertake colonization and support missionary work. This was essential because France was already behind both England and the Netherlands in developing the lands it claimed in America. By this time Virginia had a representative assembly and over 2000 colonists, New England's population was three times as great, and even New Netherland claimed more people than New France.

The prospects of commercial gain and vigorous colonization were soon dashed. First, the supply ships of 1628, with hundreds of settlers, livestock, tools, implements, and supplies, were captured at sea. Then Quebec itself was captured by the English Kirke brothers and occupied from 1629 to 1632. Thus, by the time of Champlain's death in 1635, the Canadian colony still had only a few hundred people, and the prospects of deriving great wealth from its resources were considerably dampened. By 1645, it still had only about 600 settlers and the company was heavily indebted, having never made any profits. The Company of One Hundred Associates then transferred its trade monopoly to the Community of *Habitants*, a group of about a dozen colonial merchants who had no interest in colonization.[5]

DREAMS OF A HINTERLAND EMPIRE

After New France became a royal colony in 1663, ambitious colonial administrators actively promoted the idea of building a dynamic French commercial empire in America. The first intendant, Jean Talon (who served twice, in 1665–68 and 1670–72), intimated that the crown could "form a great kingdom and found a monarchy, or at least a very considerable state" in North America. He wanted more immigrants, investments in colonial industries, and permission to trade directly with other colonies. Talon wanted support for a plan to develop the upper country or hinterland and at the same time forestall English colonization by confining the English to the Atlantic seaboard. But the replies from France indicated that it was not in the king's interests to stimulate colonial industry, to detract from the power and glory of the mother country and her monarch, or to extend settlement beyond the St. Lawrence valley.

Jean Talon, intendant of New France, 1665–68 and 1670–72.

When Governor Louis de Baude, the Comte de Frontenac, sanctioned a series of trade activities and explorations in the Lake Ontario region after 1672, he had visions of commercial expansion. Frontenac may well have been promoting his own personal interests, or those of Réné-Robert Cavelier, Sieur de La Salle, and other traders of the Montreal region. The founding of Fort Frontenac (Kingston) in 1672–73 as a trading and military post brought a reprimand from Louis XIV. The king stated that he had no desire to see the colonial inhabitants "spread as much as they have done in the past" but preferred New France to remain a compact colony along the St. Lawrence valley, in "those regions closest to the sea coasts and to communication with France."

JOHN WINTHROP AND THE "CITY UPON A HILL": THE NEW ENGLAND PURITAN VISION

THE PURITANS OF NEW ENGLAND attempted to fashion political and social institutions that might realize the "perfectible society" in America. A close analysis of the Puritan doctrine and philosophy reveals much about the origins of American social order, community feeling, and religious values and, quite possibly, about the meaning of the American national experience.

Under its first governor, John Winthrop, the Puritan colony at Massachusetts Bay, established in 1630 near present-day Boston, set out to create a "City Upon a Hill" — an experiment in creating an ideal Puritan community that might serve as an example to the world. This Puritan idealism is considered to represent the predominant religious philosophy and intellectual outlook of New England's first colonists. Since the descendants of New Englanders later pioneered in the American interior and the West, the Puritan influence is sometimes identified with American civilization itself.

In American national mythology, the "City Upon a Hill" is commonly associated with a great experiment in self-government. John Winthrop and the New England Puritans are portrayed as the torchbearers of religious liberty and political freedom, the touchstones of the American liberal tradition. Yet critics point out that Massachusetts under Winthrop was more of a theocracy than a democracy, a society dominated by Puritan ministers and lay leaders who maintained a rigid religious orthodoxy and worked to strengthen their own political power. Independent-minded Puritans like Robert Williams and Anne Hutchinson, they contend, were banished from the colony for challenging the orthodox doctrines and expressing dissenting views. Elements of both interpretations can be seen in this excerpt from Winthrop's writings:

John Winthrop, an English Puritan lawyer, left England in 1630 to found the "City Upon a Hill" and became governor of the Massachusetts Bay Colony.

We have created a City upon a Hill.... The Lord will expect a strict performance from us.... There is a twofold liberty — natural (I mean as our nature is now corrupt), and civil or federal. The first is common to man, with beasts and other creatures. By this, man, as he stands in relation to man simply, hath liberty to do what he lists; it is a liberty to evil as well as to good. This liberty is incompatible and inconsistent with authority, and cannot endure the least restraint of the most just authority. The exercise and maintaining of this liberty makes men grow more evil and in time to be worse than brute beasts: *omnes sumus licentia deteriores* [we are all worse for liberty]. This is that great enemy of truth and peace, that wild beast, which all the ordinances of God are bent against to restrain and subdue it. The other kind of liberty I call civil or federal; it may also be termed moral, in reference to the covenant between God and man in the moral law, and the politic covenants and constitutions amongst men themselves. This liberty is the proper end and object of authority and cannot subsist without it; and it is a liberty to that only which is good, just, and honest. This liberty you are to stand for, with the hazard not only of your goods, but of your lives, if need be. Whatsoever crosseth this is not authority, but a distemper thereof. This liberty is maintained and exercised in a way of subjection to authority; it is of the same kind of liberty wherewith Christ hath made us free....

John Winthrop's *Journal*, excerpts (1630 and 1645).

Hopes of creating "a great and considerable" French state in America required an infusion of people. France was populous compared with her neighbours, but in the seventeenth century there were few inducements for people to leave their European homeland, endure the arduous trans-Atlantic crossing, and start anew in a somewhat inhospitable land. France's population of 16 to 18 million was not overcrowded, its agricultural base was sound, and even persecuted French Huguenots — dominant in commerce and industry — were inclined to remain at home. Jean-Baptiste Colbert, the first minister of marine and colonies, vetoed large-scale emigration on the grounds that France must not be depopulated or its commerce and industry diffused.[6]

VISIONS OF CHRISTIAN UTOPIAS

THE EARLY SEVENTEENTH CENTURY was a period of religious revival in France, which gave an impetus to foreign and domestic missions, the creation of new religious orders and lay associations, the establishment of houses of charity, hospitals, and schools, and a reformation of religious practices. In North America the militant, aggressive, highly organized, and well-supported Society of Jesus spearheaded French missionary work. The Jesuits became the chief agents for the establishment of a "New Jerusalem, blessed by God and made up of citizens destined for heaven." To achieve that result, four "holy experiments" were attempted in New France.

CHRISTIAN HURONIA

The Jesuits had visions of turning Huronia, the confederacy of the Huron nations, into a model Christian community in New France, with themselves as the intermediaries between the crown and their converts. Father Le Jeune could write in 1635 that "it seems as if God shed the dew of his grace much more abundantly upon this New France than upon the old, and that the internal consolations and the Divine infusions are much stronger here, and hearts more on fire." Some religious enthusiasts even speculated that the Native peoples were of Jewish origin, perhaps descendants of the fabled Ten Lost Tribes of Israel, and so likely candidates for immediate mass conversion to Roman Catholicism.

From their missionary headquarters at Ste. Marie (now near Midland, Ontario), established in 1639, the Jesuits visited the Huron and Neutral villages, preached the gospel, and cared as best they could for the sick and dying as epidemics ravaged the region. Some notable gains were made — an estimated quarter of the population accepted baptism — but this broke the unity of Huron society and introduced a religious factionalism that even entered the Huron Confederacy council. Although the Huron villages were concentrated in a compact area and were economically reasonably secure, the concentrated Iroquois raids of 1648–49 succeeded in terrorizing them. They abandoned their territory; as one village after another fell before the Iroquois attacks, panic set in. The Jesuits, seeing this collapse of the confederacy, set their fortified compound of Ste. Marie ablaze. Their dream of a Huron Christian community went up in smoke in 1649.[7]

THE SILLERY *RÉDUCTION*

A second experiment was the Sillery *réduction* (or reserve, as it was later called), a Native settlement near French farmers and the town of Quebec. The missionary Paul Le Jeune had become convinced during a journey among nomadic northern Algonkian bands that they could be successfully converted only if they were resettled on agricultural lands within the European community, where families would be raised in a French and Catholic milieu. It seemed essential to him that nomadic bands give up their traditional way of life and adopt a sedentary agricultural life-style as an aid to their "civilization" and Christianization. The *réduction* was a model community that the Jesuits had first established in South America. Unlike the reserves established in the English colonies, it was not designed to restrict Native habitation and make room for European settlement.

A wealthy donor, Noël Brûlart de Sillery, provided them with land near Quebec and the means to build a chapel, houses, and other buildings, as well as to hire labourers to clear the land on which Algonkian converts were settled. By 1651, Huron refugees from the Iroquois war took up residence at Sillery. They subsequently moved farther from the town of Quebec, and their descendants today are located at Wendake (Nouvelle Lorette).[8]

WILLIAM PENN'S "HAVEN IN THE WOODS"

ONE OF THE MOST REMARKABLE and unusual proprietary colonies was Pennsylvania. In 1681, Charles II gave a tract of land between New York and Maryland to William Penn (1644–1718) in payment of a debt the king owed Penn's father.* Although Charles was generally free in giving away American possessions, the grant of Pennsylvania (literally, "Penn's Woods") was unusual because Penn was a member of the Society of Friends (Quakers), and the colony was intended to provide a home in the New World for his community of worshippers.

The Society of Friends was a religious sect that had suffered much persecution in England for its beliefs and practices. It was founded by George Fox, an itinerant lay preacher who had great spiritual gifts. Appealing mostly to the English lower classes, Fox preached that all men *and women* were equal in the eyes of God. True religious faith, the Quakers believed, required no hierarchy of priests (as in the Roman Catholic Church or Church of England), nor learned ministers (as in the Puritan religion). Fox and the Friends proclaimed that every human being possessed an "inner light" — the power to communicate directly with God.

The Quaker doctrine challenged many accepted principles and practices in British society. If all people had a spark of godliness within them, then fighting wars, bearing arms against others, and even paying taxes to support armies were morally wrong. If all men and women were equal before God, then no one should be compelled to show fealty to nobles or monarchs, and women as well as men had every right to preach the faith. To many wealthy and powerful people, such Quaker beliefs threatened the very basis of society.

As the Church of England stepped up its efforts to rid society of dissenting, nonconformist groups, Penn sought a refuge for himself and his fellow believers. Not only did he seek freedom from religious persecution, he also envisioned Pennsylvania as the ideal place for a "holy experiment" in Quaker principles. In his preface to George Fox's *Journal*, he explained those principles in the Quaker idiom:

> [T]he light of Christ within, as God's gift for man's salvation. This, I say, is as the root of the goodly tree of doctrines that grew and branched out from it, which I shall now mention in their natural and experimental order.
>
> First, repentance from dead works to serve the living God. Which comprehends three operations: first, a sight of sin; secondly, a sense and godly sorrow for sin; thirdly,

* See Rufus Jones, *The Quakers in the American Colonies* (New York: W. W. Norton, 1966), chapter 3 and book 5.

an amendment for the time to come. This was the repentance they preached and pressed and a natural result from the principle they turned all people unto. For of light came sight, and of sight came sense and sorrow, and of sense and sorrow came amendment of life.... None can come to know Christ to be their sacrifice that reject Him as their sanctifier, the end of His coming being to save His people from the nature and defilement as well as guilt of sin; and...therefore those that resist His light and spirit make His coming and offering of none effect to them.

From hence sprang a second doctrine they were led to declare as the mark of the price of the high calling to all true Christians, viz., perfection from sin, according to the Scriptures of truth, which testify it to be the end of Christ's coming and the nature of His Kingdom, and for which His spirit was and is given, viz., to be perfect as our Heavenly Father is perfect, and holy because God is holy....

Thirdly, this leads to an acknowledgment of eternal rewards and punishments, as they have good reason; for else of all people certainly they must be the most miserable, who for above forty years have been exceeding great sufferers for their profession, and in some cases treated worse than the worst of men, yea, as the refuse and offscouring of all things.

This was the purport of their doctrine and ministry, which, for the most part, is what other professors of Christianity pretend to hold in words and forms, but not in the power of godliness, which, generally speaking, has been long lost by men's departing from that principle and seed of life that is in man... and by which he can only be quickened in his mind to serve the living God in newness of life....

William Penn, "For of Light Came Sight."

Penn's colony proved to be quite different from the other English colonies. Religious toleration was granted to all believers in one God. Amerindian rights were generally recognized; land was purchased from the Delaware River valley tribes, usually at a fair price. A planned city was designed and constructed as the colony's capital, Philadelphia ("city of brotherly love"). The colony's government, consisting of a bicameral elected legislature (until 1701), was the most democratic of the colonies. With Penn's active encouragement, settlers from Switzerland and Germany as well as Britain poured into Pennsylvania, often seeking freedom from religious persecution. Swiss and German Protestants, in particular, found a haven in Penn's woods and later became the so-called "Pennsylvania Dutch." With its liberal and democratic ways, Pennsylvania stood out in stark contrast to the hierarchical and ordered society of New France.

VILLE-MARIE

Another "holy experiment" was Ville-Marie, a Utopian venture on the strategic island of Montreal conceived and supported by French *dévots*. These lay zealots were members of the Company of the Holy Sacrament, who organized the Society of Notre-Dame de Montréal, which began clearing land and erecting a town on the island in 1642. Ville-Marie was dedicated to the Virgin Mary and had as its avowed purpose the conversion of the Native peoples to Roman Catholicism.

Since there were no permanent Native encampments in the immediate area, the small Ville-Marie school and hospital served primarily the French settlers. By 1663 the religious enthusiasts who had invested in this model Christian community were both indebted and discouraged. Their association was dissolved, the island became the property of a community of secular priests, the Sulpicians of Paris, and thereafter the utopian Ville-Marie gave way to a more secular Montreal.[9]

BISHOP LAVAL'S THEOCRATIC VISION

A final experiment was the attempt by the first colonial bishop, François de Laval, to fashion a kind of theocratic rule, or government dominated by the priesthood in the name of God. Arriving in New France in 1659 as Vicar Apostolic, Laval sought to live in community with his

Bishop François de Laval.

Bishop Saint-Vallier.

diocesan clergy and to control all parish appointments and finances through the centralized institution of the Seminary of Quebec. He saw in such a system, which was unusual in the framework of the national Roman Catholic church in France, a return to the organization of the church in apostolic times as well as a means of control necessary in an unorganized territory. His vision was nurtured by an idealization of the primitive church and a pragmatic sense of administration. It was shared by Mother Marie de l'Incarnation, first superior of the Ursuline sisters in the colony, whose extensive correspondence about colonial affairs and theological writings are of great interest today.

Laval's vision of creating an ideal church and revitalizing the old faith in a New World was soon destroyed. Rome and Paris were unable to agree on the terms for the creation of a diocese (bishopric) until 1674, 15 years after Laval's arrival. Furthermore, after 1663 the monarchy occasionally intervened to limit Laval's control over religious matters such as parish appointments and settling the rate of tithes. While recognizing the authority of the Papacy, the French church had little sympathy for Laval's theocratic experiment. It remained orthodox in doctrine and committed to the principle that loyal subjects ought to adopt the monarch's religion.[10]

VISIONS OF A TRANSPLANTED *ANCIEN RÉGIME*

WHILE THE ANGLO-AMERICAN COLONIES evolved slowly toward representative government and individual "rights and privileges," New France retained the paternalist, hierarchical, and stratified structure of the *ancien régime* of France. The traditional institutions of France — an authoritarian administration, a *seigneurial* landholding system, a national church, a military establishment — were all transplanted to New France. Even though they were somewhat transformed in the early stages by the new colonial environment, these four basic power structures remained essentially intact.

In New France, unlike the neighbouring Anglo-American colonies, there would be no moving frontier of settlement, and the *pays d'en haut*, or upper country, would be a key element in the survival of the European colony. In addition to providing the framework for social order, the four hierarchical institutions promoted the formation and maintenance of an élite ruling class, considered essential to the perpetuation of that order.

THE AUTHORITARIAN ADMINISTRATION

In 1663, King Louis XIV abrogated company rule and assumed direct rule over New France, which comprised Acadia, Canada, and its hinterland *pays d'en haut*. This royal government introduced the traditional organization of a French province — a governor of high military rank, an intendant with experience in law and in financial administration, and a system of royal courts. In the case of Canada, the Sovereign Council sat in Quebec to give royal edicts the force of law in the colony and to act as a court of first instance and especially as the court of appeal.

THE ORIGINS OF SELF-GOVERNMENT IN COLONIAL AMERICA

THE COMING OF THE ENGLISH in the early seventeenth century carried the seeds of self-government to America. The English people had enjoyed the "rights and privileges" of parliamentary government for centuries, so it was only natural that institutions like those in Britain would eventually spring up in the English colonies. New France moved closer to the model of old France, but the Anglo-American colonies evolved more quickly than their mother country to democracy.

Since Frederick Jackson Turner's landmark 1893 address to the American Historical Association,* it has been fashionable to attribute the rise of American democratic ideas to the frontier experience in colonial America. Although the influence of the frontier can be overestimated, the availability of a frontier of open land in America undoubtedly had an energizing effect on land-starved European colonists. Though land was not free for the taking, it was nearly so. In seventeenth-century New England, relatively few colonists were landless, and in the Chesapeake colonies to the south the fluidity of society made it possible for most colonists to aspire to move from indentured servant to freeman, from freeman to freeholder, and perhaps even to wealthy landowner. Not only did the frontier experience tend to dissolve European class divisions, it also nurtured the development of democratic ways. The advance of the frontier, according to Turner, "meant a steady movement away from the influence of Europe, a steady growth of independence on American lines."

The first sign of American self-government was probably the establishment of Virginia's House of Burgesses in 1619 and the Pilgrims' Mayflower Compact of 1620. Whether these two developments reflect early expressions of "frontier democracy" or English colonial practice is a much-debated question.

THE CREATION OF THE VIRGINIA HOUSE OF BURGESSES (1619)

The earliest instance of self-government in the English colonies occurred in the company colony of Virginia. After the colony weathered the difficulties and misfortunes of its formative years, the principal leaders in the Virginia Company initiated a series of measures to put the enterprise on a profitable footing, mainly inducements to potential investors and prospective emigrants. In a radical departure from previous policy, the company's partners — led by Sir Edwin Sandys — ordered Governor George Yeardley to convene an assembly of elected representatives from each district of Virginia. Although the governor retained the right to veto any laws and the General Court of the Company in London held the authority to disallow decisions, the establishment of the House of Burgesses did at least allow Virginia settlers to participate in governing the colony.

---

* Frederick Jackson Turner, "The Significance of the Frontier in American History," American Historical Association, *Annual Report 1893*, pp. 199–227.

A set of instructions from the Company Council, dated 1621, set out the intent of company officials in establishing this early self-governing assembly:

> To all people, to whom these presents shall come, be seen, or heard, the treasurer, council, and company of adventurers and planters for the city of London for the first colony of Virginia, send greeting. Know ye, that we, the said treasurer, council, and company, taking into our careful consideration the present state of the said colony of Virginia, and intending by the divine assistance, to settle such a form of government there, as may be to the greatest benefit and comfort of the people, and whereby all injustice, grievances, and oppression may be prevented and kept off as much as possible, from the said colony, have thought fit to make our entrance, by ordering and establishing such supreme councils, as may not only be assisting to the governor for the time being, in the administration of justice, and the executing of other duties to this office belonging, but also, by their vigilant care and prudence, may provide, as well for a remedy of all inconveniences, growing from time to time, as also for advancing of increase, strength, stability, and prosperity of the said colony....

THE MAYFLOWER COMPACT IN MASSACHUSETTS (1620)

The Pilgrims who landed at Plymouth in 1620 pioneered the development of a new political relationship between the governors and the governed. In New France and even Virginia, political authority and justice was said to flow from the crown. The Pilgrims introduced the idea that authority should be vested in a "compact" between fellow human beings, albeit under God.

In September 1620, English Puritans left the Netherlands, where they had lived in exile, and sailed for America. Their ship, the *Mayflower*, landed at Plymouth, Massachusetts, on December 4, and a pioneer colony was quickly constructed. They had no charter from the crown or a proprietary company, so they had no laws to govern them. Furthermore, they had taken on in London a few "of the ungodly sort" who boasted that once on land they would "use their own liberty." Before anyone was permitted to go ashore, the leaders drafted a compact signed by 41 adult males:

> In the name of God, Amen. We whose names are underwritten, the loyal subjects of our dread Sovereign Lord, King James, by the grace of God of Great Britain.... Having undertaken, for the glory of God and advancement of the Christian faith and honour of our king and country, a voyage to plant the first colony in the northern parts of Virginia, do, by these presents, solemnly and mutually in the presence of God and one of another, covenant and combine ourselves together into a civil body politic for our better ordering and preservation and furtherance of the ends aforesaid. And by virtue hereof to enact, constitute, and frame such just and equal laws, ordinances, acts, constitutions, and offices, from time to time, as shall be thought most meet and convenient for the general good of the colony; unto which we promise all due submission and obedience.

At the apex of the *ancien régime* society was the monarch, who ruled by divine right. Louis XIV personally attended councils, sometimes had correspondence from the colonies read to him, and dictated replies or decrees for their government. His "decisions" were often those of his officials and courtiers, and the officials in turn depended on a growing bureaucracy for their information. Correspondence from the governors and intendants of the colonies directed the bureaucrats of the Ministry of Marine and Colonies in their formulation of policy. Correspondence from Versailles reached the administrative capital at Quebec each year after the St. Lawrence river was free of ice. The governor spent the summer months in Montreal, consulting with post commanders and Amerindian delegations, then returned to Quebec in the autumn to prepare the colonial correspondence for Versailles in conjunction with the intendant, bishop, and Sovereign Council before freeze-up.

Sometimes the colonial officials declined to enforce directives that they considered unacceptable or unsuitable for local conditions, and occasionally they suggested ordinances that would be advantageous. It was from the colony, for example, that orders prohibiting the furnishing of brandy to the Native peoples, imposing severe penalties for running the woods, and regulating the payment of tithes originated. The governor and the intendant could also use their executive powers, but their ordinances were subject to royal review. Since Versailles was far across the Atlantic and there were no large standing armies in the colony, royal officials acted with discretion when dealing with signs of discontent.[11]

Several historians have portrayed New France as a tyranny or a theocracy in which the colonists were oppressed and repressed by state and church. Although the theoretical framework of government was absolutist, it was neither despotic nor tyrannical. It was, instead, paternalistic. The king's instructions in 1663 stipulated that "the general spirit of government ought to lean in the direction of gentleness" in order to encourage permanent settlement and local initiative. The emphasis on order and subordination did not result in oppressive legislation and bureaucratic callousness. Much of the legislation was intended to alleviate human misfortune, improve living conditions, and discourage anti-social behaviour. This benevolent and paternalistic attitude of a small ruling élite was bolstered by the social teachings of the Roman Catholic church.

There was no representative assembly, as in some of the Anglo-American colonies, because France itself had had no parliament since 1614 and the colonial governor had been informed that "it is good that every man speak for himself and none speak for all." But there were frequent consultative assemblies of the leading inhabitants to discuss colonial problems, as well as chambers of commerce in the two chief towns, and local representation on the Sovereign (later Superior) Council.

THE SEIGNEURIAL SYSTEM

Central to the French régime in Canada was the *seigneurial* system of land tenure, which was suited to a stratified social order. Theoretically, all the land belonged to the crown, which apportioned it out as it saw fit to the privileged orders — the nobility and clergy, who derived a major part of their income from their estates. In Canada, the *seigneurs* or owners of estates were required in turn to recruit farmers and bring their holdings into production. The farmers, who preferred to be known as *habitants* rather than *censitaires* (which denoted their requirement to pay the annual dues of *cens* and *rentes*), were owners of their plots. Land was free, in contrast to the need to purchase land in the English colonies, so no initial payment was required to enter into a contract with the *seigneur*.

In transplanting the system to New France, the French authorities ensured that it was pruned of its less desirable characteristics. The European central village, surrounded by fields worked on a threefold cycle, was not suited to conditions along the St. Lawrence valley. It was replaced in Canada by a trapezoidal *seigneury* running back from the river front, along which each farm family, and the *seigneur* in most cases, lived. Thus a thin line of settlement formed along the river bank.

During the period of early settlement this type of survey had several advantages. It was easy and inexpensive to run the survey lines, and each farmer received a variety of soil and vegetation types as his plot ran back from the river frontage. An ideal farm would include marshlands near the river for fodder, rich heavy soils for growing cereal crops, upland meadows for grazing, and wooded and rocky uplands for fuel, lumber, and building stone. The river provided water, fish, and marine life, as well as a transportation route; thus there was no great need to construct a roadway. The farmers were reasonably close to their neighbours, yet distant enough to enjoy privacy and far enough removed from the seigneurial manor to enjoy independence.

Some of the first *seigneurs* were almost as poor as their *censitaires* during the pioneering era. Many of the seigneurial dues and privileges had to be waived in the early decades in order to encourage settlement and keep the farmers from running off into the woods to take up fur trading. Some privileges, such as the *banalité*, or right of the seigneur to a grist mill and to charge milling fees, became in the early years of colonization an obligation to provide a service rather than a source of revenue. In disputes between landowners and *censitaires* regarding contract clauses, dues, and privileges, the intendant served as the arbiter. He intervened to restrain any seigneurial impositions that might discourage immigration and settlement, but he was also very careful to suppress any questioning of authority or the established order by the *censitaires*.

The seigneurial system promoted and nurtured a pattern of social stability quite different from that in the Anglo-American colonies to the south. It was radically different from the freehold tenure that had spread throughout the English colonies. English colonists had to buy their plots of land and thereafter had to pay property taxes to the state. However, as settlement progressed along the St. Lawrence valley and agricultural production increased, the system gradually moved closer to the French model, and the dues and privileges of the *seigneurs* took on greater significance. Not all the seigneurs in the colony were from the privileged class-es; bourgeois merchants and military officers bought seigneuries. In addition, after 1685 the colonial nobili-ty was permitted to engage in commerce, an activity not permitted the nobility in France until the eigh-teenth century.[12]

COLBERT'S MERCANTILIST MODEL

In promoting the colonization and settlement of New France, the French state was driven by two main imperialist motives: to gain wealth and to enhance its power. The minister of marine and colonies and other influential colonial administra-tors operated under a system of economic expansion known in the eighteenth century as mercantilism. Jean-Baptiste Colbert, who served as minister from 1669 to 1683, was almost the living embodiment of French mercantilism. He strove to make France eco-nomically self-sufficient as well as a leading com-mercial power.

Jean-Baptiste Colbert, minister of marine c colonies and proponent of French mercant

Colbert's mercantilism was never a coherent and well-defined policy of government; it was more a set of policies that embraced three basic economic prin-ciples, described as bullionist, populationist, and protectionist. Supporters of Colbertism believed that the possession of bullion — gold and silver — was the source of economic power. Nations that did not have mines producing these precious metals must obtain them through a favourable balance of trade. A large population was desirable because it meant, among other things, a greater number of producers and a greater internal market of consumers. In order to stimulate domestic industries and reduce the need for imports, the Colbertists also favoured high tariffs on imported goods.

Colonies had an essential but sub-ordinate role to play in this mercan-tilist framework. New France was

Louis XIV.

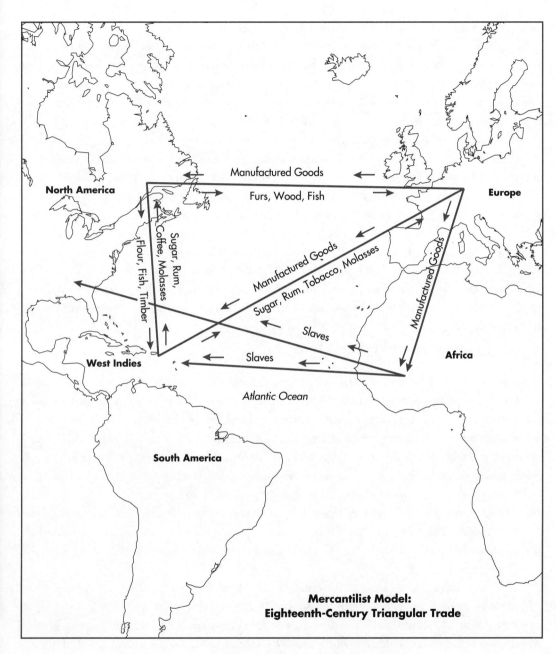

North America

Manufactured Goods

Furs, Wood, Fish

Europe

Sugar, Rum, Coffee, Molasses

Flour, Fish, Timber

Manufactured Goods

Sugar, Rum, Tobacco, Molasses

Manufactured Goods

Slaves

West Indies

Slaves

Africa

Atlantic Ocean

South America

Mercantilist Model:
Eighteenth-Century Triangular Trade

expected to trade only within the empire, and to serve both as a major source of staple products and as a ready market for French manufactured goods. Colonial enterprises and goods must never compete with metropolitan activities. Intendant Jean Talon encouraged cottage industries in New France. He had a plan to develop a shipbuilding industry and related naval production such as linen for sails, mastheads, tar, ropes, and planking, and wished to promote intercolonial trade with the West Indies. But French merchants and the royal administration strongly opposed Talon's plans, insisting that no colony should be permitted to purchase goods from another colony that it could obtain from France. Under the trade system, Newfoundland cod was carried by the French fishers to the West Indies, where sugar cane, molasses, and exotic products were loaded for the return voyage to France.

Mercantilism did more than impose restrictions on colonial development. It also provided the colonies with a degree of security and support, within a closed commercial system, that they would not have enjoyed in a free-trade situation. The mother country bought all the production of the colonies; in the case of furs, this created a problem in France when there was a glut of beaver, and new outlets had to be found to keep the Canadian merchants and their Amerindian suppliers of dressed furs happy and loyal. The metropolitan merchants also had to assure the colony the essential supplies of trade goods, foodstuffs, manufactures, arms, and ammunition. Finally, it was the metropolitan merchants who bore the costs of transport across the Atlantic, the risks of loss through natural disasters, piracy, and war, the high insurance costs, and the risks of fluctuating market conditions in Europe.[13]

THE MILITARY ESTABLISHMENT

From the beginning, settlers had to be ready to defend their families or neighbours against the threat posed by Iroquois attacks and Dutch and English trade rivals. Out of this need for self-defence grew a military tradition that marked the entire French colonial period. Local militia units were organized at first as religious units. With the advent of royal government in 1663, detachments of French regular troops arrived to carry out punitive raids on Iroquois villages. These soldiers were not only valued because of the protection they offered the colony, but also because they brought skills and money to boost the local economy. From the outset, therefore, there was a certain respect for the military under the French régime. The value of the French military presence became more evident when many discharged soldiers settled in the colony and contributed various skills as well as military expertise.[14]

The most important measure in the creation of a strong military tradition was the decree in 1669 that every male subject between the ages of 16 and 60 who was not physically disabled, or a member of the nobility, or in holy orders should report regularly for militia training and be prepared to serve anywhere in defence of the colony. Captains of the militia were appointed in each parish, not in the *seigneuries*, to distinguish the landholding system from the military organization. Their primary roles were to train the citizenry and to lead them in carrying out their responsibilities and duties to the state. Initially, many of the officers of the militia units were drawn from the *seigneurial* class and the local aristocracy because these individuals had military experience.

Militia service was universal, compulsory, and unpaid, at the call of the governor who was the commander-in-chief of the armed forces. The militia could be sent on offensive or defensive expeditions, or used for auxiliary services such as freighting goods, constructing fortifications, and scouting. The only remuneration they received was the regular provision of a musket, powder and shot, a bedroll, and perhaps a greatcoat. This patriotic obligation was apparently accepted willingly, because there were very few desertions and no mutinies. The militia became very adept at the Native style of guerrilla warfare and often fought side by side with war parties of Amerindian allies.

The French soldiers serving in New France were composed of companies of the *troupes de la Marine*, the military force organized to guard French harbours, naval bases, and outposts. Unlike the regular troops of the Ministry of War, they were organized in companies of 50 men commanded by a captain. Commissions could not be

Canadian militiaman, 1722.

purchased, but promotion depended on merit or proven ability and on seniority of service. In 1684, Louis XIV issued six commissions to Canadians to serve in the officer corps. Thereafter, the sons of the Canadian nobility eagerly pursued careers in the marine companies. This not only provided opportunities for Canadian youth to serve their country but also provided the colony with efficient officers who understood local conditions and who generally maintained excellent relations with the Amerindian allies, who were vital to French survival in the face of Anglo-American hostility.

ACTIVITIES

KEY TERMS AND CONCEPTS

Identify and briefly explain the historical significance of the following terms and concepts:

- *Nova Gallia*
- Marc Lescarbot's Acadia
- The "City Upon a Hill"
- Champlain's dream
- Company of One Hundred Associates
- Jean Talon's hinterland empire
- Christian Huronia
- Sillery *réduction*
- *Devots*
- Theocratic rule
- William Penn's "Haven in the Woods"
- *Ancien regime*
- Paternalistic government
- Seigneurial system
- French mercantilism
- Captains of militia
- Guerrilla warfare

QUESTIONS FOR DISCUSSION

1. What was the early European vision of "gold, glory, and God" in America? To what extent did the founders of New France as well as the English colonies share that vision?
2. In what ways did Acadia emerge out of a distinctly different colonial experience from that of the St. Lawrence settlement of New France? How might its early experience be compared with that of the northern frontier of Massachusetts, later Maine?
3. The visions of a Christian Utopia proposed in New France bore a striking resemblance to certain "Holy Experiments" in colonial America. Identify the main similarities of and significant differences between John Winthrop's "City Upon a Hill" and Bishop Laval's theocratic experiment, and between Ville-Marie and William Penn's colony.

4. Why did immigration to and settlement in New France lag far behind that of the Thirteen Colonies during the seventeenth century?
5. In New France, unlike the case in the Thirteen Colonies, there was no "moving frontier of settlement," but rather a compact pattern of settlement along water entrances. What influence did this settlement experience have on the colonies' differing patterns of social order, political institutions, and social and military life?
6. Why did most of the grand visions of "new societies" proposed in the seventeenth century either fade or completely evaporate in New France and the English colonies?

ANALYZING THE EVIDENCE

Comparing Visions of New Societies

Study carefully Samuel de Champlain's 1618 plan for the colonization of New France:

"[C]onsidering the advantage and profit to be derived therefrom, as well as for the glory of God as for the honour of His Majesty and for the good of his subjects, the Chamber of Commerce has passed a resolution to represent to His Majesty and to the said Lords of his Council on the measures which he should take for such a holy and glorious enterprise....

"...[T]he said Sieur de Champlain declares and proposes, subject to the good pleasure of His Majesty, should he see fit to undertake and pursue the said enterprise, to build at Quebec, the site of the Sieur de Champlain's settlement situated on the river St. Lawrence, at a narrow part of the said river, some nine hundred or a thousand yards in width, a town almost as large as St. Denis, which shall be called, if it please God and King, Ludovica, in the centre of which will be built a fair temple, dedicated to the Redeemer, and called the Church of the Redeemer, as a memorial and commemoration of the good that it shall please God to do to these poor people, who have no knowledge of His holy name, to incline the will of the King to bring them to the knowledge of His holy name, to incline the will of the King to bring them to the knowledge of the holy Christian faith and to the bosom of our holy mother Church...."

— H.P. Biggar, ed., *The Works of Samuel de Champlain,* vol.2, trans. John Squair (Toronto: Champlain Society, 1922–36), pp. 326, 337.

1. What was Samuel de Champlain's vision of "one people under God"?
2. How did his early vision of New France compare with John Winthrop's Puritan vision of the Massachusetts Bay colony?
3. To what extent did his vision differ from Winthrop's "City Upon a Hill" and William Penn's "Haven in the Woods"?
4. Which vision came closer to the perfectible society?

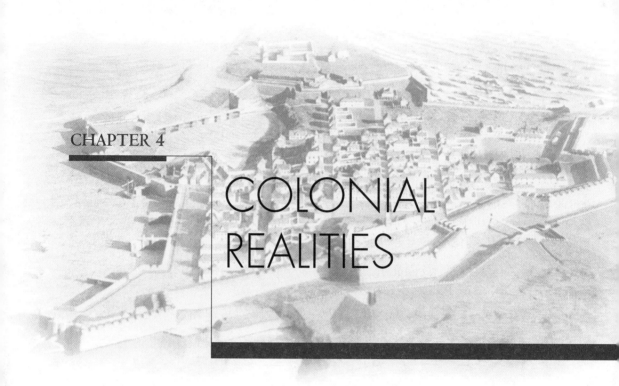

CHAPTER 4

COLONIAL
REALITIES

IN THE EIGHTEENTH CENTURY France continued under the direct royal rule of the Bourbon kings, Louis XIV (1643–1715) and Louis XV (1715–74), who governed by divine right and tolerated no parliamentary institutions. This was in sharp contrast to events in England, where in 1689 the absolute monarchy had been overturned in the "Glorious Revolution," and William III of Orange and James II's daughter Mary had been invited by a convention parliament to assume the throne with limited powers as set out in a Bill of Rights. Under Queen Anne (1702–14) the kingdoms of England and Scotland were united under the name Great Britain in 1707 and the Union Jack was adopted as the national flag. These political changes had a profound impact not only in Britain, but in the developing Anglo-American colonies.

New France and the emerging Anglo-American colonies were beginning to diverge in their patterns of colonial development. In the latter, British laws and privileges were coming increasingly under attack, long before the War of Independence. With the accession of William and Mary to the English throne, the principle was established that Parliament had to consent to all laws. News of the "Glorious Revolution" of 1689 had touched off a minor wave of rebellion in Maryland, in New York, and throughout the New England colonies. William and Mary wisely accepted the initiatives of the colonial assemblies in the 1690s to diffuse the political agitation. Even though the franchise remained limited and every colony except Rhode Island retained a high property qualification for voting, democratic ideas were percolating in the thirteen English colonies. The contests of these "lower houses" with royal governors and British officials after 1689 signified the first stirrings of representative democracy and of the eventual challenge to political power within the colonies and in the empire.

SOCIAL HIERARCHY AND ORDER

LIKE THE *ANCIEN RÉGIME* IN OLD FRANCE, the political system of New France was a hierarchy of ranks or orders. The French king, his ministers, and the higher clergy were at the top of the social pyramid. They were followed by a noble order of military origin, by the judges and state administrators, and by merchants, all of whom were commonly described as "honourable persons." The broad base of the pyramid comprised craftsmen, peasants, labourers, and vagabonds, all cruelly described as "vile persons."

Socially and religiously, New France was part of a Roman Catholic realm, and education, charity, and welfare were the responsibility of the church. Society was divided into three orders or estates — the clergy, the nobility, and the third estate, or commoners. The first two estates were privileged orders, with power, prestige, and extensive property. The upper levels of the third estate — the bourgeoisie, or middle class — held important positions in the

C.W. Jefferys' painting of the founding of Halifax.

bureaucracy, the professions, commerce, and industry. In the frontier conditions of early settlement, there had been a few notable departures from the French model. But as the colony grew and developed in the early eighteenth century it began to resemble, more and more, the *ancien régime* of France. Social distinctions became gradually more marked, and a rising privileged class began to assert its traditional rights.[1]

In this traditional, vertically hierarchical society, everyone had a superior under the king. All colonists were subject to the authority of officials holding royal commissions. The soldiers were subject to their officers, the clergy to their bishop, and wives and children to the father and head of the household. The law upheld this social order in the interest of peace, order, and good government.

LAW AND ORDER

The colony had, in its earliest days, used several different codes of custom law but had finally settled on the Custom of Paris. Not all sections of this law were used in Canada, but the provisions dealing with property, inheritance, and marriage were followed and augmented by the

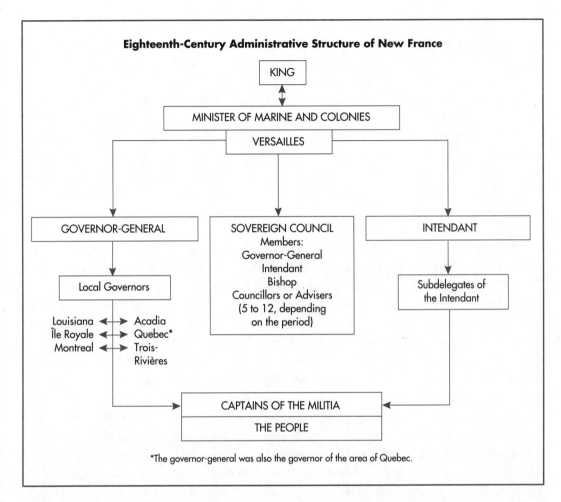

Eighteenth-Century Administrative Structure of New France

KING

MINISTER OF MARINE AND COLONIES
VERSAILLES

GOVERNOR-GENERAL

SOVEREIGN COUNCIL
Members:
Governor-General
Intendant
Bishop
Councillors or Advisers
(5 to 12, depending
on the period)

INTENDANT

Local Governors

Subdelegates of
the Intendant

Louisiana ◄──► Acadia
Île Royale ◄──► Quebec*
Montreal ◄──► Trois-
Rivières

CAPTAINS OF THE MILITIA
THE PEOPLE

*The governor-general was also the governor of the area of Quebec.

Civil Ordinance of 1667. Both *seigneurs* and *censitaires* were protected by the Custom of Paris and could not be deprived of their estates or plots so long as they lived up to their contractual agreements. Marriage law provided some protection for the property rights of women. Children were legally considered minors until 25 years of age, required curators or tutors when inheriting property, and even required parental permission to marry. Although women in New France enjoyed more rights than did those in the neighbouring British colonies, they did not have complete legal equality with men.[2]

Criminal law in the colony followed the Great Criminal Ordinance of 1670, which consolidated earlier ordinances. It was certainly harsh, as was its English counterpart in the neighbouring colonies. Yet (perhaps as a result?) the incidence of crime in New France does not appear to have been very high. Soldiers were arrested for fighting and disorderliness, as were townspeople who frequented the taverns too often. Serious crimes underwent thorough investigation involving a lengthy interrogation, the confrontation of witnesses, and, if necessary, judicial torture. Sentences ranged from fines (part payable to a charitable institution) to being publicly shamed by being made fast in a pillory or on a wooden horse, flogging, branding with the fleur-de-lis on the cheek, hanging, or even being broken on the wheel.

Sedition and rebellion against authority were severely dealt with by the courts. Individuals who dared question the existence of God, the wisdom of the king, or the integrity of some high official — and there were a few cases of such boldness in New France — brought down on themselves the full weight of the law. Swearing or using the names of God or the Virgin Mary in vain were punishable by fines or — for multiple repeat offences — cutting out the tongue. Even a tavern brawl that involved some verbal abuse of constituted authority was taken very seriously by the judges, because it represented rebellion, and sometimes attack on the class structure.[3]

The overriding desire to impose law and order was clearly reflected in regulations introduced for the townspeople of New France. Beginning as early as 1676 and extending into the 1700s, a series of urban regulations were enacted that were almost unheard of in the British colonies to the south. In Quebec, Montreal, and Louisbourg — all towns with over 4000 inhabitants — building codes, waste disposal regulations, the licensing and inspection of trades, and health regulations were enforced. Smoking in the streets was strictly forbidden, and Protestants were prohibited from public displays of their religion.

Domestic slavery in New France was regulated by an ordinance issued by Intendant Jacques Raudot in 1709 that followed the general principles laid out in the *Code Noir* of 1685 for the plantation colonies. Although the code treated slaves as chattels or property, it obliged owners to feed, clothe, and house them properly and to care for them in their old age. Slaves were also "persons" before the law, so they had rights as well as duties to their owners. They were to be instructed in the Catholic religion and encouraged to marry. Family units were not to be split up. There are records for a total of about 4000 slaves in New France between 1608 and 1760, of whom 2500 were Amerindians and 1500 came from Africa via the Caribbean. Women outnumbered men in Canada, whereas in the southern plantations men outnumbered women.[4]

Although the original intention had been to subject the Amerindians to French laws, this was soon abandoned by colonial officials on practical grounds. The Amerindian nations were left to govern themselves according to their traditional customs. In the few cases involving attacks by Amerindians on colonists, the governor had the proceedings withdrawn from the royal courts and tried under military procedures, with the consent of the Native elders. This practice flowed naturally from French colonial recognition of the independence of Amerindian nations and their status as allies, not subjects.[5]

POPULAR PROTESTS OR "THUNDER GUSTS"

The colonists were not crushed under the despotic and priestly suppression of all independence and self-expression. Popular demonstrations bordering on revolt did occur in New

France. Although these popular protests never reached the scale or frequency of those in Europe, the self-reliant and independent *habitants* occasionally vented their discontent in public. These popular protests were aimed at a redress of grievances and not at overthrowing constituted authority. They were, in fact, demands that authority be exercised, that controls be imposed. Authorities dealt with such "thunder gusts" of protest quickly, but not always with the harshness found in old France. Had the protests continued, the military would have been used to restore order, but officials preferred to compromise, redress wrongs, and maintain external order. In fact, their responses often revealed the paternalistic and benevolent side of French colonial government.

Popular disturbances in New France were not simply the spontaneous reactions of mindless people carried away by the crowd. Since there were no legislative assemblies, no press or newspapers, and petitions were forbidden, discontent could only be expressed through sullen compliance or open opposition. On at least a dozen occasions people in New France took to the streets, paraded to the walls of towns, or gathered in large groups to protest. Unlike the English colonists, who frequently demanded political reforms, the *Canadiens* and *Canadiennes* demanded social and economic justice. They protested rationing and shortages of food, sharp rises in essential commodity prices, unusual *corvées* or statute labour, and unacceptable changes in the boundaries of parishes.

One of the most remarkable collective protests was a near-riot by the women of the Quebec region in late 1757. During the food shortages caused by the Seven Years' War, the authorities had ordered butchers to sell a pound of horsemeat with every pound of beef. An irate crowd stormed the governor's residence; the women refused to buy horsemeat (which the French regular troops ate) on the grounds that it was un-Christian, saying that "the horse is the friend of man" and to eat its flesh was tantamount to cannibalism! The governor tried to appease them by offering a tour of the Quebec abattoir, but the women continued their protests over the horsemeat and subsequent attempts at bread rationing. Finally, the authorities capitulated.[6]

EIGHTEENTH-CENTURY ADMINISTRATIVE RESTRUCTURING

The beginning of the 1700s witnessed five significant changes in the history of New France. The first was the termination of the sporadic warfare that had existed between the Five Nations Iroquois and the French colonists and their Amerindian allies since 1609. By the Treaty of Montreal (1701), peace was concluded between the League of the Iroquois and the French, as well as between the Iroquois and the "domiciled" Amerindians in the colony and the nations of the Great Lakes hinterland region. The French recognized the independence of the Iroquois Confederacy, which promised in turn to remain neutral in any wars between Britain and France.

POPULAR AND VIOLENT PROTEST IN COLONIAL AMERICA*

POPULAR DISTURBANCES AND MOB VIOLENCE were not uncommon in colonial America in the late seventeenth and early eighteenth centuries. As the Anglo-American colonies evolved, class distinctions became more apparent and class lines hardened, particularly in the southern plantation colonies and northern cities and towns. By 1700, Virginia was dominated by about 50 wealthy families who owned vast plantations, controlled the court system, and employed thousands of black slaves and indentured servants. In Maryland and the Carolinas, white proprietors and slave-owners had established feudal-type aristocracies, monopolized the farmland, and driven the landless to revolt on several occasions. The leaders of early Boston, according to historian Carl Bridenbough, were "gentlemen of considerable wealth" who formed an aristocratic order by controlling trans-Atlantic commerce, asserting their authority through church and town meetings, and making careful marriage alliances among themselves. The New York aristocracy was just as prominent, and perhaps more ostentatious in its grand style of living.

The Anglo-American colonies grew rapidly in the 1700s, and over half of the newcomers were either indentured servants or black slaves. Many of America's urban immigrants struggled just to stay alive. In 1700 the New York church wardens appealed for funds because "the Crys [sic] of the poor and Impotent for want of Relief are Extreamly [sic] Grievous." All major cities were forced to erect poorhouses in the 1730s for the destitute as well as the aged, infirm, orphaned, and crippled. By mid-century the situation in Philadelphia, Boston, and New York became so bad that public complaints were regularly raised about the "beggars about the town." In colonial England, outside the towns, the "wandering poor" were also a distinct fact of life. Tax records in southeastern Pennsylvania's Chester County show that the gap in income and wealth between the rich and the poor was widening throughout the 1700s.

With such class disparities and festering discontents, outbreaks of popular protest and disorder became relatively common occurrences. A severe food shortage in Boston in 1713 led to a mass riot of over 200 people, in which the ships of a wealthy merchant were attacked, warehouses were ransacked for corn, and the lieutenant-governor was shot for interfering. In one election campaign of the 1730s, New York voters were

---

* For a detailed documentation and analysis of popular disturbances in colonial America see Gary B. Nash, "Social Change and the Growth of Prerevolutionary Urban Radicalism," in Alfred Young, ed., *The American Revolution* (Dekalb: Northern Illinois University Press, 1976); and Richard M. Brown, "Historical Patterns of Violence in America," in H.G. Graham and T.R. Gurr, eds., *Violence in America* (New York: Signet Books, 1969).

urged in an angry pamphlet to join "Shuttle" the weaver, "Plane" the joiner, "Mortar" the mason, "Smallrent" the fair-minded landlord, and "John Poor" the tenant in throwing out of office. "Gripe the Merchant, Squeeze the Shopkeeper, Spintext and Quible the Lawyer." Regular riots broke out in Boston over impressment, the British practice of dragooning colonists into naval service.

In New Jersey in the 1740s and 1750s, rioting erupted when major proprietors attempted to press their claims to disputed lands by collecting rents from the colony's poor farmers, some of whom claimed Amerindian ancestral title to the land. As in New France, the incidence of popular disturbances was closely related to war conditions and accompanying shortages. Most riots and popular protests arose while England was embroiled in its imperial wars — Queen Anne's War (the War of the Spanish Succession) in the early 1700s and King George's War (the War of the Austrian Succession) in the 1740s.

Mob violence frequently accompanied popular disturbances in colonial America. A slave uprising in New York in 1712 was put down with great cruelty. A similar rising in South Carolina in 1739 and an apprehended one in New York in 1741 resulted in whites going on rampages of burning and killing. Gangs of toughs had come into existence by the end of the seventeenth century in most colonial ports. Boston already had its infamous North End and South End gangs. Protest against British colonial policies were turned into street violence by gangs such as the Liberty Boys in all the major towns.

Lynch mobs appeared in South Carolina in the 1760s when groups of people came together spontaneously to administer corporal punishment to individuals deemed to have offended community standards. The law officers did not move to prevent this kind of mob justice. During the American Revolution in Virginia the same kind of popular vengeance instigated by a Colonel Charles Lynch (from whom lynching got its name) was turned against the Tories (Loyalists).

The second important development was the outbreak of the War of the Spanish Succession in 1702. Britain was anxious to prevent a union of the crowns of France and Spain, and thus of the colonies of Spain and France, which would have constituted a formidable world empire. France did not win this struggle but emerged from the war with the conviction that New France would henceforth play a different and more important role in the empire. New France did not have the commercial value of the West Indian colonies of Martinique, Guadeloupe, and Saint-Domingue (Haiti), but it had an important potential role in geopolitical strategy. By holding the interior of the North American continent, with the support of allied Amerindian nations, New France could hem the Anglo-American colonies along the Atlantic seaboard and force Great Britain to maintain a sizable navy and garrisons at

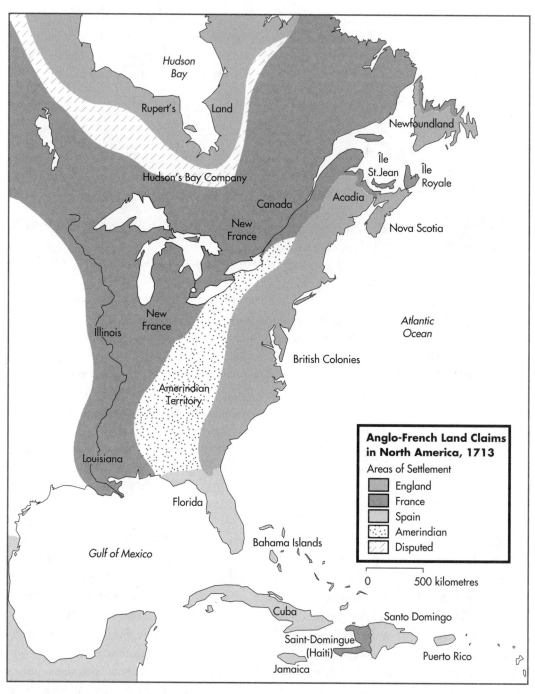

Adapted from *France in America* by William J. Eccles, published by Fitzhenry & Whiteside Ltd., Markham, Ontario.

great cost. This strategy was in the interests of the Amerindian nations as well, because they feared Anglo-American expansion into their territories and their possible displacement.

The third element forcing important changes was the Treaty of Utrecht (1713), which ended the War of the Spanish Succession. By the terms of this treaty, France surrendered to Britain the territories of Hudson Bay and Newfoundland that it had conquered, as well as much of Acadia. France retained its fishing rights off Newfoundland and retained Île-Royale (Cape Breton) and Île Saint-Jean (Prince Edward Island). The Acadians living in what became peninsular Nova Scotia would become British subjects unless they removed themselves, without most of their belongings, to French territory within one year. But all the efforts of the French to encourage them to relocate convinced only 60 families to move to Île Royale. The Acadians chose to ignore both imperial powers and to remain where they were, while resisting all British efforts to anglicize and convert them.[7]

The fourth important development was the French response to the new territorial alignments. Construction of the imposing fortress of Louisbourg began on Île Royale. The fortress would serve as a naval base and guardian of the entrance of the St. Lawrence estuary, a port of trans-shipment, and a centre for the fishery. At the mouth of the Mississippi River, the existing bases at Biloxi and Mobile were enhanced by the founding of New Orleans in 1718 and the beginnings of an important plantation economy in Louisiana. The "Illinois country" south of the Great Lakes was attached to Louisiana, settlements were developed, and an imposing fortress was built at Fort de Chartres. Detroit, which had been founded by LaMothe Cadillac in 1701, became an important link between Canada and Louisiana. Eventually a chain of forts would emerge to link the colonies.

The final development was the restoration of the fur trade and of French activity in the *pays d'en haut*, which had been interrupted first by a glut of furs on the French market in 1696 and then by the outbreak of the European war in 1702. The system of trade licences, or *congés*, was restored and the military commanders at the various posts were put in charge of the trade. La Vérendrye extended trading activities onto the western prairies in the 1730s, and by the 1740s French traders had penetrated the Missouri and Saskatchewan river systems to the foothills of the Rocky Mountains.

MERCANTILISM AND COLONIAL DEVELOPMENT

IN THE EARLY EIGHTEENTH CENTURY, French mercantilist policy took on a new imperial mission in America. Louis XIV signalled his intention to link Île Royale and Louisbourg, the St. Lawrence valley settlements, the Illinois country, the far western hinterland, and the new colony of Louisiana as a barrier to block the Anglo-American advance of trade and settlement into the North American interior. Henceforth, Canada would pursue its mercantile and military roles in co-operation with allied Amerindian nations.

NEW FRANCE, THE MERCANTILIST MAVERICK

Under the administrations of two ministers of marine, Pontchartrain (minister from 1699 to 1715) and Maurepas (minister from 1723 to 1749), an attempt was made to bring New France more into line with pure mercantilist theory. The intendant at Quebec was advised in 1702 that the colony's main role was to be "useful to the kingdom." Four years later, Pontchartrain informed Intendant Jacques Raudot (who served from 1705 to 1710) that it was improper for "manufacturing to establish itself in that country" because it would compete with metropolitan manufactures; the colony's role was to produce raw materials. Yet, in the first half of the eighteenth century, New France diverged in significant ways from the French mercantilist model. Exceptions were made to what Pontchartrain called "the general policy" when it was recognized that New France was a "maverick" in the French trading system.

At the beginning of the new century, French authorities created a council of commerce and began to renovate France's institutions of economic management. In 1717 the French government, with the consent of the business community, adopted a policy known as the *pacte colonial* or *pacte exclusif*, whereby the number of ports dealing with a colony was limited and each port was assigned specific exports. Thirteen French ports dealt with the North American possessions. Bordeaux shipped wines, Nantes sent general trade goods, Rouen exported coarse cloth, and Rochefort had the monopoly on military supplies.

Playing-card money, an ingenious invention concocted by Intendant Jacques de Meulles in 1685 to solve the currency shortage in New France.

French colonial officials permitted two notable exceptions to mercantilist restrictions. From 1716 onward an illicit fur trade between Montreal merchants and the Albany and New York traders was allowed to continue for three decades, in spite of official condemnations. A similar unsanctioned but voluminous trade was allowed to persist between Louisbourg and the New England ports. Although both these operations contravened official economic policy and ministerial instructions, they were lucrative to colonial élites and generally advantageous for the colonists. In fact, Louisbourg's chief role changed from that of a naval base to a port of commercial trans-shipment.[8]

NEW FRANCE'S SLOW ECONOMIC GROWTH

New France suffered from underpopulation in the eighteenth century, especially when compared with the English colonies, which had a rapidly expanding population. By 1730, when New France was more than 120 years old, the total French population was only 34 000, or about 5 percent of the population of the Anglo-American colonies. The economy was also retarded. Why had development been so slow? There were many reasons for the discouraging rate of economic growth. New France was far from its metropolitan centre. The journey from La Rochelle to Quebec involved a dangerous ocean crossing and navigation of the treacherous shoals of the St. Lawrence River. It usually took two months, and the return passage took about one month. The inland location of the chief area of settlement also meant that communication was virtually cut off for half the year. Climatic conditions in Canada were harsh, and the area of fertile soil was limited to the St. Lawrence valley.

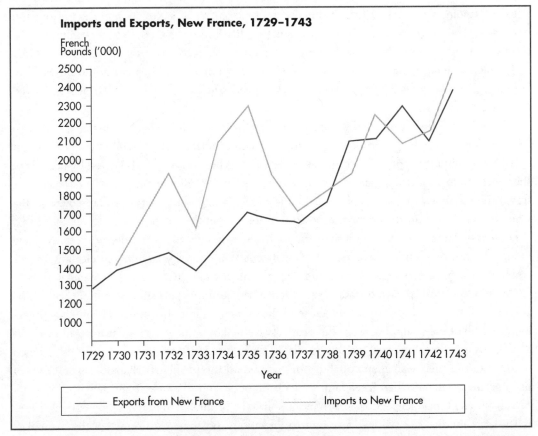

Trade in New France: Imports and Exports, 1729–43. What accounts for the favourable balance of trade in 1739 and 1741?

New France was beset by its share of monetary and financial problems. France did not have a uniform system of weights, measures, or currency before the revolution of 1789. There was never enough coinage in Canada, although the troops were a good source of currency because they were paid regularly in French money. When Intendant Jacques de Meulles found himself unable to pay administrative salaries and the wages of suppliers and artisans, he improvised by issuing a paper currency written on decks of cards cut up and suitably inscribed for the occasion. This card money circulated from 1685 to 1717, was called out of circulation, and was then reissued in 1729 and used until 1757.

New France did not have an annual budget allocated to it, in the sense of having an accounting of expenditures and revenues and an indication of profit or deficit. France did not operate by annual budgets and had no long-term economic planning. The annual *état du roy* sent to the intendant indicated the allocations for the forthcoming year but made no effort to account for actual expenses in the previous year. There was no central banking system or financial clearing house, so trading with various firms using different currencies was often complicated, slow, and expensive. The entrepreneurial class was small, with limited capital for investment in the colony, and metropolitan investors had more attractive places to invest than New France. Only cod, which brought great profits to the merchants of Granville in Normandy and St. Malo in Brittany, and furs, which brought more modest profits to La Rochelle, could be considered attractive enterprises.[9]

Since New France remained a staples economy, it had a narrow and vulnerable economic base. A crop failure due to drought, grasshopper or caterpillar plagues, or frost could wipe out a year's agricultural exports. Even the fur trade suffered periods of glut, followed by periods of shortages. An experiment in harvesting ginseng for export to China in the period 1747–52 illustrated the instability of such staple-based enterprises. The ginseng market collapsed when the Chinese found the Canadian-grown product inferior and, in the words of one French observer, "The colonists were severely punished for their excessive greed."[10] Furthermore, since New France did not develop important industries, it relied on France for cloth and clothing, wines and brandies, guns, powder and lead, utensils, salt, and a wide variety of other manufactures.

In addition to this private trade, New France had an important supply trade organized by colonial officials that was, toward the close of the French régime, the object of some profiteering. Since all of these supplies were the property of the king, the government bore all the risks of the voyage — shipwreck, piracy, spoilage, or capture in wartime — while the French merchants and their Canadian collaborators reaped all the profits. Perhaps the worst case of profiteering occurred when Intendant François Bigot organized a *Grande Société* with Bordeaux merchants and Canadian participants to monopolize the profitable military supply trade in 1755, when large numbers of troops were sent to the colony. With the connivance of the easily flattered Governor Vaudreuil the younger, an unscrupulous supplier to the ministry of war, Joseph Cadet, and greedy and corrupt underlings, the association amassed large personal fortunes for its members, wasted military appropriations, and defrauded colonists. This excessive profiteering prevented the war from stimulating the growth of the colonial economy.[11]

INDUSTRIES, ARTISANS, AND LABOURERS

New France had much more industry than might be expected in a staples-based colonial economy. In France and Britain in the early eighteenth century the only industries that employed large numbers of people were fishing, shipbuilding, and iron foundries. In New France the pattern was similar, except for the existence of the fur trade. Among the small-scale industries that developed were the naval shipyards at Quebec and the Forges du St.-Maurice near Trois-Rivières, originally established out of profits from the fur trade. Both enterprises had financial and managerial difficulties. Although the iron foundries at Trois-Rivières did not experience a strike, or "mutiny," as did the Quebec shipyards in 1741, they required periodic state subsidies and managerial changes to stay afloat.

The St. Lawrence valley industries spawned a small community of artisans. Skilled workers were imported from France, while *Canadiens* were employed mostly as unskilled workers, usually seasonally. The skilled artisans were steeped in the long-standing traditions of the European guilds, which controlled workers' training and apprenticeship, exercised the right of inspection over products, and reinforced ideas of craft solidarity among artisans. But attempts to establish craft associations or trade corporations among artisans in New France failed because of the official position of the colonial administration, which supervised all manual trades itself, and with the generally independent and self-reliant attitudes of the Canadian population.[12]

MILITARY LIFE

IN THE EIGHTEENTH CENTURY, the French military establishment assumed an even larger role in shaping both the development and the élitist class structure of New France. The military budget grew increasingly important to the economic health of the colony. Large capital investments were required to build and maintain the fortress at Louisbourg and to build a chain of forts in the interior of the continent. The large sums spent to maintain the French garrisons and the Canadian militia directly benefited both the colonists and the interior fur trade, which depended on the support of a military establishment.

THE MILITARY ESTABLISHMENT

The military establishment's influence was clearly reflected in the emergence of a new Canadian élite class in the colony's militia. By the eighteenth century French–Amerindian wars became less frequent and the role of militia officers changed from a primarily military function to a civil one, including responsibilities for enforcing state regulations, reading official decrees, maintaining civil order, and apprehending criminals. As the role of militia officers changed, so did the social composition of the group. Many sons of Canadian nobles and *seigneurs*

MILITIA STRENGTH IN NEW FRANCE, 1683–1750		
YEAR	MILITIAMEN	TOTAL POPULATION
1683	2 248	9 800*
1715	4 484	18 300*
1721	6 470	24 951
1734	8 823	37 716
1744	11 289	47 000*
1750	12 909	50 000*

* Estimate (not a census year).

sought career opportunities either in the French marine companies or in positions of command in the Canadian militia. Military service became a preferred vehicle for social advancement among New France's rising *bourgeois* class and some career officer families. The Canadian militia became less of a popular army and more of a breeding ground for New France's aspiring privileged class.

CANADIANIZATION OF THE MARINE OFFICER CORPS

The "Canadianization" of the officer corps of the marine troops was the most significant development in the creation of a colonial military establishment. The governor of New France, the Marquis de Denonville, in 1684 had deplored the lack of discipline of Canadian youth, the lack of career opportunities for the sons of the dominant class, and at the same time commented on the qualities of resourcefulness and intelligence many of these young people displayed. He thought that careers in the French regular forces might employ them usefully in the king's service and alleviate a social problem in the colony. Louis XIV, in reply, sent six commissions for Canadians in companies of the *troupes de la Marine* then stationed in the colony.

The solution to the colony's "youth problem" turned out to be beneficial. The *Canadien* officers' knowledge of the country and general competence were usually respected by their soldiers (who were French), by the colonists, and especially by the Amerindians. On the other hand, they were much feared by the Anglo-Americans and British, who sometimes characterized them — like the Native allies and citizen militia — as being courageous warriors unhampered by the conventional rules of European warfare.

Commissions in the marine troops were based upon seniority and merit or proven ability, usually on the recommendation of the colonial governor and intendant. By 1700 about 40 percent of the officers were *Canadiens*, and by 1757 they all were, except at Louisbourg, where the officers and soldiers came from France for tours of duty. The Canadian nobility was anxious to maintain its control of this military establishment. Eventually commissions were granted only to sons of serving officers, thus creating the basis for a military caste system.

Postings as military commanders in the interior fur trade country could be quite lucrative for enterprising officers. At most of the posts, except for the king's posts at Fort Frontenac and Fort Niagara, the commanding officer was given control of the trade, provided with a certain number of permits that he could either exploit or sell, and permitted a free freight allowance. The officers made good use of this opportunity to profit from their posting. Most formed partnerships with Montreal merchants, who took on the task of obtaining trade goods from France, hiring canoeists, and marketing the furs. The revenue generated by the fur trade was not widely dispersed in the colony.[13]

THE AMERINDIAN ALLIANCE SYSTEM

The French were able to rebuild their systems of alliances with the various Amerindian nations. Eventually three sets of alliances were put in place: the Three Fires Confederacy, in the upper Great Lakes region; the Mik'maq–Abenakis–Maliseet Alliance, in the Atlantic region; and the Seven Nations of Canada, in the central region.

WOMEN IN A MILITARY SOCIETY

Contrary to popular perception, women formed an integral part of New France's emerging military society. In the seventeenth century a few celebrated *guerrières*, notably Madeleine de Verchères in Canada and Madame de la Tour in Acadia, had played key roles in fighting off the Iroquois or securing the colony from armed attack. After 1700, women in New France adapted to a variety of military-related activities, such as provisioning troops, providing services, or managing farms or commercial enterprises while their husbands were away.

A few women not only accompanied their husbands to military posts in the wilderness, but also took charge of trading activities. In one case a Madame Lusignan raised a terrific row at Fort Saint Frédéric in 1752, when she completely monopolized all trade, wholesale and retail, at the post. The Catholic nuns also performed vital services, caring for the war wounded at Montreal's Hôtel-Dieu (established in 1695) and the Ursuline *hôpital militaire* at Trois-Rivières. The Sisters of the Congregation were in charge of the education of the children of the garrison at Louisbourg. At Louisbourg, Quebec, and Montreal, female tavern keepers conducted a booming business with the thirsty troops, and prostitutes plied their trade in nearby brothels.[14]

COMMUNITY AND FAMILY LIFE

WHILE THE TOWNS AND CITIES of colonial America swelled with immigrant populations, New France's rural areas showed the greater growth in population and social importance. Agriculture became more commercialized and diversified. Merchants began to set up shop outside the three major towns, villages began to grow, and artisans moved to the villages. All of these changes resulted in greater social distinctions among the common people. Also, as settlement spread, production increased, and *seigneurial* revenues multiplied, the system became more exacting and moved closer to its metropolitan model in terms of privileges and honours. Only with the passage of time did the *seigneurial* régime come to be an exploitive system, in which *habitants* lived a life of subordination to their *seigneurs*.

RURAL COLONIAL LIFE

The farms of New France represented an adaptation of the French *seigneurial* system to the North American countryside. Settlement along the St. Lawrence valley developed outward from three bridgeheads — Quebec, Trois-Rivières, and Montreal — and into the countryside away from the river frontage. Little by little, all the land between the island of Montreal and the island of Orleans was settled; new farms were carved out along a second and even a third *rang* parallel to and back from the St. Lawrence, Richelieu, and Chaudière rivers. In 1716 the crown prohibited settlement in the upper country, thus maintaining a compact *seigneurial* tract in the Laurentian lowlands.

A typical Canadian farm consisted of 100 *arpents*, about ten times the size of a peasant's holding in France. Wheat was the chief cereal crop, and some flax, oats, barley, and peas were grown. Corn, the staple crop of the agricultural Amerindian tribes, was grown by the French near the posts at Niagara, Detroit, and Michilimackinac and in the Illinois country. Most colonists ignored crop rotation and fertilization, so farms frequently suffered from soil exhaustion. Only by the mid-eighteenth century did the raising of hogs and sheep become commonplace. To the dismay of many intendants, the *habitants* preferred to raise fast horses for pleasure rather than sturdy ones for work.

Agriculture along the St. Lawrence was largely subsistence farming; surplus production was limited. Yields were reduced in certain years because of early frosts, drought, or infestations of grasshoppers and caterpillars. Poor harvests were recorded for 17 years out of 60 in the eighteenth century. Regulations against begging and vagrancy indicate that there were occasions when the towns saw an influx of the hungry from the countryside. As hungry people came into Quebec seeking employment and food in 1749, for example, Intendant Bigot issued an ordinance prohibiting anyone from coming into the city without his express permission.

Most farm families were able to carry on without additional help. Indeed, to supplement farm income, some young men continued to take to the woods in pursuit of the fur trade and adventure, either as licensed canoeists or as illicit *coureurs de bois*. *Habitants* living near the towns cut and sold firewood to the townspeople to supplement their income. Still others engaged in extensive fishing, especially downriver from Quebec, where money was to be made catching cod, herring, and porpoises. Some even took to hunting seals and whales in the Gulf of St. Lawrence.[15]

SOUTHERN PLANTATION LIFE

AMERICA'S SOUTHERN COLONIES developed into plantation societies that more closely resembled the social pattern prevailing in the British West Indies than that found in the northern English settlements. All of the southern colonies were founded as proprietary land grants, initially in the hands of private companies or major landowners. While both the southern and northern colonies were founded for essentially similar economic reasons, the religious influence in the South was not as prevalent as in New England, and the southern clergy never acquired the prestige and authority of the Puritans and Quakers in the North.

Cotton plantation in the southern United States. With the use of slave labour, huge plantations sprang up throughout the South.

While these differences were not enough to create a sharp colonial division, the differing systems of landholding and economic bases were. Land tenure in the South was marked by the accumulation of huge plantation estates producing staple agricultural products for export. To meet the shortage of plantation labour, African slaves were imported to work the fields. These developments gave rise to a remarkable disparity in income and social status between landowner and tenant, white planter and black slave. The spread of slavery after 1650 made this a society whose economic health and continuance seemed to depend on that institution. Even in the colonial period, southern life exhibited a distinctiveness and a sense of separatism that would, in the mid-nineteenth century, give rise to a nation within a nation.

THE LIFE OF THE PLANTERS

The southern planters gradually rose to wealth and power throughout the 1600s and early 1700s. In Virginia, large farm operators bought up small freeholds (20 to 200 hectares) and expanded them into huge plantations growing mostly tobacco. In Maryland, founded in 1663 with 60 manorial estates of 1200 hectares each, large landholders developed their plantations by importing thousands of tenant farmers from Europe and the northern colonies. In South Carolina huge land tracts ranging from 1200 to 20 000 hectares were bought and then subdivided very profitably. By the 1750s the colony's planters owned "plantation empires," controlled important government positions, and lived the affluent and leisured life of a colonial aristocracy.

THE LIFE OF THE SLAVES

The first Africans imported to America in 1619 came as Dutch captives; they were sold to the Jamestown colonists as indentured servants. As the tobacco, rice, and indigo plantations expanded in the southern colonies, thousands of blacks were brought from the west coast of Africa to America and sold into slavery. Those who survived the trans-Atlantic crossing in crowded slave ships became the "property" of slave owners and lived a dehumanizing life. Laws to control slaves, called *slave codes*, were passed in each southern colony. They forbade slaves from carrying weapons, holding meetings, or travelling without their owner's permission. Slaves who violated the codes could be whipped or even put to death. Although slave revolts did break out between 1712 and 1741, they were crushed by colonial authorities. Thus resistance often took other forms. For many slaves, keeping alive elements of their African culture, such as tribal names, songs, and family traditions, and passing them on to their children made life more bearable on the plantations.

WOMEN AND THE FAMILY

The most basic and essential social and economic unit in *ancien régime* society was the family. In the early eighteenth century, the family was the focus of most economic and social activities, since in a preindustrial society all pursuits were necessarily domestic industries. The family had undisputed claim to the loyalty and labour of all its members, including the children. The removal of the man from the home for most of the working day and the idea of separate spheres for men and women were developments that lay in the future.[16]

Women in New France enjoyed a comparatively favourable position; nevertheless their lot was neither easy nor pleasant. In farm work, which occupied most of the *Canadien* population, men's and women's tasks differed little. Women in New France worked in the fields alongside the men and probably — being better educated than most *Canadien* men — took up the vital role of keeping accounts and managing purchases and sales. The earlier scarcity of women in the colony in the seventeenth century, the economic hardships, and the military dangers all tended to encourage matrimony. The vast majority of girls became wives, and a surprisingly high proportion of widows remarried, usually within a short period of

An ex-voto of Madame Riverin and her four children, 1703. The portrayal of young children is a rare fact in the history of early eighteenth-century Canadian painting.

time. Because of the heightened importance of family, most women enjoyed a stronger social position than they would in an industrial society of male-dominated workshops, guilds, and professions. By the end of the French régime, women outnumbered men in the colony.[17]

French officials and visiting travellers usually described the children of the North American colony as *petits sauvages*. They deplored their rather permissive upbringing, their general lack of education and discipline, and their attitudes of self-importance. English commentators in colonial America voiced similar opinions.

Conditions in New France encouraged self-reliance and assertiveness among the colony's youth. Much of the colonial population consisted of children — averaging 40–50 percent in the later decades of French rule. The limited formal schooling, especially for boys, compelled most urban youths to seek training through craft apprenticeships. Rural people depended on their children for farm work or supplementary income from the fur trade or lumbering, and this likely made parents consider the wishes of their children in deciding family matters. Whatever the reasons, the approach to raising children and youthful behaviour did depart from the accepted Old World standards. The clergy deplored the example of Amerindians' permissive child-rearing.[18]

THE CHURCH AND RELIGIOUS LIFE

HE ROMAN CATHOLIC CHURCH in New France made few attempts in the early eighteenth century to exert undue clerical power. A succession of bishops and religious superiors concerned themselves mostly with protecting their legitimate rights. All the bishops came from privileged families in France, as did the majority of the Jesuit and Sulpician clergy. Bishop Saint-Vallier wrote a catechism for the instruction of young Canadians, and a *rituel* or service book for the guidance of his clergy. He had concerned himself since 1688 with the needs of the hospitals, charitable institutions, and schools, and he had spent his personal fortune for the poor of the colony. But long absences from his diocese and frequent quarrels with the religious communities whose affairs he attempted to direct reduced the effectiveness of his leadership. From 1722 to 1740, the three bishops who succeeded him were conspicuous more by their absence than their activity at Quebec. Only in 1740 did Bishop Pontbriand give the church vigorous leadership once again, but his death in 1760 left the colonial church without a bishop at the crucial moment of the British invasion, conquest, and military occupation of the colony.

Religious institutions in New France.
Richard Short, Vue de l'église et du collège des Jésuites, 1761. Medium: Engraving, Dimensions: 35.7 x 50.4 cm, Collection: Musée du Québec, Accession no: 54.122, Photographer:Patrick Altman

Episcopalian Church in New England.

CATHOLIC DOCTRINE AND PRACTICE

The Roman Catholic Church in New France remained — as it had been since Bishop Laval's time — attached to the national (Gallican) church of France. It struggled to indoctrinate the colonial population in the principles of Roman Catholicism, to convert the Amerindians, and to imbue state officials with a Christian social conscience. It managed to exercise effective censorship, to intervene in favour of selective immigration, to control education and social welfare institutions, and to organize a parish system over the settled areas of the colony. But it did not succeed in imbuing the colonists with the religious fervour of the early *dévots* who had played a prominent role in the establishment of the first religious institutions in the colony.

The population conformed to the externals of the faith and the conventions of the community. Officially the church condemned gambling and excessive drinking, frowned on smoking, discouraged dancing, deplored popular superstition, and exercised its right to censor reading materials and the theatre. The populace did not challenge Catholic dogma, but many continued to ignore clerical injunctions without becoming anti-clerical or even irreligious. There was a firm attachment to the rites and liturgy of the church, while at the same time people continued to believe in witchcraft, devil possession, and many traditional observances that were not in line with orthodox teaching.

Popular religious practices in New France show evidence of individual protest, independent spirits, and even an undercurrent of unbelief. For most colonists, religion seems to have been compartmentalized — church attendance, fasting, daily prayers, veneration of the saints and the Virgin Mary — without permeating daily thought and action. Thus, the state found it necessary to legislate such matters as Sunday rest, the closing of cabarets during hours of religious services, tithing, the maintenance of church properties, and respectful behaviour during sermons. The relaxed and uninhibited atmosphere of some churches gave the impression of indiscipline and nonconformity. But it must be remembered that the gregarious colonists had only limited notions of religious solemnity. Catholicism was at this time becoming less a religion of fear, as in medieval times, and more a festive and familial religion oriented toward the cult of the Virgin Mary.[19]

THE CANADIANIZATION OF THE CLERGY

A more distinctly colonial clergy began to take shape in early-eighteenth-century New France. The upper clergy, consisting of the bishop, superiors of religious communities, directors of seminaries, and canons of the cathedral, remained mostly French to the very end of the French régime. The élitist Jesuit order and the Ursuline sisters, as well as the Sulpician secular priests at Montreal, manifested a singular preference for metropolitan personnel. But the Recollets and the women's orders such as the Hospitallers, the Sisters of the Congregation of Notre Dame, and the Sisters of Charity (Grey Nuns) all began admitting colonial candidates. The secular clergy of the Seminary of Quebec showed the greatest tendency toward local recruitment.

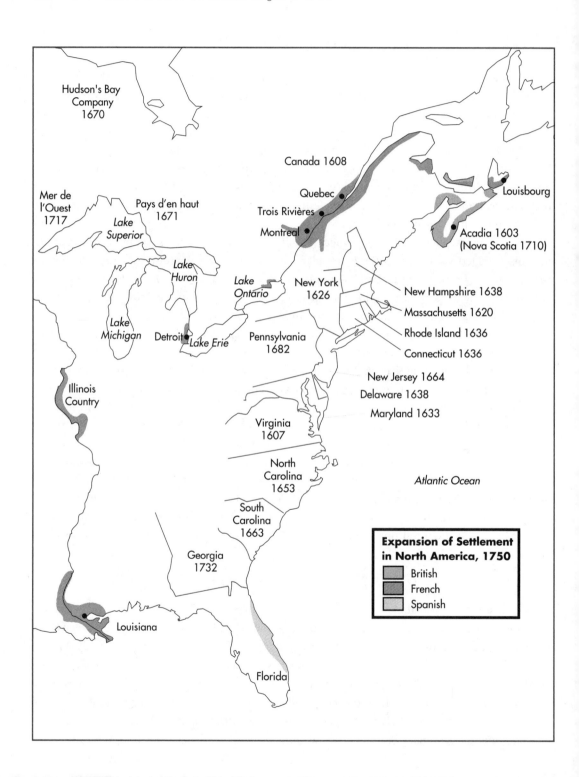

Hudson's Bay
Company
1670

Canada 1608

Mer de
l'Ouest
1717

Pays d'en haut
1671

*Lake
Superior*

Quebec

Louisbourg

Trois Rivières

Montreal

Acadia 1603
(Nova Scotia 1710)

*Lake
Huron*

*Lake
Ontario*

New York
1626

New Hampshire 1638

Massachusetts 1620

Rhode Island 1636

Connecticut 1636

*Lake
Michigan*

Detroit *Lake Erie*

Pennsylvania
1682

New Jersey 1664

Delaware 1638

Maryland 1633

Illinois
Country

Virginia
1607

North
Carolina
1653

Atlantic Ocean

South
Carolina
1663

Georgia
1732

**Expansion of Settlement
in North America, 1750**

British

French

Spanish

Louisiana

Florida

WITCHCRAFT IN MASSACHUSETTS AND NEW FRANCE

LATE IN THE SEVENTEENTH CENTURY a few young girls in Salem, Massachusetts, began suffering pains and hallucinations. When a local doctor could find nothing physically wrong with the girls, he offered a peculiar diagnosis: it was the work of "the evil hand." Unable to explain the strange occurrences, a group of Puritan community leaders charged that the girls were being tormented by witches. At first the Salem girls accused three women in the village of being witches, but as the hysteria spread other villagers were accused.

In the New England Puritan tradition, ministers offered their scriptural interpretation of the witchcraft charges, and judges applied these opinions as divine law. Puritan theologians, led by Cotton Mather and Increase Mather, gave support to the accusations and participated in the Salem witchcraft trials. Eventually, some 150 "witches" were brought to trial.

A charge of witchcraft is lodged against George Jacobs by a group of Salem girls, claiming they were "possessed" by the accused. Jacobs, condemned by the court, was hanged in August 1692.

THE ACCUSATION

Deodat Lawson, a minister visiting Salem, wrote the following account of the questioning of Martha Cory, who was accused of witchcraft.

On Monday the 21st of March, the magistrates of Salem were appointed to come to the examination of Goodwife Cory.... The worshipful Mr. Hathorne asked her why she afflicted these children. She said she did not afflict them.... The number of afflicted persons were about that time ten. Those were most of them at Goodwife Cory's examination, and did vehemently accuse her in the assembly of afflicting them, by biting, pinching, strangling, etc. And that they did in their fit see her likeness coming to them, and bringing a book to them....

It was observed several times that if she did but bite her under lip in time of examination, the persons afflicted were bitten on their arms and wrists and produced the marks before the magistrates, ministers, and others. If she did but pinch her finger, or grasp one hand hard in the other, they were pinched and produced the marks....

THE PUNISHMENT

Before the hysteria in Salem ended, many people were imprisoned, and 19 of the accused were put to death for being witches. The following is a description of the execution of some of those found guilty of witchcraft.

The court again sitting, six more were tried.... These were all brought in guilty, and condemned, and were all executed August 19 except Procter's wife, who pleaded pregnancy....

Mr. Burroughs was carried in a cart with the others through the streets of Salem to execution. When he was upon the ladder he made a speech for the clearing of his innocency with such solemn and serious expressions as were to the admiration of all present....

As soon as he was turned off, Mr. Cotton Mather, being mounted upon a horse, addressed. . . the people, partly to declare that he [Burroughs] was no ordained minister and partly to possess the people of his guilt, saying that the Devil has often been transformed into an angel of light. And this did somewhat appease the people, and the executions went on. When he was cut down, he was dragged by the halter to a hole, or grave, between the rocks, about two foot deep; his shirt and breeches being pulled off and an old pair of trousers of one executed put on his lower parts, he was so put in, together with Willard and Carrier, one of his hands and his chin and a foot of one of them being left uncovered.

Excerpted from Allen Weinstein and R.J. Wilson, *Freedom and Crisis* (New York: Random House, 1974); and Cotton Mather, *The Wonders of the Invisible World* (Boston, 1693).

Witchcraft was not unknown in New France. Thirty years before the Salem witchcraft hysteria of 1692, a Montreal tribunal convicted René Besnard of casting a spell of impotence over his former lover's husband "by incantation over a thrice-knotted string." Besnard was imprisoned. Three years later, Bishop Laval annulled the childless marriage on the grounds of "permanent impotence caused by witchcraft." The supposedly afflicted husband, Pierre Gadois, remarried and his second wife bore him 12 children, the last a set of twins!

Many French colonists continued to believe in diabolical possession, witchcraft, faith healers, soothsayers, healing waters, and a variety of other folk superstitions. Instead of stamping these superstitions out, the Roman Catholic church attempted to turn such popular beliefs to religious purposes.

Gradual "Canadianization" of the clergy began to have a marked effect on religious life. Up to 1710, over 85 percent of all new clergy had come from France. By 1755, the number of Canadian-born clergy in New France equalled the number of metropolitan-born; and by 1775, almost 70 percent would be Canadian-born. While a greater number of sons from the artisan class were entering the priesthood, it was not enough to suggest a profound change in the colony's social structure. The size and growth of the clergy suggest that certain historians' depictions of New France as a priest-ridden, church-dominated society are grossly overdrawn. The recruitment of clergy lagged well behind the colony's population growth and, by the end of the French régime, the church faced a serious shortage of clergy.

DREAMS AND REALITIES

Few of the visionary projects and dreams of empire engendered by the colonization of New France were realized. It remained a colony of very modest proportions, yet it was able to hold at bay, for a century and a half, the vastly superior Anglo-American colonies. France considered the colony useful more in strategic and military terms than in economic returns. Changes in the colony's institutions and community life seemed to suggest a growing integration into the French imperial system, not a sense of emerging French-Canadian nationalism. Perhaps the Acadians of the eighteenth century were the only people in French America who had developed a distinctive sense of identity.

The influence of the North American frontier on colonial societies is still a much-debated subject. Did independence, self-reliance, and local initiative naturally lead colonists to shed authoritarian institutions and restrictions, to develop democratic and co-operative ideas, to provide the dynamism that would fashion a new social order? The French of the eighteenth century thought otherwise. It was in metropolitan France that concepts of human rights, republicanism, and the slogan "liberty, equality, fraternity" expressed themselves, not in the colony. In New France the frontier, far from being considered an area of dynamic regeneration, was seen as the place where people escaped the social controls necessary to orderly progress and moved beyond the reach of commerce, industry, and social institutions to pursue selfish aims rather than the welfare of the whole community. New France remained very much an *ancien régime* society.[20]

ACTIVITIES

KEY TERMS AND CONCEPTS

Identify and briefly explain the historical significance of the following terms and concepts:

- Divine right of kings
- "Glorious Revolution"
- Hierarchical society
- Honourable and vile persons
- Custom of Paris
- "Thunder gusts"
- Horsemeat protest (1757)
- French–Iroquois settlement (1701)
- Treaty of Utrecht (1713)
- Mercantilist maverick
- Permitted illicit trade
- Staples-based economy
- Canadian élite class
- *Querrieres*
- *Rangs*
- *Les petits sauvages*
- Salem witch trials
- "Canadianization" of the clergy

QUESTIONS FOR DISCUSSION

1. American historian Francis Parkman offered
   this famous assessment of society in New
   France in *The Old Regime in Canada* (1887): "An
   ignorant population, sprung from a brave and
   active race, but trained to subjection and
   dependence through centuries of monarchial
   despotism, was planted in the wilderness by
   the hand of authority, and told to grow and
   flourish. Artifical stimulants were applied, but
   freedom was withheld." Did New France in
   the eighteenth century conform to this popular
   stereotype? Explain with historical examples.

2. Popular protest and rioting in early French
   Canada and colonial America took different
   forms and varied in intensity. How can this
   phenomenon be explained?

3. Acadia and the southern colony of Louisiana
   were at the "margins" of New France, separated by great distances from the "compact" St.
   Lawrence valley settlement. To what extent
   did this affect French policy and even the
   colonies' development?

4. The New France of the late seventeenth and
   eighteenth centuries has been described by historian W.J. Eccles as a "military society." Why did
   the military establishment take on an increasingly important role? How did this affect the colonial economy, women, and the class structure?

5. Historians Jan Noel and Joy Parr have argued
   that the family was the most important social
   and economic unit in New France and that
   women enjoyed a somewhat "favoured position" in *ancien régime* society. Do you accept
   this thesis? Explain your reasons.

6. The Roman Catholic church of New France
   and Puritan New England reacted differently
   and adopted different measures to control
   witchcraft and other folk superstitions. How
   can this be explained? What did the responses
   to witchcraft reveal about the societies?

ANALYZING THE EVIDENCE

Study carefully the historical evidence provided
in the accompanying table of population growth,
1710–60, and the following letter written by the
French minister of marine in 1728.

1. Compare the population growth of New
   France with that of the Thirteen Colonies,
   particularly New England.

2. Assess the validity of Maurepas's explanation
   for the difference in population and settlement patterns. What other reasons might the
   French minister have cited?

New France and New England, 1728

Letter from the French Minister of the Marine, Comte de Maurepas, to Claude Thomas Dupuy, Intendant of New France, May 24, 1728:

"It is indeed undesirable to establish new ones [settlements] and the best solution is to sit and wait, seeking to obstruct, however, the approach of the English to the trade in the *pays d'en haut*. The measures adopted for this obstruction must be disguised so as not to be discovered.

"The genius of the people of New England lies in the good farming of their lands and the step-by-step advancement of new settlement. When faced with the consideration of advancing even further, however, they would certainly refuse to do so, since they themselves would have to bear the costs.

"The residents of New France think differently. They always like to advance without burdening themselves with inland settlements, since they gain more in this way and they advance further. This difference in mentality is the reason why the English colonies are more populous and better settled than ours...."

— *Collection de manuscrits contenant lettres, mémoires et autres documents historiques relatifs a la Nouvelle-France* ([Québec: A. Coté et Cie, 1884], vol. 3, p. 142).

POPULATION OF NEW FRANCE AND THE THIRTEEN COLONIES, 1710–1760

NEW ENGLAND	1710	1720	1730	1740	1750	1760
New Hampshire	5 681	9 375	10 755	23 256	27 505	39 093
Massachusetts	62 390	91 008	114 116	151 613	188 000	222 600
Rhode Island	7 573	11 680	16 950	25 255	33 226	45 471
Connecticut	39 450	58 830	75 530	89 580	111 280	142 470
New York	21 625	36 919	48 594	63 665	76 696	117 138
New Jersey	19 872	29 818	37 510	51 373	71 393	93 813
Pennsylvania	24 450	30 062	51 707	85 637	119 666	183 703
Delaware	3 645	5 385	9 170	19 870	28 704	33 250
Maryland	42 741	66 133	91 113	116 093	141 073	162 267
Virginia	78 281	87 757	114 000	180 440	231 033	339 726
North Carolina	15 120	21 270	30 000	51 760	72 984	110 442
South Carolina	10 883	21 040	30 000	45 000	64 000	94 000
Georgia	—	—	—	2 021	5 200	9 578
TOTAL	331 711	446 185	629 445	905 563	1 170 760	1 593 625
NEW FRANCE	16 412 (1706)	24 474	34 118	43 383 (1739)	55 009 (1754)	64 041

National Archives of Canada, *Recensement du Canada, 1665–1871* (Ottawa, 1876), vol. 4; U.S. Bureau of the Census, *The Statistical History of the United States from Colonial Times to the Present* (Stamford, CT: Fairfield Publishers, 1965), p. 756. Reprinted from Virginia R. Robeson, ed., *New France, 1713–1760* (Toronto: OISE Press, 1977). Reprinted by permission of The Ontario Institute for Studies in Education.

CHAPTER 5

CONQUEST AND CONCILIATION

A<small>S THE FRENCH PRESENCE IN NORTH AMERICA</small> expanded beyond the St. Lawrence valley, west to the Great Plains, and south to the lower Mississippi valley, and as the British colonies grew strong and pushed westward, a clash between the two empires seemed inevitable. To the French, interior expansion was essential to their imperial plan of expanding the fur trade and erecting a military barrier that would limit Anglo-American expansion, particularly since the latter might stir up Native resistance and pose a threat to the small French colony in the St. Lawrence valley. To the English, who controlled 15 Atlantic colonies from Newfoundland south to Georgia, as well as the northern fur reserves, access to the vast French-held lands for settlement and trade was thought to be essential.

Not only was the looming conflict one of imperial competition, it was also a contest between two European civilizations — Catholic French and Protestant English. The prize in this struggle would be control of the continent and its peoples. Few in France or England gave any thought to what a full-scale military engagement would mean, and the problems of conciliation it would present.

Imperial rivalry between France and England had begun to intensify in the late seventeenth century. Although the main sources of conflict were Old World quarrels over monarchical succession between France, England, and Spain, eventually the North American colonies were drawn into the contest for empire. Since the defeat of the Spanish Armada in 1588, Spain's power had been waning, while that of France and England was on the rise. In North America the imperial struggle would revolve around conflicting land claims, control of the interior trade, and Amerindian policies. Between 1689 and 1763, the French and English empires would go to war four times. By the end of the decisive conflict in 1763, French rule in North America would end.[1]

THE STRUGGLE FOR EMPIRE

T<small>HE FIRST TWO FRENCH–ENGLISH WARS</small>, the War of the League of Augsburg (1689–97) and the War of the Spanish Succession (1702–13), broke out in Europe, then spread to America. In both conflicts the course of the war in the North American theatre followed a remarkably similar pattern. The French and their Native allies launched attacks on English settlements in the northern colonies, and New Englanders retaliated mostly by raiding French strongholds in Acadia. While the military results in America were inconclusive, the territorial changes effected by the Treaty of Utrecht (1713) were significant, especially for New France. By the cession of 1713, the British gained possession of peninsular Acadia (Nova Scotia), Newfoundland, and the vast Hudson Bay area.[2]

THE STRATEGIC SITUATION

By 1740, the British seemed to have a distinct strategic advantage in North America. The Thirteen Colonies were well settled and established. The population of the Anglo-American colonies (906 000) exceeded that of New France (43 000) by a ratio of 21 to 1. Most English settlements were clustered in a narrow belt of land along the Atlantic seaboard, while French settlement consisted of the small Laurentian colony and scattered pockets over half of North America.

But France was a formidable imperial foe. Economically and militarily, it was the most powerful nation in Europe. New France, united under a French royal administration, could act quickly and in co-ordinated fashion when war was in progress, in sharp contrast to the Thirteen Colonies, which seldom acted together when danger threatened. The French also enjoyed the support of most of the Amerindian nations. Only the Iroquois Confederacy and a few tribes that traded with the English refused to align themselves with the French.

THE WAR OF THE AUSTRIAN SUCCESSION

Another, more intense European war over the succession to the Austrian throne sparked renewed hostilities in North America. The French had great hopes of regaining Nova Scotia, which was not effectively garrisoned and whose Acadian and Micmac population chafed under British rule. Privateers operating out of Louisbourg were very successful in raiding New England shipping.[3] In May 1741, a small colonial force under François Duvivier launched a successful expedition against the fishing station of Canso, but a later attack by French colonials and Micmacs on Annapolis Royal (Fort Anne) was beaten back.

The New Englanders made plans to take the supposedly impregnable fortress of Louisbourg. Governor William Shirley of Massachusetts organized a volunteer militia force of 4300 from Massachusetts, Connecticut, and New Hampshire, under the command of William Pepperrell.[4] In the spring of 1745 the New England force, aided by a British naval squadron, surrounded the fortress and bombarded it for seven weeks, until the French capitulated. The New Englanders ignored European military conventions and treated the townspeople abysmally. During their occupation of Louisbourg they suffered terribly from disease and privation. An attempt by a large French squadron to retake Louisbourg ended in disaster when it was caught in a terrible hurricane, the commander Duc d'Anville died suddenly of apoplexy, and then the crew was laid low by infectious diseases.

On the Canadian frontier there was little fighting. The northern British colonies tried to organize a Mohawk attack on Montreal, but the other tribes of the Iroquois Confederacy opposed the plan, preferring to maintain their neutrality and to continue trading with both sides. The Canadians retaliated by launching an attack on New York, destroying Saratoga, and laying waste to numerous frontier settlements in Massachusetts. More threatening to New

France was the defection in 1747 of their western Native allies, who had grown disenchanted by interruptions in trade and cutbacks in French tributes (or presents) as well as military spending in the interior. The marine officers in command at the western posts averted trouble by calming the rising Amerindian resentment and then diplomatically arranging an inter-tribal defensive alliance known as the Three Fires Confederacy.

When hostilities were terminated by the Treaty of Aix-la-Chappelle (1748), New Englanders received a rude shock. In order to get back possessions in the Netherlands and the trading station of Madras in India, which the French had captured, the British government returned Louisbourg to the French. Loud outcries and bitter resentment were expressed in New England against the British diplomats who failed to consider the strategic importance of this French fortress on their northern flank.[5]

THE BRITISH IN NOVA SCOTIA

The Treaty of Aix-la-Chapelle resulted in immediate reactions from all parties in North America. The British were very aware of the

Trade and the Micmacs of Nova Scotia. What examples of cultural exchanges between Micmacs and the colonists are Illustrated? *Anonymous (Canadian): Micmac Indians (#633), National Gallery of Canada, Ottawa*

resentment and fears of their American colonists. Therefore in 1749 they began building the fortified naval base of Halifax at Chebucto Bay to counteract the threat posed by Louisbourg. It was manned by British regular troops and became the chief Atlantic naval station for the colonies. A fort was also built on the Isthmus of Chignecto facing the French Fort Beauséjour.

Concerned over the presence of an Acadian Roman Catholic majority in Nova Scotia, who steadfastly refused to swear allegiance to the British crown, British authorities encouraged Protestant colonization. Among the 3000 immigrants recruited for the colony were a number of Germans who settled at Lunenburg. Although the British promoted assimilation, the Germans held firmly to their language and Lutheran beliefs. Nova Scotia's population now consisted of British, Acadian, and German communities in addition to the Micmacs.

The Micmacs now found their ancestral lands under threat. Encroachments by the British on the Micmacs' favoured summer encampment area, and cavalier treatment by a lieutenant-governor, Edward Cornwallis, who considered them "rebellious subjects," led to hostilities. The Micmacs attacked some fishermen at Canso, raided two ships at Chignecto, burned a sawmill near Halifax, and then captured a detachment of 18 British soldiers. Cornwallis threatened to bring in troops "to root them out entirely," and his council proposed a bounty of ten guineas for every prisoner or Native scalp. The Micmacs, aided by sympathetic French missionaries, took the initiative in September 1749, formally declaring war on the British intruders.

The British–Micmac war continued until 1752, when a treaty of peace and friendship was imposed at Halifax. But the following year, after the abbé Le Loutre returned from France with promises of material support, the Micmacs resumed their raids on English establishments. A peace plan proposed by Le Loutre to create an independent Micmac hunting and fishing reserve was dismissed by British authorities, who resolved to settle the issue by force.[6]

LA GALISSONIÈRE'S PLAN FOR NEW FRANCE

After 1748, Governor La Galissonière embarked on a strategic plan to strengthen New France in areas threatened by British expansion. He extended and built up France's fortifications throughout the Ohio and Mississippi valleys as far south as Louisiana, strengthened the forts in the Lake Champlain area, and sent a detachment to the Saint John River to prevent British penetration northward through the Gaspé peninsula. In pursuing this program, La Galissonnière was really following — although more aggressively — the policies of his predecessors: establish a line of defensive forts, maintain good relations with the interior tribes, and attempt to increase the colony's lagging population. Within this overall plan, he urged a few new measures — paying gratuities to officers who learned Native languages, licensing traders to assert controls over the prices of trade goods, establishing an Abenaki buffer settlement in northern Maine, and prohibiting *métissage*, or racial intermarriage, because of its alleged bad effect on French "civility."[7]

THE DEPORTATION OF THE ACADIANS

The most adverse and controversial consequence of the war of 1744–48 was the deportation of the Acadians by British authorities in Nova Scotia. Throughout the imperial conflicts, the Acadians had attempted to remain "a people apart" and came to be known as the "neutral French." They steadfastly refused to take the British oath of allegiance because it required a virtual renunciation of an article of their Roman Catholic faith. They had also resisted French attempts to convince them to resettle on Île Royale, near Louisbourg. Furthermore, they remained aloof from the British garrisons and settlements and openly supported the Micmacs and Abenakis in their resistance to British incursions on their hunting and fishing territories. Caught in a precarious position between two rival empires, Acadians attempted to convince each party of their desire for independent cultural survival.

The intensification of the imperial struggle for control over North America in the 1750s brought matters to a head. In 1755 the lieutenant-governor of Nova Scotia, Colonel Charles Lawrence, decided to take drastic measures against the Acadians in spite of warnings from British imperial authorities to exercise caution. When a few Acadian colonists came to Halifax with a petition, Lawrence demanded that they immediately take the oath of allegiance and, when the petitioners resisted, he imprisoned them on the spot. Under considerable pressure from the government of Massachusetts and the British admiral stationed in Halifax, Lawrence and his council decided to deport the Acadians to various British colonies. The secret plan was to seize Acadian men and boys and confiscate their boats, thereby preventing women and children from fleeing with the livestock.[8]

Between 1755 and 1764, over three-quarters of Nova Scotia's Acadian population — 10 000 men, women, and children — were deported. No deliberate attempts were made to split up families, although in the confusion this did occur. Efforts were made, however, to send members of the same community to different colonies in an attempt to force assimilation on the deportees. Some escaped into the woods and took refuge with the Micmacs. Not long after, settlers from New England moved in on the abandoned farmlands. New Englanders who aided in the movement of this large number of people, such as Thomas Hancock of Boston, enjoyed profits from the sale of seized cattle, from the transport of the unfortunates, and later from the sale of some farmlands. It was a desperate act that greatly aroused the French, filled the Canadians and Native peoples with fear should the British turn on them, and even disturbed some British imperial authorities.

THE ACADIANS IN EXILE: EXPERIENCES IN THE THIRTEEN COLONIES

> You are convened this day by His Majesty's orders.
> Clement and Kind as has he been; but how you have answered his kindness,
> Let your own hearts reply! To my natural make and my temper
> Painful the task is I do, which to you I know must be grievous
> Yet I must bow and obey, and deliver the will of our monarch;
> Namely, that all your lands, and dwellings, and cattle of all kinds,
> Forfeited be to the crown; and that you yourselves from this province
> Be transported to other lands. God grant you may dwell there
> Ever as faithful subjects, a happy and peaceable people!
> Prisoners now I declare you: For such is His Majesty's pleasure!
>
> Henry Wadsworth Longfellow, "Evangeline" (1847)

Longfellow's famous poem "Evangeline" did much to immortalize the Acadian deportation of 1755.* The poem, which told a tale of heroic virtue, was loosely based on stories circulating in America almost a century later about the migration of Acadian exiles from the southern coastal colonies inland to Louisiana. Yet the "Great *Dérangement*" of 1755 was only the backdrop for the human drama of Evangeline's experience, and the real story lacked the "romance" of Longfellow's poetry.

The expulsion of the Acadians in 1755 left them a divided people, scattered in exiled groups from the shores of the St. Lawrence to the Gulf of Mexico, and as far as the ports of England and France. In the Anglo-American colonies the Acadian exiles met with a decidedly cool reception at best. Colonel Charles Lawrence, the governor responsible for their deportation, sent them away without even warning his fellow colonial administrators in the colonies to the south. As the Acadians landed at ports from Massachusetts to Georgia, the colonial authorities treated them as "refugees" and coped as best they could.

Most colonial governors and councils responded by detaining them in refugee camps and then attempting some resettlement. Massachusetts was the first colony to act, passing a law in November 1755 to place the Acadian exiles under the custody of "justices of the peace and overseers of the poor." Pennsylvania, Connecticut, and Maryland followed suit, but Virginia took a radically different approach. Governor

---

* See Naomi Griffiths, "Longfellow's Evangeline: The Birth and Acceptance of a Legend," *Acadiensis* 11 (Spring 1982): 28–41 and P.B. Waite's commentary, *Acadiensis* 12 (Autumn 1982): 186.

Robert Dinwiddie, faced with the arrival of over 1000 exiles in late 1755, saw them as "intestine enemies." He associated the Acadians with "the French people" and those who, in his words, were "mudr'g and scalp'g our frontier settlers." After first promising to settle the Acadians, he then adopted the Nova Scotia solution — loading them on ships and sending them to England!

The Acadians remaining in the American colonies, by most accounts, suffered continuing discrimination. While some assimilated and integrated into American colonial society, many — perhaps a majority — struggled to retain their "Acadianness," and some took great risks in stealing away to visit other groups dispersed to neighbouring colonies. Following the peace of 1763, significant numbers of Acadians migrated from their temporary domicile in the Anglo-American Atlantic and French ports to French-speaking areas of southern Louisiana.

The Acadian deportations continued until a year after the signing of the Treaty of Paris in 1763. Groups of Acadians were shipped in "human cargo" boats to American colonies from Massachusetts to the Carolinas, to the Poitou region of France, and even to English seaports. Their forced removal, their later incarceration in refugee camps, and the ravages of disease greatly depleted their numbers, but most held tenaciously to their Acadian identity. Of the approximately 10 000 who were deported, about 2000 managed to escape to Canada, and several hundred trekked overland from the southern coastal colonies to the lower Mississippi and Louisiana. The Acadians in the south became known as "Cajuns"; they continue to form a sizable portion of Louisiana's population.[9]

Through this mass deportation the British simply "removed" a portion of the troublesome element on the Nova Scotia frontier. Demands now arose in the Anglo-American colonies for the complete removal of the French from North America. Parallels are sometimes drawn between the deportation of the Acadians in 1755–64 and the deportation of the Japanese Canadians in British Columbia in 1942. The comparison is fitting: in both cases, citizens were the object of discriminatory legal actions, the seizure of their boats, the detention of the men, and finally mass uprooting.

THE SEVEN YEARS' WAR

WEALTHY VIRGINIANS caused a series of events that sparked the so-called French and Indian War in North America, which by 1755 became part of the international Seven Years' War. In 1749 the Ohio Land Company was organized by a group of Virginians and a few English investors who sought to promote settlement on Amerindian territory over which the French claimed sovereignty. By developing trade relations with the Amerindian tribes and building fortifications, the land company hoped to encourage settlers to purchase land and to settle in Ohio country.

To defend French claims, the governor-general of Canada placed the Ohio region under the jurisdiction of the Detroit commandant and authorized an expedition into the Allegheny, Ohio, Miami, and Maumee river areas in 1749. Lead plates bearing the coat of arms of France were buried at various points throughout the Ohio valley.

GEORGE WASHINGTON PROVOKES HOSTILITIES

Alarmed by the Ohio Land Company's activities, Governor Duquesne decided to drive the American intruders out of the Ohio region. In 1752, Captain Paul Marin was dispatched with 1500 men to build a road from Lake Erie to the headwaters of the Allegheny River, to establish a chain of forts, and to garrison them. Then, in late 1753, the governor of Virginia, Robert Dinwiddie, sent a party under a young colonial militia officer, George Washington, to Fort Le Boeuf to demand the withdrawal of the French. A letter of protest from Dinwiddie was simply disregarded. To reassert their claims of sovereignty, the French pushed on to the forks of the Ohio and erected Fort Duquesne (Pittsburgh), which gave them control over the region.

George Washington's second trip into Ohio country led to the infamous Jumonville affair. A small French diplomatic party led by Joseph Coulon de Villiers de Jumonville, while on its way to negotiate with the Virginians, was ambushed in its unguarded camp at Great Meadows, south of

The young Virginian, George Washington, on horseback during the Seven Years' War.

Fort Duquesne. The French officer and nine of his men were killed and scalped, and their unburied bodies were left to the crows. This hostile act by a small force of Virginia militia against a diplomatic mission during a period of peace on the lonely frontier led to open war.

The French laid siege to Washington's hastily constructed Fort Necessity in July 1754. They forced Washington to surrender, but allowed him to retire with his undisciplined colonial militia although he did not honour the terms of capitulation he had signed. This was also in spite of some strong demands to avenge Jumonville's death. In his haste to retire, Washington abandoned his baggage, containing his journal, which had plans for attacking the French interior posts in peacetime. The French made good use of all this in their subsequent war propaganda in Europe.[10]

The success of the French convinced the Anglo-American colonies that their principal weakness was their lack of unity. They needed a common plan of defence and integrated policy like the French. In June 1754 representatives from New York, Pennsylvania, Maryland, the New England colonies, and the Iroquois Six Nations met at Albany to draft a plan of union. Although the Albany plan fell apart, military strategy was planned in common at a conference in Alexandria, Virginia, the following year. A four-pronged military assault on New France's defence line was approved. It was also agreed that British Major General Edward Braddock would co-ordinate the military operations and that British regulars or "redcoats" would be needed to reinforce the Anglo-American militia.

VAUDREUIL'S CONTINENTAL STRATEGY

While the British and the Anglo-American colonies prepared for their campaign, the French developed a military strategy of their own, under the overall direction of Governor Vaudreuil. His plan called for the strengthening of the Canadian militia with some 3600 *troupes de terre* (French regulars), the co-ordination of large numbers of Amerindian war parties with the French force, and the launching of a series of surprise guerrilla raids at various points along the wide American frontier — a strategy markedly different from the usual European-type disciplined formation fighting. There was also a small French naval force on Lake Ontario and Lake Erie.

This military strategy, based on the assumption that hostilities would take place mostly along the "frontier," worked well in the early engagements. General Braddock, with an army of 1400 redcoats and 450 colonials, suffered a stunning defeat at the Battle of Monongahela, south of Fort Duquesne, in 1755. William Shirley's plan to attack Fort Niagara was abandoned; and the French commander, Dieskau, halted Colonel William Johnson's invasion force in the Lake Champlain area. For Britain and the Anglo-American colonies, the prospects at the end of 1755 looked bleak. But all of this occurred before war was officially declared in Europe.[11]

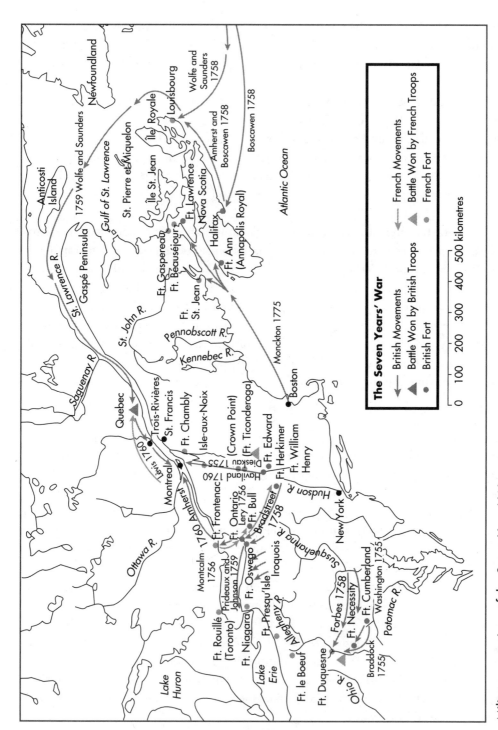

Military operations of the Seven Years' War.

THE OFFICIAL WAR

Britain's fortunes did begin to improve when the Seven Years' War (1756–63) commenced in Europe. In the autumn of 1756, William Pitt became the British prime minister and announced a more aggressive policy in the North American war. British regulars in large numbers — at least 23 000 — and the Royal Navy were directed to assume a major role in the conquest of New France. The heavy demands in Canada on food supplies — for the French regular troops, for Acadian refugees, and for large numbers of Native warriors recruited in the upper country — put a severe strain on the economy. Food shortages were rendered more acute by crop failures. Prices rose dramatically, and this inflation was worsened by the profiteering of the military suppliers. Intendant François Bigot and his associates of the *Grande Société* indulged in the excesses of the casino, the ballroom, and the banquet hall while the population faced rationing and privation. A typhus epidemic among the troops spread to the General Hospital at Quebec and to the townspeople. On the western plains the Cree had destroyed six of the eight posts of the region, leaving only Fort Dauphin and Fort La Reine (now Portage la Prairie, Manitoba) to compete with the Hudson's Bay Company.

The turning point of the war came in 1758. A massive attack was launched against Fort Carillon (Ticonderoga, New York), Fort Duquesne in the Ohio valley, and Louisbourg. Louisbourg resisted for 48 days, which saved Canada from invasion by sea. The fortress fell eventually as a result of an effective blockade by the Royal Navy and a concerted attack from the land. In July a British force of 15 000 men, the largest army amassed in North America to that time, attacked the French at Fort Carillon, now commanded by the Marquis de Montcalm. But the smaller French force of 3600 held out, albeit with heavy casualties and internal bickering over French strategy.[12]

The military quarrel pitted Canadian-born Vaudreuil against the French general, the Marquis de Montcalm. Montcalm argued for a concentration of French troops along the inner defences of the St. Lawrence and Richelieu rivers, and wanted the Canadian militia incorporated into the regular army, where they would be subject to traditional military discipline. Governor Vaudreuil insisted on strengthening the outer defence lines and keeping up the guerrilla warfare in the Ohio valley. The quarreling prompted Montcalm to request his own recall to France. Instead, he was elevated to lieutenant-general and placed in supreme command of all French forces in North America. The colonial strategy was now jettisoned and, as Governor Vaudreuil observed, "Now war is established here on the European basis…. It is no longer a matter of making a raid, but of conquering or being conquered. What a revolution! What a change." Montcalm would proceed to meet the British invaders in the same manner as they attacked — by following European tactics and conventions. The colonials were becoming marginal to the decisions determining their future.[13]

The British also had their problems. In Massachusetts a lively controversy raged between the colonial civil officials and the British military over the quartering of troops. In Virginia the governor and the elected assembly quarreled over taxation. As the financial burdens of warfare made themselves felt, the colonists refused to accept responsibility for their defence. Hopes of finally conquering New France were raised in 1758 and 1759 with British victories at Fort Frontenac and Fort Duquesne (renamed Fort Pitt), marking the collapse of the French presence in the *pays d'en haut*.[14]

BATTLES FOR QUEBEC

During 1759 the British gradually closed in on the St. Lawrence valley settlements. In June the Royal Navy, under Vice-Admiral Charles Saunders, brought General James Wolfe's 8500 British regulars up the St. Lawrence toward Quebec. They managed to navigate the river entrance, thanks to the services of captured river pilots. However, British landing attempts at Beauport proved unsuccessful, and they were soundly defeated at the battle of Montmorency on July 31, 1759. But they managed to entrench themselves at Pointe Lévis, across from Quebec, and from there they began a bombardment that lasted two months and reduced Quebec to rubble. While the city was under seige, Fort Niagara fell and the French retreated from their forts in the Lake Champlain area. Montreal was saved from direct attack in 1759 when a determined French force made a successful stand against British General Jeffrey Amherst's 11 000-strong army.

The battle for Quebec was far from a classic military engagement. The British despaired of being able to force its surrender before the navigation season closed. General Wolfe was desperately ill, but he made full use of military intimidation tactics: an army of 1600 soldiers was ordered to lay waste to the countryside along the St. Lawrence south shore, leaving buildings and ships aflame, crops and animals destroyed, and the civilian population shuddering over the destruction. The campaign was backed up by Wolfe's manifesto, threatening to see "their habitations destroyed, their sacred temples exposed to an exasperated soldiery, their harvest utterly ruined" if they answered the call to militia duty.

Quebec fell almost by accident. On September 13, 1759, just before the fleet would have to return to Europe, Wolfe managed in the night to land 4500 men at Anse au Foulon and to scale the steep cliff leading to the Plains of Abraham. Montcalm ordered a premature attack instead of awaiting the arrival of available reinforcements. In a 15-minute encounter, the French regulars and poorly trained militiamen were scattered, and the defenders ran for safety into the walled city. The fact that Wolfe fell early in the engagement and that Montcalm was mortally wounded while retreating says much about both the generalship and the tactics.[15]

Rather than attempting to break through the fortifications, the British agreed to a capitulation that allowed Vaudreuil and the French army to retreat to Montreal with full honours of war. British sentries were posted to prevent looting by the starving inhabitants of the devastated capital. The Royal Navy sailed off to England, leaving a garrison to the mercies of a

"A View of the Taking of Quebec, September 17, 1759" gives a somewhat distorted view of the military operation.

harsh winter, scurvy, and guerrilla attacks by Canadian militia and Amerindian warriors.

The capture of Quebec in 1759 did not mean the fall of New France. In April 1760, the Marquis de Lévis and the French army took the offensive, met the British under Brigadier James Murray at Sainte-Foy, and defeated them, forcing them to beat a disorderly retreat behind the walls of Quebec. A few weeks later the Royal Navy reappeared with an invasion force, and for a second time the French army retreated to Montreal.

THE CAPITULATION OF MONTREAL

Three separate British forces converged on Montreal. In August the Amerindian allies of the French signed a treaty of peace and neutrality with General Amherst at Oswegatchie, guaranteeing them "the quiet and peaceable possession of the lands we live upon." On September 5, the first allies of France in the New World, the Hurons, signed a peace treaty with General Murray at Longueuil, according to which they were guaranteed the exercise of their religion and customs and freedom of trade. Seeing that the Canadian militia had disbanded and that the Seven Nations of Canada, the traditional Amerindian allies of the French, had made peace with the invaders, Governor Vaudreuil decided to spare his disheartened French regulars further bloodshed. By the Articles of Capitulation of September 8, 1759, he surrendered the whole of New France to General Jeffrey Amherst.

New France did not surrender unconditionally. The Articles of Capitulation of Montreal were binding on the British occupation force and afforded the Canadians and their Native allies a number of important guarantees. Among the important concessions granted by the British victors were the promises not to punish the Canadian militiamen for having participated in the fighting, the free exercise of the Roman Catholic religion, the continuation of the rights and privileges of the clergy and *seigneurs*, and the guarantee of the rights enjoyed by the Native peoples under the French régime. Although the population feared the army of occupation and the consequences of British Protestant domination, there were signs that the British might retain certain aspects of an *ancien régime* society.[16]

THE AFTERMATH OF CONQUEST

The capitulation of New France was followed by a period of military occupation and martial law until a definitive peace treaty was signed in Paris in February 1763. In 1762, a French naval attack resulted in the capture of key outports in Newfoundland. This gave France an important diplomatic advantage in protecting its fishing rights. By the Treaty of Paris, New France was transformed into the British colony of Quebec. Military rule was not terminated until 1764, when James Murray was named civilian governor of the new British colony.

In the immediate aftermath of the conquest, both the French and the Canadians searched for explanations for the loss of Canada. Prominent colonials charged that France had virtually abandoned Canada until late in the war, that Montcalm and his French officers were incompetent, and that the *Grande Société* surrounding the Intendant François Bigot had bred corruption and social decay in the critical years of war with Britain. The fact that Bigot and his associates, who had amassed huge personal fortunes, were later tried and imprisoned in France for their corruption did little to soothe the resentment in Canada.

While negotiating the definitive treaty of peace in 1762, French diplomats had taken into account the

Essayist Marie Elisabeth Bégon, wife of the governor at Trois-Rivières during the last years of the French régime. Her letters, found in Paris nearly 200 years later, give a candid view of the high-living and decadent days of the régime.

economic value of their colonies and the costs of their administration and defence. It was concluded that the small island of
Guadeloupe was much more valuable than Canada. In addition, it was known that many of the Anglo-American colonies
were disgruntled and that the Amerindian nations in the hinterland were on the verge of "taking up the hatchet" to stop
further intrusion on their territories in the Ohio valley and the
Great Lakes basin. It seemed quite possible that if there were
a revolt of the British colonies and an Amerindian uprising,
Canada would serve as a Trojan horse in the British dominions.
By keeping the West Indian sugar islands and the valuable
Newfoundland fisheries, France gained immediately and
hoped to eventually regain Quebec.[17]

Mother Marie de
l'Incarnation, Ursuline, 1672.

THE BRITISH CONQUEST AND ITS CONSEQUENCES

F OREIGN INVASION, MILITARY DEFEAT, AND OCCUPATION, followed by the imposition of British rule, were a traumatic
series of events for *Canadiens*. Many of the colony's inhabitants
feared that British rule would bring repression, reduce them to
a second-rate conquered people, and lead to assimilation by
British-sponsored immigration. This "conquest mentality" of
Great Britain's "new subjects" would persist in Quebec and later
emerge to animate public debate about the place of French Canada in North America.

Yet the conquest and its immediate impact — the departure of the French administrators and troops and some Canadian merchants and officials — did not mark a complete
change for the direction of life in the colony. British rule changed some political and economic arrangements, but many aspects of Canadian life continued with little disruption. An
overemphasis on the impact of the conquest can obscure the important elements of continuity in the social and economic development of a Canadian community on the northern
half of the continent.

THE BEGINNINGS OF *LA SURVIVANCE*

Quebec was ruled as a British crown colony and was not incorporated into one of the Thirteen
Colonies. The Canadians were now forced to turn inward to their ethnic and cultural roots in
a British-dominated political and economic environment. They retained their church and its institutions and their *seigneurial* system of landholding. This system provided them with a solid bloc of

Intendant's palace and Superior Council at Quebec, 1761.

francophone settlement that could guarantee some protection from attempts at forced assimilation. On the other hand, the Roman Catholic church could no longer receive clergy or royal subsidies from France, and the expansion of its landholdings was limited, as it had been under French rule.

The conquest resulted in some social decapitation: French officials, the military establishment, and some elements of the nobility left, leaving a vacuum at the upper levels of society that the British would fill. There is little evidence of economic decapitation of a colonial *bourgeoisie* or entrepreneurial class because during the French régime the economy was controlled primarily by French metropolitan interests. Furthermore, French-Canadian merchants and investors continued to pursue the fur trade for 20 years after the conquest before a decline set in. The gradual trend among British merchants toward purchasing *seigneuries* also indicated continuity, since it had been common among French merchants to seek seigneurial status in the years before 1760.[18]

The conquest also was troublesome for the British rulers. First and foremost, they were faced with the huge military expenditures needed to maintain sizable contingents in North America. They feared an attempt by the French to regain their former colony, a general rising of the Native peoples of the interior, and the growing restlessness of their seaboard colonies, which seemed to chafe under mercantilistic restrictions and refused to accept a share of the burden of their defence in the late war. There was also the problem of incorporating a colony of "new subjects" who had no experience of representative government or English common law into the British empire. This was greatly complicated by the fact that the British army of occupation found itself enveloped by a society composed of 70 000 French-speaking, Roman Catholic *Canadiens*. These years were the germination point for *la survivance*, French Canada's struggle for cultural survival in North America.[19]

RESPONSES TO THE CONQUEST

HE CONQUEST OF CANADA by the British provoked a wide variety of responses — Amerindian, Acadian, colonial American, and *Canadien*. The conquerors themselves had to decide whether they would pursue a policy of forced assimilation or of conciliation and accommodation to local conditions. The early decades of British rule tested the limits of British assimilationist policy and French Canada's cultural identity, American territorial expansion, and Amerindian resistance.

THE AMERINDIAN REACTIONS

The Native peoples were the first to react overtly to the British conquest of Canada. Most Amerindian nations had sided with the French, who engaged in trade with them, provided annual presents to their allies, and respected their independence and their ancestral land rights. The Anglo-Americans were perceived as land-hungry intruders bent on dispossessing them. Only the Mohawk nation among the Iroquois had remained faithful to the British cause, through the Covenant Chain relationship. But even they insisted that this friendship was based on a two-row wampum agreement, whereby the Iroquois retained their independence.

On September 15–16, 1760, a week after the capitulation of the French army, delegates of the Seven Nations of Canada met with British officers and Superintendent William Johnson of the Northern Indian Department (which had been organized in 1755 to parallel French policy) to confirm earlier agreements. By the Treaty of Kahnawake they "buried the French hatchet" and entered into an alliance with the British. The British, on their part, promised them the perpetual possession of the territory they inhabited in the colony and the services the French had provided them.

In the *pays d'en haut* the situation was less settled. A movement of Amerindian resistance to relentless encroachments of Anglo-American settlement, erroneously called a "conspiracy," erupted under the leadership of Chief Pontiac of the Ottawas.

It received some moral support from traders in Louisiana, the remaining French colony west of the Mississippi, but the hope of a return of the armies of Louis XV to "liberate" the Amerindians was misplaced. In addition to the possible loss of their ancestral lands, the Amerindians faced a decline in the fur trade on which they had come to rely.[20]

THE ROYAL PROCLAMATION OF 1763

The Royal Proclamation of 1763 was designed largely to counteract Amerindian fears. In drawing the boundary line west of the Appalachians, British authorities opted to continue established French "Indian policy." Two aspects of the proclamation seemed reassuring to those threatened by the moving frontier of Anglo-American settlement. First, the entire upper country was designated a vast Native reserve, from which all unauthorized squatters and settlers were to remove themselves. Second, lands in this region could revert only to the crown, never to private individuals or land companies, in order to curb land swindling by Anglo-Americans.

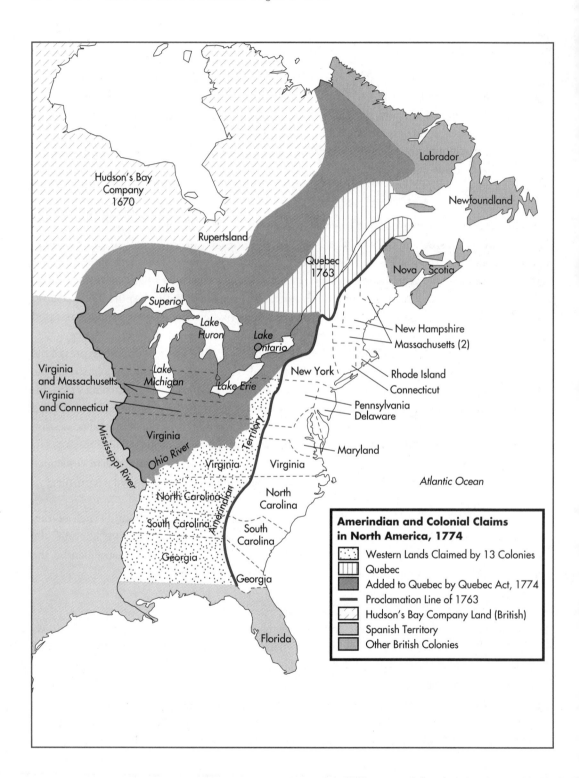

Hudson's Bay
Company
1670

Labrador

Newfoundland

Rupertsland

Quebec
1763

Nova Scotia

Lake
Superior

Lake
Huron

Lake
Ontario

New Hampshire
Massachusetts (2)

Virginia
and Massachusetts

Lake
Michigan

Lake Erie

New York

Rhode Island
Connecticut

Virginia
and Connecticut

Pennsylvania
Delaware

Virginia

Ohio River

Ohio Territory

Maryland

Mississippi River

Virginia

Virginia

North Carolina

Amerindian

North
Carolina

Atlantic Ocean

South Carolina

South
Carolina

Georgia

Georgia

Florida

**Amerindian and Colonial Claims
in North America, 1774**

Western Lands Claimed by 13 Colonies
Quebec
Added to Quebec by Quebec Act, 1774
Proclamation Line of 1763
Hudson's Bay Company Land (British)
Spanish Territory
Other British Colonies

THE AMERICAN RESPONSE: WESTERN EXPANSION AND "INDIAN REMOVAL"

THE TREATY THAT ENDED THE SEVEN YEARS' WAR in 1763 was reached between Britain and France without consulting a single Amerindian tribe. Yet, if any people had a strong claim to possession of the entire continent, it was the Native inhabitants. This Amerindian claim was stated most clearly in 1761 by a Chippewa chief. After engaging in trade with the New Jersey merchant Alexander Henry, the chief made it clear his people had no love for the British conquerors:

> Englishmen, although you have conquered the French, you have not conquered us! We are not your slaves. These lakes, these woods, and mountains were left to us by our ancestors. They are our inheritance and we will part with them to none....
>
> Englishmen, your king has never sent us any presents nor entered into any treaty with us, wherefore he and we are still at war; and until he does these things we must consider that we have no father, no friend among the white men than the King of France.

Most disturbing to the interior tribes was the growing influx of Anglo-American colonists into the Ohio country. Whereas the French had come as traders interested mostly in furs, the English intruders came as settlers to "displace" the Amerindians from their lands.

Pontiac, chief of the Ottawas, was successful in welding a confederacy of Amerindian tribes south of the Great Lakes in Ohio country and mounting an organized resistance movement. In the summer of 1763, Pontiac and the Amerindian alliance rose in rebellion. The uprising caught the British off guard at Fort Detroit, Fort Pitt, and other western posts. Under orders from British General Jeffrey Amherst, the commander of Fort Pitt gave the attacking Amerindian chiefs, with whom he was negotiating, blankets from the fort's hospital. An epidemic of smallpox did what the British soldiers had been unable to do, decimating the Amerindian forces.

Although Detroit and Fort Pitt held out, Pontiac's uprising overran most of the western posts from Michilimackinac in the northwest to Presqu'ile on Lake Erie. Soon all of the Ohio valley was enveloped in conflict, with Amerindians fighting to drive the English colonists back across the Allegheny Mountains and out of Ohio country. The uprising, however, was eventually quelled by regular British troops and colonial militia. It was a decisive clash, signifying the beginning of "Indian removal" in the western lands.

Most Anglo-American colonial leaders saw the proclamation line as a British attempt to confine their colonies' development to the Atlantic seaboard. But, for the Amerindian peoples, it was a clear recognition of their right to a share in the lands of North America. British authorities went even further in attempting to remove the sources of trade disorder on the frontier. A system of trade licences very similar to the former French *congés* system was introduced. The provision for the Ohio valley as part of the "Indian reserve" remained in place until the Treaty of Paris of 1783, which ended the War of Independence but also detached the Ohio valley from the Quebec colony.

The Royal Proclamation also instituted civil government in what was now called the colony of Quebec. The boundaries were those of the middle and lower St. Lawrence valley, roughly the seigneurial lands of the former French colony.[21]

THE ACADIAN RESPONSE

With the restoration of peace, many exiled Acadians seized the opportunity to return to their former homeland in Nova Scotia, only to find their ancestral lands occupied by New England settlers. In 1766 one group of 900 Acadians in Massachusetts gathered in Boston and tramped for four months through the wilderness, northward along the north shore of the Bay of Fundy to Chignecto and back to the Annapolis valley. Like most groups who returned there, they were met by strangers and discovered that familiar villages now bore new anglicized names.

Most returning Acadians chose to set down new roots in different parts of the Atlantic region. The largest group settled in a new homeland that in 1784 would become New Brunswick. New Acadian communities sprang up all along the Gulf of St. Lawrence, from Chignecto to the lower Gaspé peninsula. Some re-established themselves in Nova Scotia along the lower Bay of Fundy, from Digby southward. When the dikes of the marshland area were in need of repairs, they were called on to share their dike-building skills with the neighbouring New Englanders. Still other repatriated Acadians made their homes on Cape Breton's western shore and on the French islands of St. Pierre and Miquelon. Between 1764 and 1800 the Acadian population in the British Atlantic colonies jumped from a low of 2600 to 8000, and a fiercely independent Acadian community was once again thriving.[22]

ACTS OF CONCILIATION

THE BRITISH GOVERNMENT after 1763 soon recognized that attempting a rapid and forced assimilation of "His Majesty's new subjects" by legislation and large-scale immigration would be foolish. Instead it adopted a line of conduct best described as one of conciliation. Three factors seemed to dictate such a practical course of action. Growing restiveness in the Thirteen Colonies might infect the *Canadiens*, unless steps were taken to secure their allegiance. There was also the possibility of French intervention to reclaim the territories it had ceded. Finally, French-speaking Catholics with a strong military tradition, accustomed to a hierarchical, monarchical system, and with no experience of parliamentary institutions, could possibly be won over to British rule.

The British were aided in their conciliation policy by two profound external events — the American War of Independence (1775–83) and the French Revolution of the late 1780s and early 1790s. The first revolution convinced many *Canadiens* that British rule was much preferable to Anglo-American absorption. The revolution in France, with its attacks on the monarchy, privileged orders, and Roman Catholic church, left French Canada estranged, if not alienated, from its former imperial parent. British rule in Quebec could be conceived as a continuation of many French *ancien régime* institutions and practices.

CONCILIATION UNDER MURRAY AND CARLETON

Governor James Murray maintained strict discipline in the British army in Quebec, so that the Canadians came to respect it for its restrained and civil behaviour. Acts of humanity toward the civilian population also served him well. Captains of the former Canadian militia were granted new commissions and were used to aid the civil power. When there was a shortage of essential supplies in the colony, the population was issued with military stores. These measures all had their desired effect: when Murray needed *voyageurs* and other volunteers to put down Pontiac's rising in the upper country, he got all he needed.

Gradually Murray came to recognize the important role of the church in education, health and welfare services, and moral and spiritual direction. He realized that the church and its institutions might make better allies than enemies. Accordingly, grants were made to various women's institutions, to the poor parish clergy, and to the hospitals. Even the problem of finding a successor to Bishop Pontriand, who had served from 1741 to 1760, was resolved amicably. The clergy's preferred candidate was set aside, but the *abbé* Jean-Olivier Briand, a commoner (in contrast to the aristocrats who had previously monopolized high ecclesiastical offices), was secured as a reasonably acceptable replacement. With the assistance of British authorities, he was spirited across the English Channel to France, consecrated by French bishops, and returned to Quebec with the title of Superintendent of the Romish Religion. This was remarkable in

General James Murray, the first British governor of Quebec.

view of the official ban on a Roman Catholic hierarchy in the British empire at that time.

The *Canadiens* were further won over by indirect, and unexpected, benefits of British rule. Worthless French paper money was still in circulation and some goods had been hoarded, so prices after 1760 had risen sharply. The British imposed price controls, and as a result prices of hoarded goods dropped by as much as 50–80 percent. Paper money was registered, raising hopes of a fairer currency system than under the French régime, when colonial currency was regularly discounted by one-third. The fur trade was resumed in 1764. Opportunities for improved wheat exports emerged as the colony gained access to a new protected market in Britain, and traditional sources of wheat were closed off amid the rumblings of revolution in the Thirteen Colonies.

Lumber exports to Britain also grew to sizable proportions, and before long the Ottawa valley's forests were being tapped. Instead of seeking seasonal employment in the fur trade, there was now opportunity for alternative employment in the lumber camps. The population of the colony was beginning to increase rapidly, so that Murray's introduction of the potato as a popular

Sir Guy Carleton, Lord Dorchester, the successor to Governor Murray.

food was viewed favourably. These were some of the measures that resulted in what some historians have called a second conquest, or psychological conquest, of the colony.

One aspect of imperial policy was never implemented in the colony, and this lack of compliance by governors Murray and Guy Carleton did much to conciliate the "new subjects." The Royal Proclamation of 1763 provided for the introduction of English criminal and civil law and for an elected House of Assembly. Both governors ignored the implementation of English civil law, failed to call an assembly, and ruled with an appointed council. Under Governor Carleton, relations improved further. In 1771, he obtained an order that all new land grants should be conferred in *seigneurial* tenure.[23]

THE QUEBEC ACT, 1774

The culmination of the policy of conciliation was the Quebec Act of 1774, regarded by many in the Anglo-American colonies as just another of the so-called "intolerable acts." However, since the American Revolution broke out before the passing of the Quebec Act by the British parliament, it cannot have been a cause of the revolution. Under its provisions, the *Canadiens* obtained fresh guarantees for the protection of "their Property and Possessions, together with all Customs and Usages relative thereto, and all other their Civil Rights." Just as the Royal

Proclamation of 1763 has been depicted as a charter of Amerindian rights, so the Quebec Act was the charter of French-Canadian rights accorded by the British government. The seigneurial system of land tenure was continued under the property-rights clause and the French colonial civil law was maintained to regulate commerce and protect traditional forms of inheritance, including women's property rights as enjoyed under French rule.

The act also gave the Roman Catholic church the right to collect its tithes and other dues. This represented a gain in power that the church used in the following century to acquire a status and influence it had not enjoyed under French rule. The application of British criminal law, with provision for jury trials and the abolition of the French inquisitorial procedure, was widely acclaimed. The Amerindians in the upper country were reassured by the annexation of the Ohio valley, the territory south of Lakes Ontario and Erie, to the colony of Quebec. This seemed to protect them from land speculators from New York and Pennsylvania. It also pleased the Montreal fur traders, who now had undisputed access to this region.

The small British commercial minority, especially those in Montreal, whom Murray had once characterized as "merchant grab-alls," was not pleased with all provisions of the British legislation. It deplored the lack of provision for an elected legislative assembly (which it hoped to dominate), the decision not to impose English as the official language, and the failure to introduce English commercial law. Had the minority's wishes been followed by the British authorities, it is not likely that Quebec would have remained loyal to Britain during the American War of Independence.

As it was, Quebec even rebuffed metropolitan French attempts to have the former French colony join the Americans in throwing off British rule. The Quebec Act not only guaranteed the survival of the "French fact" in North America, it also helped preserve British rule in the northern half of the continent. British rule in Quebec was now based on rallying the *seigneurs* and clergy to the new order. The new order was in many ways a continuation of the old order — monarchy, "national" church, privileged orders, mercantilist policies, and conciliar government.[24]

ACTIVITIES

KEY TERMS AND CONCEPTS

Identify and briefly explain the historical significance of the following terms and concepts:

- Wars of monarchical succession
- Fortress Louisbourg
- British–Micmac War (1749–52)
- La Galissoniere's plan
- Acadian deportation
- Ohio country
- Fort Necessity
- Battle of Monongahela (1755)
- Vaudreuil's war strategy
- Battle for Quebec

- Articles of Capitulation
- Conquest mentality
- *La survivance*
- Social decapitation
- Pontiac's uprising
- Royal Proclamation line
- Acadian resettlement
- "Second conquest"
- Quebec Act (1774)

QUESTIONS FOR DISCUSSION

1. Was the struggle for the continent in the mid-eighteenth century primarily a contest of rival European empires or an epic clash of civilizations that pitted French absolutism against British democracy? Explain your position.
2. Which side — France or Britain — held the strategic advantage in the wars for empire? Explain why.
3. The deportation of the Acadians from Nova Scotia in 1755 is often considered a great "black mark" on the record of British imperial policy. On what grounds would such a claim be made?
4. What caused the outbreak of the "French and Indian War" in 1754? Which side instigated the conflict over the Ohio valley?
5. Why did New France fall in 1760? Was it due to British strategic superiority, French military incompetence, France's neglect of Canada, or some other factor?
6. Was the conquest a catastrophe or merely an incident in the evolution of French Canada? Were its consequences traumatic, and, if so, for whom?
7. Why did Britain's great act of conciliation — the Quebec Act of 1774 — meet with such hostility in the Thirteen Colonies?

ANALYZING PRIMARY EVIDENCE

1. In the critical months of the Seven Years' War, a serious quarrel broke out between Governor Vaudreuil and the Marquis de Montcalm over the proper strategy to be employed by French forces in the defence of Canada. The following statement, made by a French military aide in 1758, endorses Montcalm's position:

"Now war is established here on the European basis. Projects for the campaign, for armies, for artillery, for sieges, for battles. It no longer is a matter of making a raid, but of conquering or being conquered. What a revolution! What a change!"

— *Journals of Louis Antoine de Bougainville, 1758.*

What was Montcalm's strategy, and how did it differ from the governor's? Could the Vaudreuil military plan have saved Canada, or delayed the fall?

2. Peter Kalm, a botanist from Swedish Finland who toured widely in North America during 1748–49, offered many fascinating observations. In the following passage, identify his hypothesis (or central argument) and assess its validity:

"It is...of great advantage to the crown of England that the North American colonies are near a country under the government of the French, like Canada.... For the English colonies in this part of the world have increased so much in their number of inhabitants, and in their riches, that they almost vie with Old England.

"I have been told by Englishmen...that the English colonies in North America, in the space of thirty or fifty years, would be able to form a state by themselves, entirely independent of Old England. But as the whole country which lies along the sea-shore is unguarded, and on the land side is harassed by the French, in times of war these dangerous neighbors are sufficient to prevent the connection of the colonies with their mother country from being quite broken off. The English government has therefore sufficient reason to consider the French in North America as the best means of keeping their colonies in due submission."

ANALYZING HISTORICAL
Interpretations

Following are a few of the leading interpretations of the conquest and its consequences.
• Select the argument with which you most agree.
• Argue the case by using concrete supporting evidence.

1. "This English conquest was the grand crisis of Canadian history. It was the beginning of a new life. With England came Protestantism, and the Canadian church grew purer and better in the presence of an adverse faith. Material growth, an increased mental activity, an education real though fenced and guarded, a warm and genuine patriotism, all date from the peace of 1763. England imposed by the sword on reluctant Canada the boon of rational and ordered liberty.... A happier calamity never befell a people than the conquest of Canada by British arms."

— Francis Parkman, *The Old Regime in Canada* (Boston, 1887), pp. 400–401.

2. "Came the catastrophe of 1760–63: the Conquest confirmed by the cession. A small people with at least the beginnings of [economic] development...were introduced into a new empire....

"For the generations rising after 1760, one occupation remained above all others, cultivation of the land.... After 1760, and not before, it was more accurate to say of the *Canadien*: first and foremost, a farming man...[in a state of] economic inferiority."

— Maurice Séguin, "The Conquest and French Canadian Economic Life," *Action nationale* 28 (1947).

3. "Canadians of the upper class, who refused to submit to the victors, emigrated. They foresaw that their personal future was compromised in a colony where the principal channels of social promotion would, in future, be occupied by the British....

"Their fall...is the most striking social phenomenon of the first generation after the Conquest."

— Michel Brunet, *French Canada and the Early Decades of British Rule, 1760–1791* (1968).

4. "On the whole the Conquest was not the source of a trauma that can explain all the difficulties French-Canadian society would have to endure afterwards. The fact is that the economic, political, social, and judicial structures remained stable at least until 1791, so that the Conquest produced no basic change in the life of someone living in the St. Lawrence Valley.... The social 'decapitation' cited with such feeling by Michel Brunet was, then, not a direct result of the Conquest. Rather, it was the result of certain deficiencies in French-Canadian business. An individualist, the French-Canadian fur trader was afraid of associating with others, of diversifying his investments...."

— Fernand Ouellet, "French-Canadian Nationalism: From Its Origins to the Insurrection of 1837," *Canadian Historical Review* 45 (December 1964).

PART II

THE EMERGING NATIONS

1763–1873

With the great French–British imperial contest for the continent over, the Thirteen Colonies and the northern British colonies continued to evolve along similar paths, but in peculiarly different ways. After 1763 British economic, maritime, and defence policies came to rankle colonial authorities and mercantile interests in the Atlantic seaboard colonies. Colonial protests escalated until tension erupted into violence, and the Declaration of Independence (1776) led to the American Revolution. During the War of Independence, the British North American colonies remained loyal, or at least neutral, and became a haven for thousands of American exiles who claimed to be "Loyalists." The "Tories" of the America's Revolutionary era became Canada's "Loyalists"; and British North America remained more British than American. When the conflict was renewed between 1812 and 1814, the British northern colonies seemed to emerge from that war with a new "sense of community," distinct and different from that of the American republic.

In the wake of the War of 1812, Canadians as well as Americans showed signs of increasing national purpose and identity. The first half of the nineteenth century saw the American republic embark upon territorial expansion until the United States spanned the entire continent and asserted its "Manifest Destiny" in the hemisphere. Such expansionism, however, produced sectional conflict between North and South. Those irreconcilable divisions were settled by a bloody civil war that lasted four long years and left over 600 000 Americans dead. By contrast, British North America continued its pattern of halting, non-revolutionary change and evolution. The scattered, diverse set of colonial principalities of the late 1700s matured under British colonial administration and became, through a succession of political adjustments, a federal, self-governing state extending by 1873 from the Atlantic to the Pacific oceans.

Throughout the formative years 1763–1873, the two North American nations developed their fundamental political, economic, and social institutions. Each nation met and responded differently to the period's critical challenges: the War of American Independence, the frontier experience of settlement, the forming of national political parties, the need for effective government institutions, and the consolidation of federal power within a transcontinental state.

MAKING CONNECTIONS TIMELINE

A.D.	CANADA	NORTH AMERICA	UNITED STATES
1763	Royal Proclamation of 1763	Treaty of Paris; end of the Seven Years' War	Proclamation Line limits expansion westward
1766	•	•	The Stamp Act and American protest
1773	•	•	Boston Tea Party; Coercive Acts
1774	The Quebec Act, charter of French-Canadian rights	•	First Continental Congress
1775	American invasion of Quebec: Quebec rejects revolution. Nova Scotia remains neutral	Outbreak of the American Revolution	Lexington and Concord — start of revolution
1776	Loyalist migrations begin	•	Declaration of Independence; Thomas Paine's *Common Sense*
1783	Loss of the Ohio Valley lands by treaty	Treaty of Paris ends American Revolution	Independence achieved under Articles of Confederation
1788	•	•	Making of the U.S. Constitution
1791	Constitutional Act — Lower Canada and Upper Canada formed	•	American Bill of Rights adopted
1800	•	•	Thomas Jefferson elected president
1803	•	•	Louisiana Purchase
1809	•	•	British Non-Intercourse Act; Tecumseh forms Indian Confederacy
1812	American invasion of Upper Canada and burning of York	War of 1812	Congress enters "Second War of Independence"
1814	•	Treaty of Ghent	F.S. Key's *Star-Spangled Banner*
1823	•	•	Monroe Doctrine invoked by President James Monroe

Year	Canada		United States
1828	Upper Canadian Reformers win majority in Assembly; William Lyon Mackenzie elected; Joseph Howe joins *Nova Scotian*	•	Andrew Jackson elected president — onset of Jacksonian democracy
1832	"Montreal Massacre" stirs Lower Canadians	•	Jackson vetoes U.S. Bank Bill
1835–36	Mackenzie's Seventh Report on Grievances sent to Britian (1835)	•	War in Texas: fall of the Alamo, and Texas becomes a republic
1837–38	Rebellions in Lower Canada and Upper Canada	•	Panic of 1837
1839	Lord Durham's Report	•	•
1840–41	Act of Union — the Canadas joined in a common legislature	•	•
1844	•	•	James Polk campaigns for "54°40' or Fight" and elected president
1846–48	Repeal of Corn Laws; onset of British Free Trade	•	Mexican–American War
1849	Achievement of Responsible Government in Canadas; Lord Elgin signs Rebellion Losses Bill	•	California Gold Rush
1854	Formation of Liberal–Conservative party	Reciprocity Treaty (to 1866)	Republican party formed
1861	•	•	Confederacy formed in South; Civil War erupts at Fort Sumter
1864–65	Great Coalition formed (1864); Confederation Conferences	•	Robert E. Lee surrenders at Appomattox; Abraham Lincoln assassinated (1865)
1867	Confederation achieved; Dominion of Canada created	•	U.S. Reconstruction begins; purchase of Alaska from Russia
1870–71	Manitoba and British Columbia admitted to Dominion	•	•
1873	Entry of Prince Edward Island into Confederation	Two transcontinental nations formed	•

CHAPTER 6

REVOLUTION AND RESISTANCE

CAUSES OF THE AMERICAN REVOLUTION

REVOLUTION REJECTED: BRITISH NORTH AMERICA'S
RESPONSE TO THE REVOLUTION

THE IMPACT AND LEGACY OF THE REVOLUTION

T HE DEFEAT OF THE FRENCH in the Seven Years' War left the British in control of nearly all the settled parts of North America. The Treaty of Paris (1763) recognized British claims on the continent to all the lands east of the Mississippi River as well as Florida to the south and British North America in the north.

The jubilation that accompanied victory masked profound differences between the American colonists and British officials concerning the role of the colonies within the empire, their future development, and the rights and duties of the inhabitants. The expulsion of French power from North America removed an external threat that had bound the colonies closely to London; now these deeply rooted disagreements could surface. Within 12 short years, the Thirteen Colonies would be at war with Britain; just 20 years after the conquest of New France, Britain would lose its wealthiest and most populous colonies.

CAUSES OF THE AMERICAN REVOLUTION

B RITISH ADMINISTRATION OF THE EMPIRE was based on the economic theory known as mer-cantilism. This almost universally accepted seventeenth- and eighteenth-century theory held that the amount of wealth in the world, represented by reserves of gold and other precious metals, was relatively static. Therefore the key to economic health for any nation was a favourable balance of foreign trade. When its exports exceeded imports, a nation's reserves of gold (and thus, its percentage of the world's wealth) would increase.[1] This theory helps to explain the European powers' intense interest in colonial expansion. Colonies would enable them to have guaranteed sources of raw materials as well as markets into which they could sell their finished products. Britain's colonies in North America were to provide staple products, such as sugar and tobacco, and resource materials for British manufacturers such as timber and furs. Further, the colonies would provide a market for British goods that could not be sold elsewhere because of the mercantilist polices of other nations. In short, the colonies were to be administered primarily, if not exclusively, for the economic benefit of the mother country.

MERCANTILISM AND BRITISH COMMERCIAL POLICY

Colonial commerce was to be regulated to prevent any competition with British manufacturers and to encourage colonial dependence on Britain. As early as 1651, Britain began to put the theory of mercantilism into practice. A series of Navigation Acts passed in 1660 and 1696 stipulated that all trade had to be conducted in vessels owned and commanded by an English subject. This effectively limited competition from colonial merchant shippers. Furthermore, the 1696 statute provided that colonial staples had first to be shipped to Britain, where their re-export could be controlled and taxed. British manufacturers were protected by a variety of laws ranging from the Woollen Act of 1699, which prohibited the colonial export of any raw wool, yarn, or cloth, to the Hat Act of 1732, which forbade the colonial export of beaver hats and limited the number of hatters in the colonies.

A New England stamp master in effigy. Citizens show their extreme displeasure with the new British tax. What important conclusions about social conditions of the time can you draw from this scene?   (The Metropolitan Museum of Art, Bequest of Charles Allen Munn, 1924 (24.90.1566a). All rights reserved, The Metropolitan Museum of Art.)

These measures were entirely consistent with Britain's conception of the role of the colonies in relation to the mother country. Overseas possessions existed to serve Britain, to increase its wealth and prestige, and to provide bases from which to conduct military operations against its rivals. Yet in matters of purely local concern, the British were more prepared than the other colonial powers to grant the colonists a considerable degree of freedom and self-government. This did not mean that the British envisioned some sort of eventual partnership. Each colony was to remain totally dependent on Britain and completely subservient to its policies.

In most cases the regulation of economic life met little colonial resistance; it had assisted the development of most colonies and contributed to a steady rise in living standards. In fact, in the estimation of one historian, the colonists of North America had, by 1774, attained a standard of living that was "probably the highest achieved for the great bulk of the population in any country up to that time."[2] While certain sectors of the colonial economies — manufacturers, some exporters, and consumers — faced disadvantages from the system, others benefited from imperial subsidies for the supplies of indigo, timber, and tobacco. All colonists profited from the security and protection provided by the Royal Navy. In short, as the colonial historian Lawrence Gipson put it, "The British colonists of North America in 1763 were among the most fortunate people in the world."[3]

When restrictions were considered disadvantageous to the colonists — for example, heavy duties on Dutch tea or molasses from the French West Indies — the laws were frequently ignored. Smuggling became a routine and vital part of the American economy. Not wanting to provoke dissent, the British government had been tolerant of this flourishing illicit trade. For example, after Parliament passed the Molasses Act of 1733, which called for a duty on every gallon of molasses imported, colonial opposition was widespread. The British refused either to repeal the Act or to enforce it.

THE RISE OF NATIONAL CONSCIOUSNESS

The roots of the American Revolution lay in part in differences of opinion between the colonists and London over the nature of the imperial relationship. The British assumed the supremacy of Parliament in all matters; colonial assemblies could act only with the permission or acquiescence of Westminster. Yet the reluctance of the British government to concern itself to any great extent with the internal affairs of the American colonies encouraged the growth, however subtle, of the view that the local assemblies in the colonies enjoyed certain rights and prerogatives — most notably the right of direct taxation — that could not be interfered with by Parliament. Legally, the colonial view was groundless. However, the fact that it was widely held in all the colonies was to have serious consequences.

Furthermore, between 1609 and 1763, despite the strong attachments that most people had to their own colonies, a sense of pan-American national consciousness had begun to develop. The openness and relative social equality of North American society compared with that in Europe helped form that identity. The common frontier experiences were fashioning a new type of person — an American. Americans came to believe that the New World was somehow purer and less corrupt than the Old. They developed a belief in their innate moral superiority and possessed an abiding suspicion and mistrust of British government institutions.

THE GREAT AWAKENING

An intense religious movement known as the Great Awakening provided another major impetus to unity among the diverse colonies.[4] The brilliant Congregationalist minister Jonathan Edwards produced an impressive philosophical foundation for the movement, which was emotional, popular, egalitarian, and anti-intellectual. The spiritual, educational, and cultural impact of the movement contributed to the development of a distinctive national character. (The colony of Nova Scotia was touched by its own Great Awakening, but not until the mid-1770s, when the social consequences tended to further divide Nova Scotians from their Yankee brethren rather than unite them.)[5]

It is not surprising, then, that many Americans perceived British attempts to tighten imperial control over its colonial possessions as evidence of an old and decadent society's struggle to restrict the development of a young and dynamic one. British officials, who never abandoned their paternalistic view of the subordinate place of the colonies, reacted to American discontent and resistance with irritation at their insolence. The British Tory Edmund Burke wrote in 1769 that "the Americans have made a discovery, or think they have made a discovery, that we mean to oppress them; we have made a discovery, or think we have made a discovery, that they intend to rise up in rebellion against us. We know not how to advance; they know not how to retreat."[6]

COLONIAL DEFENCE AND TAXATION

The catalyst that brought into prominence three highly contentious and related issues was the outbreak of the Seven Years' War. One crucial issue raised by the war was the question of who was going to pay for the cost of defence. During the conflict, the colonists had irritated Britain by their reluctance to furnish troops, supplies, and money. The two most immediate problems for imperial officials after the war were the crushing debt incurred by the war and the increased costs of administering an enlarged empire. Since the welfare — if not the fate — of the colonies depended on a strong military and naval presence, it was not altogether surprising that Britain would ask the colonies to assume a greater proportion of the cost of their own defence. However, the British were making this request at the very moment that the American colonists were beginning to assert their independence.

Furthermore, if the colonists were to assume a greater share of the costs of their own defence, they would have to be taxed. The colonists objected that they were not represented in Parliament. The slogan "No taxation without representation" became the great rallying cry of the revolution. The fact that the franchise did not extend to over 90 percent of the British population, and that therefore the principle of direct taxation without representation was firmly established in Britain, was ignored by the colonists.

The Proclamation of 1763 marks the next major step in the deterioration of relations between the British and the American colonists. In order to control the Amerindians and the recently conquered French, the British government decided to close the West to settlement and create a large Amerindian reserve in the area, and to build a string of strategically located garrisons in the Northwest. These decisions angered the colonists because they wanted the rich lands of the West to be open to settlement and cultivation. To enforce the prohibition on settlement and prevent further Amerindian uprisings after Pontiac's rebellion, which had taken the British two years to suppress, a standing army of 10 000 troops was to be stationed in the colonies. With some justification, many Americans suspected that the army was being sent as much to enforce British authority over them as to protect them. Their reaction was intensified by British demands that the colonists contribute to the cost.

THE STAMP ACT CRISIS

In the next decade, a series of Acts passed by the British Parliament marked further steps on the road to revolution. The first of these was the Stamp Act, which required that special tax stamps be affixed to a variety of printed items from newspapers to legal documents.[7] Before the passage of this Act, revenue had been obtained in the colonies through indirect taxes such as customs duties. The Stamp Act was the first direct tax levied on the colonists, and although such a tax had been in effect in England since 1694, it aroused violent objections in America, particularly among the most influential members of society. In some colonies, like New England, tax officials were attacked and property was destroyed; in other areas, colonists boycotted British goods, causing a substantial drop in imports.

The Boston Massacre, 1770. Paul Revere's engraving of the Boston Massacre is a propaganda classic. In reality, the troops fired when cornered by the crowd, the officer tried to stop the soldiers (not urge them on), and the English customs house was not named Butcher's Hall.

REACTIONS OF THE CONTINENTAL CONGRESS

EXAMINE THE FOLLOWING DECLARATIONS, passed by the American Continental Congress in 1774 and 1775. What do they reveal about the motives and purposes of the American revolutionary leaders? How do these Declarations differ from the later *Common Sense* and *Declaration of Independence?*

DECLARATION AND RESOLVES (FIRST CONTINENTAL CONGRESS), 1774

...That the foundation of English liberty, and of all free government, is a right in the people to participate in their legislative council; and as the English colonists are not represented, and from their local and other circumstances cannot properly be represented, in the British Parliament, they are entitled to a free and exclusive power of legislation in their several provincial legislatures, where their right of representation can alone be preserved, in all cases of taxation and internal polity, subject only to the negative of their sovereign, in such manner as has been heretofore used and accustomed. But, from the necessity of the case, and a regard to the mutual interest of both countries, we cheerfully consent to the operation of such acts of the British Parliament as are bona fide restrained to the regulation of our external commerce, for the purpose of securing the commercial advantages of the whole empire to the mother country, and the commercial benefits of its respective members excluding every idea of taxation, internal or external, for raising a revenue on the subjects of America without their consent.

DECLARATION OF THE CAUSES AND NECESSITY OF TAKING UP ARMS, 1775

...Lest this declaration should disquiet the minds of our friends and fellow-subjects in any part of the empire, we assure them that we mean not to dissolve that union which has so long and so happily subsisted between us, and which we sincerely wish to see restored. Necessity has not yet driven us into that desperate measure, or induced us to excite any other nation to war against them. We have not raised armies with ambitious designs of separating from Great Britain, and establishing independent states....

In our own native land, in defence of the freedom that is our birth-right, and which we ever enjoyed till the late violation of it — for the protection of our property, acquired solely by the honest industry of our fore-fathers and ourselves, against violence actually offered, we have taken up arms. We shall lay them down when hostilities shall cease on the part of the aggressors, and all danger of their being renewed shall be removed, and not before....

Representatives from nine colonies met in New York in 1765 to draw up a petition against the Stamp Act. In the face of such concerted opposition, the British backed down and agreed to repeal the Act in 1766. But trouble arose a year later over new import duties on commodities that had previously been untaxed. A new round of agitation and boycott followed. British troops, sent to Boston to reinforce the garrison, opened fire on a crowd of hostile but unarmed rioters and killed three. As a result of "the Boston Massacre," radical colonial leaders[8] stirred up such agitation that almost all the taxes were repealed. Relative tranquillity ensued for the next three years.

THE FAILURE OF BRITISH CONCILIATION

Events up to this time had encouraged a growing sense of common identity in the American colonies. During the controversies, the Americans had successfully defied the imperial government, and Samuel Adams and other radical leaders had established "committees of correspondence" in several colonies. These pressure groups kept in touch with one another to maintain the agitation against grievances, real or imagined. Yet, while radicals maintained their hostility to Britain, respectable opinion in the colonies was every bit as suspicious of local radicals as of British officials. That changed in 1773 as another act of the British Parliament precipitated a new crisis.

The East India Company was given the exclusive right to sell its tea directly to American consumers without having to pay the English export tax. Conservative merchants resented this British monopoly, and were driven into an alliance with the radicals. The agitation culminated with Samuel Adams[9] and his followers staging what came to be known as the Boston Tea Party, in which a group of agitators boarded the East India Company ships and dropped the entire consignment of tea into Boston harbour, much to the delight of a large crowd of onlookers. Such open defiance of authority and wanton destruction of property might have discredited the radical cause. However, the British government's reaction to this incident was so harsh that it had the opposite effect. A series of four Acts — known in America as the Intolerable Acts and in Britain as the Coercive Acts — was passed to make an example of Massachusetts. The ill-timed passage of the Quebec Act during the same parliamentary session angered nearly all the Thirteen Colonies and helped to cement their unity against the British.

In a last-ditch attempt at reconciliation, a Continental Congress of representatives of 12 colonies met in Philadelphia in 1774. The radicals took over the proceedings and produced a strongly worded Declaration of Rights. One important result of the Congress was the creation of Committees of Safety, which laid the basis for a future colonial governmental system.

While nearly all of the colonists supported efforts to secure concessions from the British, only a minority supported the aggressive tactics of the radicals. Many were strongly opposed to any action that threatened to break the British connection. Many more were simply indifferent, confused, or ignorant. The system of Committees of Safety gave the radicals a highly effective means of committing the passive majority to their side.

THE QUEBEC ACT AND THE AMERICAN REVOLUTION

THE COMPLEXITY OF IMPERIAL POLICY for the British in North America is perhaps nowhere more evident than in the decision-making that led to the passage of the Quebec Act in 1774 and the reactions to its enactment in Britain, the English-speaking American colonies, and in Quebec itself.

The conquest of a community as large, established, and fundamentally different as New France was bound to raise difficult problems for the new masters. Opinion was divided within the British government about whether to extend toleration to the king's new French-speaking subjects, to deport them, to attempt to assimilate them into British laws and customs, or to overwhelm them, if possible, with waves of Anglo-Saxon immigration. By the early 1770s, it was clear that the colony was too expensive to maintain and of limited economic value, that the French population, far from being assimilated, was growing in size and diligent in maintaining its distinct culture, and that English immigration was too insignificant to flood the colony, but just great enough to create a small but vocal group whose presence could create friction between French and English.

The political dilemma for the British after the conquest was whether Quebec, populated largely by French Roman Catholics, should be granted English political institutions. Britain's answer in 1774 was that Quebec would not be an English colony, but rather a French one attached to Britain until such time as some other solution could be developed. The retention of the *seigneurial* system, the enforcement of church tithes, and the legal recognition of the French language, the Roman Catholic church, and other institutions of the old régime were aimed at rewarding and retaining the loyalty of the local aristocracy and clergy. The Quebec Act was accompanied by secret instructions to Governor-General Guy Carleton to undermine many of the Act's provisions by gradually introducing English legal practices through various orders-in-council and placing restrictions on the colony's religious orders. Carleton, however, kept his instructions secret and never fully implemented them.

The Quebec Act was effective in securing the support of the church and the *seigneurs*. In fact, Michel Brunet argues in his "decapitation thesis" that a kind of unholy alliance was formed between the church and the British conquerors in the wake of the departure of the economic leaders of French-Canadian society. It was less successful in winning over the *habitants*, most of whom resented the re-imposition of burdensome taxes, duties, and controls. The Act failed to create among most of the population any desire to fight for British interests. However, by cementing an alliance with the traditional leadership of Quebec society, it prevented the outbreak of serious or threatening discontent in the colony.

Among the small but ambitious and influential English merchant community, the political, religious, and even legal provisions of the Act were seen to be objectionable. On the other hand, the extension of the colony's boundaries and a variety of economic concessions to local fur traders and merchants satisfied the more moderate pro-English activists in the community. While they were prohibited from having an assembly through which they might exercise formal political power, they were able to count on the opportunity to exercise, through the governor and his council, political influence out of all proportion to their numbers. The Act not only agitated Quebec's English-speaking merchants, it also left a residue of suspicion and distrust that proved difficult to dissolve.

In the short run, however, the Quebec Act was more significant for its impact on the relationship between Britain and its other North American colonies. There is little doubt that the framers of the Act intended to send a message to the rebellious and fractious Americans that colonial assemblies were not a right, but a privilege, and that Britain was prepared to maintain a secure and permanent imperial base in North America, independent of the whims of local assemblies. In the atmosphere of suspicion and resistance that had developed by the mid-1770s, however, the effect of the Act was not to dampen the spirit of the rebelliousness in the older colonies, but to stiffen it.

Despite paper guarantees of the right of the original colonies to westward expansion, the legislation's major territorial provision, the annexation of the West to Quebec, seemed to rob those assurances of meaning. Americans might settle in the coveted western lands, but they would lack the accustomed liberties and would be subject, in part, to French civil law. Furthermore, the privileges of the Roman Catholic church had been extended and enhanced at a time when the practice of that faith in public in England still carried severe civil penalties. Finally, the decision to forbid an assembly in Quebec was taken by the suspicious Anglo-Americans, not wholly without reason, as a threat to the continued local autonomy of the other assemblies. Thus, in July 1775, the Continental Congress declared that the Act established in a neighbouring province "a despotism dangerous to our very existence." One historian has claimed that most of the colonists "probably feared the long-term consequences of the Quebec Act even more than the Townshend Duties and the Coercive Acts."

THE FIRST SHOTS OF THE REVOLUTION

On the evening of April 18, 1775, the royal governor, General Thomas Gage, moved against the rebel leaders at Lexington and Concord. He ordered British troops from Boston to seize the arms that had been stored at nearby Concord and to arrest Samuel Adams and another radical leader, John Hancock. Warned by Paul Revere and William Dawes, the "minutemen" of

Lexington and Concord challenged the British soldiers. No one knows for certain who fired the first shot, described by Ralph Waldo Emerson as "the shot heard round the world." Fighting was unexpectedly fierce but even as it continued, both sides groped clumsily for some sort of compromise to prevent a complete break. However, highly exaggerated accounts of massacres of innocent farmers produced a burst of patriotic indignation, enabling the Committees of Safety to gain control. Although the hastily assembled Second Continental Congress authorized raising an army under George Washington, only the most radical leaders seemed eager for independence. That same congress issued an invitation to the citizens of Quebec to become the fourteenth colony in revolt against Britain — an invitation that was rejected. A number of factors pushed the Congress in the direction of full-fledged independence. Significant among them was the appearance in January 1776 of *Common Sense*, a passionate 46-page pamphlet by Thomas Paine, an English radical who had recently come to America.

The final catalyst of the revolution was the declaration approved by Congress on July 4, 1775.

The Battle of Lexington, April 19, 1775. The first battle of the American Revolution saw the British redcoats rout the American revolutionaries.

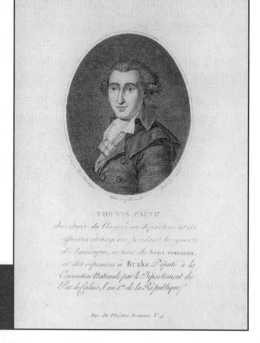

THOMAS PAINE

Thomas Paine, author of the influential pamphlet *Common Sense*, published in January 1776.

The famous painting of George Washington crossing the Delaware River in December 1776. Artistic interpretations like this do much to mythologize America's first president.

It was drafted by the young Virginia politician, Thomas Jefferson, with the help of Benjamin Franklin and John Adams. Basing his argument on John Locke's *Two Treatises on Government*, Jefferson provided the most trenchant justification for revolution on the basis of the doctrine of natural rights. The declaration severed the Thirteen Colonies not only from "all allegiance to the British Crown," but also from its neighbour colonies to the north.[10] Having declared their independence, Americans now had to win it on the battlefield — a grim struggle that would last from 1776 to 1783.

REVOLUTION REJECTED: BRITISH NORTH AMERICA'S RESPONSE TO THE AMERICAN REVOLUTION

DISSATISFACTION WITH THE BRITISH AUTHORITIES diminished in direct proportion to distance from the centre of the North American empire. Georgia, for example, the southernmost colony to join the rebellion and one of the least developed, never generated a great deal of enthusiasm for the American Revolution, in part because of the colony's dependence on British soldiers to guard its border with the Spanish Floridas. In the colonies that would later become part of Canada, a similar dependence, as well as isolation and economic underdevelopment, contributed to their rejection of the revolutionary cause.

THE REACTION OF THE ATLANTIC COLONIES

Britain's northern Atlantic colonies were unmoved by the call to arms. In St. John's Island, later Prince Edward Island, underpopulated and governed by 67 largely absentee landowners, the conflict produced little interest. The largest number of settlers were Highland Scots, loyal to their landlords and patrons, who directed the settlers to ignore the urgings of the Continental Congress. A few hundred Acadians, who had either escaped the 1755 expulsion from the island or had made their way back to it, expressed some sympathy for those who were fighting Britain. However, they were too few, too powerless, and too prudent to take any active part in the revolution. In November 1775, two American privateers sailed to Charlottetown from Massachusetts, but there was no popular rising, and thereafter St. John's Island was left to the protection of the British navy.

In Newfoundland, the population was small, poor, and scattered, and divided on ethnic, religious, and class lines. Totally dependent on the cod fishery off the Grand Banks, the island's permanent residents and a large population of visiting fishermen had little interest in American affairs. Newfoundland discontent stemmed from internal causes, notably the formal discrimination against the large Irish Catholic population, and the iron economic grip in which most fishers were held by the merchants and tavern keepers of St. John's. American privateers attacked some Newfoundland settlements during the revolutionary, but except for a degree of economic improvement as a result of the British military presence at St. John's, the colony remained largely untouched by the revolution.

QUEBEC AND THE AMERICAN REVOLUTION

In Quebec, sections of both the French and English population were upset with the policies of the British government in general and its passage of the Quebec Act in particular. While the Act pleased most of the *seigneurial* class and the Catholic hierarchy, to many of the *habitants* it signalled a reinforcement of the economic power of both church and landlord to wring added taxes from the farmers. Some in the British merchant community were irritated by the British refusal to provide a colonial assembly and by the Quebec Act's concessions to French law and the Roman Catholic church. This discontent, however, never developed widely or deeply enough to pose a serious threat to British authority in the colony, and during the revolutionary war American policy tended to alienate the little support the revolutionaries had within Quebec.

Ultimately, most of the British determined that their interests were best served either by supporting the imperial authorities or by cautious neutrality. Those in the fur

A contemporary cartoonist depicts the split between England and America, between the moderates and the radicals, and between the Loyalists and revolutionaries.

trade appreciated the extension of Quebec's boundaries in 1774 and saw their chief rivals in the western trade, the merchants of New York's Hudson River valley, take a leading role in the revolution. Others simply calculated the advantages of selling to both sides in a fluid military situation. Among the French, the upper classes and the church were firm in their loyalty. Not only had British policy protected their interests by the Quebec Act, but the whole social outlook of the *seigneurs* and the hierarchy was one of co-operation with constituted authority.

Among the mass of *Canadiens*, however, the response was one of steadfast neutrality. Most farmers were understandably interested in preserving their lives and livelihoods rather than going to war on behalf of either of two groups of bickering Englishmen. Several *seigneurs* tried to raise militia among their tenants, but had only moderate success. Bishop Briand in 1775, after American incursions into Quebec, called upon the faithful to "[defend] your country and your King with all the strength you possess." Yet while most *Canadiens* were attached to their church, their loyalty was never blind, and few French Catholics rallied to the British colours. Even as General Richard Montgomery was on the verge of capturing the last hold-out of Quebec City on the last day of 1775, the *habitants* refused to take up arms against the invaders. They remained on their farms, prepared to trade with both British and American soldiers as long as the soldiers could pay in hard cash.

At the war's outset, when British forces seemed too weak to resist American incursions into Quebec and American forces paid well for supplies, ordinary *Canadiens* were more receptive to the invader. Later on, when it became clear that the British could withstand the American military pressure, that they were not secretly organizing a mass deportation of *Canadiens* (a widespread fear among the *habitants*), and that they were more reliable customers than the Americans, French-Canadian loyalty to the crown was more evident.[11]

NOVA SCOTIA AND THE "NEUTRAL YANKEES"

The colony of Nova Scotia might have proven more susceptible to American enticement. Almost half the population of farmers and fishermen had come from New England, and many retained close family connections in those colonies. Furthermore, serious hostility had been growing between the settlers in the outlying villages in Nova Scotia and the ruling élite of the colony's capital, Halifax. There, a corrupt and mean-spirited clique of merchants, military officers, and Anglican clergy ran the colony's affairs in their own interest, frustrating the desire of rural communities to be represented fairly or merely to be left alone. Two abortive rebellions arose in the western sections of the colony during the revolutionary war. However, in the end, Nova Scotia remained in the British fold.

Critical to this outcome was the loyalty of Halifax. While some residents had publicly objected to the Stamp Act and other British policies, the city was far too dependent on the British military establishment for its livelihood ever to challenge that relationship. Its Yankee population was relatively small, and its economic position was too tied, as were those of other communities, to trade with New England. Outside Halifax, despite a common antipathy to the capital, the settlements had little contact with each other, partly because of the absence of roads.

In addition to including communities of New England emigrants, Nova Scotia was also home to several villages of German, Scottish, and Irish settlers, with whom the Yankees had little to do. Also, the neutral French of the colony, numbering nearly 6000, had remained after the 1755 expulsion and were reluctant to draw attention to themselves by being anti-British. Even if some sympathy existed within some districts for the American cause, no co-ordinated support within Nova Scotia was likely.

NOVA SCOTIA'S GREAT AWAKENING

As the war proceeded, rural Nova Scotia was caught up in its own delayed version of the Great Awakening.[12] The outlying communities turned their attention away from political activity, which seemed increasingly fruitless and frustrating, to religious revival. In so doing, many colonists lost interest in the conflict between the Americans and the British, seeking only to maintain their neutrality and independence. The war did touch Nova Scotia, as its shores were attacked and plundered by American privateers. Many turned against the Americans for these activities; others blamed the British for the failure of the imperial government to protect them. Yet with each passing year, it became clearer that Nova Scotia would not join the rebellion.

Loyalists, regarded as the enemy by American revolutionaries, often had to suffer at the hands of a patriotic mob. Here a crowd has tarred and feathered a Loyalist and is forcing him to drink tea.

Joseph Brant (1742–1807), as portrayed by William Berczy. A Mohawk chief, Brant remained a faithful ally of the British. He led the Six Nations against the French in the Seven Years' War, against Pontiac in the Amerindian uprising, and against the Americans in the Revolutionary War. (William Berczy [Canadian], Thayendanegea [Joseph Brant], #5777, National Gallery of Canada, Ottawa.)

WOMEN AND THE AMERICAN REVOLUTION

POLITICAL LIFE AND MILITARY AFFAIRS in the eighteenth-century British colonies were technically male domains. Women were not expected to attend political gatherings at courthouses, taverns, and militia meetings, which were the places where political ideas were exchanged and debated. Furthermore, as political concepts of rights and freedoms spread through the colonies in pamphlets and newspapers, women's lower literacy rates (regardless of their rank or race) meant that they could not participate in these debates as fully as did their more literate male counterparts. Those women who could read this material would have noticed that much of it depicted the colonists as embodying virtues their society associated with men and masculinity: manly self-sacrifice for the public good, manly virtue in the political arena, and male willingness to take up arms for the republic. In contrast, Britain was portrayed as the source of effeminacy, corruption, luxury and extravagance, qualities that colonial society associated with women and femininity.

Nevertheless, women were affected by the American Revolution in a variety of ways. Boycotts of British consumer goods, a strategy that has been described as the most important tactic, short of warfare, possessed by the Patriots, could not have taken place without the active support of women, the customary managers of the household economy. In these activities many women were supporting campaigns led by men, but some mounted their own boycotts and circulated petitions opposed to the importation of British goods. These women made herbal tea and spun and wove cloth and, as they did so, they pointed out that they too had a part to play in political life.

Women with husbands and other family members in the military found their daily lives greatly affected by the revolution. Women whose livelihood came from a farm or family business frequently had to assume sole responsibility for these enterprises. At first, many found this a daunting and lonely task, but as the war progressed they developed new skills and a sense of self-sufficiency. Others followed their husbands to the battleground. Known as "camp followers," they were not popular with army officials, but they provided necessary services such as cooking, laundry, and nursing.

Although the vast majority of women did not take up arms, historians have discovered that a few did disguise themselves as men and fought in the Patriot army. The most famous of these women, Deborah Sampson, fought for two and a half years before being found out. After her death, her husband was granted a pension as a soldier's widower.

Other Loyalist women found that the war brought few improvements in their daily lives. As the conflict wore on and their male relatives joined the British troops in Canada, these women found themselves isolated behind enemy lines. They often faced increased hostility and harassment from their Patriot neighbours, and their homes and property were sometimes looted and seized. Those without family support were forced to make the hazardous journey north, often with small children in tow. Although Loyalist women often performed tasks similar to those of Patriot women — becoming more self-sufficient, provisioning and sheltering troops, and sometimes acting as spies for the British — at the war's end they found themselves uprooted from their homes and communities.

Unlike their husbands, brothers, fathers, and sons, the contributions Loyalist women had made to the British cause were not highly valued by the British authorities. Women and children were regarded as a burden when they first arrived in the refugee camps in Quebec. Loyalist women found themselves confronted with a British government determined to build a society based on deference to authority and hierarchical social and political relations. In this vision, women were viewed as subject to patriarchal authority.

This cartoon captures the cultural force of the nineteenth century women's moral crusade.

The status of women in the new republic, however, was the subject of some discussion and debate. Could women be citizens and take up full political membership in the republic? The answer, it seems, was "not entirely." For the most part women were not to be admitted to the republican polity, as they could not lay claim to the republican tradition of the arms-bearing male. Married women were still considered to be subject to the British common-law tradition of *coverture*, whereby their identities were subsumed by those of their husbands.

Women's most important contribution to the new republic, it was thought, was in their role as "republican mothers." They had the important tasks of bearing, rearing, and educating the country's citizenry, shaping America's destiny by inculcating their children with morality and virtue. Thus, the ideological changes of the revolution gave American women a new civic role and an identity in the nation.

As in Quebec, however, most Nova Scotians did not express any profound loyalty to British authorities either. A brisk illegal trade with the Americans supplemented a growing prosperity brought about by Britain's increased military presence in Halifax, and British authorities were no more successful in raising volunteers than were the rebel leaders. Cut off from New England by distance and the raids of privateers and from each other by a lack of roads, the Yankees of Nova Scotia, like the Amerindians before them, chose neutrality. They were largely sympathetic to the Americans, but in no position to join or actively support their rebellion.

THE IMPACT AND LEGACY OF THE REVOLUTION

LOYALISTS AND REVOLUTIONARIES

THE DIVISION OF AMERICAN SOCIETY into those who supported the revolution and those who opposed it foreshadowed the ultimate establishment of two different societies astride the 49th parallel. While almost all Americans favoured efforts to secure concessions from the imperial government, most did not agree with the tactics employed by a handful of radicals: some were hostile to any action that threatened to sever the tie with Britain; others were simply indifferent.

The revolutionaries were not, for the most part, extremists. "They made speeches, not bombs; they wrote learned pamphlets, not manifestos. They were not abstract theorists and they were not social levelers. They did not kill one another, they did not devour themselves."[13] Some, like Thomas Paine, Thomas Jefferson, John Dickinson, and James Otis, may well have been inspired by philosophical principles, but most patriots were more practical and pragmatic. Oftentimes, as with individuals such as Samuel Adams and Patrick Henry,[14] they combined their hostility toward Britain with a powerful resentment toward their aristocratic fellow Americans.

Not all Loyalists were members of the upper class; neither were all revolutionaries economically disadvantaged. Both groups drew their adherents from every religious, social, and professional group. Both groups were represented in every region. Certainly the leading Loyalists were frequently drawn from the ranks of the Anglican clergy and from those who held offices or jobs dependent on the imperial government. Although Loyalists were fewer in New England than in New York, Pennsylvania, and Georgia, every colony was divided. Every ethnic group, too, was split over the issue, although among those born outside North America and among the Amerindians, support for the crown was much stronger. Most tribes of the Iroquois nation remained loyal, persuaded by the Mohawk Chief Joseph Brant that their interests would be better served by British officials than by land-hungry American colonists.

What led people to support one side or the other in the conflict? For many, if not most, a calculation of self-interest, as in the case of the Iroquois, determined the response to the revolution. Longstanding local political rivalries were also carried into the war. Thus, in the Carolinas, where the ruling élite backed the Continental Congress, the poor farmers on the frontier remained loyal to the crown. Furthermore, in those colonies that had actually declared independence, the option of neutrality, which may have appealed to most people, was less easy to exercise than in Quebec or Nova Scotia. Those who could not be won over by friendly persuasion were often silenced by attacks on themselves or their property. Revolutionary committees harassed and intimidated those suspected of loyalism or neutrality.

Prior to the Declaration of Independence, most opponents of British policy proclaimed their loyalty to the king even while engaged in legal and illegal anti-government activities. Later on, Americans became less interested in asserting the traditional rights of the English under the parliamentary system and more intent on establishing a new, pure, and unique society in America. The declaration confirmed the triumph of the ideal of an independent republic, without kings or aristocrats and directed by the will of its people.

THE LEGACY OF THE REVOLUTION IN THE UNITED STATES AND BRITISH NORTH AMERICA

The American Revolution produced a unique society founded on liberal, republican, and individualistic values. Those who resisted it, the Loyalists, formed the backbone of a very different society to the north. Revolution and resistance led to the partition of English-speaking North America into two distinct societies.

The northern colonies were to reflect the outlook of the Loyalists, who were attached to the monarchy and content to let their interests be represented by the British Parliament. They were hostile to the democratic and social levelling ideas of their southern neighbour. Their societies were consciously British — even in Quebec — and placed great value on British ancestry and connection. They were both more conservative and more communal. In rejecting the American Revolution and in becoming home to more than 40 000 people who fled the United States, the fabric of British North American society began to take on a very different political, social, and ideological hue from that of its southern neighbour. "The Loyalists transformed one nation and scarred another; they fled as losers and arrived as heroes. They built, out of their own despair, a land of hope."[15]

The Americans, on the other hand, came to see themselves more and more as a "gathered" community, based not on ties of blood or ethnicity, but on a common acceptance and reverence of liberal, republican, and individualistic ideas and values. A secular religion, comprising the Declaration of Independence, the Founding Fathers, and the heroes of the revolutionary war, took deep root in the newly created nation. Being born of fire, it became easy for Americans to develop their own national mythologies. Although traditionally viewed as a conservative movement, the American Revolution was in fact radical, particularly within the context and sense of the eighteenth century.[16]

Historians have begun to focus on the degree to which the revolutionaries realized that slavery and the principles that underlay their struggle against England were not only incompatible, but completely opposite.[17] The differences between the newly created nation and the remaining British colonies would shape the future histories of the United States and Canada and dominate relations between the two and with Great Britain for two centuries.

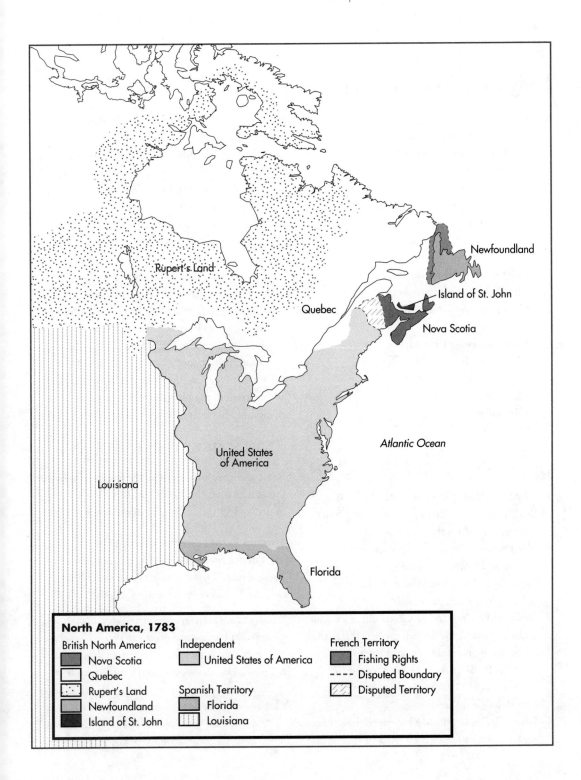

Newfoundland

Rupert's Land

Island of St. John

Quebec

Nova Scotia

Atlantic Ocean

United States
of America

Louisiana

Florida

North America, 1783

British North America
- Nova Scotia
- Quebec
- Rupert's Land
- Newfoundland
- Island of St. John

Independent
- United States of America

Spanish Territory
- Florida
- Louisiana

French Territory
- Fishing Rights
- - - - Disputed Boundary
- Disputed Territory

ACTIVITIES

KEY TERMS AND CONCEPTS

Identify and briefly explain the historical significance of the following terms and concepts:

- Mercantilism/bullionism
- Proclamation of 1763
- Quebec Act
- Great Awakening
- Stamp Act
- Taxation without representation
- Natural rights
- Committees of correspondence
- Intolerable/Coercive Acts
- Declaration of Independence
- *Common Sense*
- Patriots/revolutionaries
- Loyalists/Tories
- Gathered community
- Liberalism
- Privateers
- Coverture

QUESTIONS FOR DISCUSSION

1. To what extent did a conception of a distinct British-American society exist among North Americans before the Revolution?
2. What role did Britain see for its North American colonies in the eighteenth century? How did it differ from the role that the colonies saw for themselves?
3. How did Patriots and Loyalists differ in their attitude toward the British crown, the authority of the representatives, and their own rights as British subjects? Are those differences reflected in any way in contemporary Americans and Canadians?
4. Does the Declaration of Independence represent a restatement of the rights of British subjects or a totally new vision of society? Explain.
5. Which of its audiences — fellow Americans, the British, the international community, or history — did the Declaration of Independence address most successfully?
6. Why did Britain's northern colonies fail to join the revolution? Are there are any characteristics common to the colonies that remained loyal?
7. How did the French Canadians' perception of their role in British North America alter during the years between the conquest and the end of the eighteenth century? What factors caused this change?
8. In what ways can the American Revolution be regarded as the pivotal event defining the relationship between Canada and the United States?

ANALYZING THE EVIDENCE

Read and carefully analyze the main arguments for and against the American Revolution expressed in the following documents.

Thomas Paine, *Common Sense*, 1776

The case for revolution was forcefully presented in Thomas Paine's *Common Sense*. Paine was an English radical who had come to Philadelphia only in 1774.

"Volumes have been written on the subject of the struggle between England and America. Men of all ranks have embarked in the controversy, from different motives, and with various designs: but all have been ineffectual, and the period of debate is closed. Arms as a last resource decide the contest....

"Alas! we have been long led away by ancient prejudices, and made large sacrifices to superstition. We have boasted the protection of Great Britain without considering that her motive was *interest*, not attachment; and that she did not protect us from our enemies on our account, but from her enemies on her own account....

"...Everything that is right or natural pleads for separation. The blood of the slain, the weeping voice of nature cries, 'TIS TIME TO PART. Even the distance at which the Almighty hath placed England and America is a strong and natural proof that the authority of one over the other, was never the design of heaven....

"...[I]n America THE LAW IS KING. For as in absolute governments the King is law, so in free countries the law ought to be king, and there ought to be no other....

"A government of our own is our natural right...."

Charles Inglis, *The True Interest of America,* **1776** The Anglican clergyman Charles Inglis appealed for reconciliation and eventually went into exile in England in 1783:

"I think it no difficult matter to point out many advantages which will certainly attend our reconciliation and connection with Great Britain, on a firm, constitutional plan....

"The Americans are properly Britons. They have the manners, habits and ideas of Britons; and have been accustomed to a similar form of government. But Britons never could bear the extremes, either of monarchy or of republicanism....

"Besides the unsuitableness of the republican form to the genius of the people, America is too extensive for it....

"...[A] Declaration for Independency on the part of America, would preclude treaty intirely [*sic*]; and could answer no good purpose. We actually have already every advantage of Independency, without its inconveniences. By a Declaration of Independency, we should instantly lose all assistance from our friends in England...would be deemed rebels, and treated accordingly....

"America is far from being yet in a desperate situation. I am confident she may obtain honourable and advantageous terms from Great Britain. A few years of peace will soon retrieve all her losses. She will rapidly advance to a state of maturity, whereby she may not only repay the parent state amply for all past benefits; but also lay under the greatest obligations...."

DEBATE AND DISCUSS

Take a position on this historical issue. Argue for or against the following proposition:

"The United States is the country of the revolution, Canada of the counterrevolution. These very different formative events set indelible marks on the two nations."

— Seymour Martin Lipset, *Continental Divide* (Toronto: C.D. Howe Institute, 1989), p. 1.

CHAPTER 7

FRONTIER EXPERIENCES OF SETTLEMENT

As THE FIRST BRITISH EMPIRE in North America came crashing down with the conclusion of the American Revolution in 1783, a second British empire was born to the north. The loss of the Thirteen Colonies radically upset the entire balance of the older mercantilist system. Combined with that loss, Britain faced massive social, political, and economic changes brought about by the combination of the Industrial Revolution and the Enclosure Movement. With large numbers of immigrants coming to British North America, from both the newly created United States and Britain, the era between the American Revolution and the mid-nineteenth century was a time of "adjustment and consolidation" and a "formative" period in the emergence of pre-industrial colonial society.[1]

LOYALIST MIGRATIONS

THE INFLUX OF 30 000 UNITED EMPIRE LOYALISTS into Nova Scotia and the further addition of almost another 10 000 into Quebec produced profound political and social changes. The exodus and plight of the Loyalists has been viewed as an epic struggle in Canadian history.[2] The hardships they endured in attempting to eke out a subsistence living on a harsh frontier is a testimony to their perseverance and courage.

When the American Revolution broke out, many people living south of the border found themselves in an untenable situation. Thousands discovered that their continuing loyalty to British customs, laws, and traditions was anathema to the growing patriot movement. The American rebels contemptuously branded them "Tories," although they themselves much preferred the label "Loyalists." They were singled out for special harassment. Their stores were boycotted, their parties shunned, and their children ridiculed. Eventually, the rebels began to take stronger action against these Loyalists by inflicting corporal punishment on them. Most popularly they were tarred and feathered and run out of town, as well as being forced to give up their possessions. This kind of activity occurred with increasing frequency after sizable numbers of Loyalists joined Major General John Burgoyne's British army. However, disaster struck the British side in 1777, when Burgoyne surrendered. The thousand Loyalists in his army were in an impossible situation. American resentment against what they regarded as traitors had now reached fever pitch.

Four years later, in 1781, British general Charles Cornwallis and his 9000 men were blocked in Chesapeake Bay by a battery of French warships. Cornwallis, after stalling for some time, was forced to surrender. This defeat at Yorktown, like the one four years earlier at Saratoga, put a sizable number of Loyalist troops with the British army in grave jeopardy. They could scarcely return to their homes, as most Americans agreed with George Washington's assessment of them as traitors. Emigration was the only viable option.

They were a mixed lot, to say the least. Almost 100 000 Americans emigrated by the end of the revolutionary war in 1783. Some left for England or islands in the Caribbean. However, close to half of them migrated north. They left with a variety of emotions. Some felt acute bitterness; some suffered from hurt pride; some felt deeply indignant; while a few departed with unbridled optimism. They were rich and poor, educated and illiterate, loyal and opportunist. They came from every level of society, from the richest town merchant to the poorest backwoods farmer. They came from every colony from Maine to Georgia. Just as their backgrounds as well as their motivations in departing were different, so too was their degree of loyalty. Some were active and aggressive in demonstrating it, while others were passive and reluctant supporters of the crown. They were, for the most part, conservative. Included in their number were some pacifists — Mennonites and Quakers, for example.[3] In short, the Loyalists were an utterly heterogeneous group — differing in background, motivation, class, and aspirations.

FRONTIER EXPERIENCES OF SETTLEMENT: THE MARITIMES AND THE CANADAS

WHILE WAVES OF LOYALISTS EMIGRATED with each successive British defeat during the revolutionary war, the main push came in the aftermath of the publication of the Treaty of Paris (1783), which ended the war. During the negotiations, the British had attempted to gain some protection as well as compensation for the Loyalists. The new American government, however, had neither the power nor the desire to ease the plight of people still regarded as traitors. Further, as well-intentioned as the American negotiators may have been, they were hamstrung by the limited authority of the central government created by the Articles of Confederation. All they could do was promise to recommend that the individual states should refrain from punitive measures. In fact, Egerton Ryerson, leader of the Upper Canadian Methodists in the 1830s, would later write that fewer than 10 percent of the dispossessed Loyalists received any kind of compensation.[4]

Many Loyalists might have found the idea of sailing to England attractive, but most lacked the financial means to do so. Therefore, owing to the colonies' proximity, large numbers of Loyalists began to emigrate to Canada and Nova Scotia, the latter being the preferred choice. The colony of Canada was more distant, colder, and significantly, French. Thus, 30 000 Loyalists came to Nova Scotia, more than doubling the pre-revolution population of 17 000.

LOYALISTS IN THE MARITIMES

The Loyalists distributed themselves along the coastal regions at the mouth of the Saint John River. The commercially inclined gravitated to Halifax; the majority, however, ranged eastward

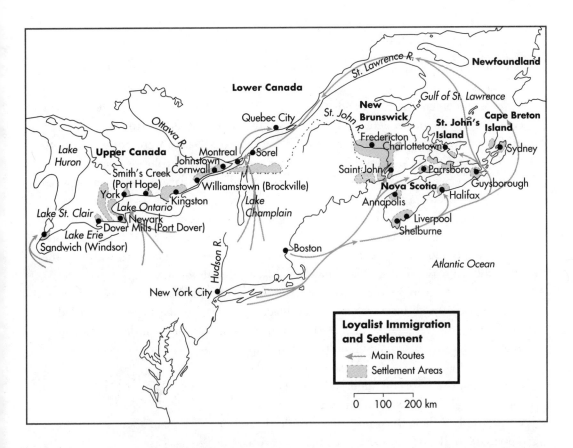

to Canso. A few ventured to Cape Breton and the Island of St. John, later Prince Edward Island. In some localities, the Loyalists joined up with previous settlers, but in most areas they found themselves in a pioneer environment. The largest group, numbering almost 10 000, went to Port Roseway, which was on the south shore of the Bay of Fundy, 250 km from Halifax; it was later renamed Shelburne.[5]

The hardships they endured during the first years have become part of the Loyalist myth. Ryerson's description would be echoed for the next century and a half: "[They] were driven from the homes of their birth and of their forefathers, to wilderness of everlasting snow."[6] The demands on the newcomers were immense. They had to obtain legal title to their land; clear that land and put in a crop; construct a dwelling, sometimes with the most primitive tools; and build communal establishments that would serve the entire regional population. All provisions were in short supply. Some endured winters living in tents. Others fashioned crude houses by dismantling the ships that had brought them. Food rations were meagre, and it was not uncommon for them to be infested with insects. Money was practically non-existent.

THE BLACK LOYALISTS

BLACKS FIRST ARRIVED IN NORTH AMERICA as early as 1619, when the first boatload landed at Jamestown, Virginia. Most came as slaves, although a handful came as freedmen. The thousands that came after did so under the most horrendous conditions. Their subsequent lives, whether on the large southern cotton plantations or on the small subsistence farms, were harsh and onerous. Slaves were not exclusive to the Thirteen Colonies. Before the outbreak of the American Revolution, they could be found in every British colony. In fact, a lucrative and active slave trade began between Halifax and Boston as early as 1751.

Although slaves were not an unusual sight in either Quebec or Nova Scotia before the revolution, they were relatively few in number. For example, in 1767, out of a total population of more than 13 000 in Nova Scotia, only 100 were black. However, in the years following the war, sizable numbers of blacks moved north.

In all, more than 3000 blacks migrated into Nova Scotia. Many came as slaves with their owners. An all-black regiment, the Black Pioneers, numbering 1500, settled in Birchtown, just outside the main settlement of Shelburne. Not all of these three thou-

sand could really be called "Loyalists" in the true sense of the word, since they came north with their owners. However, several hundred freed blacks had joined British and Loyalist regiments after having been promised their freedom if they would do so. About 500 of the free blacks settled in Nova Scotia, mostly in and around the Annapolis Valley. Many of the blacks who settled in Halifax were escaped slaves who feared reprisals from their former owners after the British troops departed.

Life for blacks in the Maritimes was hard. Invariably they were given the poorest land and the least assistance. They found themselves in bleak and isolated communities such as Birchtown. In addition, they faced the added burden of widespread discrimination. Both the native Bluenosers and the newcomers looked on the blacks with disdain and distrust.

Black Loyalists were far less numerous in the colony of Quebec than they were in the Maritimes. That was partially a result of the fact that slavery was

Watercolour by Caroline Bucknall Estcourt, *The Good "Woman of Colour" of Lundy's Lane, Upper Canada, 1839.*

uncommon in upstate New York and the Mohawk Valley, from where most of the Loyalists had come. When Lieutenant-Governor John Graves Simcoe abolished slavery in Upper Canada in 1793, the small numbers diminished even further. (His bill permitted people to hold slaves but made it illegal to import any more slaves into the colony. In addition, all those born to female slaves were freed on reaching the age of 25.) That is not to say that blacks were non-existent in Upper Canada. Particularly when the Underground Railway began in the 1850s, regional pockets of black settlement sprang up along the Detroit frontier of Canada West.

Blacks found life in Canada only marginally easier than the servitude they had been forced to endure in the United States. Many who saw an opportunity to leave Canada did so. Unlike the case for white settlers, the possibility of returning to the United States did not exist for them. Thus, when the anti-slave movements in Britain formed the Sierra Leone Company in 1791, their prayers appeared to have been answered. Almost 1200 black Nova Scotians left Halifax in the middle of January 1792 to relocate in the new nation of Sierra Leone, which had been founded on the principle of white/black equality.

Those who remained behind formed a unique nucleus. They were the first generation of black Canadians who, like most visible minorities in Canada, would travel an arduous route toward acceptance and integration. They came not so much out of loyalty as out of self-preservation. Hope had been their solace. Courage and perseverance had been their chief attributes. Theirs would be both a distinctive and an enduring history.

But as glorious as the Loyalist myth of struggle and survival may indeed be, what was perhaps equally remarkable — and essential — was the efficiency of the British army in furnishing the needed supplies. It provided food, seeds, tools, and expertise, without which the Loyalist experience would have been an unmitigated disaster. In addition, the government of Nova Scotia administered a very generous system of land grants. The government was also commissioned to assist in the establishment of Loyalist homesteads. However, the need far exceeded the supply, and surveyors were not plentiful. The demand for food, clothing, tools, and farm implements overwhelmed the governor, John Parr.

UNITED EMPIRE LOYALIST MYTH AND REALITY

In many ways, the plight of the Loyalists was intensified by their own ignorance and lack of judgement. Many had formerly been town dwellers, and some had enjoyed positions of wealth and privilege. Thus they were ill-prepared for a rugged pioneer existence. Their sense of despair and frustration began a cycle of recriminations. They appealed for assistance to a well-meaning but inefficient government. Fewer and fewer of the requests were answered, and the government, in turn, began to view the Loyalists as demanding and incompetent.

As the initial zeal disappeared and hope was replaced by despair, Loyalists began to describe their new home as "Nova Scarcity." Some gave up the struggle and sailed to England. Three-quarters of those who left drifted back to the United States after feelings there had subsided. Some departed for the West Indies. Some, believing that Nova Scotia itself was to blame for their plight, left for the Island of St. John. However, their sense of disillusionment was rekindled as they met the same fate in that colony.

There were many divisions between the Loyalists and the established citizens of Nova Scotia. The Loyalists were suspicious of the old-stock New Englanders' loyalty. Leaders within the Loyalist group harboured ambitions to hold positions of political power like those they had enjoyed in the Thirteen Colonies. That caused a strong sense of resentment on the part of the original inhabitants. Within Loyalist ranks, there was a deep division between those who had served in the regiments and those who had simply emigrated. The former were indignant that the best parcels of land were being awarded to civilians who had done nothing for the imperial cause. Perhaps the deepest division was between the 12 000 Loyalists who settled on the shores of the Bay of Fundy and the smaller group that migrated to Halifax. The former felt that the government in Halifax was distant and unresponsive and catered only to the needs of the people in the capital. Not surprisingly, a movement for a separate provincial government developed. People like Colonel Edward Winslow and Ward Chipman were quick to realize that the project promised substantial rewards, both political and economic.

The British government came to the same conclusion, but for very different reasons. The chief lesson

Encampment of the Loyalists at Johnstown (1784), located up the St. Lawrence River from Montreal. Upon viewing the site an Englishman exclaimed, "The settling of the Loyalists is one of the best things George III ever did."

that Westminster derived from the American Revolution was that in order to keep colonies weak, the best policy was to divide them, and the colony of New Brunswick was therefore established in 1784 by dividing Nova Scotia along the Missiquash River. Colonel Thomas Carleton was appointed New Brunswick's first governor, and the new province was made independent of Nova Scotia, with its own appointed council and elected assembly. Thus New Brunswick was largely a Loyalist creation: over 80 percent of its residents were Loyalists.

The coming of the United Empire Loyalists into the Maritimes had more than doubled the population; had led to the clearing of substantial portions of previously uncultivated land; and had improved the economy. Ultimately it had led to the creation of a new province that was fiercely anti-American. Given the conflicts and recriminations, the final legacy of the Loyalists in the Maritimes is ambivalent. They received less than they expected, but they produced more than they intended.

THE UNITED EMPIRE LOYALISTS IN THE CANADAS

The experiences and consequences of the United Empire Loyalists' arrival in Quebec was decidedly different from those in the Maritimes. About 10 000 Loyalists migrated into Quebec. Whereas the migration into Nova Scotia tended to come from the more substantial classes of the eastern seaport towns, the exodus into Quebec was drawn from the western frontier regions of New England, New York, and Pennsylvania. These Loyalists were pioneer farmers, well suited to establishing homes in the wilderness. Whereas the movement into the Atlantic region had come by sea, that into Quebec took the overland route. And while loyalty was the initial impulse that motivated the movement into Quebec, it was also part of a natural expansion into the interior of the continent.[7]

The Loyalists initially came into Canada in the wake of Burgoyne's defeat at Saratoga in 1777. Small numbers came with whatever they could carry across the border. By 1781, there were 3000; after the battle of Yorktown and the eventual ending of hostilities, there would be another 7000. At first, Governor Frederick Haldimand, Guy Carleton's able and humane successor, set up temporary refugee camps on the *seigneury* of Sorel. He believed it best to keep the newcomers, with their notions of liberty and representative government, separated from the existing population, which held much more traditional views.

Initially, Haldimand was rather reluctant to settle the newcomers in the western part of the province because he was concerned about trouble with the Amerindians. Added to that difficulty, he had the troublesome and sensitive question of what to do with the Mohawk and other Iroquois tribes who, under Joseph Brant's influence, had supported Britain during the revolutionary war. However, when he became aware of the potential buffer that the Loyalists, if settled in large blocks in the western reaches of the province, could provide against the Americans, he reversed his decision. His hand was also forced by Carleton's decision to send a group of 200 families to the eastern end of Lake Ontario.

Haldimand had to equip the newcomers with provisions: tents, muskets, seeds, clothes for three years, and an axe and a hoe for each man. When he left in 1784, over 6000 refugees had been settled; all except 500 were drawing full provisions.

THE LOYALIST LAND GRANTS

Land allotment in Canada followed the same pattern as in Nova Scotia. In order to keep the peace and prevent a lawless Amerindian frontier, the British government was adamant that private purchases of land from the Amerindians were prohibited, and the government concluded formal treaties with the various Amerindian tribes to the west. After that, Governor Haldimand had the land surveyed. The actual award of land was done by a lottery. The officers were very displeased because the governor would not allow them to select the best lots for themselves. As early as 1783, more than 3 million acres had been given to the Loyalists, who were not the least bit reluctant to use their loyalty as a justification for their land claims. It has been argued that social and economic factors, rather than emotional and psychological ones, were at the root of the Loyalist migrations. This was particularly true of the "late Loyalists," whose loyalty was to be found more in their pocketbooks than in their hearts.[8]

Nevertheless, the hardships that give credence to the Loyalist myth appeared. As in Nova Scotia, a shortage of surveyors meant troublesome delays. Shortages of tools, clothing, and other necessary implements made things worse. When the government's three-year support program ended in 1786, the hardships were intensified. The climax came in 1788 with the so-called "hungry year": a combination of drought and cutworms devastated Loyalist crops. It is estimated that about 50 percent of the population would have died of starvation without the importation of food from the Mohawk Valley. However, the lesson was learned — the settlers could no longer count on government handouts. They cleared huge areas of land, built roads, and established communities and services.

A very different lifestyle from Loyalist farmers was enjoyed by William McGillivray and his family. Representing the elite of fur-trading society, he played an instrumental role in negotiating the 1821 Hudson's Bay Company – North West Company merger. (M18683, William McGillivray and His Family, 1805–1806, William Van Moll Berczy, painting, oil on canvas, McCord Museum of Canadian History, Montreal.)

THE FOUNDING OF UPPER AND LOWER CANADA

Thousands had initially come out of loyalty — in varying degrees — to British customs and institutions. Even though that sentiment may indeed have waned over time, it was still strong. Thus, the Loyalists could not long tolerate living under the confines of the terms of the Quebec Act. As early as April 1785, Sir John Johnson proposed the establishment of a wholly Loyalist colony. Guy Carleton, now Lord Dorchester, the governor, was placed in a difficult position. What policy could possibly satisfy both the French and the English? How could he meet the demands of one group without seriously upsetting the other?

When William Grenville became the new secretary of state, the British government slowly realized that a new constitutional arrangement was required.[9] Such changes would "promote the prosperity" of Canada. In addition, it would confer upon the Loyalists the type of institutions — most particularly an elected assembly — they most desired. Furthermore, by dividing the colony, it would potentially avoid the errors the British had committed in dealing with the Thirteen Colonies. Dorchester's draft bill arrived too late for the 1790 parliamentary session. With some re-working on the part of Grenville, the Constitutional Act passed through the British Parliament and was given royal assent in June 1791.

Amelia Douglas, the mixed-blood wife of James Douglas. Inter-marriage between fur traders and Amerindian women helped to promote harmonious Natve – white relations and a mutual trading relationship.

Parallel representative governments with elected assemblies were established for the two colonies that were carved out of Quebec. There would be an appointed governor, an executive council, and a legislative council (which could be hereditary), where the real power resided. The actual division of Quebec into Upper and Lower Canada (the former English and the latter French) was not actually contained in the Act; it was carried out through executive action, as this would avoid public debate and discussion over boundaries. The Ottawa River was eventually decided on as the dividing line. The Act further ordered that one-seventh of all the crown lands be set aside for the maintenance of "a Protestant clergy."

The Constitutional Act was highly significant for the future of Canada. It attempted to establish two separate colonies, one French and one English.

Although the French were allowed to retain their civil law, their language in their courts, the *seigneurial* system, and their Roman Catholic church, the intent was not to create an enduring "French" colony in Lower Canada. It was assumed that, given English control over commerce, coupled with expected British immigration, both colonies would be English (if not Protestant). Finally, both the English in Upper Canada and the French in Lower Canada were given their own separate representative government. That government was to last, imperfectly, for the next 50 years.

THE BRITISH MIGRATION AND SETTLEMENT EXPERIENCE

THE LOYALISTS PROVIDED ONLY THE BEGINNINGS of English settlement in parts of British North America. In the early 1800s, the greatest movement of people in the history of Europe began. During the nineteenth century, millions of people moved from the countryside to the towns, from one country to another, or from the continent across the seas to many areas of the world. As part of this "Great Migration," European peoples flooded across the Atlantic Ocean to the American republic and the British North American colonies.[10] British North America — like the United States — was profoundly affected by the great trans-Atlantic migration. In 1806, the colonies of Nova Scotia, New Brunswick, Lower Canada, Upper Canada, and Newfoundland had a total population of 461 000. By 1821, the population totalled 750 000; and by mid-century, it reached 2 300 000. The flood of new immigrants was a mixed group of well-to-do and impoverished English emigrants, Catholic and Protestant Irish, Highland and Lowland Scots, and even a group of Lutherans from Germany. All through the 1820s, 1830s, and 1840s they poured into Britain's northern colonies, in spite of a long and arduous Atlantic crossing and great hardships on their arrival in the "new country."

THE GREAT EXODUS

Why did millions of British people emigrate to the New World? Most British emigrants were poor and their future in Ireland, Scotland, or England looked bleaker than the prospects of a new life in the wilderness of British North America. In England, the rise of industrialism had attracted many from the rural farmlands to the cities. The developing factories seemed to offer unlimited urban unemployment. Unfortunately, this was not the case. Tens of thousands were unsuccessful in their search, which resulted in the creation of a swelling unemployed and impoverished urban population. A similar movement of people had occurred in Scotland, where many Highlanders had been forced off the land by "clearances" to make way for the sheep needed by the growing wool industry. In Ireland, the population had exploded from 6 million in 1815 to 8 million in 1841, and had then been struck by a terrible potato famine that sent thousands fleeing to other countries.

At various times the British government assisted emigrants. Groups of disbanded military units after 1815, and later small colonies of destitute Scots and Irish, were helped. Many more were financially assisted by British emigration societies determined to rid their home countries of undesirable groups, from the 1846–48 Irish potato famine victims to "the outcasts of London." Emigration was also supported by various British voluntary societies that organized and paid for the resettlement of

British emigrants leaving their homeland during the Great Exodus.

thousands of poor men, women, and orphaned children. One such humanitarian effort, headed by Maria S. Rye, rescued and transported more than 1600 orphan girls to Upper Canada.[11]

THE CROSSING AND ARRIVAL

For most penniless Irish, Scots, and English, the ocean voyage to British North America was a horrible ordeal. Fleeing disease, famine, and poverty, they boarded cargo ships sailing with empty holds that would take on timber in Quebec for the return voyage. So many emigrants died on the trans-Atlantic voyage that the cargo vessels were known as "coffin ships." After crossing the North Atlantic, the ships sailed around Newfoundland and entered the St. Lawrence River. Since many on board were diseased or dying, the first stop after 1831 was Grosse Isle (the "Isle of Death"), just below Quebec. Sick passengers were removed from the ships and placed in quarantine in wooden sheds that passed for a makeshift hospital.[12] Once an immigrant ship was given a clean bill of health, it sailed on to Quebec or Montreal. There the surviving immigrants disembarked for life in a new land.

The end of the Atlantic crossing was for most newcomers the beginning of an overland journey. Most of the British emigrants moved on to Montreal and then to Upper Canada in search of cultivable land or employment. For thousands, British North America was only a way station on the route to the United States. Since the St. Lawrence was still the main avenue of transport, most immigrants went by bateaux or Durham boats to Prescott or Kingston, where they boarded Lake Ontario steamers to ports farther inland. Some new arrivals in Upper Canada settled and took up employment in towns like Toronto or Hamilton. The vast majority, however, sought to settle in more remote parts of the province, taking advantage of land grants or cheaper-priced lots. Immigrants who arrived with sufficient capital or who had saved up enough money by doing odd labouring jobs were able to purchase a "location ticket." Ticket in hand, they set off on foot or in carts to take up their land in the backwoods.

PIONEER EXPERIENCES IN UPPER CANADA

The experiences of settlement in British North America varied considerably from colony to colony, from towns and villages to backwoods farm communities. For most newcomers, both in Upper Canada and elsewhere in the colonies, the first home was a primitive shelter in the backwoods. Upon arrival, the pioneer family faced the formidable task of clearing the land, building a wooden shelter, and preparing for its first Canadian winter. In parts of Upper Canada, clearing the land was an occasion for frontier co-operative efforts. It was quite common for farm neighbours to join in land-clearing and barn-raising bees to help the family get established in the backwoods country.[13]

Pioneering in Upper Canada evoked a wide range of responses from the early settlers. The English gentlewoman Anne Langton expressed hopeful optimism after her arrival in 1837 at her brother's farm near Sturgeon Lake, Upper Canada:

Two of Upper Canada's women pioneers: Susanna Moodie (left) and Anne Langton (right).

What most strikes me is a greater degree of roughness in farming, buildings, gardens, fences and especially roads, than I had expected. But when one looks at the wild woods around, and thinks that from such a wilderness the present state of things has been brought out by a few hands...one's surprise vanishes, and one rather wonders that so much has been done....[14]

Typical of the thousands of poor British settlers who found new economic opportunities in Upper Canada was Philip Annett, an English day-labourer. In 1830, he reported that it was "a good country for poor folk," with "excellent land" bearing crops of wheat and corn. "Here you have no rent to pay, no poor-rates, and scarcely any taxes. No game-keepers or Lords over you.... A man can earn enough in three days to last him all the week."[15]

A few Upper Canadian settlers saw an invigorating, enterprising impulse at work similar to that of American frontierism. Catherine Parr Traill, an Englishwoman who arrived in Upper Canada in 1832, was one who believed that the pioneer experience bred strength, vigour, and optimism:

Canada is the land of hope; here everything is new; everything going forward; it is scarcely possible for arts, sciences, agriculture, manufactures, to retrograde; they must keep advancing; though in some situations the progress may seem slow, in others they are...rapid.

She marvelled at the spirit of frontier co-operation, most evident in the work bee. "In spite of the differences of rank among those that assisted at the bee," she reported, "the greatest possible harmony prevailed."[16]

Not all British observers were so enchanted with their early experiences in British North America. Susanna Moodie, an English gentlewoman who left England in 1832 and settled with her husband in Upper Canada, despaired about pioneer life. Settling first near Cobourg, the Moodies moved two years later to a homestead near Peterborough so that Susanna could be nearer her brother and her sister, Catharine Parr Traill. With her upper-class birth and rearing, Susanna found pioneer life full of crudity, discomfort, and endless toil. The immigration pamphlets, she wrote in *Roughing It in the Bush* (1852), "prominently set forth all the *good* to be derived from a settlement in the Backwoods of Canada; while they carefully concealed the toil and hardship to be endured in order to secure these advantages."[17] For Susanna, the frontier life in Upper Canada was anything but an energizing experience. "My love for Canada," Moodie remarked bitterly, "was a feeling very nearly allied to that which the condemned criminal entertains for his cell."

The arrival of tens of thousands of British and European settlers had its most dramatic effect on the Native peoples of Upper Canada and the other colonies. The Amerindian tribes initially granted the use of their ancestral lands to the European newcomers, then found themselves crowded out of the more favoured parts of Upper Canada. In the district around York (Toronto), for example, the Mississaugas conceded land rights in the Toronto Purchase in 1788, were gradually driven away by expanding white settlement, and in 1847 resettled on the New

Credit reserve with the Six Nations at Brantford. According to Lieutenant-Governor Sir Francis Bond Head, the treatment of the Native peoples in Upper Canada was part of "the most sinful story recorded in the history of the human race." After taking possession of "their country" and driving them from "vast regions of land," he pointed out in 1836, "nothing…remains of the poor Indian but the unnoticed bones of his ancestors…the race barely lingers in existence."[18]

LEGACIES OF SETTLEMENT

British immigration after 1815 dramatically altered the character of Britain's northern colonies in America. Between 1815 and 1855, about 1 million British emigrants landed in British North American ports. Although a significant proportion of the newcomers drifted south to the United States, the thousands who remained set the cultural character of all the colonies, except French-speaking Lower Canada, for the next two generations. Most of the flood of British emigrants chose to settle in the English-speaking province of Upper Canada. But the Maritime colonies had also received British-born newcomers, and the vast expanses of Rupert's Land — the Northwest — also acquired sizable communities of English-speaking inhabitants.

Few British North Americans in the early nineteenth century experienced the romance of the frontier. From the colonial beginnings, the first large waves of white settlers — Loyalist and later British — endured hardships and tests of endurance. Settlements were built more on practical principles of survival and order than on the "forest-born" ideals of democracy. By mid-century, a new but distinctly British colonial order had taken shape. Raw pioneering had given way to rising settlements boasting churches, schools, taverns, stores, and small workshop industries. Railways had begun hauling freight and passengers from Halifax to Rivière du Loup on the St. Lawrence, and west to the border with the United States in Canada West (formerly Upper Canada). In one lifetime, the British settlers had passed from a rough pioneer experience to life in a pre-industrial colonial society. In their essential "Britishness," the inhabitants of the northern colonies, including Lower Canada (later Canada East), differed in outlook from their American neighbours.

Toronto's King Street, 1836. By the mid-1830s, "Muddy York" had become a small provincial city with an ordered social life and a commercial centre that would soon rival Montreal's.

THE FRONTIER MYTH OF THE AMERICAN WEST

MYTHS PLAY A POWERFUL ROLE in a country's identity. They provide a communal focus, a point of reference, and a vehicle for unification and patriotism. They become the seeds for popular folklore, heroes, and legends. They are crucial in a country's early history as they provide the "ties that bind." Whether they are absolutely true, somewhat embellished, or grossly exaggerated, myths are necessary elements of a nation's identity.

American popular literature since the early 1800s produced a host of symbols and myths associated with the "Wild West" beyond the frontier. In his *Leatherstocking Tales*, the novelist James Fenimore Cooper fashioned the image of a heroic frontiersman who roamed among the Amerindians in the western wilderness. Cooper's hero was a fighter and hunter and demonstrated a natural nobility born of the wilderness. Yet *Leatherstocking Tales* celebrated the exploits of those outside settled society, beyond the frontier. Poetic ideas of the agricultural West as the garden and of its cultivation were much slower to develop in popular fiction.

The American frontier farmer had few of the attributes of a hero. His settled and laborious ways contrasted sharply with the "exotic glamour" of the hunters, scouts, and outlaws of the Wild West. While the western hero evoked an image of noble savagery and freedom from restraints, the yeoman farmer was commonly depicted as part of the lower order of colonial society.

In American popular thinking after the 1820s, the agricultural West was clearly differentiated from the Wild West beyond the line of settlement. The frontier of agricultural settlement was depicted as the limit of "civilized society," where social order and the class system governed status relations among people. Notions of social equality and agrarian freedom espoused by Thomas Jefferson and his disciples found little expression in fictional literature. According to historian Henry Nash Smith, the author of *Virgin Land: The American West as Symbol and Myth* (1950),* "no coherent literary tradition" existed before the late 1870s that embodied egalitarian ideals of the American frontier. If novels were any guide, Americans in the frontier period may have lacked a "whole image of the West."

The standard interpretation in Smith's *Virgin Land* has not gone unchallenged. Historian Rush Welter was one who questioned the Smith thesis.† The themes traced by Smith, according to Welter, were "too nearly poetic in their inspiration, too nearly conventional in their application," to be entirely convincing. Americans probably held a

---

* See Henry Nash Smith, *Virgin Land: The American West as Symbol and Myth* (Cambridge, MA: Harvard University Press, 1950).
† Rush Welter, "The Frontier West as Image of American Society," *Pacific Northwest Quarterly* 52 (January 1961).

wider variety of images of the West and may not have always distinguished between the romance and the reality of frontier experiences. Welter concludes that the Turnerian theory still has validity. Between 1776 and 1860, far from being bound by literary images, Americans came to see in the West what Welter termed "an almost limitless extension of the social and economic and political values they associated with their country at large."

THE FRONTIER THESIS

PERHAPS THE DYNAMO that moved everything from politics to demographics during this "formative" period of "adjustment and consolidation" was the frontier.[19] While the legitimacy of this concept is hotly disputed, there can be little argument that the frontier was of paramount importance to the growing colonies. Not only did the frontier have a profound influence on the evolution of American history, it had an equally significant — albeit different — impact on Canadian development. In short, the frontier was the backdrop against which most of the political, demographic, and economic changes of the decades between the end of the American Revolution and mid-century were fashioned.

THE FRONTIER MYTH

The origins of the frontier thesis lie in American historian Frederick Jackson Turner's watershed paper delivered to the 1893 meeting of the American Historical Association. Turner pronounced that "the frontier is the outer edge of the wave — the meeting point between savagery and civilization." Although not blind to the negative aspects of the frontier, Turner attempted to analyze what in his estimation was the frontier-born greatness of America. It was on the frontier, he argued, that all the great American virtues — self-reliance, egalitarianism, co-operation, individuality, and democracy — were born.[20] It was the constantly expanding frontier of settlement moving into unoccupied land that shaped the nature, pattern, and dynamism of American development.

Turner was not without his critics, particularly later American historians such as Arthur Schlesinger, Jr. and Richard Hofstadter. The latter commented: "The notion of an aggressive pioneering national spirit nurtured by repeated exposure to primitive conditions became a means to national self-glorification." He also attacked Turner's use of vague terms — the West, the frontier, individualism, and the American character. Turner himself had earlier conceded that even the central concept of the frontier "is an elastic one." The fundamental weakness of the theory, Hofstadter claimed, lay in its intellectual isolation and its obsession with the uniqueness of the frontier. In a similar fashion, writing from a radical revisionist perspective, William Appleman Williams damned the theory as a "romantic flight from reality."[21]

Even though Turner's analysis exaggerated the uniqueness of American development, the frontier thesis became an integral part of American historiography. Furthermore, it developed its own self-sustaining myth; in fact, it exerted an influence far beyond the realm of pure historical debate and became a vital aspect of American thought. Because people believed that the American frontier was closing up around the turn of the century, American politicians felt that frontier values could be recaptured by pursuing an international frontier and embarked on an aggressive policy of overseas expansion.

President Franklin D. Roosevelt employed the Turner thesis in his famous 1932 Commonwealth Club speech, in which he provided a historical justification of his New Deal program. "Our last frontier has long since been reached, and there is practically no more free land.... There is no safety valve in the form of a western prairie to which those thrown out of work by the eastern machine can go for a new start." Thirty years later, President John F. Kennedy and his "New Frontiersmen" spoke of outer space as the "last frontier" that remained to be conquered. Clearly the frontier myth has exerted a powerful influence on the American psyche.

CANADIANS AND THE FRONTIER THESIS

The debate in Canada regarding the validity of the frontier thesis has been far less acrimonious than that waged in the United States.[22] Arthur M. Lower, a Harvard student of Turner's, attempted to follow the Turnerian analysis and apply it to the Canadian context.[23] Although he did not discount the role played by the English aristocratic tradition, he nevertheless saw Canadian development as primarily an outgrowth of the influence of the frontier. "Both in Canada and the United States, democracy has been a condition, not a theory. It has been the spontaneous product of the frontier and the forest." He further argued that "the frontier environment, or life lived on the margin of civilization, tends to bring about an equality of which the political expression is democracy."

In a scathing attack, historian John L. McDougall seriously questioned the theory's validity.[24] In examining the society of French Canada, he came to the conclusion that "it could be little short of a calamity if Canadian historians were to attempt to deform the story of our own development to fit the Procrustes bed of the frontier thesis." He argued that the *habitants*, living in a decidedly frontier society, failed to manifest any of the characteristics — individualism, acquisitiveness, love of democracy — that Turner's theory ascribed to them.

Frederick Jackson Turner (second from right) conducting a graduate class at Harvard.

Other Canadian historians have offered a qualified acceptance of the frontier thesis as it applies to Canada. Harold Innis, in his study of the fur trade in Canada, was influenced by Turner's analysis.[25] Donald Creighton's Laurentian interpretation of Canadian history, clearly related to Innis's "staple thesis," also is in part a derivation of the frontier concept.[26] In arguing the primacy of the St. Lawrence River system in both economics and politics, Creighton advanced an environmentalist analysis. However, he reversed the frontier thesis, as did J.M.S. Careless in his metropolitan thesis. These historians argued that commercial, metropolitan centres, rather than the frontier, provided the impetus for Canadian development. After the 1930s, frontierism passed out of fashion in Canada.

The historical debate notwithstanding, the frontier experience occupied a significant place in Canadian development. The pattern and order of settlement in the two "Wests" was very different. In the United States, individual settlers, very much in a random fashion, went west in advance of any legal and/or governmental institutions. The pattern in British North America was quite different. The unsettled West was normally first penetrated by trappers and traders who exploited the natural wealth of the area. They were followed by government institutions, which organized the new territory. Finally came the settlers, who would usually be engaged in agriculture. The fact that governmental and legal institutions preceded settlement in Canada, whereas the opposite was the case in the United States, had a profound impact on the subsequent development of both nations.

ACTIVITIES

KEY TERMS AND CONCEPTS

Identify and briefly explain the historical significance of the following terms and concepts:

- United Empire Loyalists
- American frontier
- Staple thesis
- Late Loyalists
- Constitutional Act (1791)
- Black pioneers
- Great Migration
- Irish famine
- "Isle of Death"
- Location ticket
- Barn-raising bee
- *Roughing It in the Bush*
- Removal of the Mississaugas

QUESTIONS FOR DISCUSSION

1. Why did millions of people move to the North American frontier in the period from the American Revolution to the mid-nineteenth century? Which factors — push or pull — were greater?

2. Compare and contrast the United Empire Loyalists and the late Loyalists. Are they and their exile experiences similar or different?

3. Were the British wise in passing the Constitutional Act of 1791? Justify your answer.

4. To what extent were the migrants from the Old World and the American Loyalists who emigrated to British North America motivated by different influences and pressures?

5. How did the immigrants' actual experiences in the Maritimes and the Canadas compare with their expectations?

6. To what degree did the frontier experience enhance or diminish the role of Native women in North American society?

7. Is the frontier thesis more applicable to American history than to the Canadian experience? Explain your reasoning.

8. Myths are an integral feature of any nation. Identify the significant myths of Canadian and American history from this era. How are those myths different from today's myths?

ANALYZING THE EVIDENCE

Analyze carefully the accompanying two graphs, showing population growth in British North America, 1806–51, and British immigrant arrivals at Quebec in the peak period of the Great Migration. Based on the graphs' statistical evidence, answer the following questions:

1. How did Upper Canada's population growth compare with that of the other British North American colonies in the early nineteenth century? What factors might explain the variations in growth?

2. Why did British emigration peak in 1832, 1841–42, and 1846–47? Try to identify the factors in each case.

3. From which part of the British Isles did most of the immigrants entering at Quebec come? Explain the reasons for this development.

4. Which British North American colony had the greatest population growth between 1806 and 1825? Between 1825 and 1838? Between 1838 and 1851? Suggest some reasons in each case.

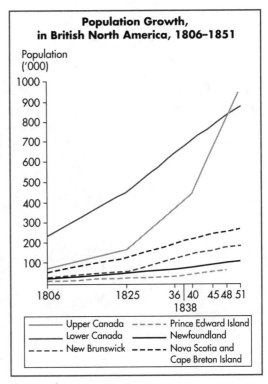

Population Growth, in British North America, 1806–1851

Upper Canada
Lower Canada
New Brunswick
Prince Edward Island
Newfoundland
Nova Scotia and Cape Breton Island

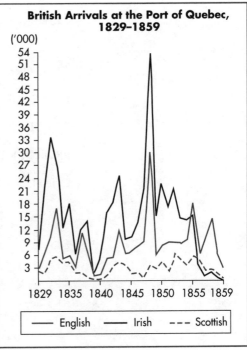

British Arrivals at the Port of Quebec, 1829–1859

English   Irish   Scottish

IDENTITY AND NATIONHOOD

THE 30-YEAR PERIOD between the end of the American revolutionary war and the War of 1812 was one of great change for both British North America and the United States. In British North America, the immigration of the Loyalists and others substantially increased the population, and as a result had a major economic and commercial impact. In addition, the arrival of the Loyalists led to the creation of new provinces — New Brunswick and Upper Canada — and the institution of representative government. Finally, the newcomers provided an early form of nationalism, based largely on a deep sense of anti-Americanism.

In the new republic of the United States, these three decades were ones of growth and expansion. The constitution was rewritten; the national government was remade; and the balance of power between the states and the central government was radically altered. The economy was put on a stable foundation; the land area was virtually doubled; and the reputation of the fledgling nation was aided by the work of its first president, George Washington.

In Canada, there were many adjustments and some consolidation; in the United States, in addition, there was tremendous expansion — in territory, in the influence of the national government, and in international reputation. The Americans were beginning their meteoric rise; they were soon to flex their muscles by challenging the major power, Britain. The War of 1812 would test the strength of America's Manifest Destiny and the loyalties of the British North American colonies.

THE FORMING OF THE AMERICAN REPUBLIC

DURING THE REVOLUTIONARY WAR, local state governments had to conduct the war, collect taxes, supply their troops, and maintain order. Not surprisingly, these governments resembled British colonial governments in several respects: they were democratic, representative, and bicameral. However, they did differ in some significant aspects. First, one of the roots of the revolution had been the absence of a written constitution. The Americans corrected this shortcoming by insisting that all constitutions be formally written. There was a break with the British past in the American insistence on the separation between church and state. In the newly created United States, there would be no established church. Naturally, the new governments would be republican. Finally, another force behind the revolution had been the Americans' view that their rights and liberties had been trampled by an overbearing British establishment. Thus, a written bill of rights was a consistent feature of all state constitutions.

CREATION OF A NATIONAL DOMAIN

Creating the state governments was a relatively easy matter. Yet, most Americans clearly saw the need for a national government. Thus, the Second Continental Congress met in 1776 to draft a national constitution. The delegates to this congress faced a formidable challenge. They had to design a government that would bind the new nation together, yet they were adamantly loyal to their own states. At the same time, having the abuses of the British Parliament fresh in their minds, the delegates recognized the dangers of granting too much power to the central authority. It took approximately a year and a half before the Continental Congress could agree on the final constitutional draft. It was not until 1781, when the last state ratified this new constitution, that the articles became the law of the land.[1]

Although the national government was given certain specified powers (to declare war, make treaties, borrow money, and the like), the articles placed strict limitations on the authority of Congress. For example, it could not collect taxes, which severely curtailed its power. In addition, Congress could not regulate foreign or domestic trade. Even more significant was the clause that assured each state that it would keep its sovereignty, freedom, and independence, and that it would retain "every power, jurisdiction, and right" not expressly given to the central government. In addition, the absence of a chief executive (a president) and a national system of justice seriously restricted the power of the central authority. As if this was not enough to cement the superiority of the local governments over Congress, one final point confirmed it. Major decisions had to be approved by nine of the thirteen states, and any amendment to the articles had to be agreed on unanimously.

PROBLEMS UNDER THE ARTICLES OF CONFEDERATION

The fact that the system was unworkable was clear by the middle of the 1780s.[2] Congress was too hamstrung to deal with several vexing problems — foreign relations, the Northwest Territory, trade, and tariffs. Furthermore, hard-pressed Massachusetts farmers demanded that paper money be issued so that they could meet their debts more easily. When wealthy creditors refused, not wanting to accept payment in depreciated currency, an abortive revolt of Massachusetts farmers and mechanics, led by Daniel Shays and aimed at relieving the debtor classes, broke out in 1786. Shays's Rebellion frightened men of property into the realization that a stronger central government was a necessity.

THE MAKING OF THE U.S. CONSTITUTION

Twelve states responded to Congress's call in February 1787 to send delegates for "the sole and express purpose of revising the Articles of Confederation." The group of prominent colonial notables assembled on May 25, 1787, included George Washington, Benjamin Franklin, Alexander Hamilton, Thomas Jefferson, and James Madison.[3] Since the state governments

E PLURIBUS UNUM/ OUT OF MANY, ONE

AMERICA UNDER THE ARTICLES OF CONFEDERATION	FROM CONFEDERATION TO THE CONSTITUTION
No president, executive power	President to be chosen indirectly by the people and given executive power. Made commander in chief of the army and navy, and takes all steps necessary to ensure that laws are faithfully executed.
No federal courts	Federal judges established with authority to enforce laws and annul state laws that are inconsistent with the federal constitution or laws.
No taxation powers	Congress given powers to raise funds through "taxes, duties, imposts, and exercises."
No regulation of commerce	Congress to regulate commerce with foreign powers, between states, and with the Amerindians.
States were sovereign	A federal union was formed from which secession was impossible. Federal constitution and laws made supreme in all states.
Unanimous consent required to amend articles	Constitution can be amended with the approval of three-quarters of the states.

would not relinquish their ultimate sovereignty, Roger Sherman devised the Connecticut Compromise, which protected the identities of the smaller states through equal representation in the Senate. Had James Madison and Edmund Randolph had their way, the Virginia Plan would have been adopted, which would have allocated seats in both houses on the basis of a state's population. Now Sherman, building on Benjamin Franklin's "Great Compromise" (representation by population in the lower house and equal representation in the upper house), guaranteed every state that it would have two senators regardless of its size.

The national government was given a longer list of delegated powers, while the state governments retained a powerful list of reserved powers. The central government received power over foreign affairs, war and peace, the regulation of interstate commerce, foreign trade, and the admission of new states. Importantly, the so-called "elastic" clause (empowering Congress to "make all laws which shall be necessary and proper for carrying into execution" its enumerated powers) would, along with the power to regulate interstate commerce, be interpreted by the Supreme Court in such a way as to greatly enlarge the power of the central government. Nevertheless, the states still retained considerable power (such as civil and criminal law, intrastate commerce, and municipal governments).

Significant state power was added with the passage of the Tenth Amendment, ratified in 1791. It limited the effectiveness of the "elastic" clause by stipulating that "the powers not delegated to the United States by the Constitution, nor prohibited by it to the States, are reserved to the States respectively, or to the people." It lent considerable credence to the argument

George Washington presiding over the Federal Convention, during which the proposed constitution was debated.

that states retained their sovereignty and had merely delegated some powers to the federal government. Although a more equitable balance between the power of the national and local governments had been struck, the scale still tipped in favour of the states. Years later, John A. Macdonald of Canada would see this as the major shortcoming of the American system.

Another issue concerned the election of the president. Since the president would wield tremendous influence through his veto, his power over appointments as well as his duties as commander-in-chief and head of government, this was a sensitive issue. The crucial compromise involved the creation of an electoral college, which would result in an indirect election of the chief executive.

Just as a compromise was essential between the large and small states, a similar resolution was needed between North and South. The major question concerned the status of slaves. The South wanted them counted as part of the population, as this would obviously increase the power of the southern states. However, the North argued that since slaves were considered chattel, they should not be counted. The controversy was solved with the "three-fifths rule," which determined that for the purposes of representation and taxation a slave would be counted as 60 percent of a white man. The massive contradiction posed by slavery and republicanism, recognized and acknowledged by the Founding Fathers, was something that, although legislatively compromised, would haunt American society for decades to come.[4]

By strengthening the power of the central government, the delegates had created an effective structure. Without the changes, the national government would have been paralyzed into irrelevancy. With the new constitution and the first ten amendments (the Bill of Rights), the framers of the document proved their farsightedness. They had constructed a document that was modified little more than a dozen times over the next two centuries and had developed a government system that, in its fairness and balance, became the model for many nations. *E Pluribus Unum* was more than the motto of the new American republic. The framers of the constitution had managed to bring the emerging American community of 3 million people together as "one nation, indivisible."[5]

CAUSES OF THE WAR OF 1812

A RENEWAL OF HOSTILITIES BETWEEN BRITAIN and her former colonists came about for a number of reasons.[6] Neither Britain nor the United States had fully absorbed the meaning of the results of the American Revolution. The British never gave their former colonists the respect that the Americans believed they deserved; the Americans distrusted Britain and had an exaggerated sense of their own power and significance in international affairs.

A series of issues led to a deteriorating relationship. Both sides failed to fulfil key provisions of the Treaty of Versailles of 1783. Most prominently, the British retained a number of forts in the Ohio Valley, from Oswego to Michilimackinac, which were to have been ceded to the Americans. Second, the issue of maritime rights, including impressment, blockade, and contraband, arising out of the Napoleonic Wars, contributed significantly to the slide to war. For the Americans, alleged British violations in this area were both an affront and a challenge to the American claim to national status. Third, the influence of the vocal War Hawks — such as Henry Clay from Kentucky and John C. Calhoun of South Carolina — whipped up American anger against Britain and British North America.

RETENTION OF THE WESTERN POSTS

On the festering issue of the western forts, the British claimed that they had kept the outposts because of the inability or unwillingness of the weak American federal government to force individual states to compensate the Loyalists for their property losses during the revolution. It had been agreed that each state would offer some compensation to Loyalists whose property had been confiscated and should allow exiled Loyalists to return to settle personal business without fear of arrest or attack. However, until 1789 the union was governed by the Articles of Confederation, which gave the federal government no power to enforce its decisions within the states. Most states simply ignored the wishes of the federal authorities and refused to give any consideration to the unfortunate Loyalists.

THE AMERINDIAN QUESTION

The British colonial authorities also hoped to encourage the creation of an Amerindian territory in the region, both to serve as a buffer between Canada and the United States and to prevent reprisals against Canada by Britain's Amerindian allies, whose interests were ignored by the Treaty of Versailles. For their part, the Americans suspected that the British were using the Amerindians merely to frustrate the new nation's expansion and development. When Amerindians involved in several battles with American troops in the 1790s were found to have been supplied with weapons and ammunition from the British-occupied forts, those suspicions were confirmed. Anglo-American relations in general and the issue of the western forts in particular improved with the 1794 signing of Jay's Treaty. It called for the British to withdraw from the western outposts by 1796 in exchange for allowing British merchants to carry on trade in the area. Chief Justice John Jay also agreed that the United States would pay the old claims of British merchants against American citizens.

NAPOLEONIC WARS AND IMPRESSMENT IN THE BRITISH NAVY

That slight improvement in British–U.S. relations was dramatically altered with the outbreak of the Napoleonic Wars in Europe at the start of the nineteenth century. The outbreak of those wars heightened the degree of mutual suspicion as well as introducing new areas of conflict. In a profound way, the War of 1812 was the North American phase of the Napoleonic Wars.

The British had vigorously pursued the questionable policy of impressment since 1803. Life for the ordinary sailor in the British navy had always been hard. Low pay, long and dangerous voyages, and often brutal discipline made navy life sufficiently unappealing that naval officers, especially during wartime, often sent gangs into the streets to kidnap — or "press into service" — vagrants or other able-bodied men who happened to get in their way. With the outbreak of war, many sailors sought refuge in American ports or on American merchant ships, where they would not be involved in hostilities and where wages for seamen were far better.

The British navy, faced with thousands of desertions[7] from its ranks and chronically short of men, stopped and boarded American vessels and forcibly removed sailors who claimed to have American citizenship. British authorities reasoned that they had a right to recover deserters and to do so by force if American captains would not co-operate. Frequently, however, the British navy did not just recover deserters. Often, it simply kidnapped American citizens — for example, Herman Melville's *Billy Budd* became popular in the United States largely because of the horrors of impressment that it outlined. Americans failed to appreciate the technical right of the British navy to seize British subjects who had deserted. British officers, on the other hand, did not appreciate the impact of their actions on the Americans, who felt their sovereignty and independence were being violated by their former colonial master.

THE CHESAPEAKE AFFAIR

In 1807, the two nations nearly went to war over the "Chesapeake Affair," in which the American ship of that name was attacked by a British frigate, the *Leopard*, with the loss of over 20 American lives and the seizure by the British of four American citizens, one of whom was later hanged in Halifax. "No nation," said John Quincy Adams, later president of the United States, "can be independent which suffers her citizens to be stolen from her at the discretion of the naval or military officers of another." Anti-British sentiments were expressed throughout the United States, and even President Thomas Jefferson is reported to have threatened an invasion of Canada in retaliation.

Another cause of friction was the British government's interference with American commercial shipping. The United States pursued a policy of neutrality in the Napoleonic Wars and traded freely with all parties in the European conflict. Both Britain and France attempted to enforce economic blockades against each other. Furthermore, the British considerably expanded the definition of "contraband." Whereas formerly it had been limited to "accoutrements of war," now it was expanded to include virtually anything that could assist the enemy. Both belligerents also seized neutral ships on the open seas, especially those ships suspected of doing business with their enemies. During Jefferson's first administration, American shippers had been able to accumulate substantial profits that more than offset their losses from such seizures. However, in 1805, British courts outlawed the lucrative trade involving goods shipped from the French West Indies to France by way of the United States.

The French showed no more regard for American neutrality than did the British. However, given the dominant position of the British navy after Admiral Horatio Nelson's victory at Trafalgar in 1805, the most serious violations came from that quarter. Furthermore, both Jefferson and James Madison suspected, probably with good reason, that the system of blockades and restrictions on trade passed by the British cabinet was aimed more at eliminating American competition with British trading and shipping companies than at weakening France.

SUSPICION OF AMERINDIAN INTRIGUES

In the western areas of the United States, especially, suspicion of Britain's Amerindian agents was the primary source of pro-war sentiment. While it is most likely that Britain's influence over its former allies declined after 1795 and that the periodic uprisings by various tribes in defence of their traditional lands owed little to British encouragement, it was difficult for most Americans to understand Amerindian resistance in other terms. American leaders believed that the Amerindians could be persuaded to give up their traditional lives as hunters in order to pursue small-scale farming in the manner of the whites. Unable to comprehend why the Amerindians would fight to retain their way of life, many Americans could see only the sinister influence of the British.

American settlers continued to flood into the Northwest. On the eve of the War of 1812, Ohio's population was over 230 000; Kentucky's about 400 000. The Shawnee warrior Tecumseh and his brother, known as The Prophet, formed an alliance of several tribes whose lands were being threatened by the expansion of American settlement.[8] In 1811 they led an uprising. Although Tecumseh's forces were defeated at the Battle of Tippecanoe in Indiana, public opinion in the western United States held the British responsible for arming and encouraging the Amerindians. This appeared to be confirmed by Tecumseh's decision not to go to Washington to negotiate with American officials but to contact British agents in Upper Canada, where he pledged his loyalty to the crown.

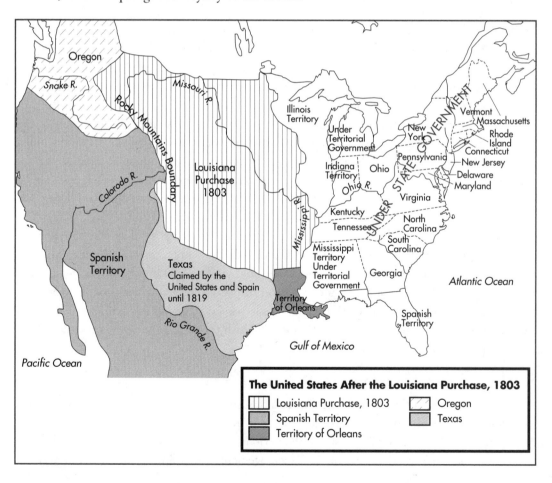

The United States After the Louisiana Purchase, 1803

Louisiana Purchase, 1803
Spanish Territory
Territory of Orleans
Oregon
Texas

AGITATION OF THE WAR HAWKS

A final cause for the outbreak of the War of 1812 lies in the aggressive Republican nationalism espoused by a new group in Congress. Many Republicans, first elected in 1810, were eager to wrest leadership from Madison and his contemporaries. Led by the powerful Kentuckian Henry Clay and the intellectual John C. Calhoun from South Carolina, they came to be known as the War Hawks. They clamoured for war both as a means for land acquisition and as a means of avenging national honour. They demanded the expulsion of British power from the continent as a step in securing peace and favourable terms from the Native peoples. With their allies driven out of Canada, the War Hawks reasoned that the Amerindians would be unable to defend their lands. In addition, there would be no obstacles to the American settlement of Upper Canada. This meant an invasion of Canada, and Clay and Calhoun were anything but reluctant in urging such a course of action. The former succinctly summarized the prime goal of the movement in 1810: "I am not for stopping at Quebec, but would take the whole continent."

The diplomatic efforts and economic pressure employed by the Jefferson and Madison administrations had failed to solve any of the deep-seated American grievances against Britain. Early in his term as president, Madison opened negotiations with the British representative in Washington. Just when it seemed that the two sides had reached a compromise, the British foreign secretary, George Canning, rejected any relaxation of Britain's naval policies. This rebuff and the election in 1810 of a large number of militantly anti-British congressmen undermined the president's efforts to preserve peace. Faced with growing opposition within his own Republican party over his apparent weakness in defending American rights and interests, Madison decided on war.[9]

DECLARATION OF WAR

Militarily, the United States was ill-prepared for war. The legacy of the American Revolution and the American suspicion of powerful standing armies and navies kept the regular army of the United States small. Its navy was no match for its powerful British counterpart. The Republican-controlled Congress voted only a small increase in the army, from 10 000 to 35 000 men. Land defence was left to individual state militias, while naval operations, after Congress's rejection of a major tax increase, had to be carried out largely by privateers. After 1810, Madison's government began to build up its regular forces in response to unrest among the Amerindians and worsening relations with Britain. However, the American military lacked the numbers, the training, and the leadership, as well as the equipment of their opponent. Furthermore, the United States had a much smaller population than Britain, was less developed economically, and, despite the unifying effects of the recently but narrowly ratified American constitution, was politically unstable and divided by regional interests.

THE "INCREDIBLE" WAR OF 1812

THE WAR ITSELF WAS A DISAPPOINTING COMEDY OF ERRORS for the United States. It was little short of a military debacle.[10] If not for the British preoccupation with Napoleon, it would have been an unmitigated disaster. The most sensible plan for the Americans would have been to attack Montreal or Quebec, thereby cutting off the scattered settlements of Upper Canada from the support of the British navy's powerful base at Halifax. Such a course would have required the support of state officials and the citizens of New York and the New England states. However, majority opinion in the Northeast remained absolutely opposed to the war. In April 1812, for example, Massachusetts elected a strongly anti-war governor, Federalist Caleb Strong. In neighbouring Connecticut and Rhode Island, too, the state governments made use of every plausible excuse to avoid supporting the war effort. In fact, although New Englanders refused to lend money to their own federal government, they did lend it to the British. New England farmers readily sold supplies to the British army in British North America without blinking an eye.

THE INVASION OF CANADA

American General William Hull surrenders Detroit to British General Isaac Brock in 1812. Brock was knighted for his military achievement; Hull was sent to prison in Quebec.

The feeble American leadership opted for an attack on Upper Canada, the most sparsely populated and least well-defended colony. Many of the War Hawks hoped the invasion in the West would cut off the Amerindian tribes from their sources of military supplies. Others hoped to annex the area to the United States to allow future expansion. Some thought that the large number of American-born residents in the colony might offer little resistance to a campaign of "liberation" by United States' forces. But the population in Upper Canada had been

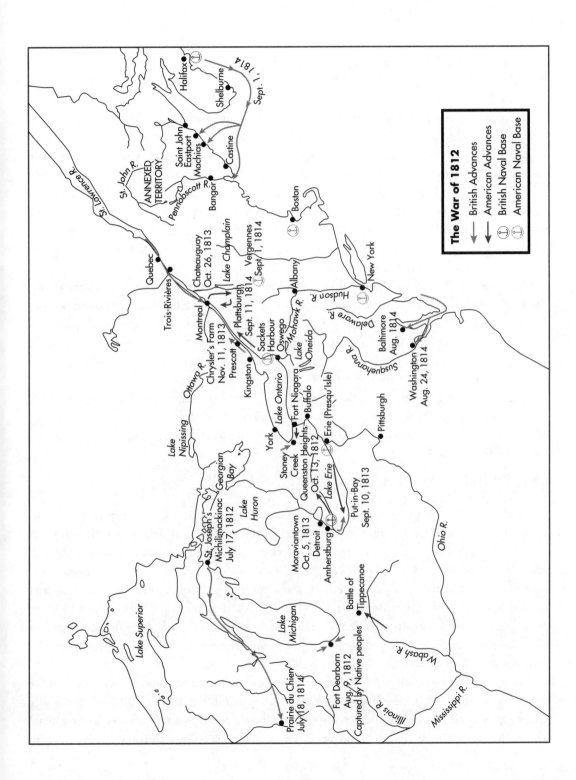

The War of 1812

Legend:
- British Advances
- American Advances
- British Naval Base
- American Naval Base

Halifax
Shelburne
Sept. 1, 1814
Saint John
Easport
Machias
Castine
St. John R.
ANNEXED TERRITORY
Penobscott R.
Bangor
Boston
St. Lawrence R.
Quebec
Trois-Rivières
Chateauguay Oct. 26, 1813
Lake Champlain
Vergennes
Sept. 1, 1814
Albany
Montreal
Plattsburgh Sept. 11, 1814
Hudson R.
New York
Ottawa R.
Chrysler's Farm Nov. 11, 1813
Prescott
Kingston
Sackets Harbour
Oswego
Mohawk R.
Lake Oneida
Delaware R.
Susquehanna R.
Baltimore Aug. 1814
Washington Aug. 24, 1814
Lake Nipissing
Lake Ontario
York
Fort Niagara
Buffalo
Erie (Presqu'Isle)
Pittsburgh
Stoney Creek
Queenston Heights Oct. 13, 1812
Lake Erie
Put-in-Bay Sept. 10, 1813
Ohio R.
Georgian Bay
St. Joseph's
Michilimackinac July 17, 1812
Lake Huron
Moraviantown Oct. 5, 1813
Detroit
Amherstburg
Battle of Tippecanoe
Wabash R.
Lake Superior
Lake Michigan
Fort Dearborn Aug. 9, 1812 Captured by Native peoples
Prairie du Chien July 18, 1814
Illinois R.
Mississippi R.

swollen not just by Loyalists but by thousands of non-Loyalist immigrants who had crossed the border in search of less expensive farmland, or for protection from the Amerindians. In 1792 the colony's governor, John Graves Simcoe, had actually invited Americans to take up residence in the new territory.

General William Hull commanded a force of 2200 men drawn from the regular American army and the Ohio militia. He was a cautious leader; in the eyes of many, he was indecisive. Supplied with the names of over 100 supposedly pro-American settlers, Hull invaded Upper Canada in early July and issued a boastful proclamation to the residents. Only a few settlers responded, and while Hull's army met no resistance, neither did he mount an attack against Amherstburg, the centre of British military power in the area. After 30 days, running short of provisions, afraid of Amerindian attacks, and concerned about rumours of British reinforcements from the Niagara region, Hull abandoned the invasion. The welcome that he had expected from the colony's settlers never materialized.

Incompetent American military leadership, personal rivalries in the ranks, and the opposition of many New England state officials to the war enabled Lieutenant-Governor Isaac Brock to seize the initiative. First, he sent a force to surprise and capture the small American garrison at Michilimackinac, near the head of Lake Huron. The victory, won without a shot, was minor, but it strengthened Amerindian confidence in Britain's value as an ally and won most of the northwestern tribes to the British cause. It also persuaded General Hull to retreat to the relative safety of Detroit. Gathering a force of over 400 men, mostly local militia, Brock then made a dash to Amherstburg in mid-August and resolved to attack Detroit. With the aid of Tecumseh's warriors and the confusion and dissension in Hull's army, he secured the surrender of Detroit in August.

BRITISH TRIUMPH AT QUEENSTON HEIGHTS

Brock then led his troops back to the Niagara frontier to recapture Queenston Heights from a second American invasion force in October.[11] In this battle, in which British regulars and colonial militia were joined by Amerindian warriors and a group of black volunteers, Brock was killed. A more cautious subordinate, Major-General Roger Sheaffe, took command after Brock fell and directed the rout of the Americans. Yet Brock's name remains the one associated with the victory at Queenston, where he acquired a reputation for heroism and military genius that would grow after his death.[12] His two victories had also clearly demonstrated to the Americans that Upper Canada could not be conquered easily. Nor would the invaders be welcomed as liberators.

In 1813, the Americans made further ineffective attempts at invasion. Plans were laid for an attack on Fort York (present-day Toronto) as soon as the ice disappeared from the lower Great Lakes. York was less well defended than the larger town of Kingston and, as provincial capital, had a certain symbolic importance. On April 27 an American force landed at York,

A British view of the battle of Queenston Heights, October 1812. The picture is a composite rendering of the battle, depicting events that occurred over a three-day period.

An American painting of the death of Tecumseh, 1813. The Shawnee leader tried to incite the Amerindian tribes to resist U.S. territorial expansion and its disruptive effects on trade alliances.

backed up by naval guns. General Sheaffe chose to abandon the town, but not before ordering the destruction of the fort's magazine. Local officials, including the Rev. John Strachan and the commanders of the militia, were left to arrange a surrender. Angered at the escape of Sheaffe's troops and the destruction of the arms and ammunition they had hoped to capture, the American commanders permitted widespread looting and burning by their troops.

At the end of May another force, under General Henry Dearborn, captured Fort George and Fort Erie on the Canadian side of the Niagara River. The Americans, however, suffered two defeats: at Stoney Creek (near present-day Hamilton), and at Beaver Dam, the battle associated with the alleged heroism of Laura Secord.

The first major American success came with the Battle of Lake Erie in September 1813. An American naval force defeated a smaller British fleet at Put-in-Bay in Ohio, perhaps the first time that an entire British fleet had been captured. This victory gave the United States effective control over the lower lakes and the inland coasts. British troops occupying Detroit were compelled to retreat into Upper Canada, where they could establish a defensible position.

This decision did not sit well with Britain's Amerindian allies. Tecumseh accused the British community of cowardice, but joined in the retreat. A large American force defeated the British and their Amerindian allies at Moraviantown (near modern-day Stratford, Ontario). The Amerindian leader Tecumseh was killed in this battle, and with him died the hope of an independent Amerindian territory between the American and Canadian borders.[13]

ATTEMPTED INVASIONS OF 1813–1814

The Americans did not, however, take advantage of their victory. United States authorities chose to return to their original military plans, centred on the capture of Montreal, thereby dividing the Canadas and securing a base from which to attack Quebec. In October 1813, a two-pronged invasion was aimed at Montreal, but both armies were defeated by much smaller forces — at Chateauguay, near Montreal, and at the battle of Crysler's Farm, near Cornwall. The losses were sufficient to persuade the Americans to abandon their invasion and retreat back into New York State.

The defeat of Napoleon in the spring of 1814 strengthened the British position. With peace near at hand in Europe, Britain could transfer both soldiers and supplies from there to North America. In Washington, the war department decided on a direct attack on the British naval base at Kingston. However, the field commander, perhaps mistakenly, chose to invade the Niagara region. After an initial victory at Chippewa Plains in early July, but hampered by inter-service rivalry and personal jealousies within the American command, lacking artillery, and outmanoeuvred by British and Canadian troops, the American advance was halted in a bloody battle at Lundy's Lane at the end of the month. By November, the Americans had withdrawn completely from Upper Canada. A second invasion into Lower Canada in March had also been beaten back with little difficulty.

BRITISH RETALIATION AND THE COMING OF PEACE

IN THE SUMMER OF 1814, weariness on both sides led to the opening of peace negotiations at Ghent, Belgium. In the United States, there were moves toward secession by several New England states, and many of the former War Hawks were now prepared for peace. The British, who had been engaged in almost continuous warfare with France for a generation, wanted a settlement.

THE BRITISH CAMPAIGNS OF 1814

To weaken the American government's negotiating position, the British planned attacks on American territory at several points. In August 1814, British troops landed in Maryland to carry out a raid on Washington, the American capital. The White House, the Capitol, and other public buildings were burned. More serious destruction was probably prevented by the effects of a late summer hurricane, whose torrential rains dampened the flames. Then the British moved on toward the major port of Baltimore. There, despite heavy naval bombardment of Fort McHenry, which defended the city, American soldiers and Maryland militia were able to hold off the attackers.

At the beginning of September 1814, Lieutenant-General Sir John Sherbrooke led an expedition from Nova Scotia to northern Maine. This territory, a part of old Acadia, had been given to the United States in 1782. Its reclamation by the British would provide a shorter route for commercial and military traffic from the Maritimes to Montreal. Sherbrooke won an easy victory and occupied the strategic port of Castine in Penobscot Bay. The local population were well treated by British authorities and seemed quite content to live under British administration, which they did until the war's end.

THE PEACE SETTLEMENT

The failure of Sir George Prevost's attack on Plattsburg, New York, and the stubborn refusal of the American diplomats to make any territorial concessions persuaded the British to agree, in December 1814, to a treaty that restored the *status quo ante bellum* and referred outstanding issues to commissioners for more detailed negotiations. The issues of impressment and interference with neutral shipping were no longer of immediate importance with the return of peace in Europe, and they were left unsettled. Ironically, what was for the Americans their most successful military operation — the rout of British forces by General Andrew Jackson at New Orleans — took place two weeks after the signing of the Treaty of Ghent but before word of the agreement could reach the armies.

Two further settlements completed the peace negotiations. In April 1817, the two sides concluded the Rush–Bagot Agreement — later hailed by American president Lyndon Johnson as the world's "oldest arms-limitation treaty" — which limited the number of armed ships on the Great Lakes. In 1818, the boundary between the United States and British North America was set at the 49th parallel from the Lake of the Woods to the Rocky Mountains, and the Americans agreed to the loss of the inshore fishing rights in New Brunswick and Nova Scotia.

CONSEQUENCES OF THE WAR OF 1812

THE WAR OCCUPIES A RELATIVELY INSIGNIFICANT PLACE in British history given that, in the words of Canadian historian A.R.M. Lower, the British "did most of the fighting" and "their navy was the major instrument in ending the war." In the years after 1815, however, British authorities strengthened defences and encouraged immigration and economic development in the colonies, while at the same time pursuing a policy of peace and expanded trade with the Americans.[14]

"DEEDS SPEAK": MILITIAMEN, MEDALS, AND THE INVENTED TRADITIONS OF 1812

THE ROLE OF THE UPPER CANADIAN militia during the War of 1812 has never been investigated adequately. During the conflict John Strachan accurately predicted that future historians would tell of the heroic exertions of a militia that had "saved the country" with only "a handful of regular troops." Later writers did make such claims — often because they relied on Strachan and other colonial officials for information on the conduct of the war. In 1862, for example, Gilbert Auchinleck noted that with the help of "a mere handful of British troops the Canadian militia achieved the expulsion of the invading foe." By relying on propaganda statements, which glossed over widespread evidence of desertion and treasonable conduct, early Canadian writers could assert routinely that the militia "came out of the war covered in glory." *This "militia myth" gained widespread acceptance and was not seriously challenged until the 1950s, when professional historians, such as C.P. Stacey and G.F.G. Stanley, showed that citizen-soldiers had played only a secondary role in the defence of Upper Canada. After examining accounts of battles, these historians revealed that British regulars had done most of the actual fighting, but they still maintained that the efforts of the inhabitants had been essential and important. That view, however, placed too much stress on the activities of those who did serve, and both historians failed to note that those who did were not typical.† In fact, militia returns, diaries, and confidential correspondence reveal that most colonists exhibited very little enthusiasm to shoulder arms. Although all able-bodied adult males were expected to serve in the militia, only a minority of them accepted that obligation willingly....

Whether they remained at home through legal or illegal means, the majority of Upper Canadians managed to avoid serving in the militia. After the Battle of Queenston Heights on October 13, Sheaffe had summoned 5000 colonists to duty on the front lines, but on October 24, the paymaster recorded the presence of only 846 militia officers and privates in the Niagara Peninsula. Instead of increasing as time passed, the number of men on duty actually declined. Sheaffe was sure that most of the desertions were prompted by the miserable camp conditions....

The emphasis on the activities of non-combatants, such as [William] Green and [Laura] Secord, is understandable since the militia myth, though offering subsequent

*Strachan's prediction is quoted in C.P. Stacey, "The War of 1812 in Canadian History," *Ontario History* 50 (1958): 155–156. Gilbert Auchinleck, *A History of the War Between Great Britain and the United States of America During the Years 1812, 1813, and 1814* (Toronto, 1862)

†C.P. Stacey, "The War of 1812 in Canadian History," *Ontario History* 50 (1958): 153–159; G.F.G. Stanley, "The Contribution of the Canadian Militia During the War," in Philip Mason, ed., *After Tippecanoe* (Toronto: Ryerson, 1963), pp. 28–48.

generations of Canadians the opportunity to bask in the reflected glory of their fore-bears, failed to offer prominent examples of superlative deeds. Canadian writers who were anxious to celebrate the actions of their ancestors did not know of the existence of the Upper Canada Preserved Medal nominees. Early nineteenth-century authors relied on the militia myth to fill the void, but later writers discovered that the activities of some truly exceptional non-combatants could serve the same purpose. Thus, in the pages of many Canadian books, Green and Secord are the most important participants at Stoney Creek and Beaver Dams, although in fact, only British regulars saw action in the former battle and the latter was fought by Caughnawaga and Six Nations warriors.

Other Upper Canadians, such as John Strachan and William Allan, have also gained recognition for their wartime deeds. Not all individuals, however, have deserved their fame. For instance, John Strachan, "the fighting bishop," has erroneously been credited with saving York from "wholesale burning" in April 1813. In fact, Strachan was conveniently engaged in "looking after the Ladies" while the battle raged....

George Sheppard, "'Deeds Speak': Militiamen, Medals, and the Invented Traditions of 1812," *Ontario History* 83(3) (September 1990): 207–232.

AMERICAN SOVEREIGNTY REAFFIRMED

In the United States, Jackson's victory in the war's final battle and the success of American diplomacy at Ghent helped to erase the memory of earlier failures. The war confirmed the nation's determination to defend its sovereignty, its citizens, and its trade and commerce. The Federalist party, the major national opposition party and the dominant political force in the Northeast, which had become identified with almost treasonable opposition to the war, was discredited and faded from the political scene. The era following the war witnessed a growth in Americans' pride in their national experiment, accompanied by territorial, demographic, and economic expansion. It is not surprising, then, that when the United States chose a national anthem in 1931, it looked back to the War of 1812 and selected Francis Scott Key's "The Star-Spangled Banner," written in honour of the successful defence of Baltimore in 1814.

IMPACT ON THE NORTHERN BRITISH COLONIES

The British North American colonies also felt the effects of war in different ways.[15] In the Maritimes, the war brought increased prosperity and enhanced the military importance of the garrison at Halifax. Under the shrewd leadership of Sir John Sherbrooke, the colonies of Nova Scotia and New Brunswick became centres for a vast and profitable illegal trade between the United States and Britain. The region grew wealthier from the demand for timber from its woodlots and the sale of the spoils captured by the privateers that sailed from its ports. The war years laid a foundation for future economic growth and were remembered as a "golden age" in Maritime history.[16]

Although French Canadians in Lower Canada were no more enthusiastic about the war than were their neighbours in New York, their defence of the colony helped to persuade British authorities to give greater attention to the rights set out in the Quebec Act. By 1818, they recognized Roman Catholicism as the established religion in the colony. The war, and particularly the battle of Chateauguay, enhanced the feeling of French-Canadian nationalism. The response of the French Canadians during the war won a measure of respect from their anglophone neighbours and helped to foster a myth of bicultural co-operation in defence of a common Canadian homeland.

The major impact of the war and of the myths and memories it inspired was felt in Upper Canada.[17] Prior to 1812, the colony was thinly populated, and the majority of settlers were American immigrants who had little sense of loyalty to Britain or British institutions. During the war, those of doubtful allegiance were driven out. The anti-Americanism of Upper Canada's Loyalist élite became official policy and, in time, part of the colony's cultural life. Further immigration from the United States was officially discouraged. Instead, the authorities promoted immigration from Great Britain, offering free passage to the colony, 100 acres of land, and rations for eight months.

The War of 1812 has been commonly portrayed as the "seedtime" of British-Canadian nationalism, especially in Upper Canada.[18] The war gave the young colony of Upper Canada its own folklore, which held that its Loyalist population turned back the American threat almost single-handedly in the face of treasonable behaviour by non-Loyalist settlers and the indifference or incompetence of British authorities. This Loyalist mythology unified and helped to legitimize the authority of the small Loyalist élite. However, serious doubts exist about the veracity of this myth. It has been pointed out that not only were some of the Upper Canadian leaders undeserving of their reputation but that most of the general population refused to volunteer for active service.[19] Nevertheless, the men who had led Upper Canada during the war — Bishop John Strachan, William Allan, J.B. Robinson, and others — believed they should continue to lead it afterward. Known as the "Family Compact," they would use loyalty as a powerful political weapon.

A DEVELOPING SENSE OF NATIONHOOD

As in the United States, by the latter part of the nineteenth century the War of 1812 had become for many Canadians a crucial event in the birth of a national community. Perhaps unfortunately, the defining characteristics of that emerging national identity were too often formulated in negative terms and rooted in anti-Americanism. To be truly Canadian meant to be opposed to American ideas of republicanism, democracy, equality, and liberty. Nationalist literature portrayed Americans — the detested Yankees — as crude, vulgar, and violent, and this tendency has not completely disappeared even to this day.

"OF SLENDER AND DELICATE FRAME": THE PLACING OF LAURA SECORD IN THE NARRATIVE OF CANADIAN LOYALIST HISTORY

TO MOST CANADIANS, Laura Secord is best-known today as the figurehead of a candy company, her image that of a young, attractive woman wearing a low-cut, ruffled white gown. Some may have a vague knowledge of her walk in 1813, from Queenston to Beaver Dams, to warn the British troops of an impending American attack. From the mid-nineteenth century, the story of that walk has been told by a number of Canadian historians of the War of 1812 in Upper Canada.

Secord became part of the narrative of Loyalist self-sacrifice and duty to country and crown primarily — although not solely — because of the attempts of female historians and writers of the period. They strove to incorporate women into Canadian history and to dislodge the masculine emphasis of the nineteenth-century Loyalist myth of suffering and sacrifice. Women such as Sarah Curzon, the feminist writer, historian, and temperance advocate, insisted that white Canadian women, past and present, had something of value to offer the nation and empire and that their contribution as women to the record of Canadian history be acknowledged and valued. Secord, she (and others like her) argued, was not outside the narrative of Canadian history, and she (and other women) therefore had a place in shaping the "imagined communities" of Canadian nationalist and imperialist discourse.

Unlike that of other potentially unruly and disruptive women in Canadian history, Laura's Secord's image could be more easily domesticated to accord with late-Victorian notions of white, middle-class femininity. It could also be moulded by feminists to argue for a greater recognition of the importance of such femininity to Canadian society. Moreover, Laura Secord was not an isolated figure. Ranged behind and about her was a whole gallery of women in Canadian history, from Madeleine de Verchères of New France to the anonymous pioneer woman of the backwoods of Upper Canada.

In Upper Canadians' commemorations of the War of 1812, the important sacrifices for country and monarch were made by Upper Canadian men, frequently in their capacity as members of the militia who risked life and limb to protect women and children, homes and hearths, from the brutal rampages of hordes of bloodthirsty Americans. During the war, and in its aftermath, women's contributions to the defence of the colony were either downplayed or ignored, in favour of the image of the helpless Upper Canadian wife and mother who entrusted her own and her children's safety to the gallant militia and British troops.

In addition to that of the militia, an extremely significant masculine figure was that of the British commander General Isaac Brock, who made the ultimate sacrifice

Laura Secord.

for the colony by dying at the Battle of Queenston Heights in 1812. Brock provided those who shaped the history of the war with a Christ-like figure, a man who had given both his troops and the colony beneficent paternal guidance and wisdom but who had not spared himself from the physical dangers of war — dangers that really only threatened men in the military. Those who contributed to the glorification of Brock claimed that he had provided an invaluable means whereby the colonists might resist the enemy's encroachments. Brock had inspired Upper Canadian men, who might emulate his deed of manly patriotism, and he had reassured Upper Canadian women that, come what may, they could look to their husbands, fathers, sons, and brothers for protection.

The walk of Laura Secord meant that certain women could be written into the record of loyalty and patriotic duty in Canadian history and that female heroines could gain recognition for the deeds they committed. In the context of late-nineteenth- and early-twentieth-century debates about gender relations in Canadian society, Secord was a persuasive symbol of how certain women might breach the division between "private" and "public," the family and the state, and do so for entirely unselfish and thus patriotic reasons. The narratives of Laura Secord's walk helped shape an image of Canadian womanhood in the past that provided an inspiration for turn-of-the-century feminists. These women could invoke memory and tradition when calling for their own inclusion in the "imagined community" of the Canadian nation of the late nineteenth century.

On the other hand, more visionary nationalists saw in British North America's response to invasion the birth of a people who could develop their own distinctive future. "The people of Canada," wrote historian William Coffin, "feel that the War of 1812 is an episode in the story of a young people, glorious in itself and full of promise. They believe that the infant which, in its cradle, could strangle invasion…is capable of a nobler development, if God wills further trial."[20]

A symbol of patriotism from the War of 1812. The Loyal and Patriotic Society of Upper Canada issued this medal depicting the British lion saving the Canadian beaver from the American eagle.

Both sides can rightly claim that they "won" — or at least, did not lose — the war. The Americans won several major land battles and control of two lakes, and respect. The Canadians won many battles when they were badly outnumbered and withstood the American attempt to conquer them. Ultimately, the war enhanced feelings of nationalism, through the vehicles of dozens of celebrated heroes, battles, and myths, in both the United States and British North America.

ACTIVITIES

KEY TERMS AND CONCEPTS

Identify and briefly explain the historical significance of the following terms and concepts:
- Manifest Destiny
- Articles of Confederation
- Connecticut Compromise
- Bill of Rights
- Bicameralism
- Three-fifths rule
- "Massive contradiction"
- "Elastic clause"
- *E Pluribus Unum*
- Impressment
- Contraband
- War Hawks
- *The Star-Spangled Banner*
- "Seed time" of nationalism
- "Militia myth"
- Upper Canada Preserved medals

QUESTIONS FOR DISCUSSION

1. What did the making of the U.S. Constitution reveal about America's emerging sense of national purpose? Where did British North America fit into the American vision of the continent?
2. Was the American Constitution "a bundle of compromises"? Justify your decision with historical evidence.
3. How did conflicting political philosophies and patriotic goals lead to the War of 1812?
4. What was the *fundamental* cause of the War of 1812? Justify your choice with historical evidence.
5. What effect did the war have on the development of a national feeling in Canada and the United States? What forms did such expressions of identity take?

6. The Upper Canadian militia has been credited with "saving the country" during the War of 1812 since Bishop John Strachan made that claim. To what extent were the Canadian militia heroics of 1812 part of an invented nationalist military tradition?

7. Did Canada's sense of nationhood find its roots in the War of 1812? Justify your answer with concrete historical evidence.

8. Myths are central to the establishment of a nation's identity. What lessons does the War of 1812 provide about the way in which myths are created, given legitimacy, and believed?

ASSESSING FACT AND INTERPRETATION

In assessing the validity of interpretations in history, the facts must be weighed carefully. Do the facts support the judgements being made by the historian, popular writer, or textbook author? Following is a small example taken from popular interpretations of the War of 1812's impact on Canadian "nationality." Read the documentary evidence and then study the excerpts from two popular historical interpretations.

1. Assess the reliability of the document. Is it a reliable account? How much weight should it be assigned?

2. Which of the interpretations is supported by the document? Should the historians' judgements be revised? Explain your answers.

The Document

"My situation is most critical, not from anything the enemy can do, but from the disposition of the people — the population, believe me, is essentially bad — and full belief possesses them all that this Province must inevitably succumb. This pre-possession is fatal to every exertion — Legislators, Magistrates, Militia Officers, all, have imbibed the idea, and are so sluggish and indifferent in their respective offices that the artful and active scoundrel is allowed to parade the Country without interruption, and commit all imaginable mischief.

"…There can be no doubt that a large proportion of the population in this neighborhood are sincere in their professions to defend the country, but it appears likewise evident to me that the greater part are either indifferent to what is passing, or so completely American as to rejoice in the prospects of a change of Governments…."

— Major-General Isaac Brock, *Personal Correspondence,* July 1812.

Interpretation 1

"The sense of Canadian nationality, which has radiated out from Upper Canada…through all the west and to some degree into the Maritime provinces, dates from the War of 1812. It gave to Upper Canada an official tradition of military glory. It did not matter that this was rather insecurely based; people believed in it and it influenced their loyalties. It accentuated Upper Canada's dominant hatred, whose incidence it changed slightly, from hatred of 'republicanism' to hatred of 'the Americans' or 'the damn Yankees'"

— From *Colony to Nation*, by Arthur Lower. Used by permission of the Canadian Publishers, McClelland & Stewart, Toronto.

Interpretation 2

"Traditionally, a common enemy unites a people in a common cause, especially when family farms are overrun, crops despoiled, homesteads gutted, livestock dispersed. But…there is little evidence of a united front against the enemy on the part of the people who suffered these disasters; it is doubtful if they were any angrier at the Americans than at the

British and Indians, who actually caused a third of the devastation....

"Yet, in an odd way, the war did help to change Upper Canada from a loose aggregation of village states into something approaching a political entity. The war, or more properly the myth of the war, gave the rootless new settlers a sense of community. In the end, the myth became the reality.... For the first time, Upper Canadians shared a common tradition."

— Pierre Berton, *The Invasion of Canada, 1812–1813* (1980), p. 29. Reprinted by permission of *My Country Productions.*

CHAPTER 9

POPULAR DEMOCRACY AND THE REFORM TRADITION

B ETWEEN 1820 AND 1850, movements of democratic reform arose in both the United States and British North America. In the American republic, the widespread democratic impulse reached its peak after the election of Andrew Jackson to the presidency in 1828. Jackson's election seemed to signify the triumph of a new liberal reform tradition. Not since the bloodless "Revolution of 1800," which brought the Jeffersonians to power, had America experienced such a profound political change. Jackson and his supporters, the advance guard of American democratic reform, pledged government *by* the "common people," not just government *of* and *for* the people. During the "Age of Jackson," the struggle for political equality and economic reform would move to the centre of American politics.

British North America experienced a similar political ferment. Reform movements emerged after 1820 in Upper and Lower Canada and in the Maritimes. While the British North American movements sprang from local colonial conditions and contained elements of British parliamentary reformism, they were undoubtedly influenced by democratic experiments underway in the United States at that time. The rebellions of 1837–38 in the Canadas and the later struggles of the 1840s to achieve responsible government drew some inspiration and political rhetoric from movements in Jacksonian America. Yet many British North Americans retained a strong disdain for republican democratic ideas and remained unmoved by Jackson's "age of the common man." To them, Jacksonian democracy smacked of mediocrity, levelling, patronage, and the distribution of political spoils. More democratic, responsible government would come, but by different means. The British North American colonies proceeded along another, more British and more evolutionary route to popular democratic government.

SOURCES OF REFORM AND REBELLION

W ITH THE END OF THE WAR OF 1812, the colonies of British North America experienced renewed economic growth: wheat and lumber emerged as the new staples of the St. Lawrence colonial economy, and the Montreal-based fur trade pushed farther into the Northwest.[1] Large-scale migration of people from Britain and the United States created a sizable population of immigrants struggling to get established in a new land. By the 1820s, each of the colonies faced growing problems with the land grant system, and the colonial governments were in need of increasing revenues for road building, education, and settlement assistance to the thousands of poor immigrants. But these massive social and economic changes were not accompanied by political or constitutional change.

At the end of the American Revolution, the almost 50 000 United Empire Loyalists who arrived in British North America discovered the inhabitants still living under the Quebec Act. The British Colonial Office had therefore passed the Constitutional Act of 1791 to address the concerns of the newly arrived English-speaking immigrants, as well as to confirm the position of the large French-Canadian population. That legislation had divided Quebec at the Ottawa River into Upper and Lower Canada, each with a separate government. These governments consisted of a legislative assembly elected on a limited franchise and an appointed governor assisted by executive and legislative councils whose members were appointed.[2] This system may have been representative, but it was neither democratic nor responsible, and it proved to be incapable of responding to the demands for reform.

THE COLONIAL OLIGARCHIES

In all the colonies, the real governing power resided in the appointed councils, whose members came to believe that they constituted a perpetual governing class. This idea was supported by their own appointments for life, compared with the appointed terms of a long series of governors. The governors were transitory rulers in a strange and foreign land who came increasingly to rely on the councils; their advice became law.[3] Rather rapidly these councils fell into the hands of a minority of powerful and well-connected propertied and commercial interests. This small minority of well-entrenched and inter-related élites developed into an oligarchy that dominated the largely agrarian population.

The Family Compact in Upper Canada and the Chateau Clique in Lower Canada exercised a stranglehold over the commercial and political life of their respective colonies because they could use the authority, patronage, and power of their governmental positions to perpetuate themselves and

"The Three Robinson Sisters." The daughters of the chief justice of Upper Canada, John Beverly Robinson, seemed to epitomize the affluence and privilege enjoyed by prominent Toronto families associated with the Family Compact.

control the economy.[4] The term "Chateau Clique" came from the meeting place of this powerful group. The term "Family Compact" was coined by 1830s Upper Canadian reformers. William Lyon Mackenzie published an article in 1833 that demonstrated the stranglehold on the colony by a small group linked by ties of kinship and marriage. Recent historians have argued that although the latter term has been widely used for more than a century and a half, it is more of a symbolic label than an accurate description.[5]

Naturally the members of the councils used their considerable political power to formulate policies favourable to their own cause. Their control over public expenditures allowed them to spend tax money on canals that would promote their business interests, rather than the roads needed by the settlers. Because they controlled the Clergy Reserves, they were able to preserve the Anglican church as the dominant Protestant denomination. Both councils — along with the governor — had a veto power that enabled them to frustrate the will of the elected assembly. Through their power over appointments, the compacts were able to control the legal, religious, and educational systems in the colonies. Since the ruling élites remained staunchly pro-British, they branded any opposition as dangerously republican and disloyal.

In the face of this inequitable system, demand for reform was predictable and the reform movement in all the colonies began to attract increasing support. Although the reformers repeatedly won majorities in the legislative assemblies, their wants and needs were no closer to realization. Funding for improved roads — a virtual necessity for the pioneer farmers — was consistently vetoed by the legislative council. An improved land-grant system would be impossible while the Canada Land Company continued to operate. A farmer could spend years clearing his own piece of land, only to run into a wild clergy or crown reserve, held for speculation by the oligarchy. An improved system of schools remained almost impossible unless the revenues could be raised through the sale of clergy or crown reserves.

THE ROOTS OF CONFLICT IN UPPER CANADA: THE LAND-GRANT SYSTEM

Land distribution and ownership emerged as one of the earliest reform issues, particularly in Upper Canada. In 1817, Robert Gourlay, a Scottish-born land agent, tried to obtain land grants to settle families from Scotland. When the province's executive council repeatedly blocked him, he circulated a questionnaire and held township meetings. The public response revealed acute dissatisfaction with the land-grant system.[6] Branded a radical, Gourlay attacked the Family Compact and became its most celebrated victim. Twice acquitted of libel charges, he was banished from Upper Canada in 1819 on charges of sedition.

The Gourlay episode drew attention to — and aroused popular protest over — the land question. At precisely the time when land was needed by a growing population of newcomers, it was being monopolized by large land companies and the governing councils. Demands continued to arise for changes in the restrictive system of crown and clergy reserves and in the land distribution practices of the Canada Land Company.

THE ALIEN QUESTION

Another major source of conflict in the Canadas was the "alien question." At the centre of the controversy in Upper Canada was Barnabas Bidwell, an American immigrant who had sworn an oath of allegiance to the crown and who was elected in 1821 as a Reform member of the assembly. The Tories demanded that he be ousted from the chamber for improprieties he had committed in his native Massachusetts. The assembly rejected the legal charge of embezzlement but did vote to expel him for want of moral character. His son, Marshall Spring Bidwell, a leading reformer and a future speaker of the assembly, initially faced the same Tory challenge.[7] The Bidwell affair revealed the Tory tactic of branding opponents as disloyal and republican. Further, the incident brought into question the status of American immigrants — the majority of the population of the colony —

The Reverend John Strachan, Anglican Archdeacon of York (Toronto).[o]

and the validity of their land titles, since aliens could not hold land. Finally, the alien question brought the younger Bidwell to the fore as a new Reform leader.

THE CLERGY RESERVES

The Church of England had been able, partly because of its tie to Britain and more significantly because of the work of people such as Archdeacon John Strachan of York, to become the established church within the colony. Just as one-seventh of all the land was held for the crown, another one-seventh was set aside for the maintenance of the church. The principle of the separation of church and state was clearly being violated, as the clergy reserves were reserved exclusively for the Anglican church.[8] Only the Anglican church was entitled to solemnize marriages and burials. In 1824, the Reformers captured a majority in the assembly and attempted to pass a bill entitling the Methodists to perform the same rites. The bill was instantly vetoed by the legislative council. In addition, education was firmly under the control of the Church of England. The Methodists, the fastest-growing Protestant denomination, sought to minimize that control.[9]

AMERICAN INFLUENCES IN UPPER CANADA

A CRUCIAL QUESTION IN UPPER CANADA in the 1820s and 1830s was the role and influence of American settlers. By the outbreak of the War of 1812, American settlers heavily outnumbered the original Loyalist inhabitants. After the war, British policy officially discouraged further immigration from the United States. Then, in the 1820s, the issue erupted into the so-called "alien" controversy. Some Upper Canadians charged that provincial authorities and the British government were working together to deprive American settlers of their political rights and even their land titles; people of American origin found that their "loyalty" was often called into question.

Here are a variety of views on the American presence and the "alien" question. What do they reveal about Upper Canadian society in the 1820s and 1830s?

A few deep and designing politicians, who have long nestled about the Colonial Executive — and who...the moment they have been warmed into existence by the fruits and the toils and the industry of the American emigrant farmers — the early pioneers of our forests — turned round upon their benefactors, and shed upon them the deadly poison of their political malice.

...The Alien Question has been nothing but a snare — a hidden trap, with which to destroy the civil rights of the American emigrants in this colony — an apple of discord, with which first to divide the people, and then rule them with an iron rod....

Editorial in the *Canadian Freeman,* York, 1826.

In many parts of the Province the teachers are Americans, for the sake of obtaining employment they have swallowed the oath of allegiance which agrees so ill with them that the rest of their lives is spent in attempts to disgorge it. These men are utterly ignorant of everything English and could not if they tried instruct their pupils in any of the duties which the connection of the Province with England casts upon them. The books they use are all American, filled with inflated accounts of American independence and the glorious wars with England. The exploits of General Jackson and the heroes of '76 fill the youthful mind to the exclusion of everything glorious or interesting in English history.

R.B. Sullivan, Memorandum to Sir George Arthur, June 1, 1838. Public Archives of Canada, Upper Canada Sundries, June 1838.

The Canadians are neither British nor American: the local circumstances and situation of the country (which are among the most powerful influences which form national character) tend towards the latter; and the tendency is increased by the vicinity of, and intercourse with the States: on the other hand, early habits and associations, communication with their friends in the old country, political and ecclesiastical institutions, and the antipathy produced by rivalry and collision with their American neighbours, unite them to Great Britain. I think they are more American than they believe themselves to be, or would like to be considered.

John R. Godley, 1842.

RELIGION AND SOCIETY IN BRITISH NORTH AMERICA

HISTORIANS OF BRITISH NORTH AMERICA have long been aware of the importance of religion in colonial politics, particularly debates that took place in Upper Canada between supporters of different Protestant denominations. Issues such as the clergy reserves, the future of a state-supported university, and the relationship of religion to colonial education involved a number of colonial officials, politicians, and clerics, all of whom had very strong ideas concerning the relationship of religion to the state and society.

To British officials, such as Lieutenant-Governor John Graves Simcoe, and to many supporters of the colonial élite the establishment of the Anglican church in British North America was essential to the maintenance of colonial political and social stability. They felt that the lack of such a church in the American colonies had played an important role in Britain's defeat and that an established church would help ward off incipient republicanism by teaching loyalty, deference to authority, and respect for social and political hierarchy. With the exception of Quebec, where a succession of governors felt it would be inappropriate and misguided to attempt to strengthen the Anglican church's position, colonial authorities attempted to implement the imperial government's plan.

Their strategy, though, was not a huge success. In Nova Scotia, the Anglican church was relatively small, its presence in the colony weak and not well-supported by the majority of Nova Scotians, especially those who lived outside Halifax. While the church was a much stronger presence in Upper Canada, it found itself continually forced to defend many of its assumptions of privileged status. To a great extent, this situation arose out of the diversity and fragmentation of the religious landscape of Upper Canada. The number of settlers who belonged to many other denominations — Baptists, Presbyterians, Methodists, Quakers, Mennonites, and members of the Roman Catholic church — made it very difficult for the Anglican hierarchy to claim congregational support. To John Strachan, Methodism in particular threatened established political and social order because its supporters were prone to political dissent and possibly republicanism.

Certainly many Methodists, as well as other religious groups that were associated with dissent, had arrived in Upper Canada from America. However, Methodism itself had originated in England, as a movement tied to the Church of England that was originally meant to stimulate and rejuvenate Anglicanism. What Strachan, and others like him, feared was not just its tie to America but the particular styles of religious worship that groups such as Methodists and Baptists encouraged.

Dubbed "enthusiastic religion," in contrast to the more staid and structured services of Anglicanism, these evangelical groups stressed the importance of the individual's experience of religious faith. Each person, they believed, needed to feel a sense of his or her own sin as acutely as possible and to accordingly struggle to renounce it, experiencing a thorough and sometimes dramatic conversion to Christ's love and salvation in this process. To some government officials, the Baptist preachers of the Maritimes and the Methodists of Upper Canada were dangerous because of their lack of formal education and their ability to appeal to people's emotions.

While their methods of spreading religion might have seemed suspicious to the authorities, in fact they were particularly well-suited to colonial conditions. The strategy of sending out ministers as itinerants who would ride around a circuit (an assigned area), preaching and holding services, was most effective in areas with small and scattered populations who often could not sustain a church on their own. Camp meetings and revivals, where people would gather in a secluded area for a few days and listen to forcefully delivered sermons that would exhort them to seek repentance and salvation, also helped remind settlers of the role of religion in their lives.

Religious observances might combine both personal piety and the chance to socialize; they gave settlers the opportunity to see their neighbours and develop the kind of ties that were important to community-building. These activities could cut across denominations, as in the early nineteenth century many pioneer churches frequently shared the same wooden buildings for their services. By mid-century, as more denominations began to build their own permanent structures out of stone or brick, such sharing became less important. Nevertheless, some of Upper Canada's more important interdenominational voluntary institutions and movements, such as Sunday schools and the temperance movement, had their start in religious bodies.

Public disenchantment with the privileged position of the Church of England strengthened the reform movement. By calling for the secularization of the clergy reserves and funding for public education as well as championing the cause of true religious freedom, the Reformers gained the invaluable support of Egerton Ryerson and the Methodists.

ROOTS OF CONFLICT IN LOWER CANADA

The trouble in Lower Canada had its origins in political and racial cleavages that reinforced one another and was much more serious. The Reformers wanted governmental reform not simply for structural change, but also to ensure the cultural survival of the French-Canadian majority by providing them with real political power. Thus, the campaign in Lower Canada manifested serious racial overtones as the French-controlled assembly waged battle against the British-dominated councils.[10]

THE RACIAL ISSUE

While the population of Lower Canada in 1822 was almost 430 000, in Upper Canada it was under 150 000. Upper Canada was almost exclusively English-speaking, with a strong Loyalist strain, but in Lower Canada a French-speaking majority, largely rural and agrarian, found itself subordinate to the English-speaking minority. That minority came to form the same kind of oligarchic régime as its counterpart in Upper Canada. The Chateau Clique, like the Family Compact, was able to translate its commercial control into political domination.

The reform movement in Lower Canada was both conservative and nationalist. It aimed to institute a responsible system of government so that the majority, the French Canadians, could have a more active say in their own lives. But in seeking to change the system, the fundamental aim was to preserve the French-Canadian culture and way of life.[11] The reformers were not, for the most part, attempting to imitate the liberal ideology of the French and American revolutions. They were not doctrinaire idealists, but nationalists hoping to defend their way of life against onslaughts from a belligerent and entrenched British ruling oligarchy.

THE RISE OF THE *PATRIOTES*

The reform crusade was conservative in another, perhaps more fundamental, sense, best personified by the movement's undisputed champion and spokesman, Louis Joseph Papineau.[12] Papineau sought to defend traditional Roman Catholic society. He was also a representative of a new, emerging intellectual élite who were being denied real political power. Papineau was articulate, intelligent, and well-educated, and should have achieved a political position of significance and substance. Yet, having first been elected to the assembly in 1808 at the age of 26, he could rise no further than speaker, a position that he held continuously from 1815 until 1837.

Louis Joseph Papineau. First elected to the assembly of Lower Canada in 1810, Papineau emerged as the parliamentary leader of the Lower Canadian reformers and served as speaker of the house intermittently from 1815 to 1837.

Papineau's situation was scarcely unique. The *colleges classiques* were graduating lawyers, journalists, doctors, priests, and administrators who could not be absorbed into the public service. Virtually none of a long string of governors, with the exception of Sir George Prevost, was willing to grant offices to the members of this rising class.[13] Thus, the reform movement was, in part, a function of a repressed nationality seeking its just rewards. These men were conservative nationalists who sought firstly to guarantee the survival of their race, and secondly to gain entry into the corridors of power. If they were to be successful in obtaining the latter, it would go a long way to ensuring the former.

THE QUESTION OF FINANCIAL CONTROL

Papineau was convinced that he could successfully press for changes by using the assembly's power of the purse, following the British custom that recognized the right of the lower house to authorize the spending of public monies.[14] He worked in close association with John Neilson, the leader of a small but vocal group of English-Canadian reformers. However, Papineau's association with Neilson was inherently unstable and was terminated in 1834.

Up to 1818, permanent crown revenues and monies raised through duties imposed under the Quebec Revenue Act of 1774 had proved sufficient for the governor to carry on the administration of the colony. However, in 1818 Sir John Sherbrooke found himself in the novel and uncomfortable position of not having enough money to meet government expenses. He asked the assembly to vote him the difference. Not realizing its opportunity, the assembly acceded to the request.

The following year, the assembly began to flex its muscles by refusing the identical petition unless it was given total control over all government revenues. The new governor, the Duke of Richmond, and his more celebrated successor, Lord Dalhousie, refused this demand. They argued that the assembly was attempting to gain complete government power under the thinly veiled pretext of trying to gain control over revenues. They added that the executive administration of the colonial government was to be independent of popular control. The legislative council answered by refusing the budget proposed by the assembly.

The council's reasoning was that it was willing to surrender control of all revenues in return for a permanent civil list. Such a list would ensure the salaries of the governor and his appointed officials, thereby eliminating the necessity of calling the assembly into session. The assembly, under Papineau's leadership, escalated the controversy by rejecting the proposal. Thus, over the next decade the battle was renewed annually and the debate worsened. Frustration and bitterness built up on both sides as council and assembly stubbornly held to their respective positions. The controversy intensified as the French-Canadian–controlled assembly continually voted down English requests for funds to expand and improve transportation facilities.

THE JACKSONIAN DEMOCRATIC EXPERIENCE

AT THE SAME TIME as the Canadian reform movements were gaining ground, Andrew Jackson emerged at the head of a rising democratic reform wave that revolutionized the American party system. Before 1810, the right to vote in the United States was mainly restricted to the propertied and well-to-do. Gradually, property requirements to qualify for the vote were set at increasingly lower levels, and new western states with no property qualifications for voting were admitted.

The most dramatic increase in democratic participation occurred between 1824 and 1828. In the controversial presidential election of 1824, only 335 000 voters had cast ballots, and the disputed result was decided when the House of Representatives chose John Quincy Adams. Four years later, over 1 155 000 Americans voted, and Andrew Jackson of Tennessee was swept into the White House. In many states, voter turnout more than tripled, and Jackson's supporters — the Democratic Republicans — hailed the victory as a triumph for "the common people."[15]

ANDREW JACKSON AND THE MYTH

Andrew Jackson's election in 1828 marked, in many ways, a watershed in American politics. Until then, the men who occupied the presidency had come from either Virginia or Massachusetts, were closely identified with the nation's aristocratic élite, and seemed far removed from the great mass of citizens. Jackson seemed to symbolize the common, self-made man. He had sprung from humble Tennessee origins, distinguished himself as a hero in the War of 1812–14, and earned the popular nickname "Old Hickory." To many Americans, his election appeared to represent the triumph of democracy in American society.[16] At his inauguration in March 1829, the crowd of admirers surged into the White House, tracked mud on the carpets, knocked over tables, stood on chairs, and only dispersed when the liquid refreshments were

Andrew Jackson, nicknamed "Old Hickory," served two terms as president of the United States. Not one to shy away from controversy, he adopted a highly individualistic style.

gone. As Supreme Court Justice Joseph Story remarked at the time, "The reign of King Mob seemed triumphant."

Jackson was far from an ideal representative of American frontier democracy. After gambling away an inheritance from an Irish grandparent, he became rich as a land speculator and trader in Nashville. His brutal suppression of the Creek Indians in 1813–14 and his virulent anti-Amerindian attitudes were legendary. On the eve of assuming the presidency, Jackson was not only wealthy but owned a large Tennessee plantation with over 150 slaves.[17]

THE JACKSONIAN APPEAL

Jackson's rhetoric of liberal democratic reform won a widespread following that extended far beyond the western frontier states. He attracted support from urban mechanics, labourers, professionals, and even businesspeople, as well as western farmers. Large numbers of working people were drawn to Jackson, even though he offered little for the labouring classes and had shown no sympathy for rebellious workers during a labour dispute on the Chesapeake and Ohio Canal. Under Jackson's leadership, the emerging Democratic party won the backing of organized labour. Through prudent and moderate reform, it also won the enduring loyalty of "the middling interest" — the yeoman class of small producers and independent farmers.[18]

One of Jackson's campaign promises was to open up government to the masses of people rather than keeping it the preserve of the privileged. The guiding philosophy was "to the victor belong the spoils." He dismissed 40 percent (252 out of 612) of his predecessors' appointees. He justified his policy on the grounds that anyone possessed the ability to execute the duties of government service. In addition, he claimed that his political allies should be rewarded. Finally, he noted that if political officeholders were not periodically replaced, an entrenched class of federal bureaucrats would arise — an unpalatable development for "Old Hickory."

THE TARIFF AND STATES' RIGHTS

In the early years of Jackson's administration, the tariff emerged as a highly divisive political issue. By the mid-1820s, it had become apparent that tariff policy favoured the northern rather than the southern states. The bulk of American industry had developed in the North, while the South continued to depend on revenues from the export of agricultural products. The tariff question came to a head in 1828, shortly before Jackson assumed office. In response to demands from northern manufacturers and western farmers, Congress enacted a new and substantial tariff. Duties were as high as 45 to 50 percent on some imports, and critics in the South branded the measure the "Tariff of Abominations."

The high tariff of 1828 not only aggravated sectional discontent, but fuelled the movement for states' rights in the South. The vice-president, John C. Calhoun of South Carolina, wrote an anonymous article entitled "The South Carolina Exposition and Protest," which expressed the view that the Union was a compact of sovereign states. The federal government, established through the constitution, was a mere agent of those states. Thus, any state could rule on the constitutionality of any federal statute and, if it deemed a law unconstitutional, it could nullify the law within its borders.

Jackson's position on states' rights and nullification was unclear. Southern planters, seeing Jackson as one of their own, hoped he would support their cause. Jackson's true feelings on states' rights became clear during a dinner in 1830 honouring Thomas Jefferson's birthday. After many toasts were offered in favour of states' rights, Jackson's turn came. Staring coldly at Calhoun, Jackson declared, "Our *federal* union: it must be preserved." The vice-president could only respond weakly: "The union, next to our liberty, most dear!"

The tariff issue continued to simmer for the next two years. In 1832, a presidential election year, Jackson persuaded Congress to lower the duties on a selected range of products. But the reductions did not go far enough. Calhoun called for nullification, and South Carolina responded by calling for a special convention. By a vote of 136 to 26, the delegates voted to declare the tariffs of 1828 and 1832 null and void. In addition, the South Carolina legislature called up the state militia and voted funds for its mobilization. If the federal authorities attempted to intervene, South Carolina was prepared to use force to secure its point.

President Jackson, who had just won easy re-election, moved swiftly to quell the South Carolina protest. In February 1833, Congress passed the Force Bill, which empowered the president to use the army to collect revenues. Jackson left little doubt as to how he planned to respond to the crisis. He said he would "hang the first man of them [the nullifiers] I can get my hands on to the first tree I can find." A compromise bill was passed in March 1833, which saw a slight lowering of the tariffs. South Carolina responded in an ambivalent fashion. On the one hand, it repealed the Ordinance of Nullification; on the other hand, it nullified the Force Bill.

JACKSON AND THE BANK WAR

Jackson's egalitarian and reform impulses were dramatically revealed in his "war" against the Bank of the United States.[19] Like most westerners, he saw the Bank as an unhealthy concentration of economic power. Jackson was suspicious of all banks and distrustful of paper money. According to the president, the bank was a "hydra-headed monster" that "impaired the morals of our people [and] threatened our liberty." In addition, in his eyes, the bank was dominated and controlled by one man — Nicholas Biddle, its president.

The bank's charter did not expire until 1836. However, in 1832 Daniel Webster and Henry Clay persuaded Biddle to ask Congress for an early renewal of the bank's charter. Clay hoped to force Jackson's hand. If he signed the renewal bill, he would lose support in the South and West. If he vetoed it, it would cost him votes in the North, where voters generally saw the bank as a stabilizing mechanism. In July, Congress passed the bank bill, whereupon Jackson promptly vetoed it. He said that it favoured the rich, was unconstitutional, and was controlled by foreign investors. He wrote to his vice-president, Martin Van Buren, "The bank is trying to kill me, but I will kill it!"

Jackson's bank veto was the central issue of the 1832 election. But "Old Hickory's" popular appeal and strong public sentiments against the bank gave him a landslide victory. Jackson continued his war on the bank by removing government funds from it and depositing them in state ("pet") banks. Facing steadily decreasing deposits, Biddle decided to restrict credit and to call in loans. In an attempt to embarrass his rival, Biddle embarked on a tight-money policy that led to a severe constriction of land speculation and business investment in 1833–34. The bank's charter was allowed to expire in 1836 and — true to Jacksonian principles — the United States remained without a national bank until 1913, when the Federal Reserve System was established.

JACKSONIAN AMERICA

Many of the reforms of the Jacksonian era were more effective in achieving stability and control than in alleviating social inequalities. With the rapid growth of America had come waves of new immigrants and signs of an emerging industrial order — canals, telegraph lines, and railways. In 1790, fewer than 1 million Americans lived in cities; in 1840, 11 million did so. New York had only 130 000 people in 1820, but 1 million by 1860.

In some respects, the Jacksonians were the champions of an older, more conservative bourgeois order seeking to contain and to control the changes wrought by the onset of urban, industrial society.[20] Typical of the Jacksonian democrats was Martin Van Buren, who succeeded Jackson as president. Under his political leadership in New York and later Washington, a coalition of rising businessmen, yeoman farmers, southern planters, and northern mechanics was welded together into an organized political party, and any possibility of social disorder was effectively banished from the United States.[21]

REBELLIONS AND REFORM IN BRITISH NORTH AMERICA

ALMOST A DECADE after Andrew Jackson's election triumph of 1828, armed revolts broke out in Upper and Lower Canada, the two largest colonies in British North America. Demands for political reform were voiced in all of Britain's remaining North American colonies, but only in the two Canadas did rebellions actually occur. In both cases the problems of the 1820s and 1830s still festered. Colonial government remained remote from popular concerns; appointed councils and the elected assemblies were deadlocked. Both Lower and Upper Canada were suffering economic dislocations that pitted rural agrarian interests against the commercial élites of the colonies. In Lower Canada, language and race were also a major component in the unfolding conflict, as the English-dominated oligarchy increasingly became a target of French-Canadian nationalist leaders.

LOWER CANADA: THE PRECONDITIONS FOR REBELLION

The revolt in Lower Canada grew out of an intense political struggle for control over colonial affairs. The requisite leadership came from Louis Joseph Papineau (1786–1871), the speaker of the Lower Canadian assembly.[22] At issue was the right of the elected assembly to control

A society divided: two views of Lower Canada in the 1830s. Compare the scenes of life in these two towns, the French-speaking town of Point Levis *(above)* and the English-speaking town of Sherbrooke *(below).* To what extent was Lower Canada already divided into two societies or "two nations"?

revenues and the general conduct of government. At Papineau's urging, the lower chamber consistently refused to vote supply, hoping to bring the councils to their knees.

In 1827, after yet another assembly refusal, the governor, Lord Dalhousie, dissolved the assembly and appealed directly to the voters. Hoping to capture enough seats to obtain the coveted permanent civil list, the governor campaigned actively in the bitter election. The reformers won in a landslide, and Papineau was re-elected speaker by the new assembly. Giving vent to his displeasure, Dalhousie vetoed the nomination on the grounds that Papineau had uttered slanderous criticisms of the government during the campaign. He also prorogued the assembly a scant two days after it met.

A select committee of the British House of Commons was established in 1828 to investigate the woeful state of affairs in the Canadian colonies. The committee made a number of innovative recommendations, the most important of which was that in return for a permanent civil list, the assemblies be given control over crown revenues, a measure embodied in an Act of Parliament in 1831. The committee also suggested that relations between the assembly and the councils be harmonized by appointing more French Canadians to the latter.

In Lower Canada, the political and racial climate was too unstable to allow for successful piecemeal reforms. Papineau was thoroughly disenchanted with the select committee's insistence on a permanent civil list. His disillusionment was increased when, during an election riot of 1832, government troops killed three French Canadians. The "Montreal massacre" further deepened his feelings of resentment toward the British authorities.

Papineau used the incident to stir up support for his reform movement. In 1834, the assembly voted to approve the 92 resolutions he had drawn up. The document was a protracted criticism of the oligarchic system of government and included a long list of grievances. It recommended that the assembly have total control over finances; that the legislative council be made elective; and that the executive council be made "responsible." The apparently radical and republican tone frightened many of the moderate reformers, including John Neilson.

Following Papineau's victory in the 1834 election, the British, wanting to find an appropriate compromise without having to surrender, despatched Lord Gosford as the new governor. Prevented by the British government from making substantive concessions, Gosford found himself in an untenable position. The assembly once again refused the British proposal of exchanging control over all revenues in return for a permanent civil list. On this occasion, the lower house limited its grant of supply to only six months. In addition, for the first time, the assembly demanded that the executive council be made responsible to it. The councils refused both the restricted grant as well as the constitutional reform proposal.

Frustration within the reform ranks increased sharply. The radicals of the *Parti Patriote* despaired of achieving constitutional changes through the established system, because the

British government was unshakable in its opposition to the granting of responsible government to the colonies. Their political frustration was heightened by economic circumstances. The "agricultural crisis"[23] set the radicals on a path that could only culminate in violence.

Overpopulation, coupled with overfarming, had exhausted the soil, forcing farmers to shift from wheat production to potatoes. A wheat-fly infestation in 1831 further reduced production and eliminated surpluses for export. Farmers were reduced to a subsistence level and were unable to act as consumers of products made in the urban centres. Unemployment became widespread as the ensuing 1837 depression cast an increasingly wider net.

Papineau began echoing the slogans of the American Revolution. Yet, he was never really genuine in his imitation of American principles or institutions. It was simply a manifestation of his frustration, which had risen to new heights in the wake of the proroguing of the assembly in late August 1837. He was losing control of the reform movement, which was falling increasingly into the hands of extremists.

THE INSURRECTIONS OF 1837–1838

The growing extremism found expression in the creation of the *Fils de la Liberté*, modelled on the American Sons of Liberty. The extremists on the British side created their own organization — the Doric Club. On November 7, 1837, an altercation took place between representatives from each group. From that point on, misunderstanding was heaped upon ignorance. Papineau and his leading lieutenants, hoping to quiet the situation, left Montreal. The government, believing that they had gone to the countryside to incite the disgruntled farmers, issued warrants for their arrest.

Government troops tried to execute the warrants but were repulsed by armed *patriotes* at St. Denis on November 23. That was the signal for open rebellion.[24] However, it was leaderless and sporadic.

A famous painting of an armed *patriote* of 1837–38, later to become a powerful symbol of Quebec nationalism.

Papineau fled to the United States. Two days after the battle at St. Denis, a second clash took place at St. Charles, which was easily won by the government side. In December, in a final bloody stand at St. Eustache, just north of Montreal, the rebels were mercilessly dispersed by over 2000 government troops.

A second insurrection erupted in November 1838. Unlike the rising of 1837, it was a *patriote* revolt undertaken with the aid of Canadian sympathizers in exile in the United States. The plan for rebellion was never really hatched, however. A crowd of several thousand *patriotes* from the parishes of Lower Canada gathered at Napierville, where the radical leaders, Robert Nelson and Cyrille H.O. Coté, issued calls for independence from British rule. But the uprising collapsed in confusion — and government forces encountered no serious opposition. The dreams of the radical *patriotes* would not come to pass. Reform would take place through established British colonial channels.

UPPER CANADA: THE DRIFT TO REBELLION

In Upper Canada the Reformers won majorities in the 1824 and 1828 elections, but achieved few political changes. The 1828 contest, however, brought into prominence William Lyon Mackenzie, who assumed the leadership of the radical Reform movement.[25] After founding his newspaper the *Colonial Advocate* in 1824, he had almost continually been at the centre of controversy. His fiery and biting editorials had earned him the wrath of the Tories. When a Tory mob reacted by raiding his office and dumping his presses into Toronto harbour in 1828, Mackenzie not only obtained financial compensation from the courts, but also attained a popular reputation as the champion of the underdog, or the "common people."

In the 1830s, the Reformers made little headway. Mackenzie's call for an elected legislative council and a responsible executive council in the 1830 election so enraged the governor, Sir John Colborne, that he branded the Reform leader a traitor and rallied Tory support to defeat the Reformers. In 1831, the assembly voted to support Colborne by granting him a permanent civil list in return for full control over government revenues. The Reformers were outraged, so much so that Mackenzie became increasingly radical in his pronouncements.[26] His harangues against the Family Compact mixed elements of agrarian protest and Jacksonian moral reformism with notions of republicanism and democracy.

During the 1834 election, Mackenzie's drift to radicalism split the Upper Canadian Reform movement. The Reverend Egerton Ryerson and the more moderate Reformers broke with Mackenzie and his radical faction. While Ryerson accused Mackenzie's radicals of being atheists and republicans, the rebel leader implied that Ryerson and his Methodist followers had sold out to the Family Compact for a share of the clergy reserves.

Despite the internal divisions, the Reformers managed to capture a majority in the assembly in 1834. When the councils again resorted to obstructionist tactics, frustration again mounted in Reform ranks. Their only recourse was a select committee on grievances, which in 1835,

Reverend Egerton Ryerson, leader of Upper Canadian Methodists and the father of public education in Ontario.

Upper Canadian Reform leader William Lyon Mackenzie.

under Mackenzie's leadership, drew up a far-reaching report documenting numerous abuses of power and recommending political reforms. The radical Reformers like Mackenzie and the moderates led by Robert Baldwin gradually drifted farther apart. Baldwin's group favoured reforms based on the British cabinet system, wherein the government was responsible to the majority in the elected assembly. For his part, Mackenzie began to advocate an American-style democracy in which the councils as well as the assembly would be elected by the people.[27]

After the appointment of Sir Francis Bond Head as lieutenant-governor in 1836, the political situation deteriorated further. An initial attempt was made to broaden representation on the executive council by appointing Baldwin and two other moderate Reformers to the six-person council. But the good-will and co-operation soon evaporated. Bond Head believed he could govern quite capably without either the councils or the assembly, and he made several public appointments without consulting his executive council.[28] This breach of custom led to a dramatic turn of events: the council resigned *en masse*; the assembly voted non-confidence and refused to grant funds; and Bond Head dissolved the assembly and called an election. The election campaign featured widespread bribery and intimidation at open polling stations, and Bond Head and the Tories dealt the divided Reformers a crushing defeat.

The election defeat of 1836 radicalized Mackenzie's Reform faction and pushed it to the point of rebellion. Seeing the impossibility of change through democratic channels, the movement looked to Mackenzie for leadership and drew strength from the radical ideas in his new journal, *The Constitution*. The mounting sense of injustice was only heightened by the depression of 1837, which gripped the rural countryside. This "agricultural crisis" had a serious effect, causing farm exports to drop and prices to plummet. Bond Head's refusal to allow the Bank of Upper Canada to suspend *specie* payment made conditions worse. When the bank attempted to call its loans, bankruptcies and foreclosures resulted. The final nudge came from Papineau and the *patriotes* of Lower Canada. After receiving word that armed resistance had erupted in the rural areas outside Montreal, Mackenzie gave the signal to take up arms.

THE YONGE STREET REBELLION

The Mackenzie rebellion was poorly led, disorganized, and short-lived. Mackenzie's "plan" was to over-run the city hall, seize the arms stored there, and overthrow the government. The actual fighting was over almost before it began. On December 7, 1837, a motley collection of a few hundred armed rebels marched from Montgomery's Tavern in the north end of Toronto and were met by Colonel James Fitzgibbon and his force of 1000 volunteers. Fitzgibbon, an adjutant-general and veteran of the War of 1812, had taken matters into his own hands when Bond Head had vacillated on a plan of action. A few volleys were fired, the rebels fled, and the Yonge Street rebellion was over. Shortly thereafter, another radical member of the assembly, Dr. Charles Duncombe, launched a similar uprising in the Western District of Upper Canada. Like the Yonge Street rebellion, it was easily quelled by "loyalist" forces.[29]

The skirmish at Montgomery's Tavern, Toronto, in1837. Colonel Robert Moodie is shot dead on his horse as he attempts to warn the Tories at Toronto.

Mackenzie fled to Navy Island, outside Buffalo, where he organized a government-in-exile and contemplated an invasion assisted by American sympathizers. The scheme quickly died. The Tories felt vindicated by their December victory. To them, it was proof positive that the Reform movement was merely a front for republican conspiracy. They set out to rid themselves of any last vestiges of challenge. Only two men, Samuel Lount and Peter Matthews, were actually executed for their part in the rebellions. However, almost 100 prisoners, both from the rebellion and from arrests of later frontier raiders, were banished to Van Diemen's Land (Tasmania). Simultaneously, many Reform leaders found it a convenient time to leave the colony voluntarily. Bidwell and others departed, seeing arbitrary arrests as evidence of the conquering Tories' reign of vindictiveness. For the Tories of Upper Canada, however, it was a short-lived victory.

THE MARITIMES AND REFORM

Comparatively, political reform in the Maritimes came without the rancour and strife that accompanied the process in Upper and Lower Canada.[30] First, the Maritimes lacked the volatile racial dimension that was a vital component of the process in Lower Canada. Second, the oligarchies in the Maritimes were not as entrenched as were their counterparts in the Canadas. In addition, they did not employ loyalty to the crown and the stigma of "republicanism" as political weapons to keep the wayward in line.

In Nova Scotia, for example, both Tories and Reformers could legitimately claim Loyalist ancestry. As Joseph Howe, one of the leading agitators for responsible government, said in the Nova Scotia Assembly: "The idea of republicanism, of independence, of severance from the mother country, never crosses my mind…. I wish to live and die a British subject." Finally, the Maritime assemblies had given the councils the permanent civil list in return for control over government revenues early on, so this never arose as a reform issue.

That is not say, however, that Maritime reform was completely peaceful. In Prince Edward Island, reformers in the Escheat Movement demanded the cancellation of absentee landowners' proprietary grants. Because of the extent of agrarian and political discontent, rebellion might have broken out on the island had not the rebellions in the Canadas been put down firmly. In New Brunswick, a major controversy over revenue from crown lands, particularly timber rights, ended in 1837 with the reformers managing to regain control of them. In Nova Scotia, reformers, most notably Joseph Howe, were extremely angry with many appointed government officials in the colony. Despite these incidents of incipient rebellion, compared with what had transpired in the Canadas, Maritime reform was accomplished with much less vehemence.

LORD DURHAM'S MISSION AND REPORT

Faced with rebellion in the Canadas, the British government acted quickly. Governor Lord Gosford was recalled; Bond Head's resignation was accepted with relief. That left the way clear to appoint someone who could govern the colonies, investigate the root of their problems, and recommend long-term solutions. The choice fell on John George Lambton, the Earl of Durham, nicknamed "Radical Jack." Arriving at Quebec in May 1838, Lord Durham was invested with wide powers as high commissioner and governor-in-chief of British North America.[31]

Durham initially undertook two separate but inter-related tasks: to govern Lower Canada, and to make arrangements for the establishment of his inquiry. After dismissing the council, he appointed five members of his own staff. This prevented either the English or the French from feeling alienated. His immediate problem was what to do with the more than 150 prisoners from the rebellion who were languishing in jail. Realizing that no French-Canadian jury would ever return a guilty verdict, he obtained confessions from nine of the principals, whom he exiled to Bermuda, and pardoned the remainder. The problem was that he had no authority to do either. He exacerbated the situation when he declared, again with no jurisdiction, that Papineau and several of his chief lieutenants were to be permanent exiles. When the British government react-

Lord Durham, author of the *Report on the Affairs of British North America* (1839). Although credited with proposing responsible government, he most likely appropriated the idea from Robert Baldwin, a moderate Reform leader in Upper Canada.

ed by disallowing his exile ordinance, Durham interpreted the decision as an indictment, resigned his post, and returned to England after only five months in Canada.

Durham's famous report, issued in 1839, offered an incisive, albeit racist, analysis of the causes of the unrest and proposed major reforms in the political and constitutional structure of the colonies. Durham identified two fundamental sources of discontent in the Canadas. The first was that the friction between the legislative councils and the legislative assemblies was the underlying cause of the rebellions. Second, he believed that the root cause of the political struggle in Lower Canada could be ascribed to what he saw as the backward nature of the French-Canadian population.

To ameliorate these and other difficulties, Durham made a host of recommendations, three of them of paramount importance for constitutional reform. All were inter-related and mutually reinforcing. One was that the two Canadas be reunited in a common assembly based upon the principle of representation by population. The second was that responsible government based on the British cabinet system be instituted. The third was that jurisdiction over imperial and local matters be separated.

THE "PAPER-STREWN PATH" TO RESPONSIBLE GOVERNMENT

The road to responsible government in the Canadas proved to be a long and arduous one.[32] Strong as the desire for reform was in Upper and Lower Canada, the traditions of British constitutionalism and loyalty were far stronger. Only a few hundred in Upper Canada and perhaps slightly more in Lower Canada had actually joined in the rebellions. Most British North Americans, it appeared, favoured the approach recommended by Lord Durham — orderly evolution to colonial self-government.

It took almost a decade after the appearance of Lord Durham's report before the practice of responsible government was recognized and accepted by the British authorities. In 1840–41, the two Canadas were united in a common legislative system and renamed Canada East (Lower Canada) and Canada West (Upper Canada). A succession of colonial governors attempted, with varying degrees of determination, to overcome the entrenched oligarchies' resistance to constitutional reforms. Until the mid-1840s, the British government and the Colonial Office pursued a cautious and piecemeal policy of reform.

Within the Reform movement in the Canadas, internal divisions arose and hampered the determined efforts of its public leaders, Louis Hippolyte Lafontaine and Robert Baldwin. Finally, the Reformers gained with their ballots in 1848 what the rebels had failed to achieve with arms in 1837. Baldwin, the Reform leader in Canada West, and Lafontaine, his counterpart in Canada East, each secured a majority of members in their respective parts of the assembly. This double majority enabled the Reformers to impose their demands for constitutional reform. A year later, in 1849, the principle of responsible government was demonstrated when the governor-general, Lord Elgin, signed into law a major bill with which he personally disagreed, because it had been passed by a majority in the assembly. The Rebellion Losses Bill compensated those in Lower Canada who had suffered property damage during the rebellions.

Constitutional reform came earlier in Nova Scotia.[33] As early as 1839, Lieutenant-Governor Sir Colin Campbell had shown reform inclinations when, at the urging of Governor-General Lord Sydenham, he invited three Reformers, including Joseph Howe, into the council. The vital precedent had been established that members of the executive council did not necessarily come exclusively from the oligarchy. In the three years after 1843, Governor Falkland was consistently rebuffed in his attempts to bring Reformers into the coalition government; he was therefore replaced by Sir John Harvey in 1846.

The burning of the Parliament buildings in Montreal, 1849. Riots followed Lord Elgin's signing of the Rebellion Losses Bill in 1849. The Tory faction in Montreal interpreted his action as a betrayal of the British empire and an acceptance of French domination.

When Harvey was again unsuccessful in attracting Reformers into the government in 1847, he called an election. The Reformers won a large victory and, in keeping with the new endorsement of self-government in the British Colonial Office, the Reformers were called upon to form the new government. The "premier" was J.B. Uniacke, the leader of the majority party in the assembly. As such, he was empowered to select his executive councillors from the ranks of his own Reform party. Thus responsible government became a reality in Nova Scotia one year before it was achieved in the Canadas.

The spirit of constitutional reform soon spread to the other Maritime colonies. In New Brunswick and Prince Edward Island, the conflict between the council and the assembly centred on ownership of valuable crown lands. The issue was never as contentious as that of the clergy or crown reserves in the Canadas. In fact, once Nova Scotia showed the way, the other Atlantic colonies followed — New Brunswick in 1848, Prince Edward Island in 1851, and Newfoundland in 1855.

THE TWO REFORM TRADITIONS

ALTHOUGH THE REFORM MOVEMENTS in the Canadas spawned armed revolts, they did not win widespread support. When political reform did come to the Canadas and the Maritimes, it took the form of orderly British colonial evolution. The reform movements of the 1820s, 1830s, and 1840s in British North America were essentially conservative in their spirit. Although leaders like Mackenzie and Papineau did at times express radical republican or liberal democratic slogans and ideals, the vast majority of Canadian reformers might be described as "conservative revolutionaries." They sought in many ways to reform the colonial system in order to preserve older, agrarian values threatened by changing economic and social conditions.[34]

CHANGES IN GOVERNMENT IN THE CANADAS, 1791–1849

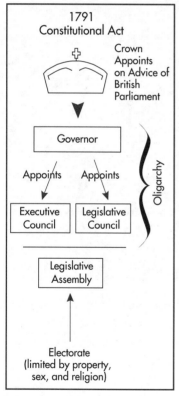

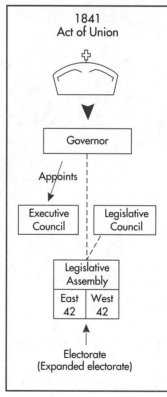

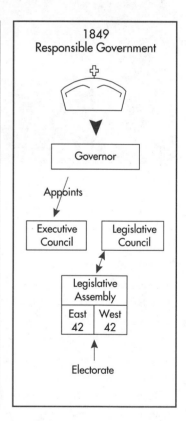

The Constitutional Act, 1791, establishes oligarchic rule in both Upper and Lower Canada.

The governor begins the practice of appointing members to the Legislative Council who have the support of the Legislative Assembly.

Lord Elgin asks the Legislative Assembly leader to appoint the Legislative Council. It becomes, in effect, a cabinet.

The reformers in Lower Canada, in particular, sought alterations in the colonial system that might preserve and protect French-Canadian culture in the face of economic and social change. A recent interpretation sees the inhabitants of Lower Canada not as passive victims of events but rather as actively responding to the democratic appeals of their leaders because the language of reform was congruent with their experience and outlook.[35]

The Jacksonian experiment in popular democracy undoubtedly exerted some influence on British North American reform movements. Both Mackenzie and Papineau borrowed somewhat from Jacksonian ideas to fashion their own political program. Both saw in the democratization and opening up of the political system models that they could emulate. In their eyes, the members of the oligarchic Family Compact and Chateau Clique were British colonial versions of the aristocratic order that Jackson was challenging. The Upper Canadian radical reformer William Lyon Mackenzie saw in the American Democratic president a kindred spirit, although that impression soured in later years. To some degree, Papineau's speeches of the 1830s reflected American republican ideas. And Dr. Duncombe's 1837 rising in western Upper Canada attracted most of its support from mature, well-settled farmers of American birth or origin, which may well have made them more receptive to radical republican ideas.

But that is probably the limit of American influence. In the Canadas, as in the Maritimes, most segments of the Reform movement were moderate reformers who favoured British colonial institutions over American elective ones. Any hint of American "republican influences" was enough to arouse the emotional loyalism of both conservative and moderate reform elements in any of the colonies. Compared with the Jacksonian democrats of the 1830s, radical reformers in the Canadas never commanded such widespread public support. The failure of the rebellions of 1837–38 led, in fact, to a period of reaction in the Canadas. The most radical reform demands, which bore a resemblance to Jacksonianism, were snuffed out and gave way to calls for an orderly transition to British colonial self-government.

ACTIVITIES

KEY TERMS AND CONCEPTS

Identify and briefly explain the historical significance of the following terms and concepts:

- Ruling oligarchies
- Legislated assimilation
- The "alien question"
- Clergy reserves
- *Chateau Clique*
- Permanent civil list
- Franchise

- Union Bill of 1822
- "Jacksonian democracy"
- Spoils system
- The Bank War
- Ninety-Two Resolutions (1834)
- Insurrections of 1837–38
- Republicanism
- *Colonial Advocate* and *The Constitution*
- Duncombe's Rising

• Lord Durham's Report (1839)
• Rebellion Losses Bill
• *The Novascotian*
• Conservative revolutionaries
• Liberal

QUESTIONS FOR DISCUSSION

1. What were the main sources of political discontent in Upper and Lower Canada in the years between 1820 and mid-century? To what degree were those grievances shared by British North Americans in the Maritimes?

2. The Jacksonian reform movement of the late 1820s and early 1830s erupted at a time when reform agitation was gaining support in the northern British colonies. Did the Jacksonian movement have an influence on British North American reform movements? If so, in what respects?

3. Compare the rebellions in Upper Canada and Lower Canada in the 1830s. To what extent were they "separate but inter-related events"?

4. In *The Patriots and the People* (1993), Allan Greer argued that Lower Canada during 1837–38 experienced "a classic revolutionary crisis." The old order, according to Greer, lost its legitimacy and rural peasants sought to "reconstitute rule on new foundations." To what extent did the Lower Canadian risings of 1837–38 constitute a popular revolution that was quelled by British colonial authorities?

5. Why was constitutional reform achieved earlier and with less strife in the Maritimes than in the Canadas?

6. To what extent did Jacksonian democracy and the British North American reform movements contribute to the formation of the modern "party system" in both the United States and Canada?

ASSESSING HISTORICAL INTERPRETATIONS

Following is a variety of viewpoints expressed by historians on the major issues in North American reform from 1820 to 1850.

1. Analyze each historian's viewpoint or interpretation. Identify the thesis.
2. Assess the validity of the interpretation on the basis of your reading of the evidence.

Issue A: The Nature of Jacksonian Democracy

"In order to understand the means by which this leader [Andrew Jackson], trained on the frontier, expressing its militant quality and its democracy, won the presidency, we must draw a distinction between the Jackson men and the Jacksonian Democrats in 1828. The 'Jackson men' included, not only the trans-Allegheny followers of the 'Old Hero,' and the kindred people of Pennsylvania, but also the New York democracy and the tidewater aristocracy of the southern seaboard. Nevertheless, Jacksonian Democracy was based primarily upon the characteristics of the back country. Jackson was himself a product of the frontier West — that West which was born of the southern upland in the days when a sharp contrast existed between the interior farmers and the tidewater planters...."

— Frederick Jackson Turner, *The United States 1830–1850: The Nation and Its Sections* (New York: Henry Holt, 1935). Reprinted by permission of the publisher.

"The leadership of the New York Democratic Party [in the Jacksonian era] does not appear to have been recruited from the...sections of society that struggled 'to restrain the power of the business community.'...

"...[F]armers, mechanics and 'working classes' did not form the 'main-stay of the Democratic party.' Instead of low-status economic groups, the Jacksonian's strongest support came from relatively high-status socioeconomic groups in the eastern counties, and relatively low-status ethnocultural and religious groups in all sections of New York."

— Lee Benson, *The Concept of Jacksonian Democracy: New York as a Test Case* (Princeton, NJ: Princeton University Press). Excerpt reprinted with permission of Princeton University Press.

Issue B: Was Mackenzie a Jacksonian Reformer?

"It has become a cliché of Canadian historiography that the political thought of William Lyon Mackenzie was deeply influenced by the values and objectives of Jacksonian Democracy. As in all clichés there is a kernel of truth in this observation."

— J.E. Rea, "William Lyon Mackenzie — Jacksonian?" *Mid-America* 50 (1968).

"Mr. Mackenzie spoke of 'agriculture, the most innocent, happy, and important of all human pursuits'; and he voiced the traditionary [*sic*] agrarian view…which associated monopoly with speculation and depreciation — not with restraints upon enterprise."

— Bray Hammond, *Banks and Politics in America* (Princeton, NJ: Princeton University Press, 1957).

CHAPTER 10

AMERICAN CONFLICT AND CANADIAN CONFEDERATION, 1860–1867

THE RISE OF THE CONFEDERATION MOVEMENT

THE COMING OF THE AMERICAN CIVIL WAR

EXTERNAL PRESSURES AND INFLUENCES

THE AMERICAN IMPACT ON CONFEDERATION

T

HE ACHIEVEMENT OF CONFEDERATION has traditionally been viewed as the shining moment of triumph when farsighted statesmen transformed a dream into a reality. It was, in fact, far more practical and pragmatic. Confederation was born out of the ashes of the failure of two unions — the Union of the Canadas and Maritime Union. It was more the result of external pressures impinging on the British North American colonies than the orchestrations of nation-building politicians. The new Dominion was formed, in historian J.C. Bonenfant's words, "not by people who desired intensely to live together, but rather by people who could not live separately."[1]

Many internal factors argued against Confederation. The instability inherent in the governmental system established under the Act of Union of 1840–41 made the passage of Confederation — and much other legislation — doubtful at best. The political and personal rivalries of the principal leaders mitigated against a federal union. The continuing racial animosity between the French and English resulted in the deep distrust of the French for any large scheme that appeared to imperil their continued cultural survival. The suspicion of the Maritimers — distant, isolated, and small in population — did not augur well for the chances of a federal union. The constant controversy surrounding the Intercolonial and Grand Trunk railways added further division within the northern colonies.

External pressures were critically important as a catalyst in the movement for British North American Confederation. Donald Creighton wrote, "The anxious encouragement of Great Britain was the first of the external forces hastening national expansion; the second was the pressure of a resentful and predatory United States."[2] One might quibble with the order of influences identified by Creighton, but the strength of those American and British pressures cannot be denied.

British influences on the Confederation movement were many and varied. Since the late 1840s the colonies had enjoyed a larger measure of self-government under the principle of responsible cabinet government. The adoption of free trade through the repeal of the mercantilist Corn Laws in 1846 forced British North America to compete for international markets. The refusal of the British government, in the early 1860s, to appropriate substantial sums for the defence of its colony was a telling demonstration of its growing indifference to British North America. The British refusal to provide the requisite bond guarantee for the construction of the Grand Trunk Railway was a further prod to Confederation. In addition, the regular and open attempts on the part of the Colonial Office to influence Maritime politicians in favour of Confederation indicate clearly that the British government was taking more than a passive interest in the movement.[3]

Confederation took place amid an atmosphere of North American conflict. The American Civil War (1861–65) and its immediate aftermath affected not only the union of the British North American colonies, but directly determined the form that their government ultimately took. A series of American events — the *Trent* Affair, the St. Albans Raid, the cancellation of the Reciprocity Treaty, the end of the Civil War, and the Fenian Raids — were the propelling forces behind Confederation. Because of British sympathy for the Confederate cause, the danger that the victorious northern states might attack the thinly defended British North American colonies remained a real possibility in the 1860s. Against such a backdrop, the Fathers of Confederation frequently pointed to — and in some cases exaggerated — the American threat in order to stir British North Americans in support of federal union.

THE RISE OF THE CONFEDERATION MOVEMENT

IN 1858, Abraham Lincoln uttered his famous dictum, "A House divided against itself cannot stand." He was saying that the United States could not long endure being half-slave and half-free. His maxim could apply with equal legitimacy to the colonies of British North America: they could not continue to endure the sectional and racial hostility that had paralyzed them into deadlock by the early 1860s. It is no mere coincidence of history that, just as the American union was being fractured by a bloody civil war, the British North American colonies were awakening to the advantages of union.

POLITICAL DEADLOCK IN THE CANADAS

In little more than a decade and a half, the united Province of Canada suffered through 15 different ministries and more than half a dozen elections.[4] In establishing equal representation for the two Canadas, East and West, within the united legislature, the Act of Union had perpetuated the sectional and racial divisions inherent in British North America. That problem was exacerbated by population trends. The 1861 census revealed that Canada West had almost 300 000 more people than Canada East. As the English, led by George Brown, raised the cry of "rep by pop," the French feared the old bogey-man of assimilation. The principle of "double majority" — that a majority was needed in each assembly of the Canadas before legislation could be passed — became a major stumbling block to the passage of legislation. The presence of many independent members prevented most ministries from commanding the support of the majority in the assembly. The result was dissolution and deadlock.

The *Canadien* reformers who followed Louis H. Lafontaine sought constitutional concessions that would give them greater political strength. Already Canada East enjoyed its own system of civil law, special privileges in matters of religion, as well as its own unique system of education and landholding. Continuing the pattern established by the Robert Baldwin–Louis H. Lafontaine ministry, a series of dual administrations based on French and English joint premiers attempted to govern in ways acceptable to both sections of the fragile union.

The French-Canadian politicians adopted a conservative approach to politics. Economic and liberal reform schemes held little attraction. Rather, their aim was to create political structures that promised to guarantee their cultural survival in the face of what they interpreted as English hostility. They had little in common with the Reformers of Canada West. The onset of "revolving door ministries" really began in 1854 when Augustin Morin united with the champion of Canada West Toryism, Sir Allan McNab. This ministry, like almost every one that would follow it, was unstable. The Morin–McNab government forced the Tories to accept the continuance of the French-Canadian culture. For their part, the French had to assent to commercial expansion. Politics did indeed make strange bedfellows.

SHIFTING POLITICAL ALIGNMENTS

A new ingredient was added to the political cauldron in the 1850s — George Brown and the Clear Grits. As editor of the *Globe*, Brown was able to publicize — and popularize — his views.[5] Being strongly anti-French, Brown felt that the Morin–McNab ministry was too conservative and overly dominated by Canada East. Furthermore, he wanted to liberalize the politics of the day by imitating many aspects of the republican system of the United States. The Grits wanted to institute universal suffrage, free trade, and a secret ballot. In addition, Brown's Grits wanted to open up the Northwest for their agrarian constituency.

However, their most crucial proposal was a response to the changing population pattern of the province. Because the population of Canada West was growing far faster than that of Canada East and would soon surpass it, as early as 1853 Brown and the Grits raised the cry of "rep by pop." The English saw it as a means of accomplishing what was justly theirs and ending French intransigence and domination; the French, on the other hand, seeing that it was a thinly veiled attempt at assimilation, entrenched themselves in their opposition. The battle lines were now drawn over questions of representation, taxation, religion, and language.

The Charlottetown Conference, 1864. The delegates gathered to consider proposals for British North American union while the Civil War rumbled on in the United States.

Francis Hincks, an old champion in the fight for responsible government, replaced McNab, and even though the new Hincks–Morin ministry was able to survive the 1854 election, its fortunes were on the decline. There was widespread criticism of the government for being unable to resolve the age-old problem of the clergy reserves. Fuelling that criticism was the 1853 passage of the Separate School Bill, which had been voted down by a large majority in Canada West but which had been carried because of the votes of the members from Canada East.[6]

THE GREAT COALITION

The Hincks–Morin government was defeated on a motion of non-confidence in June 1854. Their lack of strength, substantially reduced in the subsequent election, forced them to resign amid disorder and disintegration. Their loss was John A. Macdonald's opportunity.[7] With the political acumen that was to become his trademark, the lawyer from Kingston was able to engineer the creation of the "Liberal–Conservative" party, which united his own moderate conservatives from Ontario, McNab's radical conservatives, and George Cartier's moderate conservative *Bleus* from Quebec.

After a series of changes in leadership, a lasting political partnership — the Macdonald–Cartier ministry — emerged. The central role that the Liberal–Conservatives played can be seen in the fact that of more than a dozen ministries in the decade after 1854, all but three were drawn from their ranks. Their true status was confirmed with their election victory in 1857, which saw the lines of sectionalism hardening as Brown's Grits won a majority in Canada West but were held in a position of opposition because of the larger plurality captured by *les Bleus* in Canada East.

The symbolic death knell for the existing political system came with the June 1864 defeat of the Taché–Macdonald government after only a three-month tenure. In May 1864, a legislative committee was struck, headed by George Brown, to investigate a way out of the political impasse. In a neat historical irony, the very day — June 14 — that the committee reported back marked the collapse of the Taché–Macdonald government. The seeds of Brown's idea of a larger federal union had landed on anything but fertile soil, leaving, as Edgar McInnis has noted, "no assurance that the project would not expire with it."[8]

Clashes of personality — over and above political instability — were another important obstacle to achieving Confederation. Given George Brown's dislike of the French, it was not surprising that virtually all French-Canadian leaders regarded him with a jaundiced eye. Macdonald, ever the politician, based his alliance with Cartier and the French on pragmatism. Cartier, for his part, saw Macdonald as a bulwark against Brown's demand for "rep by pop," which threatened to extinguish the French culture. Finally, Brown and Macdonald had a mutual dislike, bordering on hatred, for one another. Macdonald saw his rival as disloyal, pro-American, and dangerously radical. The publisher of the *Globe* criticized the Conservative leader as an opportunist, a procrastinator, and a dissembler.

LESSONS OF THE AMERICAN UNION

ONE OF THE FATHERS OF CONFEDERATION who drew lessons from the American experience was John A. Macdonald. Determined to avoid the difficulties associated with "states' rights" agitation in the United States, he initially argued for a legislative form of union, based upon a single central government and no provinces. Only when Macdonald's preferred scheme met with resistance and proved impracticable did he endorse the alternative of federal union. Even then, Macdonald favoured a scheme that, he felt, conferred on the central government and Parliament all the powers "which are incident to sovereignty."

Macdonald's speeches and comments during the Confederation debates indicate that he was mindful of the dangers of "states' rights." What lesson did Macdonald draw from the American experience?

We should concentrate the power in the Federal Government, and not adopt the decentralization of the United States. [Some] would give sovereign power to the Local Legislatures, just where the United States failed. Canada would be infinitely stronger as she is than under such a system.... It is said that the tariff is one of the causes of difficulty in the United States. So it would be with us. Looking at the agricultural interests of Upper Canada, manufacturing of Lower Canada, and maritime interests of Lower Provinces, in respect to a tariff, a Federal Government would be a mediator. No general feeling of patriotism exists in the United States. In occasions of difficulty each man sticks to his individual State. Mr. Stephens, the present Vice-President, was a strong Union man, yet when the time came, he went with his State. Similarly we should stick to our Province and not be British Americans. It would be introducing a source of radical weakness. It would ruin us in the eyes of the civilized world. All writers point out the errors of the United States. All the failings prognosticated by De Tocqueville are shown to be fulfilled.

John A. Macdonald, a key supporter of British North American union.

John A. Macdonald, Discussion by the Fathers of Confederation, October 24, 1864.

Ever since the [American] union was formed the difficulty of what is called "states' rights" has existed, and this had much to do in bringing on the present unhappy war in the United States. They commenced, in fact, at the wrong end. They declared by their Constitution that each state was a sovereignty in itself, and that all the powers incident to a sovereignty belonged to each state, except those powers which, by the Constitution, were conferred upon the General Government and Congress. Here we have adopted a different system. We have strengthened the General Government. We have given the General Legislature all the great subjects of legislation. We have conferred on them, not only specifically and in detail, all the powers which are incident to sovereignty, but we have expressly declared that all subjects of general interest not distinctly and exclusively conferred upon the local governments and local legislatures, shall be conferred upon the General Government and Legislature. —— We have thus avoided that great source of weakness which has been the cause of the disruption of the United States.

Speech of John A. Macdonald, *Parliamentary Debates*, 1865.

These men were able to put aside their personal feelings in 1864 to form the Great Coalition,[9] which had as its single goal the creation of a federal union. It did not inspire their contemporaries with optimism. Brown's view of coalitions was that they resulted from the "machinations of weak men with an itch for power."[10] Macdonald was initially opposed to the federal scheme but accepted the idea of a coalition to keep some semblance of political stability. Ultimately, given their poor personal relations and the strongly partisan sectional constituency that each represented, Confederation was still a distant prospect.

THE MARITIMES AND CONFEDERATION

The tension between the two Canadas was not the only sectionalism that threatened Confederation's chances. If a larger federal union was to become a reality, it was imperative that the Maritimes —— especially New Brunswick —— be included.[11] Maritimers had every reason to be sceptical of any program that promised to join their destiny with that of their western neighbours. They were reluctant to relinquish their lucrative trade with the New England states, which any union with the Canadas would have forced them to do. Given their small population, they felt that they would be swamped in any united parliament. Clearly, any union proposal threatened what they regarded as their unique identity. They saw themselves as distant and isolated from the Canadas. There was, at that time, no physical link between the Maritimes and the Canadas. Furthermore, they saw no necessity to save the Canadians from their own follies. Why should they become embroiled in the seemingly insoluble conflict between the French and the English? They saw that their tax money would be used to benefit the Canadians, who were eager to open up the Northwest. Finally, through the urgings of Governor Arthur Gordon of New Brunswick, the old idea of a Maritime union was being resurrected in the mid-1860s.

Maritime leaders initially greeted the idea of Confederation with ambivalence. To many, the Canadian scheme seemed vaguely threatening and did not promise to resolve their difficulties.[12] Traditionally, their lack of enthusiasm has been taken as proof of their innate conservatism, but this view oversimplifies and trivializes the Maritime objections to the Confederation scheme.[13] If the Maritime politicians were to be won over to Confederation, it would take powerful arguments as well as ample amounts of eloquent speechmaking and champagne to melt away their reluctance.

However, there was a more decisive factor in Maritime opposition. Confederation arrived at a critical juncture. Many Maritimers were fearful that as the age of steam and steel arrived, their traditional economy, based on wooden shipbuilding and fishing, would relegate them to perpetual second-class status. Apprehensive about the economic transition, Maritimers felt that Confederation presented yet another menacing challenge.

Within the context of change and dislocation, and influenced by a sense of common Atlantic identity, it was natural that Maritime leaders turned first to the idea of Maritime union. The concept went back half a century but took on renewed interest as financial and political difficulties appeared to jeopardize the Maritime hope for an Intercolonial Railway. However, despite the fact that by 1863 several of the provincial legislatures were seriously debating the proposal, it died quickly. Once the Intercolonial was revived and the Canadians announced that they would cover all surveying costs for the line, Maritime union was never spoken of again.

Two unions — one that had been proposed but never implemented and one that had been tried and found severely wanting — clearly demonstrated the weakness of a domestic initiative behind Confederation. In sum, the internal situation in British North America made the prospects for a federal union slim indeed. Many political issues — such as funding for the Grand Trunk Railway, economic expansion, secularization of the clergy reserves, and separate schools — could not be resolved. If they could not, what chances did a far more encompassing plan for a federal union have?

Sectionalism, both between the Canadas and between the Maritimes and the Canadas, was a clear hindrance in the movement toward Confederation. The state of political deadlock in which the Canadas found themselves made the achievement that much more difficult. Given the domestic limitations, if a federal union was to be achieved, the impetus would have to come from outside.

THE COMING OF THE AMERICAN CIVIL WAR

THE ROOTS OF THE AMERICAN CIVIL WAR went back almost to the birth of the nation.[14] In adopting the Articles of Confederation in 1781, the Americans sowed the seeds of their own destruction. They recognized the necessity of providing Congress with some legal basis for its authority. However, because of the fear of a central power coupled with the desire of the states to retain their sovereignty, the articles created a national government that was subordinate to the power of the state governments. The ultimate superiority of the state governments lay in the fact that any amendment to the articles required the unanimous consent of the states. Herein lay the crucial weakness that in 80 years would lead to war.

ROOTS OF THE SECESSION MOVEMENT

As the northern and southern states grew, they developed remarkably different economies and cultures.[15] The North was mainly industrial and urban, while the South was largely agrarian and rural. These basic difference could not be ignored, and sectionalism became the major political reality — much as it would be in British North America — for almost half a century. Since the Nullification Crisis of President Andrew Jackson's administration of the 1830s, the divisions between the sections had been hardening.

Southern opinion was inflamed by the abolitionist movement[16] headed by William Lloyd Garrison, the Nat Turner insurrection, and the heated debates in the Virginia legislature over the issue of slavery. Slavery lay at the heart of the sectional split. Yet it was as much an effect as a cause of the difference. As important and emotional an issue as it undoubtedly was, slavery was caught up in the larger controversy of sectionalism. Lincoln was to make clear on many occasions that the Civil War was not fought over the issue of slavery. Rather, it was to preserve the union. The issue of states' rights, rather than slavery, was the fundamental cause of the Civil War.

SLAVERY AND WESTERN EXPANSION

The sectional crisis heated up considerably as the United States began expanding rapidly toward the Pacific. The question arose as to what should be done with the lands acquired from Mexico. The extreme northern position was advanced by David Wilmot, who called for the exclusion of slavery from that area. The radical southern position was put forth best by John Calhoun of South Carolina, who argued, on the grounds of the property rights set out in the Fifth Amendment, that slavery should be permitted in all territories. Two moderate positions emerged between the two extremes. One was that of President James Polk, who argued that the Missouri Compromise line should be extended to the Pacific Ocean. The other was that of Senator Stephen Douglas of Illinois, who championed the idea of popular sovereignty, whereby the voters in each territory, irrespective of its location, would vote to allow or to exclude slavery in their territory.

With the passage of the Compromise of 1850, California was admitted as a free state.[17] This upset the precarious balance of 15 free and 15 slave states. Henry Clay — "The Great Compromiser" — had fashioned this compromise, as he had done 30 years earlier with Missouri.[18] The other side of the 1850 accord was that in the remainder of the Mexican cession, slavery would be determined by popular sovereignty. In violating the basic provision of the Missouri Compromise, which prevented slavery north of the 36°30' line, Congress opened the door to a host of problems.

THE UNDERGROUND RAILWAY

THE ROAD TO FREEDOM for more than 30 000 American blacks was the legendary Underground Railway. Originally started by the Quakers of Pennsylvania in the early years of the nineteenth century, the "railway" was as much an idea as a physical fact; as much a hope as a reality. There were no stations; no track; no cars; no engines; no rolling stock. The idea of the Underground Railway was a clandestine operation carried on by thousands of courageous individuals who were linked by their hatred of slavery and their love of freedom. Perhaps foremost among them was Harriet Tubman, nicknamed "the Black Moses," who led more than 2000 slaves to freedom and who had an unheard-of $40 000 price on her head. Another prominent leader in the movement was the Quaker abolitionist Levi Coffin, known as the "president" of the Underground Railway, who hid more than 100 escaped slaves in his Cincinnati home every year.

In order to deceive bounty hunters, runaway slaves and the "conductors" on the Underground Railway used many railroad terms. In addition, the Underground Railway, which more accurately was a long series of safe havens, developed an intricate system of connection "lines" that included many routes into Upper Canada. Those safe stops — or "stations" — were seldom direct. More often than not they zig-zagged, changed direction, or even doubled back — all to throw off the pursuers.

By the 1820s, the Underground Railway had established definite routes into Upper Canada. Runaway slaves were passed through a network of "stations" throughout Ohio, Michigan, New York, and Pennsylvania. Cities such as Buffalo, Rochester, Cincinnati, and Detroit were prominent jumping-off points. The ends of the road to freedom in Upper Canada were numerous. Many were concentrated on the shores of Lake Erie, in towns such as Windsor, Amherstburg, and Sandwich. Moving further away from the border, places such as Chatham, St. Catharines, Hamilton, Brantford,

Harriet Tubman was called "the Black Moses" because she led more than 2000 slaves out of bondage on the Underground Railway. Slaveowners offered an unheard-of reward of $40 000 for her capture.

Oakville, and Toronto became home for hundreds of fugitives. Moving further east, Ottawa, Montreal, and Saint John all became end points for large numbers of runaways.

Hiding in cellars, in swamps, and on steamers, and travelling mostly at night, made for an incredibly arduous journey. Not only the physical realities — little food or water; few, if any, possessions; long and dangerous marches — but the emotional terror of being stalked and the psychological pain of leaving behind loved ones made it a nightmarish experience. But through it all there was a beacon of freedom that provided the needed comfort.

> I'm on my way to Canada
> That cold and distant land
> The dire effects of slavery
> I can no longer stand —
> Farewell, old master,
> Don't come after me.
> I'm on my way to Canada
> Where coloured men are free.

"The Free Slave," by George W. Clark, an early abolitionist.

Within a short time a small group of southern legislators began the fateful attempt to establish slavery in that part of the Louisiana Purchase previously recognized as free soil. They allied themselves with Douglas, who hoped to pass a bill establishing local government for Kansas and Nebraska. Douglas saw the admission of these states as a means of facilitating the construction of a transcontinental railway whose eastern terminus might be in his home town of Chicago. Southern political allies supported Calhoun's position that slavery ought to be permitted in all territories, and that the part of the Missouri Compromise that prohibited it should be struck down.

Douglas attempted a compromise through the passage of the Kansas–Nebraska Act (1854), which repealed the Missouri Compromise and replaced it with the doctrine of popular sovereignty. Northern critics rose in protest against the upsetting of the Missouri Compromise and raised fears that under the Kansas–Nebraska Act any territory could potentially be opened up to slavery. With the Kansas–Nebraska controversy, the free soilers were now pitted against the defenders of slavery.

DEEPENING SECTIONALISM

In demanding the repeal of the Missouri Compromise, southern politicians had put their northern Democratic allies in an untenable position in their home constituencies. Their action was doubly counterproductive because it helped create a powerful anti-slavery party that threatened to destroy southern control of the federal government. Those who opposed the extension of slavery could find little solace in either the Whig or Democratic parties. Thus, the Republican party was born in the mid-1850s out of an amalgam of protectionist Whigs, disgruntled Democrats, and Free Soilers.

The 1856 election dramatically revealed just how sectionally divided the nation was. James Buchanan, the Democratic standard-bearer, won by carrying every southern state with the exception of Maryland, while the Republican nominee, John Fremont, carried all but five of the free states. Increasingly, the Republican party spoke for the North while the Democrats represented the South.

In the late 1850s, the Dred Scott decision aggravated the conflict.[19] Scott had been a slave in the state of Missouri. He had moved with a new owner to Illinois, then sued for his freedom. The Supreme Court not only denied the contention that residence in a free territory made a slave free, but furthermore denied the right of a slave, as less than a full citizen, to petition the court. Northerners, even those of a moderate stripe, were shocked. The decision upheld the southern argument that Congress could not ban slavery from any territory. By implication, it denied the legitimacy of Douglas's theory of popular sovereignty: if Congress could not prohibit slavery, then neither could a state legislature. Republicans were outraged as their position — that Congress had the right to keep slavery out of the territories — had been ruled unconstitutional.

THE SLAVERY QUESTION

The slavery question came centre stage during the Lincoln–Douglas debates of 1858. Abraham Lincoln argued that the principal difference between himself and his opponent — and between Republicans and northern Democrats — was that he and his party regarded the institution of slavery as morally repugnant, while Stephen Douglas and his party were indifferent to it. In order to defend his doctrine of popular sovereignty in light of the recent Dred Scott decision, Douglas articulated his Freeport Doctrine. This theory held that slavery could not be established and maintained in a territory unless a slave code protecting slaves as property was enacted by the local legislature. Douglas won the battle but lost the war. He narrowly defeated Lincoln in the senatorial race, but his Freeport Doctrine made him totally unacceptable to southerners as a presidential candidate.

In the famous Lincoln–Douglas debates in 1858, slavery became the key issue. Lincoln attempted to paint the crucial difference between himself and his senatorial opponent by arguing that he was morally opposed to the extension of slavery.

THE CASE OF DRED SCOTT

ONE OF THE MOST SIGNIFICANT Supreme Court decisions was *Dred Scott v. Sanford*. In deciding on the issue of Scott's citizenship and in further ruling that Congress could not prohibit slavery in the territories, this decision was a major cause of the Civil War. Dred Scott, held as a slave in Missouri, was taken by his owner into the free state of Illinois. After being brought back to Missouri, Scott was sold to Sanford, a citizen of New York. Scott then brought suit against Sanford, claiming that he had become a free man by residing in Illinois. The case went up the judicial ladder, with the final appeal being launched by Scott in the Supreme Court. Chief Justice Tawney delivered the opinion of the court.

> The question is simply this: can a Negro, whose ancestors were imported into this country and sold as slaves, become a member of the political community formed and brought into existence by the Constitution of the United States, and as such become entitled to all the rights, and privileges, and immunities, guaranteed by that instrument to the citizen. One of these rights is the privilege of suing in the court of the United States....
>
> The words "people of the United States" and "citizens" are synonymous terms.... They both describe the political body who, according to our republican institutions, form the sovereignty, and who hold the power and conduct the government through their representatives. They are what we familiarly call the "sovereign people," and every citizen is one of this people, and a constituent member of this sovereignty. The question before us is, whether the class of persons described in the plea of abatement compose a portion of this people, and are constituent members of this sovereignty. We think they are not, and that they are not included, and were not intended to be included, under the word "citizens" in the Constitution, and can, therefore, claim none of the rights and privileges which that instrument provides for and secures to citizens of the United States. On the contrary, they were at that time considered as a subordinate and inferior class of beings, who had been subjugated by the dominant race, and whether emancipated or not, yet remained subject to their authority, and had no rights or privileges but such as those who held the power and the government might choose to grant them....
>
> ...But it is too clear for dispute, that the enslaved African race were not intended to be included, and formed no part of the people who framed and adopted this Declaration; for if the language, as understood in that day, would embrace them, the conduct of the distinguished men who framed the Declaration of Independence would have been utterly and flagrantly inconsistent with the principles they asserted; and instead of the sympathy of mankind, to which they so confidently appealed, they would have deserved and received universal rebuke and reprobation.
>
> No one of that race had ever migrated to the United States voluntarily; all of them had been brought here as articles of merchandise. The number that had been emancipated at

that time were but few in comparison with those held in slavery; and they were identified in the public mind with the race to which they belonged, and regarded as part of the slave population rather than the free. It is obvious that they were not even in the minds of the framers of the Constitution when they were conferring special rights and privileges upon the citizens of a State in every other part of the Union.

And upon a full and careful consideration of the subject, the court is of the opinion that, upon the facts stated in the plea of abatement, Dred Scott was not a citizen of Missouri within the meaning of the Constitution of the United States, and not entitled as such to sue in its courts....

Upon these considerations, it is the opinion of the court that the Act of Congress which prohibited a citizen from holding and owning property of this kind in the territory of the United States north of the line therein mentioned [36 − 30], is not warranted by the Constitution, and is therefore void; and that neither Dred Scott himself, nor any of his family, were made free by being carried into this territory; even if they have been carried there by the owner, with the intention of becoming a permanent resident.

Emotions boiled over with the re-emergence of the unstable abolitionist John Brown.[20] He had first gained national prominence in 1856 during the "Bleeding Kansas" controversy, when he led a raid at Pottawattomie Creek. Brown again aroused southern hostility in October 1859 when he led another raid against the federal arsenal at Harper's Ferry, Virginia. Southerners' panic quickly became outrage as they learned that respectable northerners had backed the plot.

THE 1860 ELECTION AND SOUTHERN SECESSION

The climax was reached in the terminally divisive election of 1860. By sweeping almost all the free states, Lincoln was able to capture a slim plurality. However, his opponents polled over 1 million votes more than he did. John Breckingridge, representing the southern wing of the Democratic party, easily carried most of the South. The fractured Democrats also ran Douglas, who won only the electoral votes of Missouri and half of New Jersey. John Bell, running under the Constitutional Union party, won three border states.

South Carolina interpreted Lincoln's election as an incitement to secession from the union. At a hastily called state convention in December 1860, South Carolina delegates repealed their ratification of the U.S. constitution. In less than six months, their lead was followed by the six gulf states. Organizing themselves at a convention in Montgomery, Alabama, they established the Confederate States of America and selected Jefferson Davis of Mississippi as their president. The Civil War that followed was a bloody sectional and ideological conflict that would have serious repercussions not only for the United States but also for British North America.

EXTERNAL PRESSURES AND INFLUENCES

B Y THE 1860s, developments in Great Britain as well as the United States were influencing events in British North America. Since the mid-1840s, Britain had been following a policy of free trade, and the colonies were no longer regarded as precious economic assets to the imperial metropolis. A few British imperial critics, such as Benjamin Disraeli, went so far as to declare the colonies "millstones around the Mother Country's neck." And when the united Province of Canada erected a tariff in 1859 to protect Canadian manufactures against British as well as other foreign imports, it raised questions in Britain about the value of the colonies as markets.

THE IMPERIAL NUDGE

British colonial policy gradually came to reflect changes in thinking about the colonies. A group of British anti-imperialists, known as "little Englanders," questioned the need to maintain colonies at all. Troubled by the continual efforts of the Canadian colonies to secure financing for railways and works of defence, one English Liberal proposed that they "become an independent state…and build up their own future without relying upon us." While such extreme views never won full acceptance, they did signal a change in imperial policy. British authorities in the 1860s indicated a growing desire to have colonies, such as those in North America, assume a greater financial responsibility for their own defence in order to reduce the burden on the British taxpaying public.

Proposals for federation, such as that suggested for British North America, won increasing sympathy in Britain. Many British officials welcomed any scheme that might permit the colonies to stand on their own feet and reduce the need for continued financial and military support. Edward Cardwell, the head of the Colonial Office, put the matter succinctly in a June 1864 dispatch to the governor of New Brunswick. The Confederation scheme, he wrote, was "in the strong and deliberate opinion of the British government an object much to be desired." Britain's desire to cut costs was evident by the 1860s, particularly when it came to dealing with requests for the financing of intercolonial railways. When trouble broke out in the United States, Britain showed even more interest in bringing about some form of British North American union.

VISIONS OF MANIFEST DESTINY

For much of the nineteenth century, the United States had been expanding and spreading its influence. By the 1840s, the Americans' conviction that it was their "manifest destiny" to control North America was deeply rooted.[21] A vociferous American expansionist expressed the widespread sentiment in an 1844 address to the Democratic Convention:

> Land enough — land enough! Make way, I say, for the young American Buffalo — he has not yet got land enough…. I tell you, we will give him Oregon for his summer shade, and the region of Texas as his winter pasture. [*Applause*] Like all his race he wants salt, too. Well, he shall have the use of the two oceans — the mighty Pacific and the turbulent Atlantic shall be his…. He shall not stop his career until he slakes his thirst in the frozen ocean. [*Cheers*]

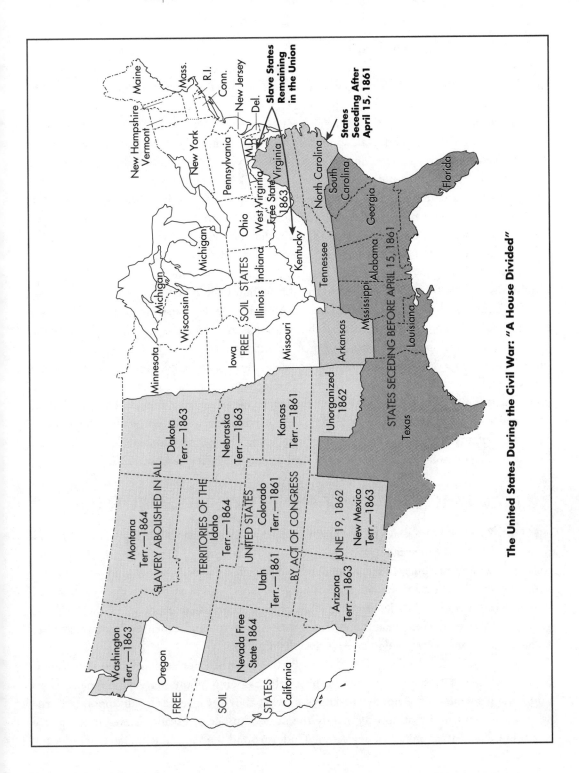

The United States During the Civil War: "A House Divided"

Many thought that continental expansion was becoming part of God's plan for the American republic. American expansion had a great appeal to frontier expansionists in Congress and their business supporters. It would open up markets for northeastern manufacturers, provide rich sources of raw staples, and give fresh impetus to American commerce abroad.

American continental expansion in the 1840s had brought a series of frictions with Great Britain. In the Aroostook Valley along the Maine–New Brunswick border, American lumber interests had succeeded in 1842 in winning a boundary settlement favourable to the United States' claims. The Democratic president, James K. Polk, had been instrumental in this acquisition. After campaigning in 1844 on the slogan "fifty-four forty or fight," he had secured the Oregon Territory as far north as the 49th parallel in 1846. America's southwestern territories had been acquired through war (1846–48) with the country's southern neighbour, Mexico. After that scattered and decisive conflict, Mexico not only gave up all claims to Texas, but ceded the whole of New Mexico and California to the United States for $15 million. By that acquisition, 1 300 000 km^2 was added to the continental United States.

The outbreak of the American Civil War in April 1861 only resurrected calls for "Manifest Destiny." Many leading northerners shared the conviction that Britain's sympathies were with the Confederacy. A small but vocal group of American expansionists in the North began urging that once the southern secessionist movement was quelled, the country should turn its attention to the annexation of British North America. Although President Abraham Lincoln showed no interest in such annexationist schemes, the idea was trumpeted by his secretary of state, William Seward. In one famous statement, Seward declared: "Nature designs that this whole continent…shall be sooner or later within the magic circle of the American Union." The vision was more fanciful than real, but it undoubtedly weighed on the minds of the leaders of British North America.

THE AMERICAN IMPACT ON CONFEDERATION

THE CIVIL WAR ushered in a period of crisis in Anglo–American relations. A series of events raised fears of American aggression and imparted a sense of urgency to the movement for federal union. Although the fears were unfounded, many British North Americans continued to believe that a victorious and perhaps vengeful North posed a threat to the weak and disunited British colonies. In a landmark 1865 speech, George-Étienne Cartier of the *Parti Bleu* went so far as to declare that the colonies had either "to obtain British North American Confederation or be absorbed in an American Confederation."[22]

On the surface, it appeared as though British North America supported the North. Many in Canada saw the war rather simplistically as being "about slavery." As many as 40 000 Canadians joined the northern armies in what they regarded as a self-appointed crusade.[23] It is estimated that approximately the same number of escaped slaves found a safe haven in Canada after their journey on the Underground Railway. In less than a decade, the number of blacks in the province more than doubled from the 1850 level of 30 000. However, these facts could not disguise the reality: because of diplomatic pressure, Canada was forced into the uncomfortable position of siding with the South.

Britain, requiring southern cotton for its textile industry, found it expedient to support the Confederate cause. That support was substantial, and the victorious North would subsequently demand compensation in the so-called "Alabama claims," which involved a suit for damages inflicted by British-made ships sold to the Confederacy. Being a colony, British North America had little choice but to follow the British lead. Furthermore, as the war was gradually seen not as a campaign to end slavery but rather as a military attempt to preserve the union, sympathy for the South, especially in conservative circles, was heightened.

THE *TRENT* AFFAIR

The first incident to worsen relations between the United States and British North America was the short-lived *Trent* affair of 1861. The Civil War had just broken out when two delegates of the Confederacy boarded a British steamer, the *Trent*, which was bound for England. Their purpose was to negotiate an alliance between the Confederacy and England. The North wanted to forestall any assistance from across the Atlantic, so northern naval personnel stopped the *Trent* in international waters, boarded it, and took away the two southerners at gunpoint. The British were outraged.

In late 1861, about 14 000 British troops were sent to British North America. The St. Lawrence was frozen over, and the eastern end of the Grand Trunk Railway was inaccessible. Thus the troops landed at Saint John and began a horrendous overland journey of over 1000 km through the snow. This event did much to rekindle the desire to build the Intercolonial Railway, which would provide the Maritimes with some physical link to the Canadas. It also produced a great imperial–colonial debate over the question of defence. The British argued that the Canadians must tax themselves to raise a militia for their own defence. The Canadians responded that war would be the result of rivalry between Britain and the United States, and that therefore the British should bear most of the burden for defence. When the British refused to vote a major increase in defence expenditures, the Province of Canada attempted to pass a Militia Bill in 1862. It called for the raising of a militia of 50 000 men at a cost of almost $500 000. But the French-Canadian members voted against the proposal, and the Macdonald–Cartier government went down to defeat.

THE ST. ALBANS RAID

The next major irritant in the relations between British North America and its southern neighbour again arose as a result of the Civil War. By a quirk of good timing it took place in October 1864, at the very moment when the delegates were assembling in Quebec to hammer out the specific terms of Confederation. The South was becoming increasingly desperate, particularly after the battles of Gettysburg and Vicksburg, which underscored the certainty of their ultimate defeat. Thus, they came to embrace wild and daring schemes that might forestall their demise. A band of 23 Confederate troops led by a former Confederate officer, Bennett H. Young, launched a raid on St. Albans in northern Vermont. The raiders started from Canada, and after robbing three American banks of over $250 000 and killing two Americans, escaped back across the border to Canada.

The raiders were apprehended by Canadian authorities and brought to trial in Montreal. Judge C.J. Coursol released them, arguing that he had no jurisdiction because they had done nothing wrong in the eyes of Canadian law. A number of them were subsequently re-arrested and charged in Superior Court. However, again they were acquitted. This time the court accepted the defence that they had acted as belligerents. The North was outraged. They claimed that the Canadians were failing to act neutrally as well as failing to police their borders adequately.[24]

The Americans were quick to respond. By a strange coincidence, on the very day that the Montreal court released the raiders, the House of Representatives passed a motion calling for the abrogation of the Reciprocity Treaty. In addition, an executive order was passed requiring Canadians to carry passports when travelling to the United States. Further, the U.S. gave six months' notice of its intention to terminate the Rush–Bagot agreement. Finally, the U.S. general in charge of the northeast frontier was given orders to pursue all raiders "into Canada if necessary and destroy them." In spite of all this, the crisis was not viewed as being as serious as the *Trent* affair three years earlier.

THE THREAT OF A MOBILIZED NORTH

When the Civil War drew to a close in 1865, new fears arose in British North America. Influenced by the rhetoric of Secretary of State William Seward, prominent Canadians like Thomas D'Arcy McGee of Montreal West warned that "the acquisition of Canada" remained "the first ambition of the American Confederacy [*sic*]." The presence of a mobilized Union army so close to the British North American border only added to the apprehensions. Out of a population of 18.9 million in 1861, the Union had mustered an army of some 2 million — one of the largest in the world at that time. By the war's end, they were battle-trained veterans. Given British North America's grave state of disunity, the miserable state of its defences, and British indifference, what chance would it have against the vast might of the United States?

THE FENIAN SCARE

The Fenian Raids of 1866 were an added prod to Confederation, and also came at a critical juncture. If a federal union was to become a reality, the Maritimes had to be included. If they were not, then it was back to the old system of political deadlock within the united Province of Canada. If the Maritimes were to be part of the scheme, then, given New Brunswick's geographical position, its acceptance was crucial. However, in the 1865 New Brunswick election, Leonard Tilley and the Unionists had gone down to defeat, and A.J. Smith had been swept into office on an anti-Confederation platform.

A dramatic portrayal of the Battle of Ridgeway, June 1866. This painting tends to glorify the small skirmish. The short encounter was marked by much confusion; it ended when the British regular soldiers approached and the Fenian raiders took flight.

The Fenian raiders made several incursions into Canada in 1866. While the Fenians appeared to be members of a dangerous Irish-American brotherhood, they were really a rag-tag band of extremists who constituted no real threat to British North America. In the spring of 1866, the Fenians held a "convention" in Eastport and Portland, Maine, and then launched a small "strike" in neighbouring New Brunswick. Five Fenians crossed the border, held up a customs officer on Indian Island, tore down the Union Jack, and then beat a hasty retreat. The June 1866 Battle of Ridgeway in the Niagara peninsula of Canada West was more of a minor skirmish than a battle. About 800 Fenians were met and thrown back by a slightly larger force of Canadian militia, leaving six Canadians dead and another 30 wounded. As soon as the Fenians crossed back to the American side, government authorities arrested the ringleaders and took away their stock of weapons.[25]

The Fenian threat had its greatest effect in New Brunswick. Shortly after the election of Smith's anti-unionist government, fears of Fenian actions had been stirred by the Fenian convention at nearby Portland in April 1865. A few months later, Lieutenant-Governor Arthur Gordon succeeded in convincing the anti-unionists to accept a new election early in 1866. The looming threat of Fenian raids added much to Leonard Tilley's argument for federal union. With the support of the governor, timely appeals to defence and loyalty, and some lavish promises of financial aid from Canada, Tilley and the Unionists were returned to office. In certain critically important New Brunswick localities — notably Charlotte County — the Unionists won over the populace with a combination of appeals to loyalty and promises of greater material progress.[26]

THE FENIAN BROTHERHOOD

FENIAN WAS THE POPULAR NAME for members of the Irish Republican Brotherhood (IRB), a secret society formed in Ireland in 1858 to secure Irish independence from Britain. Its titular head was James Stephens, who organized the underground network with the help of funds collected by his American deputy, John O'Mahony. That American wing became quite powerful, amassing a war chest of half a million dollars and an army of 10 000 American Civil War veterans.

In 1865, a major rift occurred within Fenian ranks. One group, led by O'Mahony, favoured an uprising in Ireland. The other, headed by William Roberts, wanted to invade British North America and use it as a base of operations. When the British government took stiff preventive measures against a possible Irish uprising, all North American Fenians, including a minuscule group in Toronto headed by Michael Murphy, embraced the Roberts plan. In a September 1865 convention in Cincinnati, the Fenians adopted the slogan of "On to Canada."

Grandiose plans of repeated invasions of various points between Windsor and Nova Scotia were drawn up. Funds were accumulated, supplies obtained, and troops marshalled. By the end of 1865, the Fenian Brotherhood stood poised to attack Canada.

One Fenian ditty captured well the spirit of the movement:

We are the Fenian Brotherhood
Skilled in the arts of war.
And we're going to fight for Ireland
The land that we adore.
Many battles we have won
Along with the boys in blue.
And we'll go and capture Canada
For we've nothing else to do.

The attacks did indeed come. On June 1, 1866, a force of Fenians led by John O'Neil took Fort Erie. The following day they were met and defeated by a larger Canadian force at Ridgeway. Less than a week later, almost 2000 Fenians crossed over into Canada East at Pigeon Hill and Frelighsburg. After plundering, they retreated without a fight. Other sporadic raids occurred. O'Mahony himself led an earlier border raid against New Brunswick in April 1866. The Fenians tested the Canadian defences at Prescott. Even after Confederation, the Fenians persisted. O'Neill, then president of the organization, launched two small raids against the Quebec border in 1870, the most prominent of which was at Eccles Hill. In the following year the Fenians attempted to attack in the area around Pembina, Manitoba. Perhaps their most noteworthy accomplishment in the post-Confederation era was James Whelan's assassination of D'Arcy McGee.

The movement itself seemed doomed to expire. The Roman Catholic church condemned it because of its secret nature. Its organization, never strong, collapsed when most of the leaders found their way into jail. After the Washington Treaty (1870), the American government made an attempt to curb the movement's more blatant activities. Finally, the Canadian government commissioned more than 30 000 soldiers to meet the challenge. After the movement expired, most Irish-American republicans drifted into the more tightly disciplined *Clan-an-Gael* organization. The Clan contributed men and money to the campaign for Irish Home Rule. The IRB attempted to continue as an underground organization into the twentieth century.

THE ENDING OF RECIPROCITY

An outside economic influence was added to this long list of military and political factors that nudged Canadians along the path to union. In the spring of 1866, after considerable debate, the United States cancelled the ten-year-old Reciprocity Treaty. The Americans cited several reasons for the decision. They argued that existing tariffs, and particularly the A.T. Galt tariff of 1859, were protectionist measures that violated the spirit of free trade. Some American congressmen and trade authorities claimed that Canadians were benefiting more from the 1854 treaty than the Americans were. A few advocates of Manifest Destiny envisioned cancellation leaving British North America economically crippled, thus inviting annexation.

The impact of the cancellation of the treaty was difficult to gauge.[27] The experience of losing American reciprocity evoked for some colonial politicians memories of 1846, when Britain embraced free trade and left Canada almost economically abandoned. While it probably played a small role in the defeat of Smith's anti-unionists in New Brunswick, the action came too late to have much impact on the overall movement for Confederation. Growing numbers of British North Americans, however, now recognized that some new form of economic union was imperative.

THE MEANING OF CONFEDERATION

Canadian Confederation, like the American Civil War, has often been interpreted as a heroic episode in nation-building. Macdonald, Cartier, Brown, and the other British North American leaders were certainly important in assembling the building blocks of the Canadian national edifice. Yet external pressures and influences — emanating from the United States and Britain — were as crucial in the creation of the nation as the constitution-making efforts of the

Fathers of Confederation. Perhaps historian P.B. Waite was correct when he wrote: "Confederation was not, except in Canada West, what is usually referred to as a popular movement. It was imposed on British North America by ingenuity, luck, courage, and sheer force."[28] The story of Confederation was largely one of American pressures, political coalitions, and Colonial Office blandishments.

ACTIVITIES

KEY TERMS AND CONCEPTS

Identify and briefly explain the historical significance of the following terms and concepts:

- Political deadlock
- Sectionalism
- Double majority
- Revolving ministries
- "Little Englanders"
- "Rep by pop"
- Great Coalition
- Maritime union
- Fenianism
- Reciprocity
- "Fifty-four forty or fight"
- States' rights
- Abolitionism
- The *Trent* affair
- Popular sovereignty
- Secession
- Legislative/federal union
- Manifest Destiny

QUESTIONS FOR DISCUSSION

1. In his writings on political deadlock in the 1850s and 1860s, Paul G. Cornell has argued that the Great Coalition of 1864 was "the main spring of the Confederation movement." How valid is this common assessment? To what extent does it ignore the role of the Maritimers in the coming of the union?

2. Why did the American Civil War erupt in the 1860s? Assess the relative importance of various factors in the development of the conflict.

3. It is often argued that Britain showed "apparent indifference" to British North America's fate in the early 1860s. Did Britain aid the Confederation movement? If so, how?

4. In 1865, George-Étienne Cartier claimed that the British North American colonies faced a choice between Confederation or absorption into the American union. How valid or, indeed, accurate was this claim?

5. "The great majority of nations have been formed, not by people who desired intensely to live together, but rather by people who could not live separately." Assess this statement, made by French-Canadian historian Jean Charles Bonenfant in 1966. To what extent does the analysis apply to French Canadians, Maritimers, and Upper Canadians in the 1860s?

6. Compare the British attitude toward British North America in the decade before Confederation with the British attitude toward the Thirteen Colonies a century earlier.

7. Is there any evidence that the Maritimes were dragged into Confederation? Does their

subsequent history indicate that they made a wise decision in joining the federal union in 1867?

8. Which twentieth-century leaders considered themselves to be John A. Macdonald's heirs? How valid are their respective claims?

MAKING HISTORICAL CONNECTIONS

Timelines can be very useful in organizing and establishing the sequence of historical events. A series of events or chronology can also be used to establish historical cause-and-effect relationships. This exercise tests your ability to establish a chronology and to draw connections between related events.

Following are two sets of events occurring in the United States and British North America from the 1840s to 1878.

United States

(1) Secession of South Carolina
(2) Kansas–Nebraska Act
(3) Dred Scott Decision
(4) Ending of Reciprocity Treaty
(5) Missouri Compromise
(6) Lincoln Elected President
(7) St. Albans Raid
(8) Lincoln–Douglas Debates
(9) Fenian Raids
(10) Outbreak of Civil War
(11) Trent Affair
(12) Compromise of 1850

British North America

(1) London Conference
(2) Granting of Responsible Government
(3) Queen Victoria Signs British North America Act
(4) Morin–McNab Ministry
(5) Prince Edward Island Enters Confederation
(6) Defeat of Taché–Macdonald Ministry
(7) Charlottetown Conference
(8) Manitoba Enters Confederation
(9) Formation of Great Coalition
(10) Britain Adopts Free Trade
(11) British Columbia Enters Confederation
(12) Quebec Resolutions

Using the lists, complete the following exercise.

1. Date accurately each of the events or items listed for the United States and British North America.

2. Arrange the assorted events in chronological order in two timelines.

3. Cross-reference the events in the United States with those in British North America. Try to identify related events and any connections between them. Assess the impact of one event on another in the sequence of events.

4. Develop one or two hypotheses concerning events that are directly related to one another.

CHANGING FORMS OF FEDERALISM

THE DECADE FOLLOWING 1864 was a momentous one in Canada's history. During those years, one achievement followed another as British North American politicians began to take greater responsibility for managing their colonies' affairs. By an Act of the British Parliament, the Dominion of Canada came officially into being on July 1, 1867. Through the acquisition of Rupert's Land from the Hudson's Bay Company two years later, the Canadian government was able to increase the land area of the young nation by more than 300 percent. Also within that decade, three additional provinces — Manitoba (1870), British Columbia (1871), and Prince Edward Island (1873) — were added to the original four.

In designing the government, the Fathers of Confederation encountered perhaps their most challenging task. Fundamentally, what they were addressing was the question of power. Who would have it? How would it be divided? How would it be administered? How would it be controlled? In addition, they had many other weighty issues to resolve. What would they utilize from the British parliamentary system and the American republican system? Would Canada be a federal or a unitary state? If it were the former, would it be centralized or decentralized? What would be the method of representation — regional, equal, by population, or by appointment — in the bicameral legislature? Or would it even be a bicameral legislature? How would power be apportioned between those two houses? Would Confederation be a "compact" between the joining provinces as well as between the "two founding races"? Where would ultimate sovereignty reside? In selecting as well as rejecting aspects of both the British and American systems, the hope was that Canada would obtain "the best of both worlds."

The birth of the Dominion was marked by a fair measure of genuine foresight, but also by political expediency and fundamental economic considerations. For some of the leading Canadian statesmen, Confederation promised new political opportunities and an escape from what John A. Macdonald called "the dreary wastes of colonial politics." That they were acting in the interests of the dominant commercial and financial interests of the colonies need hardly be debated. The rising industrial and financial élites of Montreal, Toronto, and Nova Scotia were not only among the strongest supporters of union; they were also among its most obvious beneficiaries.[1]

Whatever their motivations and interests, the Fathers of Confederation created a viable and durable structure. It was a federal union based on the British parliamentary model but incorporating elements of the newer American federal system. It would prove to be a flexible form of union, one that addressed the need of the time as well as providing a framework for growth, development, and change. Over the first 25 years of its existence, Canadian federalism would evolve in ways markedly different from the American version. The Dominion would be rounded out, expanding territorially to the Pacific. Yet continuing economic depression, and the consequent failure of Macdonald's national policies to produce the expected results, helped to promote a rising tide of provincialism; and a series of British constitutional decisions had a decentralizing effect on the overall federal system.[2]

CONFEDERATION ACHIEVED, 1864–1867

THE ROAD TO CONFEDERATION was paved with diplomacy and compromise. In August 1864, the Canadian leaders were able to pry an invitation from the Maritimes to attend a conference to be held in Charlottetown.[3] The original purpose of the meeting was to discuss the old Atlantic idea of a Maritime union. The reality, however, was that such a combination was never a serious possibility — a fact underscored by Newfoundland's refusal to send delegates. Given Prince Edward Island's lukewarm support for the scheme, it was felt most propitious to convene the conference in Charlottetown to increase the likelihood that the island's leaders would attend. In fact, so reluctant were the Maritimers that in the words of historian P.B. Waite, "It was only by Canadian initiative — interference perhaps — that the Charlottetown Conference was held at all."[4]

THE CHARLOTTETOWN CONFERENCE

The premier of Prince Edward Island, John Gray, was elected chairman as the proceedings opened on September 1, 1864. The 15 delegates from the three Atlantic colonies quickly decided to postpone the discussion of Maritime union until they heard what the Canadians had to say. The leading members of the Canadian delegation were well rehearsed and briefed. They impressed their hosts with their forceful arguments. Macdonald and Cartier both talked persuasively about the benefits of a British North American union. Galt explained the financial arrangements of Confederation, whereby the central government would assume the debts of the provinces that joined as well as some of their revenue-raising powers, and would also pay them an annual per capita subsidy.

The warmth of the gregarious Canadians did much to dissolve Maritime reticence. In fact, after George Brown's speech on the constitutional aspects of Confederation on the following Monday, the Maritime delegates were "unanimous in believing Confederation to be highly desirable, if satisfactory terms could be agreed on." During that third session, Brown outlined the two fundamental problems of federalism. The first concerned the structure and composition of the bicameral legislature, while the second involved the crucial division of powers between the central and local governments.

The Charlottetown Conference was a watershed in Canadian history. Without having entered the realm of specifics, the delegates had been successful in obtaining a general consensus on the principle of a federal union. Certainly there were many vexing issues, ranging from the nature of representation in the Upper House to how federal appointments would be made, that begged for resolution. In fact, other than Brown and perhaps Galt, the Canadians, by and large, had dealt only in generalities. But they had developed a common direction, a united purpose, and a genuine national spirit.

THE QUEBEC CONFERENCE

On October 10, 1864, 33 delegates, including two from Newfoundland, met in Quebec City to flesh out the specifics of the new federation.[5] Significantly, almost all of them had extensive business interests in banking, timber, land, or railways. A note of urgency pervaded their deliberations because of the St. Albans Raid, which occurred only nine days after the conference opened. Like the discussions of the preceding month, these too were held in private.

Using Brown's ideas of federation that he had outlined in Charlottetown as a basis, the politicians began the laborious task of establishing a constitution for the new nation. On some issues there was easy agreement, while on others there was great disagreement. All agreed that ties with Britain would be retained and that "the well-understood principles of the British constitution" would be adhered to "as far as our circumstances will permit."[6] There was also consensus about the fact that it would be a "federation" — meaning that there would be more than one level of government.[7] There would be a national government that would address the needs common to all, and there would also be local or provincial governments that would look after regional concerns. There was also agreement that the federal parliament would be bicameral.

Delegates to the Quebec Conference, October 1864, which produced the 72 Resolutions, the basis of the British North America Act.

However, many issues caused serious dissension and division. How power would be shared between the two levels of government caused considerable debate. The question of representation, both in the lower and the upper house, brought on a debate of crisis proportions. The financial terms of Confederation also took much time to resolve. The same could be said of the question of federal appointments.

The Fathers of Confederation were definitely not radical. They were highly suspicious of both abstract principles and wholesale change. As Donald Creighton pointed out, "They were mid-Victorian British colonials who had grown up in a political system which they valued, and which they had not the slightest intention of trying to change by revolution."[8] They strongly embraced the nineteenth-century belief in material progress while rejecting the eighteenth-century political values of the American and French revolutions as irrelevant and idealistic. These men wished to deal with the prosaic concerns of expansion and enterprise, not matters of the social contract and the inalienable rights of man. Thus, not surprisingly, they fashioned through a series of compromises a government that would meet and hopefully expand their interests. The resolutions, taken as a whole, are inherently conservative in nature.[9]

Each one of the main delegates at Quebec obtained something that he thought essential. As Brown was to note afterward, the Quebec scheme was "necessarily the work of concession." But, in being forced to make mutual concessions, the end product did not reflect any one of the principals' objectives exactly. Macdonald got his strong central government, but he did not obtain a legislative union that would have extinguished local governments. He outlined his two fundamental requirements: parliamentary institutions must be at the core of the new federation, and the central government must be made overwhelmingly powerful in order to offset the centrifugal tendency inherent within the new nation.

Cartier obtained provincial governments that would have control over civil and property rights, religion, and education — the things most necessary for cultural survival. Brown obtained his long-coveted aim of "rep by pop" within the House of Commons through his ingenious plan of awarding Canada East 65 seats and the other provinces seats in proportion, according to the population in the 1861 census.[10] Nevertheless, certain guarantees ensured the continuation of "French power" in the government. Furthermore, Brown took exception to the Intercolonial Railway, which he regarded as a burdensome expense on the Canadian people. He only acquiesced when he saw that Quebec insisted on the inclusion of the Maritimes in order to adjust the balance in their favour against Canada West, and Maritime acceptance could only be gained with the promise to build the railway.

STATES' AND PROVINCIAL RIGHTS ADVOCATES: JOHN C. CALHOUN AND A.A. DORION

BOTH THE UNITED STATES AND CANADA have produced a succession of public figures committed to the assertion or defence of states' or provincial rights. Two of the most prominent were John C. Calhoun of South Carolina and Antoine-Aimé Dorion of Lower Canada. While these two figures rose to prominence at different times and reflected radically different cultural traditions, they espoused some ideas that had a similar ring.

Read the following statements by Calhoun and Dorion. Compare their arguments for states' and provincial rights. Identify the main similarities and differences.

JOHN C. CALHOUN, "THE RIGHTS OF THE SOUTH" (1850)

John C. Calhoun (1782–1850) was a South Carolinian who emerged in the 1830s and 1840s as the leading spokesman for the interests of the American South. He analyzed the South's position in the Union and foresaw this agrarian, debtor region being relegated to a minor role in the national economy. As a political thinker, he formulated two doctrines of great significance: nullification and concurrent majorities. His philosophy of minority rights was aimed at preventing a northern-controlled majority from imposing its will on the South. The following passage, illustrating that philosophy, is from his final speech to Congress in 1850, referring specifically to the slavery question.

> How can the Union be saved? There is but one way by which it can with any certainty; and that is, by a full and final settlement, on the principle of justice, of all the questions at issue between the two sections. The South asks for justice, simple justice, and less she ought not to take. She has no compromise to offer, but the Constitution; and no concession or surrender to make. She has already surrendered so much that she has little left to surrender. Such a settlement would go to the root of the evil, and remove all cause of discontent, by satisfying the South she could remain honorably and safely in the Union, and thereby restore the harmony and fraternal feelings between the sections which existed anterior to the Missouri agitation. Nothing else can, with any certainty, finally and forever settle the questions at issue, terminate agitation, and save the Union.
>
> But can this be done? Yes, easily; not by the weaker party, for it can of itself do nothing — not even protect itself — but by the stronger. The North has only to will it to accomplish it — to do justice by conceding to the South an equal right in the acquired territory, and to do her duty by causing the stipulations relative to fugitive slaves to be faithfully fulfilled — to cease the agitation of the slave question, and to provide for the insertion of a provision in the Constitution, by an amendment, which will restore to the South, in substance, the power she possessed of protecting herself, before the equilibrium

between the sections was destroyed by the action of this Government. There will be no difficulty in devising such a provision — one that will protect the South, and which, at the same time, will improve and strengthen the Government, instead of impairing and weakening it....

...I have been governed by the motives which have governed me in all the stages of the agitation of the slavery question since its commencement. I have exerted myself, during the whole period, to arrest it, with the intention of saving the Union, if it could be done; and if it could not, to save the section where it has pleased Providence to cast my lot, and which I sincerely believe has justice and the Constitution on its side.

Speech to Congress, March 4, 1850.

A.A. DORION, "CONFEDERATION AND FRENCH-CANADIAN RIGHTS" (1865)

Antoine-Aimé Dorion (1818–91) of the *Parti Rouge* led the Lower Canadian opposition to Confederation in the legislative assembly. Dorion's *rouges* feared the power granted to the central government and argued that the province would have such "small power" that it would not be respected in the federal union. He also contended that federal disallowance put Lower Canada (French Canadians) at the mercy of the central government.

Antoine-Aimé Dorion was a staunch defender of cultural-minority interests.

South Carolinian John C. Calhoun, like Dorion, sought to safeguard the interests of his region.

Members from Lower Canada are made aware that the delegates all desired a legislative union but it could not be accomplished at once. This Confederation is the first necessary step towards it.

I know there is an apprehension among the British population in Lower Canada that, with even the small power that the Local Government will possess, their rights will not be respected. How, then, can it be expected that the French population can anticipate any more favorable result from the General Government, when it is to possess such enormous powers over the destinies of their section of the country? Experience shows that majorities are always aggressive, and it cannot well be otherwise in this instance.

It therefore need not be wondered at that the people of Lower Canada, of British origin, are ready to make use of every means to prevent their being placed at the mercy of a preponderating population of a different origin.

I agree with them in thinking that they ought to take nothing on trust...and neither ought we of French origin to do so, in relation to the General Government, however happy our relations to each other may be at present.

I will simply content myself with saying that...I strongly fear it would be a dark day for Canada when she adopted such a scheme as this.

CHALLENGES TO CONFEDERATION

The delegates at Quebec had no legal standing. They did not officially represent their respective provinces. After they had worked out the details for their new government, a number of the delegates experienced a sense of euphoria. Some rashly suggested that they might submit their draft constitution to the electorate for approval. More sober heads prevailed and the delegates concurred with the British proposal that ratification should be obtained from the provincial legislatures. This course would involve the delegates in a difficult and acrimonious battle that would delay the establishment of the new federal union for almost three long years.[11]

Half a year after the Quebec Conference, Confederation was at a standstill. Only one colony — Canada — clearly supported it, and even then, French Canadians were divided. The only colony that had allowed its electorate to vote on the proposal — New Brunswick — rejected it. In fact, every one of the Atlantic colonies had either opposed Confederation or simply demonstrated its indifference to the scheme.[12]

At this point, external influences began to assert themselves. Britain let it be known that it strongly approved of the union scheme, would convene a conference to expedite it, and would quickly pass the necessary legislation to implement it. The American cancellation of the reciprocity treaty left New Brunswick without a viable alternative to Confederation and in open defiance of the mother country's wishes. The greatly exaggerated Fenian raids further led to New Brunswick's reversal in the June 1866 election. On the last day of June, the new assembly voted in favour of Confederation. A similar change of heart took place in Nova Scotia as its assembly approved Confederation.

THE LONDON CONFERENCE

The final act in the drama was the December 1866 London Conference, at which delegates from Canada, New Brunswick, and Nova Scotia drew up the legislation for the British Parliament to create the new nation. Macdonald was the conference chairman. The work was uneventful and involved only minor tinkering. Remembering the line from Psalm 72 of the Bible, Samuel Leonard Tilley provided the name "Dominion of Canada" as an alternative to "Kingdom," which was deemed to be too offensive to the Americans. The British North America Act passed through both British Houses of Parliament with virtually no major changes or even serious debate. Queen Victoria signed the bill into law on March 29, 1867, and it was agreed that it would become effective on the first day of July. Confederation was now a reality.

CANADIAN GOVERNMENT — A BLEND OF TRADITIONS

THE CANADIAN GOVERNMENT that was created at the time of Confederation was an interesting amalgam.[13] It was the product of various compromises — political, cultural, and regional; it

The draft of the British North America Act, with corrections, notations, and doodles by Sir John A. Macdonald.

attempted to combine aspects of both the British and the American systems; and it tried to address the needs of two different cultures and several different regions. The governmental structure attempted to preserve the link with Britain while forging a uniquely Canadian system. Finally, this new system had to be dynamic enough to solve the immediate problems and provide for growth, development, and change. It had to be specific and yet general. It had to allow for the expression of the majority while providing safeguards for various minorities.

THE DIVISION OF POWERS

A number of significant compromises made Confederation acceptable to most interests. Critically, the union would be a federal rather than a legislative one. Given the size and diversity of British North America, coupled with the existence of two "founding races," it would have to be a federal system of government. Otherwise it was virtually certain that Cartier and Quebec would not have joined the union, and highly dubious whether Nova Scotia and New Brunswick would have done so. In such a federal system, a central government would address national concerns, while provincial governments would look after local concerns.[14] Such a system would allow for the retention of local identities while providing jointly for trade and defence.

When it came to the distribution of power within the federal structure, Macdonald reiterated that the central government had to be the dominant body. Cartier was concerned because he was joining the future of his people to an English majority. Minority status in a legislative union would put the survival of the French way of life severely in jeopardy. Although he was unable to obtain a true legislative union, Macdonald was successful through a variety of means in making the central government the dominant body.

Pointing to the American Civil War — and pointing out that its prime cause was states' rights and not slavery — Macdonald convinced his colleagues. Under section 91 of the British North America Act, the central government was assigned significant powers over all matters of a "general nature," ranging from trade and commerce to defence. It also was given so-called residual powers — the right to make laws "in all areas not expressly reserved" for the legislatures of the provinces.

The provincial governments were given some important "enumerated powers." Control over property and civil rights, as well as language and religion, were deemed essential by Cartier and the Quebec delegates.[15] They were assigned to the provinces so as to enable French Canadians to preserve and protect their unique cultural traditions, and to soothe the fears of Maritimers that Confederation would see local ways swallowed up. Provincial governments, it was hoped, would manage those "matters of a local nature" so essential to the maintenance of regional identities.

Mindful of the American example of "states' rights," the clear intent of the Fathers of Confederation was to establish the central government as the dominant body.[16] The federal government was given a far more extensive list of enumerated powers — 37, compared with the provinces' 15 — as well as responsibility for "peace, order and good government" in the Dominion. To add economic clout to political power, only the central government was given the right to levy both direct and indirect taxes. The central government was given the power to appoint provincial lieutenant-governors. Finally, to demonstrate the central government's superior position over the provincial governments, it was given the right to disallow any provincial law that it deemed in contravention of a federal statute.[17]

THE CANADIAN AND AMERICAN SYSTEMS: FORMS OF GOVERNMENT AND FOUNDING PRINCIPLES

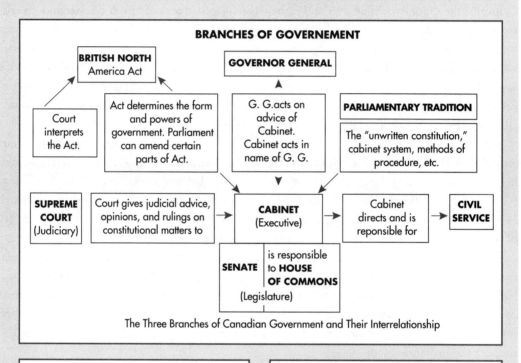

BRANCHES OF GOVERNEMENT

BRITISH NORTH America Act

Court interprets the Act.

Act determines the form and powers of government. Parliament can amend certain parts of Act.

GOVERNOR GENERAL

G. G.acts on advice of Cabinet. Cabinet acts in name of G. G.

PARLIAMENTARY TRADITION

The "unwritten constitution," cabinet system, methods of procedure, etc.

SUPREME COURT (Judiciary)

Court gives judicial advice, opinions, and rulings on constitutional matters to

CABINET (Executive)

Cabinet directs and is reponsible for

CIVIL SERVICE

SENATE is responsible to **HOUSE OF COMMONS** (Legislature)

The Three Branches of Canadian Government and Their Interrelationship

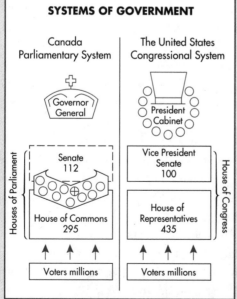

SYSTEMS OF GOVERNMENT

Canada Parliamentary System	The United States Congressional System
Governor General	President Cabinet
Senate 112	Vice President Senate 100
House of Commons 295	House of Representatives 435
Voters millions	Voters millions

Houses of Parliament

House of Congress

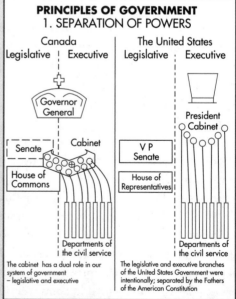

PRINCIPLES OF GOVERNMENT
1. SEPARATION OF POWERS

Canada Legislative	Executive	The United States Legislative	Executive
	Governor General		President Cabinet
Senate	Cabinet	V P Senate	
House of Commons		House of Representatives	
	Departments of the civil service		Departments of the civil service

The cabinet has a dual role in our system of government – legislative and executive

The legislative and executive branches of the United States Government were intentionally; separated by the Fathers of the American Constitution

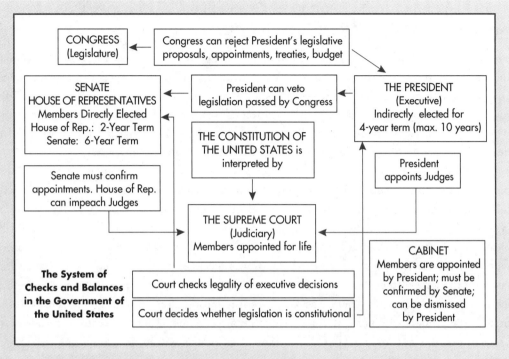

CONGRESS
(Legislature)

Congress can reject President's legislative proposals, appointments, treaties, budget

THE PRESIDENT
(Executive)
Indirectly elected for
4-year term (max. 10 years)

SENATE
HOUSE OF REPRESENTATIVES
Members Directly Elected
House of Rep.: 2-Year Term
Senate: 6-Year Term

President can veto legislation passed by Congress

THE CONSTITUTION OF THE UNITED STATES is interpreted by

President appoints Judges

Senate must confirm appointments. House of Rep. can impeach Judges

THE SUPREME COURT
(Judiciary)
Members appointed for life

The System of Checks and Balances in the Government of the United States

Court checks legality of executive decisions

Court decides whether legislation is constitutional

CABINET
Members are appointed by President; must be confirmed by Senate; can be dismissed by President

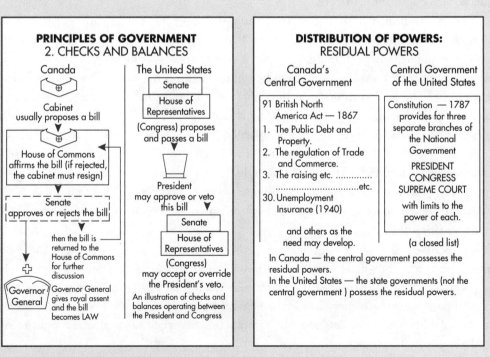

PRINCIPLES OF GOVERNMENT
2. CHECKS AND BALANCES

Canada

Cabinet usually proposes a bill

House of Commons affirms the bill (if rejected, the cabinet must resign)

Senate approves or rejects the bill

then the bill is returned to the House of Commons for further discussion

Governor General gives royal assent and the bill becomes LAW

The United States

Senate

House of Representatives

(Congress) proposes and passes a bill

President may approve or veto this bill

Senate

House of Representatives

(Congress) may accept or override the President's veto.

An illustration of checks and balances operating between the President and Congress

DISTRIBUTION OF POWERS:
RESIDUAL POWERS

Canada's Central Government

91 British North America Act — 1867
1. The Public Debt and Property.
2. The regulation of Trade and Commerce.
3. The raising etc. ....
.................................etc.
30. Unemployment Insurance (1940)

and others as the need may develop.

Central Government of the United States

Constitution — 1787 provides for three separate branches of the National Government

PRESIDENT
CONGRESS
SUPREME COURT

with limits to the power of each.

(a closed list)

In Canada — the central government possesses the residual powers.
In the United States — the state governments (not the central government) possess the residual powers.

THE BRITISH TRADITION: CONSTITUTIONAL MONARCHY AND PARLIAMENTARY GOVERNMENT

The Fathers of Confederation all accepted the necessity of retaining the connection with Britain. Thus, the Dominion would have a constitutional monarchy. Such a monarchy would rule in accordance with the principles of responsible, cabinet government. The powers of the monarch would be severely limited by a written constitution. The retention of the monarchy would be a source of stability as well as providing a bulwark against the unbridled kind of democracy (labelled "mob rule" by its critics) to be found in the United States.

Further cementing the link with the British tradition, the Fathers opted for a parliamentary system of government. They had enjoyed almost a quarter of a century of experience with this form of government. In addition, they were dubious about the efficacy of the American system of "checks and balances." They further agreed that this federal Parliament would be bicameral. Representation within the lower house, the House of Commons, was agreed upon with relative ease. Brown's idea of "rep by pop" was accepted by all, although with some reluctance on the part of the Maritimes. Elections, based on a limited franchise, would be held at least once every five years. There was to be a redistribution after each decennial census. Of its first 181 members, 45 percent came from Ontario. When Quebec's seats were added to Ontario's contingent, over 80 percent of the voting power within the Commons was lodged in those two dominant provinces.

The question of representation in the upper house, the Senate, brought up a host of questions. Should it be patterned after the British House of Lords? Or should the upper house resemble the American Senate, which at that time was elected by the members of the lower house? Would representation be determined on the basis of region, population, or province? The final resolution of the debate was a long time in coming. It would be an appointed body, nominally federal in its representation. There would be a total of 72 senators. Ontario and Quebec were each awarded 24 members, while New Brunswick and Nova Scotia each had twelve. Ostensibly, the Senate was intended to provide a second review of legislation (a "sober second thought"). In actuality, because senators had to have a property qualification of $4000, the Senate became the protector and guardian of property rights. It was to be a conservative check on any radical tendencies emanating from the House of Commons.

The Senate was originally intended to protect provincial rights, particularly those of the smaller provinces. But having the federal government appoint senators severely diminished their status as representatives of the provinces. Making the office a lifetime tenure further reduced the senators' effectiveness as guardians of provincial rights. In theory the Senate could initiate any bills other than "money bills"; in practice that right, as well as the right to revise legislation, would be little used.

BRANCHES OF GOVERNMENT

The real power in the system lay not in the Senate, or even in the Commons. The exercise of substantive governmental power would be accomplished within the executive branch of government.[18] The cabinet — selected by the leader of the majority party in the Commons — would wield the real power, and particularly the prime minister. The Canadians decided to reject the American idea of vesting within one person — the president — the powers and functions of head of government and head of state. In Canada the monarch would be head of state.

The judicial system was also the result of compromise, with the result once again favouring the central government. While the administration of justice and the organization of the courts remained within provincial jurisdiction, all judges above the level of county court were appointed and paid by the central government. The system of popularly elected judges (with the exception of the Supreme Court) was yet another American concept rejected by the Canadians. Further, criminal law would be the exclusive preserve of the federal government. In addition, a uniform civil law for all the English-speaking provinces, subject to their ratification, would be determined by the central government. Finally, the Dominion government had the right to establish the highest court of appeal and any other courts "for the better administration of the laws of Canada."

THE FINANCIAL TERMS

The financial terms of Confederation, like everything else, revealed the supremacy of the central government as well as the favoured position of Quebec and Ontario. All customs revenue (with the exception of that on timber) would go to the federal government. The provincial governments gave up other taxing powers to the central government; only Ottawa was empowered to levy both direct and indirect taxes. To placate the provinces, the central government agreed to pay an annual per capita subsidy of 80 cents as well as to assume provincial debts. The firm commitment to complete the Intercolonial Railway was the final "carrot" held out to the reluctant Maritimers.

THE BEST OF BOTH WORLDS?

Confederation was the most dramatic change in Canadian history since 1760. However, it was brought about for fundamentally conservative aims and instituted in the most conservative manner possible. There was no break with the principle of British parliamentary supremacy. The tradition of the rule of law was maintained. So was the principle of responsible government, with the executive being held accountable to the legislative branch. The tradition of the independence of the judiciary (through appointment rather than election) was maintained. The monarchical system was preserved as a source of authority and stability. Radical American-style notions were rejected: there would be no statement of charter principles through a bill of rights; there would be no widening of the franchise. In short, the British North America Act was an inherently conservative document, through which the framers were attempting to preserve, protect, and expand their interests.

Clearly, some features of the government structure were taken from the United States, particularly the concept of federalism. Along with the name of the upper house, Canadians also borrowed the system of equal representation from the American example. Thus, the Canadian bicameral Parliament would mirror the American bicameral Congress (lower house elected on the basis of representation by population and upper house selected on the basis of equal regional representation).[19]

Nevertheless, a host of American governmental features were deemed unwise or impracticable. Few Canadians in the 1860s approved of the American republican system. Also rejected was the concept of the separation of powers, which the Americans had established in order to prevent any one branch of government from becoming overly powerful. Rather, Canada continued the British principle of responsible government whereby the cabinet (or executive) was generally drawn from, and held accountable to, the legislative branch. Rejected finally was the powerful Senate, which by subsequent constitutional amendment in the United States would be elected. In America, the Senate could not only initiate legislation but also, with a two-thirds majority, override presidential wishes, and could even, in theory, remove a chief executive from office.

To substantiate the notion that there was no radical break with the past, one need only look at the many British features incorporated into the Canadian governmental structure. Maintained was the concept of the crown as the head of the government; a responsible parliamentary system; and a bicameral legislature modelled on the British example. Although Canada rejected the British notion of a titled, hereditary nobility as well as the British name for the upper house, the Canadian Senate, in terms of powers and responsibilities, was patterned far more on the House of Lords than on the American Senate. In tradition, custom, and practice, the new Dominion government was far more British than American.

THE ROUNDING OUT OF CONFEDERATION, 1867–1873

FOUR MONTHS AFTER CANADA had officially come into being, John A. Macdonald felt confident enough to face the electorate. Recently knighted for his work in bringing Confederation to a successful conclusion, he knew well enough that the election, conducted over a six-week period, would reflect the public's view on the federal union. Not only did Macdonald wish to see the ratification of the plan; he wished to gauge public support for an expanded British North American nation.

In the 1867 federal election, the Conservative government carried the election by capturing 108 seats, while the mixed opposition of Reformers, anti-Confederates from the Maritimes, and *Rouges* from Quebec took 72. It was scarcely a ringing endorsement of Confederation. In light of the fact that Macdonald won fully 99 of his seats in Quebec and Ontario, it truly was a "victory with a question mark."[20]

"BETTER TERMS" FOR NOVA SCOTIA

Macdonald now faced the problem of solidifying his Confederation structure. The first order of business was to get the reluctant Nova Scotians back in the fold. Joseph Howe and the other anti-Confederates had failed to convince the British government to exclude their province from the new federal union.[21] However, they did not regard that as the final statement on the issue. Rather, the election results merely rekindled their fire. Basing his argument on the overwhelming anti-Confederate successes, both in the federal and provincial elections, Howe led a second delegation to Britain in order to pry his province from the clutches of the Canadians. The British took the same tack as Macdonald. "Repeal is not even a matter of discussion" was the official response.

Although the repeal movement had stalled, something had to be done to rectify the troubles in Nova Scotia. Howe considered but quickly abandoned the extreme alternatives of annexation to the United States or open rebellion, and accepted that submission, on the best available terms, was the only rational route. Macdonald held out an olive branch

CROSS ROADS.

Nova Scotia at the crossroads. Sir Charles Tupper (left) attempts to win the favour of Miss Acadia, unsure of which direction to take — to Ottawa or Washington? In the shadows is Joseph Howe, the anti-Confederation leader.

of "better terms": the federal subsidy to Nova Scotia was increased from the original $63 000 annually to $82 000 a year for the next ten years. As part of the accord, Howe negotiated a cabinet position for himself. Thus, Macdonald effectively co-opted his chief Maritime critic.

Now that Nova Scotia was safely in the fold, along with its sister province, New Brunswick, Macdonald attempted to steer the remaining Atlantic provinces into Canada. Newfoundland resisted his appeals in the provincial election of 1869, which brought the anti-Confederates into power.[22] With its deep British roots and Atlantic outlook, that colony would resist Confederation for another eight decades.

PRINCE EDWARD ISLAND'S ENTRY

Prince Edward Island proved to be an easier catch. A strong fight was being waged between the forces supporting Confederation and those opposing it. The split had taken a critical turn

Heart's Content, Newfoundland: the arrival of the trans-Atlantic cable in 1866.

when the island entered the 1870s and the economy suffered a sharp downturn. Economic difficulties were intensified by the islanders' attempt to construct their own railway. The costs greatly exceeded the estimates, and the result was that they were saddled with a heavy debt. Islanders had seen their provincial deficit mushroom from $250 000 in 1863 to $4 million a decade later. Not wanting to increase their taxes to discharge the debt, the option of joining Canada and having the federal government assume the debt began to look increasingly attractive.

Further worsening the economic picture was the high number of absentee landowners, which limited the available tax base. Prince Edward Islanders could not long hold out by themselves. Ottawa promised to provide a grant of $800 000 to buy out the absentee landowners. Furthermore, the Dominion government would take over the island railway, pay a generous subsidy, and guarantee communication between the island and the mainland. Thus, on July 1, 1873, the seventh anniversary of the birth of Canada, Prince Edward Island became the seventh province to join the Dominion.[23]

AMERICAN EXPANSION AND THE NORTHWEST

No less difficult and in many ways far more potentially lucrative for Macdonald was the problem of holding on to the West. That was the area that many in Central Canada eyed with the hope of future advantage. In fact, some had accepted Confederation precisely because of the commercial gain offered by the future exploitation of the West. The danger was the American concept of Manifest Destiny. If the Canadians were slow to seize control of the area, then certainly the Americans would not be so reluctant. The very real threat of American encirclement was brought home to many Canadians with the American purchase of Alaska from the Russians. Negotiated by Secretary of State William Seward for a price of $7.2 million, the deal was loudly jeered by many Americans. (The American press labelled it "Seward's folly.") However, to Macdonald and his fellow Canadians, it was a source of serious concern. In addition, the United States had despatched a consul to Red River in the hope of annexing the area.

For almost two centuries, the Hudson's Bay Company had carried on a highly lucrative fur trade in the area known as Rupert's Land, which included all the land that drained into Hudson Bay.[24] The company was reorganized in 1863, and its focus shifted from fur trading to land sales and control of communications. The Canadians wanted to share in these developments. Complicating the situation was the fact that the Hudson's Bay Company insisted on retaining considerable tracts of arable land as part of any final deal. Finally, a new government in Britain dictated the terms of settlement. The Canadian government agreed to pay £300 000 (approximately $1.5 million) and to grant the company one-twentieth of all the land in the territory. The official date of transfer was to be December 1, 1869. With one stroke of the pen, Macdonald had expanded his new country to six times its original size.

However, in annexing the Northwest, no provision for — or mention of — the inhabitants of the area had been made. (Louis Riel would later speak of them "being bartered away like common cattle.") The inhabitants consisted of a few white settlers, some Amerindians, and the Métis, who lived in the Red River area and numbered about 10 000. The Métis were the product of mixed marriages between white fur traders and Amerindian women. They had originally been nomadic and dependent on the annual buffalo hunts, but had begun to settle and engage in agriculture. They were fearful about the survival of their culture. This concern was intensified by suspicions about an influx of white settlers from Ontario. The Métis held no paper title to their land and were anxious about the sale of the territory to the Dominion government.

Given the prevailing expansionist attitude in Ottawa, it was not surprising that the government bungled the Métis problem almost from start to finish.

This 1871 painting by Frances Ann Hopkins shows government troops on their way west to put down Louis Riel's Red River Rebellion.

Macdonald, hoping to rid himself of a political rival in Ottawa, nominated William McDougall as the first lieutenant-governor of the Northwest. It was McDougall who had helped to negotiate the purchase of the area from the Hudson's Bay Company and had championed the acquisition of the area for the land-hungry farmers of Canada. He was scarcely an impartial choice. McDougall further inflamed passions by setting out for the Northwest well ahead of the official date of transfer.

THE RED RIVER RESISTANCE

Survey crews had been sent from Ontario to organize the land before the expected flood of settlers from Ontario arrived. They surveyed the land on the American square-section system instead of the long, narrow, rectangular strips that the Métis had adopted from the old seigneurial system of New France. After he was elected secretary of a Red River council, the 24-year-old Louis Riel moved swiftly. In October 1869, he and a band of Métis stopped the survey, arguing that the Canadian government exercised no authority in the territory.[25] William McDougall was stopped from entering the territory just outside Pembina, south of the border. The Métis argued that he had no jurisdiction in the Northwest prior to December. Two days later the Métis, in a bloodless coup, seized the main Hudson's Bay Company base at Fort Garry. Still proclaiming his loyalty to the crown, Riel prepared a bill of rights and attempted to unite the colony under his leadership. A provisional government was established that opposed the transfer of the territory and promised to negotiate the entrance of the Northwest into Confederation.

Macdonald was in no hurry to negotiate. In British law, neither Riel's council nor his later provisional government had any authority. However, because after December 1 the power of the Hudson's Bay Company ended, and British authority was not directly represented within the area, a political void existed. In addition, Riel's military position was impregnable during the winter.

Macdonald wanted to find an accommodation. Bishop Taché, who was the spiritual leader of the Red River area, was recalled from a meeting in Rome. The Roman Catholic priests in Red River, fearing an influx of Protestant farmers, had united under Riel's banner. Donald A. Smith, head of the Hudson's Bay Company, was sent to Fort Garry to hear the Métis Bill of Rights and offer the possibility of compromise. Matters were proceeding well; Smith held two large public meetings on January 19 and 20, and the people appointed delegates to negotiate in Ottawa.

Just as tranquillity loomed on the horizon, Riel committed his one grave blunder. The Canadian party, led by John Schultz, was opposed to Riel's growing status and power. The party wanted to open up the Northwest to Canadian settlement and exploitation. However, they had incurred the wrath and suspicion of virtually everyone in the colony — the Métis, the Roman Catholic priests, and the officials of the Hudson's Bay Company. A number had already been arrested and imprisoned by Riel's provisional government. A few had escaped and organized an operation at Portage la Prairie to free their colleagues.

AMERICAN WESTWARD EXPANSION AND AMERINDIAN REMOVAL

AS NORTH AMERICAN WHITE SETTLEMENT advanced westward over the Great Plains, so did the process of Amerindian removal and subjugation. The idea that the American plains were a "Great Desert" was gradually dispelled in the 1850s. Traders and settlers who crossed the West on their way to California and the Pacific coast reported that much of the western plains and northern prairie was potentially good for settlement. When the Civil War ended and Canadian Confederation came into being, waves of white settlers began to occupy large sections of the region. For the Amerindian peoples, western settlement led to a series of retreats, periodic conflict, and eventual subjugation.*

THE SUBJUGATION POLICY

At the very time that the Canadian government began to assume control over Amerindian lands in the Northwest, United States authorities were fully embarked on their own, more extensive "peace policy." Leading members of Congress, disturbed over the prospects for continuing and expanded conflict between whites and Native peoples, proposed policies to prevent, or at least reduce, it in the years ahead. A major government commission, with the encouragement of President Ulysses S. Grant (1869–77), negotiated treaties to remove the plains Native peoples to reservations, chiefly in South Dakota and in Amerindian territory. Many tribes resisted dispossession and removal, however, and many Amerindians confined to reservations rebelled against the restrictions of the reserves and the unscrupulous activities of civilian agents employed by the Bureau of Indian Affairs.

With the breakdown of the pacification policy, the United States Army was sent in to take over. Its mission was to keep the Plains peoples on the reservations, to round up those who had fled, to provide security for white settlers, and to intervene in cases of severe injustice. The intervention of the U.S. Army's cavalry did little to reduce white–Amerindian conflict and, in some cases, aggravated the problem. Clashes arose between white settlers and land speculators determined to occupy the land and Amerindian tribes resisting the destruction of their ancestral hunting grounds. Many Amerindians fiercely objected to the severe restrictions and "Americanization" practices imposed on them on the reservations. As in the past, treaties were broken and the

---

* For fuller treatments see Dee Brown, *Bury My Heart at Wounded Knee* (New York: Bantam Books, 1970); and John L. Tobias, "Canada's Subjugation of the Plains Cree, 1879–1885," *Canadian Historical Review* 64 (December 1983): 519–548. An excellent recent treatment is Anthony F.C. Wallace, *The Long Bitter Trail: Andrew Jackson and the Indians* (New York: Hill and Wang, 1993). The Hollywood perspective is portrayed in the film *Dances With Wolves*.

better lands of the reservations were reallocated to greedy white settlers. The coming of the railroads brought more white settlers and the gradual destruction of the buffalo herds. By 1883 the completion of the Northern Pacific Railway sealed the fate of the final, northernmost herd in the United States.

THE DISPOSSESSION OF THE UTES

The impact of American Amerindian policy was graphically revealed in the experience of the Utes, an Amerindian tribe native to the arid foothills, mesas, and mountain slopes of present-day Colorado. From the time of the arrival of the first whites in Cherry Creek in the 1850s, the tribe sought friendly relations. In 1868, a treaty was signed and ratified by the U.S. Senate, giving the Utes over 6 million ha of land, most of it in Colorado west of the Continental Divide, "forever." After the coming of the Transcontinental Railroad in 1869, however, thousands of settlers arrived and white encroachment threatened the Ute landholdings. Finally, with the Ute lands virtually enveloped by Colorado settlers, the tribe signed a treaty to avert widespread bloodshed. By the terms of the 1881 settlement, the Utes gave up over 4 million ha of land, containing valuable mines, for $50 000 a year, and land grants of 150 ha to each Indian in an unspecified area.

The sad story of the removal of the Utes was told by an eyewitness, Captain James Parker of the Fourth U.S. Cavalry:

> After a debate lasting several hours, they sent for [Colonel] Mackenzie. They proposed a compromise. They said they had concluded they must go, but first they wished to go back to their camp and talk with their old men. "No," said Mackenzie. "If you have not moved by nine o'clock tomorrow morning, I will be at your camp and *make* you move."
>
> The next morning, shortly after sunrise, we saw a thrilling and pitiful sight. The whole Ute nation on horseback and on foot was streaming by.
>
> As they passed our camps their gait broke into a run. Sheep were abandoned, blankets and personal possessions strewn along the road, women and children were loudly wailing. Poor things! They were leaving the land which had been theirs for centuries, their home, their country, for an unknown destination hundreds of miles away.
>
> James Parker, *The Old Army: 1872–1918* (Philadelphia: Dorrance, 1929), p. 153.

THE CLIMAX OF AMERINDIAN RESISTANCE

The experience of the Utes was repeated numerous times in the history of the American West. Eventually, the entire western plains of the United States were cleared for white settlement and occupation. On a cold winter day in 1890, the sad history of the Amerindians reached its dramatic climax when U.S. Army soldiers attacked an encampment of 350 Amerindians at Wounded Knee, South Dakota, and left 300 men, women, and children strewn across the battlefield.

In the Canadian Northwest, the Plains Cree and the Métis suffered a markedly similar, albeit less bloody, fate. The advance of settlement and the dispossession of the Native peoples contributed greatly to the Métis Northwest Rebellion of 1885. During the rebellion, the Cree attacks on Battleford and Frog Lake were very much the acts of a desperate, starving people. By the end of the decade, the Plains Cree had not only been subdued, but were broken up and confined to reserves administered by others.

Riel, who had shown much restraint up to this point and was in fact preparing to release the men, regarded this as an act of open defiance. He was determined to uphold his authority by making an example of one of the conspirators. Thomas Scott, an Orangeman from Ontario who had escaped imprisonment in December, was selected. His conduct had been consistently insulting, rude, and provocative. Riel remained impervious to appeals both to humanity and reason after a Métis jury found Scott guilty of insubordination. Scott himself never believed that the Métis would go ahead with his execution. However, on March 4, a Métis firing squad carried out the order. The ramifications of Riel's decision were to be immense for the future of Canada.

THE CREATION OF THE "POSTAGE STAMP" PROVINCE

Protestants in Ontario were outraged at Scott's execution. They demanded the end of a negotiated settlement and insisted that a military expedition be sent out to the Red River. Macdonald, recognizing the necessity of appeasing Ontario, despatched a force under the command of Colonel Garnet Wolseley. Final settlement of the Manitoba problem came when Parliament passed the Manitoba Act. Under its terms, Manitoba became the fifth province of Confederation in 1870. The "postage stamp" province was to be officially bilingual, and existing property rights were respected. Manitoba was to be represented by four members in the House of Commons and two members in the Senate. The rest of the West was to be administered as the Northwest Territories under an appointed governor and council.

BRITISH COLUMBIA AND THE RAILWAY PROMISE

The entrance of British Columbia into Confederation, compared with that of Manitoba, proved to be far less violent and much simpler.[26] A gold rush in the 1850s had swelled the colony's population to 30 000. The accompanying prosperity ended in the following decade as the gold disappeared, and a serious economic recession hit the colony. (Vancouver Island and British Columbia had been united into one colony in 1866.) As the population shrank, the debt, which had been incurred during better times, became increasingly onerous. Fully half the provincial revenues went to discharge the interest on the deficit of over $1 million.

The colony had few alternatives. While a dwindling number of merchants agitated for annexation with their southern neighbours, increasing support was found for union with Canada. Neither alternative seemed attractive. The communication and transportation difficulties inherent in any union with Canada appeared insurmountable. In addition, the Canadian market seemed too small to ensure prosperity for British Columbia. The entrenched British officialdom, personified by the governor, Frederick Seymour, regarded union with Canada as bordering on treason.

Annexation to the United States was not without its advocates. Entrepreneurs saw new trade links being opened up if they aligned themselves with the United States. Financial interests dreamed of Victoria becoming the chief port for trade between the United States and the Orient. The annexationist group received much encouragement from the Americans, led by William Seward and Charles Sumner. A petition from the legislature was for-

Cutting out the 49th Parallel, on the right bank of the Mooyie River, B.C., looking west.

warded to President Ulysses S. Grant to negotiate the transfer of the colony to the United States. However, given the "Britishness" of British Columbia, along with a host of other difficulties, annexation remained the idle dream of a small minority.

There was little that Macdonald could do directly during this debate. He kept the imperial government informed about threatening American moves. A major obstacle to union with Canada was removed with the death of Governor Seymour in late 1869. His replacement, Anthony Musgrave, worked tirelessly to bring British Columbia into Canada. Musgrave published a dispatch from the British colonial secretary stating that Britain supported the joining of British Columbia to Canada because it promised the best prospects for the colony. The last barrier to union was removed when the Canadian government purchased Rupert's Land.

ANNEXATION COMPLETED

British Columbians were surprised by the favourable terms: Ottawa would assume the province's debt; the standard provincial subsidies would be paid, depending on population; and the province was given control over most of its public lands. The final act of generosity was the commitment

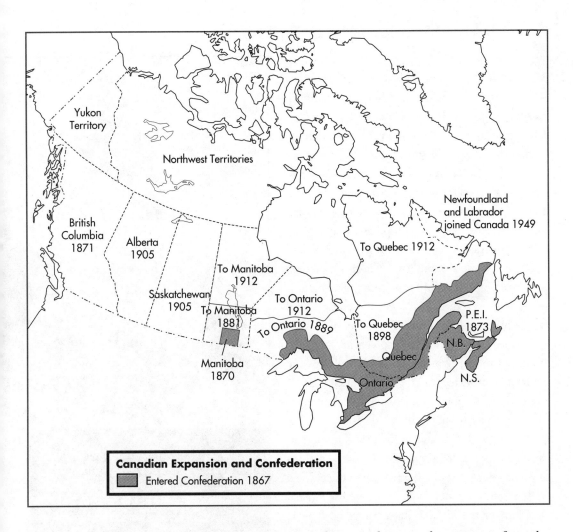

Canadian Expansion and Confederation

Entered Confederation 1867

Yukon Territory

Northwest Territories

Newfoundland and Labrador joined Canada 1949

British Columbia 1871

Alberta 1905

Saskatchewan 1905

To Quebec 1912

To Manitoba 1912

To Manitoba 1881

To Ontario 1912

To Ontario 1889

Manitoba 1870

To Quebec 1898

P.E.I. 1873

N.B.

Quebec

Ontario

N.S.

to start a transcontinental railway within two years and to complete it within ten years from the date of union. Because of the unexpected generosity of the Canadians, opposition to union died down, and in January 1871 the legislative assembly unanimously accepted the terms of union. On July 20, 1871, the sixth province was added to the Dominion.

With the annexation of the West completed, Dominion authorities founded and despatched to the region the North-West Mounted Police. From 1873 onward, the Mounties constituted an effective federal presence on the Prairies. They policed the Amerindians and the Métis, chased American traders out of southern Alberta, and symbolized the stability and order desired by white settlers in the Northwest. Under federal rule, the lightly populated region enjoyed little political representation in Ottawa. Until 1887, Manitoba's handful of members of Parliament were the only representatives of the Prairies in Parliament.[27]

FEDERALISM AND THE COURTS

IN THE FIRST 25 YEARS OF CONFEDERATION, Macdonald's centralized federalism faced a succession of challenges. When the glow of Confederation faded and Dominion policies failed to bring relief from the prolonged depression of the late nineteenth century, the provinces voiced deeply felt regional and local concerns. The practical realities of administering a diverse, transcontinental nation, raising and spending public monies, and even implementing legislation, inevitably led to interprovincial and federal–provincial conflicts. Clashes between provinces, assertions of French-Canadian nationalism, and even threats of secession complicated the politics of federalism. Whenever Canadian politicians were unable to resolve their jurisdictional disputes, which was quite often, the Judicial Committee of the Privy Council (JCPC) in Britain was appealed to for final settlement.

On balance, the judicial decisions of the JCPC in the 1880s and early 1890s tended to favour the provinces at the expense of the national government — quite the reverse of the pattern in the American federal system. There the judicial decisions of the United States Supreme Court, especially during Chief Justice John Marshall's tenure (1801–35), had the effect of strengthening federal power in relation to states' power.

"Centralization, or Provincial Autonomy Abolished." A critical view of John A. Macdonald's centralized form of federalism. The sympathies of the famous cartoonist J.W. Bengough are clearly evident.

Champions of Canadian provincial rights did not take long in coming to centre stage. As early as 1868, Joseph Howe and other Nova Scotians had obtained better financial terms by threatening to withdraw from the one-year-old union. Perhaps the most articulate and forceful of the advocates of the provincial cause in the 1880s was Oliver Mowat, Ontario's premier for almost a quarter of a century. He emerged as the leader of the "provincial rights movement."[28] A particular source of discomfort for Mowat and other provincial premiers was the federal power of disallowance, by which provincial laws could be struck down if the federal government deemed them to be harmful to the country as a whole.

JOHN MARSHALL AND THE RISE OF AMERICAN FEDERAL POWER

A T ITS CREATION, the United States was a decentralized federation of former colonies. Under the original Articles of Confederation (1783–87), the American founders established a system based on the principle of state sovereignty and a limited national government. Their unhappy experience with Britain before 1776 made them suspicious of central authority and anxious to guard their hard-won popular form of self-government. This tradition of decentralized federalism did not last, however.

Two major constitutional developments significantly altered the American federal system. First, the adoption of the new constitution in 1787 to replace the former articles made for a substantially changed distribution of power. Under the constitution, the national government was empowered to do far more: it could now conclude treaties, regulate interstate commerce, and raise and maintain armies. In addition, the chief executive, the president, was given far more power as well. A second critically important development in the transition to more central authority was the work of John Marshall, the chief justice of the U.S. Supreme Court from 1801 to 1835.

John Marshall arrived at the Supreme Court at a time when the United States was undergoing a major political realignment. The Republicans led by Thomas Jefferson had toppled the ruling Federalists in a presidential election termed "the revolution of 1800." Having lost control of the White House and Congress, the outgoing president, John Adams, took steps to strengthen Federalist influence in the judicial branch. The most significant court appointment of the handful made by Adams was that of John Marshall of Virginia as chief justice. Probably no single act of Adams's administration had more far-reaching results.

A staunch federalist, Chief Justice Marshall almost completely dominated the other justices on the court during his 35-year tenure. In more than 500 legal opinions, he reshaped the political and economic structure of the American nation. Marshall's decisions established fundamental American legal principles and invariably enlarged federal powers. As early as 1803, in the case of *Marbury v. Madison*, Marshall established the principle of judicial review, whereby the court was the final interpreter of the constitution.

The powers of the legislature are defined and limited; and that those limits may not be mistaken, or forgotten, the Constitution is written. To what purpose are powers limited, and to what purpose is that limitation committed to writing, if these limits may, at any time, be passed by those intended to be restrained?... It is a proposition too plain to be contested that the Constitution controls any legislative act repugnant to it.... A legislative act contrary to the Constitution is not law.... It is emphatically the province and duty of the judicial department to say what the law is.

Marbury v. Madison, United States Supreme Court, 1803.

In *Fletcher v. Peck* (1810), the court held for the first time that a state law was unconstitutional. That case, as well as the 1819 *Dartmouth College v. Woodward* decision, upheld the sanctity of contracts. Also in 1819, in the famous *McCulloch v. Maryland* case, Marshall upheld the constitutionality of the second Bank of the United States, basing his ruling on a loose construction of the constitution. He wrote: "Let the end be legitimate, let it be within the scope of the Constitution, and all means which are appropriate, which are plainly adapted to that end, which are not prohibited, but consistent with the letter and spirit of the Constitution, are constitutional."

The authority of the national government was further enlarged in the 1824 *Gibbons v. Ogden* decision, in which the court struck down a New York state law that had awarded a steamboat company a monopoly on passenger service across the Hudson River between New Jersey and New York. The court held that a state could regulate commerce only within its borders and that only Congress was empowered to regulate interstate commerce.

In these important rulings, the Marshall court strengthened the central government at the expense of the states. His decisions generally weakened the legal basis for the states' rights. As the years passed by, the former president, Thomas Jefferson, expressed alarm over Marshall's impact. "The great object of my fear is the federal judiciary," he once wrote. "That body...ever acting, with noiseless foot...gaining ground step by step, and holding what it gains, is engulfing insidiously the special [state] governments." Despite his fears, Jefferson could not alter the course of events. The Marshall court succeeded in shaping a loose collection of states into a more centralized union.

THE JCPC DECISIONS

At the centre of the federal–provincial struggles of the 1880s were two thorny issues: liquor licensing and provincial boundaries.[29] In a border dispute between Manitoba and Ontario in 1881, the Dominion government legislated a boundary between the two. Ontario successfully petitioned the JCPC for a ruling more favourable to itself. Ottawa's power over liquor licensing was upheld in *Russell v. The Queen* (1882) on the grounds that the Dominion possessed the "residual power" to legislate for peace, order and good government. Then, in 1883, the Dominion government disallowed Ontario's temperance bill, by which the province claimed exclusive control over the sale of beer, wine, and liquor within the province.

The landmark case in Canada began innocently enough in Archibald Hodge's Toronto tavern and billiard hall. The local liquor licence commission, claiming powers under an Ontario law, forbade games to be played in a licensed drinking establishment after the official 7 p.m. closing time. On May 7, 1881, Hodge closed up the bar at the St. James Hotel, but his patrons continued playing billiards. The owner was charged and fined $20 for the offence. On the advice of his lawyers, Hodge appealed, confident that the courts would find the Ontario law an encroachment on federal authority.

The momentous decision went against Hodge and federal authorities. In 1883, only a year after *Russell v. The Queen*, the JCPC insisted that Ontario's right to make police regulations under section 92 of the British North America Act was supreme. Provinces were not mere "municipalities," as Macdonald had once contended. Within their sphere, the court found them fully equal to the federal power. The precedent had been set. The *Hodge v. The Queen* decision in 1883 proved to be the first of many such rulings that overrode Macdonald's conception of federalism.

PROVINCIAL RIGHTS AND FEDERAL POWER

Provincial resentment against federal transgressions intensified, and many provincial politicians began to follow Mowat's lead. Growing disenchantment with national policies led many provinces to elect administrations dedicated to provincial autonomy. In Quebec, Honoré Mercier led his newly created *Parti National* to victory in 1887. Exploiting Quebec anger at the 1885 execution of Louis Riel, Mercier portrayed himself as a defender of French-Canadian rights and Roman Catholicism. Maritime disaffection was largely economic, as the region experienced a rapid decline in the demand for its products. Many Maritimers, most notably Premier W.S. Fielding of Nova Scotia, blamed Confederation for their persistent economic woes. The climax of their

Honoré Mercier, Quebec premier from 1887 to 1891 and leader of the *Parti National*.

"Ontario has played the part of an uncomplaining milch cow for all the other provinces since 1867, but patience must soon cease to be a virtue." The Toronto *Mail*, March 18, 1887.

resentment was reached in 1886, when the Nova Scotia legislature passed a resolution favouring the Atlantic provinces "withdrawing from the Canadian federation and uniting under one government."[30]

West of Ontario, things were scarcely better. British Columbia was upset over the continual delays in the construction of the transcontinental railway. The Conservative government of John Norquay in Manitoba was angered by Ottawa's cancellation of charters for the construction of railway lines. The premier attempted to enact various bills that cut into the Canadian Pacific Railway's monopoly privilege. In every case, Macdonald invoked the power of disallowance. Furthermore, the people of Manitoba resented the federal government's ownership of provincial public lands. All of this rising discontent came to a head in 1887 when, at the invitation of Mercier, the provincial premiers met at an interprovincial conference in Quebec City.[31]

Macdonald dismissed the premiers' conference as nothing more than a partisan gathering — all but one of the premiers attending was a Liberal. However, the writing was on the wall. Macdonald's preferred form of federalism was being severely challenged by the decisions of the JCPC and the growing provincial autonomy movement. A vibrant Canadian provincial-rights tradition had arisen and would not go away.

ACTIVITIES

KEY TERMS AND CONCEPTS

Identify and briefly explain the historical significance of the following terms and concepts:

- Federalism
- Constitutional monarchy
- Responsible government
- Bicameralism
- Unitary state
- "Checks and balances" (separation of powers)
- Executive/legislative/judicial branch
- Direct/indirect taxes
- Power of disallowance
- Enumerated/residual powers
- Annexation
- Métis
- Orangeism
- *In camera* meetings
- Judicial review

QUESTIONS FOR DISCUSSION

1. What kind of a federal system did the Fathers of Confederation create at the conferences of the 1860s? Why did it evolve into a federal rather than a legislative union?

2. To what extent were the Quebec Resolutions and the plan of federal union "imposed" on the people of the various British North American colonies?

3. In the formation of Canadian government, which influences were stronger — British or American? Justify your answer with examples.

4. Compare the Canadian and the American systems of government. How were regional, state, or provincial interests protected in the two federal systems?

5. To what extent did the American Constitution and the British North America Act embrace the notion of "perpetual union"? How flexible were the two federal systems?

6. Compare the Judicial Committee of the Privy Council decisions of the 1880s with the rulings of John Marshall's Supreme Court from 1801 to 1835. To what extent did judicial review have opposite effects in Canada and the United States?

7. Compile an organizer that lists the governmental elements that the Fathers of Confederation selected and rejected from both the British and American systems.

8. The Fathers of Confederation conducted their deliberations *in camera*. What are the advantages and disadvantages of "closed-door" meetings?

9. Over the last decade and a half, Canadians have witnessed a plethora of constitutional conferences. In what ways were these conferences similar to, and different from, those of the nineteenth century?

ANALYZING THE EVIDENCE

Canada's first prime minister, John A. Macdonald, envisioned a centralized form of federalism. During his terms in office (1867–73 and 1878–91), he took steps to promote such a system. In 1868, he clearly summarized his view of Canadian federalism:

"I fully concur with you as to the apprehension that a conflict may, ere long, arise between the Dominion and the 'States' Rights' people. We must meet it however as best we may. By a firm yet patient course, I think the Dominion must win in the long run. The powers of the General Government are so much greater than those of the United States, in its relations with the local Governments, that the central power must win....

"My own opinion is that the General Government or Parliament should pay no more regard to the status or position of the Local Governments than they would to the prospects of the ruling party in the corporation of Quebec or Montreal. So long as the dual system exists, a certain sympathy will also exist. This was beneficial at the commencement of matters and should be kept up, at all events for this parliament, until the new constitution shall have *stiffened in the mould*."

— Sir John A. Macdonald to Brown Chamberlin, October 26, 1868.

1. Identify the key elements of John A. Macdonald's conception of federalism. Summarize the key points briefly.

2. For each point, compare Macdonald's *ideal* with the *reality* of Canadian federalism from 1867 to 1891.

3. Nationalist historians like Arthur Lower and Donald Creighton have interpreted the rise of provincialism in the 1880s as an obstacle to national progress and a low point of "national spirit." In fact, was Macdonald's vision of federalism beneficial to all parts of the new Dominion? To what extent were provincial-rights advocates such as Oliver Mowat and W.S. Fielding far wiser in their assessment of what Canada really needed?

4. Brian Mulroney and John A. Macdonald are the only Conservative prime ministers to have won back-to-back majority governments. How would Mulroney view Macdonald's conception of nineteenth-century Canada? What factors account for that view?

The Most Extensive and Best Appointed Establishment in Canada
FOR MANUFACTURING HARVESTING MACHINERY.

Works of The Massey Manufacturing Co., Toronto, Ont.

PART III

THE INDUSTRIAL STATE

1873–1939

F rom Canadian Confederation to the onset of World War II, Canada and the United States
were transformed into modern industrial states and experienced dramatic changes in social
conditions. The two North American peoples witnessed the rise and expansion of modern
industry and grew preoccupied with debates over the proper role of both the state and the
individual in an emerging corporate-dominated economy. In response to rising industrial capitalism, workers and farmers organized to protect themselves and to advance their interests.
Industrial growth was accompanied by waves of immigration and the emergence of North
American cities and great metropolitan centres. The millions of immigrants brought not only
fresh infusions of human energy, but also demands for assimilation and the difficulties of social
adjustment in North American industrial society.

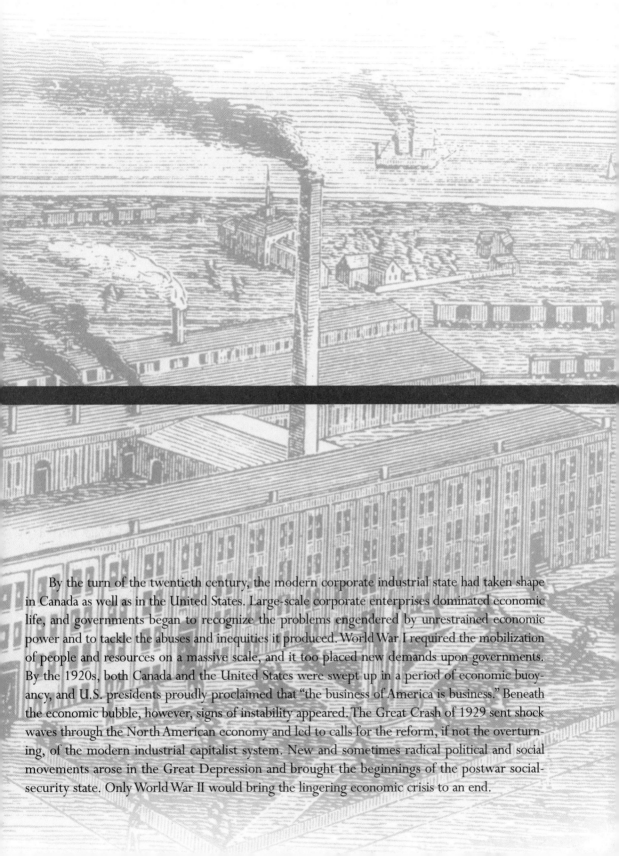

By the turn of the twentieth century, the modern corporate industrial state had taken shape in Canada as well as in the United States. Large-scale corporate enterprises dominated economic life, and governments began to recognize the problems engendered by unrestrained economic power and to tackle the abuses and inequities it produced. World War I required the mobilization of people and resources on a massive scale, and it too placed new demands upon governments. By the 1920s, both Canada and the United States were swept up in a period of economic buoyancy, and U.S. presidents proudly proclaimed that "the business of America is business." Beneath the economic bubble, however, signs of instability appeared. The Great Crash of 1929 sent shock waves through the North American economy and led to calls for the reform, if not the overturning, of the modern industrial capitalist system. New and sometimes radical political and social movements arose in the Great Depression and brought the beginnings of the postwar social-security state. Only World War II would bring the lingering economic crisis to an end.

MAKING CONNECTIONS TIMELINE

A.D.	CANADA	NORTH AMERICA	UNITED STATES
1873	Prince Edward Island enters Confederation	Onset of world depression	Closing of American frontier; dawn of "New Industrialism"
1879	John A. Macdonald's National Policy tariff	•	Thomas Edison invents light bulb; Terence V. Powderly heads Knights of Labor
1886	•	•	Haymarket Bombing; American Federation of Labor founded; Interstate Commerce Act
1887	"Commercial Union" rejected in federal election; first interprovincial conference at Quebec	•	Dawes Act breaks up Indian reservations
1889	Labour and Capital Commission Report; Patrons of Industry enter Ontario	•	Jane Addams founds Hull House
1890–91	Macdonald era ends	•	Sherman Antitrust Act; McKinley Tariff; shootings at Wounded Knee (1890)
1892	•	•	Homestead Strike; Populist Party founded at Omaha
1896	Wilfred Laurier and Liberals elected to power; Sifton's "Last Best West" immigration drive	Economic boom begins	William McKinley elected president; William Jennings Bryan's "Cross of Gold" speech
1898–99	Canadian contingent sent to Boer War; AFL enters Canada	•	Spanish-American War (1898); First Open Door Note (1899)
1901	•	•	Teddy Roosevelt succeeds assassinated president; U.S. Steel founded
1903	Cobalt mining boom	Alaska Boundary decision	•
1904–05	Alberta and Saskatchewan enter Confederation	•	Roosevelt's "Fair Deal," Lincoln Steffens's *The Shame of the Cities*
1906	Ontario Hydro established	•	Hepburn Act; Pure Food and Drug Act
1908	•	•	General Motors formed; Ford produces first Model T

1910–11	Laurier and Reciprocity Treaty rejected in 1911 federal election	Reciprocity Agreement	•
1912	•	•	Woodrow Wilson's "New Freedom" triumphs over Teddy Roosevelt's Progressive party
1914	Britain and Canada enter the war	World War I	United States remains neutral; Federal Trade Commission; Clayton Antitrust Act
1917	Canadian Corps capture Vimy Ridge; conscription and federal income tax introduced	•	United States enters World War I
1918–19	Prime Minister R. L. Borden at Versailles; Women's Suffrage; Winnipeg General Strike and sympathy strikes	Armistice ends war	Wilson's Fourteen Points; Prohibition begins
1920	National Progressive party formed at Winnipeg; origin of three-party system; rise of Maritime Rights agitation	•	Senate rejects Versailles Treaty and League of Nations membership; women granted the vote
1923	Cape Breton coal strike at Sydney; Halibut Treaty signed	•	Teapot Dome scandal; Calvin Coolidge becomes president
1926	King–Byng Crisis; Duncan Commission Report on Maritime claims	•	•
1929	Winnipeg Grain Exchange and stock exchanges collapse	Onset of the Great Depression	"Great Crash" on Wall Street and panic
1932	R. B. Bennett's Relief Camps opened; Canadian Radio Broadcasting Commission founded	•	Bonus Army; banking panic; F. D. Roosevelt elected president
1933	Dust Bowl; Regina Convention of the CCF	Depth of the Great Depression	"Hundred Days" of the New Deal
1935	On-to-Ottawa Trek; Bennett's New Deal; Alberta Social Credit phenomenon	•	Second New Deal: Wagner Act, Social Security Act
1937–38	Oshawa GM Strike; Rowell–Sirois Commission formed	•	Recession of 1937
1939	Mackenzie King's government enters war	World War II begins	United States maintains neutrality

INDUSTRIALISM AND ITS IMPACT

IN THE DECADES FOLLOWING CONFEDERATION and the American Civil War, Canada was transformed into a modern industrial state. The Industrial Revolution, which began in Great Britain in the eighteenth century, was slow in coming to North America. But when it arrived in the United States after 1815 and in Canada by the 1840s and 1850s, myriad economic and political changes followed in its wake. From about 1850 onward, the signs of industrialization — railway tracks, telegraph lines, and factories — sprang up in central Canada and the Maritimes. The traditional British North American economy, based on the export of staple products — fish, fur, timber, and wheat — to Britain and the United States, grew more diversified. In the last third of the nineteenth century, British North America was remade, both physically and psychologically, from a largely pre-industrial community, based on farming, fishing, and lumbering, into an emerging industrial capitalist society.

With the rise of industrialism came a peculiar Canadian development strategy, in which the growth of the state and economic growth went hand in hand. Successive Canadian governments, from the time of John A. Macdonald forward, departed from traditional laissez faire philosophy and pursued national-development policies designed to facilitate business growth and expansion. Of these measures, the protective tariff policy, instituted by Macdonald's Conservative government in 1879 and popularly known as the "National Policy," was the most visible, dramatic, and influential. Together these policies formed a kind of national development strategy of "defensive expansion" based on an east–west axis of trade distinct from trade with the United States.[1]

THE RISE OF THE INDUSTRIAL STATE

ORIGINS OF INDUSTRIALISM

THE FIRST REAL SPURT OF CANADIAN INDUSTRIALIZATION came after 1850, several decades later than in the United States. The canal system of the Canadas, which had been completed in 1848, greatly improved the quality and speed of communications and transport. A large wave of British immigration between 1840 and 1857 substantially increased the size of the domestic market and provided newly emerging industries with a pool of cheap and abundant labour.

With the arrival of steam and iron technology, Canadian industries began to multiply in number and to shift from small-scale craft production to mechanized factory production. Flour mills and sawmills, now more frequently powered by steam than by water, remained the principal manufacturing establishments, but new mechanized factories and mills began to spring up in larger Canadian cities and towns. At first these establishments were concentrated in Montreal, where mechanized operations started in boot and shoe making, milling, and the manufacture of iron and wood products. Other manufacturers in cities and towns like Toronto, Hamilton, London, and Brantford soon followed, making items such as mill gears, steam pipes, paint, soap, and woollen goods. Canada's largest manufacturer of farm machinery, the Massey Manufacturing Company, began in 1847 as a family-run iron foundry in Newcastle, Canada West, and expanded rapidly. By 1860, Canadian-made goods and machines were beginning to replace American- and British-manufactured items in Canada's shops and general stores.

THE RAILWAY-BUILDING CRAZE

Railways came to symbolize the new industrial age in the 1850s. In 1850, only 120 km of railway track had been laid; by 1865, over 3300 km of track was in use. Wood-burning steam engines hauled farm produce to market and brought machine-made products to the farm. They transported not only necessities like stoves and glassware, but also luxury items such as parlour pianos and buggies. With generous government subsidies, the St. Lawrence and Atlantic Railway opened for traffic in 1853, the Great

From craft to mechanized production in the boot and shoe industry. (M930.50.8.79 Untitled [Boot and Shoe Industry], 1850–1899, John Henry Walker, Wood engraving, Ink on paper, McCord Museum of Canadian History, Montreal.)

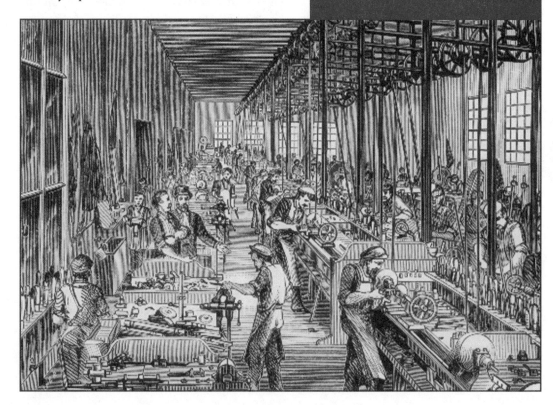

Western Railway in 1854, and the Northern Railway in 1855. Each line was intended to link an emerging metropolitan centre with a hinterland area. For example, railways were built to improve Montreal's communications with the Eastern Townships, to secure for Hamilton the trade of the Niagara peninsula, and to open up the area north of Toronto for settlement. The most ambitious railway scheme, the Grand Trunk, was chartered in 1853 and linked Montreal with Sarnia, but it soon became mired in financial troubles and teetered on the brink of bankruptcy.

Despite these financial woes, the railway boom brought significant economic benefits. The railway companies, financed largely by British investors, attracted infusions of capital, which then became available for other investments. A host of metal-producing workshops and foundries emerged in central Canada in the 1850s to meet the needs of the railways. Indeed, the large railway companies began to resemble modern integrated industrial corporations, producing a wide variety of goods needed by the transportation system.

A CHANGING ECONOMIC ORDER

Much of the Canadian economic growth and prosperity in the years preceding Confederation resulted from international factors. In the 1840s, Great Britain began to dismantle the old colonial system of imperial preferential tariffs on timber and grain. To offset this loss of British preferential trade, in 1854 the Canadian colonies entered into a reciprocity treaty with the United States. The agreement was a bargain: British North America gained a reciprocity of trade in natural products in return for opening its inshore fisheries to the Americans. Indeed, reciprocity contributed, in part, to the return of colonial prosperity and the railway-building mania of the 1850s. As a result, although trade with Britain continued to expand in the 1850s, a new trade pattern emerged as Canadian imports from the United States exceeded imports from Britain between 1852 and 1855. During that period, Canadian exports to the United States quadrupled and equalled exports to Britain.

In the wake of the Crimean War (1854–56), grain prices rose, benefiting British North American wheat producers. Both American western settlement and the Civil War (1861–65) generated healthy demands for Canadian food products and lumber. In addition, the steady infusion of British capital for the railways provided additional development capital for Canadian industries.

UNEVEN DEVELOPMENT

The Maritime provinces had heartily welcomed reciprocity; it seemed that increased trade with both the provinces of Canada and with the United States had resulted in a "golden age." But these provinces' economies had some fundamental weaknesses. The meagre progress of railway building in the 1850s indicated the Maritimes' shortage of capital, native or imported, to promote growth. Only 400 km of track had been laid in the Maritimes, compared with nearly 4000 km in the Province of Canada.

THE ORIGINS OF AMERICAN CHILD AND WOMEN'S LABOUR

THE RISE OF INDUSTRIAL AMERICA created a demand for a new type of labour force. Most white Americans in the 1820s were farmers who worked their own land, so few were interested in factory work at first. Factory owners could not turn to artisans or craftsmen, who had little interest in factory employment. In the early American textile industry, factory owners recruited most of their labour force from the ranks of women and children. Children were particularly favoured in the early Rhode Island mills. Their small size enabled them to move nimbly around dangerous machinery. Boys and girls ranging in age from 7 to 12 came cheap, receiving wages of 33–67 cents per week, compared with adult earnings of $2 and $3 a week. Women also worked for low wages; one reason was their relative lack of skills, compared with those of artisans who had apprenticed and trained for many years.

THE LOWELL SYSTEM

Employing young women as textile workers became known as the "Lowell system." Most of the female labourers recruited were young girls from neighbouring farms who were willing to work before settling down. New England's major cotton merchants, the Boston Associates, sought to attract industrious women from respectable families, so they closely supervised the women's everyday lives. At Waltham and Lowell, Massachusetts, the company provided boarding houses, schools, amusement facilities, religious instruction, and land for gardening.

Life was hard for the women in the Lowell mills. Although in the company's early years the girls were well treated and paid relatively good wages, the working hours were long and conditions

Women shoemakers march, Lynn, Massachusetts, 1860. Led by the city guards, 800 women shoemakers marched along with working men proclaiming their refusal to be "slaves."

inside the factory were damp, dark, and noisy. The poet and millworker Lucy Larcom contended that Lowell workers were oppressed and often unhappy:

> Poor lone Hannah,
> Sitting at the window, binding shoes:
>   faded, wrinkled,
> Sitting, stitching, in a mournful muse.
> Bright-eyed beauty once was she,
> When the bloom was on the tree:
>   Spring and winter,
> Hannah's at the window, binding shoes.

Some women were not content to remain "sitting at the window." In the 1830s, women millworkers went on strike over wage reductions, and in the 1840s, they mounted annual campaigns that petitioned state legislatures to reduce the length of the working day.

Commerce in the Maritimes depended on wooden sailing ships, yet the days of the Lunenberg schooner were numbered in a new age of steam and iron technology. The ocean-going steamship, which by 1868 accounted for a third of the tonnage in St. Lawrence ports, signalled the end of Maritime shipping and shipbuilding. The region's transition to industrialism did not occur until at least the 1870s.[2]

The veil of prosperity barely concealed British North America's underlying economic problems. The "infant industries" created during the railway boom of the 1850s faced stiff American and British competition in the domestic market. When the heavy American demand for foodstuffs and lumber ceased at the end of the Civil War and the United States cancelled the Reciprocity Treaty in 1866, many economic difficulties returned. Without preferred access to Britain's market and without reciprocity, the new Dominion of Canada was in an economic quandary. It was forced to rely on its limited home market and its uncertain position in an international market where European nations were beginning to erect high protective tariffs against all trading nations.

THE ADVENT OF NATIONAL POLICIES

Late in 1873, a disastrous worldwide economic depression hit both Canada and the United States. In Ontario, Quebec, and the Maritimes, businesses closed their doors and banks failed. By the mid-1870s, thousands of men "tramped" the roads looking for work. Deepening depression and the failure of Prime Minister Alexander Mackenzie's Liberal administration (1873–78) to alleviate its economic effects led to a revival of protectionist sentiment. Prominent central Canadian business leaders and politicians came to feel that the federal union was beginning to resemble a "bundle of sticks loosely tied together." To growing numbers of Canadian businesspeople, particularly the leaders of the fledgling Manufacturers' Association of Ontario, tariff protection seemed to be their economic salvation.

THE NATIONAL POLICY TARIFF

In his quest for improved Canadian trade opportunities, John A. Macdonald had sought on several occasions to negotiate a new reciprocity agreement providing for freer trade with the United States, but without success. By the mid-1870s, he had taken a different tack. Writing to a Conservative newspaper editor as early as 1872, he came out for "a National Policy in tariff matters" that avoided the unpopular word "protection," yet effected "a readjustment of the tariff in such a manner as incidentally to aid our manufacturing and industrial interests." By using the term "National Policy," Macdonald appealed to "Canada for Canadians" sentiment and attempted to capitalize on public disenchantment with the Liberals' cautious approach to building the Canadian Pacific Railway and opening the West.

Macdonald's triumph in the 1878 general election marked the cementing of a new business–government partnership in defence of the National Policy. Ontario manufacturers and protectionists, who had organized a National Policy League to promote "protectionism" during the 1878 campaign, were rewarded for their efforts. With very few exceptions, the tariff presented in the federal government's 1879 budget conformed with the schedule of duties proposed by Toronto and Montreal manufacturers. Import duties on manufactured goods were raised to levels ranging from 10

A Canadian business view of the economic problems of the 1870s. The cartoonist makes the case for increased protection for "infant" Canadian factories.

percent on semi-manufactured goods to 25–41.4 percent on items such as carriages, agricultural implements, screws, paint, railway cars, and woollen clothing. One of the primary principles behind such a tariff policy, Macdonald claimed in March 1881, was to establish "a permanent policy" and thereby maintain economic stability for "capitalists…investing their capital in new enterprise." But the close ties forged between central Canadian manufacturers and the Canadian state would anger western farmers and Maritime-rights advocates for years to come.

HENRY CLAY'S AMERICAN SYSTEM

JOHN A. MACDONALD'S NATIONAL POLICY tariff could hardly be considered a Canadian invention. High protective tariffs had played an integral part in building up the industrial economies of both Britain and the United States. Although the protective tariff of 1879 was framed largely in response to the unregulated flow of American-produced goods into the Dominion, Macdonald was likely influenced by American precedent and practice. For, in some respects, Macdonald's National Policy of tariff protection, railway building, and western settlement bore a striking resemblance to the development strategy of the "American System," promoted by Senator Henry Clay of Kentucky after 1815, which was a three-pronged program based on a protective tariff, a national bank, and "internal improvements" or better canals and roads to aid interstate commerce. Whether or not Clay's American System influenced the promoters of Canada's National Policy is a fascinating question.*

Henry Clay, the originator of the American System. A Republican from Kentucky, he voiced the concerns of many people in the new western states.

* See Melville H. Watkins, "The American System and Canada's National Policy," Canadian Association for American Studies *Bulletin* 3 (Winter 1967): 26–42.

While Macdonald and the manufacturers may not at first have conceived of the National Policy as part of a grand national design, the tariff of 1879 did produce some tangible economic benefits. Raising tariff levels encouraged a minor industrial boom, especially in textiles, and helped sustain steady expansion in some industries, notably those producing boots and shoes, furniture, agricultural implements, foundry products, tobacco, and wood products. Nor was this industrial growth limited to central Canada; the Maritimes also experienced a spurt of industrialization. Along with this Maritime industrial expansion, however, came the seeds of potential difficulty, as economic control of the region was gradually passing to central Canadian commercial interests in Montreal.

THE CPR: THE TIES THAT BIND

The harmony of national interest between the Canadian government and the business class, so evident in the National Policy tariff, was even clearer in Macdonald's resurrection of the Canadian Pacific Railway (CPR). The transcontinental railway scheme, first proposed by Macdonald in the early 1870s, had been stalled by the Pacific Scandal of 1873 and carried forward on a more modest, staged-construction basis by Mackenzie's Liberal government. But Macdonald claimed that a transcontinental railway was urgently needed because the American "wolf" was at the door. A Pacific railway, according to Macdonald, must be built immediately, by enterprising businessmen operating an all-Canadian company over an all-Canadian route, if the West was to be secured against the imminent threat of annexation. Only through the building of the CPR could industrialized central Canada be bound together with the western resource hinterlands in fulfilment of Macdonald's "National Dream."[3]

Building the CPR was presented by Macdonald's government as a do-or-die challenge. Not surprisingly, the contract was awarded in 1880 to a private syndicate headed by two wealthy businessmen: George Stephen, president of the Bank of Montreal; and Donald A. Smith, a senior official with the Hudson's Bay

The indispensable buiders: Chinese navvies at work on the Canadian Pacific Railway.

Company. Under the terms of the lucrative and somewhat reckless contract, Stephen and the syndicate received an immediate cash subsidy of $25 million (roughly equivalent to the annual national revenue); one-half the arable land in a belt 40 km wide on either side of the proposed CPR line from Winnipeg to the Rocky Mountains; some 1200 km of railway, already constructed under public ownership and valued at $31.5 million; a monopoly on rail traffic for 20 years; and perpetual exemption from all taxation. In return, the CPR syndicate undertook to complete the transcontinental within 10 years by laying 3000 km of track in northern Ontario and the West.

Brushing aside the Liberal criticisms that the CPR deal was a "reckless" giveaway scheme, Macdonald and the Conservatives pressed ahead with their ambitious plans for construction. An American railway builder, William Cornelius Van Horne, was engaged as chief engineer. The project was pursued at a frantic pace through the rock and muskeg of northern Ontario and the steep grades of the Rockies. Although the CPR was initially promoted as an all-Canadian enterprise, much of the financing for the project came from the United States, so that by 1883 almost 53 percent of the company's shares were held by Americans. The line itself was built mainly by Chinese and Irish immigrant labour. Many of the 15 700 Chinese brought to British Columbia for the CPR worked long hours at very low pay, performing difficult and dangerous tasks such as blasting rock and ballasting the line. In pursuit of Macdonald's scheme, hundreds of Chinese "navvies" were reportedly left behind, buried in unmarked graves by the side of the track.

The building of the CPR has often been heralded as the realization of Macdonald's "National Dream," linking east and west with bonds of steel. Yet the epic story may contain elements of delusion.[4] Although Macdonald contended that the CPR was urgently needed to meet the challenge of American expansion into the West, few Americans — with the notable exception of railway promoter Jay Cooke — threatened Canadian territorial ambitions, and the only serious American railway competitor, the financially troubled Northern Pacific, was in no economic position to invade the West in a big way.

After waiting 10 years for a Pacific railway, there seemed no good reason why British Columbia could not have been persuaded, possibly through annual subsidies, to forgo the line for another decade without jeopardizing national economic development. Furthermore, the Liberal program of staged construction under public financing, consisting of short links to waterways, had considerable merit because the CPR's eventual main role became that of moving western wheat to the nearest navigable water. In short, there might have been, in the words of historian H.V. Nelles, "other equally legitimate National Dreams."

WESTERN SETTLEMENT POSTPONED

The population growth and western settlement envisioned by Macdonald and supporters of his national policies never materialized. In spite of an extremely high rate of natural increase and a steady, though unspectacular, inflow of newcomers from Britain, the Dominion grew only slowly. Even with the introduction of the American system of free quarter-section homesteads and the completion of the CPR in 1885, the population of the West only grew from about 73 000 in 1871 to 251 000 in 1891.

Why did Macdonald's dreams of population growth go largely unfulfilled? In 1873, the worldwide depression dried up world markets for wheat and other Canadian staple products and effectively discouraged the migration of peoples to the Dominion. Land was still available on easy terms in the American West, and many potential settlers — Canadians from the East as well as immigrants — opted to take up homesteads there rather than journey on to Manitoba or the Northwest Territories. In addition, after the end of the Civil War the United States had experienced booming industrialization in the North and national growth unmatched in its history. People and capital from Europe and Latin America were drawn to the United States for its widely known employment and investment opportunities. It seemed that while American western states like Minnesota, Nebraska, Iowa, and the Dakotas were growing by leaps and bounds, the Canadian West lagged behind.

Throughout most of the late nineteenth century, Canada's population growth was slowed by continuing emigration to the United States. In the two decades 1871–91, the Dominion experienced a net outmigration of people — more than 1.5 million immigrants entered the country, but almost 2 million left. Maritimers went in large numbers to New England (the "Boston States"); Quebeckers to the New Hampshire, Vermont, and Massachusetts mill towns; Ontario farmers to the Midwest farming frontier; and central Canadian artisans to the burgeoning American industrial cities. Only in the late 1890s and early 1900s, with the return of world prosperity, the closing of the American frontier to settlement, and the arrival of thousands of new European immigrants, would the dreams of extensive western settlement and rapidly expanding industrial cities come to fruition in Canada.

THE CHALLENGE OF COMMERCIAL UNION AND UNRESTRICTED RECIPROCITY

Macdonald's tariff and railway policies may have brought some respite from the economic depression of the mid-1870s, but the results were shortlived. Another economic slowdown set in after 1883, marked by a new round of falling prices and a decline in Canada's exports of such leading staples as lumber and wheat. Thus, even though the protective tariff stimulated some growth in domestic manufacturing, the overall rise in Canadian production remained frustratingly slow in the 20 years after 1873 and the pattern of heavy emigration to the United States continued almost unabated. And as economic conditions worsened throughout the Dominion in the 1880s, groups of English-Canadian public figures began to talk of re-establishing closer political, economic, and military ties with Britain in an "imperial federation," while others resurrected the old notion of commercial union with the United States.

Building a protective wall around Canada's domestic market was not enough to remedy the commercial problem. The Dominion needed increased trade abroad, particularly with the

United States. Thus, in spite of repeated rebuffs, the renewal of some form of reciprocity remained an objective of both Macdonald and the opposition Liberals, and efforts by U.S. President Grover Cleveland (1884–88) to reduce the American protective tariff aroused new hopes that prospects were becoming more favourable. An organized political movement emerged in the late 1880s to actively promote a commercial union between Canada and the United States, led by Erastus Wiman, a Canadian-born Wall Street financier, and J.W. Longley, a prominent Maritime newspaper editor.

THE TRIUMPH OF PROTECTIONISM

As a possible solution to economic depression and as a means to ensure its political survival, the Liberal party flirted with the idea of a freer trade policy. The Liberals after 1887, under their new leader Wilfrid Laurier, were far from agreed on the issue. Laurier himself favoured merely lower tariffs, but a free-trade section in the party led by Sir Richard Cartwright carried the day in 1888, committing the Liberals to a policy of "unrestricted reciprocity" with the United States — a form of commercial union under a politically less damaging name.

Even though Macdonald was the father of the Canadian protective tariff system, he tried once again in 1887 to steal his opponents' thunder by securing his own reciprocal trade agreement with the United States. Only when his initiative failed did he mount a stirring defence of the National Policy of tariff protection. In the climactic election of 1891, fought largely on the trade issue, Macdonald attacked unrestricted reciprocity as "the veiled treason," resorted to the loyalty cry with his slogan, "The Old Man, the Old Flag, and the Old Policy," and appealed to patriotism with phrases such as, "A British subject I was born, a British subject I will die."

The campaign strategy worked, and Macdonald won his final election battle. A new, high-tariff Republican administration in Washington under President Benjamin Harrison was faced with a surplus of American agricultural produce and implemented the "McKinley tariff" of 1890, inaugurating protection for American farm products. The Liberals gradually backed away from unrestricted reciprocity, and by 1893 the policy was quietly dropped from the Liberal economic platform.

THE AGE OF INDUSTRY

WHILE PUBLIC DEBATES SWIRLED AROUND POLITICAL AND ECONOMIC QUESTIONS, industrialism was slowly remaking society in both the United States and Canada. In the years from the American Civil War to the end of the century, the United States underwent phenomenal industrial growth. While its population and returns from agriculture tripled after 1850, its industrial production increased elevenfold. Ten times as much capital was being invested in American manufacturing in 1900 as in 1860, and more than four times as many workers were being employed. Such expansion allowed the United States to overtake Britain in manufacturing output and to become the world's leading industrial power by the mid-1890s.

In the United States, industrial growth was greatly fostered by the prevailing economic philosophy of laissez faire, in which government exercised little control over business. Yet American administrations and Congress did not remain completely aloof from economic life. While few restrictions were placed on business, much was done to assist business through massive land grants to railways and protective tariffs. The United States after 1860, in fact, was a gigantic consumer market, free of interstate tariffs and guarded from foreign competition by a wall of protectionist duties. Under such conditions, American industries like iron and steel, meatpacking, and machine-shop production flourished and grew to dominate the U.S. economy.

Industrial America. The Carnegie steel works in Pittsburgh contributed to pollution in both the air and the water, earning Pittsburgh the nickname "The Smoky City" by the end of the nineteenth century.

THE RISE OF AMERICAN BIG BUSINESS

In spite of the differences in the scale and pattern of industrialization, economic growth after 1865 in both the United States and Canada was marked by a strong trend toward consolidation in business. The U.S. economy, which had previously consisted mainly of thousands of small business establishments, became dominated by a smaller number of large industrial enterprises. American "big business" appeared for many reasons. Technological advances made possible increases in the scale and speed of production that, in turn, necessitated substantial amounts of capital. Such capital was more easily secured by the business that promised greater dividends through the efficiencies of mass production. In addition, large-scale industry offered many advantages: the centralization of control, the elimination of potentially wasteful competition, and the orderly division of markets.

Yet bigness also had its drawbacks. Giant American combines and mergers defied the historic laissez faire principles of American individualism and equal opportunity. Small producers could not compete against giant corporations or attract the necessary capital to establish new businesses. American consumers also suffered, for few received the full benefits of mass production in the form of lower prices. Instead, increased profits went to the capitalist or were simply reinvested in expanded production.

The rise of American "big business" in the late nineteenth century led to the virtual monopolization of the country's wealth by a group of enterprising industrialists. Before the Civil War, the United States had probably fewer than 20 millionaires; by 1892, it had at least 4000. In that year, it was estimated that some 71 percent of the country's wealth lay in the hands of 9 percent of its families. Such wealth not only commanded political power and influence, it often produced entrepreneurs who were indifferent to the material welfare of their workers and prepared to resort to immoral methods in the pursuit of personal gain.

CANADA'S AGE OF ENTERPRISE

Governments in the second half of the nineteenth and the early part of the twentieth centuries were generally friendly to private enterprise, providing a protected Canadian market and combining generous subsidies with limited social control over business. Signs of this close working relationship between government and business could be seen in the two dominant issues of the period — the National Policy tariff and the CPR. The protective tariff of 1879 was created largely at the instigation of Canadian manufacturers and, as its chief beneficiaries, they remained its staunchest defenders. On the railway issue in the 1880s, the CPR syndicate was what Macdonald once called the "sleeping partner" of the Conservative government. Not surprisingly, the CPR syndicate and its supporters poured an estimated $1 million into Conservative election coffers between 1878 and 1890.

Despite this close collaboration, Canadian business leaders exhibited a strong "protective impulse," in contrast to their American counterparts. From Confederation onward, Canada's emerging business class sought forms of protection from the insecurities and instabilities of free and open competition. For most Canadian manufacturers, the National Policy tariff was essential: it guaranteed a sheltered market for home industry and almost assured business success. Throughout the latter decades of the nineteenth century, protective tariffs and price-fixing combines were sought in order to stabilize business life or to relieve an insecurity and fear of failure that the *Commercial* magazine once called "dyspepsia of the mind." Competition may have been the life of trade, but the bottom line was making a "living profit." To a greater extent than American and even European businessmen, Canada's men of capital joined against the destructive forces of laissez faire and the free market.[5]

The rise of Canadian industrial capitalism produced a business class diverse in its interests and motivations. The ranks of the new generation of businesspeople included "self-made men," sons of inherited wealth, and aspiring scientific managers. Two prime examples were Frederic Nicholls, president of Canadian General Electric and a staunch tariff protectionist, and Jean-Baptiste Rolland, a Montreal bookseller who expanded in 1882 into the pulp and paper industry.

AMERICAN TRUSTS AND ROBBER BARONS

AMERICA'S CAPTAINS OF INDUSTRY and their giant enterprises swallowed up corporations throughout the 1870s and 1880s until many of the nation's largest industries were controlled by "trusts" — giant firms holding a monopoly or near-monopoly on trade. The threat posed by the trusts to freedom of enterprise aroused much public alarm, but U.S. governments — federal, state, and local — seemed powerless to act. One major attempt to regulate the trusts, the Sherman Antitrust Act of 1890, passed by Congress during the Benjamin Harrison administration, had little effect. The Act was loosely worded and proved difficult to enforce. The government lost seven of the first eight cases that it brought against the trusts under this legislation.

Furthermore, a U.S. Supreme Court decision in the case of *U.S. v. E.C. Knight Company* (1895) rendered the anti-trust law almost impotent. The court ruled that the company in question, which had secured control of 98 percent of the U.S. sugar-refining business, was not guilty of violating the Sherman Act because its actions did not involve "restraint of interstate trade." This and other decisions by the Supreme Court convinced many big businesses that they were free to consolidate. Thus the U.S. anti-trust law actually may have sanctioned and speeded up the movement in U.S. industry to form trusts.

Among the products of America's new industrial order in the later nineteenth century, three individuals stood out: Andrew Carnegie, John D. Rockefeller, and J. Pierpont Morgan. Each man rose to prominence in a different field and came to be labelled a "robber baron" of American industry.

An immigrant Scot of poor parentage, Carnegie rose "from rags to riches" in the American tradition of Horatio Alger. Between 1864 and 1901, he built the U.S. Steel

Left to right: Andrew Carnegie, John D. Rockefeller, and J.P. Morgan.

Corporation, which at its height produced one-quarter of the nation's steel. If Carnegie was the leading figure in steel, Rockefeller was his counterpart in the American oil industry. Through cut-throat competition and ruthless business practices, he transformed a small Ohio oil company into the Standard Oil Trust, which by the early 1880s owned 95 percent of all U.S. oil refining and completely controlled commodity pricing. The same passion for efficiency and profits marked the career of J.P. Morgan, the dominant figure in the shaping of American finance capitalism. Morgan specialized in buying railway companies, insurance firms, and banks; reorganizing their financial and managerial structures; and then placing them under the control of J.P. Morgan and Co. Morgan's wealth and power were legendary in American financial circles.

Toward the end of Morgan's life, when the House of Morgan entered into an association with a financial group controlled by Rockefeller, it was estimated that persons associated with the two interests held a total of 341 directorships in 112 corporations and possessed resources valued at over $22 billion. This shocking concentration of economic power not only supported their claim to be captains of industry; it also seemed to contradict the ideals of equal opportunity in a democratic state.

For some Canadian businessmen, dependence on the state for aid in development produced its share of uncertainties as well as satisfactions. George Stephen of the CPR was closely aligned with John A. Macdonald in one of the cosiest business–government friendships in North American history. Yet Stephen was rarely satisfied with this apparently happy working relationship. In his heavy correspondence with Macdonald throughout the 1880s, he regularly complained about the alleged failure of the Dominion government to provide additional financial subsidies or to safeguard the property interests of the CPR. This alliance was far from one of two equal partners sharing the reins of power — the alliance that Stephen always hoped for and Liberal opposition critics thought existed in the 1880s. Still, many Canadian business leaders shared the view that the government's proper role was that of aiding development, primarily through tariff and railway policies. What industrial growth did occur in the period was spurred, not by laissez faire, but rather by a business class operating largely under the aegis of an expansive, interventionist, paternalist government.

THE PROBLEMS OF INDUSTRIALISM

CONFRONTING THE NEW INDUSTRIAL ORDER

The advance of industrialism not only produced great new concentrations of wealth, but also challenged the institutions and values of Canada's predominantly rural and agricultural society. In the last third of the nineteenth century, the rise of large-scale mechanized industry and the expansion of Canada's rail network stimulated the growth of the Canadian industrial city.

Although most Canadians still lived in villages and rural areas, increasing numbers of people were gathering in cities and towns. A modern urban industrial society was in the making. This fundamental change brought to the fore a new, often bewildering, set of social and political problems.

For the late-nineteenth-century Canadian working man and woman, the industrial system was fraught with difficulties. Men and women, fresh from Canadian or Old World farms, often did not adjust easily to the new system of machines and factories. From Nova Scotia coal mines to Montreal's cigar and tobacco industry, and from Quebec City docks to Ontario textile mills, Canadian workers confronted new industrial modes of working and of living.

The *Report of the Royal Commission on the Relations of Labor and Capital* (1889) was published 10 years after the adoption of Macdonald's National Policy tariff. The commission had investigated conditions in Canada's factories and touched on many of the problems facing workers. One of the greatest evils accompanying the new factory system, according to the commission's report, was the effect of large-scale industry, with its mass production methods, on traditional employer-worker relations. The desire of employers to "acquire vast fortunes in the shortest possible interval of time," the report contended, had caused employers to demand "a very large percentage of work with the smallest possible outlay of wages."[6] As factories grew larger, the workplace became increasingly impersonal. Since employees could easily be replaced, it became harder for individual working people or groups of workers to "bargain" with their employers over wages and working conditions.

The Toronto Rolling Mills, typical of many nineteenth-century factories investigated by the Royal Commission on Labor and Capital, 1889.

LONG HOURS AND MEAGRE WAGES

For Canadian workers, long hours and low wages were the companions of industrialization. In the 1880s, 10–12 hours was the normal working day, and some workers logged up to 75 hours per week. In cotton textile mills, some children under 10 years of age worked continuously from 6:30 a.m. until noon and from 12:45 till 7:30 p.m. each day.

Wages were not only very low, but inequitable. In Ontario knitting mills, for example, adult male workers earned $7.75 for a 59-hour week, while women and children of 10–12 years worked just as long for $1.65 to $3 a week. Skilled male workers — those with apprenticeship training or education — might earn no more than $10–$15 a week. Even though industrial expansion in the 1880s brought a general increase in real wages, many workers in large cities like Toronto and Montreal found that the cost of rents and coal left little margin for survival. There were mining and textile-mill districts in Nova Scotia, northern Ontario, and Quebec where companies owned entire towns and controlled all the houses, schools, stores, and most other social institutions. One Glace Bay, Nova Scotia, coal miner testified before the 1889 royal commission that after charges for the company doctor, the school, the tallyman, blasting powder, and company store purchases, his pay account often showed no cash at month's end. Little wonder that miners dubbed the local company supply depot the "Pluck Me Store."

THE EROSION OF CRAFT SKILLS

Work in the large factories of Victorian Canada grew more specialized and monotonous as workers increasingly became machine tenders. Groups of skilled artisans such as Toronto shoemakers tried in vain to resist the onslaught of power-driven machines and mass production, which threatened their tradition of craftsmanship, imposed new forms of work discipline, and reduced a worker's control over the pace and quality of production. The installation of new machines, particularly in the printing, shoemaking, and iron moulding trades, also reduced the need for hand labour, throwing workers out of jobs and creating technological unemployment. Many displaced working men and women simply found it difficult to master new skills and to get new jobs.

INDUSTRIAL CONDITIONS

Although working conditions in Canadian factories did not approach the horrors found in the British and American "dark Satanic mills" of the mid-nineteenth century, they often were dirty, hazardous, and even inhumane. The worst of all conditions were probably those discovered by the 1889 royal commission in cotton mills and cigar factories. In one flagrant case, which exploded into a well-publicized scandal in 1889, the owner of a Montreal cigar factory punished his employees for misconduct by cuffing child apprentices, locking up male journeymen in a "black hole" in the factory cellar, and — in one instance — pinning a young female worker on the floor and clubbing her with a cigar mould.

"HIDDEN WORKERS": WOMEN, WORK, AND THE FAMILY IN THE NEW INDUSTRIAL ORDER

ALTHOUGH CANADA EXPERIENCED INDUSTRIALIZATION at a much slower rate and on a much smaller scale than did the United States, nevertheless men, women, and children in fast-growing cities such as Toronto and Montreal were greatly affected by the economic and social changes of the late nineteenth century. Historians have argued that the various strategies adopted by working-class families in their struggle to survive involved all members of the household: mothers, fathers, children, and any other relatives who might have shared their accommodation. These "family survival strategies" were not entirely new but drew on pre-industrial patterns of family life and work in central and eastern rural Canada.

For pioneer women, this meant unpaid labour and child-rearing, as well as preparing food and providing the clothing necessary to the family's daily survival. While rural life could be daunting in its round of back-breaking, ceaseless labour, families who lived in cities and towns faced a range of different problems. Not only did they have to cope with overcrowding, poor housing, unhealthy water, and inadequate sanitation, urban families were more likely to be dependent on wage labour and to need cash than were rural families. However, waged work could be difficult to come by and might fluctuate on a seasonal basis, and it usually was not paid enough to support a family adequately.

Children gathering coal cinders from a Toronto rail yard.

Very few working-class families were in a position to save in order to protect themselves against accidents, illnesses, or the death of the primary wage-earner. The loss of a husband and father could be a disaster for his survivors, as women's work was generally paid even less than that of men. Furthermore, women workers in the 1870s–1890s were consigned to a much narrower range of occupations, most often textile and garment-making, shoe and boot making, and domestic service.

How, then, did urban working-class families survive? Some families were left hungry, cold, and destitute by changes in the economy; most found ways of coping. Those families with sufficient living space to squeeze in a few more people took in boarders to augment their cash income, particularly when their children were too young to work. Wives and mothers might perform odd jobs for neighbours: taking in laundry, ironing, mending, and babysitting. Women who lived in cities that had garment industries often worked as seamstresses in their homes, although the pay for the piecework they performed was very low.

Children's labour was also quite important to the family's survival. In Montreal, a city where many industries depended on child labour in the 1870s and 1880s, whole families might go to work in textile, cigar, and boot and shoe factories. Even when children were not involved in factory work, they still performed a wide range of tasks around the home, including sweeping steps, scrubbing floors, gathering fuel, and looking after younger children. Families who took in piecework frequently relied on children's labour, both in the construction of items and to carry raw materials and finished products between home and contractor.

But all this work barely assured family survival. Urban families thus resorted to other methods of supporting themselves, such as growing small gardens and, before the introduction of municipal ordinances that prohibited such practices, keeping a cow, a pig, or some poultry (either to supplement their food supply or to sell). In times of crisis, especially during winter, families might turn to charities run by middle-class benevolent groups or trade unions for assistance. A number of Protestant charitable organizations were formed across the country during the nineteenth century and, particularly in Quebec, Roman Catholic religious orders also played a central role in providing social welfare and relief and dispensing fuel, clothing, blankets, provisions, and shelter to the poor.

In spite of such industrial discipline, competition for factory work was at times fierce. Macdonald's government-supported immigration wave never really materialized, but even modest numbers of newcomers were enough to cause surplus workers in a slow-growing, and periodically stagnating, Canadian economy. While Canadian manufacturers enjoyed the benefit of high protective tariffs, working people complained about employment competition from hungry, desperate immigrants, brought to Canada at the workers' expense. Increasing numbers of people, mostly sons of farmers, were moving from rural Ontario, Quebec, and the Maritimes to the industrial towns and cities. They were creating additional pressure in the urban labour market and helping to drive down factory wages.

THE PROBLEMS OF CANADIAN FARMERS

Farmers were also profoundly affected by the new industrialism. Once dependent almost entirely upon hand tools — axes, saws, pitchforks, scythes, and rakes — they began to turn increasingly to steel ploughs, reapers, and threshers in tilling their land. The use of farm machines boosted production, but it also greatly increased farm costs and reduced the need for farm labour, driving many people to the industrial towns and cities.

Falling prices for farm produce were a persistent problem for Canadian farmers throughout the 1880s and 1890s. Prices fell mostly because of overproduction, particularly in wheat. The increase was largely the result of the opening of farmlands in the prairie West and the U.S. Midwest and the combined effects of new farm methods and new machinery. By 1896, the *Farmer's Advocate* was moved to describe the previous summer as "one of the most trying seasons" ever for Ontario agriculture.[7]

Many Canadian farmers, attracted to the agrarian way of life by the dream of an independent farming existence, found themselves as bound to the local merchant and money lender as industrial labourers were to their employers. Farmers in rural Ontario often charged that some local merchants were "cunning exactors" who gouged farmers and then took possession of their property in payment of debt. Trust and loan companies that held farm mortgages were regularly blamed for squeezing farmers of the fruits of their labours.

A frequent complaint of farmers was that the National Policy tariff system favoured business combines and special interests. Under the tariff, Canadian consumers, including all farmers, were compelled to pay 25–55 percent more for necessary imported goods than was their natural value in the world's markets. Many farmers felt that the small, propertied, agrarian class was being eliminated. Instead of popular government, the *Canadian Farmers' Sun* observed in 1892, "we have a government of the people, by the representatives, for the classes who can pull the string." The string pullers kept the tariff — a tax on the people — high, while taxes on capital were held low.

RAILWAYS AND FREIGHT RATES

Farmers, especially in rural Ontario and the prairie West, reserved their strongest criticism for the railways. Railways were vital transportation links built with the financial support of governments, and many farmers failed to see why they had been turned over to "private corporations to charge toll on." Farmers particularly objected to the CPR's monopoly, which permitted that company to set all freight rates for shipments to and from communities served by only one line.

"Our parliaments," one farmer protested in 1886, "are composed largely of the hirelings of railway companies, and the laws are made to suit the purposes of their employers."

Farmers who began to fill in the Prairies in the 1880s and 1890s encountered the worst problems of a farm frontier. Many homesteaders in the early stages of western settlement came with little capital; suffered through periodic droughts, flooding, and hail storms; and eventually abandoned their land. One Moosomin, Saskatchewan, farmer who took up land in 1884 spent 20 years paying off his debts to an investment company and seed grain suppliers before gaining clear title to his property. Reports in the *Manitoba Free Press* in the early 1890s told of a growing exodus of prairie farm boys to cities and towns in the East and the United States.

CHALLENGING THE NEW ORDER

In Canada and the United States the late nineteenth century was an age of social criticism and speculation, of stirring public debates over the nature, benefits, and perils of the emerging capitalist order. Hundreds of intellectuals (called "brainworkers"), activists, editors, lecturers, people's poets, labour leaders, and farm organizers emerged in Canada after 1870 to make varied critiques of the emerging industrial system and often to espouse visions of a better world.[8] As both the initiators and products of Canada's working class and farm movements, they mounted platforms to speak at labour rallies and farmers' assemblies, promoted their ideas through the "people's press," and penned social criticism that attacked the inequities of industrial society. The pages of reform newspapers such as the *Ontario Workman*, the *Palladium of Labor*, the *Canadian Farmers' Sun*, and Victoria's *Industrial News* testified to the emergence of a freely germinating radicalism, surprising in its scope and sense of urgency.

VISIONS OF REFORM

One of the earliest Canadian labour papers to question the emerging industrial order was J.S. Williams's *Ontario Workman*, a radical weekly promoting shorter working hours in the 1870s. It was mild, however, compared with the labour-reform voices of the 1880s. Strongly influenced by an upsurge in working-class activism and the powerful ideas of Henry George's book *Progress and Poverty* (1879), radical social critics began to speak out.

The most prominent radical critic of the 1880s in Canada was probably T. Phillips Thompson, a Toronto journalist of independent mind, satirical humour, and visionary socialist ideas. He criticized the "unearned wealth" accumulated by landowners and monopolies and advocated a "single tax" on land, patterned after that proposed by Henry George. A series of *Palladium of Labor* articles written by Thompson under the pseudonym "Enjolras" from 1883 to 1886 attacked the "Gospel of Greed and Grab," lambasted the so-called "uppertendom" of Canadian society, and set out a utopian socialist vision of a better world. He dreamed of a world that "might be," based upon "SOCIAL REORGANIZATION — Universal Democracy and Co-operation — No Wars or Monopolies."

AMERICAN CRITICS OF THE NEW INDUSTRIAL ORDER

DURING THE LAST THIRD of the nineteenth century, the ideas generated by leading American social critics were central to the discussion of social questions in the United States, Canada, and Great Britain. Daring social critics were not new to America, but the rise of the North American industrial capitalism after 1860, it seemed, had created social evils so contentious and so pressing that far-reaching critiques and solutions were advanced with a new sense of urgency.

In the United States, the most effective and widely read of the new generation of social critics was Henry George, a struggling San Francisco journalist. His *Progress and Poverty*, published in 1879, was not merely a tract for the times but a major work of American radical thought. In his impassioned opening lines, he identified the central problem of the age:

> The present century has been marked by a prodigious increase in wealth-producing power.... It was natural to expect, and it was expected, that...the enormous increase in the power of producing wealth would make real poverty a thing of the past...[but] disappointment has followed disappointment.... We plow new fields, we open new mines, we found new cities; we drive back the Indian and exterminate the buffalo; we girdle the land with iron rods and lace the air with telegraph wires; we add knowledge to knowledge, and utilize invention after invention.... Yet it becomes no easier for the masses of our people to make a living. On the contrary, it is becoming harder.... The gulf between the employed and the employer is growing wider; social contrasts are becoming sharper; as liveried carriages appear, so do barefooted children.

Industrial progress, according to George, had been accompanied by searing poverty. And, with deep Christian passion, he protested against the suffering wrought by unrestrained industrialism. George's solution was a new tax policy, which later became known as the "single tax." A tax on land values was necessary, he explained in 1884, because "the private ownership of land has been the great cause of serfdom" and "an equal right to land is an inalienable right that attaches to every human being that comes into the world."

What George attempted in a major book of social criticism, his American contemporary Edward Bellamy tried to do in a novel. In *Looking Backward* (1888), Bellamy pictured a future utopia in A.D. 2000 in which human society was managed by a single public trust in the interests of the common people. The disorderly world of competitive capitalism had given way to a rationalized system of labour and distribution and a nationalized system of production. *Looking Backward* sparked the emergence of a "nationalist" movement in the 1890s aimed at promoting Bellamy's ideas. In Canada as in the United States, small groups of reformers and socialists organized both "nationalist societies" and "single tax clubs" to propagate the labour reform message.

Other prominent labour reformers attempted to "spread the light" in other parts of the Dominion. In Montreal, activists like A.T. Lépine, William Darlington, and Richard Kerrigan rose to prominence, while in the Maritimes Robert Drummond of the Provincial Workmen's Association and Martin Butler of Fredericton championed the labouring class's cause in the 1880s and 1890s.

Labour reformers were not alone in challenging the new industrial order. Spokesmen for Canada's farmers developed their own critique of industrial society and actively resisted the encroachments of industrialization on their agrarian way of life. From the early days of the Dominion Grange Association in the 1870s onward, farm leaders affirmed their strong faith in agrarian ideals and expressed growing fears over the social cost imposed by industrialism on rural communities. Agriculture was "the first and most noble of all occupations," according to the Grange manual of 1875, "but where it has been neglected, degeneracy began." Instead of merely giving in and bemoaning their lost status, agrarian reform leaders openly attacked the domination of business combines and monopolies and sought to build a counter-organization of all "common peoples," toilers as well as tillers, to carry forward that struggle.

THE WORKING-CLASS RESPONSE

LABOUR ORGANIZATIONS had existed in Canada since the War of 1812, when unions of skilled workers first appeared in Saint John, New Brunswick. A host of small, struggling unions had grown up since the 1830s, mostly in highly skilled trades such as printing, shoemaking, and carpentry. But the rise of large-scale industry after 1860 presented such a multitude of problems for workers that larger, more permanent trade unions began to appear. These new organizations remained limited largely to skilled and semi-skilled craftsmen. Common labourers, struggling to keep above the subsistence level, frequently unemployed, and "tramping" from place to place to look for work, were mostly beyond the reach of union activity. For many of these itinerant labourers, the border between Canada and the United States barely existed. Union ideas frequently spread into Canada from Britain and the United States, where labour organizations had a much longer history.

THE NINE-HOUR MOVEMENT

The drive for shorter hours of work was an international idea that swept into the industrial cities of central Canada and stirred the leaders of Canada's fledgling unions into action. In 1859, the struggle for a nine-hour day achieved its first breakthrough, after a five-month struggle, among engineers in Newcastle, England. The subsequent triumph of British nine-hour leagues led to similar agitation in the United States for the eight-hour day, from 1866 into the early 1870s. The movement arrived in Canada in January 1872, when a co-ordinated nine-hour campaign was launched with great enthusiasm at Hamilton. Soon, with the energetic efforts of Great Western Railway machinist James Ryan, nine-hour leagues sprang up in railway towns like Montreal, Stratford, and London, and the *Ontario Workman* emerged in Toronto as labour's newspaper.

A massive nine-hour procession held in Hamilton in May 1872 drew 1500 committed marchers. The ambitious plan of Canada's nine-hour pioneers for the country's first co-ordinated strike ended in failure, however. In April 1872, Toronto printers launched their own strike for a nine-hour work day, upsetting Ryan's plan to make Hamilton the centre of strike action. They were vigorously opposed by the newspaper publishers, led by George Brown of the *Globe*. Brown had 24 strike leaders arrested for seditious conspiracy under a law forbidding union organization, but the Toronto printers won impressive backing from fellow unionists and the public — and gained additional support from an unexpected source. In a bid to win labour sympathy and outmanoeuvre George Brown and the Grits, the Tory prime minister, Macdonald, hurriedly passed the Trade Union Act, a law modelled after 1871 British legislation legalizing registered trade unions. The appeal of Macdonald's trade-union law, combined with growing disunity in labour ranks, gradually undermined the co-ordinated nine-hour campaign. Striking Hamilton workers returned to work without gaining a reduction in hours. Many Canadians still questioned the very right of organized labour to exist.

THE CANADIAN TRADES AND LABOUR CONGRESS

During the nine-hour agitation of 1872, labour leaders resolved to organize for independent political action and formed the Canadian Labour Union (CLU), patterned after a similar American national union launched in 1866. The CLU, however, did not survive the decade. Like most Canadian unions, it was hard hit by the disastrous depression after 1873 and struggled in vain against a devastating round of wage cuts and dismissals. It was also the victim of internal divisions, mainly centred on the question of immigration and the growing competition from immigrant labour for scarce jobs. In 1886, a national association was finally formed, based largely in Ontario and Quebec, which became the Canadian Trades and Labour Congress.

THE RISE OF THE KNIGHTS OF LABOR

During the 1880s, Canadian workers were caught up in a labour whirlwind. A vibrant and dramatic American-based movement swept into Canada, which challenged the rules of conventional unionism and attempted to transform many established institutions, ideas, and values in late-nineteenth-century North American society. The main force behind this labour upsurge was the Noble and Holy Order of the Knights of Labor (KOL).[9]

The KOL was born in Philadelphia in 1869, when a small group of garment workers joined together under the leadership of Uriah Stephens. The order was a secret society, bound by oaths, passwords, and elaborate rituals, which attempted to unite all workers in one great organization — native-born and foreign-born, skilled and unskilled, blacks and whites, women as well as men.

T.V. Powderly in 1879.
(The Granger Collection, New York.)

Only those classified by the KOL as non-producers — such as lawyers, doctors, bankers, and bartenders — were excluded from its ranks. Unlike traditional craft-based unions, it combined aspects of a religious brotherhood, a labour-reform society, a fraternal order, and an orthodox union. The KOL's original ideology favoured peaceful labour negotiation over strikes and envisioned a future co-operative society in which labour was treated with dignity and honour, while capitalists, who lived off the production of workers, were considered social parasites.

The KOL grew slowly in the 1870s, expanding from Pennsylvania coal mines to Pittsburgh shops to New York factories. Only after Terence V. Powderly succeeded Stephens as leader did the KOL throw off its cloak of secrecy and begin appealing to the broad mass of workers throughout North America and even parts of Europe. The results of the new appeal were spectacular. In 1881, the first-known KOL local assembly was formed in Hamilton. Within six years, the Dominion was dotted with 168 local assemblies, numbering at least 12 250 members. In the United States, the KOL scored a major victory in an 1885 strike against Jay Gould's Union Pacific Railroad, and membership soared from 500 000 to over 1 million American workers. During the decade, hundreds of Canadian assemblies were formed and dissolved, and thousands of workers came into contact with the KOL.

THE KNIGHTS CRUSADE IN CANADA

In Ontario the Knights of Labor experienced their greatest successes and defeats. Although strongest in rapidly expanding cities like Toronto and Hamilton, the KOL made great inroads in the province's smaller communities and claimed 21 800 members in 83 localities. But in its "people's strikes" and other ventures, it was not so successful. A series of mass strikes spearheaded by the KOL between 1886 and 1881 in communities from Chatham and Merritton to Gravenhurst and Ottawa–Hull provoked turbulent class conflict and met stiff employer resistance. A temporary labour victory in the Toronto Street Railway strikes of 1886 was undermined by company dismissals and the prosecution of KOL leaders. A co-operative bus company set up by the Toronto KOL to compete with the street railway failed. Such was the fate of all other Ontario attempts at co-operative management, including a Norwich knitting-mill and a Chatham biscuit factory.

Outside of Ontario, the KOL upsurge met with an uneven reception. In Quebec in the 1880s, where

Haymarket Square Panic, May 4, 1886. A bomb thrown by an unknown person caused the Chicago police to intervene to disperse the Knights of Labor rally. (The Granger Collection, New York.)

the order was known as *Les Chevaliers du Travail*, it gained significant support in the Montreal, Quebec City, and Hull regions as an alternative to the more secular, materialistic craft unions. To the west, the KOL established a scattering of local assemblies, mainly in expanding railway towns like Winnipeg and Calgary. On the East Coast, the KOL enjoyed little success because most of the region's mine, shop, and dock workers rallied to the Nova Scotia-based Provincial Workmen's Association. In British Columbia, the KOL challenged head-on the coal empire of Robert Dunsmuir, a ruthless Scot with a hatred of unions, who operated mines at Wellington and Nanaimo. After entering British Columbia in 1883, the KOL joined with the shortlived Miner's Mutual Protective Association in opposing Dunsmuir's efforts to crush unions by importing Oriental labourers as strike breakers. Whereas the KOL elsewhere battled prejudice against women and blacks, in British Columbia as well as California it flourished on anti-Chinese feeling.

The KOL's decline was almost as meteoric as its rise. In the United States, it was blamed, quite unfairly, for bombing a group of Chicago police who were attempting to break up a labour rally at Haymarket Square in 1886. The Haymarket explosion, which left

10 dead and 50 more injured, shattered the American KOL by turning public opinion strongly against unions. In Canada, the Noble Order survived longer. Internal divisions were patched up, and particularly in Quebec and eastern Ontario the KOL continued to wage the workers' struggle into the early 1900s. But drained of its organizing vitality, the KOL slowly faded until 1902, when remnants of the order were purged from the Canadian Trades and Labour Congress.

THE PROVINCIAL WORKMEN'S ASSOCIATION

In the 1880s, East Coast labourers rallied to the cause of the Provincial Workmen's Association (PWA). Originally formed near the Springhill Mining Company, the PWA started its first lodge in 1879 and slowly expanded its organizational base under the leadership of Robert Drummond. Throughout the 1880s, the PWA organized lodges with the same enthusiasm as the Knights of Labor, bringing Granton wharfmen, mainland and Cape Breton miners, New Glasgow and Pictou glass and foundry workers, and Amherst shoemakers into the fold. After 1890, Drummond adopted a policy of conciliation with the Nova Scotia coal mining companies and the PWA eventually split apart. Surviving into the new century, the association continued to pursue a moderate approach and was eventually "used" by the companies to keep the more radical United Mine Workers of America out of the region's mines.

"PURE AND SIMPLEDOM": GOMPERS AND THE AFL

The Knights of Labor faced a challenge not just from capital, but also from within the ranks of labour. Started as a federation of craft unions in 1881 and reorganized in 1886, the American Federation of Labor (AFL) gradually rose to replace the KOL as the dominant labour organization in the United States. Its principal founder and leader was a New York cigarmaker, Sam Gompers. In sharp contrast to the KOL, Gompers's AFL espoused a practical, clear-eyed philosophy of unionism that came to influence trade unionism not only in the United States but also in Canada.

Unlike the KOL, the AFL was a federation of separate national craft unions, each representing a group of skilled workers in a trade or craft, such as printers, carpenters, and cigarmakers. For the most part, the AFL sought to organize skilled workers by their craft rather than by the industry in which they worked. The organization concentrated on practical economic issues — higher wages, shorter hours, and better working conditions — and pursued the goals of "pure and simple" unionism. The way to obtain a larger slice of the "capitalist pie," Gompers and other AFL leaders insisted, was through collective bargaining with employers. Strikes should be used primarily as a means of securing union demands, not of overturning the whole system.

The AFL's brand of unionism eventually spread into Canada. When American business enterprises began expanding their operations beyond the United States, the AFL followed.[10]

Starting in the 1890s, AFL unions welcomed Canadian locals, encouraged voluntary organizing, and often took on the name "international." In 1899, the AFL launched a major
organizing drive in the American South, the Rocky Mountain region, and Canada. Before
the year's end, the union had 12 volunteer organizers at work in Canada and claimed 10 450
members. A full-time Canadian organizer, Hamilton carpenter John Flett, was appointed
by Gompers in 1900, and he stimulated the organization of a host of AFL-affiliated international unions in towns scattered from rural Ontario to Prince Edward Island. Between
1898 and 1902, more than 700 AFL locals were chartered and 86 federal labour unions
were established, raising the number of organized workers in Canada from roughly 20 000
to over 70 000.

At the Trades and Labour Congress (TLC) annual convention held at Berlin, Ontario, in
September 1902, the triumph of Gompersism over Canadian unionism was completed. AFL-affiliated unions voted to expel rival organizations from the TLC, and the majority of Canada's organized workers were welded firmly into the AFL international system. In line with Gompers's
thinking, dual unionism — two unions competing for membership in a single jurisdiction — was
stamped out in Canada. But the struggle of Canadian labour went on, as craft unionists continued to fight for union recognition in the workplace and were increasingly driven into socialist reform politics.

THE AGRARIAN RESPONSE

FARMERS IN CANADA AND THE UNITED STATES, like other North American workers, came to
recognize the need in the late 1800s for co-operative action in tackling the problems posed
by advancing industrialism. Their organizational response took the form of agrarian movements aimed at protecting established rural values and at securing a larger political role for
farmers. This Canadian agrarian response closely paralleled, in many respects, the rise and fall
of American Populism during the same period.

THE CO-OPERATIVE PIONEERS

The earliest organization formed for the defence of Canadian agrarian life was the Grange,
an offshoot of the American movement of the same name. The American National Grange,
or Patrons of Husbandry, had been established in 1867 as a fraternal society for farmers. In
the United States the Grange had emerged as a kind of cultural organization and had local
chapters in many farm communities; farm families met regularly for recreation and discussed ways of improving farm methods. By 1875, however, the Grange had swelled to some
1.5 million American members, mainly in the U.S. Midwest, and its leaders had turned to
proposing co-operative solutions to the economic problems posed by falling farm prices and
business monopolies.

THE "AGRARIAN MYTH" OF THE GRANGE

THE AMERICAN NATIONAL GRANGE, founded in 1867 by Oliver Hudson Kelley, was originally a friendly society, or social club, which limited its membership to farmers. Like other fraternal orders, the Grange developed its own ritual, held ceremonial meetings, and evolved a kind of mythology. At its meetings in local lodges and its out-of-doors picnics, Grangers and their families often celebrated the nature and value of the rural, agrarian way of life.

The Grange ritual was an attempt to describe in mythical terms the social experience of the agriculturalist. The Grange ordered agrarian society according to a hierarchy of agricultural "callings." The various "degrees" of the Grange callings paralleled the evolution of the farmer from the station of Labourer, who used an axe to clear the forest; to Cultivator, who raised crops; to Harvester, who gathered and stored them; and finally to Husbandman, who tended animals — a stage thought by Grangers to be the most settled state of agriculture.

A lithograph mural dated 1875, which depicts the "Agrarian Myth" of the Grange. "I Pay For All" says the inscription below the central figure, a sturdy Granger. The ideal farmer is surrounded by rural pastoral scenes, including the Biblical Ruth and Boaz (lower right); a harvest dance (lower left); a farmer's fireside (upper left); and the Grange in session (upper right).

The Grange ideology has often been considered a form of arcadianism, or a celebration of a disappearing agrarian age. Examining the Grange ritual in the context of advancing late nineteenth-century industrialism may suggest other interpretations.

The Grange entered Ontario and Manitoba in 1874. By 1876, the Canadian organization had grown so rapidly in Ontario that the American Grange granted it full autonomy. Like its American counterpart, the Dominion Grange began to involve itself in politics. During the winter of 1875–76, for example, the organization publicly advocated tariff protection for agriculture after one-third of its 15 000 Canadian members signed a petition supporting such a policy.

The Grange championed co-operative action among farmers. Working together through the Grange, farmers in Ontario and Manitoba organized farm co-operatives, which were economic associations owned and managed by

Grange meeting in the woods, Scott County, Illinois. Some Grange lodges held meetings in the woods and called for "equal rights" for farmers.
(The Granger Collection, New York.)

farmers. These co-ops were designed to reduce the control of agricultural distributing companies, and to promote the economic well-being of farmers. In Ontario, the Grangers set up a wholesale supply company, a fire insurance company, and a trust company, while on the Prairies they established buying clubs and independent farmers' elevators. Some of these early co-operative ventures succeeded, like the Ontario People's Salt and Soda Company, but most failed. Many farm co-operators lacked business experience, but the most important reason for their failure was the lack of capital to compete successfully with established businesses.

Like its urban counterpart, the Knights of Labor, the Grange saw its promising beginning turn into a precipitous decline by the mid-1880s. The Dominion Grange pressured governments for legislation controlling freight rates, similar to the so-called "Granger laws" passed in the states of Illinois, Minnesota, Iowa, and Wisconsin, but without much success. Torn by internal squabbling, the Grange lost the support of the farm newspapers essential to promoting its cause. By 1886, Grange records revealed that over two-thirds of its local lodges had gone inactive.

THE RISE AND FALL OF POLITICAL AGRARIANISM

Out of the ashes of the Dominion Grange grew another offshoot of an American farm organization, the Grand Association of the Patrons of Industry. The Patrons had originated in 1887 at

Port Huron, Michigan, as a secret rural lodge. But shortly after the Patrons organization arrived at Sarnia in 1889, it began to take on a strong "Canadian," and even a highly localized, outlook. Very quickly the Patrons supplanted the more staid and conservative Grange as the dominant force among organized farmers in Ontario. By 1891, the Ontario Patrons had severed all ties with the parent organization, and two years later it claimed 100 000 members organized in 2000 clubs. In Manitoba and Quebec, the Patrons had started up in 1894 and experienced a similar growth.

Unlike the Grange, the Patrons engaged in political action from the outset. The Ontario Patrons began by developing a political platform in an attempt to exert influence on the Liberal and Conservative parties. The Patrons' platform, drawn up in London in 1891, addressed agrarian concerns over land policy, railway monopolies, tariff rates, and government inefficiency. Noticeably absent from the Patrons' program were more radical policies like silver coinage, the graduated income tax, and the nationalization of private utilities, all of which were being promoted by American populists at this time. Indeed, the Patrons' political energies were mostly concentrated on a vehement condemnation of Canada's national policies, particularly the protective tariff, extravagant railway building, and expensive immigration schemes. Its program aimed primarily at reducing urban, corporate control over government and eliminating corruption from Ontario's system of party politics.[11]

The Patrons in Ontario evolved from a rural fraternal society into a formal political party. This political transformation was spurred by three main factors: a rapid decline in farm prices, rural depopulation, and the continuing neglect of agrarian interests by Ontario's established parties. In the 1894 provincial election, the Patrons captured 17 of 94 seats in the legislature, rocked Oliver Mowat's Liberal regime, and threatened to upset the province's two-party system.

THE PATRONS IN DECLINE

Leaders of the Ontario Patrons attempted to forge a farmer–labour populist alliance. George W. Wrigley, founder of the Patrons' weekly newspaper, *Canadian Farmers' Sun*, envisioned a union of the "tillers and toilers" dedicated to toppling the monopolies and combines in the name of justice. Working together with Patron Grand President Caleb Mallory, Wrigley's group made some headway, forging links between the TLC unions and Patron lodges in Toronto, Cornwall, and elsewhere. However, the editor of the *Sun* tried in vain to persuade the Patrons to adopt such measures as initiative, referendum, the single tax, and reducing the power of monopolies. While the Patrons' co-operative ventures in Ontario and Manitoba, including wholesaling and binder-twine operations, continued to survive after 1900, the movement itself faded out of existence.

The response of Ontario agrarian reform leaders to the advance of industrialism showed that the Patrons' vision of a better society consisted of more than rugged individualism and a return to some arcadian past. Assailing private monopolies and combines as terrible social evils, promoting co-operation instead of competition, and fostering unity between tillers and toilers were all ideas strikingly similar to those associated with the American Populist movement of the 1890s.

LOOKING FORWARD — AND BACKWARD

For Canadian workers and farmers, confronting and tackling the problems posed by the emerging industrial state produced more defeats than triumphs. Various movements, from the Grange and the Knights of Labor to the Patrons of Industry and the Provincial Workmen's Association, illustrated the dilemma faced by urban workers and farmers in a society in transition. Caught in the process of industrial change, reformers and activists — urban and rural — had looked both forward and backward. Some had attempted to promote the economic well-being of their class or to build a more equitable society. Others had struggled to protect established values and cherished institutions or to restore lost status.

Industrialism and the impact of prolonged depression had made many Canadians question the nature and purpose of the emerging industrial capitalist order. American social critics like Henry George and Edward Bellamy had won considerable popularity in Canada and helped shape radical reform ideas espoused by Canadian labour and agrarian reform groups. Such ideas would have a lasting significance: they provided Canadian labour with a political program, laid the foundations for a farm co-operative movement, and set many radical workers on the path to Canadian socialism in the twentieth century.

Yet few Canadians entering the new century realized that the Dominion stood on the threshold of worldwide economic recovery and a massive Canadian immigration boom that was laden with its own challenges and problems.

ACTIVITIES

KEY TERMS AND CONCEPTS

Identify and briefly explain the historical significance of each of the following terms and concepts:

- Industrial capitalism
- The factory system
- The railway-building craze
- The Lowell system
- Protective tariff
- Commercial union and unrestricted reciprocity

- Captains of Industry
- Family survival strategies
- Henry George's single tax
- Edward Bellamy's utopia
- Agrarianism
- Factory discipline
- The company store
- Nine-hour movement
- "Pure and simpledom"
- Patrons of Industry

QUESTIONS FOR DISCUSSION

1. What role did the state play in the industrialization of Canada and the United States in the late nineteenth century? Did the Canadian government of John A. Macdonald, through its National Policy tariff and railway policies, provide greater aid to national development than its American counterpart did?

2. Who were the leading industrialists in late-nineteenth-century North America, and what values did they hold? Were there any significant differences in attitudes, ideology, or action between Canadian and American businesspeople?

3. Which industrial abuses in the "dark Satanic mills" of Britain and the United States did the 1889 Labour and Capital Commission unearth in Canada?

4. What did the radical thought and solutions of Canadian labour and agrarian reformers owe to the ideas of America's leading social critics, Henry George and Edward Bellamy?

5. How did the Knights of Labor and Patrons of Industry challenge the new industrial capitalist order in the 1880s and 1890s? Why did they fail to bring about a new society? Can they be simply dismissed as "lost causes"?

ASSESSING HISTORICAL INTERPRETATIONS

Compare the competing interpretations for each of the following issues, and offer your own analysis:

1. Businessmen and the Industrial State

"[A] small class of men...more or less knowingly played the leading roles in an age of industrial revolution.... Under their hands the renovation of our economic life proceeded relentlessly: large-scale production replaced the scattered, decentralized mode of production; industrial enterprises became more concentrated, more 'efficient' technically, and essentially 'co-operative,' where they had been purely individualistic and lamentably wasteful. But all this revolutionizing effort is branded with the motive of private gain on the part of the new captains of industry. To organize and exploit the resources of a nation upon a gigantic scale, to regiment its farmers and workers into harmonious corps of producers, and to do this only in the name of an uncontrolled appetite for private profit — here surely is the great inherent contradiction whence so much disaster, outrage and misery has flowed."

— Excerpts from *The Robber Barons: The Great American Capitalists 1861–1901,* copyright 1934 and renewed 1961 by Matthew Josephson. Reprinted by permission of Harcourt Brace & Company.

"[T]he intervention of the federal government not only failed to damage the interests of the railroads, but was positively welcomed by them since the railroads never really had the power over the economy, and their own industry, often ascribed to them. Indeed, the railroads, not the farmers and shippers, were the most important single advocates of federal regulation from 1877 to 1916....

"From the 1870s until the end of the century American railroad history moved in a crude cycle of voluntary or, alternately, political attempts to solve economic problems.... In their desire to establish stability and control over rates and competition, the railroad executives often resorted to voluntary, cooperative efforts involving rate agreements and the division of traffic. When these efforts failed, as they inevitably did, the railway men turned to political solutions to rationalize their increasingly chaotic industry."

— Gabriel Kolko, *Railroads and Regulation 1877–1916.* Copyright © 1965 by Princeton University Press. Excerpt reprinted with permission of Princeton University Press.

"Few businessmen ever like dangling on the strings held by the invisible hand of the free market. They looked to government to cut those strings, to liberate them from the harsh discipline of competition by taking them under its protective wing. Since the 1870s the dominant tradition in Canadian business has been to reject free enterprise laissez faire liberalism in favour of sheltering under the wing of an expansive, interventionist, paternalist government."

— Michael Bliss, "'Rich by Nature, Poor by Policy': The State and Economic Life in Canada," in R. Kenneth Carty and W. Peter Ward, eds., *Entering the Eighties: Canada in Crisis* (Toronto: Oxford University Press, 1980), pp. 86–87. Note: This statement was written in 1980 and therefore does not reflect the remarkable change in Canadian business attitudes in the 1980s. — Michael Bliss, March 1988.

2. The Meaning of Agrarian and Labour Reform

"The Patron crusade illustrated the dilemma of the farmer in a society in transition. The accelerated shift from a predominantly agricultural economy towards an urban industrial society produced a vocal response from the small propertied interests of rural Ontario. These farmers were caught in what contemporary observers referred to as the 'Social Crisis.'… But, unlike urban dwellers, Ontario farmers were unable to abandon classical economic liberalism in favour of collectivist action. Awed by the growth of monopoly capitalism, big government, and organized labour, the farmers, through the Patron organization, stood committed to an 'anti-protective impulse.' Marshalling both laissez faire economic arguments and the rhetoric of democratic politics, their protests represented the dying cries of old Ontario agriculture. After a brief flirtation with independent political action, a final attempt to defend anachronistic rural values, the farmers of Ontario conceded the struggle."

— S.E.D. Shortt, "Social Change and Political Crisis in Rural Ontario: The Patrons of Industry, 1889–1896," in Donald Swainson, ed., *Oliver Mowat's Ontario* (Toronto: Macmillan, 1972), pp. 211–212. Reprinted by permission of S.E.D. Shortt.

"We…argue that the Noble and Holy Order of the Knights of Labor represented a dramatic shift away from past practices within the history of Ontario workers. Although the Knights built on the accumulated experience of the working class, they channeled that experience in new directions. In the words of Raymond Williams, they took a whole series of residual aspects of the class experience, built upon them, and erected a structural and intellectual apparatus that was the beginning of emergent purpose; they moved beyond limited forms of class conflict, always present in industrial capitalist society, to a more thoroughgoing orchestration of class struggle. In short, the Knights of Labor in Ontario created, for the first time, what Lawrence Goodwyn has called a movement culture of alternative, opposition, and potential. In the breadth of their vision, the scope of their organization, and their unique refusal to collapse the cause of workers into this or that reform or amelioration, or restrict entry to the movement to this stratum or that group, the Knights of Labor hinted at the potential and possibility that are at the foundation of the making of a class."

— Gregory S. Kealey and Bryan D. Palmer, *Dreaming of What Might Be: The Knights of Labor in Ontario, 1880–1900* (Toronto: New Hogtown Press, 1987), pp. 16–17.

"A crisis of faith confronted many Canadian Protestants in the late nineteenth century. Their religious beliefs were challenged by the new biological sciences and by historical criticism of the Bible. Personal salvation, for centuries the central concern of Christianity, no longer seemed an adequate focus in an age that gave rise to industrial cities and grave social problems.…

"No single word more accurately caught the spirit of the developing reform movement of late nineteenth-century English Canada than 'regeneration'. It was, of course, a religious concept meaning to be born again. Once applied to individuals, it was increasingly used to describe social rebirth. For Phillips Thompson, as for many contemporary social critics whom he admired and read — Henry George, Edward Bellamy, William Morris, H.M. Hyndman, Edward Carpenter — socialism was, if not a new religion, then the philosophy of a 'new life' similar in its regenerative function to traditional Christianity. Its aim was not born-again individuals but born-again societies, where men and women would love one another in perfection...."

— Ramsay Cook, *The Regenerators: Social Criticism in Late Victorian English Canada* (Toronto: University of Toronto Press, 1985), frontispiece and p. 173. Reprinted by permission of the publisher.

IMMIGRATION AND NATIVISM

A VAST TIDE OF IMMIGRATION WASHED upon the shores of North America in the years between 1880 and the mid-1920s. This flow of immigrants was part of a great exodus from Europe, described as "the mightiest movement of people in modern history." Added to the European migration was a wave of Asian immigration that swept ashore mainly in California and British Columbia. Attracted by the lure of new opportunities in a "promised land," or driven by hardships in Europe and Asia, they came in the millions — in all, 11 million men, women, and children entered the United States between 1870 and 1900, and another 18 million migrants followed between 1900 and 1930.

Until the turn of the century, the vast majority of European and Asian emigrants headed for the United States. America provided a powerful magnet for people, attracting millions of Europeans and many Canadian-born as well. Its lure as the "promised land" was so strong that in its first three decades Canada barely maintained its population. But with the return of world prosperity, the discovery of gold in the Yukon, the gradual closing of the American frontier to settlement, and the advent of Canada's first massive immigration promotion campaign, many immigrants began to flood into the newly opened land of western Canada in the late 1890s. During the first major Canadian wave of immigration between 1896 and 1914, some 3 million immigrants, including large numbers of British labourers, American farmers, and eastern European peasants, came to the Dominion.

RELUCTANT HOSTS

NEWCOMERS TO CANADA during the immigration boom were often received by reluctant hosts. In English-speaking Canada, they encountered the prevailing social attitude that historian Howard Palmer termed "Anglo-conformity."[1] Most Canadian political leaders, journalists, and commentators believed that it was the obligation of new arrivals to conform to the culture and institutions of Canadian society and to its already firmly established ways. If the immigrant proved unwilling or unable to conform, he or she should be excluded.

Much like Americans of the period, English-Canadians tended to classify immigrants according to their nationalities. British immigrants were considered more desirable in the Dominion than in the United States, and white northern Europeans were readily welcomed as the most compatible and assimilable newcomers. As in the United States, central, southern, and eastern Europeans, and especially Asians and blacks, found few welcome mats. Appreciation for the emerging multi-ethnic cultural mosaic would take time to develop in the Dominion.

WELCOME TO AMERICA — THE PROMISED LAND

INSCRIBED ON A PLAQUE at the Statue of Liberty in New York harbour is a sonnet entitled "The New Colossus," written in 1886 by Emma Lazarus, a New York social reformer.

> Not like the brazen giant* of Greek fame,
> With conquering limbs astride from land to land;
> Here at our sea-washed, sunset gates shall stand
> A mighty woman with a torch, whose flame
> Is the imprisoned lightning, and her name
> Mother of Exiles. From her beacon-hand
> Glows world-wide welcome; her mild eyes command
> The air-bridged harbor that twin cities frame.
> "Keep, ancient lands, your storied pomp!" cries she,
> With silent lips. "Give me your tired, your poor,
> Your huddled masses yearning to breathe free,
> The wretched refuse of your teeming shore,
> Send these, the homeless, tempest-tost to me,
> I lift my lamp beside the golden door!"

Lazarus's "The New Colossus" interpreted the Statue of Liberty, facing toward the Old World, as a beacon of hope for all immigrants uprooted from the land of their birth. But the message must have seemed more mythical than real for millions of late-nineteenth-century newcomers to America. Many entered the "Land of Promise" with a glimpse of the Statue of Liberty, then found themselves swallowed up by the suffocating world of the tenements in America's great cities. Still others faced untold prejudice, discrimination, and even hostility from Americans increasingly alarmed by the "huddled masses" flooding through that "golden door."

Generations of American immigrants, arriving year after year, later gave the statue the meaning Lazarus's poem attached to it. And, for some, the personal dream of freedom and economic opportunity did find fulfilment in America.

* The "brazen giant" is the Colossus of Rhodes, which once stood in the harbour of Rhodes and was regarded as one of the "seven wonders" of the ancient world.

The celebration of the unveiling of the Statue of Liberty, 1886. This symbol of American liberty was a gift from France.

Canada's immigration boom took place from 1896 to 1914. Like the American boom in earlier decades, it dramatically altered the basic settlement patterns, ethnic composition, and class structure of the Dominion. It brought to the country its first large infusion of people of other than British, French, or Native origin. For, while two out of every three immigrants were from Britain or the United States, tens of thousands came directly from many parts of continental Europe, embracing different cultures and speaking in a multitude of tongues.

Immigrants to Canada between 1896 and the mid-1920s were often greeted with distrust and suspicion. Nativism — intense opposition to internal minority groups because of their "foreign" connection — had reached its most virulent and violent form in the United States. But in Canada too after 1880 it reared its ugly head, particularly among Anglo-Canadians in western Canada. Even after prosperity came to Canada at the turn of the century, ethnic conflict often simmered close to the surface, and stereotypes abounded as people from diverse backgrounds attempted to make sense of one another and to establish relationships in a new society.[2]

THE IMMIGRATION BOOM

CANADA EXPERIENCED PHENOMENAL IMMIGRATION and population growth in the years 1896–1921, much like that recorded in the United States in earlier decades. The Dominion's population crept ahead by only 24 percent between 1881 and 1891; in the next 20 years it jumped by 64 percent. In the first 20 years of the century, the number of people who lived in Canada almost doubled, from 5.4 million to 10.4 million. Of those who immigrated between 1896 and World War I, 1 250 000 came from Britain, 1 million from the United States, and thousands more from continental Europe. In Canada, population shifts occurred, as thousands of eastern Canadians joined in the rush to the Prairies. Yet, in spite of the fact that official Canadian policy sought immigrant agriculturalists, many who entered Canada as farmers and farm labourers quickly found their way into railway camps, mines, and factories.

European immigrants bound for Canada, circa 1910. Thousands came by steamship, sailing from European ports.

THE WHEAT BOOM AND THE OPENING OF THE WEST

With the lifting of the global economic depression, there were new markets and higher prices for western staple products. A "wheat boom" was generated and sustained by a healthy demand for foodstuffs to supply the increasingly urban populations of industrial Europe and the United States. Transportation costs to Europe were falling, and the Canadian Pacific Railway (CPR) was clamouring for traffic and freight, particularly in the prairie West. New advances in dry-farming techniques, pioneered in the American West and Northwest in the 1880s and 1890s, and the introduction from the United States of new inventions in farm machinery like the chilled-steel plough, made the vast expanses of prairie soil more cultivable for farmers. The advent of early-maturing Red Fife and Marquis wheat strains and the appearance of mechanical grain elevators made it possible to cultivate seed during a short growing season, to expand cultivation into potentially fertile lands farther north on the Prairies, and then to market the grain more efficiently. With the American frontier largely settled by the mid-1890s, a swelling tide of European agriculturalists and land-hungry American farmers began heading for the Canadian Prairies, the "Last, Best West."

CLIFFORD SIFTON'S IMMIGRATION CAMPAIGN

An aggressive immigration promotion policy initiated by Wilfrid Laurier's Liberal government and under the leadership of its minister of the interior, Clifford Sifton, did much to facilitate the upsurge of immigration. Under Sifton, the interior department's immigration branch launched a massive promotional blitz to "sell" Canada to prospective immigrants in Britain, the United States, and continental Europe, and to "settle the empty West" with hardy, self-reliant agriculturalists. In the determined drive to "get results," Sifton's immigration officials poured over $1 million into extensive advertising and recruitment campaigns in the United States and Europe, organized tours of the West for trainloads of foreign newspaper editors and journalists, published and distributed millions of pamphlets extolling the virtues of "The Land of Opportunity," and paid generous bonuses to a group of German steamship agents, the North Atlantic Trading Company, in return for directing suitable settlers to the Dominion.[3]

THE "PUSH" FACTOR: ESCAPING HARDSHIPS IN EUROPE

Important as Sifton's organizational and promotional efforts were in stimulating immigration, many European immigrants were driven to Canada by economic and political hardships. Prominent among those fleeing the Old World were thousands of peasant farmers from central and eastern Europe. For many of them, Canada meant escape from overcrowding on small plots of land, relief from heavy land taxes, and freedom from political harassment under the rule of the crumbling Austro–Hungarian empire. A great number of Ukrainians, according to Ukrainian emigration promoter Dr. Joseph Oleskiw in 1895, desired "to quit their native

Selling Canada to prospective immigrants was a major part of Clifford Sifton's massive immigration promotion campaign.

country, due to overpopulation, subdivision of land holdings, heavy taxation, and unfavourable political conditions." Some emigrants sought to avoid compulsory military service in imperial armies. Other groups of emigrants, like the Jews, Mennonites, and Doukhobors of Russia, were fleeing from religious persecution. Compared with the estimated 1.5 million Jewish emigrés from Russia and Poland who moved to the United States between 1899 and 1914, however, relatively small numbers of this persecuted group entered Canada.

ARRIVING IN THE PROMISED LAND

During the peak immigration years, thousands of newcomers converged on Canada from all directions and headed in all directions. Once the new immigrants arrived, Immigration Branch officials took over, from the moment they disembarked from the steamship to the time they reached their destination. The officials processed the new arrivals in the Halifax or Quebec immigration sheds ("cattle pens"), and medical officers inspected their health. Other agents shepherded them onto CPR colonist car trains, often accompanying large parties as interpreters. Immigrants reached the West by colonist trains from the East Coast and by Pullman sleeper and in railway boxcars from Minnesota and Iowa. They also came in freight trains from Ontario and North Dakota, and in covered wagons from Utah and Idaho.

Breaking ground in the prairie West. Prairie women shared in the work, from raking hay to helping seed the turnips.

Winnipeg was the major western Canadian distribution point for immigration traffic from eastern Canada and overseas. Here a steady stream of immigrants took shelter in the immigration halls or, when the halls overflowed, bedded down on the cold floors of a skating rink or local hospital. From Winnipeg, they travelled in different directions by rail branch lines to their planned destinations. Frequently, new arrivals lacking much money spent their first night in government-provided bell tents, pitched beside many a prairie railway station.

Under Sifton's immigration policy, the responsibility of the state ended when new arrivals reached their destination. Officials were assigned to help immigrants locate their homesteads or to provide the names of local farmers seeking hired hands. But, once this was done, settlers were left, in Sifton's words, to "shift for themselves." Yet thousands of peasant farmers known as "sod busters" came to Canada with almost empty pockets — and were forced to work as farm labourers until they acquired sufficient starting capital. Still other settlers were driven in the winter season to tramp across the Prairies in search of wage work on the railways, in lumber and mining camps, to earn money for oxen or a plough. Little was done for those settlers who, despite energetic efforts, failed. Many of the almost 1 million American immigrants did, in fact, quit the Canadian West and return to their homeland.

IMMIGRANT WOMEN

The immigration wave also included surprising numbers of single women, mostly from Britain. Most of these women migrated to Ontario, although smaller numbers settled in

Manitoba and the West. Governments since the 1870s had sponsored single women to immigrate in response to the so-called "servant problem." In the early 1900s the problem became more acute as Canadian-born women increasingly shunned domestic service to take up factory, retail, or clerical work. Many domestic servants were single women, and large numbers of them were Finnish. The urban working-class women who answered the call often found working conditions difficult in isolated rural areas. They were driven by isolation and loneliness to change positions regularly, leaving domestic service for other kinds of employment. More and more single women migrated north and west during the immigration boom, abandoning domestic service to work in lumber camps, run boarding houses, or work in restaurants.[4]

THE URBAN IMMIGRANT EXPERIENCE

A large proportion of the poor farmers and farm labourers recruited by the Dominion government did not become agricultural-ists. While the official slogan of Sifton's immigration drive was "Only Farmers Need Apply," thousands of new immigrants congregated in the swelling, slum-ridden districts of Canadian cities. Large numbers of these urban immigrants were Italians, Jews, Greeks, and Chinese who came to settle in the ethnic ghettos of Toronto, Montreal, Winnipeg, and Victoria. There, amid overcrowding, unsanitary conditions, and extreme poverty, they became objects of curiosity, hostility, and often prejudice. To many middle-class Canadian social reformers, these "Little Italies," "Jewish quarters," and "Chinatowns" seemed like breeding grounds for disease and crime and cesspools of social vice. Yet these eth-nic communities showed great cultural vitality and aided thousands of newcomers to make the adjustment to a strange land. For the urban immigrant, the ethnic ghet-tos offered familiar Old World churches or synagogues, fraternal societies, and family

Newly arrived maids on the steps of the Finnish Immigrant Home in Montreal, Qubec, c.1929.

contacts, which eased the trauma of dealing with alien Canadian institutions, a new language, and a dramatically different way of life.

WEST COAST IMMIGRATION: ASIANS

Asian immigration into Canada had always been, and continued to be, essentially a West Coast phenomenon. In 1881 there were 4400 Asians in Canada, mainly Chinese who had entered from California during the gold rush. Between 1881 and 1884, some 15 700 more Chinese were brought in from Canton and Hong Kong as contract labourers to work on the CPR. When the railway was completed, the CPR disclaimed all responsibility for the Chinese workers, and neither the federal nor the provincial governments offered much assistance. By 1901 the number of Asians had risen to 23 700, including 4700 Japanese and about 1700 East Indians. Most Asians settled in British Columbia, where they made up 11 percent of the population and, since they were mostly adult males, a much higher proportion of the workforce.

Economic expansion in the early 1900s created a new demand for industrial labour and spurred a fresh infusion of Chinese, Japanese, and East Indian immigrants. An organization known as the Nippon Supply Company, working in association with the CPR and possibly with the tacit support of the Japanese government, was engaged in importing Japanese immigrants in a clandestine operation. In 1907–08 the number of Asians entering Canada increased dramatically: the figure jumped from 400 in 1904–05 to 12 000 four years later. In spite of a head tax of $500 imposed in 1903 on every Chinese immigrant, the influx of Chinese continued to increase, reaching a record high of nearly 7500 in 1912–13. While the Chinese immigrants were predominantly male, the women who came were either married to non-Chinese men or brought over by British Columbia businessmen who paid their head tax and employed them as domestics, waitresses, and even prostitutes. Asian immigrants working on railways or in mines and fisheries made a significant contribution to British Columbia's economic development. But many residents of British Columbia and scattered communities in the prairie West would come to see these immigrants as an economic and cultural threat.

RECEPTION IN THE PROMISED LAND

THE ARRIVAL OF HUNDREDS OF THOUSANDS of newcomers from all over the globe touched off a raging debate over immigration policy and the future shape of Canadian society. To the vast majority of Anglo-Canadians, the new arrivals, particularly central and eastern Europeans and Asians, seemed mysterious, culturally incompatible, and perhaps even threatening because of their sheer numbers. As immigration figures grew, public tensions mounted. Popular reactions among the host population ranged from grudging acceptance to outright prejudice until World War I, when the public debate assumed a new focus and urgency.

THE "FOREIGN PROBLEM"

Throughout the peak years of immigration, Anglo-Canadians confronted most non-British, non-French immigrants with the attitudes of Anglo-conformity. Members of the Anglo-Canadian élite were, with few exceptions, Anglo-Saxon Protestants who had grown up in a period when the British empire was on the rise. They gloried in the triumphs of the empire and believed firmly in loyalty to God, king, and country. In their view, the Anglo–Saxon peoples and the British principles of government represented the height of biological evolution and human achievement — and much of Canada's greatness stemmed from its Anglo–Saxon heritage.

How the multitude of new ethnic minorities could be assimilated or absorbed into English-Canadian or French-Canadian society was a question that troubled many Canadian journalists, reformers, and public officials.[5] As superintendent of All Peoples' Mission in north-end Winnipeg, the Methodist minister J.S. Woodsworth knew the immigrant problem at first hand. In 1908, when a quarter to a third of Winnipeg's population were "foreigners," he expressed a deep concern about overcrowding and commingling among the "tens of thousands of non–English-speaking immigrants." Seeing all the newcomers "poured into the same crucible," Woodsworth raised questions about what he called "the resultant product."

Conservative-minded English-Canadian writers and intellectuals like Stephen Leacock saw the problem differently: the new European and Asian immigrants were a threat to Anglo–Saxon values and institutions. The new arrivals were, in Leacock's view, impoverished, illiterate "proletarians" who lacked "experience with self-government" and were "unfit material from which to build the commonwealth of the future." Canada, Leacock contended in 1911, had followed the American method of "cheap and easy nation-making," and now confronted a greater problem of assimilating immigrants than did the United States.

The idea that Canada should be turned into a "melting-pot" had some advocates. The popular Presbyterian minister and writer Ralph Connor saw that out of the infusion of diverse races "one people is being made." In *The Foreigner* (1909), he wrote: "The blood strains will mingle in the blood of a race greater than the greatest of them all." Yet even those who espoused such a "melting-pot" ideology tended, in practice, to urge new immigrants to conform with Anglo–Canadian values and traditions.

The French-Canadian attitude toward immigration was mixed. Certainly the Liberal party, the major proponent of mass immigration, enjoyed the support of most Quebec voters after 1896. But some, like Quebec nationalist Henri Bourassa, who initially supported Sifton's immigration policy, grew alarmed over the shift in population balance. "Our partly French and partly English country," he told Parliament in 1906, was becoming "a land of refuge for the scum of all nations." The great fear was that the small French-Canadian populace in the West, unassisted by any significant immigration from Quebec or France, would be drowned in the flood of newcomers.

THE AMERICAN "MELTING POT"

THE POPULAR VIEW OF AMERICA as a "melting pot" is deeply rooted in the historical experience of the United States. From the eighteenth century onward, European and American social observers and writers expressed the belief that America was a "new nation" in which all immigrants could be absorbed and all would contribute to an "emerging national character." Even Frederick Jackson Turner, the American historian who developed the "frontier thesis" in the 1890s, gave credence to the melting pot idea. "In the crucible of the frontier," he asserted in 1920, "the immigrants were Americanized, liberated, and fused into a fixed race, English in neither nationality nor characteristics."

The conception of America as a "melting pot," however, was really popularized by Israel Zangwill, an English-Jewish writer who, at the turn of the century, saw the United States as a haven for the poor and oppressed of Europe. In 1908, Zangwill's drama, *The Melting Pot*, was produced for the first time; it became an American popular success. It is a play dominated by the dream of a composer, a young Russian-Jewish immigrant to America, whose goal is to create a vast "American" symphony, which expresses his love for an adopted homeland that serves as a model of ethnic harmony and brotherhood for all of humankind. In the process of writing the symphony, he falls in love with, and proposes to marry, a beautiful and cultured Gentile girl. Here the protagonist, David Zuixano, expounds his symphonic vision.

> America is God's crucible, the great Melting Pot where all the races of Europe are melting and re-forming! Here you stand, good folk, think I, when I see them at Ellis Island, here you stand in your fifty groups, with your fifty languages and histories, and your fifty hatreds and rivalries. But you won't be long like that, brothers, for these are the fires of God you've come to — these are the fires of God. A fig for your feuds and vendettas! Germans and Frenchmen, Irishmen and Englishmen, Jews and Russians — into the Crucible with you all! God is making the American.*

Zangwill's imagery was more than just a literary rhapsody. *The Melting Pot* gained wide popularity precisely because it gave voice to, and harmonized with, deeply held American nationalist, egalitarian ideas.

* Israel Zangwill, *The Melting Pot* (New York: Macmillan, 1909), p.37.

Immigration officials and most Anglo-Canadians had an "ethnic pecking order" for immigrants; they found British and American immigrants the most desirable, followed closely by western Europeans and Scandinavians, who were regarded as culturally similar and thus assimilable. Considerable opposition emerged over the entry of central and eastern Europeans, Asians, and three particular religious sects — Mennonites, Hutterites, and Doukhobors. Antipathy toward American blacks ran so deep that they were systematically barred from entering Canada. Because these groups were all considered "unmeltable," they suffered from racism and discrimination, along with the usual pressures for conformity to Anglo-Canadian ways.

OPEN DOOR VERSUS SELECTIVE IMMIGRATION

Open immigration was strongly supported by most industrialists and businesspeople. The remarkable growth of the booming agricultural and industrial sectors between 1896 and 1914 produced a demand for labour, both skilled and unskilled, that seemed insatiable. Two transcontinental railways were being built across the West. New mines and smelters were opening up all over the country. Factories were booming with record production levels. Settling the West was opening up new markets for eastern manufactures and new sources of valuable raw materials. What industrialists and other business interests desired — and sought — was a ready supply of cheap, pliant labour. But British immigrants, often highly skilled and union-oriented, could not fill the bill. So Canada's "captains of industry" urged the importation of more eastern Europeans. They were regarded as obedient and industrious, willing to work for low wages under "rough" conditions in mining, railway-building, and lumbering, and an important ingredient in sustaining a growing economy.[6]

Immigrant miners packed into rail cars at Donkin Mine, Cape Breton. The cargo includes Italians and a least one black miner.

Few Canadians endorsed such an open-door immigration policy. Frank Oliver, the minister of the interior who succeeded Sifton in 1905, favoured a more restrictive approach. To Oliver, what was at stake was the kind of society Canada wanted to build. For it to be one of the "great civilizations of the world," a policy of selective immigration was necessary, based on racial and cultural considerations. As minister of the interior, Oliver acted to tighten up the Immigration Act and made regular use of immigration procedures to exclude both Jews and blacks, whom he considered "undesirable." By 1911, he could assert with accuracy that his policy was "restrictive, exclusive, and selective" in comparison with Sifton's approach. But even the selective immigration measures undertaken by Oliver did little to dampen the flood of newcomers at the height of the immigration boom.

NATIVISM: THE TREATMENT OF UKRAINIANS AND DOUKHOBORS

The immigrant groups most often singled out for hostility on the Prairies were two central and eastern European communities of newcomers — Ukrainians and Doukhobors. Ukrainians were the most conspicuous and numerous eastern European group to arrive in western Canada after 1896. In all, some 170 000 land-starved Ukrainian peasants came to Canada between 1896 and 1914, settling primarily in groups in the parkland areas of Manitoba, Saskatchewan, and Alberta. Some immigration critics stereotyped Ukrainians as poor "men in sheepskin coats" and ascribed to them undesirable racial and cultural characteristics; others expressed deep-felt Anglo-Saxon nativist fears. The poverty of the new arrivals and reports of smallpox raised much public alarm. Further anxiety was aroused by the "isolation" of Ukrainians in their settlements and their tendency to resist adopting Anglo-Canadian ways. Anti-Ukrainian sentiment was taken up with great relish, mainly by Conservative newspapers and politicians, which flailed away at "promiscuous foreign immigration."

The arrival of the Doukhobors aroused even more anxiety. This immigrant group of 7400 peasants belonging to a Russian pacifist religious sect received a very unfriendly welcome in western Canada. Immigration officials encouraged them to settle near Prince Albert and Yorkton, Saskatchewan, where they might practice their pacifist, communal-living beliefs free from persecution. But friction developed between the sect and both Dominion and provincial governments over the granting of final title to their homestead lands. When the Doukhobors refused to give up communal land ownership and to swear the oath of allegiance to the crown, over half of their Saskatchewan lands were confiscated in 1907 by government authorities. As a result, many Doukhobors, under the spiritual leadership of Peter Veregin, moved in 1912 to the Kootenay region of British Columbia, where new lands were purchased and the sect continued to practise its non-conformist beliefs.

EXCLUSIONISM: ANTI-ASIAN SENTIMENT IN BRITISH COLUMBIA

Central and eastern European immigrants aroused nativist anxiety largely because of their numbers, but Asians suffered blatant discrimination for other reasons. In the Anglo-Canadian hierarchy of races, Chinese, Japanese, and East Indian immigrants, because they were non-white, were considered less desirable than the Slavs of Europe. Public debate over groups like the Ukrainians and the Doukhobors focused mostly on how they could be assimilated or made to conform with Anglo-Canadian ways. But public arguments over Asians — like that over American blacks — centred on whether they should be allowed to enter Canada at all. And debate over the non-white Chinese, Japanese, and East Indians already in Canada was not primarily about "Canadianizing" them, since this was widely regarded as both impossible and undesirable, but about whether or not they should be extended the same voting, residential, and occupational rights as other citizens.

A Chinese store and its patrons, British Columbia, 1890–1910. Storekeeping was a common Chinese occcupation in the West; those who moved east turned mainly to operating laundries and restaurants.

Asian immigration was not part of the Canadian government's plan to settle western Canada. Demands for the exclusion of Chinese immigrants had begun well before the turn of the century and resulted in legislative restrictions on their immigration. In response to these restrictions, the province's business leaders, led by the CPR, began in the early 1900s to import large numbers of Japanese and East Indians to perform the heavy labour once done by the Chinese.

"YELLOW PERIL" FEARS IN CALIFORNIA

SIZABLE NUMBERS OF ASIANS had come to America, known to the Chinese as the "Mountain of Gold," between 1850 and the turn of the century. Chinese first landed on the West Coast during the California gold rush, and thousands more followed in the late 1860s to work as "coolies" in the building of the Central Pacific Railroad. By 1880 some 75 000 had settled in California, and they made up some 20 percent of the labour force. Many enterprising Chinese, who had left their homeland for mainly economic reasons, enjoyed material success in California and other states. The Japanese were slower in migrating to the United States.

Asians faced great prejudice, hostility, and even violence in California, where most of them lived. The first public outcries against the Chinese were heard in the 1850s, but violent anti-Chinese feeling came to a head when economic depression struck California around 1873. The decline of rail construction caused Chinese to flood the labour market and intensified hostility among California workers. Ill-feeling, already running high, was fanned into violence by labour leader Dennis Kearney as crowds of unemployed California workers rallied on street corners and sand lots. The "sand lotters" soon attacked the unfortunate Chinese, lynching some in city streets and burning the homes and premises of others.

Public pressure from unemployed workers, distressed farmers, and American nativists resulted in restrictive legislation against the Chinese. California's new state constitution of 1879 enacted into law the slogan "Keep California White," prohibiting Chinese from owning property and working in certain occupations. Demands for immigration restriction built up among Californians, and Congress responded in 1882 by enacting the Chinese Exclusion Act. It prohibited Chinese workers from entering the United States, a policy renewed by later legislation every ten years until 1965. Faced with such hostility and discrimination, thousands of Chinese left the United States, and the entire population dwindled to some 61 000 by 1920.

The very success of enterprising Japanese in California led to anti-Japanese actions. Organized labour, fearful of competition from low-paid Japanese, and American nativists, crusading against an alleged "Yellow Peril," pressed for restrictive legislation. After the Chinese were excluded, pressure for further action against the Japanese resulted in a "gentleman's agreement" (1908) by which the government of Japan denied passage to all labourers, except "former residents" and their immediate families. It was an arrangement markedly similar to the one negotiated between Japan and Ottawa. Japanese students were also segregated in the schools of America's Far West, and in 1913 California prohibited Japanese ownership of land and restricted leasing to a three-year period. Japanese immigration slowed to a trickle, and thousands returned to their homeland.

The arrival of increasing numbers of Japanese and East Indians inflamed nativist feeling in British Columbia. Trade unionists regarded the Japanese as a more serious economic threat than the Chinese, since they were more aggressive in pursuing skilled jobs. Led by the extremist Asiatic Exclusion League, a series of demonstrations and parades were held in Vancouver in 1907 to protest the increasing inflow of Asian immigrants in a time of economic recession. Sparked by several emotional anti-Asiatic speeches, a march in June 1907 turned into a full-scale riot as mobs descended on Vancouver's "Chinatown" and "Little Tokyo," attacking Asians, breaking windows, and destroying business properties. A similar citizens' uprising occurred in Lethbridge, Alberta, in December 1907, when an angry crowd attacked two Chinese-owned restaurants and "roughed up" a few Chinese. In the aftermath of these riots, the Laurier government bowed to public pressure for immigration restrictions in 1908.

BARRING THE DOOR: THE *KOMAGATA MARU* INCIDENT

Canada's restrictive immigration policy faced its severest challenge during a controversial May 1914 incident. A Japanese-registered immigrant ship, the *Komagata Maru*, arrived in Vancouver harbour carrying 376 East Indians, apparently in an attempt to test regulations barring these British subjects from Canada. Port authorities, supported by Ottawa, refused to allow the vessel to dock. If these immigrants were accepted, the Vancouver *News–Advertiser* claimed, the remaining 300 million "natives of India…who have the same rights as these…would have the same claim." For over two months the ship, laden with immigrants, lay anchored offshore, while anti-Asian sentiment rose again in British Columbia.

To allow these Indians in, H.H. Stevens, Vancouver's Conservative M.P., told a huge rally of West Coast nativists, would threaten to eradicate "the civilization which finds its highest exemplification in Anglo-Saxon British rule." Canada must go as far as possible, he urged his enthusiastic audience, "to keep [itself] pure and free from the taint of other peoples." Finally, Robert Borden's Conservative government ordered the Canadian navy into action. The training ship *Rainbow* pulled alongside the *Komagata Maru* and escorted it out to sea, while cheering British Columbians lined the waterfront. The Pacific coast province would remain true to its name — British.

Asians refused entry. Some 376 South Asians brought to Vancouver on the *Komagata Maru* in 1914 were turned away by civic and immigration officials.

WARTIME NATIVISM AND THE "RADICAL ALIEN" SCARE

THE OUTBREAK OF WORLD WAR I in August 1914 brought dramatic changes in public attitudes toward immigrants and ethnic minorities. The Germans, who formerly had been regarded as among Canada's most desirable immigrant groups, almost overnight became the most undesirable. Immigrants from the Austro-Hungarian empire, including Ukrainians, Austrians, Poles, Czechs, and Slovaks, also found themselves under intense suspicion, though few felt any loyalty to their former imperial masters. These "enemy aliens," as all immigrants from enemy countries were called, became the objects of widespread persecution and hostility.[7]

THE THREAT OF THE "ENEMY ALIEN"

Canada's "enemy aliens," like their counterparts in the United States, faced a barrage of unofficial and official restrictions. Across the Dominion, German, Ukrainian, Austrian, and other "suspicious" eastern European workers were fired from their jobs and placed under police surveillance for what were termed "patriotic reasons." German- and Austrian-language schools and many of their churches were closed; their newspapers were first censored and then ordered to print in English only. In Berlin, Ontario, a German-Canadian community founded in the late 1700s, anti-German feeling ran so high that citizens voted to change the city's German name to "Kitchener," after Lord Kitchener, British secretary of state for war.

At critical times during the war, German-Canadian homes, clubs, and businesses were subjected to violent attacks. Rioting soldiers and civilians defaced, wrecked, and even looted German premises hotels and social clubs in Victoria, Calgary, and Berlin. In Calgary, the Alberta city with the largest German population, mobs of 500–1500 soldiers and civilians went on the rampage for two consecutive nights in February 1916, completely wrecking a German-owned restaurant and a hotel in the German-speaking district. In all three cities, local German-speaking residents (many of whom were naturalized citizens or German-speaking immigrants from Russia) barricaded themselves in their homes, hoping the fury would pass.

Government policy toward "enemy aliens" was as much a response to public pressure as an attempt to provide for Canada's security. Each enemy alien was required to register with a local magistrate, to report on a monthly basis, and to turn in all his or her firearms. Those declared "dangerous enemy aliens" after October 1914 were removed from cities and mining camps and placed in internment camps, simply because of suspect loyalty. In many cases, immigrant workmen who had been dismissed from jobs were interned to relieve the high unemployment rate. Over 8000 aliens were eventually interned, yet very few acts of sabotage or espionage were uncovered. Indeed, security risks were considered so minimal that all but a few of the internees were paroled in mid-1916 when a shortage of manpower arose during the war.

In 1917, concerns raised by Conservative–Unionists that the "foreign population" opposed conscription and would vote Liberal *en masse* met with a swift response. Under the Wartime

Elections Act of 1917, "enemy aliens" who were born in an enemy country, whose mother tongue was the language of an enemy country, and who had not been naturalized before 1902, were disfranchised. Unlike wartime registration and internment, the Act was directed primarily at naturalized Canadian citizens. Although some Liberal politicians and the Liberal press charged that taking the vote away from recognized Canadian citizens was both unfair and un-British, ethnic leaders, possibly sensing the weight of Anglo-Canadian opinion against "enemy aliens," merely accepted their fate.

RESTRICTIONS ON PACIFISTS

Immigrants from "enemy" countries were not alone in suffering the effects of wartime nativism. Similar treatment was meted out to three pacifist religious sects: Doukhobors, Mennonites, and Hutterites. Even though these groups came to Canada with specific guarantees from the federal government permitting them to maintain their autonomy, educational freedom, and exemption from military service, such formalities were easily forgotten in the atmosphere of wartime. As the casualty lists lengthened in World War I, increasing numbers of Canadians, particularly in western Canada, grew resentful of the exemptions from military service, which they felt were allowing many Mennonite and Doukhobor farmers to prosper. In Manitoba, the provincial government reacted to public pressure by making public school attendance compulsory, ending bilingual German–English language teaching in public schools, and closing Mennonite private schools. By 1919, agitation against the three groups by patriotic campaigners and veterans' groups finally bore fruit. The federal cabinet issued an order-in-council in June 1919 specifically barring the entry of members of these groups into the Dominion.

ANTI-RADICAL SENTIMENT AND THE 1919 LABOUR CRISIS

Canadian trade unions, capitalizing on expanding wartime industrial production, had bolstered their memberships by enlisting the support of thousands of immigrant workers. The newly potent union movement had flexed its muscles in a wave of strikes that swept the Dominion in 1917 and 1918. Most of the strikes were fought for higher wages to keep pace with wartime inflation. With the war's end had come new sources of tension and anxiety — the return of the veterans and a postwar economic recession.

Out of these postwar conditions emerged a relatively new and virulent form of anti-immigrant sentiment — anti-radical nativism. Much of the public hostility toward strikes in 1917 and 1918 assumed a nationalistic form because radical activity was identified in the public mind as the work of "foreigners." The fact that labour radicalism flourished in mines and frontier camps where the majority of workers were European immigrants, and that some radical labour leaders were class-conscious Slavs, gave rise to an image of the Slavic immigrant as dangerous revolutionary. To most employers and many Canadians, "foreigners" had no right to disrupt the harmony of Canadian society, and class conflict had no place in a Canada where there was ample opportunity for all.

A band of "Loyalist" Winnipeg veterans march in opposition to the General Strike and blame the "alien enemy" for stirring up labour unrest.

The connection between immigrants and radicalism was cemented in the public's mind by the dramatic events of 1919, a year of labour crisis in Canada. The most serious labour dispute, the Winnipeg General Strike of June 1919, enjoyed considerable support among Slavic immigrant labourers. Government leaders and businesspeople attempted to discredit the Winnipeg strike and strikes in other Canadian centres by charging that they were the work of alien revolutionaries.

A full-scale "Red Scare" ignited by the 1919 strikes claimed many victims. Foreign-born radicals were deported; police agents infiltrated left-wing political organizations; companies routinely fired suspected foreign radicals; and mobs of war veterans ransacked Winnipeg's Ukrainian Labour Temple and clashed openly with European immigrants in other western Canadian cities. Borden's government responded to the public indignation with new federal laws preventing the entry of immigrant radicals and strengthening the government's powers of deportation.

CANADIANIZATION IN THE 1920s

ATTITUDES TOWARD IMMIGRANTS IN CANADA during the early 1920s differed markedly from those in the United States. Between 1920 and 1924 there was an upsurge of nativist ferment across America, best exemplified by the rise of the Ku Klux Klan, which harassed blacks, Jews, Roman Catholics, and everyone it considered "dangerous" and "un-American." Economic depression, resumed immigration, and immigrant resistance to Prohibition laws all contributed to this revived Anglo-Saxon and anti-Catholic nativism. Yet nativist feeling seemed to wane almost everywhere in Canada except on the Pacific coast.

Anglo-Canadian assimilation in the 1920s was promoted under the guise of "Canadianization." Most influential Anglo-Canadians viewed the "melting pot" experience in the United States as a failure. In 1928 R.B. Bennett, then the Conservative opposition leader in Parliament, told the House of Commons that Canada would not allow itself to repeat the American mistake of becoming "a polyglot population without any distinctive civilization." By welcoming greater British immigration, it would make sure to "assimilate these people to British institutions." British civilization, he stressed, was "the test by which all other civilized nations are measured."

Efforts by Protestant churches and patriotic groups to Canadianize newcomers, which had begun at the turn of the century, were continued. Provincial governments, the churches, and voluntary organizations promoted the extension of the public school system as society's primary force for the assimilation of "foreigners." But assimilationist pressures in Canada were much milder than those exerted in the United States because English Canadians, wary of flag-waving nationalism, often could not agree on the norm to which immigrants were to be assimilated. For many ethnic minorities, however, the pressures of Anglo-conformity remained real.

RESPONSES TO ASSIMILATIONIST PRESSURES

Campaigns to Canadianize the large immigrant population were not completely successful; many ethnic and religious minorities preferred to maintain their own traditions, beliefs, language, and way of life. A few immigrant groups, mostly Mennonites and Doukhobors, continued to live in ethnic bloc settlements and to resist all attempts to impose Anglo-Canadian values and institutions. Immigrant groups simply refused to melt away as much in Canada as they had in the United States.

Nowhere was the conflict between tradition and assimilation more evident than in the experiences of many European families in the 1920s. Here the conflict was played out in the personal interaction between the "old" and the "new" generation in many families. A young Hungarian featured in John Marlyn's Winnipeg-based novel *Under the Ribs of Death* found himself torn between maintaining his old customs and trying to look and act English-Canadian.[8] Being different was rarely easy in a Canadian society that pointed fingers at "foreigners."

BOOSTERISM AND RENEWED IMMIGRATION

Restrictionist immigration policies initiated during the war and immediate postwar period did not last much beyond the early 1920s. Hoping to recapture the turn-of-the-century "boom" spirit, leading businesspeople, newspaper editors, and Liberal politicians began vigorously promoting new immigration.

AMERICANIZATION IN THE SCHOOLS

MANY AMERICAN EDUCATIONAL REFORMERS saw the schools as the principal solution to the "immigrant problem." Like most American nativists, they believed that if the new non-British immigrants could not be excluded, then everything must be done to instil Anglo-Saxon values in the allegedly "inferior breeds" of "foreigners" in their midst. Expressing this view, in 1909, American educator Ellwood P. Cubberly wrote that the task facing American institutions was to

> break up these people as a part of our American race, and to implant in their children, so far as can be done, the Anglo-Saxon conception of righteousness, law and order, and popular government, and to awaken in them a reverence for our democratic institutions and for those things in our national life which we as a people hold to be of abiding worth.*

Saluting the flag in the Mott Street Industrial School, New York, 1890.

*Ellwood P. Cubberley, *Changing Conceptions of Education* (Boston: Houghton Mifflin, 1909), pp.15–16.

This American assimilationist impulse, combining intense nationalism with Anglo-conformist ideas, contributed to the rise of the "Americanization" movement that gripped the United States during and after World War I. While "Americanization" had many varieties, in its crudest form it was a patriotic movement aimed at stripping immigrants of their traditions, culture, and language, and making them over into "Americans," steeped in Anglo–Saxon values and cherishing national ideals.

America's immigrant children who meant to better themselves learned the importance of "becoming American." In schools, settlement houses, and playground activities, the immigrant child was gradually "Americanized." But the process was far from painless. In many American families, the desire of immigrant children to gain acceptance in the majority culture drove a wedge between the generations. Immigrant parents watched with a mixture of pride and dismay as their children gradually turned into "Americans."

With the return of prosperity in 1925, Mackenzie King's Liberal government yielded to the pressure. Under the Railways Agreement of 1925, the Canadian National Railways (CNR) and the CPR were given permission to recruit agricultural immigrants from "non-preferred" countries in central and eastern Europe in order to meet the insistent demands of business for more settlers to boost western railway traffic, stimulate export trade, and open up larger markets for domestic manufacturers. Under this scheme, the railways brought some 200 000 central and eastern Europeans, including Ukrainians, Russian-Germans, Poles, Hungarians, and Mennonites, to Canada. Many of these newcomers came because a strict American quota system prevented them from entering the land of their first choice, the United States.

THE REVIVAL OF NATIVISM

The new wave of European immigration in the mid-1920s led again to a rise in nativist feeling and loud calls for "foreigners" to conform with "Anglo-Saxon" values and traditions. Public anxiety and fear was whipped up by western Canadian nativists, who charged that the Liberal government was attempting, through open immigration, to populate the nation with "Roman Catholics" from Europe. Nativist sentiment was perhaps strongest in Saskatchewan, where an Anglican bishop and Barr Colony founder, George Exton Lloyd, spouted anti-foreign ideas.

The Ku Klux Klan (KKK) was one patriotic organization that capitalized on this upsurge of Anglo-Saxon, anti-Catholic nativism. In a campaign to spread its influence beyond the southern and midwestern United States, the Klan had moved into Toronto and Montreal in 1921 and organized branches in southern Ontario, British Columbia, and Manitoba. Although the KKK had little success recruiting in Ontario and the Maritimes, western Canadians responded in alarming numbers to the Klan slogan of "One Flag, One Language, One School, One Race, One Religion."

THE KU KLUX KLAN REVIVAL IN THE 1920s

AMERICAN RACIAL INTOLERANCE after World War I was strongly reflected in the amazing revival of the Ku Klux Klan. The new Klan was formed in Georgia in 1915, and the organization spread quickly from its base in the South to parts of the Midwest and West. While the original Klan, founded in the post–Civil War Reconstruction era, had terrorized freed slaves and their white sympathizers, the new Klan emphasized broader nativist goals: the defence of Americanism, Protestant Christianity, and white supremacy. Consequently, the Klan harassed not only blacks, but also "foreigners," Roman Catholics, and Jews. Anti-Semitism, based on the belief that Jews were the root of urban corruption, now became a major part of their message of hate.

Between 1920 and 1923, Klan membership in the United States jumped from 5000 to 3 million. The new Klan emerged as a powerful political force in Texas, Oregon, Georgia, Oklahoma, Alabama, and especially Indiana. Candidates supported by the Klan were elected governors in Oklahoma and Oregon. The political strength of the Klan declined after 1924, however, when Klan leaders became embroiled in corrupt and illegal activities and the organization's lynchings and violence provoked a public backlash.

Ku Klux Klan meeting in Kingston, Ontario, 1927.

Unlike the American parent organization, which espoused Americanism, white supremacy, and anti-Semitism, the Canadian offshoot emphasized anti-Catholicism and moral rectitude. Klan leaders found their most fertile ground in Saskatchewan: in four months during 1927, the KKK's Saskatchewan following jumped from fewer than 50 to more than 15 000, and local branches sprouted up in the cities and towns of Alberta and Manitoba. Despite firm opposition from the Liberal press and from Saskatchewan premier Jimmy Gardiner, KKK membership reached a peak of 20 000 in the summer of 1928. In Saskatchewan and Manitoba, the KKK vanished almost as suddenly as it had appeared, but in Alberta the movement survived in various forms for almost a decade.

The growth of the Klan in Canada seemed, on the surface, to be an expression of American cultural attitudes. Yet the principal KKK organizers in Saskatchewan and Alberta both came from predominantly anti-Catholic, rural Ontario. Like most major social and institutional forces in western Canada during the 1920s, the KKK reflected cross-influences from Britain, Ontario, and the United States, the West's three main sources of immigration.

THE CHALLENGE OF ETHNIC DIVERSITY

Canadian society in the 1920s remained marked by stubborn ethnic and cultural differences. Confronted with this reality, many Canadians began to show sympathy for "melting pot" ideas. As the anxious wartime nativist impulse faded and Anglo-Canadian assimilation efforts started to falter, the "melting pot" approach to Canadianization won much more popular favour.

Signs of the growing acceptance of "melting pot" ideas could be found in many places. A new generation of writers, such as Kate Foster, author of *Our Canadian Mosaic* (1926), argued that immigrant assimilation was indeed occurring, but the end product was a new "Canadian" type. Not only were some of these Canadian writers confident that non–Anglo-Saxon immigrants could be assimilated, they even conceded that the immigrants in question might have some valuable cultural contributions to make. A few influential English-Canadian leaders, like John W. Dafoe, editor of the *Winnipeg Free Press*, and John S. Ewart, a prominent nationalist spokesman, recognized that non-British immigrants could not be expected to feel loyalty to the British empire and publicly discussed the need for conformity to exclusively "Canadian" institutions and values.

Between 1880 and the mid-1920s Canada, like the United States, had absorbed its first major waves of European and Asian immigration and confronted critical questions concerning immigration policy and the future shape of society. Throughout the period, English Canadians and French Canadians showed little inclination to create a "mosaic" society by encouraging the cultural survival of ethnic minorities. If such a multicultural society was beginning to form, it owed much to powerful historical and social forces and little to consciously pursued immigration and cultural policies. In Canada, the historic English–French duality continued to inhibit the development of a strong, concrete nationalism, and the relative size of the immigrant intake in relation to the host population helped make complete cultural assimilation a virtual impossibility. And Canada's recurrent pattern of Anglo-Canadian nativism, anti-Asian sentiment, and racially "selective" immigration policies calls into question the popular assumption that Canadians have been notably more tolerant toward ethnic minorities than have Americans.

ACTIVITIES

KEY TERMS AND CONCEPTS

Identify and briefly explain the historical significance of each of the following terms and concepts:

- The immigration boom
- Reluctant hosts
- Nativism
- "The Last, Best West"
- "Servant problem"
- Ethnic ghettos
- Melting pot
- Anglo-conformity
- Selective immigration
- Exclusionism
- *Komagata Maru* incident
- Enemy aliens
- Anti-radical nativism
- Canadianization and Americanization
- John Marlyn's *Under the Ribs of Death*

QUESTIONS FOR DISCUSSION

1. What were the major causes of the massive
   immigration to North America that began in
   the last half of the nineteenth century? Why
   did Canada not experience the "immigration
   boom" until the late 1890s?
2. How did men and women differ in their
   immigration and settlement experiences?
   How were women, single as well as married,
   affected by those experiences?
3. In what ways was the "new immigration" to
   the United States and Canada different
   from previous movements of people to
   North America?
4. How did the host populations of Canada and
   the United States react to the new arrivals?
   Were there any differences in the way the
   two countries received the new European and
   Asian immigrants?

5. What form did Anglo-Canadian "nativism"
   take in connection with: (a) eastern and central Europeans, (b) Asians, (c) wartime
   enemy aliens, (d) pacifist religious sects, (e)
   radical labour leaders? Was it more or less
   hostile than the prevailing American attitude?
6. The United States has long been considered a
   "melting-pot" society, while Canada has a reputation as a "mosaic" or cultural pluralist society. Do either of those popular metaphoric
   descriptions "fit" in the immigration boom
   period from 1880 to the 1920s?

ASSESSING HISTORICAL INTERPRETATIONS

Assess each of the following conflicting interpretations of immigration and nativism in
Canada and the United States. Nativism is a
concept of American origin that has been identified as a major factor in the history of immigration and ethnic relations. Is this concept
applicable to the Canadian experience? Weigh
each of the following views in explaining your
answer.

"The concept of 'nativism' is inapplicable to Canada
in view of the very different historical development
of Canada and the United States and the particular
context within which nativism arose in the United
States…. American nativism…while witnessing strong
regional variations, reflected the revolutionary experience and the consensus approach to nation-building;
it embodied the ideals of homogeneity and uniformity which underpinned the notions of the 'American
way of life' based on the dominance of the largely
Anglo-Protestant host society. Canada, with its dual
colonial past (French and English experiences) and its

lack of a revolutionary tradition, has had a more amorphous national identity and Canadians have found it more difficult than Americans to articulate and legitimate a national ideal."

— A synopsis of Cornelius Jaenen, "The Unique Qualities of Canadian Ethnic Studies," University of Toronto lecture, October 5, 1978.

"That nationalism has been significantly different in Canada does not mean that nativism has not existed; rather it simply means that in Canada the types of nationalism which allied themselves with prejudice were different from those in the United States. The all-pervasive fact of two major societies in Canada — one English-speaking and one French-speaking — has not prevented each of them from developing its own model or ideal by which newcomers are judged and its standards to which newcomers are expected to conform. Although Canada's dualism has admittedly prevented the development of one national consensus like that which generated nativism in the United States, both English-speaking and French-speaking Canada developed their own nationalistic norms....

"While a comparison between Canadian and American nativism reveals some differences, it does show that...three strains of nativism (Anglo-Saxon, anti-Catholic, and anti-radical)...had considerable influence in western Canada prior to World War II."

— Howard Palmer, *Patterns of Prejudice: A History of Nativism in Alberta* (Toronto: McClelland and Stewart, 1982), pp. 8–9. Used by permission of the Canadian publishers, McClelland and Stewart, Toronto.

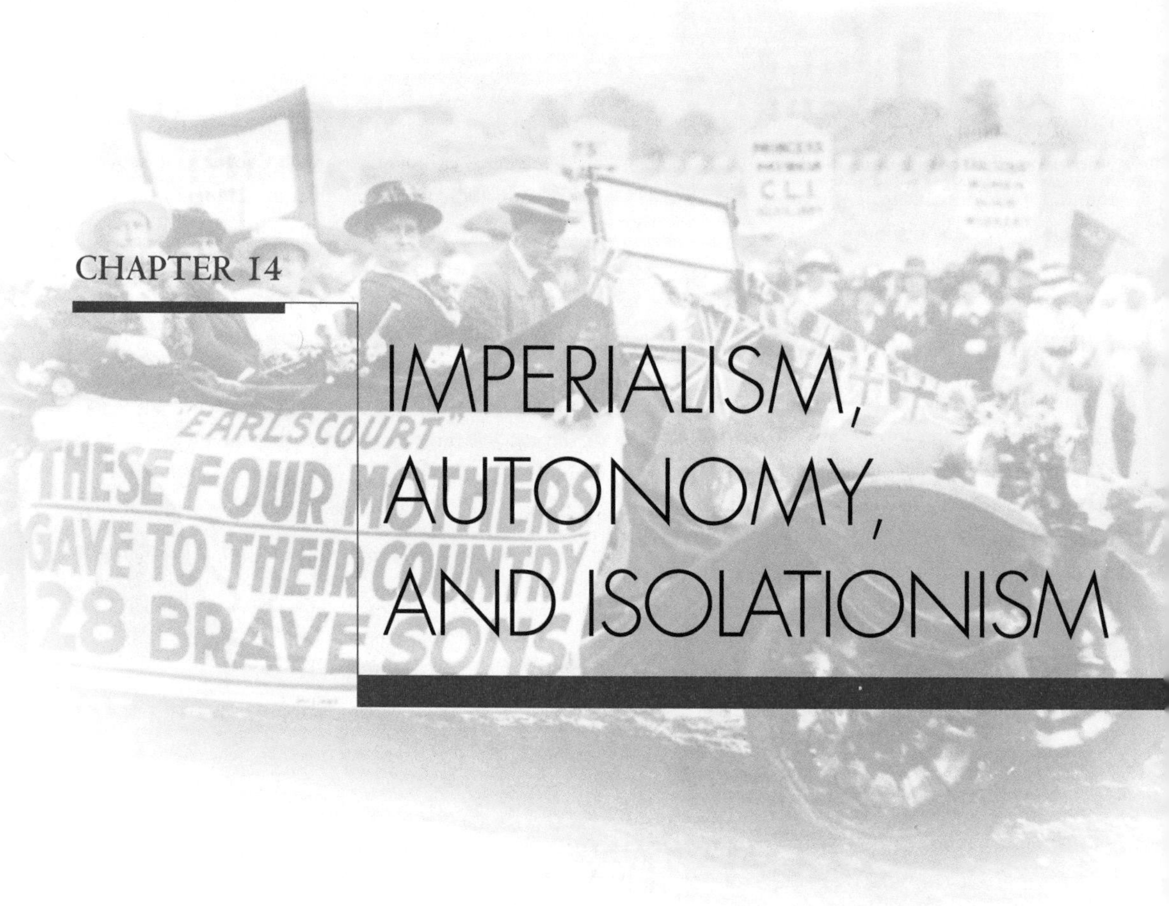

CHAPTER 14

IMPERIALISM, AUTONOMY, AND ISOLATIONISM

CANADA AND THE NEW IMPERIALISM

THE CLASH OF EMPIRES

RESPONSES TO THE GREAT WAR

ISOLATIONISM IN THE INTERWAR YEARS

AT THE TURN OF THE TWENTIETH CENTURY, a new age of imperialism was profoundly altering relations among the world's nations. A revival of world prosperity was accompanied by intensified trade rivalries and imperial competition. The world's great nation-states, particularly Great Britain, Germany, and their newest rival — the United States — dominated international relations. As their interests and entanglements became worldwide, few nations were untouched by the effects of their imperial rivalries.

In the new imperialist age, Canadians had to tread a careful path. Just as Canada began to emerge as a full-fledged, autonomous nation, Britain appealed to Canada and other self-governing dominions to embrace closer imperial federation, to rally to the defence of empire in South Africa, and then to honour military commitments in a major European war. Meanwhile, the United States rose to become a world power through the acquisition of an empire of its own in the Caribbean Sea, the Pacific Ocean, and the Far East. Thus, good relations with this North American neighbour were obviously desirable for Canada, while American "Manifest Destiny" had to be closely watched.[1]

CANADA AND THE NEW IMPERIALISM

WHEN WILFRID LAURIER'S GOVERNMENT took office in 1896, imperialism was clearly on the rise. Great Britain, the United States, and the powerful European nation-states were pursuing overseas territories and shifting the world balance of power in the process. The main reason for this expansionism was economic: industrializing countries sought new outlets for products and new sources of raw materials. In Great Britain in the 1860s, the colonies had been treated as "millstones"; now, at the end of the nineteenth century, they were celebrated as jewels in the imperial crown. This dramatic shift in British thinking about the empire was in large part a response to the rise of imperial Germany; Britain and Germany were rivals in a fierce competition over naval building and overseas expansion.

The new imperialism was supported by social arguments. Political leaders and imperialist thinkers claimed that the developed European and American nations were engaged in a "civilizing mission." The imperial spirit in Great Britain, the United States, and nearly every European country stressed the superiority of one "race" over another. It was considered the "white man's burden" to civilize less developed colonies. The new imperialism often found expression in "jingoism" (extreme nationalism), but it also infused new industrial societies like Britain and the United States with a spirit of progressive social reform. In the United States, as in Britain, the imperial mission was usually championed by progressive reformers like America's president, Theodore Roosevelt.

THE IMPERIAL FEDERATION MOVEMENT

The dawning of the new imperialism brought an end to Canada's exclusion from crises beyond its borders. Alarmed by the growth of military power in Europe and by increasing competition in commerce and industry, British politicians turned to the empire for support. The Imperial Federation League was founded in 1884. A young British businessman turned politician, Joseph Chamberlain, said in Toronto in 1888: "It may be that the Confederation of Canada may be the lamp lighting our path to the federation of the British Empire.... Let us do all in our power to promote it and enlarge the relations and goodwill which ought always to exist between the sons of England throughout the world and the old folks at home."

To many English-speaking Canadians, the appeal to Anglo-Saxon superiority aroused strong loyalties. But for those nationalists wanting greater Dominion autonomy, it seemed to imply a centralized federation in which Canada's growing nationalism would be stifled. And among anti-imperialists, especially those of French-Canadian origin, these visions of Anglo-Saxon greatness produced outright hostility or at best indifference.

In the late 1880s and early 1890s, imperialist ideas took strong root in Canada at a time

Colonial Conference, London, 1897. The colonial secretary, Joseph Chamberlain, is seated, surrounded by colonial prime ministers and governors, including Sir Wilfrid Laurier.

when prolonged economic depression, growing English–French antagonisms, and the threat of American commercial union raised fears of Canada's imminent dissolution. Canadian imperialists, as a countermeasure to reciprocity with the United States, advocated the idea of an economic union of the empire through preferential tariffs.

THE CANADIAN VARIETY OF IMPERIAL NATIONALISM

Leading Canadian imperialists promoted imperial unity as a unique form of Anglo-Canadian nationalism. The prominent spokesmen for the movement were Colonel George T. Denison of Toronto, a police magistrate and military enthusiast; George R. Parkin, the headmaster of Upper Canada College in Toronto; and the Reverend George M. Grant, principal of Queen's University. They believed that Canada could survive and grow only if it maintained the imperial connection. They were convinced that though unrestricted reciprocity might bring temporary prosperity, it would also lead to the gradual assimilation of Canada into the United States. As Grant observed, "We are Canadian, and in order to be Canadian we must be British." To leading imperialists, support for the British in economic and defence matters was a means to attain fuller Canadian nationhood and a way to play a larger role in the world.[2]

Even though the imperial unity movement never secured a British imperial preferential trading system, the movement gathered fresh strength and new adherents and exerted a powerful influence on Ottawa after the mid-1890s. Its most ardent supporters came from the older regions of Ontario and the Maritimes, particularly from areas peopled by descendants of the United Empire Loyalists. Toronto retained its late-nineteenth-century reputation as the country's most imperialistic city. One measure of the movement's appeal could be seen in the public schools of Ontario and other English-speaking provinces. Here the greatness of the empire was described in "approved" school readers and illustrated in classroom displays; Empire Day — Queen Victoria's birthday — was celebrated with children's parades, patriotic songs, and essay-writing contests. In local communities, the Imperial Order Daughters of the Empire (IODE) took the lead in organizing many imperial nationalist events.

WILFRID LAURIER'S IMPERIALISM

Wilfrid Laurier became prime minister in 1896. To Laurier and his supporters, the main concern was to preserve and promote racial harmony between English Canadians and French Canadians. As Laurier wrote in 1904: "My object is to consolidate Confederation, and to bring our people, long estranged from each other, gradually to become a nation." But much like John A. Macdonald before him, Canada's first French-Canadian prime minister claimed in 1897 that he was "British to the core." His imperialism was based on respect for British political traditions and a belief that the empire was the bulwark of justice and liberty in the world.

TWO VOICES OF IMPERIALISM

THE TWO IMPERIALIST THINKERS of the late nineteenth century who exerted the greatest influence on Canada and the United States were Joseph Chamberlain, British colonial secretary from 1895 to 1903, and Alfred T. Mahan, whose volumes on the role of sea power in history made a profound impression on American expansionists. Chamberlain argued that Britain's empire represented a source of strength and vitality and made a great contribution to the civilization of the world. Captain Mahan argued that America's honour and prestige, as well as her defence and trade, depended on the acquisition of overseas naval bases, the control of the Caribbean and trade routes to the Far East, and the creation of an unassailable naval force.

JOSEPH CHAMBERLAIN ON IMPERIAL UNION IN 1903

In a famous speech delivered at Glasgow in October 1903, Chamberlain extolled the practical advantages of empire to Britain and the colonies alike:

> I appeal to you as fellow-citizens of the greatest Empire that the world has ever known; I appeal to you to recognize that the privileges of Empire bring with them great responsibilities. [*Cheers*] I want to ask you to think what this Empire means, what it is to you and your descendants. I will not speak, or, at least, I will not dwell, on its area, greater than that which has been under one dominion in the history of the world. I will not speak of its population, of the hundreds of millions of men for whom we have made ourselves responsible. But I will speak of its variety, and of the fact that here we have an Empire which with decent organization and consolidation might be absolutely self-sustaining.[*Loud cheers*]...
>
> And when I speak of our colonies, it is an expression; they are not ours — they are not ours in a possessory sense. They are sister States, able to treat with us from an equal position, able to hold to us, willing to hold to us, but also able to break with us. I have had eight years' experience.[*Cheers*] I have been in communication with many of the men, statesmen, orators, writers, distinguished in our Colonies. I have had intimate conversation with them. I have tried to understand them and I think I do understand them [*Cheers*], and I say that none of them desire separation. There are none of them who are not loyal to this idea of Empire which they say they wish us to accept more fully in the future, but I have found none who do not believe that our present colonial relations cannot be permanent. We must either draw closer together or we shall drift apart.

ALFRED T. MAHAN ON "LOOKING OUTWARD," 1890

In this passage from *The Interest of America in Sea Power* (1890), Alfred T. Mahan emphasizes the importance of sea power in achieving national greatness. His expansionist doctrines won many converts. Foremost among his disciples was Theodore Roosevelt, who became assistant secretary of the navy in 1897 and later an expansionist president of the United States.

> Indications are not wanting of an approaching change in the thoughts and policy of Americans as to their relations with the world outside their own borders.... It is safe to predict that, when the opportunities for gain abroad are understood, the course of American enterprise will cleave a channel by which to reach them....
>
> The interesting and significant feature of this changing attitude is the turning of the eyes outward, instead of inward only, to seek the welfare of the country. To affirm the importance of distant markets, and the relation to them of our own immense powers of production, implies logically the recognition of the link that joins the products and the markets — that is, the carrying trade; the three together constituting that chain of maritime power to which Great Britain owes her wealth and greatness.... We shall not follow far this line of thought before there will dawn the realization of America's unique position, facing the older worlds of the East and West, her shores washed by the oceans which touch the one or the other, but which are common to her alone....
>
> To protect and develop its own, each nation will seek points of support and means of influence in a quarter where the United States always has been jealously sensitive to the intrusion of European powers. The precise value of the Monroe Doctrine is understood very loosely by most Americans, but the effect of the familiar phrase has been to develop a national sensitiveness, which is a more frequent cause of war than material interests; and over disputes caused by such feelings there will preside none of the calming influence due to the moral authority of international law, with its recognized principles, for the points in dispute will be of policy, of interest, not of conceded right....
>
> Whether they will or no, Americans must now begin to look outward....
>
> Alfred T. Mahan, *The Interest of America in Sea Power* (Boston: Little, Brown, 1890).

While Laurier sympathized with Canada's evolution toward dominion self-government within the empire, he did surprisingly little to advance the process. At the 1897 colonial conference, the British colonial secretary, Joseph Chamberlain, put forward a strong appeal for imperial federation. Chamberlain proposed a "great council of the empire," free trade, and a single imperial navy. Like other colonial prime ministers, Laurier saw this as an association to be dominated and guided by Britain for its own purposes. In an 1897 conference in London he rebuffed Chamberlain's scheme, declaring himself "quite satisfied with the conditions of things as they are," and he continued to insist that imperial ties should neither be formalized nor strengthened. Canada's contribution to the empire would be determined in Canada, by Canadians, and according to Canadian needs. His position amounted to what John Dafoe, editor of the *Winnipeg Free Press*, once called "fifteen years of saying no" to most appeals for closer imperial unity.

ANTI-IMPERIALISM IN CANADA

The aggressive imperialism of late Victorian Britain was not without its critics in Canada. After 1900, anti-imperialism became a major force, particularly in French Canada, and came to be symbolized there by one man — Henri Bourassa. Bourassa, a former Quebec Liberal, broke with Laurier over the South African war, and from 1899 onward mounted, with his associates Olivar Asselin and Armand Lavergne, a stinging critique of British imperialism as reactionary, anti-Canadian, and racist.

Opposition to imperialism did not come from French Canada alone. Among the leading English-Canadian critics were political economist Adam Shortt, lawyer John S. Ewart, and poet Charles Mair. These nationalists were determined to be "more British than American," more monarchical than republican. The "kingly function," to use Mair's phrase, was an important foundation of Canadian life, and one that defined the tone and style of the emerging Canadian community.

THE CLASH OF EMPIRES

CANADA AT THE TURN OF THE CENTURY confronted a world undergoing dramatic shifts in power relations. By the late 1890s, the new imperialism was becoming more bellicose and threatening. New strains were being placed on relations within the historic North Atlantic triangle of Canada, Britain, and the United States. The British empire, which now covered over one-quarter of the globe, seemed to be entering its twilight in spite of Joseph Chamberlain's attempts to create a centralized imperial federation. While British hegemony faced increasing challenges, America was fast rising to become a world power.

AMERICA'S NEW IMPERIALISM

Since the 1860s, the United States had shown a growing interest in foreign markets. By the 1890s, the American frontier was closing for settlement. The United States was now the world's leading industrial power and needed new sources of raw materials and more extensive markets abroad. American capital poured first into Hawaii and Cuba, and then into other distant, underdeveloped areas of the globe.[3] To many American expansionists, the Manifest Destiny impulse that inspired westward expansion now extended beyond the continent and across the seas.

The assertiveness of the new American imperialism was clearly demonstrated in the 1895 Venezuelan boundary crisis. Britain and Venezuela had haggled for eight years over the boundary line separating Venezuela and British Guiana, a small British colony on the north-ern coast of South America. After the British refused to settle the matter by arbitration, the American administration intervened directly with Secretary of State Richard Olney's diplo-matic note, reaffirming the Monroe Doctrine. The British prime minister, Lord Salisbury, stood firm, accusing the United States of "twisting the tail of the British lion." But the war scare that followed produced a negotiated settlement in 1897.

During America's expansionism in the late nineteenth century, the flag often followed the dollar. American trade and investment in the Caribbean, the Pacific, and the Far East brought extensive overseas possessions and spurred the development of a large naval fleet to protect new territories, or "spheres of influence." Even though the United States was a relative late-comer to the scramble for empire, its territorial gains after 1898 were extensive. In short order, the United States became a full-fledged colonial power. It annexed the Hawaiian Islands and humbled Spain in the Spanish–American War, quickly acquiring Puerto Rico, the Philippines, and Guam, and establishing a protectorate over Cuba.

"BIG STICK" DIPLOMACY

Under President Theodore ("Teddy") Roosevelt, the United States began to assert its imperial power and influence in the world. Roosevelt actively promoted commerce abroad, championed the Monroe Doctrine, and stood ready to meet any challenge to America's national interest. His brash philosophy of American assertionism was clearly expressed in 1900 when he declared, "Speak softly and carry a big stick, you will go far." Roosevelt's policy embodied a view, held by many Americans, that it was the "mission" of "superior" countries such as the United States to carry out the "most regrettable but necessary international policy duty which must be performed for the sake of the welfare of mankind."

Roosevelt's imperial methods were perhaps most starkly revealed in the taking of the Panama Canal. A canal through the Isthmus of Panama would consolidate U.S. control of the Caribbean Sea and shorten the shipping route between the Atlantic and the Pacific oceans. After a U.S. offer to purchase the canal site for $10 million from Colombia was rebuffed, Roosevelt urged Panamanians to rise in revolt. American canal lobbyists succeeded in incit-ing a revolution in November 1903, and the president sent the warship U.S.S. *Nashville* to ensure that Colombia did not interfere. He quickly recognized the rebel Panamanian gov-ernment, finalized the canal deal, and turned the new nation of Panama into another American protectorate. Years later Roosevelt boasted, "I took the Canal Zone and let Congress debate." When the canal opened in 1914, its official motto was "The Land Divided, the World United," and the U.S. navy enjoyed easy access between the Atlantic and the Pacific oceans.

The growing imperialism of Teddy Roosevelt's foreign policy did not go uncriticized: here Roosevelt is depicted as the policeman of the world.

THE ALASKA BOUNDARY DISPUTE

In this imperialist age, Canada could be forgiven for treading carefully. Good relations with Washington were obviously desirable, but America's designs on the continent needed watching. For many Canadians a sense of "nationality" was aroused by the fear, real or imagined, of absorption by the rising American empire. This feeling of nationality, rooted in loyalty to the "British connection," was only reinforced by the unease and suspicion engendered by what Governor-General Lord Minto once called "the Yankee bluff and swagger."

Getting along with the Americans was a challenge for Wilfrid Laurier's government. Since 1896 Ottawa had quarrelled with Washington over a series of issues, including the high U.S. tariff, the inshore Atlantic fisheries, and an American law barring "alien" Canadian labour. But none was as serious as the Alaska boundary dispute in 1903. At stake was the international boundary between Canada and Alaska, stretching some 1000 km down the coast beside the Yukon and British Columbia in the "Alaska Panhandle." This boundary had not been defined since the Anglo–Russian Treaty of 1825.

The Alaska boundary became an urgent matter in the late 1890s, when gold was discovered in the Klondike region of the Yukon and thousands of gold miners rushed there. Canadian and American merchants on the Pacific coast fought for the lucrative trade of bringing in supplies for the gold seekers. In the intense commercial rivalry that arose between Vancouver and Seattle especially, the boundary line became vital. Canada clearly had the rich gold fields in its territory, but the Americans claimed ownership of the coastal inlets leading to the fields from the Pacific. The crux of the question was the division of the Lynn Canal, the best route to the Klondike, on which lay the ports of Skagway and Dyea. If the head of the Lynn Canal was designated Canadian territory, goods from Vancouver could enter freely; otherwise they must pass through American customs houses, to the economic benefit of Seattle.

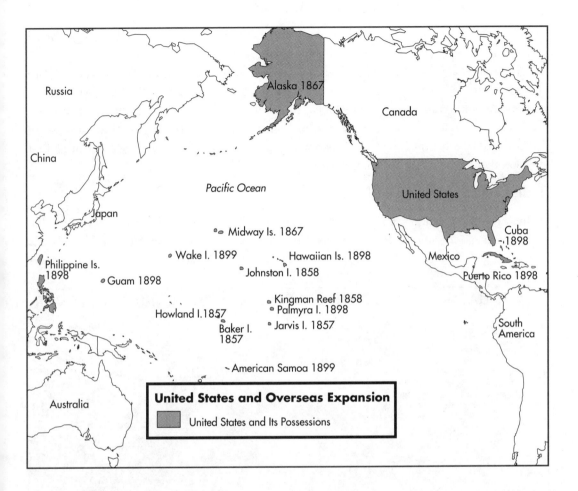

THE ALASKA DECISION

President Roosevelt adopted a tough stance to persuade Britain to let the United States have its way in the Alaska dispute. The dispute was referred to a joint commission of six officials, three from the United States and three appointed by Great Britain. The British government named two Canadians and the lord chief justice of England, Lord Alverstone, to the tribunal. Although the arbitration agreement stipulated that each side would appoint "impartial jurists of repute," Roosevelt named his secretary of war and two senators well known for their hard-line positions on the Alaska question. Furthermore, Roosevelt warned the British privately that if the tribunal failed to uphold the American claim, he would send U.S. marines to "run the line."

In the end, rather than risk offending Roosevelt and possibly upsetting Anglo–American relations, Lord Alverstone supported the U.S. claim, giving the Americans almost all they had demanded. His decision resulted in an outpouring of bitterness in Canada. Many Canadians, including the two Canadian commissioners and most newspaper editorialists, denounced Britain and its representatives for sacrificing the interests of Canada.

After the Alaska decision, Laurier came slowly to recognize that the Dominion's welfare could be better served if Canada assumed responsibility for its own diplomatic negotiations, particularly with Washington. Accordingly, the Laurier government in 1909 authorized the creation of a modest department of external affairs, and joined with the United States to establish the International Joint Commission to deal with mutual disputes — two halting first steps on the long road to Canadian autonomy.

THE SOUTH AFRICAN CRISIS

At the turn of the century, Canada was also confronted with critical choices in its relationship with Britain and the empire. Public pressures for closer imperial unity came to a head in Canada during the Boer War of 1899–1902. In early October 1899, Britain declared war on the Boers

PEACE HATH HER VICTORIES NO LESS RENOWNED THAN WAR.

A harshly critical view of Wilfrid Laurier's South African policy. On the eve of the Boer War in October 1899, Julien of the *Montreal Star* drew a sharp contrast between the prime minister's professions of imperial solidarity and his response to an appeal for Canadian participation in the South African conflict. When war broke out a week later, Laurier's government dispatched a contingent of volunteers.

in South Africa, allegedly to end persecution against British subjects in the Transvaal and to protect the interests of all non-Africans, known as *Uitlanders*, in the colony. The British considered it a serious military emergency, and the colonial secretary requested Canadian military units to fight alongside the British in defence of the empire.

Britain's intervention in South Africa opened bitter racial divisions in Canada. Most English-speaking Canadians, led by prominent imperial-nationalists and spurred on by a jingoistic English-language press, responded to Chamberlain's call for Canadian troops with enthusiasm.[4] To them, contributing to the defence of the empire was an opportunity for Canadians to demonstrate nationhood by aiding Britain in its "hour of need." Lord Minto, Canada's governor-general, and General Edward Hutton, the British commander of the Canadian militia, pressed the Laurier government to make a contribution in keeping with "the importance of Canada."

The Boer War not only brought Canadian imperial sentiment to a fever pitch, it also galvanized anti-imperialists into action. In French Canada the struggle of the Boers for their "national" rights aroused some sympathy, and proposals for Canadian participation were greeted with vehement opposition. To Bourassa and his fellow anti-imperialists, it was "Britain's colonial war," a far-off conflict that had little to do with Canada. Sending troops to South Africa, they charged, would set a dangerous precedent for further demands from Britain.

Caught between the conflicting demands of English Canadians for troops and the stiff resistance of his French-speaking ministers, Laurier attempted a compromise to avert a racial crisis. Canada would raise a volunteer contingent of 1000 troops and transport them to South Africa, where the British government would provide for their financial support. To placate French-Canadian critics, Laurier made it clear that such a policy should not be considered as a "precedent for future action." The initial Canadian volunteer force, commanded by Lieutenant-Colonel William Otter, was quickly dispatched to South Africa and later was joined by other military units. By war's end, about 7000 Canadians had served in South Africa.

Like most compromises, the Boer War decision failed to satisfy everyone. Laurier's policy of using volunteers was condemned by many English-speaking imperial nationalists as a clever but unworthy evasion of Canadian responsibility. A few Canadian patriots chastised Laurier for not insisting on independent Canadian participation. Some French-Canadian critics charged — in spite of Laurier's assurances to the contrary — that the policy constituted a binding commitment to future participation in all of the empire's military adventures. The highly principled and idealistic Henri Bourassa broke with Laurier on the issue, resigning his House of Commons seat in protest. "To govern," he snapped angrily, "is to have courage…to risk power to save a principle."

THE NAVAL QUESTION

In spite of concerted efforts to avoid further entanglements after the Boer War, Laurier found it impossible to remain aloof from questions of imperial defence. Growing tensions in Europe and the dangers posed by an escalating Anglo–German rivalry caused an agitation for greater colonial participation in the naval race. This reached a peak in the winter of 1908–09, when it was rumoured that Germany's secret naval power threatened to overtake that of Britain. In 1909, pressure on Laurier's government mounted as Britain doubled its naval building program and appealed to the empire for immediate cash contributions.

Though Laurier had been promising to develop a Canadian naval defence policy since 1902, little had been done. Now the "naval scare" forced Laurier's hand. With the tacit support of opposition leader Robert Borden, the Liberal government endorsed a resolution favouring the building of a Canadian navy, yet rejecting *regular* financial contributions to the British admiralty. By leaving open the possibility of a temporary *emergency* contribution, Laurier secured Parliament's unanimous support.

Laurier's Naval Service Bill, introduced in January 1910, was typically cautious. A Canadian navy was established, and provision was made for a naval college to train officers. The navy, like the militia, was under Canadian command but, in case of war, it could — with the consent of Parliament — be placed at the disposal of Britain. "The position we take," Laurier stated, "is that it is for the Parliament of Canada, which created the navy, to say when and where it shall go to war."

Robert Borden and the Conservative opposition denounced the Naval Service Bill as a feeble proposal offering only half-hearted support for the empire. In an impassioned address to the House of Commons, Borden claimed that the British were already facing "an emergency which may rend the empire asunder." Urged on by Tory imperialists, he appealed for a "free and loyal contribution" to meet the present crisis. While Borden's Conservatives mocked the idea of a "tinpot navy," Henri Bourassa and the *nationalistes* attacked the policy for completely different reasons. They claimed that Laurier's assurances of Canadian control were meaningless, since the prime minister was bound to cave in under imperialist pressure in an emergency, just as he had done in 1899 over the Boer War.

THE 1911 ELECTION: A TRIUMPH FOR IMPERIAL NATIONALISM

Most of the critical issues facing Canada in the Laurier years were brought into sharp focus during the general election of 1911. After 15 years in office, Wilfrid Laurier's government set aside its support of the National Policy tariff system and proposed a reciprocal trade agreement with the United States. In Quebec the crucial debate centred on the Naval Service Bill, a measure condemned by Bourassa's *nationalistes* and federal Conservatives alike. On both of these questions, the campaign of 1911 served to crystallize opinion in the raging public debate over Canada's destiny. Imperial nationalists in English-speaking Canada mounted an effective anti-reciprocity campaign, arguing that the agreement was "the thin edge" of a wedge leading to economic and political union with the United States.[5]

Laurier's Liberal government and the reciprocity agreement went down to a crashing defeat in the 1911 election. Opponents of reciprocity agreed with Borden that the issue was

"Canadianism or Continentalism," and charged that Laurier was soft on the imperial connection; for them, the defeat of reciprocity was necessary to preserve their economic interests as well as their nationality. In Quebec, the naval question proved decisive. Bourassa's *nationalistes* pointed to Laurier's naval policy as one that would commit Canada in advance to future British wars; they joined with Borden's Conservatives in an "unholy alliance" to bring Laurier's government down. The election verdict was clear: Borden and the Conservatives won 134 seats, while Laurier's Liberals were reduced to 87. The issue of reciprocity with the United States was laid to rest for years to come.

The United States took the 1911 defeat of freer trade in stride. Although there were signs of private bewilderment, Washington did not officially crit-

An anti-reciprocity cartoon commenting on America's historical expansionist policies, and entitled "LOOKING OUR WAY."

icize the decision or attempt retaliation. America's strategic goal of strengthening North American economic links may have suffered a temporary check, but it was being advanced nonetheless, even without reciprocity.[6] The United States was gradually gaining ground on Great Britain as a market for Canadian exports; the American republic provided 60 percent of Canada's imports; and over 400 American branch factories had already sprung up in the Dominion. With the onset of World War I, Prime Minister Borden's government made pilgrimages to Washington to secure access to U.S. resources and reported in 1918 that President Woodrow Wilson regarded "the boundary line" as having "little or no significance" when considering the most effective wartime pooling of resources.

RESPONSES TO THE GREAT WAR

ON THE EVE OF "THE GREAT WAR," Canada seemed a serene and isolated place, somehow remote from the quarrels and rivalries of Europe. Its tranquillity and peacefulness was captured well in Stephen Leacock's 1912 novel, *Sunshine Sketches of a Little Town*. Even though the Canadian militia had been upgraded since the South African war, Canada was a decidedly unmilitary society.

Beneath the seeming serenity, however, there was unhappiness and racial division. Economic prosperity diminished in 1913, and all was not well between French-speaking and English-speaking sections of the Dominion. The two cultural communities ignored each other except when some crisis arose — as in 1912, when the Ontario government issued Regulation 17, limiting French both as a language of instruction and as a subject of study in the province's schools. French-speaking Ontarians took offence, and they received vociferous support from the outraged Bourassa and his followers. Thus, as war approached, fissures were appearing in the country's facade of unity.

CANADA'S RESPONSE TO WAR

The outbreak of war in August 1914 shattered Canada's tranquillity. When the German armies invaded neutral Belgium, King George V of Britain issued a declaration of war on behalf of all his subjects. As a colony in the empire, Canada was bound by this declaration, and Prime Minister Borden reacted to the call with predictable enthusiasm: he pledged that Canada would "put forth every effort" and "make every sacrifice" to honour the responsibility to the empire. The show of support in 1914 was remarkable. Laurier, now opposition leader, spoke for many Canadians when he proclaimed that, in Britain's hour of danger, Canada's only possible answer was "Ready, aye ready." Crowds of people in Montreal, Toronto, and Quebec roared their approval. Even Henri Bourassa, who narrowly escaped German internment in the French province of Alsace, returned to add his blessing to the war effort.

Canada may have had no choice about participating in the war, but the extent of its involvement was an entirely different matter. Borden was so impressed with the initial Canadian excitement that in December 1914 he confidently promised that there would "not be compulsion or conscription" for overseas service. Most Canadians probably shared Laurier's conviction that their country should give "assistance to the fullest extent of [its] power." Such confidence was well-placed in the early war years. Like most Britons, Canadians expected the war in Europe to be short and glorious. A majority of the country's population was either British-born or of British origin and retained strong emotional ties to Britain.

Canada fought strongly beside Britain in World War I. Just two months after the outbreak of hostilities, the first contingent of 30 000 Canadian troops landed in England, and by February 1915 the Canadian Division, as it was designated, took its place in the trenches on the Western Front. The original call for 25 000 troops was expanded to 250 000 in 1915, and to half a million in the following year. Eventually more than 600 000 men and women were raised to form an army corps of four divisions; naval strength expanded to 8000 personnel with the development of a coastal patrol service. Another 8000 served in the Royal Air Force and added a particularly heroic chapter to Canada's World War I fighting record. The Canadians in khaki, according to British Prime Minister Lloyd George,

Canadians soldiers returning from the Battle of the Somme, November 1916.

distinguished themselves as the best "storm troops," and soon were used to "head the assault in one great battle after another." Certainly the price paid for that Canadian reputation was high — in the first poison-gas attack at Ypres, in the bloody disaster of the Somme, and even in the glow of victory at Vimy Ridge in 1917. By war's end, more than 60 000 Canadians had been killed in action — 7000 more soldiers than were lost by the United States.

AMERICA'S RESPONSE: ATTEMPTED NEUTRALITY

When armed hostilities broke out in the summer of 1914, Americans responded quite differently. Most Americans remained remarkably detached from the events in Europe and showed little or no inclination to become involved. President Woodrow Wilson echoed the desires of most of his fellow citizens when he called upon Americans to stay "neutral in fact as well as in name during these days that are to try men's souls."

For the first three years of the war, Wilson's administration kept the United States out of the conflict. But for a major world power with extensive economic and political interests abroad, observing a course of neutrality and avoiding direct involvement in World War I was not easy. As Wilson soon discovered, the long-established rules of neutrality could not be easily applied to a "total war" fought on several continents and using modern technological weapons. Britain and Germany conspired to compel the United States to adopt a policy of ostensible neutrality that was, in fact, beneficial to their own national interests. Britain imposed a naval blockade around Germany and actively sought to restrict the trade of the United States and other neutrals with the Central Powers (Germany and its allies). Germany sought to counter the British blockade in the North Atlantic with a variety of means, including a blockade around the British Isles; German submarines attacked all enemy vessels in the area.

American intervention in Mexico, 1917: General John J. ("Blackjack") Pershing led an army of 6000 men across the Rio Grande into Mexico, as part of President Wilson's futile attempt to control the Mexican Revolution.

As the war dragged on in Europe, the military struggle of Britain and its allies won increasing sympathy from the American public. Support for neutrality began to erode. Wilson's refusal to impose a total American embargo on North Atlantic trade with the belligerent nations, which would have penalized Britain more than its enemies, was interpreted by the Germans as proof that the United States favoured the Allied cause. Only after Germany waged unrestricted submarine warfare on belligerent and neutral shipping at the end of 1916, however, did Wilson abandon his formal position of neutrality. Following the sinking of four American merchant vessels in March 1917, the U.S president asked Congress for a declaration of war. In spite of some opposition, Congress agreed, and on April 7, 1917, the United States officially entered the war.[7]

America's entry into the war proved decisive. By December 1917, the U.S. commander, General John "Blackjack" Pershing, had landed in France with 176 000 troops. The American expeditionary force grew to 722 000 in June 1918, and reached a peak of almost 2 million by Armistice Day, November 11, 1918. Combined with U.S. war appropriations of over $35 billion and the deterrent power of an American naval force in European waters, U.S. military strength contributed greatly to the defeat of the Central Powers.

OPPOSITION TO CONSCRIPTION

At the outset of the war, most Canadians embraced the view that "Canada was at war when Britain was at war." But as the fighting dragged on into 1916, enthusiasm for Canada's involvement waned and — with the appearance of ever-lengthening casualty lists — voluntary enlistment dropped. Popular demands for a national or "union" government were already being voiced when the question of reinforcements for the armed forces became urgent. The sense of crisis arose from the sharp decline in voluntary recruitment throughout 1916, part from Borden's insistence that Canada maintain four full divisions on the Western Front. Whatever the reasons, Borden moved reluctantly toward conscription in the face of bitter opposition from most French Canadians and sizable numbers of farmers and workers in Ontario and the prairie West. But he knew also that many English Canadians were behind him. Thus, in May 1917, the government endorsed conscription for overseas service and pursued negotiations with leading opposition Liberals for the formation of a union government.

The Military Service Act of 1917 divided Canadians. Liberal leader Wilfrid Laurier, who refused to join a union government, led the opposition to the compulsory military service measure. He charged Borden's government with bad faith, called for a referendum on conscription, and defended his home province of Quebec against the vicious attacks of many English Canadians. Another irritant was Manitoba's decision in 1916 to eliminate bilingual schools entirely in the province. Many *Canadiens* asked why they should fight for an empire whose supporters denied them equal rights at home. According to Bourassa and his followers, the Borden government had violated its earlier promise of no conscription and bowed to the will of the English-Canadian Protestant majority.

French-speaking Quebeckers were not alone in opposing conscription in Canada in 1917. Farmers in Ontario and the prairie West made clear their strong resistance to a measure that would take their sons and cause labour shortages on the farm. Trade unionists organized opposition among factory workers, railway workers, and the coal miners of Cape Breton and the West. Still other minority groups, including Ontario Mennonites, Ukrainian immigrants, Quakers, and Jehovah's Witnesses, either openly opposed compulsory military service or appealed for exemptions on grounds of pacifism.[8]

MOBILIZATION FOR WAR

The Military Service Act carried in Parliament after a bitter, divisive struggle, in which 20 of Laurier's Liberals deserted to support conscription, and a unionist coalition was formed. The results of the 1917 general election, fought largely on the conscription issue, were conclusive: Borden's unionist government received 153 seats and the Liberals were reduced to 82, all but 20 of them in Quebec. Canada's most divisive election revealed the price of an enlarged Canadian role in the imperial war effort.

CRITICS OF THE GREAT WAR AT HOME

THE SPEECHES AND WRITINGS of the prominent critics of involvement in World War I provide much insight into their motives. Compare and contrast the various anti-war arguments raised on both sides of the North American border during the war years 1914–18.

J.S. WOODSWORTH, 1914

The Reverend James Shaver Woodsworth was a Methodist Church mission worker and pacifist. In 1918, having lost a Manitoba government welfare post for openly opposing conscription, he resigned from the church and bitterly criticized it for its support of the war.

J.S. Woodsworth, Methodist minister and social reformer, and later founder of the Co-operative Commonwealth Federation.

> Many are going to the front or are supporting the war in the belief that in this way they may help to bring about the triumph of right and the reign of peace. Some of us have not so learned Christ, yet we dare not dogmatize. We confess that we walk with uncertain steps. We plead that no one demand of us absolute consistency.... More and more we must think not so much of the persons engaged in the war as of the causes that led to the war — the great social and moral wrongs that inevitably lead to disaster. These are our real foes rather than the Germans and the Austrians, and they are found not alone in the enemy's camp....

HENRI BOURASSA, 1916

In 1916, Henri Bourassa's cousin, Talbot Papineau, wrote Bourassa an open letter disparaging the lack of enthusiasm for the war shown by French Canadians. Bourassa's spirited reply contended that the refusal of French Canadians to enlist in overwhelming numbers sprang from essentially patriotic motives.

> There is among the French-Canadians a larger proportion of farmers, fathers of large families, than among any other ethnical element in Canada. Above all, the French-Canadians

are the only group exclusively Canadian.... They look upon the perturbations of Europe, even those of England or France, as foreign events. Their sympathies naturally go to France against Germany; but they do not think they have an obligation to fight for France, no more than the French of Europe would hold themselves bound to fight for Canada against the United States or Japan, or even against Germany, in case Germany should attack Canada without threatening France.

If English-speaking Canadians have a right to blame the French-Canadians for the small number of their recruits, the newcomers from the United Kingdom, who have supplied a much larger proportion of recruits than any other element of the population, would be equally justified in branding the Anglo-Canadians with disloyalty and treason. Enlistment for the European war is supposed to be absolutely free and voluntary. This has been stated right and left from beginning to end. If that statement is honest and sincere, all provocations from one part of the population against the other, and exclusive attacks against the French-Canadians, should cease. Instead of reviling unjustly one-third of the Canadian people — a population so remarkably characterized by its constant loyalty to national institutions and its respect for public order — those men who claim a right to enlighten and lead public opinion should have enough good faith and intelligence to see facts as they are and to respect the motives of those who persist in their determination to remain more Canadian than English or French.

In short, English-speaking Canadians enlist in much smaller number than the newcomers from England, because they are more Canadian; French-Canadians enlist less than English-Canadians because they are totally and exclusively Canadian. To claim that their abstention is due to the "baneful" influence of the Nationalists is a pure nonsense.

Henri Bourassa, *Canadian Nationalism and the War* (Montreal, 1916), pp. 27–30.

A POPULAR AMERICAN SONG: "I DIDN'T RAISE MY BOY TO BE A SOLDIER," 1915

Alfred Bryan wrote the lyrics, and Al Piantadosi the music, for the hit song of 1915, "I Didn't Raise My Boy to Be a Soldier." The words captured the American public's desire to stay out of the war underway in Europe:

Ten million soldiers to the war have gone
Who may never return again.
Ten million mothers' hearts must break
For the ones who died in vain.
Head bowed down in sorrow
In her lonely years,
I heard a mother murmur thro' her tears.

CHORUS:

I didn't raise my boy to be a soldier,
I brought him up to be my pride and joy,
Who dares to put a musket on his shoulder,
To shoot some other mother's darling boy?
Let nations arbitrate their future troubles,
It's time to lay the sword and gun away,
There'd be no war today,
If mothers all would say,
I didn't raise my boy to be a soldier.
What victory can cheer a mother's heart,
When she looks at her blighted home?
What victory can bring her back
All she cared to call her own?
Let each mother answer
In the year to be,
Remember that my boy belongs to me!

"I DIDN'T RAISE MY SON TO BE A SOLDIER," words by Alfred Bryan and music by Al Piantadosi. © 1915 (Renewed) EMI First Catalog Inc. All Rights Reserved. Used by Permission of WARNER BROS. PUBLICATIONS INC., Miami, Fl. 33014

In the United States, the resistance to wartime mobilization was different. President Wilson's attempts to defend American neutrality between 1914 and 1917 were supported by a network of anti-militarist, pacifist, and peace organizations. Once America entered the war, however, the public response changed radically. Under the Selective Service Act of 1917, all able-bodied young men had to register with the local draft boards. More than 24 million Americans were enrolled, of whom almost 3 million were trained for the armed forces in 32 great camps throughout the country. The Wilson administration mounted a vigorous campaign to sell the war to the people and clamped down on dissent. Under the Espionage Act (June 1917) and the Sedition Act (May 1918), hundreds of American socialists and pacifists, including the former U.S. Socialist party candidate for president, Eugene V. Debs, were imprisoned for "obstructing the war."

THE IMPACT OF THE GREAT WAR

When the guns fell silent on November 11, 1918, the Canadian losses totalled over 60 000. For Canada, the Great War was a kind of "baptism of fire" not unlike America's War of Independence. A separate Canadian Corps had been created and commanded by a Canadian, and Canadians could take pride in their battle honours and in their material contributions to the war. Borden's efforts to promote Canadian autonomy and enlarge Canada's role in imperial councils had resulted in a place for the Dominion in the Imperial War Cabinet. Participation in World War I had significantly enhanced the Dominion's status in the empire. Yet, perhaps less obviously, Britain's weakened financial position was beginning to nudge Canada into closer economic relations with her North American neighbour.

ISOLATIONISM IN THE INTERWAR YEARS

IN THE IMMEDIATE AFTERMATH OF THE GREAT WAR, isolationism from European affairs was a natural response to the four-year ordeal. Although World War I remade the map of Europe and the world, it did little to change Canadian perspectives. It brought, in the words of political scientist James Eayrs, "half a million Canadians to Europe but Europe no closer to Canada." To the traditional security provided by membership in the British empire might now be added the protection afforded by sharing a continent with a friendly guardian, the United States. For all intents and purposes, Canada seemed to be, in Senator Raoul Dandurand's famous 1924 phrasing, "a fire-proof house, far from inflammable materials."[9]

SOURCES OF ISOLATIONISM

Postwar isolationism may have been a product of geography, but it was primarily shaped by a sense of disillusionment and distrust. Policy-makers in both Washington and Ottawa tended to blame European policies, European statesmen, and European ambitions for the carnage of the war years. While few publicly broadcast this North American feeling, Prime Minister Mackenzie King and others privately expressed the view that the Canadian sacrifice in lives was part of "the price the world has paid for the European diplomacy of the last hundred years."

American disillusionment sprang directly from a sense of rejection. In January 1918, President Woodrow Wilson had unveiled a plan for

Signing of the Treaty of Versailles, 1919. Seated at the centre from left to right are America's Woodrow Wilson, France's Georges Clemenceau, and Britain's David Lloyd George. Sir George Foster (standing fourth from left) was Canada's delegate after Robert Borden returned to Canada.

a peaceful postwar world order. His Fourteen Points promised no revenge on the defeated powers, national self-determination for subject peoples, freedom of the seas, and the formation of an international peace organization, later known as the League of Nations. At the Paris Peace Conference at Versailles in 1919, Wilson made little headway with his peace plan during the closed-door sessions among the "Big Four" postwar leaders. In the end, he was forced to make major concessions on many of his points in order to secure a peace treaty and his cherished covenant for the League of Nations.

Wilson's vision of a new world order was dealt a second rebuff when the U.S. president returned home from Versailles. Many questions were raised about the effect of American membership in the proposed League of Nations on the nation's freedom of action in the world. A group of senators, led by Henry Cabot Lodge of Massachusetts, argued that article 10 of the league's covenant would threaten U.S. sovereignty by prescribing collective security and thereby compelling America to involve itself in settling disputes around the world. The president battled the league's detractors in a vigorous national debate, but the U.S. Senate defeated American membership in the league in November 1919 and again in March 1920. Isolationism had triumphed, and American determination to avoid becoming involved in war would last well into the 1930s.

TRANSITION TO COMMONWEALTH

Canada emerged from the war with a new status in the British empire. Prime Minister Borden used Canada's military contribution to secure recognition of the nation's status as a separate and equal member of the empire. He insisted on, and obtained, separate Canadian representation at the Paris Peace Conference, the right to sign the peace treaty, and full membership in the League of Nations. In spite of reservations about the "severity" of the Treaty of Versailles and concerns about the effect of league membership on imperial relations, Borden's government ratified the treaty and Canada entered the league.

Mackenzie King's election to office in December 1921 ushered in a curious, almost puzzling, era in Canadian foreign relations. Prime Minister King was a "closet nationalist," someone who saw Canada as "a North American nation under the crown."[10] Instead of asserting Canada's role in the shaping of common imperial policies, as Robert Borden and his successor Arthur Meighen had done, King worked in a cautious, non-committal fashion to transform Canada into a more self-governing Dominion within an evolving British commonwealth of nations. To King, keeping domestic peace between English and French Canadians, and avoiding the bitter divisions of 1917, took precedence over new initiatives in imperial relations.

King's approach to external relations was to attempt to resolve opposing viewpoints while closely guarding his own opinions. Although nationalist by inclination, he contented himself with steering a cautious middle course, avoiding commitments that might threaten Canada's autonomy within the empire–commonwealth. His approach was symbolized in the Chanak crisis of 1922: British troops were threatened with attack by nationalist Turks near Chanak on the Dardanelles, and the British government issued a public appeal for the military support of the dominions. Canadian Conservative leader Arthur Meighen responded quickly with the bold pledge of imperial loyalty: "Ready, aye, ready, we stand by you." King stayed silent and then stated, "Parliament will decide." This would remain King's political credo throughout the 1920s and 1930s. In almost every external crisis, Canada would wait and see, and any decision would be made by the people's elected representatives in Parliament.

FROM "BRITISH" TO "NORTH AMERICAN"

King slowly disengaged Canadian external policy from that of Great Britain and reduced Canada's international commitments. Much of this change could be attributed to the strong influence of King's closest adviser, the under-secretary of state for external relations, O.D. Skelton, who saw the British connection as an impediment to Canada's evolving autonomy. Eventually King convinced the British foreign office to relinquish its control over Canada's external policy by the Statute of Westminster in 1931. The British empire became an empire no longer, but more of a decentralized association of co-equals, the Commonwealth of Nations.

After 1919, the Dominion was no longer simply a British colony. Situated next to the world's largest and most prosperous democracy, Canada had slowly been transformed into a North American nation. A steady stream of young Canadians had begun migrating south to the land of opportunity, while Canadian governments struggled to maintain moderate tariffs and reasonable prices to prevent a larger exodus. By 1922, American capital investment exceeded British investment in Canada's economy, and soon American radio, movies, and automobiles reflected a growing Americanization of cultural life and consumer tastes. In 1926, King's government sent Vincent Massey to Washington to head Canada's first permanent diplomatic mission. A year later, the U.S. State Department officially acknowledged that Canada–U.S. relations were "of vital importance to both countries" and set up its own embassy in Ottawa.

CANADA AND THE LEAGUE OF NATIONS

After joining the League of Nations in 1919, Canada followed a curious policy of lukewarm commitment to its purposes and actions. From the beginning, King seemed to share the view of Canadian external affairs officials that the world peace body was really "a European league with the non-Europeans tacked on," particularly since U.S. membership had been rejected in 1919; King's attitude to the body in its formative years was, according to his official biographer, "one of studied neglect." Ever conscious of the damage another war could do to Canadian national unity, King sought to avoid commitments and to encourage the possibilities of peace.[11]

In the 1930s, Canada contributed its share to the gradual collapse of the League of Nations as an institution for the prevention of war. The most graphic illustration of Canada's confused and ambivalent policy occurred during the league's debate in the fall of 1935 over the Italian invasion of Abyssinia, a clear act of wanton aggression by Mussolini's Italy against an independent African nation. In this case the acting Canadian delegate to the league, Dr. Walter Riddell, proceeded without instructions from Ottawa to urge fellow members to apply stiff sanctions on the supply of oil to Italy. Although the proposed oil sanctions would likely have had little effect on Italy, Benito Mussolini responded with the angry threat, "Oil means war!" Unwilling to force such a conflict over Abyssinia, Ottawa repudiated Riddell's unauthorized statement and joined other league members in backing down. It was an inglorious episode, not only for Canada but for the league itself, since it demonstrated that few governments in the mid-1930s were willing to take any risks for the sake of collective resistance to aggression. The league was thus rendered virtually impotent in the face of rising fascism in Europe.

AMERICA'S ISOLATIONISM AND NEUTRALITY

The results of World War I had not brought what many Americans had hoped for — peace, disarmament, and a world made "safe for democracy." Instead the war was followed by a new set of disappointments. In spite of repeated efforts in the 1920s, the United States was unable to secure repayment for the over $10 billion that Americans had loaned to Allied governments during and immediately after the war. The American administration participated in a series of world conferences on disarmament between 1921 and 1932, but aside from the goodwill, little was accomplished.

American disillusionment over World War I was revived in the 1930s by Senate investigations carried out by North Dakota Senator Gerald Nye between 1934 and 1936. Nye probed the role of the munitions industry and international investment banks in America's entry into the war. His findings showed that the "merchants of death" — munitions makers and bankers — not only strongly favoured American war participation, but also reaped rich profits from the conflict. Many people concluded from Nye's investigation that the arms-makers and bankers were largely responsible for drawing the United States into the war. Whatever the validity of these conclusions, it fed the nation's anti-war sentiment.

American isolationism reached its peak in the mid-1930s. Between 1935 and 1937, isolationist forces in Congress succeeded in passing four Neutrality Acts. These laws, reflecting widespread American public sentiment against war, were precipitated by fears of rising Italian and German fascism and the deteriorating European situation.[12] In general terms, the Neutrality Acts prohibited the shipment of munitions to belligerents, or warring nations; authorized the president to list commodities that could be sold to belligerents only on a "cash-and-carry" basis and on their ships; and made it unlawful for Americans to travel on the vessels of belligerent nations. The intention of the legislation was clear: to keep the United States out of war and to prevent American citizens from becoming involved in incidents like those that led to Wilson's declaration of war in 1917.

ROOSEVELT, ISOLATIONISTS, AND AMERICAN NEUTRALITY, 1935–1941

ISOLATIONIST ATTITUDES FLOURISHED in the United States during the 1930s, reflecting the considered response of a large, responsible, and perhaps shrinking segment of the American public. The rise of European aggression after 1935 had brought alive, once again, the threat of involvement in war. Congress passed Neutrality Acts in 1935–37 to insulate the United States from the crises in Europe, and President Franklin D. Roosevelt publicly concurred with the passage of neutrality legislation. Remembering the Great War with horror and beset by a crippling depression at home, much of the American public embraced what was known as isolationism.

American anti-war sentiments peaked in the mid-1930s. Senator Gerald P. Nye headed an investigation into the misdeeds of munitions makers in World War I, and his report, in large part, led to the enactment of neutrality legislation. Only after the outbreak of full-scale war in 1939 did Roosevelt gradually move toward an interventionist posture, repealing an earlier arms embargo and entering into a Lend–Lease agreement to supply Britain with vital military supplies.

THE HISTORIANS' DEBATE

American isolationist policy in the 1930s, and especially the diplomacy of President Roosevelt, has generated intense debate among historians. Why was Washington, unlike Ottawa, so cautious about acting to aid Britain in resisting European fascist aggression? Was President Roosevelt really a committed "storm cellar" isolationist? What role did political considerations play in his decisions?

A POPULAR EXPRESSION OF AMERICAN UNILATERALISM: MANFRED JONAS, 1966

American isolationism during the thirties was basically "the nation's insistence upon the sole authorship of its legal acts" and thus "the non-judicial counterpart of sovereignty," combined with a policy of subordinating virtually all other interests to that of avoiding war. It was a general American sentiment; not, as sometimes pictured, simply a Midwestern phenomenon born of the insularity of the American interior. Nor was it merely a partisan movement aimed at undermining the popularity and prestige of President Franklin D. Roosevelt. Isolationist leaders had diverse backgrounds, advocated varied courses of action, and shared few domestic interests. But men from New York and California, from Idaho and Texas, men whose political creeds ranged from the socialism of Norman Thomas to the conservative Republicanism of Herbert Hoover, made common cause in the field of foreign policy because they believed in unilateralism and feared the effects of war on the United States.

Geographic insularity and political partisanship help to explain why anti-intervention-ist sentiment was more prevalent in the Republican Middle West than in any other section of the country, and why a disproportionate number of spokesmen for isolationism came from that region. At the same time, the affinity between the tenets of isolationism and the presuppositions underlying various forms of agrarian radicalism colored the Midwestern response to the wars in Europe and Asia. In the final analysis, however, the basic assump-tions of those who opposed greater American participation in world affairs were more comprehensive and more complex, transcending both regional and partisan interests.

THE ILLUSION OF NEUTRALITY: ROBERT A. DIVINE, 1968

From the beginning of the neutrality struggle, [President Roosevelt] had played an equiv-ocal role. Failing to realize the strength of the isolationist forces, he had first encouraged the Nye committee to enter into the subject of neutrality legislation. When he belatedly discovered the overpowering desire of the American people to avoid war at all costs in 1935, he shrank from an open contest, contenting himself with a cryptic warning that neu-trality legislation might encourage rather than deter war. Working toward the goal of exec-utive discretion, he had tried to moderate the isolationist impulse in 1936 and 1937 with little success. As his own realization of American responsibility for European stability grad-ually developed, he attempted to educate Congress in his new understanding. But his efforts, both in the quarantine speech and in the more concrete attempt to repeal the arms embargo early in 1939, were handicapped by his domestic political reverses and his resul-tant unwillingness to state his views forthrightly. Only when the reality of war finally began transforming public opinion did he move effectively to revise the neutrality legisla-tion. And even then he had to compromise, accepting the cash-and-carry restrictions as the necessary price for repeal of the arms embargo....

Cash-and-carry neutrality was an illogical policy, yet it was exactly what the nation wanted. In the course of the next two years, the American people, reacting to the succes-sion of German triumphs in the battlefield, moved closer and closer to war, but they still maintained their fierce determination to avoid the final plunge....

Robert A. Divine, *The Illusion of Neutrality: Franklin D. Roosevelt and the Struggle over the Arms Embargo* (Chicago: Quadrangle Books, 1968), pp. 333–335.

Though the Neutrality Acts prescribed an antidote to war, they failed to have the desired effect. Between 1933 and 1937, President Franklin D. Roosevelt did not take a firm stand and wavered according to public opinion: at times he sided with the isolationists, at other times with their opponents, the internationalists. Most Americans mouthed sentiments of neutrality and favoured a policy that allowed them to render aid to the Allies through "cash and carry" trade without directly committing themselves to intervention in the war.

THE IMPACT OF CANADIAN ISOLATIONISM

While Americans experimented with neutrality, Canadians found solace in the British policy of appeasement. Just as Canadian distrust of European politics had fuelled isolationist sentiment in the immediate postwar years, it also helped to cloud understanding of what was happening inside Europe during the worsening crisis of the later 1930s. Most Canadian policy-makers failed to recognize the dangers to world peace posed by Fascist Italy and Nazi Germany until it was too late. The rise of the totalitarian dictators Benito Mussolini and Adolf Hitler was mostly regarded by Canadians as merely another chapter in a familiar story of European instabilities. That prevailing attitude may help to explain why Ottawa did so little to aid or welcome Jewish refugees fleeing from Nazi bestiality in Europe.[13]

Like British Prime Minister Neville Chamberlain and most western leaders, Mackenzie King came to believe that Hitler could be placated by a policy of appeasement. King's faith in the wisdom of such an approach was reinforced by personal meetings he had with Hitler and key Third Reich officials during a trip to Germany in 1937. According to a well-known Canadian journalist, King came away believing that Hitler's desires to reunify all German peoples was "a natural feeling"; his "ambitions were centred entirely" in Germany and its neighbouring provinces, and therefore there would be "no early trouble in Europe." In a July 1937 CBC radio broadcast he went even further, claiming that despite all appearances "neither the governments nor the peoples of any of the countries I have visited desire war." In Ottawa, the prime minister was not alone in his judgements.[14]

Canada's external policies in the interwar years were, for all intents and purposes, those of Mackenzie King, and they set new standards of caution and fluidity. At a time that cried out for bold and courageous statecraft, King preferred hesitation for the sake of unity, believing that a unified Canada was a stronger member of the empire–commonwealth. In that "in-between time" of the 1930s, Canada's policies, like those of the United States, were heavily influenced by isolationism.

ACTIVITIES

KEY TERMS AND CONCEPTS

Identify and explain the historical significance of each of the following terms and concepts:

- The new imperialism
- Manifest Destiny
- Imperial federation movement
- Imperial nationalists
- Dominion autonomy
- North Atlantic triangle
- Spanish–American War
- "Big Stick" diplomacy
- "Tinpot navy"
- "Ready, Aye Ready"
- Isolationism
- "Fireproof house" policy
- Fourteen Points
- Chanak Crisis, 1922
- Commonwealth of Nations
- Riddell incident
- Neutrality Acts

QUESTIONS FOR DISCUSSION

1. Why was Canada caught up in the new imperialism of the late nineteenth century?
2. What lay behind the growth of imperialism in the United States in the late nineteenth century? Was American expansionism rooted in ideology, economic motives, or a sense of mission?
3. The imperial debate took different forms in Canada and the United States in the years from 1890 to 1914. Identify the common notions and explain the crucial differences.
4. How did the great imperial powers, Britain and the United States, view the role of the colonies? How did they treat subject peoples in dominions like Canada and in colonial possessions of the "uncivilized" world?
5. How did Canada and the United States differ in their perceptions of, attitudes toward, and participation in the Great War?
6. In what ways did World War I contribute to a North American distrust and disillusionment with the affairs of Europe and the rest of the world?
7. Historian C.P. Stacey once described the United States and Canada between the wars as two "hermit kingdoms." How accurately did this metaphor describe the two nations' external relations policies between 1919 and 1939?

INTERPRETING THE EVIDENCE

Each of the following passages provides an interpretation of Canadian and American external policies from the 1890s to the 1930s. Assess the validity of the interpretations in light of your reading of the evidence.

1. The Imperial Debate in Canada

"It was the Imperialists in the old country and in Canada who...believed, apparently with good reason, that a little urgency was all that was needed to make Canada the very forefront of the drive for the consolidation of the empire.... The hereditary devotion to the British Crown...threw into eclipse the corresponding sentiment in England. English-speaking Canadians were more British than the British; they were more loyal than the queen."

— John W. Dafoe, *Laurier: A Study in Canadian Politics* (Toronto: McClelland and Stewart, 1963), p. 55.

"Imperialism was one form of Canadian nationalism. This sense of nationality was grounded upon a definite conception of Canada's past, her national character, and her mission in the future, and in its heart was a yearning for significance and a desire to obliterate the stigma of colonialism."

— Carl Berger, *The Sense of Power* (Toronto: University of Toronto Press, 1970), p. 259.

2. The Roots of American Imperialism

"[America's] engagement in overseas imperialism was so abrupt and unpremeditated...and we were so little prepared for it, that our thinking could not adjust itself.... For almost half a century after our isolation was gone we still clung to the isolationist policy. Only a nation with such vast reserves of strength as we had could have survived this failure of understanding to keep up with change."

— Louis J. Halle, *Dream and Reality* (New York: Harper & Row, 1958), p. 176.

"[In the history of American territorial expansion] it has been found possible to fit each successive acquisition of territory into the pattern of things decreed by divine will or inescapable destiny. The avowal of need or greed, coupled with the power to take, has never satisfied our national conscience."

— Julius W. Pratt, "The Ideology of American Expansion," in Avery O. Craven, ed., *Essays in Honor of William E. Dodd* (Chicago: University of Chicago Press, 1935), pp. 335–353.

"[When President William McKinley issued his war message in 1898] many business spokesmen who had opposed war had recently changed their minds.... Business boomed after McKinley signed the declaration of war.... A new type of American empire, temporarily clothed in armor, stepped out on the international stage after a half of century of preparation to make its claim as one of the great world powers."

— Walter LaFeber, *The New Empire* (Ithaca, NY: Cornell University Press, 1963), p. 406.

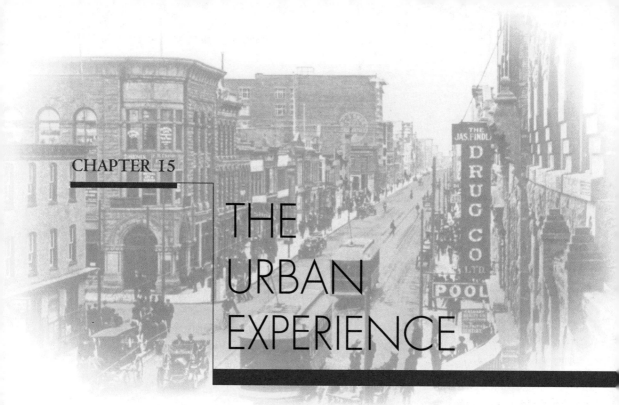

CHAPTER 15

THE URBAN EXPERIENCE

CITIES HAVE HAD A PROFOUND INFLUENCE on North American development. Urban communities have existed since the beginning of European settlement, serving as centres of growth and focal points of identity in both Canada and the United States. As settlement grew, cities and towns began to exert ever-stronger metropolitan influences over their surrounding hinterland regions. The rate of growth of these urban centres varied, but after 1860 some of them grew into substantial cities. With the rise of the modern industrial city, the United States and Canada entered an urban age.

From 1860 to 1914, a period of rapid urbanization occurred in North America. In 1860, less than 20 percent of all Americans lived in cities; by 1900, some 40 percent of them did so. For Canada, the pattern of urban growth was similar, but occurred slightly later and was not as extensive. By World War I, 40 percent of Canada's population was urban; and by 1921, the census showed that more Canadians lived in urban centres than in rural areas.

The rise of cities strengthened — and accelerated — a significant trend toward metropolitanism in North America. Large urban communities, like New York and Chicago, Montreal and Toronto, came to dominate their hinterland regions by providing a variety of functions. The new urban metropolises were centres of industrial enterprise, commercial facilities, transport services, financial establishments, and political power, where critical decisions were made and from which influence was diffused through smaller hinterland centres to all parts of the continent. Such metropolitan dominance, according to historian J.M.S. Careless, constituted a "feudal-like chain of vassalage" whereby major cities exerted profound influences over smaller centres and whole regions, shaping their identities as well as their economic life.[1]

The rapid growth of cities brought new social and political problems — overcrowding, corruption, social disorder, and lack of municipal services. Concerns over water quality, transportation, poverty, disease, crime, and inefficient government produced a sense of urban crisis — and inspired civic-reform movements in both the United States and Canada. While urban reformers were driven by a variety of motives, most set out to remedy the ills of the big city and to bring regeneration, order, or social purity to urban life. It was this early urban-reform movement that, for better or worse, laid the initial foundations for the institutions and social services of the modern city.

THE RISE OF THE URBAN METROPOLIS

THE URBAN EXPLOSION IN THE UNITED STATES began in the 1850s and reached its peak between 1880 and 1900. During this period, New York City grew from fewer than 2 million people in 1880 to 3.5 million in 1900; Chicago rose from 440 000 to 1.7 million; and

Philadelphia climbed from 847 000 to 1.3 million. A host of smaller cities like St. Louis, San Francisco, and Cleveland also expanded rapidly.

Canada's urban growth after 1860 differed in scale, but generally followed the pattern in the United States. In the Atlantic region, growth was more pronounced in the earlier decades. Although the leading Atlantic centres — Saint John, Halifax, and St. John's — had populations of only 25 000 to 50 000, each city had a large influence. Only in these cities were labour and capital sufficiently concentrated to support metropolitan functions for the surrounding region.

In central Canada, rapid metropolitan growth occurred between 1880 and World War I. Montreal early emerged as Canada's first national transportation metropolis. Toronto, with a rich agricultural and resource hinterland, developed banking and investment institutions and new manufacturing through the 1870s and 1880s, and by the late 1890s and early twentieth century was challenging Montreal for business and trade in western Canada.

Before 1900, only 20 percent of the prairie population of 400 000 lived in urban centres, and Winnipeg and Vancouver were the West's only major urban centres. In the new century, the dramatic growth of prairie settlement led to the development of Edmonton, Calgary, Regina, and Saskatoon, and the prairie West's urban population increased fourfold in the first decade. After the peak of expansion in 1913, the growth of prairie urban centres tapered off considerably. Drought and the Great Depression in 1929–30 brought an end to this era of urban expansion, both in the Prairies and elsewhere.

FRONTIER, METROPOLIS, AND REGION

From its earliest beginnings until at least 1920, Canada evolved largely through the spreading of frontiers across the continent. These expanding frontier areas developed into distinctive regions primarily through the growth of cities, especially the largest, most powerful kind of city, the metropolis. Up until the 1860s and 1870s, Atlantic cities like Halifax and Saint John flourished in a commercial age dominated by "wood, wind, and sail." Montreal, the greatest metropolis of Canada, probably reached its height of influence between 1860 and 1900 as the nation's pre-eminent financial and manufacturing centre, and home to two of Canada's largest business enterprises, the Canadian Pacific Railway and the Bank of Montreal. As the frontier of development moved westward, Toronto emerged after 1900 as a rising metropolis fuelled by a northern Ontario mining and forestry boom, cheap hydro-electric power, and the northwestern expansion of "empire Ontario."[2]

The prairie West's main railway distribution point, Winnipeg, became its earliest metropolitan centre and ranked third in population among Canada's cities by 1911. With the onset of the Great War, the Manitoba city experienced recession and sluggish growth, and there was a gradual westward shift in population to newer prairie cities like Calgary and Edmonton. In this way, the interplay of metropolis and frontier, seeming opposites, actually shaped much of Canada's social development. Behind the rise of the frontier, hinterland, or region in Canada — as in the United States — lay the formidable influence of successive metropolitan centres.

THE RISE OF NORTH AMERICAN CITIES

MASSIVE IMMIGRATION had much to do with the explosive growth of American cities. If the native-born children of the new immigrants were counted, most big cities were largely "foreign" at the turn of the century. The vast majority of new immigrants settled in New York, Philadelphia, Boston, and other eastern ports of disembarkation for European newcomers. New York City by 1900, for example, was the largest Irish and Jewish city in the world, and the second-largest Polish city.

TABLE I   POPULATION OF MAJOR AMERICAN CITIES, 1860–1900

CITY	1860	1880	1900
New York City	1 174 800	1 912 000	3 437 000
Philadelphia	565 500	847 000	1 294 000
Boston	177 800	363 000	561 000
Baltimore	212 400	332 000	509 000
Cincinnati	161 000	255 000	326 000
St. Louis	160 800	350 000	575 000
Chicago	109 300	503 000	1 698 000

TABLE 2   COMPARATIVE POPULATION OF CANADIAN CITIES, 1861–1921

CITY	1861	1901	1921
Montreal	90 300	328 200	618 600
Toronto	44 800	209 900	521 900
Vancouver	—	29 400	163 200
Winnipeg	—	42 400	179 100
Hamilton	19 100	52 600	114 150
Quebec	51 100	68 800	95 200
Ottawa	14 700	59 900	107 800
Calgary	—	4 400	63 300
Edmonton	—	4 200	58 800
Halifax	25 000	40 800	58 400

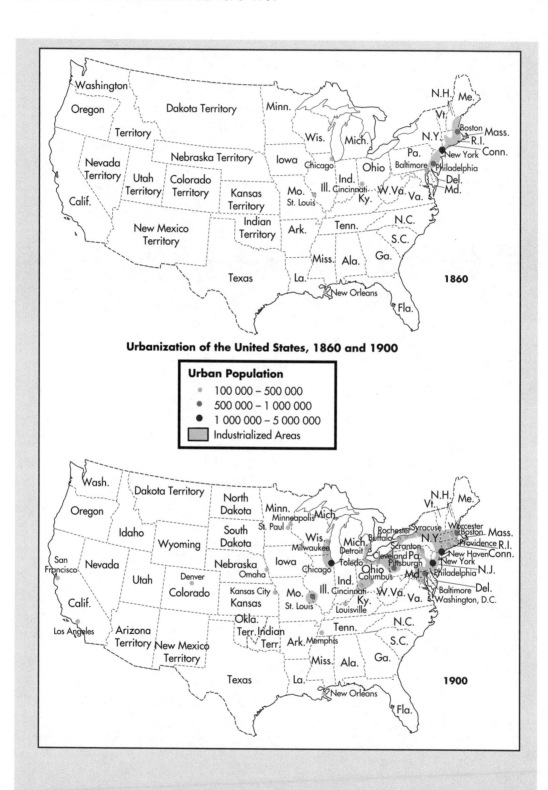

Urbanization of the United States, 1860 and 1900

Urban Population

- 100 000 – 500 000
- 500 000 – 1 000 000
- 1 000 000 – 5 000 000
- Industrialized Areas

The influx of immigrants alone was not responsible for rapid American urbanization. Throughout the late nineteenth century, growing numbers of men and women from America's farms and rural areas flowed into the cities. Some Americans left the farms to escape the isolation of rural life or the tedium and often meagre material rewards of farm labour; others were attracted to the big cities by the lure of better-paying factory jobs or the prospect of making their fortunes in business.

While rapid growth affected cities large and small, the most remarkable aspect of American urbanization was the emergence of the nation's gigantic metropolises. The accompanying statistical tables on page 405 and map on page 406 demonstrate the pattern of urban growth in America. They also provide some basis for comparing urbanization in the United States and Canada from 1860 to 1920.

LIFE IN THE CITIES

THOUSANDS OF PEOPLE were drawn into the cities to take up work. But the lure of the cities was not just employment. New buildings, new services, and new amenities caused profound changes in Canadian society, and more importantly, in the everyday lives of Canadians. For many people, these were a source of pride and wonder. An 1891 volume published by the Toronto *Mail* testified to the "recent phenomenal growth" of the city and boasted of "vast building enterprises underway, which soon will add immensely to the artistic beauty as well as to the substantial wealth of the city."

Nowhere in the West was the boom more in evidence than in Winnipeg, where one marvelled at the "handsome and commodious railroad station" and "all the modern conveniences of street railways [and] electric light" that were "furnished in abundance" in 1906. Even Edmonton, in 1913 a frontier city of 30 000, was a fascinating place for wide-eyed homesteaders struck by its impressive street signs "painted in large letters, some illuminated and all overhanging the street in bewildering confusion."

THE CHANGING FACE OF THE CITY

Rapid, unplanned growth in the cities transformed urban life. As more people gravitated to the cities and more businesses grew up, land prices rose sharply, especially in downtown areas. Cities like Montreal, Toronto, Halifax, and Winnipeg built street railways to open the surrounding suburbs for housing developments. The horse trolley and later the electric trolley revolutionized urban transport. The directions taken by the public transportation lines charted the direction of a city's growth. Shops, housing, and businesses followed the transit lines from the centre of the city. Many cities, like Winnipeg, Toronto, and Montreal, were divided by a network of rail lines into definable residential districts, rich or poor.

Two faces of Winnipeg. The commercial bustle of downtown and a huddle of immigrant children outside All People's Mission in the North End.

Street lighting provided an important indicator of the relative economic status of city districts. Lighting was installed first in the central commercial areas and then on the streets servicing the homes of the well-to-do. In Vancouver, one observer reported in 1916, lighting was still poor in most residential sections, with arc lamps generally placed only at street intersections. Downtown in the poorer districts, behind the great stores and hotels, the lighting was poor or non-existent, and on narrow back streets and laneways hydro and telephone lines added to the ugliness of the dingy, crowded tenement areas.

PROBLEMS IN THE CITIES

Canada's new industrial cities, particularly Montreal, Hamilton, and Toronto, like many in North America at the time, could be grimy, smoky, and unpleasant places to live. "Industrial smoke" from the factory chimneys, a 1915 report noted, "disfigures buildings, impairs the health of the population, renders the whole city filthy, destroys any beauty with which it may naturally be endowed and tends, therefore, to make it a squalid and undesirable place of residence."

HOUSING CONDITIONS

Canadian cities presented stark contrasts in their housing districts. Every major city had its affluent residential districts, where "captains of industry" lived in ornate villas with well-kept grounds on tree-lined avenues. In Toronto, Jarvis and Sherbourne streets were the favoured areas; in Montreal, some 40 millionaires reportedly lived in one "Golden Mile" along Sherbrooke Street. Montreal reformer Herbert B. Ames described this area as "the city above the hill" — "the exclusive habitat of the rich and the well-to-do."

But every Canadian city at the turn of the century also had areas of poor housing. Ames called this poor housing district in Montreal "the city below the hill," the "home of the craftsman, of the manual wage-earner, of the mechanic and the clerk...the real industrial class" and "a submerged tenth" making its "claims upon neighborly sympathy." Montreal's slum district had its counterpart in Toronto, known as "The Ward." This area — clearly visible from the T. Eaton Company Factory and the Toronto City Hall — was condemned regularly in the press for its disgraceful housing, particularly its ramshackle outhouses and alleyways littered with refuse. Winnipeg's North End was another crowded district of dilapidated rooming houses bursting with recent immigrants, located on "the other side" of the CPR tracks.

Back alley in "The Ward," Toronto, 1914. The rear of 210 Chestnut Street, photographed by the Toronto Department of Health. A slum area described by Rev. H.S. Magee in the *Christian Guardian* (1911) as "the festery sore of city life."

PUBLIC HEALTH AND SANITATION

Cities like Toronto suffered from inadequate water-supply and sewage-disposal systems. In 1906, the provincial board of health tested Toronto's water and found 14 percent of the samples infected. In spite of warnings that supplying such infected water was "nothing short of criminal negligence," city council delayed action for years. Faced with an outbreak of typhoid fever in February 1910, the city finally arranged for the water supply to be chlorinated, and in 1911 it discontinued the practice of dumping raw sewage into Toronto Bay, a short distance from the city's water intake. There was a dramatic reduction in the number of deaths from typhus, and typhoid was never again a major killer in Toronto.

There were other health hazards for city dwellers. Another major problem in Toronto was contaminated milk, which was partly responsible for the city's high infant mortality rate. In April 1909, an Ontario milk commission classified about 40 percent of Toronto's milk supply as "substandard." In Montreal, tuberculosis was the biggest health problem. Between 1900 and 1918, the mortality rates from tuberculosis in Montreal averaged over 200 deaths per 100 000 population, considerably higher than that of any other large North American city.

THE COST OF LIVING

Assessing the living standards of Canada's urban working class in the early twentieth century is difficult because there were significant income variations within the working class, usually reflecting differences between skilled, unskilled, and seasonal labour. City dwellers experienced inflation and periodic recessions accompanied by unemployment, and they faced a massive influx of immigrant labour competing for jobs, housing, and municipal services.

Recent studies of the Montreal and Toronto working-class communities suggest that living standards were static, perhaps even eroded, during the "boom" years from 1900 to 1921. While the wage rates of Toronto's skilled workers rose steadily before 1912, a Toronto Board of Trade report noted that the cost of living was "higher in Toronto than it is in the smaller towns of Ontario." At the end of 1916, an official in the Quebec Department of Labour reported that the wages of Montreal workers were so low that children at 14 or 15 years of age were compelled to leave school to help provide for the family's support. Rents for housing were so exorbitant in Toronto and Montreal that, as the Ontario Housing Committee pointed out in 1919, "the low paid wage-earner, with a family dependent solely on his earnings, rarely can afford to pay the rental charged for adequate accommodation, and must resort to sub-letting."

VISIONS AND REFORMERS

IN THESE YEARS THE INDUSTRIAL CITIES OF TORONTO, Montreal, Winnipeg, and elsewhere were home to both the very affluent and the destitute. They were places of conspicuous expenditure and abject poverty. These conditions gave rise to a movement for reform of the cities in

Canada and the United States. It seemed to growing numbers of social critics and reformers that the city had become the repository for all the most visible — and disturbing — ills of modern industrial society, where poverty, crime, disease, prostitution, and all sorts of miseries flourished.

Canada's urban-reform movement got underway in the late 1880s and 1890s. Like its American counterpart, the urban Progressive movement, it was born amid a sense of crisis. It was feared that excessive industrialization and massive overcrowding from rural and external immigration to the cities would produce desperate social problems similar to those existing in New York, Chicago, and other American industrial centres. After the turn of the century, public concern intensified, as social critics and journalists unearthed and publicized mounds of evidence detailing the sorry state of life in Canada's cities. The movement probably peaked during the Great War and its aftermath, when a wave of social regeneration swept across Canada. By the 1920s, the movement was spent. Its legacy, though, was the host of civic services and municipal institutions still in existence today in the metropolitan centres.

THE REGENERATORS

Who were Canada's first urban reformers, and what motivated their campaigns for social improvement and municipal reform? Most of the leaders of the first wave of urban reform were representatives of a predominantly white, Anglo–Saxon Protestant rising middle class in the big cities of English-speaking Canada. The well-educated middle-class reformers who led the various movements were influenced first by their counterparts in Britain and, in the twentieth century, by sources in the United States. They frequently borrowed ideas from England or the United States, while asserting that Canadian cities were different — less corrupt, healthier, and freer of serious social ills. Many social critics and urban reformers, according to historian Ramsay Cook, were seeking to reform their whole society by laying the foundations for a new, prosperous social order not unlike "God's kingdom on earth." They envisioned reform not as a series of small, isolated measures but as a grand project to "regenerate" society as well as the human soul.[3]

A significant number of municipal reformers, particularly in Montreal, Toronto, and Winnipeg, were drawn from the ranks of the well-to-do business and professional class. Among them were Herbert B. Ames, a Montreal businessman and author of *The City Below the Hill* (1897), an exposé of the city's poorest housing district; and S. Morley Wickett, a Toronto businessman closely affiliated with the Canadian Manufacturers' Association, who in 1914 helped found the Toronto Bureau of Municipal Research (a Canadian offshoot of the U.S. Research Bureau movement, started in 1906 in New York City). These well-heeled reformers were giving voice to upper-class disgust over the disorder, inefficiency, and dishonesty in civic affairs and sought to make the city run more like the modern business corporation.

THE MUCKRAKERS

THE AMERICAN PROGRESSIVE MOVEMENT in the years 1900–16 was strongly supported by many scholars, journalists, and novelists. Theodore Roosevelt applied the name "muckrakers" to writers who persistently exposed evil and corruption wherever they found them — in civic, state, and national governments, and in the business world. Although Roosevelt used the term in a pejorative sense, writers and social critics bore the label "muckraker" with pride and popularized it in the press.

Jacob Riis, a Danish-born police reporter turned social reformer and tireless campaigner for the elimination of slum conditions on New York's Lower East Side, did much to expose the horrid living conditions in the late nineteenth century. His first book on the subject, *How the Other Half Lives* (1890), seared the social conscience of prominent New Yorkers, including Teddy Roosevelt, and helped eventually to force reforms on the city's often greedy landlords. Life in the tenements of New York was graphically revealed in Riis's haunting words and photographs. To concerned Americans, they spoke volumes.

The journalist Lincoln Steffens did most to identify and publicize the problems and abuses in America's cities. He specialized in exposing corrupt city governments. In 1904, Steffens published some of his best articles in a book, *The Shame of the Cities.* He contended that urban rot was the direct consequence of an American system of special "privilege," sanctioned by public apathy.

Bandits' Roost, Mulberry Street, Lower East Side, New York City.

Rear tenements in Roosevelt Street, New York City.

Now, the typical American citizen is the business man. The typical business man is a bad citizen; he is busy. If he is a "big business man" and very busy, he does not neglect, he is busy with politics, oh, very busy and very businesslike. I found him buying boodlers in St. Louis, defending grafters in Minneapolis, originating corruption in Pittsburgh, sharing with bosses in Philadelphia, deploring reform in Chicago, and beating good government with corruption funds in New York. He is a self-righteous fraud, this big business man. He is the chief source of corruption, and it were a boon if he would neglect politics....

We Americans may have failed. We may be mercenary and selfish. Democracy with us may be impossible and corruption inevitable, but these articles, if they have proved nothing else, have demonstrated beyond doubt that we can stand the truth; that there is pride in the character of American citizenship; and that this pride may be a power in the land. So this little volume, a record of shame and yet of self-respect, a disgraceful confession, yet a declaration of honor, is dedicated, in all good faith, to the accused — to all the citizens of all the cities in the United States.

Lincoln Steffens, *The Shame of the Cities* (New York, 1904), "Introduction."

Women as well as men rallied to the cause of civic and moral reform. Factory conditions, congestion, disorder, drinking and intemperance, food and water impurities, contagious diseases, prostitution, and immigration were all identified as worthy targets of reform. This great wave of moral fervour was, in the words of sociologist Mariana Valverde, "not completely repressive or puritanical," but rather part of a broader effort to promote "a common vision of the pure life" and to "abolish urban slums" by means of the symbolic as well as practical use of "light, soap, and water."[4]

SAVING THE CITY

Leading urban reformers in English-speaking Canada were also intent on spreading the "social gospel." The rise of cities and the accompanying grave social problems sparked efforts by concerned clergy, social workers, journalists, and civic officials to bring a Christianizing influence to bear on the ills of urban, industrial-capitalist society. Daily newspapers and "people's journals" like the Toronto *World* and the Hamilton *Herald* began in the 1880s to draw attention to urban ills, to criticize the civic establishment, and to champion the causes of "clean government," fresh air children's camps, and juvenile delinquent reform.

Journalist John J. Kelso turned his attention to child welfare and was appointed in 1893 as Ontario's first superintendent of neglected and dependent children. He closed the Penetanguishene juvenile reformatory in 1905, turned the care of delinquent and dependent children over to foster homes, and organized children's-aid societies all over Ontario. In Winnipeg, J.S. Woodsworth, the superintendent of All People's Mission, applied the social gospel to the

John Kelso on an outing to the Fresh Air Fund Farm with wards of the Children's Aid Society.

problems of immigrants and the poverty-stricken in the city's North End. His book, *My Neighbor*, published in 1911, graphically described the plight of the poor in Canada's cities and made an impassioned plea for social action.

WOMEN, GENDER RELATIONS, AND SOCIAL REFORM

As Canadian society became more urban and industrialized, the separation of the workplace from the home became increasingly evident, as did the distinction between the public, or "work," sphere and the private sphere of the home. In Victorian Canada, the home was considered the woman's "proper sphere." The majority of women were confined to working at home at household tasks. Although by the late nineteenth century Canadian women were entering the workforce, they were few in number — only 11 percent of women in 1891 — and they were mostly young and single. But even these few women seemed to some to threaten the existence of the family, and clergymen, doctors, and other male opinion leaders wrote and spoke at length on the "woman question." Women, these men asserted, were to have only one role in life — that of wife and mother.

JANE ADDAMS AND THE SETTLEMENT HOUSE MOVEMENT

T HE STAGGERING PROBLEMS OF AMERICA'S CITY SLUMS did not go completely unattended in the late nineteenth and early twentieth centuries. Small groups of hardheaded idealists and social activists moved into slum neighbourhoods and established "settlement houses," or community mission centres that provided a wide range of social services to the city's poor and disadvantaged. The best known of these settlement houses was the legendary Hull House in Chicago's West Side, founded in September 1889 by Jane Addams and a group of other well-educated women.

In 1883, Addams had visited the founders of Toynbee Hall, a community mission house in the poverty-stricken East End of London, England. Moved by the conditions of human wretchedness there and the work being done by the mission house, Addams returned to the United States and spearheaded a settlement project of her own: she arranged to purchase a decaying mansion in one of Chicago's slum neighbourhoods, and opened Hull House.

Jane Addams managed the work of Hull House with determination, humanity, and compassion — an apparent model of Christian charity. Yet she did not conceive of Hull House as a form of charity or philanthropy. Rather, Addams sought to help her Chicago "neighbours" through nursery programs, adult education classes in English, assistance with job placement, and other tangible ways. "Working people," she wrote in 1892, "require only that their aspirations be recognized and stimulated, and the means of attaining them put at their disposal."

Under Addams's direction, Hull House grew into a great complex of buildings: a coffee house, a gymnasium, a woman's club, a boarding house for working girls, the Hull House Apartments, a boy's club, an art gallery, and a day nursery. The Hull House "experiment" attracted so

An ardent feminist and pacifist, Jane Addams received the Nobel Peace Prize in 1931 for her leadership of the Women's International League for Peace and Freedom.

much notoriety from the 1890s onward that visitors and pilgrims were attracted from around the world.

The women of Hull House documented the urgent problems of their West Side Chicago neighbourhood. Then, armed with the facts, they took on the city's "ward bosses" and began to propose major legislative changes. Alice Hamilton, a physician based at Hull House, treated the neighbourhood's sick and debilitated. She soon grew alarmed over the ravages of infectious diseases and became a vigorous campaigner for public health reform. Florence Kelly studied slum housing and working conditions in the factories. Her reform agitation helped to establish a new housing code in Chicago and to bring about an eight-hour day for Illinois workers, even though the eight-hour work day was later struck down.

The settlement idea pioneered in North America at Hull House caught on in many cities. By 1895, at least 50 settlement houses existed in American cities, and missions were beginning to be established in Canada's big urban centres. Despite their concrete successes, settlement house reformers came to recognize that private efforts barely made a dent in the problems of slum life. "Private beneficence," Jane Addams asserted, "is totally inadequate to deal with the vast numbers of the city's disinherited."

This idealization of women's role failed to take account of a number of factors that made it impossible to realize. First, the ideal assumed that every woman was financially dependent on a male breadwinner. This overlooked the large proportion of single, widowed, and divorced women. Second, the ideal assumed that every male was able to earn enough to support his family. The reality was very different; married women combined household duties with other tasks to supplement the family income. In urban slums like Toronto's "The Ward" and lower Montreal, working-class wives took in sewing at pitifully low piece rates.

Women had long been active in charitable institutions dealing with social problems. In the late nineteenth century, women's growing dissatisfaction with their role in the private sphere led many to an increased awareness of and involvement with issues such as temperance, public health, and child welfare. When these women were publicly criticized for their activism, they prepared a defence of their goals, which provided a foundation for the woman's movement. Two arguments were developed. One was that of "maternal" or "social" feminism. Women's special experience in caring for their families should be extended to responsibility for establishing order in society; and, unless women had the vote, social conditions would not be improved and society reformed. The other argument was that of "equal rights" or "equity" feminism. This argument was based on a concept of simple justice: women were human beings, endowed with the same abilities as men. Yet men only, and elected only by men, made decisions for women.

THE URBAN SUFFRAGE MOVEMENT

BY THE LATE NINETEENTH CENTURY, when Canadian women's suffrage societies were first being founded, the social conditions that produced the North American urban reform movement — industrialism, urban congestion, city slums — were much in evidence. Canada's first suffrage societies, to a greater degree than their American counterparts, emerged as part of a broad reform movement encompassing temperance, child welfare, public health, and other social issues. Canadian suffragists used "equal rights" and "maternal" feminist arguments in equal measure to promote their causes.

THE FIRST SUFFRAGE GROUP

Compared with the suffrage campaigns in the United States and Great Britain, Canada's suffrage movement started late and resembled, in the words of one of its pioneers, "a struggle, never a fight." The first suffrage association, the Toronto Women's Literary Club, was established in Toronto in 1877 by Dr. Emily Howard Stowe. It was a small group of mainly middle-class women who were interested in promoting women's access to the professions and in discussing "women's higher education, including her moral and physical welfare." In 1883, the Toronto group became more open about its aims and changed its name to the Toronto Women's Suffrage Association.

Born into a Quaker family in Norwich, Ontario, in 1832, Stowe earned a medical degree in New York in 1868, after being denied admission to the University of Toronto medical school because she was a woman. While in New York, she met two leading American feminists, Elizabeth Cady Stanton and Susan B. Anthony. Stowe became a confirmed feminist as a result of her struggle to earn her medical qualifications and the right to practise medicine.

The 1890s saw considerable activity in the woman's movement. The Woman's Christian Temperance Union (WCTU) and other social organizations became established as national associations, and suffrage societies sprang up in Nova Scotia, New Brunswick, and Manitoba. In Manitoba, a unique group of Icelandic suffragists under the leadership of Margaret Benedictssen had agitated for

Dr. Emily Stowe.

women's suffrage since arriving in Canada in the 1870s and were later joined in their efforts by the Manitoba WCTU, which included some leading Canadian suffragists. Several of the members of the British Columbia WCTU emerged as suffrage leaders also. In Quebec, two English-speaking associations, the Montreal Local Council of Women and the Montreal Women's Club, acted as incubators for the movement.

The National Council of Women of Canada (NCWC) was founded in 1893 as an umbrella organization of reform associations. Lady Ishbel Aberdeen, the wife of Canada's governor-general, was a leading spirit in the organization. Affiliated local councils served as umbrella organizations for the various local associations in their communities. Under Lady Aberdeen's leadership, the so-called "Parliament of Women" stressed the "grand woman's mission of 'mothering'" pursued through "women's work," with charitable organizations caring for the sick, aged, inebriate and insane. Not until 1910, when women's suffrage was gaining social acceptance, did the council endorse the principle of voting rights for women.

THE WOMEN'S TEMPERANCE CRUSADE

The single most popular route to Canadian women's suffrage activity, however, was the temperance crusade. The largest temperance society, the WCTU — founded in Canada in 1874 by Letitia Youmans — was dedicated to eradicating social and family problems by eliminating alcoholism. By 1891, the WCTU claimed over 9000 members in locals across Canada and, in 1900, it was organized into 26 departments, each addressing a separate aspect of social reform. Eventually, when governments refused to introduce temperance legislation, the WCTU turned to political action to fight for suffrage as a means to achieve its ends. Temperance crusaders believed that the enfranchisement of women would swing the political balance in favour of prohibition.

Also underlying the suffrage movement and much of late-nineteenth-century urban reform was a growing concern over the future of the Anglo-Saxon race. The influx of immigrants into Canada, combined with declining birth rates among white Anglo-Saxon Protestants, fed fears of "race degeneration" and the weakening of the "British component" in Canada.[5] Because most late-nineteenth-century suffragists were equally committed to the regeneration of the Anglo-Saxon race, they placed considerable emphasis on the home in rearing healthy, moral children. To many Canadian suffragists, female enfranchisement was pursued not so much to challenge accepted female roles, but to add "good Christian women" to the electorate.

THE FIRST BREAKTHROUGHS

Two developments with quite contradictory effects seemed to push the campaign into action in 1910. The sensationalist tactics adopted by militant British "suffragettes" — particularly hunger strikes and "votes for women" public marches — attracted the attention of the Canadian public. But perhaps most important, the National Council of Women formally

The Canadian suffragist delegation to the American Suffrage Parade, Washington, 1913. The Canadian suffrage movement was closely linked with those of the United States and Great Britain. Here, the Canadian delegation takes its place at the rally planned to coincide with President Woodrow Wilson's inauguration.

endorsed a women's suffrage resolution, signalling the growing public acceptance of female enfranchisement. After 1910, suffrage societies again began to spring up across the country. One of Canada's most vigorous suffrage organizations, the Manitoba Political Equality League, led by Lillian Beynon Thomas, Dr. Mary Crawford, and Nellie McClung, formed in 1912, was followed in succeeding years by the Montreal Suffrage Association (1913), and the Saskatchewan Equal Franchise Board (1915). By 1916, Toronto alone had eight suffrage associations.

The new suffragists were also social reformers. Many of them turned to public affairs and suffragism out of concern for an apparent disintegration of traditional family life and believed that a woman's primary duty lay within the home. However, many suffragists also believed that men had proven themselves unfit to make decisions for society's welfare and that public life needed an application of maternal skills to clean up the ills of urban society.

DIVISIONS WITHIN THE MOVEMENT

The movement after 1910 was divided over its allegiances, strategy, and priorities. Regional, urban–rural, and class differences caused additional problems. The established suffrage societies generally ignored female workers and their problems, since they had neither the contacts nor the political strength to mobilize them. Canadian suffragists shied away from supporting strikes by women workers, made little attempt to recruit working-class women into their associations, and were not above shunning working-class women who attended their meetings. A few suffrage leaders, such as Flora McDonald Denison and Alice Chown in Ontario, and British Columbia trade-union activist Helena Gutteridge, displayed an empathy for working-class women's problems and a desire to work with them. However, they were hampered by the attitudes of other suffrage leaders and the indifference of the organized labour movement.

The militant tactics of British and American suffragettes had little appeal in Canada; only a handful of more radical feminists like Dr. Augusta Stowe-Gullen and Flora Denison were in favour of such strategies. In keeping with the country's reputed character, the Canadian suffragists generally waged what was once described as a "wholly dignified campaign." "Votes for women" petitions were the favoured method of persuasion, although Canadian suffragists staged mock parliaments, sponsored plays, arranged exhibits, and sold postcards. One of the most effective reform weapons was the Manitoba mock parliament, staged in 1914 by Nellie McClung and the Winnipeg Political Equality League, in which women legislators debated the merits of extending the franchise to men and turned all the usual arguments on end.

Finnish women in Northern Ontario march for voting rights.

SOURCES OF URBAN REFORM IDEAS

Since urban problems were common to all industrialized nations, reformers naturally looked to Europe and the United States for solutions to urban problems. Guillaume Nantel, a journalist and cabinet minister in the Quebec government, wanted to apply Baron Hausseman's ideas for laying out boulevards in Paris to the island of Montreal. Thomas Adams, a Scottish-born town planner, promoted practical town plans and the concept of garden cities popularized in Britain by Ebenezer Howard.

But most of the influence on urban reform came from the United States. At the All People's Mission in Winnipeg, J.S. Woodsworth drew on the settlement work of Jane Addams at Chicago's Hull House. His book *My Neighbor* dealt with the social problems in Winnipeg, but many of its ideas and suggestions for reform were already being promoted by urban progressives in the United States. H.B. Ames's low-cost housing projects for Montreal working-class families were modelled on American experiments in Philadelphia and elsewhere. Schemes for providing good city government in American cities were closely monitored by municipal reformers in Canada. One plan, based on a scheme pioneered in Galveston, Texas, was to abolish city council and replace it with a four- or five-person executive commission elected at large. It was seriously debated by Canadian urban reformers in Calgary, Toronto, and Saint John, New Brunswick. In the end only Saint John adopted the plan, in 1907.

The American progressive reform movement provided many ideas, such as government by a commission without a city council and management by civic experts. But most municipal reformers had an underlying commitment to British parliamentary practice, and Canadian cities established or retained elected city councils, even though these bodies did not provide model civic government. In its formal structures, if not in its social direction, Canadian civic reform differed from that in the United States.

ACHIEVEMENTS OF URBAN REFORM

URBAN REFORMERS HAD VARIOUS AIMS: some wanted beautiful cities filled with parks, tree-lined boulevards, and stately buildings, or garden cities where development was controlled and citizens were provided with a full range of services and amenities; others sought to create model municipal governments based on principles of economy and efficiency; still others hoped to convert the city into a humane Christian community that provided a decent life for all, including the poor and the dependent children.

The achievements of progressive urban reform, in Canada as in the United States, fell far short of these idealized visions. Many Canadian civic reformers persisted in believing that voluntary action would be sufficient to transform municipal government into an effective instrument of reform. But the experience of the 1880s and 1890s convinced most reformers otherwise. So, by 1900, reformers came to place more emphasis on concrete structural changes, such as the achievement of women's suffrage, the modernization of municipal government, the establishment of improved health and welfare services, stricter controls on housing development, and even the takeover of municipal utilities.

PUBLIC HEALTH AND SOCIAL WELFARE

Public health regulations were passed in many cities after 1880 to deal with the problems of disease control, contaminated food, sanitation, and substandard housing. Campaigners like Toronto's Dr. Helen MacMurchy attempted in the years after 1910 to impose a strict code of public health on all city dwellers; they were supported by the city's middle and upper classes, who feared the spread of infectious diseases to their neighbourhoods. These efforts were not always appreciated by the poor of the cities. In 1885, Montreal civic officials initiated a vaccination program during a severe smallpox epidemic, which was claiming the lives of 2500 Montrealers. Some members of the French-speaking urban working class, not perhaps fully understanding the scheme, rioted, and militia units were called in to control them. In Toronto, in addition to improvements in the water supply, sewage disposal, and milk processing, public health nursing programs were started, and school dental and medical examinations were expanded.

Yet public health standards remained low. Toronto's medical officer of health reported in 1919 that over half of the children examined in the city's schools suffered from "physical defects" requiring medical attention. Montreal failed to develop a systematic control program for tuberculosis or diphtheria. A 1927 health survey concluded that the city's official and voluntary health services still lagged far behind those in other North American cities of comparable size.

Toronto's campaign for public health reform. A public health nurse making a school visit.

Moral reform was championed by the churches and various women's organizations. At their urging, municipal and provincial authorities passed laws aimed at stamping out juvenile crime, intemperance, immorality, and civic corruption. Not only were most moral-reform measures less than successful, they also drew the anger of many citizens, who viewed these laws as attempts to force city dwellers to conform to middle-class values.

Closely connected with health care and moral reform were the problems of social welfare and housing. Traditionally the care of the urban poor had been the task of the churches and private charities, while welfare relief was provided by municipal and provincial authorities. In the years 1880 to 1920, however, rapid urban growth completely overloaded this system. A new generation of social reformers sought an expanded role for the state in the provision of much-needed welfare services. Among the services provided were children's-aid societies, city playgrounds, juvenile courts, asylums, unemployment relief, food inspection, and limited workers' compensation. Little progress was made, however, in improving working-class housing, particularly in Montreal and Toronto, where housing codes were not enforced, public monies

were scarce, and owners resisted the costs of upgrading the housing. Even Toronto's municipal housing program, started in the war years by the city's housing commission, barely made
a dent in the lack of adequate, low-cost rental housing for the working classes.

THE ENFRANCHISEMENT OF WOMEN

Women's suffrage owed as much to World War I as it did to the determined efforts of the suffrage campaigners. Canada's entry into the conflict in 1914 opened up new opportunities for
women in voluntary patriotic service outside the home and employment in the booming
munitions industry. During the war, Canadian women demonstrated the organizing skills and
expertise they had acquired in their suffrage and reform organizations. Women's contributions
were evident in a variety of wartime innovations and projects, such as mothers' pensions, the
Canadian Patriotic Fund (for assisting soldiers' families), public health inspection, day nurs-
eries, and Canadianization programs for immigrant children. Grudgingly, Canadian men came
to recognize the nation's debt to its women. The appointment of women to judgeships and
government commissions, and the election in 1917 of the first woman to a provincial legislature (in Alberta), seemed to testify to a change in public attitudes toward women. Suffragists
like Nellie McClung, in her best-selling book *In Times Like These* (1915), predicted optimistically that female enfranchisement would usher in a new era of political equality.

Manitoba was the first province to enact a bill extending the vote to women. Female suffrage
came in January 1916, shortly after Winnipeg suffragists presented two petitions containing over
43 800 names and helped to topple the Roblin government. Buoyed by the popular sympathy won
by prairie suffragists and strongly supported by the farmers' organizations, similar women's suffrage bills were passed in Saskatchewan (1916) and Alberta (1916). Provincial governments in
Ontario (1917), British Columbia (1917), Nova Scotia (1918), New Brunswick (1919), and
Prince Edward Island (1922) all followed suit, motivated in some cases by the notion that it would
solidify support for Prohibition.

Women's contributions to the war effort, and the conscription crisis of 1917, overcame
the resistance of the federal politicians. The Wartime Elections Act, passed shortly after Robert
Borden's government introduced conscription in the spring of 1917, enfranchised the female
relatives of men serving overseas. In March 1918, a bill for full female franchise was introduced; and in 1919, women won the right to a seat in the House of Commons.

Resistance to female enfranchisement died hard in Quebec. During the 1918 debate on the
women's suffrage bill, several French-Canadian members of Parliament, spurred on by a series of
anti-suffrage articles written by Henri Bourassa in *Le Devoir*, voiced their strong opposition. Female
enfranchisement, they insisted, would prove disastrous for the traditional Roman Catholic, French-
Canadian way of life — disrupting homes, destroying marriage ties, lowering the birth rate, and
weakening both parental authority and public respect for women. For another 22 years these arguments continued to frustrate Quebec women in their struggle for the provincial vote.

"A MORE MILITANT TRADITION":
THE AMERICAN SUFFRAGE DRIVE

MOST COMPARISONS OF THE EARLY WOMEN'S RIGHTS MOVEMENTS in the United States and Canada indicate that the American struggle displayed a more vibrant, militant tradition. Catherine L. Cleverdon, in her 1950 study, *The Women Suffrage Movement in Canada*, stated that by waging a "wholly dignified campaign" for the right to vote, Canadian feminists had "robbed" the story of "the colour" found in "American women's efforts to attain equality." Cleverdon asserted that "at no stage of the campaign was there anything remotely resembling militant tactics" such as those used by American and particularly British suffragettes.

During America's first women's enfranchisement drive between 1870 and 1900, the National Woman Suffrage Association took the lead in asserting the "right" of American women, under the existing U.S. Constitution, to cast a vote. According to leaders of that organization, the U.S. constitution's guarantee of the vote to "citizens" and "persons" included women. To test their legal claims, the association urged its members to register a protest by attempting to vote in elections. By 1872, about 150 women in eleven states, including a few in the South, had gone to the polls to confront often puzzled election officials; some of the incidents ended up in the courts. Perhaps the most highly publicized attempt took place in Rochester, New York, in 1872, when women's rights leader Susan B. Anthony bravely cast her vote and then incurred the wrath of the New York daily press.

THE FINAL PHASE

The American women's suffrage campaign, like the Canadian one, peaked as a major political force in the first two decades of the twentieth century. The passage of the nineteenth amendment to the U.S. Constitution in 1920 was a triumph for a whole network of women's organizations that had doggedly maintained the struggle for the ballot. In the forefront of that bitter and at times acrimonious fight were the National American Woman Suffrage Association (NAWSA) and its affiliated state societies, and the National Woman's Party; but a host of independent suffrage groups, women's clubs, and labour reform organizations like the National Women's Trade Union League played their part in stirring up what NAWSA president Carrie Chapman Catt called the "suffrage noise."

For a country that led the world in pushing for universal *manhood* suffrage throughout the nineteenth century, the failure to extend the franchise to women was a striking anomaly. Although the U.S. voting public expanded through the removal of property qualifications, the enfranchisement of male blacks, and state laws enfranchising the foreign-born, the vote was still denied to half of the nation's population: women. The resistance to women's suffrage, according to historian Eleanor Flexner, "instead of weakening (over the

70-year struggle)...actually stiffened, becoming more active and more articulate." Only after 1900 did a breakthrough come, as the original temperance leaders were gradually superseded by increasing numbers of mostly middle-class, college-educated suffragists.

BANNER WAVING AND PICKETING: THE CONGRESSIONAL UNION STRATEGY

Of all the American suffrage organizations, the most militant and effective was probably the Congressional Union, later reconstituted as the National Woman's Party (founded 1917). The main target of the union's suffrage efforts was Woodrow Wilson, U.S. president from 1912 to 1920. After repeated appeals for a suffrage amendment were rebuffed by Wilson, the union resorted to a variety of public tactics in the hope of goading the president into action. Once, in December 1917, a delegation disrupted Wilson's State of the Union address to Congress by unfurling a huge yellow banner, reading, "*Mr. President, What Will You Do For Woman Suffrage?*" Beginning in January 1917 and lasting for one and a half years, the union picketed the White House. Enduring jeers and abuse, two teams of "silent sentinels" (maintained by a thousand volunteers) stood staunchly at the White House gates, holding up "*Votes for Women*" banners.

CONTROL OF MUNICIPAL UTILITIES

The utilities question loomed large in debates over Canadian urban reform from the 1880s onward, particularly in the years after 1900. Waterworks, street railways, electric power, and telephone systems formed the utilities base considered essential to urban life and growth. Most of the utilities in Canadian cities had been developed by private capitalists (often with generous public subsidies), and there were concerns about whether they were being managed in the public interest. Even though few questioned the efficiency of privately owned utilities, civic reformers contended that their pursuit of business profits prevented the provision of standardized, low-cost services to industry and the population.

Municipal reformers advocated civic control, or outright civic ownership, of utilities, as in the United States and Britain. They argued that utilities should be run as monopolies to prevent wasteful and expensive private competition and the exploitation of a captive market, with little regard for the interests of the city.[6] Municipal ownership would allow the city to extend utilities to suburban communities, reduce rates, and increase civic revenues. The idea met with stiff resistance. Even though campaigns for municipal ownership were supported by most consumers, including progressive businesspeople, powerful private owners of utility companies fought the assault on their right to private enterprise and unimpeded profits to the bitter end.

The struggle for municipal ownership was not an immediate success. In Montreal between 1904 and 1909, the private utility companies withstood an attempt at municipal takeover and remained in private hands for another three decades. Moncton, New Brunswick, which had controlled its own power and transportation utilities for 15 years, returned them to a private company, ostensibly to save the taxpayers money. But these cases were the exceptions. As early as 1893, civic authorities in Guelph, Ontario, had taken over the city's gasworks and the electric light and power company. The Union of Canadian Municipalities was founded in 1901 by civic officials from Ontario and Quebec cities specifically to assert democratic control over the powerful utility companies. The principle of public control, if not municipal ownership, received strong support in 1905 when Adam Beck and the Ontario government established the Ontario Hydro-Electric Power Commission, and in 1907 when the Manitoba government purchased a privately owned telephone system and expanded it across the province.

TOWN PLANNING AND URBAN DEVELOPMENT

In the years before World War I, influential Canadian businesspeople and public figures were converted to the concept of planned community development. Many Canadian cities enacted special zoning laws to protect residential areas. Halifax undertook a massive reconstruction scheme after the great 1917 explosion. Toronto developed the city's waterfront as a multiple-use site, with improved harbour and warehouse facilities, land serviced for industry, better housing for workers, and a recreational area of beaches, all joined to the rest of the city by an expanded streetcar system.

Town planners were much less effective in addressing the problems of urban congestion in the city's slum areas and immigrant ghettoes. Ames, Kelso, Woodsworth, and others had alerted planners to the dilapidated tenements in crowded slums. Eventually new housing laws were passed to control tenements and to set minimum standards, but these measures merely limited the spread of city slums.

MUNICIPAL GOVERNMENT REFORMS

No aspect of the reform movement attracted as much public attention as the "fight for clean government." Like major American cities, many Canadian urban centres from Halifax to Vancouver had come to be controlled by corrupt party machines or untrained and incompetent aldermen. Too often, city councils were dominated by party or ward bosses more concerned with private gain, local interests, and political survival than with the city's welfare.

In the years after 1890, civic reformers attacked municipal corruption and inefficiency and attempted to turn "old guard" politicians out of office. In Montreal, Ames and business-minded civic leaders put together a reform coalition, supported by most English-speaking voters, key businessmen, and French-Canadian progressives like Henri Bourassa and Oliver Asselin. The battle against the old guard raged for two decades until 1914, when the reform alliance was crushed by a French-Canadian party boss. Montreal's ward politicians had won popular support by attempting to deal with the miseries of their mainly francophone constituents.

TAMMANY HALL: BOSSISM IN NEW YORK CITY

A MERICA'S CITIES SEEMED TO OUTGROW their governments in the years after 1860. The electorate became too large and fragmented to function as a community. New strains were placed on traditional town government, with its elected mayor and a small group of aldermen. The tremendous responsibilities of supervising massive fire and police departments, sanitation, tax assessment, housing standards, and public health called for political organization on a larger scale. Such organization was provided by powerful and efficient political machines.

As the industrial cities grew, so did the tax revenues and the size of city contracts. Nearly all of the wealthy and socially prominent citizens supported the Republican party, so most newcomers to a city were excluded from civic affairs. Soon ambitious politicians, mostly Democrats, realized that, by winning the loyalty of the majority of people in a ward or city neighbourhood and by forming alliances with other ward bosses like themselves, they could take control of municipal government and use it for their own private gain. Politics, to these party bosses, was like a business — the business of securing the retaining votes.

The most notorious political machine was the New York City Democratic machine known as Tammany Hall. Under "Boss" William Tweed in the late 1860s and 1870s, Tammany Hall indulged in corruption on a massive scale: bribery was used freely to control judges and law-enforcement officials, public works contracts provided for kickbacks to the machine, political influence was peddled to Cornelius Vanderbilt and other business barons, and Tammany officials were hired in great numbers for civic positions on the public payroll.

In spite of the indictments of urban reformers, Tammany Hall and other machines had some redeeming qualities; they performed very personalized social services among the poor of the cities. During the winter of 1870, for example, Boss Tweed spent $50 000 on coal, which was dumped by the tonne on street corners in the poorest parts of New York City. Most ward bosses made it their business to see that, when marriages and births occurred in their neighbourhood, the events were recognized with gifts. The party bosses, then, delivered on their promises — a lesson often lost on the city's "do-good" social reformers.

Although the American idea of commission government did not take root in most Canadian cities, urban centres like Toronto, Montreal, and Vancouver gradually did establish commissions as adjuncts to their city councils. These commissions were responsible for managing hydro-electric power distribution, municipal parks, harbour facilities, and public transportation.

Other municipal-government reforms were purely Canadian, following neither American progressive ideas nor British policies of democratic control over civic affairs.[7] Impressed by the successes of Canadian business and firmly committed to corporate ideals of managerial efficiency, structural reformers attempted to establish greater civic efficiency by establishing boards of control. Unlike American-style city-manager systems, these boards were composed of elected councillors and functioned as a kind of municipal cabinet, working in conjunction with the city's chief executive, the mayor.

URBAN REFORM AND ILLUSIONS OF PROGRESS

Canada's first phase of urban reform arose in the 1880s, peaked in the years after 1900, and gradually declined in the 1920s. Like its American counterpart, the Canadian movement aroused public interest but did not always translate reform ideas into genuine social and economic improvements. Most municipal reformers focused narrowly on administrative changes and did not cure the social and economic problems that accompanied the urban industrial revolution.

The basic features of the modern Canadian city — mass transit systems, public utilities, official plans, civic boards and commissions, and a range of social services — took shape in the years 1880–1920. Only four decades later, the main achievements of this first wave of reform would come under attack from a new generation of urban reformers.

ACTIVITIES

KEY TERMS AND CONCEPTS

Identify and explain the historical significance of each of the following terms and concepts:

- North American metropolitanism
- Metropolitan dominance
- The "regenerators"
- Age of "light, soap, and water"
- Social gospel
- The "City Below the Hill"
- Toronto's "The Ward"
- The "proper sphere"
- Maternal feminism
- Hull House
- Woman's Christian Temperance Union
- Winnipeg mock parliament
- Commission government
- Muckrakers
- Clean government
- Tammany Hall

QUESTIONS FOR DISCUSSION

1. Why was North American society transformed by a wave of explosive urban growth from 1860 to the early 1920s? In what ways was the process of urbanization different in Canada than in the United States?

2. What were Canadian cities like in the late nineteenth and early twentieth centuries? What accounted for the violent contrasts between rich and poor districts in cities like Toronto and Winnipeg, New York and Chicago?

3. Who were Canada's early urban reformers, and what were their prime motivations? Distinguish between the social regenerators, the business-progressives, and the structural reformers.

4. What impact did the rise of a North American urban–industrial order have on gender relations? Why did educated,

middle-class, Anglo–Saxon women come to the fore in the urban reform movement?

5. How did the women's suffrage movement evolve in the United States and in Canada? Why did women's-rights agitation tend to take more militant forms in the United States than in Canada?

6. What did civic reformers in Canada and the United States achieve? Did the actual reforms in social services and municipal government match the ideas of the reformers?

INTERPRETING TABLES AND THEMATIC MAPS

Statistical tables and maps can be valuable tools for analysis, particularly in the historical study of cities. For each of the following statistical tables and maps, identify the pattern of urban growth shown, analyze the data, and draw some conclusions that can be supported by the facts.

RANK OF SELECTED CANADIAN CITIES BY SIZE, 1901–1931*

RANK	1901	1911	1921	1931
1	Montreal	Montreal	Montreal	Montreal
2	Toronto	Toronto	Toronto	Toronto
3	Quebec	WINNIPEG	WINNIPEG	Vancouver
4	Ottawa	Vancouver	Vancouver	WINNIPEG
5	Hamilton	Ottawa	Hamilton	Hamilton
6	WINNIPEG	Hamilton	Ottawa	Quebec
7	Halifax	Quebec	Quebec	Ottawa
8	Saint John	Halifax	CALGARY	CALGARY
9	London	London	London	EDMONTON
10	Vancouver	CALGARY	EDMONTON	London
11	Victoria	Saint John	Halifax	Windsor
12	Kingston	Victoria	Saint John	Verdun
13	Brantford	REGINA	Victoria	Halifax
14	Hull	EDMONTON	Windsor	REGINA
15	Windsor	Brantford	REGINA	Saint John
16	Sherbrooke	Kingston	Brantford	SASKATOON
17	Guelph	Peterborough	SASKATOON	Victoria
18	Charlottetown	Hull	Verdun	Trois-Rivières
19	Trois-Rivières	Windsor	Hull	Kitchener
36	—	SASKATOON	—	—
73	CALGARY	—	—	—
77	EDMONTON	—	—	—
97	REGINA	—	—	—
110	SASKATOON	—	—	—

*Cities in the prairie West are highlighted in capital letters.

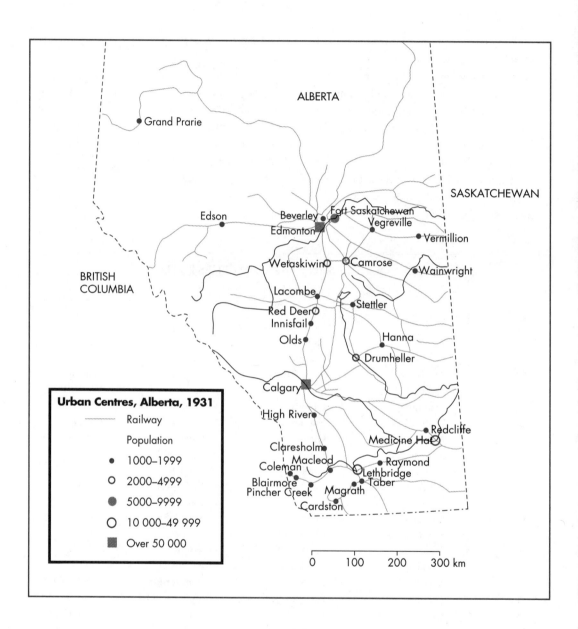

ALBERTA

SASKATCHEWAN

BRITISH
COLUMBIA

• Grand Prarie

Edson •

Beverley
Edmonton
Fort Saskatchewan
Vegreville
• Vermillion

Wetaskiwin○ ○Camrose   •Wainwright

Lacombe•
Red Deer○   •Stettler
Innisfail•
Olds•   Hanna•
○ Drumheller

Calgary

High River•

Claresholm•   Redcliffe•
Medicine Hat○

Macleod
Coleman•   •Raymond
Blairmore•   •Lethbridge
Pincher Creek•   Magrath•   •Taber
Cardston•

Urban Centres, Alberta, 1931

	Railway
	Population
•	1000–1999
○	2000–4999
◉	5000–9999
○	10 000–49 999
■	Over 50 000

0   100   200   300 km

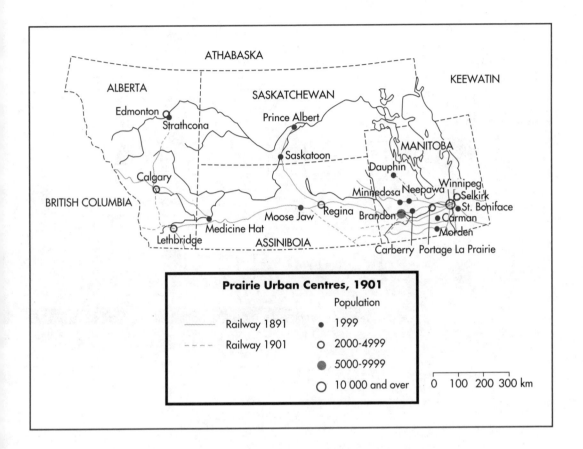

Prairie Urban Centres, 1901

Population

——— Railway 1891   ● 1999

- - - - Railway 1901   ○ 2000–4999

     ◉ 5000–9999

     ○ 10 000 and over

0   100   200   300 km

CHAPTER 16

THE INDUSTRIAL STATE TRANSFORMED, 1896–1929

THE AGE OF BUSINESS ENTERPRISE

REFORMING THE MODERN CORPORATE INDUSTRIAL STATE

THE GREAT WAR AND LABOUR RADICALISM

HINTERLAND REVOLTS OF THE 1920s

A NEW INDUSTRIAL AGE DAWNED IN NORTH AMERICA at the close of the nineteenth century. In Canada, as in the United States, crucial changes occurred in the economy with the emergence of large-scale corporate business and the reshaping of the industrial state. The Canadian economy entered a phase of expansion, industrial consolidation, and increased economic concentration, which might be described as "monopoly capitalism."[1] Yet, out of this period would emerge Canada's unique mixture of capitalist business enterprise and positive state intervention in promoting economic development.

Prime Minister Wilfrid Laurier boasted that "the twentieth century will belong to Canada," and his wishful boast seemed to strike a responsive chord in many Canadians. These buoyant hopes at the turn of the century owed much to the return of prosperity to North America after years of economic depression. The growth came largely from the rise of the wheat economy in the West; massive mineral discoveries in the Klondike, the interior of British Columbia, and northern Ontario; and new infusions of American capital into Canada. Two new transcontinental railways were launched, factories expanded behind protective tariff walls, and completely new industries were started, such as steel, automobiles, chemicals, pulp and paper, and electrical goods. Capital and industry became more centralized in Montreal and Toronto, and the regional economies were integrated under the strong influence of these central Canadian metropolises. Although in 1900 three out of every five Canadians still depended on the land for their livelihood, urbanization was increasing in conjunction with industrialization.

Yet the emerging Canadian corporate industrial state, like its American counterpart, was erected on a fragile economic base. By the late 1920s, it would be clear that the consolidation of capitalism carried with it some inherent weaknesses and the seeds of potential economic disaster.

THE AGE OF BUSINESS ENTERPRISE

AT THE TURN OF THE CENTURY Canada entered a period of development strikingly similar to America's "Gilded Age" in the late nineteenth century. Powerful industrial and financial capitalists headed multimillion-dollar corporations created in a wave of business mergers and combinations after 1900. In the popular press and literature of the time, these Canadian entrepreneurs were depicted as towering figures who were building a nation by driving steel rails through the wilderness, erecting booming new factories, blasting metals out of the Canadian Shield, or harnessing the power of Niagara. An opinion poll in 1909 named four railway presidents among "Canada's ten biggest men," and many Canadian school children dreamed of one day becoming millionaires.

But the rise of powerful captains of industry did not win universal praise. American big businessmen were publicly rebuked as "robber barons"; in Canada, leaders of labour and agrarian

Business magnate Hart Massey and his family epitomized the Toronto business and social establishment. Massey's business interests grew into the Massey-Harris Company, the largest farm machinery manufacturer in the British empire.

movements criticized Canadian plutocrats as oppressors of industrial workers, grain farmers, and small homesteaders. Leading intellectuals and clergy — English Protestant and French Roman Catholic — questioned the predominant social approval of "business values" and unrestrained acquisitiveness. Stephen Leacock's popular satirical book, *Arcadian Adventures of the Idle Rich* (1914), reinforced in the public mind images of ruthless and ostentatious tyrants whose self-interested behaviour eroded the basis of religion, politics, and common morality.

FUSION OF PRIVATE AND PUBLIC ENTERPRISE

Most American businessmen strongly espoused rugged individualism and the Horatio Alger model of "rags to riches" economic success. Canadian business leaders equally professed to be followers of unfettered free enterprise and laissez faire. Many of their actions, however, suggested otherwise. In their search for security of investment, relief from potentially disastrous competition, or stability in the market, they not only accepted, but at times actively sought out, government involvement in business. In turn, Canada's enormous size, small population, and scarcity of entrepreneurs combined to force governments to provide generous subsidies to business ventures. In addition, taxation was light or non-existent. Canadian business operated in a protective, supportive, and usually favourable environment and flourished from this hot-house effect.

Nowhere was this clearer than in the fields of railway construction and hydro-electric power development. Canada's second wave of railway building was heavily supported by governments. Both of the new transcontinental lines constructed after 1903 — the Canadian Northern and the Grand Trunk — were built with over $200 million in funds from Laurier's government and became railway empires floating on government bonds. When both railway companies failed in 1915–16 because of overbuilding and ruinous competition, government again came to their rescue. Temporary assistance was given by the Conservative–Unionist government of Robert Borden at first. Then, in 1919, Dominion authorities took over the two railways and merged them into a single, publicly owned system known as the Canadian National Railways. Free-wheeling free enterprise gave way to state regulation, then government ownership, and eventually to a "new era" of capital, labour, and state co-operation.[2]

Sizable groups of enterprising businessmen played a crucial role in the early establishment of publicly owned hydro systems. During the decade around 1900, a popular Ontario public power movement arose. It was spearheaded by London businessman and mayor Adam Beck and supported by a disparate group of manufacturers, board of trade activists, and social reformers. A Toronto-based syndicate of private electrical interests threatened to gain a monopoly over the distribution of water-generated electricity. Advocates of public control of power, with strong support in western Ontario centres, pressed for government ownership to prevent the production, delivery, and sale of electricity from falling into the hands of private, profit-seeking monopolies. The Conservative government of James P. Whitney responded by setting up the Hydro-Electric Power Commission of Ontario in 1906, placing all electrical power under its control and ensuring a secure, relatively cheap supply of power to industry and consumers. A similar experiment in the public ownership of hydro began in Manitoba that year, although it faced more persistent opposition from private competition.

THE RISE OF NORTHERN ENTERPRISE

In the twentieth century, electricity and gasoline replaced steam as the driving force for industry and gave birth to a new generation of factory machines. These technological advances boosted production and brought far-reaching changes to the scale and organization of industrial enterprises. Between the early 1890s and 1914, large industrial and financial corporations all but supplanted small-scale, owner-operated businesses. A great wave of business mergers and consolidations, which reached a crest between 1909 and 1912, gave birth to such giants as Dominion Steel, Canada Bread, Dominion Canners, and Canada Cement.

American capital added to this industrial growth as U.S.-owned multinational enterprises expanded into Canada. The number of American branch factories in Canada jumped from about 70 in 1900 to 215 in 1909 and reached 450 by 1914. Coca-Cola, Westinghouse, Quaker Oats, Sherwin-Williams Paints, Gillette Safety Razor, and General Motors, to name only a few, set up Canadian subsidiaries in this period. American investment was concentrated in southern Ontario and Montreal, especially in border frontier areas. Such investment meant employment, and soon towns in Ontario and the prairie West were competing with each other, offering "bonus" schemes to attract American branch plants. Building sites were sometimes given free, tax incentives were offered, and services such as water, sewers, and electrical lines were subsidized.

Canadian and American entrepreneurs erected industrial empires in the resource hinterlands. F.H. Clergue, an American entrepreneur, expanded a small power plant in Sault Ste. Marie into Consolidated Lake Superior Corporation, which before its collapse in 1903 owned and operated the Algoma Steel Company, power companies, railways, steamships, a telegraph company, and nickel, iron, and gold mines. Equally notorious were the exploits of Henry Melville Whitney, a Boston financier, who wooed the support of Nova Scotia premier W.S. Fielding in consolidating Cape Breton coal mines into the Dominion Coal Company in 1893. Six years later Whitney persuaded a new Liberal premier, George Murray, to help create the Dominion Iron and Steel Company (DISCO) with government bounties and royalty concessions on coal. Whitney was eventually edged out of business by rival entrepreneurs, but Dominion Coal and DISCO went on to dominate the lives of miners and steelworkers in Cape Breton's "company towns."

LABOUR AND THE NEW INDUSTRIAL SYSTEM

The rise of large-scale corporate enterprise had widespread effects on labour. As they mechanized, these vast business organizations revolutionized the work process. Sophisticated electricity- and gasoline-driven machinery and technology led to the introduction of assembly-line production in Henry Ford's automobile assembly plants in the United States and in the Canadian branch plants. Industrial engineers were needed rather than artisans and craftspeople, and by the 1920s the vast majority of industrial wage earners were machine operators, clerical workers, and maintenance staff. Skilled workers were not so much eliminated as shifted out of production into new jobs as machine operators or low-level administrative staff.

Along with the assembly line, centralized co-ordination of production was introduced to promote efficiency and reduce operating costs. Industrial production not only became more "scientific" in its methods but increasingly regimented. Frederick Winslow Taylor, the American father of "scientific management" or Taylorism, developed new techniques for more

A brand new Model A Ford rolled off the assembly line every three minutes in an attempt to put North America on wheels.

centralized, cost-efficient management control. Employers set high production standards; they sent management staff onto the shop floor armed with stop watches to time the rate at which workers performed operations and to speed them up. Under such "drive" systems workers lived in fear of dismissal; any attempts to resist were viewed as "troublemaking."

CONTESTED TERRAIN: GENDER AND SKILL

The corporate industrial transformation fundamentally altered gender relations as well as class and ethnic relations in the workplace. In the printing, hosiery, and garment trades, candy factories, and urban telegraph industry, skill classifications stemmed from deeply held patriarchal values. "Rough work" was mostly reserved for so-called "rugged men" and higher-paying

A needle-trades sweatshop, Toronto, around the 1890s. Toronto's garment industry employed mainly immigrant Jewish women in sweatshops along Spadina Avenue.

skilled jobs for the male "breadwinners." Male workers, according to historians Joy Parr and Christina Burr, were mostly employed in "skilled crafts," while "women's work" was invariably considered unskilled and expendable in tough times.[3]

The Toronto printing trades were a case in point. With the widespread introduction of machine typesetting in the 1890s, the gender division of labour became a contested terrain. When the employers threatened to employ cheaper female labour, the male hand-compositors faced a "crisis of masculinity" and vigorously defended their craft-based notions of skill. The male dominated Toronto Typographical Union (TTU) finally succeeded in gaining jurisdiction over the operation of the new typesetting machines and in virtually excluding women from the trade and better-paying jobs.

Men and women workers responded to the new world of mechanized work with suspicion, if not outright hostility. Many wage earners reacted by quitting frequently and moving on to other jobs; some immigrants from Europe returned home. Widespread labour turnover meant that many men and women drifted from one job to another, from mills to construction camps to mines; from the textile industry to clerical work. The conditions spawned by this new industrial system led many factory workers to turn to unions and radical labour movements.

REFORMING THE MODERN CORPORATE INDUSTRIAL STATE

THE RISE OF LARGE-SCALE CORPORATE BUSINESS in the United States challenged many deeply rooted values and beliefs about individual economic liberty and the ideal of the "self-made man." Prevailing beliefs about the gospel of individual economic success collided head-on with the realities of a modern industrial state dominated by large corporations and a new, powerful class of wealthy capitalists. By 1900, more and more Americans were awakening to the fact that these large corporate enterprises were not only curtailing economic competition but threatening the very basis of America's prized traditions of individualism and economic freedom.

The forces of American liberal reform that had been gathering momentum since the 1870s culminated in the Progressive movement in America from 1900 to 1917. Aimed primarily at reforming — not replacing — the corporate industrial system, the movement generated a series of impulses for change in society and in local, state, and national government. Out of the welter of reform impulses, a loose coalition of American "Progressives" emerged. They pursued a variety of goals: economic reforms, such as the control or "busting" of the giant trusts, and the regulation of utilities; political reforms like the dismantling of urban political machines and the eradication of civic corruption; and social reforms, such as relief for the urban poor, the regulation of child and female factory labour, and the "Americanization" of immigrants. Among the symbolic leaders of Progressivism were two American presidents, Theodore Roosevelt (president 1901–08) and Woodrow Wilson (president 1912–20). Both not only took up the slogans and rhetoric of Progressivism but enacted a series of measures aimed at reforming business, protecting ordinary Americans, and cleaning up the system.

THE "COMBINES QUESTION" IN CANADA

A broad wave of Progressivism aimed at controlling the trusts and reforming corporate business never really materialized in Canada. Nothing comparable to the famous U.S. Sherman Anti-Trust Act of 1889, Teddy Roosevelt's later "trust-busting" campaigns, and Wilson's regulatory reforms occurred in Canada. The Canadian anti-combines tradition from 1889 to 1920 resembled more closely British industrial policy than American.

Canadian efforts to regulate big business were sporadic at best. Complaints about "rings" and "trusts" operating in Canada had been raised since the 1870s, but little was done until a select committee of the House of Commons was appointed in 1888. It investigated charges of price fixing, but the resulting anti-combines bill (1889) was never enforced because of vehement protests that price arrangements were necessary to ensure "the reasonable right to make a small profit." With the election of Laurier and the Liberals in 1896, Canadian policy seemed to recognize tacitly the right of business to combine and to accept modest price fixing as essential for some businesses to make a "living profit."

The wave of Canadian mergers created mounting pressure on Laurier's government in 1909–10 to take some form of action against the combines. In swallowing up other enterprises and fixing prices to restrict competition, Canadian combines were behaving much like the bad "trusts" in the United States. Mackenzie King, now minister of labour, responded with the Combines Investigation Act of 1910. In the bill, King closely followed American developments, and even went so far as to distinguish between good and bad trusts. King supported the argument that mergers were generally beneficial because they improved efficiency and hence made prices reasonable; he had trouble finding examples of bad trusts. The Anti-Combines Act was so ineffectual that it was used only once before being repealed in 1919.

TIMES OF INDUSTRIAL CONFLICT

Booming economic times in North America brought intensified labour unrest because the fruits of prosperity did not reach the city slums or the frontier bunkhouse camps. From the late 1890s into the new century, prices rose dramatically and wages lagged behind. While capitalists amassed fortunes, workers had to fight for a fair share of the expanding pie. The result was seething discontent that erupted into industrial conflict and even workplace violence.

Growing numbers of workers turned to unions for protection and security and transformed Canada's small and fragmented labour movement. The American Federation of Labour (AFL) under Samuel Gompers had demonstrated its strength in 1902 when, at the Trades and Labour Congress, dissenting locals were forced to form their own rival Canadian Federation of Labour (CFL). Many workers were against the craft-based AFL-type of union. The Western Federation of Miners (WFM) and other American unions, which had fought some hard battles against ruthless employers, believed in organizing on a much wider base. This spirit of militant industrial unionism spread into Canada in the 1890s after giant American mining corporations started operations in British Columbia, and American-born and seasoned WFM members moved into the mines and camps of the province. Although the WFM local of

The militia confront striking B.C. fishers. A standoff between the 6th Duke of Connaught's Own Rifles and strikers at Steveston near the Fraser River salmon fishery, July 1900.

smelter workers was crushed in the Rossland Strike of 1901, a surge of labour radicalism among workers helped elect two unionists to the British Columbia legislature — the first socialists elected anywhere in the British empire.

Labour radicalism in British Columbia reached its peak with the rise of the International Workers of the World (IWW), nicknamed "the Wobblies." Formed in June 1905 in Chicago to counter Gompers's craft unionism, the IWW sought to organize all industrial workers into One Big Union and to prepare for a general strike that would pave the way for radical social change. Under the colourful leadership of "Big Bill" Haywood, the Wobblies took their campaign against what they called the AFL's "pure and simple" unionism into the railway camps, mines, and mills of British Columbia. After 1908, the IWW won considerable support among unskilled, itinerant workers, including loggers, longshoremen, and railway construction workers on the Canadian Northern and Grand Trunk Pacific lines. Unlike the craft unions, the Wobblies welcomed transient workers of every ethnic background. By 1912, the union had 12 locals and 5000 members, and claimed the allegiance of nearly 40 percent of all railway construction workers.

The IWW won much respect from the labouring classes for its courageous fights for "free speech" in many western American cities and in Vancouver and Edmonton. But others saw it as a threat to the capitalist system, and it was resisted by all the weapons of the system — the press, the courts, the police, the army. At its peak in the United States, the IWW, led by Haywood and Elizabeth Gurley Flynn, mounted a mass strike in 1912 against the mills of the American Woolen Company, and forced the huge company to give in to its wage demands. The legendary Mother Mary Jones, a white-haired United Mine Workers organizer in her eighties, even carried the IWW message to the B.C. mining frontier, firing up the miners with her oratory. Yet the idea of organizing transient labour ultimately proved futile. When the railway construction ended, the IWW faded as a force in western Canada. South of the border, Haywood and the IWW leaders experienced regular arrests and were eventually subdued in 1918 by laws imposed to limit wartime dissent.

THE CAPE BRETON MINERS' STRUGGLE

The craft-based union in the Maritimes was the Nova Scotia Provincial Workermen's Association (PWA). Unlike its western counterparts, the PWA favoured negotiating better working conditions over striking. After a bitter seven-week strike against the giant combine Dominion Steel and Coal at the Sydney mill in 1904, it was reduced to a so-called "company union."

American-style unionism came to Nova Scotia with the United Mine Workers of America (UMW), an AFL-affiliate. Both Dominion Steel and the PWA fought a lengthy strike called by the UMW in 1909–10, which threatened to bring Cape Breton to the brink of civil war. During the conflict, strikers were evicted from their company-owned houses and the Canadian militia was called in to aid the civil authorities. When Dominion Steel finally worked out a contract with the PWA, UMW supporters went underground. After seven years, they re-emerged to capture the leadership of the miners' union. By 1918, 11 000 Cape Breton miners had been absorbed by the UMW international union, leaving the PWA in tatters.

MACKENZIE KING'S LIBERAL CORPORATISM

The Liberal government in Ottawa sought to dampen industrial conflict through a new "liberal corporatist"* approach to labour relations. The chief architect of this policy, William Lyon Mackenzie King, was a young labour-relations specialist who had joined the newly formed federal Department of Labour in 1900 as editor of the *Labour Gazette*. King was a Harvard-trained labour expert who espoused the liberal corporatist notion of "conciliation" in labour disputes. Central to his conception of labour relations was the principle of maintaining industrial peace at all costs. Business, labour, and government, King believed, could coexist and resolve any dispute if the facts were examined and a "cooling-off" period was permitted. As deputy minister of labour, he resisted calls for compulsory arbitration, pursuing instead a general policy of conciliation aimed at "compelling compromise."[4]

Under King's direction, the federal labour department attempted conciliation in a series of industrial disputes. Out of almost 700 disputes between 1900 and 1907, 41 were referred to federal conciliators and 33 were settled. Although the department claimed to be acting impartially, on many occasions it upheld company interests. King was openly hostile to radical industrial organizations such as the WFM and the IWW and had little sympathy for "union recognition" strikes, preferring to deal with tamer "company unions."

Two ugly and disruptive labour disputes in 1906 in the Alberta coal fields and the Quebec lumber town of Buckingham forced the Laurier government to take action. The Industrial Disputes Investigation Act was enacted in 1907. True to King's liberal corporatist ideology, it stressed "investigations" and provided for a compulsory delay of work stoppages during them. By the standards of labour policy at that time, the Act was progressive legislation.

Yet it was not without its drawbacks for labour. In two highly charged disputes — the Toronto Bell Telephone operators strike of 1907, and the Grand Trunk Railway strike of 1910 — the Act clearly worked to the benefit of the employers. Since the investigation stage interrupted the strike, employers used the time to train replacement workers and plan countermeasures for the next work stoppage. The Act did not compel employers to negotiate, and since public opinion was shaped largely by wealthy newspaper owners, the cooling-off period was used to bring external pressure to bear on labour. King's labour policies may have helped defuse industrial conflict, but they hampered labour far more than they did capital.

---

* Liberal corporatism is an ideology rooted in the acceptance of a new industrial order shaped by the emerging corporate business organizations and their desire for a stabilized, rationalized, and ever-expanding economic society.

"SERVANT OF POWER":
MACKENZIE KING AND THE ROCKEFELLER FOUNDATION*

IN HIS YEARS WITH THE FEDERAL LABOUR DEPARTMENT, Mackenzie King earned a reputation as an astute conciliator in labour relations, who upheld liberal principles of fair play and equity. Yet, during World War I, with Wilfrid Laurier and the Liberals out of power, King worked as a key labour-relations consultant to the Rockefeller Foundation in New York. The Rockefellers, at that time, were widely known as the greatest "robber barons" of American capitalism. And in the wake of the "Ludlow Massacre" of 1914 in the Colorado coal fields, they were known as the most hard-fisted, anti-labour capitalists of them all.

The Colorado Coal Strike of 1913–14 had been brutally suppressed by the Rockefeller-owned Colorado Fuel and Iron Corporation at a high cost. The striking miners had been evicted from their company-owned shacks, set upon and attacked in their tent encampments by Rockefeller-hired detectives, replaced in the mines by "scab labour," and raided in a surprise machine-gun attack by the National Guard at Ludlow. The Rockefellers' interests may have won the battle for the Colorado coal fields, but they lost the larger war for American public opinion. Outrage over the "Ludlow Massacre" and the Rockefeller company's tactics spread across the United States, spurred on by Congressional investigations of the "Colorado coal war."

The Rockefellers responded to the public wrath with a campaign to improve their corporate public image. To this end John D. Rockefeller, Jr., hired Mackenzie King as a technical expert in labour relations. King saw the position as an opportunity to tackle a major labour problem and perhaps convince the Rockefellers to set things right in their companies. In the process, however, he joined a new breed of American scientific managers and technocrats employed as "servants of power."

A different King was starkly revealed during this Rockefeller period. In accepting the position, he basically concurred with the Rockefellers, John Sr. and son, on the issue of union recognition. The Rockefellers were adamant that they would never bargain with the United Mine Workers (UMW), the union representing most Colorado coal miners. Although King went along with this, he did try to impress upon them the critical need to improve the abysmal working conditions prevailing in the Colorado mines. King's strategy had three main elements: organize a "company union" to encourage worker participation in the mine's affairs; win the workers over with modest improvements in wages and conditions; and break the "illegitimate" union (the militant UMW) by refusing to recognize it for bargaining purposes. This became the so-called

---

* For a fuller treatment see Reginald Whitaker, "The Liberal Corporatist Ideas of Mackenzie King," *Labour/Le Travailleur* 2 (1977): 154–158.

Rockefeller "Colorado Plan," a strategy later widely used to undermine independent trade unionism. King emerged from the Rockefeller period convinced that the Rockefellers were "enlightened capitalists," and decried those who hurled "nothing but abuse" at the family and its corporate consultants.

William Lyon Mackenzie King (centre) and John D. Rockefeller Jr. (right) inspect the mines, 1915. The future prime minister was employed as a labour-relations specialist by the Rockefellers.

THE GREAT WAR AND LABOUR RADICALISM

DURING THE FOUR LONG YEARS OF WORLD WAR I, Canada was plunged into a period of drastic economic and social change. Hardly any economic or social institution remained unaffected by it. The war years (1914–18) brought voting rights for women; the first, "temporary" income tax; and even the beginnings of Prohibition. The manufacture of munitions for the war produced a great expansion of production. But wartime inflation and stories of corruption and profiteering among the business class made Canadians more critical than ever of the philosophy, practices, and morality of those who controlled the modern industrial system.

The Great War brought a gradual recovery from an economic depression that began in 1912 and dragged on into the first year of the war. During this period unemployment had depleted the ranks of organized labour. Many in the first wave of recruits for the Canadian expeditionary force in 1914 were driven to enlist as much by unemployment as by patriotism. Slowly, wartime contracts for supplies, uniforms, and materials pulled the economy out of recession. In western Canada, which had recently been suffering from drought and depressed wheat prices, wartime wheat demand caused farm commodity prices to rise faster than costs, and wheat cultivation expanded from 4 to 6 million hectares. By 1916, army recruiters and munitions factories were competing for labour, producing a serious labour shortage that was eventually filled by women entering the workforce in large numbers. Boosted by wartime employment, union membership in Canada reached 378 000 by 1919.

WAR AND THE INDUSTRIAL SYSTEM

At the beginning of the war, Canadian manufacturers expected large orders and profitable business from Britain. But the ill-designed, shoddy uniforms, equipment, and weapons supplied to the first Canadian contingent overseas did nothing to attract British orders for goods. Most of the Allied orders went to the United States, even though it remained officially neutral until 1917.

Canada's first attempt at war manufacturing was an ill-conceived fiasco. Sam Hughes, minister of militia in the Borden government, hastily assembled a group of his cronies in the Shell Committee to bid for British artillery contracts. When orders began pouring in late in 1914 and early in 1915, the Shell Committee suppliers failed to deliver. By the summer of 1915, Britain faced a desperate shortage of artillery ammunition. Britain's new minister of munitions, Lloyd George, reacted with a clear policy: no more orders until Canada's munitions industry was totally reorganized.

J.W. Flavelle, a self-made Toronto millionaire, was called on to head the Imperial Munitions Board (IMB), set up as an agency of the British government. Flavelle remade the munitions industry. Utilizing the business leadership skills he had developed in his own business, Flavelle recruited a team of efficient managers, clamped down on outrageous profiteering, and imposed quality control on manufacturers. The Imperial Munitions Board and its head were not loved by all. Many in the prairie West, with its high unemployment and limited manufacturing capacity, complained that Flavelle was favouring eastern business. Flavelle responded, with characteristic bluntness,

While men were at the front, women assumed skilled positions in manufacturing, especially in the munitions industry. But when peace came, munitions factories closed, the men returned, and female workers found themselves unemployed.

that western contractors had not delivered. Trade unions charged that the IMB's contracts failed to contain the "fair wage" provisions found in British and Canadian government contracts. Workers, Flavelle declared, should be thankful for a job.

The IMB was autocratic and powerful — and successful. By the war's end it had 600 factories employing 300 000 workers, including 40 000 women, and had branched out into the production of ships, aircraft, flying boats, chemicals, and explosives. When, in 1917, Britain announced that it could no longer afford to purchase the IMB's products, the financial crisis was resolved by Flavelle's ingenuity. He temporarily floated the IMB's finances on the federal treasury, bank loans, and Victory loan proceeds, and then secured important new purchase orders from the United States.

THE RESURGENCE OF LABOUR MILITANCY

The war produced a bitter harvest of labour discontent. Wartime inflation caused prices to outpace wage increases. Borden's Conservative–Unionist government appealed for a total national war effort and sacrifices by all, yet the business class managed to reap material benefits from Canada's wartime industrial mobilization. Excluded from wartime consultation and influence, many labour leaders became openly critical of the Borden government, the Trades and Labour Congress, and in some cases the whole industrial system. Fighting the prolonged war in Europe necessitated an unprecedented mobilization of human and material resources by the state; it also unleashed a number of repressive innovations, such as the establishment of Royal Canadian Mounted Police security operations, the internment of citizens deemed "enemy aliens," the enforcement of wartime censorship, and the imposition of compulsory military service overseas.[5] Rising Canadian labour militancy was not an isolated phenomenon, but part of a broader working-class upheaval that found expression in the Russian Revolution of 1917 and was spreading rapidly through the industrialized countries of Europe and the Americas.

However, the Great War was not the only cause of postwar working-class unrest. New groups of workers had joined the labour movement — public service workers, West Coast loggers, and previously unorganized workers in Toronto's and Montreal's packing houses and garment shops. Prewar immigrants from eastern and southern Europe, including Finns, Jews, and Ukrainians with Old World socialist backgrounds, were now adding their energies and skills to the movement. Labour's strength was also augmented by increasing numbers of unionized women, ranging from telephone operators to store clerks to garment workers. By the early postwar years, the working-class districts of the large cities were rife with discontent.[6] Poor and relatively expensive housing and abysmal living conditions in immigrant districts contributed to working-class unrest and helped widen concerns beyond those of the workplace. This explains why the wave of postwar unrest bred general and sympathetic strikes that even involved working people outside the unions.

ORGANIZING FOR WAR: THE AMERICAN EXAMPLE*

WORLD WAR I brought a marked expansion of governmental activity in the United States as well as in Canada. America's entry into the war in April 1917 led the Woodrow Wilson administration to create a series of specialized agencies. As part of this government expansion during the war, leading businessmen, technocrats, and scientific managers were recruited to head the war mobilization agencies. Business leaders were particularly favoured for their capacity to tap the vast resources of large business corporations and to harness private interests on behalf of the administration.

Under the Wilson war administration, a number of powerful "dollar-a-year men" joined the federal government establishment. Among those recruited were:

- *Bernard Baruch*, Wall Street financier: Appointed chairman of the War Industries Board.
- *Walter Gifford*, AT & T executive: Appointed director of the Council of National Defense.
- *Howard Coffin*, vice-president of the Hudson Motor Company: Appointed chairman of the Aircraft Production Board.
- *Herbert Hoover*, corporate engineer and entrepreneur: Appointed chairman of the Ford Administration.
- *Edward Hurley*, machine-tool manufacturer: Appointed president of the U.S. Shipping Board.
- *Eugene Meyer, Jr.,* Wall Street banker: Appointed director of the War Finance Corporation.

All these "corporate volunteers" were reputed to be men who placed the public interest above narrower private motives. In fact, however, many of the dollar-a-year men saw great opportunities, perhaps advantages, in playing a direct role in the shaping of a new military–business–government order, not just for wartime but for peacetime.

The chairman of the Wartime Industries Board, Bernard Baruch, headed an agency similar to J.W. Flavelle's Imperial Munitions Board. Of all of President Wilson's wartime administrators, Baruch became one of the strongest advocates of economic consolidation, of an end to anti-trust laws, and of corporate leadership in conjunction with a friendly government in Washington. Historian Michael Bliss has argued that in spite of the superficial similarities between Baruch and Flavelle, the Canadian businessman-turned-administrator never shared Baruch's commitment to a permanent form of state capitalism based on the wartime model.

* For a more detailed study see Robert D. Cuff, "Business, the State, and World War I: The American Experience," in J.L. Granatstein and R.D. Cuff, eds., *War and Society in North America* (Toronto: Thomas Nelson, 1971), pp. 1–19.

1919: THE YEAR OF LABOUR REVOLT

Militant industrial unionism boiled over in 1919. A new western radical and socialist move-ment convened a western labour conference at Calgary in March 1919. The conference endorsed secession from the TLC and the formation of a Canadian "One Big Union." Spearheaded by the Vancouver trade unionist and socialist Victor Midgely, and with the strong support of the British Columbia delegates, a series of radical resolutions were passed: to make common cause with the Bolshevik revolution, to endorse the strategy of the general strike, and to cast off the craft unionism of the AFL and create a new labour organization. In the weeks following the convention, although the One Big Union idea met with stiff resistance among Alberta and Saskatchewan craft unionists in TLC strongholds, it won significant sup-port from miners in Alberta, organized loggers, and trades councils in Victoria, Vancouver, and Winnipeg. Such was the response in the West that Canada experienced a "Red scare," as mid-dle-class Canadians grew fearful that the "virus" of Bolshevism or Russian communism was spreading to North America.

The year 1919 was the year of strikes in Canada. The biggest confrontation was the Winnipeg General Strike, which broke out in May among metal-trades workers, claimed the support of 30 000–35 000 working people, and tied up the city for six weeks. The strike occurred amid an unprecedented wave of strikes across Canada, totalling over 320 by the end of 1919. Among the numerous work stoppages were major general strikes at Amherst, Nova Scotia, and Toronto, where the local trades and labour council led 5000–15 000 work-ers from 40 unions to walk off their jobs for six days.

Winnipeg divided, 1919. An anti-strike rally organized by the Committee of 1000.

The Winnipeg General Strike ended in defeat for labour. Only one member of the Winnipeg Central Strike Committee had advocated the One Big Union idea, yet Borden's cabinet shared the view held by most middle-class Canadians that the strike was the work of "foreign Bolsheviks." An anti-strike citizens' committee of 1000 swept aside labour's key demand for the right to collective bargaining and urged firm action to suppress the "deliberate, criminal, and fantastic attempt to make a revolution." The general strike came to a head when some 1800 "special police" were hired by the anti-strike committee. The Royal North West Mounted Police raided labour halls and the homes of the strike leaders to arrest them, and a silent parade of strikers were attacked by police authorities on "Bloody Sunday," June 21, 1919, leaving two strikers dead and 30 people injured. With the strike's leaders jailed and the city under virtual military occupation, the strike committee capitulated.

FRAGMENTATION AND CORPORATE WELFARISM

The breaking of the Winnipeg General Strike and the sympathy strikes led to a fragmentation of the union movement. J.S. Woodsworth, the Methodist minister and editor of the Winnipeg strikers' paper, was elected to Parliament in 1921, and a few other Labourites and socialists won election to the Manitoba legislature. But otherwise, Canada's labour unionists found little cause for optimism as they entered the 1920s.

The 1919 wave of labour revolt ushered in not a revolution, but a period of uneasy harmony between capital and labour. Business fears of a Bolshevik uprising proved groundless, as strike activity subsided and union membership went into decline. More advanced, forward-thinking business leaders seized the opportunity to win back labour–capital co-operation through a variety of employee-benefit schemes known as "corporate welfarism."[7] Whether for reasons of business self-interest or paternalism, firms began in the 1920s to offer employees a number of modest benefit plans, including company medical insurance and pension plans, holiday or year-end cash bonuses, and even company-assisted or -subsidized housing, most often provided in the mining, lumbering, and pulp and paper enterprises carried on in remote or isolated areas. Branch plants of American companies such as International Harvester, Imperial Oil, and General Motors generally led the way with the most elaborate plans, but even small family firms catered to the health and happiness of employees by sponsoring family picnics and providing some company recreation facilities.

Corporate welfare measures were not the only, or even the most popular, business tactic for securing workers' compliance with the new corporate industrial order. If, despite all of these welfare-like antidotes, some workers still succumbed to labour militancy, employers did not hesitate to dismiss the union "ringleaders" or to call on the police, militia, or the courts to uphold their management property rights. One maker of steel-mesh fencing in 1921 and 1922 advertised his product, partly in jest, as the perfect way to keep out "Thieves, Firebugs, Bolshevists, Peddlers, Organizers, and undesirables of every kind."

HINTERLAND REVOLTS OF THE 1920s

D URING THE PERIOD POPULARLY KNOWN AS THE "ROARING TWENTIES," the prosperity of industrialization seemed to many in the West and the Maritimes to benefit only the central Canadian regions. Feeling bypassed by national development, alienated by wartime policies, and increasingly dominated by central Canadian economic institutions, westerners and Maritimers turned to protest movements.

THE WESTERN FARMERS' MOVEMENT

Western protest was not new. It dated back to the entry of Manitoba into Confederation, the Red River resistance of 1869–70, and the North West Rebellion in 1885. John A. Macdonald's National Policy tariff persisted as a major target of western discontent. Regional dissatisfaction grew during the war years and into the immediate postwar depression, until it emerged after 1919 as a full-scale protest movement and a powerful third party, the National Progressives. During World War I, wheat farmers had had a captive market for their crops. In order to control prices and make the delivery system as even and predictable as possible, the federal government established the Canadian Wheat Board in 1917. Although some farmers were displeased with these controls on prices, most accepted the wheat board as a progressive step in wheat marketing. When the war ended, few farmers wanted to see the board disbanded. But in 1921, the new Liberal government under Mackenzie King was determined to avoid "any interference of a serious character with the business of the country." To placate western farmers, a Canadian Wheat Board was reinstituted, but it had little power, and its implementation was shunted off to the provinces.

Ploughing by steam tractor in Alberta, 1910.

THE CO-OP RESPONSE

The new Canadian Wheat Board proved totally ineffectual in marketing the bumper wheat crop of 1922. For many farmers in the West, as in other parts of English-speaking Canada, the co-operative movement seemed to be the answer. The "co-op" idea had taken root in the West in the early 1900s, and had spread from grain growers to livestock producers, poultry and egg producers, and dairy operators. Many of the political leaders of the National Progressive Party, notably Manitoba's T.A. Crerar and the American-born Henry Wise Wood of Alberta, had emerged out of this early wave of farm co-operatives.

The National Progressive party, based in the West, scored a breakthrough in the 1921 federal election, when it sent 64 members to Parliament. But the national success was shortlived; the party slowly disintegrated, torn by internal division and robbed of its leadership and policies by Mackenzie King's Liberal government. But in the midst of this disintegration, prairie farmers found another co-operative remedy — the idea of pooling.* An American pool advocate, Aaron Sapiro, urged grain farmers in 1923 and 1924 to bind together to secure their rightful share of the benefits of their labours by joining pools.

Farmers found that pooling improved their returns, and after 1923 wheat pools were organized on a co-operative basis in Alberta, Saskatchewan, and Manitoba. The sudden successes of the grain farmers were not just a matter of co-operative organization; they were aided by reduced federal tariffs on agricultural implements and by lower rail freight rates. For some enthusiasts, the co-operative pools pointed the way toward a political program based on a "co-operative commonwealth" among all producers and consumers.

SOURCES OF MARITIME AGITATION

As in the West, agitation in the Maritimes was closely related to the rise of farmer and labour reform protest. After World War I, many in the Maritimes seemed to share the economic and political frustrations of the western Progressives. The takeover and closure by central Canadian companies of Maritime manufacturing operations was roundly condemned as evidence of the decline in status and influence of the region. Labour journals such as the Halifax *Citizen* advocated independent political action. In the 1918–20 period Maritime farmers not only participated in western co-operative organizations, but also joined their western counterparts in the Progressive political movement.

The Maritime alliance with western Progressivism did not last, however. Western Progressive leaders showed little sympathy for the Maritimers' position on key economic questions, including transportation policy and tariff protection. The Maritime Progressives peaked in the 1920 Nova Scotia provincial election, winning 11 of 43 seats; but within a year the Maritime Progressive parties in Nova Scotia and New Brunswick were in a serious decline; party organization was reduced to a hollow shell, and the movement's journal was dependent on regular injections of funds from its Winnipeg parent.

---

* Pooling refers to arrangements for the collective handling, storage, and marketing of farm produce, particularly wheat and grain products. Producers combine to "pool" their production for mutual benefits.

AMERICA'S FARMER–LABOUR MOVEMENT AND ITS DEMISE

THE END OF WORLD WAR I produced an economic collapse that brought American farmers to the brink of ruin. Much of the decline could be traced to the wartime inflation of land prices and Washington's May 1920 decision to end price supports for wheat. After the government's move, the bottom fell out of wheat prices and grain farming was thrown into a severe economic crisis. To make matters worse, the agricultural market in Europe began drying up as European farmers resumed production, and other countries flooded the market with their produce. The results for American agriculture were catastrophic. Bankruptcies and foreclosures multiplied to an avalanche — and over 450 000 American farmers lost their properties in the worst agricultural crash up to that time.

To meet the agricultural crisis of the early 1920s, American farmers turned to organizing producer associations in a fashion similar to their Canadian counterparts. Of all American farm movements in the 1920s, the one with the most specific and coherent program was the National Non-Partisan League. Founded in 1916, it operated in North Dakota, Minnesota, and other midwestern states bordering on Canada. Like the Canadian western Progressives, the Non-Partisan League advocated the expansion of farm co-operative organization and control of local state governments. Like its Canadian counterpart, the league set out a "progressive" political platform, demanding

- public ownership of terminal elevators, flour mills, packing-houses, and cold-storage plants;
- state inspection of grain and grain dockage;
- government hail insurance;
- state-run rural credit banks.

Under the leadership of Arthur C. Townley, the league exerted tremendous influence in North Dakota, where it pressured state authorities to place most agricultural facilities under state control. The rapid introduction of such reform, however, led to a strong reaction, beginning in 1921, and gradually the league declined in influence. One of the prominent leaders of Canada's Progressive movement, Henry Wise Wood, had been born in Wisconsin and derived many of his co-operative ideas from the Non-Partisan League program.

The American Farmer–Labor movement met with much less success in national politics. An attempt was made in the late summer of 1919 to launch a national Farmer–Labor party and to draft Wisconsin senator Robert M. ("Fighting Bob") La Follette as its presidential candidate in the 1920 election. There was friction between radical labourites and the organized farmers; La Follette declined the invitation to run under the Farmer–Labor banner, and the national party eventually disappeared after 1920.

"MARITIME RIGHTS"

Maritime discontent did not disappear with the collapse of the Progressive movement. Maritimers objected to the patronizing attitudes of both central Canadians and westerners, and the Maritimers' sense of regional loyalty was only reinforced when they became the butt of sarcastic jokes. Not surprisingly, Maritimers came to share a common resentment against the source of these disparaging comments, and this combined with Maritime resentment over the Conservative government's lack of response to the region's complaints to give the Liberals 25 of the Maritimes' 31 seats in the 1921 federal election.

The Maritime bloc of Liberals that came to Ottawa in 1921 made little headway in pressing regional concerns. Preoccupied with wooing the West, Prime Minister King generally ignored the Maritimers. Repeated delegations to Ottawa by politicians, businesspeople, and union and farm leaders met with little response. A popular "Maritime Rights" campaign waged by the Halifax *Herald*, the Saint John *Telegraph-Journal*, and local boards of trade culminated in a noisy demonstration by 300 protesters before the federal cabinet in early 1925.

Eventually the King government was compelled to act. The early 1920s were a time of lingering depression in the Maritimes. Cut off from traditional markets by freight rates and hampered by inflation and tariff reductions, Maritime factories were shut down in Amherst and Saint John by their parent firms. The British Empire Steel Corporation, operating the financially troubled Cape Breton coal mines, faced strikes every year from 1922 to 1925 until its iron and steel operations became bankrupt. Between 1920 and 1926, 42 percent of the region's manufacturing jobs disappeared, and thousands left to seek opportunities in central Canada and elsewhere.

Woman and Family in a Mining Town, Glace Bay, Nova Scotia, 1925. This work by Lawren Harris reveals another side of the twenties—not all shared in the prosperity.

In the federal election of 1925, the Conservatives, the new champions of Maritime rights, took a majority of the seats in Nova Scotia and New Brunswick. Reduced to a minority, the Liberal government finally reacted by appointing a Royal Commission on Maritime Claims. Through an adroit policy of study, delay, and a few minor concessions in 1927, King managed to defuse the protest.

SIGNS OF INSTABILITY

Between 1896 and the late 1920s, the economies of Canada and the United States were transformed into a new stage of capitalist development. Through business mergers and consolidations, private corporations and a few public enterprises grew large enough to secure monopolistic control of key economic sectors. Throughout this period, the Canadian state — like its American counterpart — ensured that business would enjoy security and periodic support without much interference or regulation. Economic growth was achieved, but competition was eroded by price-fixing and other restraints of trade. By the 1920s, signs of instability began to appear — unevenness of economic development, from region to region and from class to class; rampant stock market and land speculation; and unprecedented risk-taking by banks and other business institutions.

Capital did not go unchallenged. Protest movements arose to assert the interests of labour, farmers, and regions. Industrial unionism, western Progressivism, and Maritime rights were all, in part, responses to economic changes associated with the consolidation of corporate capitalism. None of these movements were able to check the slow drift of the corporate state into profound economic crisis.

ACTIVITIES

KEY TERMS AND CONCEPTS

Identify and briefly explain the historical significance of each of the following terms and concepts:

- Corporate industrial state
- Monopoly capitalism
- America's "Gilded Age"
- Plutocrats
- Public enterprise
- "Drive System"
- Gender division of labour
- American Progressive Movement
- Combines Investigation Act
- AFL unionism
- "The Wobblies"
- Company unions
- Shell Committee
- IMB and WIB
- One Big Union
- Year of Labour Revolt
- Welfare capitalism
- Unroaring Twenties
- Co-operative movement
- Maritime Rights movement

QUESTIONS FOR DISCUSSION

1. Historians of the radical working-class school of Canadian history, like Gregory S. Kealey and Michael Cross, contend that Canada between 1896 and 1929 experienced "the consolidation of monopoly capitalism." Can Canadian history be explained most effectively in terms of stages of capitalist development, or in terms of periods of government and politics? Explain fully your position.

2. Canadian economic expansion was so dramatic from 1896 to 1914 that the period is known variously as the "Boom Years," the "Age of Enterprise," or the "Great Business Barbecue."

To what extent was Canada's Age of Enterprise a small-scale, later version of America's "Gilded Age" of capitalism? What were the differences between the two experiences?

3. How did the organization of the modern industrial workplace reflect a gender division of labour? To what extent were craft-based skills and better-paying jobs considered the preserve of male "breadwinners"?

4. What movements emerged to challenge the dominance of corporate business and business values in the modern industrial state? How did each of these labour, class, and regional movements eventually fare?

5. The 1920s in North America are often portrayed as a "roaring" prosperous age in popular texts and fictional works. What evidence is there that this popular image distorts the reality of Canada in the 1920s?

6. What signs of weakness appeared in the Canadian and American economic systems in the 1920s? Why were they largely ignored by governments and most politicians?

ANALYZING POLITICAL CARTOON INTERPRETATIONS

Examine carefully the political cartoon below dealing with an aspect of Canadian economic development from 1896 to 1929.

1. Identify the central issue or theme, the figures represented, and the time period.

2. Outline the cartoonist's interpretation of the key issue or question.

3. Explain the importance of the issue raised in the evolution of the Canadian corporate–industrial state.

CHAPTER 17

RESPONSES TO ECONOMIC CRISIS, 1929–1939

CAPITALISM IN CRISIS

LAISSEZ FAIRE POLICIES ON TRIAL

FRANKLIN D. ROOSEVELT, THE NEW DEAL, AND
R.B. BENNETT'S RECOVERY PLAN

THE SOCIAL AND POLITICAL RESPONSES TO DEPRESSION

THE GREAT DEPRESSION hit most Canadians and Americans with an unexpected jolt. While campaigning for the United States presidency in October 1928, Herbert Hoover had boasted that "our American experiment in human welfare has yielded a degree of well-being unparalleled in the world. It has come nearer to the abolition of poverty, to the abolition of fear and want, than humanity has ever reached before." Robert McKee, president of the Vancouver Board of Trade, spoke for many leading businesspeople when he assured a 1929 audience that "prosperity was so broad, so sound, so hopeful for the future" that it inspired "a new confidence in their country." Similar optimism was expressed by merchants, managers, small manufacturers, and professionals who believed that North America had achieved "eternal prosperity."

But the unthinkable happened. Within a year, the New York Stock Exchange crashed. The whole North American economic system faltered, then teetered on the brink of collapse. The horrible Great Depression would not lift until the outbreak of World War II in 1939. In between were what has been popularly described as "Hard Times" or the "Dirty Thirties," a decade of desperation, anger, broken dreams, and political ferment.[1] What had gone wrong?

CAPITALISM IN CRISIS

THE GREAT DEPRESSION in many parts of Canada did not start with the New York crash of October 1929. World wheat prices began declining from highs in 1927, and both the price and demand for newsprint had slipped as well. In western Canada the economy had begun to shake in 1928, with the onset of unstable markets for wheat and a severe drought in Saskatchewan. The Winnipeg Grain Exchange, in fact, collapsed amid tumbling wheat prices a few days before the New York stock-market panic. Since the growth of the 1920s had hinged largely on American demand for, and consumption of, Canadian resources such as lumber, newsprint, and base metals, the downturn in the American economy soon reverberated in Canada among the nation's export industries.

Once the great crash hit Wall Street, Canadian stock markets followed New York and plummeted dramatically. International Nickel, Noranda Mines, Canada Power and Paper, Ford Motor Company — the cornerstones of Canadian corporate capitalism — suffered massive losses in the general collapse of stock prices. On October 29, 1929, "Black Tuesday," over 850 000 shares were sold off on the Montreal and Toronto exchanges. The Toronto *Daily Star's* index of 16 key stocks fell $300 million — a million dollars a minute on that fateful day of trading. In New York, the crash took an even heavier toll. More than 16 million shares were traded, investors lost their shirts as stocks lost half their value, and the *New York Times* estimated total

The Wall Street panic of October 29, 1929.

one-day losses at up to $9 billion. After a brief, shaky recovery in June 1930, the market turned down again, and then went down relentlessly for the next two years.

CAUSES OF THE GREAT DEPRESSION

The crash was more a symptom than a cause of the instabilities in the North American and western industrial economies. Only a small percentage of Canadians and Americans "played the market" and suffered personal ruination in the stock market collapse. The roots of the instability ran deeper, into the very foundations of the capitalist system. After the Great War, the Peace Settlement of 1919 had ushered in a new economic era, but one based on a rickety economic structure and potentially ruinous German reparations debts. High tariffs, erected in a wave of 1920s protectionism, set up barriers that impeded the flow of trade. After a cycle of unrestrained financial speculation, an abrupt tightening of credit in 1929–30 delivered a shock the structure could not stand, and it came tumbling down.[2]

SPECULATION GONE WILD:
EARLY SIGNS OF THE COMING CRISIS

TWO EPISODES IN THE UNITED STATES OF THE 1920s illustrated clearly the dangers of massive, traditional speculation: the Florida Land Boom of 1924–25 and the Goldman Sachs Stock Promotion.

THE FLORIDA LAND BOOM

Suddenly in the mid-1920s, interest in buying Florida real estate reached epidemic proportions. Florida's favourable climate, its accessibility to big cities in the northeastern United States, and the increased mobility brought by the automobile all made the sunshine state an attractive place to buy land. As word spread that purchasing real estate in Florida was a foolproof investment, a "speculative bubble" was created. In the rush to buy land, fortune seekers purchased swampland, bogs, and common scrubland for prices far in excess of their true value. For most buyers, the land was a speculative investment to be sold for a quick turnaround profit.

Just as the Florida Land Boom passed its peak in 1926, two disastrous hurricanes hit. The worst one, in September 1926, left 400 dead, tore the roofs off thousands of homes, and flooded the streets of Miami. Millions of dollars were lost as previously valuable properties plummeted in value and thousands of speculators lost their investments.

THE GOLDMAN SACHS STOCK PROMOTION

The Goldman Sachs Trading Corporation was formed on December 4, 1928, and for the next 11 months it became a major player in the Wall Street market. The original corporation was an "investment trust" worth $100 million; its only function was to invest in other companies. In rapid succession, it merged with Financial and Securities Corporation, thus doubling its assets, and then launched Shenandoah Corporation, which in turn established Blue Ridge Corporation. In August 1929, Goldman Sachs further expanded by issuing $71.4 million more in securities, and then buying another investment firm and a West Coast bank.

The Goldman Sachs financial empire was built on a precarious house of cards. Shenandoah's stock, issued at $17.50 a share, rose to $36, then dropped to 50 cents. The parent Trading Corporation did worse. In February 1929, its stock had inflated in value to $222.50 per share; two years later it was being sold off for a dollar or two. For Goldman Sachs, as for other less flamboyant companies, the bubble burst on Black Thursday, October 4, 1929.

Canada's resource-dependent economy was particularly vulnerable to instability in the world economic system. From 1930 onward, Canada was caught in the grip of a downward economic spiral. Demand for Canadian staples — wheat, wood, paper, fish, minerals, coal, and to an extent base metals — fell off sharply as buyers around the world cut back on purchasing. Where markets could be found, there were drastic drops in prices. Prairie wheat farmers were the most seriously affected. Just when the bottom fell out of the world wheat market because of overproduction, a horrible drought struck the plains of southern Alberta and Saskatchewan, reducing the land to "dust bowl" conditions.

Linked to the decline in resource industries were dramatic drops in other economic sectors. The major railways, which had provided a sizable proportion of business investment since the 1850s, reacted to declines in freight traffic by cutting back on purchases of rolling stock and cancelling planned construction projects. Although sheltered somewhat by high protective tariffs, manufacturing production fell by one-third between 1929 and 1932 as demand for farm implements, automobiles, and steel products plummeted. This drop in business spending in response to the major decline in demand for export staples turned a severe recession into the Great Depression, which gripped Canada until World War II.

An unemployed blacksmith and his family in Alberta. Not finding employment at home, many packed up their possessions and searched the country for work.

"HARD TIMES" IN CANADA

For tens of thousands of ordinary Canadians, living during the Great Depression was a matter of surviving. In the early years, Canadian newspapers carried news of collapsing wheat prices, shrinking newsprint markets, business bankruptcies, factory closings, and abandoned building projects. Mass unemployment struck Canada: 27 percent of workers were jobless in 1933, the Depression's worst year. Young men and women just out of school were unable to find work. Some 15 to 20 percent of Canadians were compelled to live on direct government relief, at a time when only the most destitute were eligible for assistance. Able-bodied young men rode the rails from place to place, and older Canadians moved from job to job looking for work or hoping to find better economic conditions. "The struggle for jobs [was] uppermost in everybody's mind," one of the unemployed recalled. "If you didn't work you went short on groceries."[3]

THE HARDEST HIT

Farmers on the Prairies or in rural Canada were hurting before the Great Depression; after 1929 their situation worsened. Costs of farm production exceeded income, forcing thousands of farmers into bankruptcy. In 1928, the net worth of prairie farms was an estimated $363 million; by 1933, the figure was *minus* $10 728 000. Drought, heat, dust, and grasshoppers also struck the Canadian West, forcing nearly 250 000 westerners to leave the Prairies between 1931 and 1941. Driving across rural Saskatchewan in the summer of 1936, James Gray of the *Winnipeg Free Press* reported passing through "village after village without sign of life, past empty farm after empty farm and watched the son of a garage-owner work for two hours to clean grasshoppers off our car for a dollar." Doctors in rural Ontario as well as the prairie West found that once-prosperous farmers could no longer pay medical fees; the doctors regularly accepted poultry, potatoes, and cord wood to settle accounts.

Life was little better for the poor and jobless in Canada's cities. Long lines of Canadians assembled outside missions or "soup kitchens," waiting for a serving of bread, a bowl of soup, or a hot meal. There was a stigma attached to accepting handouts or "going on the dole," but many down-and-outers in the cities had little choice. Most cities operated relief offices that "doled" out whatever assistance was available. However, the rules for being eligible for relief were stringent, and the amount of relief woefully inadequate. In most cases, only those facing starvation were given relief, and the assistance came in the form of food vouchers redeemable at local stores. Rarely was there enough for a family to buy clothing, so many improvised by fashioning clothes out of curtains, bed sheets, and even flour bags. Working women, who had become better-established in the workforce during the 1920s, found themselves either squeezed out of jobs in favour of unemployed men or forced to accept cuts in pay to maintain their positions.

"THE LUCKY ONES"

The Great Depression did not distribute its suffering evenly. Canadians with steady jobs managed quite well because of the deflation. Prices remained low, meaning that the dollar went further. With bread at 5¢ a loaf, hamburger at 10¢ a pound, and a good brick house valued at $4000, a family with a wage earner employed at decent wages of $20–$30 a week got along quite nicely. Some factory workers, civil servants, and teachers with a steady income actually enjoyed slight increases in their living standards. For many Canadians, the 1930s were the time to buy that first automobile, new radio, or first mechanical refrigerator at reasonable prices. A few at the top of the economic ladder remained immune or sheltered from the full force of the Depression, and some, like the John David Eaton family of Toronto, found themselves on "Easy Street." But these people were the lucky ones.

EUGENICS AND DEGENERACY

The Great Depression also produced some bizarre social mutations. The eugenics theory of "race betterment" had arisen in the early 1900s, but not until the 1930s did it gain some legitimacy.[4] In 1930, at the onset of the Depression, the Eugenics Society of Canada was formed by a group of respectable citizens, including doctors and public health professionals, who declared

This colourful poster attracted thousands of Canadians to the Canadian National Exhibition, held annually in Toronto since 1879. The CNE was especially important in the 1930s because it offered an escape from the hardship of the Depression.

that heredity and "defective genes" were the single most important cause of the nation's social problems. An anxious and distressed Canadian middle class was susceptible to the claim that poverty, crime, delinquency, and intellectual disabilities were primarily the products of defective genes, not a defective social system. In 1933, Alberta and British Columbia passed legislation permitting the sterilization of people with mental and intellectual disabilities. The case in favour of sterilization was based as much on the economic fears generated by the Depression as on the logic of the mental hygienists. However, the campaign for sterilization and the eugenics movement itself died a quick death once the knowledge of the Nazis' "Final Solution" spread to North America.

LAISSEZ FAIRE POLICIES ON TRIAL

AT THE OUTSET OF THE GREAT DEPRESSION, Canada's two major political leaders — Prime Minister Mackenzie King and Conservative opposition leader R.B. Bennett — took a laissez faire, "wait-and-see" attitude and continued to prescribe orthodox economic remedies. King urged Canadians to remain calm and voiced the expectation that good times would arrive soon. Like his American counterpart, President Herbert Hoover (1928–32), King saw the 1929 stock-market crash and the ensuing cycle of price collapses, layoffs, and plant closures as part of the natural order of things in a capitalist economy, where economic freedom occasionally led to periods of overproduction and short-term unemployment.

Even though the 1929 "recession" was particularly bad, King and Hoover believed it would not last very long. When cornered in the House of Commons, the prime minister argued alternately that the Dominion was "already recovering from the seasonal slackness" of late 1929 and that unemployment was a provincial matter. But, since five of the provincial governments were run by Conservatives, King was leery of giving them grants to pay for unemployment relief in case they made political gains. King, under intense fire from the Conservative opposition and from Labour member of Parliament J.S. Woodsworth for his cold-hearted laissez faire approach, shot back that he might be persuaded to give some support to the Progressive (Farmers') governments in Manitoba and Alberta, but would not give any Tory government "a five-cent piece."

R.B. BENNETT AND THE DEPRESSION

In the 1930 federal election, R.B. Bennett and the Conservatives took a more activist stance. The newly chosen Conservative leader was a Calgary corporation lawyer and self-made millionaire who made ample use of his spell-binding oratory in Canada's first radio-dominated election. Bennett succeeded in making the Liberals' neglect of unemployment and the need for higher tariffs the central election issues. "Mackenzie King promises you conferences," he declared, "I promise you action." American workers, Bennett told a group of unemployed Sydney steelworkers, still had their jobs because of the U.S. Smoot–Hawley high tariff. "I will make [tariffs] fight for you. I will use them to blast a way into markets that have been closed."

The Conservatives won a clear majority of seats in the 1930 election, so R.B. Bennett, not King, bore the brunt of the Depression. He quickly swung into legislative action with two emergency measures: a bill providing for $20 million in relief for the unemployed during the winter of 1930, which marked a departure from pure laissez faire policy; and a hefty increase in the tariff, which he confidently predicted would create some 25 000 jobs for unemployed Canadians. Both initiatives were introduced as "emergency" measures; Bennett had only a vague idea of the economic consequences. At the 1930 imperial conference in London, Bennett and three cabinet colleagues appealed to Britain and the other colonies to boost trade by a new imperial preference system, only to be rebuffed.

"WAITING OUT" THE CRISIS

Like U.S. President Hoover and Mackenzie King, Bennett believed that the economic recession of 1929–30 was a temporary phenomenon. The problem, however, was that the "temporary recession" refused to lift. In fact, the economic situation deteriorated further in 1931 and 1932, in spite of Bennett's measures. His instinctive reaction was to counsel patience. It would take time for the tariff increase to take effect, he insisted, and Canadians would have to "wait out" the economic chaos.

Until 1932, the Bennett government held firm in its Depression policies. The Relief Acts of 1930 and 1931, described by Bennett as "palliative" measures, did little to ease the plight of the unemployed. The federal money earmarked for public works was divided among the provinces on the basis of population rather than need. Communities like Toronto and working-class Burnaby, British Columbia, which had large unemployed populations, received much smaller grants per out-of-work citizen than did many other cities and towns. Relief administration was terribly haphazard, favoured married men and British subjects, and was given out by hastily organized charities and local committees.

The Bennett name became associated with the social ills of the 1930s. Just as American shantytowns were called "Hoovervilles," motorless cars drawn by horses to save gas were labelled "Bennett-buggies."

As the number of unemployed swelled and the number on relief reached an estimated 2 million by 1932, new measures were taken to "contain" as well as aid the growing army of unemployed. Under legislation proposed by General A.G.L. McNaughton of the Canadian army, single unemployed men were housed in relief camps scattered across the country. Administered by the defence department, these "Bennett relief camps" provided destitute young men with free board and lodging plus 20¢ a day.

Bennett's tariff policy failed to produce the expected results. The drastic upward revision of 1930 aided manufacturers in central Canada by all but eliminating foreign competition in the domestic market. But it did nothing to assist primary producers in the West and the Maritimes — the regions hardest hit by the Depression. In export markets, the high tariff was, if anything, a disadvantage, because it encouraged the United States and other countries to retain their tariff restrictions on Canadian products. Western wheat farmers, for example, were almost shut out of foreign markets and, even with widespread crop failures in 1932–33, unable to sell off huge wheat surpluses. A major imperial economic conference hosted by Bennett in Ottawa in the grim summer of 1932 raised some hopes that were eventually dashed. Although agreements reached at Ottawa establishing a reciprocal preferential trade arrangement with Britain helped raise slightly Canada's trade figures, they had little immediate impact on the country's increasingly restive 650 000 unemployed.

In the depths of the Great Depression, Bennett gained the popular reputation of a callous Olympian figure, the millionaire unmoved by the distress of the poor. Bennett denounced his radical critics as "communists," and in one ill-advised statement advocated crushing the "Reds" under "the iron heel of capitalism." Even though Bennett worked long days and responded with personal kindness to thousands of letters from ordinary Canadians in distress who requested assistance, the image of a cold, hard-hearted man remained etched in the public mind.

THE ON-TO-OTTAWA TREK

The relief camps established in 1932–33 for single unemployed men soon became a breeding ground for popular discontent. During a period of over three years, 170 000 youngish men passed through the camps; at their peak in 1935, more than 200 camps were in operation. In many camps the men complained of prison-like conditions — poor food, bedbugs, isolation, hard labour, mosquitoes, and pointless make-work projects. With no women, no democratic vote, no entertainment, no books, no recreational sports, and no alcoholic beverages, many relief-camp inmates felt like "a lost legion of youth" — rotting away out of society's sight. Amid such conditions, unrest was common. Small bands of communists became active in the camps, organizing branches of the Workers' Unity League, and in 1932–33 at least 57 serious disturbances erupted in protest over camp conditions.[5]

THE AMERICAN BONUS ARMY MARCH AND DISPERSAL, 1932

THE "ON-TO-OTTAWA TREK" launched by Canada's relief-camp strikers in 1935 was not the first mass action by the unemployed in the Dirty Thirties. In the spring of 1932, angry war veterans assembled in Portland, Oregon, to form a protest organization called the Bonus Expeditionary Force (BEF), or Bonus Army. Most of those who gathered were destitute, without work, and had families living on the edge of starvation. They held government bonus certificates that guaranteed them payment for war service — in 1945. They demanded that Congress pay them now, when the money was desperately needed.

The members of the BEF chose a former sergeant named Walter W. Waters as their spokesman. It was decided that their cause would be publicized by marching on Washington and petitioning Congress and the president for prompt payment of what was owed them. Realizing the controversy they might stir up, the marchers were careful to maintain strict discipline throughout their efforts. They advocated "no panhandling, no drinking, and no radicalism."

Many journeyed to Washington, D.C., by hitchhiking; some hopped freight trains. By

The Bonus Army on Capitol Hill, Washington, 1932.

the time Waters and his men reached the Capitol, their number had grown to about a thousand. As the days and weeks of camping out near the Capitol at Anacostia Flats went by, the BEF's forces grew to more than 15 000 veterans and their families. Among them were unemployed miners from West Virginia and sheet-metal workers from Chicago.

A bill to pay the bonus passed the House of Representatives in June 1932 but was defeated in the Senate. When Walter Waters announced the verdict to a crowd of marchers gathered outside the Capitol building, they greeted the news with an ironic display of patriotism, bursting into song with a rendition of "America." Some, discouraged by the Senate's decision, headed for home. Most stayed on, encamped on Anacostia Flats or in government buildings near the Capitol.

President Herbert Hoover had no sympathy for the Bonus Army marchers. He refused to meet the Bonus Army leaders or delegations. To Hoover, the Bonus Army was a "mob" that threatened the government, as well as an unsightly collection of misfortunates who drew public attention to the nation's unemployment problem. With his patience at an end, Hoover ordered the army to evict them from their camps. A military force commanded by army chief of staff Douglas MacArthur flushed the veterans out of old buildings with tear gas, forcibly removed the campers, and torched their makeshift cardboard and tarpaper shanties, reducing Bonus City to a field of ashes. Hoover was adamant in his defence of the army's actions. "A challenge to the authority of the United States government has been met swiftly and firmly," he declared. "Our government cannot be coerced by mob rule."

An organized Canadian movement of resistance emerged in April 1935 in British Columbia. The Relief Camp Workers' Union led half the inmates of the British Columbia camps in a mass exodus, and 1500 of them converged on Vancouver, demanding changes in the camp system. Over a two-month period in Vancouver, the strikers mounted a huge May Day demonstration, held peaceful parades, snake-danced through department stores, and clashed a few times in isolated incidents with local police. In spite of condemnations by Mayor Gerry McGeer, they won public sympathy with demands for better "work and wages," workers' control of the camps through elected committees, and the right of campers to vote. With strikers beginning to fall away in late May 1935, the organizers settled on a dramatic new tactic — a protest parade by freight train to Ottawa. Like the American Bonus Army marchers of 1932, they would take their case to the capital.

The "On-to-Ottawa" trek revived the momentum of the relief camp strike. About 1200 strikers, cheered on by a sympathetic Vancouver crowd, boarded freight trains for the gruelling trip to Ottawa. The trekkers met with a positive reception along the route and arrived in Regina in mid-June like "a proud little army." The wave of popular support generated by the relief-camp strikers, and the leadership role played by Arthur "Slim" Evans, a self-declared communist, convinced Bennett and his cabinet that a socialist revolution was imminent.

THE REGINA RIOT

Bennett ordered the trek halted in Regina. The Royal Canadian Mounted Police (RCMP) stopped the train and herded the strikers into a temporary camp; the prime minister announced that he would meet with their leaders, who were permitted to continue to Ottawa. Evans and his delegation presented a list of six demands, calling for improved wages and a reduced work week, adequate provision for first aid supplies, recognition of a democratically elected committee of relief work-

The Regina Riot, July 1, 1935. The Canadian Press reported: "For more than two hours violent fighting continued between the camp 'deserters' and the police."

ers, removal of the camps from the authority of the defence department, a system of social and unemployment insurance, and the democratic right to vote. Although the demands sounded reasonable, Bennett reacted with open hostility and tersely dismissed their demands.

The showdown was not long in coming. When the strike leaders returned to Regina and began addressing a peaceful rally in Market Square, the local police and the RCMP rushed the platform, and began making arrests and flailing away with baseball bats. The enraged crowd of 1700 strikers and sympathizers turned on the Regina authorities and a full-blown riot erupted, leaving one Regina police detective dead and over 40 police officers and trekkers injured. After the riot was quelled, most of the strikers accepted the Saskatchewan government's offer of free passage home or back to the camps. Gradually changes were made that raised the daily allowance and turned administration of the camps over to provincial authorities. For Bennett and his government, the incident proved damaging, however. The prime minister's endorsement of the RCMP tactics aroused strong recollections of Herbert Hoover's brutal order to disperse the Bonus Army marchers of 1932.

FRANKLIN D. ROOSEVELT, THE NEW DEAL, AND R.B. BENNETT'S RECOVERY PLAN

C ANADA DID NOT SUFFER ALONE in the Dirty Thirties. Between 1920 and 1932, American national income plummeted from $87.4 billion to $41.7 billion. Unemployment reached 4 million in 1930, 8 million in 1931, and 12 million in 1932. One out of four American workers had no income. More than a million impoverished Americans wandered aimlessly as hoboes, and in big cities like Chicago up to 50 percent of the population of working age was out of work. Cardboard, wood, and wire-mesh shanties, known as "Hoovervilles," sprang up along railway sidings and even inside Central Park in New York City. Desperate men and women began to voice seething discontent and to consider radical alternatives to the existing system. The time seemed ripe for bold political experimentation, and many Americans came to believe that saving the capitalist system itself required some radical departures from the orthodox policies of President Hoover and his administration.

FDR AND THE NEW DEAL

Political change came to the United States in the 1932 election, which brought Franklin Delano Roosevelt to the White House. The Democratic president had promised "a new deal for the American people," and he arrived in Washington optimistically proclaiming "the only thing we have to fear is fear itself." Beneath the confident rhetoric, there was no ideology, no reasoned analysis of the economic crisis, not even a systematic plan for implementing this New Deal. "The country demands bold, persistent experimentation," Roosevelt insisted. "It is common sense to take a method and try it. If it fails, admit it and frankly try another."[6]

Once Roosevelt assumed office in March 1933, the New Deal "experiment" was underway. In consultation with his "Brains Trust" of intellectual advisers, "FDR" launched a widely varied, almost haphazard series of legislative Acts and orders aimed at tackling the problems of depression. Within hours of his inauguration, he announced a national bank holiday — all the banks were closed — until Congress could deal with the threat of a total collapse of the banking system. Roosevelt then introduced the Emergency Banking Relief Act, and allowed only the solvent banks to reopen. He also secured an Act through Congress that took America off the gold standard and paved the way for easier credit and deficit financing, both essential to the New Deal recovery program.

During Roosevelt's first "Hundred Days," the president presided over a remarkable wave of state intervention into the economy. Fifteen major bills were passed through Congress, and the next 18 months were spent in feverish activity to put an alphabet soup of agencies and programs into operation, including the Civilian Conservation Corps (CCC), the Federal Emergency Relief Administration (FERA), and the Civil Works Administration (CWA). The Agricultural Adjustment Act (AAA) sought to cut farm production and raise prices by paying farmers to stop growing food or to dispose of livestock. General Hugh "Ironpants" Johnson was

Receiving a first welfare cheque after the passage of the U.S. Social Security Act in 1936.

placed in command of the National Recovery Administration (NRA), with the task of reviving industrial production through the adoption of NRA "codes of fair competition," a practice that, in effect, encouraged price fixing and monopoly — and forced many small competitors out of business. Another major departure was the Tennessee Valley Authority (TVA), which spent

May McCloud Bethune, director of Negro Relations for the National Youth Administration, came to the Roosevelt administration after serving as president of the National Council of Negro Women.

$145 million on a dam and electricity generating station at Muscle Shoals, Alabama, and became a publicly run power company selling cheap electric power to seven southern states.

THE NEW DEAL'S EFFECTS

In 1935, the U.S. Supreme Court ruled that the NRA and the AAA were unconstitutional because they usurped the power of Congress and encroached on areas reserved for the states. Faced with court challenges and mounting criticisms from business and labour, Roosevelt ushered in a second wave of reforms to the economic system. The Social Security Act of 1935 provided America's first national program of old-age pensions, unemployment insurance, and aid to people with disabilities. Senator Robert Wagner sponsored the National Industrial Relations Act (1935), which guaranteed the right to collective bargaining and forbade employers to discriminate against unions.

The New Deal had a permanent impact — restoring confidence in the American political and economic system, entrenching in law the rights of organized labour, and laying the initial foundations for the U.S. social security state. But, by 1939, some 9 million Americans remained jobless, millions of families lived in poverty, the national debt had doubled to over $40 billion, and average personal income was still below that of 1929. For all its frenzied activity, the New Deal had not ended the Great Depression.

THE WINDS OF NORTH AMERICAN REFORM

As Canada weathered the economic chaos of 1933 and limped into 1934, many Canadians grew impatient with Bennett's wait-and-see policies. The American example of the New Deal could not be ignored. The first Canadian government to hoist the flag of New Deal–style reform was the British Columbia Liberal administration of T.D. "Duff" Pattullo. In spite of Pattullo's statements to the contrary, the B.C. Liberal program of 1932 — with its "new deal" label and its dramatically increased public spending for relief and industrial grants — bore the strong whiff of American New Deal reform. Canada's minister to Washington and Bennett's brother-in-law, W.D. Herridge, was also an early convert to New Dealism. Beginning as early as mid-August of 1933, he started urging the Canadian prime minister to take up the New Deal idea of "pump priming" the economy. In a series of letters and memos throughout 1934, the pleas grew stronger. "We need a Pandora's box" like Roosevelt's New Deal, Herridge insisted in April 1934, and one providing "the seeds of a new order of prosperity."

Another major push in the direction of reform came from a most unlikely source within Bennett's own Conservative cabinet. Harry H. Stevens, the minister of trade and commerce, had grown increasingly frustrated over Bennett's indifference toward the plight of small manufacturers, small producers, and underpaid workers. Early in 1934, Stevens launched a blistering attack on the "unfair or unethical trading practices" of large retailers, who threatened to "destroy the system" by squeezing out small manufacturers and producers. The outburst so enraged the T. Eaton Company and the Robert Simpson Company that they pressured Bennett to extract a public retraction. Mindful of the popular support for Stevens's position, the prime minister avoided a public split by establishing a special parliamentary committee under Stevens to investigate the problem of "mass buying" and "price spreads" and later appointed him to head a royal commission inquiring into the problem.

Stevens's campaign against big-business profiteering earned him the nickname "Mr. Price Spreads," and a reputation as a champion of the "little guy" in business. When news leaked out that Stevens had accused Simpsons' executives of "milking" $10 million from the company and bilking their employees through a stock purchase plan, a cabinet crisis erupted. Stevens resigned to sit as a Tory backbencher, but Prime Minister Bennett remained uncharacteristically silent, perhaps sensing that Stevens voiced the frustrations of many small producers and businesspeople across Canada.

R.B. BENNETT'S "NEW DEAL"

Amid unrelieved economic depression, mounting public disaffection, and clamour for action, R.B. Bennett dropped a political bombshell. On January 2, 1935, in the first of five national radio broadcasts, he astounded both the public and an unsuspecting cabinet by announcing his personal conversion to "New Deal" reform. "I am for reform," he proclaimed. "And…reform means Government intervention…. It means the end of laissez faire. Reform heralds certain recovery. There can be no permanent recovery without reform." Why had he waited four long years before acting? Bennett explained that "we had first to save the ship and guide it to less troubled waters." Measures undertaken in 1934, such as the Farmers' Creditors Arrangements Act and the creation of the Bank of Canada, were only "the initial measures in the government's reform program."[7]

Over the next ten days, Bennett unveiled a Canadian version of FDR's New Deal. He proposed myriad reforms: legislation establishing a uniform wage, an 8-hour day, and a maximum work week; insurance against sickness, industrial accidents, and unemployment; an improved old-age pension scheme; and higher taxes for non-producers who derived their income from stocks or securities. Farmers' debts would be scaled down through "a far-reaching agricultural credit program." As soon as the Price Spreads Commission's report was ready, he pledged to provide protection against the exploitation of producers by "monopolistic purchasers" and "certain types of middlemen" and to act to "put a stop to these inequities." The voice belonged to Canada's millionaire prime minister, but the message — written mostly by W.D. Herridge — bore the unmistakable ring of FDR's "Hundred Days" of 1933.

The actual "New Deal" legislation fell far short of the expectations generated in Bennett's radio talks. Three Acts providing for the 8-hour day, a 6-day work week, and a federal minimum wage were routinely passed. The centrepiece of Bennett's recovery plan, the Employment and Social Insurance Act, turned out to be a limited unemployment insurance scheme that excluded 40 percent of wage earners and provided meagre weekly payments for recipients. After an attempt at reconciliation with H.H. Stevens failed, the prime minister suffered a "mild heart attack" and sank back into his pre–New Deal doldrums. Thereafter the Bennett program lost steam, and to make matters worse, it was eventually ruled *ultra vires* by the courts.

The "New Deal" experiment was really Bennett's last stand. A final clash with Stevens erupted in June 1935 over the government's unwillingness to act on the key recommendations of the Price Spreads Commission report concerning excessive business profits and unfair trade practices. Such was Stevens's frustration with the Bennett Conservatives that he launched a new federal party, the Reconstruction party, to turn "Canada's industrial, economic, and social life to the benefit of the great majority." The Stevens revolt, coupled with public reaction to the dispersing of the On-to-Ottawa relief trek, spelled political trouble for Bennett. In the ensuing 1935 general election, Bennett's Conservatives went down to crashing defeat at the hands of Mackenzie King's Liberals, campaigning with the slogan "King or Chaos." Some 390 000 protest votes were cast for Stevens and the Reconstructionists. With his "policy of no policy," it would be King, not Bennett, who rode out the Depression in Ottawa.

THE SOCIAL AND POLITICAL RESPONSES TO DEPRESSION

THE GREAT DEPRESSION was a powerful political catalyst in Canada as well as in the United States. A variety of social and political movements, of the right, left, and moderate centre, emerged in the 1930s, questioning whether the corporate industrial state was malfunctioning and challenging the very basis of the two-party political system. Each of these movements reflected a profound shift in public attitudes. The misery of the Depression had a radicalizing effect. It sparked growing demands for farmer–labour co-operation and more drastic government action, first to provide relief for the legions of unemployed, and eventually to create a buttress of security against the instabilities of the old economic order.

RADICAL LABOUR PROTEST

As early as the winter of 1929–30, signs of violent working-class protest began to surface in parts of Canada. Street demonstrations occurred in the early 1930s in such scattered places as Vancouver, Winnipeg, Sudbury, Toronto, and Sydney Mines — wherever Communist organizers could mobilize workers with the party slogan "Fight or Starve." Grass-roots organizations of the unemployed, like Toronto's East York Workers' Association, rallied relief recipients in working-class districts and fought to eliminate the degrading relief vouchers system and to prevent cuts in payments. In the summer of 1932, some 600 Communist party members and sympathizers attended a "Workers' Economic Conference" in Ottawa and held an open-air rally on Parliament Hill. It was broken up by the police, who arrested the ringleaders and scattered the remaining delegates with truncheons.[8]

"Red" trade unionists of the 1930s were spearheaded by the Workers' Unity League (WUL), a Communist-led and -controlled organization formed in 1929. The WUL quickly earned a reputation as a formidable "fighting force"; by 1933, it had sponsored 11 industrial unions and claimed responsibility for instigating three-quarters of all strikes in Canada. One remarkable WUL victory was scored in a 1933 furniture workers' strike at Stratford, Ontario. After violence flared on the picket line, the town's nervous mayor asked for military aid and turned the industrial district into a zone of military occupation. WUL organizers helped spark a support rally for the workers, which attracted 3000 indignant citizens, backed a strike action by women chicken-pluckers, and aided in a later labour takeover of the town council. The WUL's existence was short-lived, however. In 1935, the Communist International ordered it to disband and encouraged "red" unionists to redirect their energies toward penetrating the Canadian Labour Congress.

COMMUNIST SUPPRESSION AND REVIVAL

In spite of the Marxist–Leninist rhetoric and success in labour organizing, the likelihood of Communist-inspired revolutionary action was remote in the 1930s. The Communist Party of Canada (CPC) gained adherents as public faith in the capitalist system became shaken by the Depression. Campaigns of protest focused attention on the Conservative government's policy of deporting thousands of immigrants labelled as "foreign radicals." Yet the CPC, for all its notoriety, was loosely organized and badly split into two bitterly opposed factions — doctrinaire Stalinists and advocates of an independent line. Until 1936, the CPC itself was illegal under section 98 of the Criminal Code, which forbade not only revolutionary actions but their advocacy if they might lead to the use of force or violence.

Ontario police authorities raided the Toronto Communist headquarters in 1931 and arrested eight leading Communists, including an English-born machinist named Tim Buck. The defendants

Communist gathering at the corner of Dundas and Spadina in Toronto, 1931.

were convicted of membership in an illegal organization and seditious conspiracy. They were sentenced to imprisonment in Kingston Penitentiary, where Tim Buck survived an assassination attempt. Such harsh treatment aroused a surprising wave of public sympathy for the Communist "underdogs." A determined and vocal campaign to free the imprisoned leaders eventually succeeded in June 1934, when the government released them. Tim Buck's triumphant return to Toronto was marked by a "mass welcome rally" at Maple Leaf Gardens, attended by over 17 000 cheering and placard-waving supporters. The euphoria quickly died out, however. Even in the depths of the Depression, only a minority of Canadians would rally to the cause of communism.

THE ANTIGONISH MOVEMENT

In the Maritimes, economic protest took a different form. The "Antigonish Movement," led by Roman Catholic social activists at St. Francis Xavier University, called for rural reform through the creation of local co-operatives and adult-education programs. Using the extension department of the university as an organizational base, the charismatic Rev. Dr. Moses Coady and two other key leaders launched study groups and developed a rural reform program advocating co-operation in production (through local creameries, canneries, and fish plants), in purchasing, in transportation, and in the marketing of products.[9]

THE KINGFISH AND LE CHEF:
HUEY P. LONG AND MAURICE DUPLESSIS

PROBABLY THE MOST POPULAR and colourful American populist politician of the 1930s was Huey P. Long of Louisiana.* A master of oratory and homespun humour, he plunged into politics as a champion of the "little guy" and the underprivileged. Running for governor of Louisiana in 1928, Long denounced the railroads and the oil industry that controlled the state. He promised to tax them heavily in order to finance a massive hospital and road-building program, and to upgrade public education facilities in a state notorious for neglecting its schools.

After his election, Long kept his campaign promises. He introduced state-subsidized lunch programs in public schools, provided and distributed textbooks, built paved state highways, and strongly supported Louisiana State University. Long also cultivated a humorous public image by naming himself "The Kingfish," after a character in the popular *Amos n' Andy* radio show.

Beneath the veneer of folksy southern populism, Huey Long was a hard-driving politician who built a political machine that gave him dictatorial power over Louisiana. An early supporter of President Roosevelt's New Deal, he withdrew his support when the actual programs seemed too favourable to Wall Street and big business. Long then advanced his own "Share Our Wealth" program, aimed at ending the Depression in the deep South.

Long's "Share Our Wealth" program embodied a peculiar blend of rural populism and socialism. In his autobiography, *Every Man A King*, he set out a radical plan for ending the Depression and reforming the American economic system. Every American family would be given a house, an automobile, a radio, and an annual income of $2500. Young people would receive a free college education; the elderly would get pensions; and war veterans would get their long-denied bonuses. To finance all of this, Long proposed a 100 percent tax on all personal income over $1 million, so as to redistribute income from the rich to the poor.

Long's personal dynamism and his program won him a nationwide following. He was elected to the Senate in 1932, and promoted his ideas far and wide. About 4.6 million Americans joined his "Share Our Wealth" clubs around the country. With such popular support, Long announced that he would run for president in 1936. But that was not to be. He was cut down by an assassin's bullet late in 1935.

Huey Long's populist and dictatorial style bore a striking resemblance to that of Maurice Duplessis, the powerful premier of Quebec from 1936 to 1939 and again from 1944 to 1959. Like Long, Duplessis, known by friends and critics alike as "Le Chef," earned a public reputation as a benevolent autocrat with little respect for democratic principles. Both

---

* For a recent re-evaluation of Huey Long and his legacy see *The History Teacher* 27 (2) (February 1994): 119–131; and Glen Jeansonne, *Messiah for the Masses: Huey P. Long and the Great Depression* (New York, 1993).

Two powerful politicians of the 1930s: Huey P. Long, Governor of Louisiana (left), and Maurice Duplessis, Premier of Quebec.

Long and Duplessis emerged in the 1930s with rural populist political bases and a strong determination to strengthen their respective regions. But there the similarities seem to end. Long's "Share Our Wealth" program was quite unlike Duplessis's economic policies. For all his hue and cry against the "trusts" in 1936, Duplessis not only took little action, but gradually came to accept them as essential to the maintenance of economic order.

The Antigonish Movement succeeded in involving large numbers of farmers, fishers, and coal miners in many forms of co-operative enterprises. From the eastern Nova Scotia counties around Antigonish and Cape Breton, it spread in the mid-1930s to Prince Edward Island and New Brunswick, aided by federal government and American Carnegie Foundation subsidy grants. The Antigonish Movement responded to rural concerns such as impoverishment, depopulation, and the social degeneracy associated with the onslaught of urban industrialism. It offered a "middle way" between big capitalism and big socialism but was hampered by the religious gulf between the Roman Catholic and Protestant communities. By 1938, the movement claimed to involve some 50 000 Maritimers in its activities, including 42 co-operative stores, 17 lobster canneries, 10 fish-processing plants, 140 credit unions, and almost 2400 study clubs.

THE CO-OPERATIVE COMMONWEALTH FEDERATION

A related social movement that emerged from the political ferment of the early 1930s was the Co-operative Commonwealth Federation (CCF). It began as a merger of the Progressive and Labour

Delegates to the founding convention of the CCF at Regina, July 1933. J.S. Woodsworth is seated at the centre of the first row.

parties under the leadership of J.S. Woodsworth, now a Winnipeg Labour member of Parliament. At a convention in July 1932 in Calgary, the founding party members adopted the name the Co-operative Commonwealth Federation and endorsed a short program of democratic socialist principles. More than 150 delegates attended the Regina convention of July 1933, where J.S. Woodsworth was selected leader and the CCF election program was developed and approved.[10]

The Regina Manifesto of 1933 was drafted by Frank H. Underhill, F.R. Scott, and the League for Social Reconstruction, a small group of Toronto and Montreal intellectuals formed in the winter of 1931–32. "The CCF," the manifesto proclaimed, "is a democratic movement, a federation of farmer, labour and socialist organizations, financed by its own members and seeking to achieve its ends solely by constitutional methods." The essential tool for bringing about the "co-operative commonwealth" was public ownership on behalf of the people, particularly in the fields of finance, transportation, communications, and electric power.

The CCF was a unique, hybrid form of democratic socialism. Although its strongest roots were in rural Saskatchewan, the movement was more than an expression of "agrarian socialism" and the co-operative idea. It was an amalgam of different elements: Labour reformist, agrarian co-operative, Marxist socialist, and Christian social gospel. The CCF drew uneven support: the Roman Catholic church caused it to be utterly rejected in Quebec, but it won wide support in the West, and in 1944, under Baptist minister T.C. "Tommy" Douglas, it gained power in Saskatchewan.

THE SOCIAL CREDIT MOVEMENT

In Alberta the Great Depression produced a more exotic movement, with radically different answers to the economic crisis. William "Bible Bill" Aberhart, a Calgary high school principal and popular radio preacher, discovered "Social Credit" in the summer of 1932. The Social Credit doctrine had been devised by a Scottish mining engineer, Major C.H. Douglas. Deeply troubled by the suffering and hopelessness caused by the Depression, Aberhart seized on this new economic theory, which he saw as the "cure" for the Great Depression.[11] Aberhart argued that the major problem with the economic system was "a deficiency of purchasing power" among consumers that, if left uncorrected, would destroy capitalism. The solution was simple: to provide a "social dividend," or regular money payments called "prosperity certificates," to the people, and thereby increase the supply of money that could be spent. To prevent runaway inflation, a "just price" would be set by government for most if not all goods.

Aberhart's version of Social Credit spread like wildfire across Alberta. Aberhart preached the economic gospel of Social Credit in Sunday radio broadcasts that reached an estimated 300 000 listeners in the early 1930s. After attempting without success to interest Alberta's traditional parties in Social Credit, he converted the social movement into a new third party. In August 1935, Aberhart and the Social Credit party, aided by public disenchantment with the corrupt and scandal-ridden United Farmers of Alberta regime, took 56 of the 63 seats in the Alberta legislature.

In spite of the smashing 1935 election victory, Aberhart's Social Credit program was never carried out in its entirety. A series of Acts was passed to put Social Credit theories into operation, including the issuing of a cash dividend of $25 a month to every Alberta resident. However, since most Social Credit measures involved monetary matters, these laws were either disallowed by the federal government or declared unconstitutional by the courts. Aberhart responded to these setbacks by dropping the party's monetary policies and consolidating Social Credit support with a stable, pragmatic, and mildly reformist brand of government. Social Credit rule proved so durable that it lasted in Alberta from 1935 to 1971.

THE UNION NATIONALE IN QUEBEC

In Quebec, political responses to the Depression were those of a province not like the others. The long-entrenched Liberal administration of Louis-Alexandre Taschereau came under increasing attack for its corrupt patronage system and its hard-nosed free-enterprise policies between 1930 and 1935. A fiery nationalist politician born in the Montreal slums, Camillien Houde, captured the Quebec Conservative party leadership and mobilized a movement of the working class and the dispossessed against the so-called ruling "clique." A band of Quebec fascists led by Adrien Arcand and known as the "blueshirts" spouted anti-Semitic propaganda. Within the Conservative opposition, the traditional *bleu* forces, led by Maurice Duplessis, dislodged Houde from the party leadership in 1933. Another challenge came from a reformist faction of anti-Taschereau Liberals, the *Action Libérale Nationale* (ALN), which proposed a reform program aimed "against the trusts," but also against CCF-style "socialism." Duplessis's Conservatives entered into an alliance with the ALN in the fall of 1935 to form the Union Nationale party. In the 1936 Quebec election, the new party toppled the Taschereau administration by winning overwhelming support in rural and small-town Quebec.[12]

Once in power, Maurice Duplessis and the Union Nationale made a few concessions to ALN reformism, then lapsed into a defensive, conservative brand of nationalism. Duplessis extended low-cost loans to farmers, courted the support of the Roman Catholic church, and spent large amounts resurfacing rural roads. He resisted calls for the regulation of the "trusts" and rejected a proposal to create a public hydro company in competition with private electrical utilities. Instead of clamping down on the trusts, Duplessis turned on groups that might threaten the existing economic order — trade unionists, ordinary workers, socialists, and communists. The Padlock Law of 1937, strongly supported by the Quebec business élite and Roman Catholic hierarchy, struck at the basic civil rights of Quebec citizens. It gave the provincial attorney-general the right to shut down or padlock the premises of "subversive" organizations. While the law was ostensibly aimed at communist groups, it was frequently used to silence other organizations or publishing houses critical of the Union Nationale regime. The Union Nationale became so entrenched that, with the exception of the period 1939–44, it ruled Quebec until 1960.

LESSONS OF THE 1930S

Awareness of the enormity of the Great Depression came slowly. Both Mackenzie King and R.B. Bennett expected the economic crisis to solve itself. Franklin D. Roosevelt's New Deal was eventually taken up and repackaged by Bennett in 1935, but too late to rescue his government. When King returned to power, he opted to reduce trade barriers and otherwise to wait out the Depression. In spite of such weak leadership, social programs were developed, such as public relief and old-age pensions, that formed the early basis for an emerging bureaucratic, social welfare state.[13]

If governments were cautious in grappling with the Depression, other groups of Canadians were not. New political parties, social movements, and labour organizations offered solutions from all sides of the political spectrum. Ordinary Canadians embraced unique ideas for solving the Depression, ranging from mobilizing the unemployed to deporting "foreign radicals" to joining in a back-to-nature movement. But no person or party was able to solve the economic crisis: it took another world war to do that.

ACTIVITIES

KEY TERMS AND CONCEPTS

Identify and explain the historical significance of each of the following terms and concepts:

- Dirty Thirties
- Unrestrained speculation
- "Dust bowl"
- On the dole
- Eugenics movement
- Laissez faire
- Wait-and-see policy
- Regina Riot
- NRA
- "Mr. Price Spreads"
- R.B. Bennett's New Deal
- Antigonish Movement
- WUL
- Regina Manifesto
- Social Credit
- Padlock Law (1937)

QUESTIONS FOR DISCUSSION

1. Why did the Great Depression happen? To what extent were its causes in Canada different from its causes in the United States?

2. How did the Great Depression affect the lives of ordinary people? Which groups or classes of people, and which regions, suffered the most in the economic crisis of the 1930s?

3. The Great Depression has been described as a "radicalizing" experience. How did it affect class, gender and ethnic relations in Canada and the United States?

4. What orthodox or conventional economic policies were attempted in Canada and the United States? Why did they generally fail?

5. Most historians agree that Franklin D. Roosevelt's New Deal was a bold program of "experimentation." Did the New Deal represent a coherent or

properly co-ordinated plan for relieving the Great Depression? What was its impact on corporate concentration, organized labour, the unemployment rate, and the American national debt?

6. Was R.B. Bennett's New Deal of 1935 an attempt to replicate FDR's original New Deal (1933–36)? Why was it never implemented in its entirety?

7. The Great Depression served as a "political catalyst," spawning radical third parties like the Co-operative Commonwealth Federation and the Social Credit party in parts of Canada. Why did parties and movements of the radical type enjoy relatively more success in Canada than in the United States?

ANALYZING AND INTERPRETING ORAL EVIDENCE

For the history of recent times, evidence from written materials and old photographs can be supplemented by information collected through talks or oral interviews with people who lived through, or participated in, events that occurred during the period under study.

Oral evidence should be analyzed with the same careful scrutiny given to any written document. Following are extracts from popular oral histories of the 1930s in Canada and the United States. For each extract:

1. *Identify the source of the evidence*, i.e., the person's name, role or occupation, and the year or time period when the interview was conducted.

2. *Determine how reliable the evidence is.* Examine the person's role, his or her biases, truthfulness, and state of memory so long after the event.

3. *Assess the person's interpretation of events.* Is it plausible, logical, or supported by facts? How

does it fit the accepted viewpoint or the prevailing attitude at the time?

Recollections of the 1930s

A Prairie Farmer

An anonymous farmer, interviewed in the early 1970s:

"After the third bad year the missus said she wasn't going to take any more and somehow we got through that winter and lit out for the Okanagan Valley in spring.

"Sold what stock we could, gave the rest away, scrub stuff, there was nothing but scrub stuff by that time, and put two trunks on top of the car and left everything behind. Houseful of furniture, implements, crusher, harness, windmill, batteries, you couldn't give it away. The missus never looked back, just straight ahead down the road...."

— Barry Broadfoot, *Ten Lost Years* (Toronto: Doubleday, 1973).

Ed Paulsen

A drifter, born in South Dakota, who rode the freights from 1926 onward and ended up in San Francisco in 1931; interviewed in the late 1960s:

"I'd get up at five in the morning and head for the waterfront. Outside the Spreckles Sugar Refinery, outside the gates, there would be a thousand men. You know dang well there's only three or four jobs. The guy would come out with two little Pinkerton cops: 'I need two guys for the bull gang. Two guys to go into the hole.' A thousand men would fight like a pack of Alaskan dogs to get through there. Only four of us would get through, I was too young a punk.

"So you'd drift up to Skid Row. There'd be thousands of men there. Guys on baskets, making weird speeches, phony theories on economics. About eleven-thirty, the real leaders would take over. They'd say: O.K., we're going to City Hall. The Mayor was Angelo Rossi, a dapper little guy. He wore expensive boots and a tight vest. We'd shout around the steps. Finally, he'd come out and tell us nothing."

— Studs Terkel, *Hard Times* (New York: Pantheon Books, 1970), p. 30. Copyright © 1970 by Studs Terkel. Reprinted by permission of Pantheon Books, a division of Random House, Inc.

Arthur A. Robertson

A New York industrialist and investment broker who was a millionaire at age 30 in 1928 and remained active in real estate and investment circles throughout the 1930s; interviewed in a New York skyscraper, late 1960s:

"In the early Thirties, I was known as a scavenger. I used to buy broken-down businesses that banks took over. That was one of my best eras of prosperity. The whole period was characterized by men who were legends. When you talked about $1 million you were talking about loose change. Three or four of these men would get together, run up a stock to ridiculous prices and unload it on the unsuspecting public. The minute you heard of a man like Durant or Jesse Livermore buying stock, everybody followed. They knew it was going to go up. The only problem was to get out before they dumped it....

"We talked of all their holdings. Livermore said: 'I own what I believe to be the controlling stock of IBM and Philip Morris.' So I asked, 'Why do you bother with anything else?' He answered, 'I only understand stock. I can't bother with businesses.' So I asked, 'Do men of your kind put away $10 million where nobody can ever touch it?' He looked at me and answered, 'Young man, what's the use of having ten million if you can't have big money?'

"In 1934 — after he went through two bankruptcies in succession — my accountant asked if I'd back Livermore. He was broke and wanted to make a comeback in the market. He always made a comeback and paid everybody off with interest. I agreed to do it. I put up $400 000. By 1939, we made enough money so that each of us could have $1 300 000 profit after taxes...."

— Studs Terkel, *Hard Times* (New York: Pantheon Books, 1970), pp. 66, 67. Copyright © 1970 by Studs Terkel. Reprinted by permission of Pantheon Books, a division of Random House, Inc.

PART IV

MODERN CHALLENGES

Since the onset of World War II, Canada and the United States have experienced rapid and startling changes. Developments at home and in world affairs have posed challenges to long-held political, economic, and social values. The two nations emerged from World War II strengthened, relatively unscathed, and determined to play active, though differing, roles in shaping the postwar world order. In this era, Canadians and Americans entered a period of prosperity only dreamed of by past generations. Through the Cold War, the postwar boom, the immigration wave, the women's movement, and the technological revolution, the forces of change have been overwhelming. Coming to grips with these developments has tested governments in both nations.

For North Americans, the postwar years have been dominated by the search for stability abroad and security at home. Canada and the United States sought guarantees against the

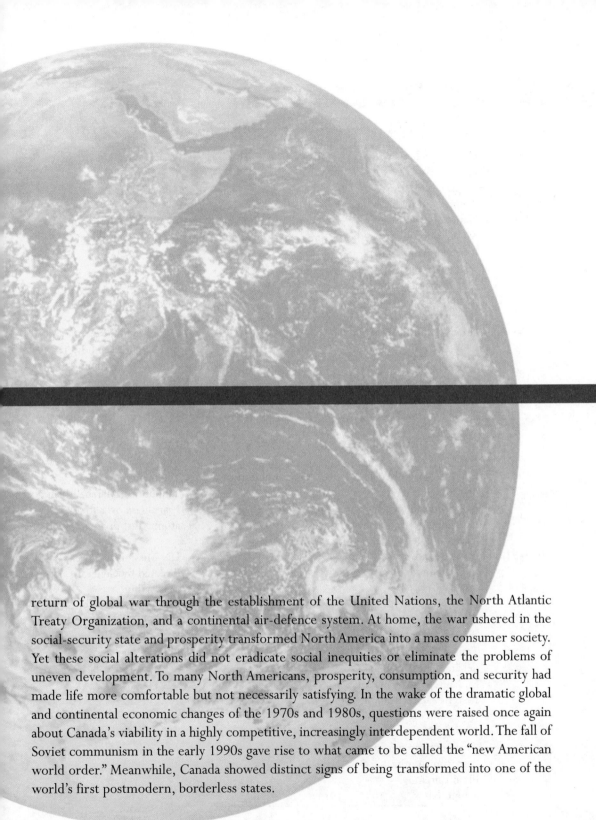

return of global war through the establishment of the United Nations, the North Atlantic Treaty Organization, and a continental air-defence system. At home, the war ushered in the social-security state and prosperity transformed North America into a mass consumer society. Yet these social alterations did not eradicate social inequities or eliminate the problems of uneven development. To many North Americans, prosperity, consumption, and security had made life more comfortable but not necessarily satisfying. In the wake of the dramatic global and continental economic changes of the 1970s and 1980s, questions were raised once again about Canada's viability in a highly competitive, increasingly interdependent world. The fall of Soviet communism in the early 1990s gave rise to what came to be called the "new American world order." Meanwhile, Canada showed distinct signs of being transformed into one of the world's first postmodern, borderless states.

MAKING CONNECTIONS TIMELINE

	CANADA	NORTH AMERICA	UNITED STATES
1939	Canada declares war on Germany (September 10); Troops sent overseas	Outbreak of World War II	War begins; United States maintains neutrality; *Gone with the Wind* released
1940	National Resources Mobilization Act passed; federal unemployment insurance enacted	Ogdensburg agreement	Franklin D. Roosevelt re-elected president
1941	Wartime wage controls; troops sent to Pacific (Hong Kong)	Hyde Park declaration	Japanese attack on Pearl Harbor; United States enters the war
1944	Family Allowances Act; CCF elected in Saskatchewan; conscription crisis	•	D-Day landings commanded by Dwight Eisenhower; U.S. "island hopping" in in Pacific war
1945	Mackenzie King's "New Social Order" program; Igor Gouzenko spy case; Canada joins United Nations	End of the war and dawn of the nuclear age	Harry Truman succeeds President Roosevelt; atomic bomb dropped on Japan; United Nations founded at San Francisco
1947	Imperial Oil's discovery of Leduc No. 1	Baby boom underway	Truman Doctrine announced; Marshall Plan
1949	Newfoundland enters Confederation; Asbestos strike in Quebec	Formation of NATO	Fears arise over first atomic test in Soviet Union
1950–53	Canada sends military aid to U.N. force in Korea	Korean War	UN Mission to Korea, directed by General MacArthur
1952	CBC-TV goes on the air; Canada joins Columbo Plan	•	Dwight D. Eisenhower elected president
1956	Trans-Canada Pipeline debate; defeat of Louis St. Laurent government; Lester Pearson's Suez Crisis initiative	•	Elvis Presley craze; age of "Rock 'n' Roll" begins
1957	John G. Diefenbaker elected prime minister; first woman minister — Ellen Fairclough — appointed	NORAD agreement	Race riots in Little Rock, Arkansas

1959	Cancellation of the Avro Arrow	St. Lawrence Seaway completed	Statehood for Alaska and Hawaii
1960	Dawn of Quebec's Quiet Revolution	•	John F. Kennedy elected president; birth control pill put on the market
1961	Founding of the New Democratic Party; CTV Network established	President Kennedy visits Canadian Parliament	Bay of Pigs disaster
1962	Diefenbaker questions Kennedy's missile crisis actions; U.S. State Department intervenes in election	Cuban missile crisis	Kennedy imposes naval quarantine and scores strategic victory
1963	Fall of Diefenbaker government; establishment of "Bi and Bi" Commission	•	Kennedy assassinated in Dallas, Texas; Martin Luther King's "I Have a Dream" rally in Washington
1964	"Go Home Liz" protests in Quebec	•	President Lyndon Johnston launches "Great Society" program; Gulf of Tonkin resolution
1965	Adoption of Maple Leaf flag	•	•
1967	Centennial year celebration; Expo '67; Charles de Gaulle's state visit to Quebec	• •	Summer riots in black ghettos of American cities
1968	Trudeaumania; Pierre Trudeau government elected; formation of Parti Québécois; Watkins report on foreign ownership	•	Protests at Democratic National Convention; trial of "Chicago 7"; assassinations of Robert F. Kennedy, Martin Luther King, and Malcolm X; Richard M. Nixon elected president
1970	FLQ October Crisis; Royal Commission on Status of Women report	•	Shooting of students at Kent State Vietnam protest
1972	Canada–USSR hockey series	•	Nixon re-elected; Watergate scandal; Nixon's China visit
1973	Trudeau's national oil-pricing policy; Foreign Investment Review Act; Mackenzie Valley Pipeline Inquiry	Arab oil embargo and oil price shock	U.S. energy-supply crisis; Vietnam ceasefire arranged, fighting continues

MAKING CONNECTIONS TIMELINE   continued

1976	René Lévesque and P.Q. achieve power; Montreal Olympic Games	•	Jimmy Carter elected president
1979	Trudeau era interrupted by election of Joe Clark's Progressive Conservative government	•	Camp David peace accord; Iran hostage crisis begins (lasts 444 days)
1980	Trudeau returned to power; "Non" side triumphs in Quebec referendum; Terry Fox's Marathon of Hope launched	•	Ronald Reagan elected president on "Make America Strong" platform; John Lennon assassinated in New York City
1982	National Energy Program implemented; patriation of the Canadian Constitution (April 17); anti-Cruise missile-testing protests	Economic recession	Reagan administration pursues "Reaganomics" and boosts defence budget
1984	First woman governor-general, Jeanne Sauvé; Brian Mulroney's PCs elected in a landslide	•	Reagan re-elected, committed to "New Conservatism"
1985	FIRA becomes Investment Canada; Rick Hansen's "Man in Motion" world tour	Launching of Mulroney–Reagan free-trade initiative;	Geneva summit between Reagan and Mikhail Gorbachev
1988	Mulroney government re-elected on free-trade issue	FTA takes effect January 1, 1989	George Bush elected president
1989	Canada joins Organization of American States	Fall of Berlin Wall alters North American defence priorities	U.S. intervention in Panama deposes Manuel Noriega

1990–91	Meech Lake Accord fails (June 1990); Canada joins coalition forces in Persian Gulf War; General Lewis Mackenzie leads UN peacekeeping force into Bosnia and Croatia	•	United States leads "Desert Storm" operation against Iraq in Persian Gulf War; Anita Hill testifies at Clarence Thomas Supreme Court confirmation hearings (October 1991)
1992	Charlottetown Accord defeated in October 1992 referendum; Canada participates in UN mission to Somalia (December 1992); Miss Canada pageant cancelled	North American Free Trade Agreement (NAFTA) under negotiation	Democrat Bill Clinton elected president, ending Republican rule in Washington
1993	Kim Campbell becomes first woman prime minister, then is defeated by Jean Chrétien's Liberals in October 1993 federal election	NAFTA concluded with Mexico; Cigarette smuggling crisis at Akwesasne Reserve on Canada–U.S. border	U.S. health-care reforms stalled in Congress
1995	Prime Minister Chrétien hosts Ottawa summit meeting with President Bill Clinton (March)	Wal-Mart retail chain enters Canada after takeover of Woolco stores	Republicans in Congress propose "Contract with America" reforms

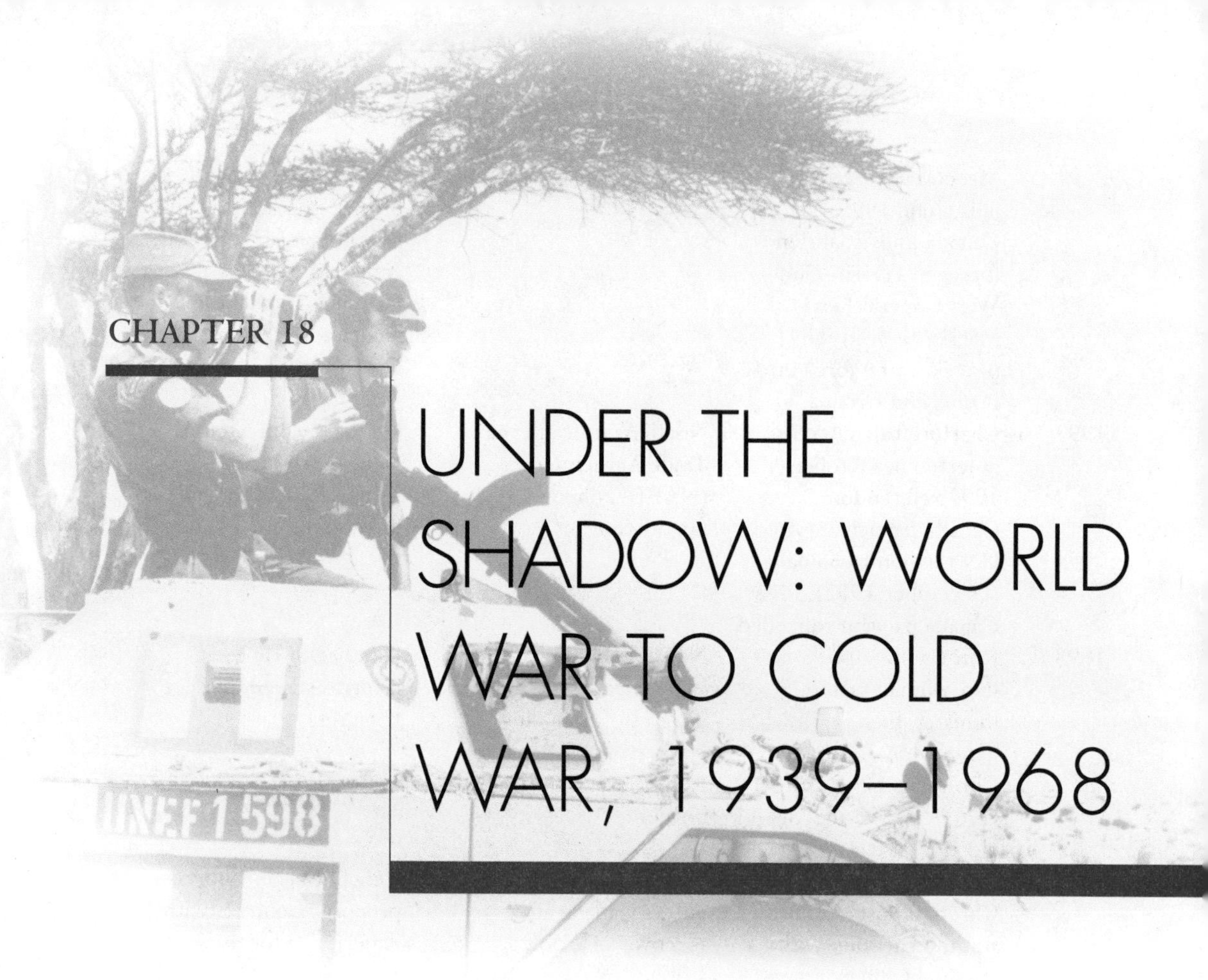

CHAPTER 18

UNDER THE SHADOW: WORLD WAR TO COLD WAR, 1939–1968

THE NORTH AMERICAN ALLIES AT WAR

THE SOCIAL-SECURITY STATE

TOWARD A PEACEFUL INTERNATIONAL ORDER

CANADA AND THE NEW AMERICAN EMPIRE

THE TURBULENT 1960s

WORLD WAR II WAS, in many ways, a "total war," with far-reaching consequences for Europe and the old international order. It left Europe in ruins and produced a revolution in thinking that worked profound changes in societies and institutions. For North Americans, the 1939–45 war against European fascism and imperial Japan posed unrivalled challenges of mobilization, wartime sacrifice, and production. Canada plunged into the war in September 1939, one week after Britain. Although both Canada and the United States made significant human and material sacrifices in the war, they emerged relatively unscathed by the horrible devastation. Neither country experienced foreign invasion or suffered battle losses comparable to those of the Soviet Union and most European states.

Nevertheless, both Canada and the United States were greatly and permanently affected by World War II. The two societies emerged with modern factories, highly skilled and trained workforces, and the highest living standards in the world. The war also completed what the Great Depression had started — a virtual revolution in social and economic policy. Amid the hothouse atmosphere of wartime, governments dramatically increased their spending and extended their activities. Government initiatives sowed the seeds for a new postwar social order. Out of the war emerged the beginnings of the modern "social-security state," in Canada as in the United States.

World War II also marked a watershed in both countries' foreign policies. After having guided Canada to autonomous status in the British Commonwealth, Mackenzie King's foreign policy before the war had been careful and tentative and was characterized by a certain North American isolationism. Most Canadians' first loyalty was to Britain, and King's favoured role was that of a North American "linchpin," keeping the United States and the mother country in harmony. The United States, for its part, pursued overseas trade with vigour. Yet it remained reluctant to participate in the struggles of Europe, especially after the experience of World War I.

World War II changed almost everything. Six years of world conflict

Mackenzie King with American President Franklin Roosevelt and British Prime Minister Winston Churchill at the Quebec Conference in 1943. Though host to the conference, King was not a participant in the discussions about the postwar order.

devastated the peoples and economies of Europe and left Great Britain severely weakened and almost bankrupt. The United States was thrust upon the world stage as a superpower with global aims and responsibilities, with a huge budget for aid and arms, and with rapidly expanding national interests. The effect of war on Canada was no less pronounced: the nation emerged from the war as a ranking industrial power prepared to play a constructive role in shaping a new world order. The United States and Canada were not only largely unscathed by the war, but were stronger and infused with a new — though different — sense of mission.

THE NORTH AMERICAN ALLIES AT WAR

CANADA DECLARED WAR ON NAZI GERMANY on September 10, 1939, one week and a House of Commons debate after Britain's entry into the conflict. Fighting alongside British forces, Canadian troops joined in the defence of Europe against the Nazi armies. Royal Canadian Air Force (RCAF) squadrons were transferred overseas, and Canadian airmen assumed a larger role in the monumental struggle known as the Battle of Britain. Under the British Commonwealth Air Training Plan (BCATP), established in late 1939, Canada became the chief training base for British and Commonwealth flyers. Vigorous recruitment and mobilization of the military reserves produced over 60 000 soldiers by the end of September 1939. During the war, Canada enlisted 1.1 million men and women

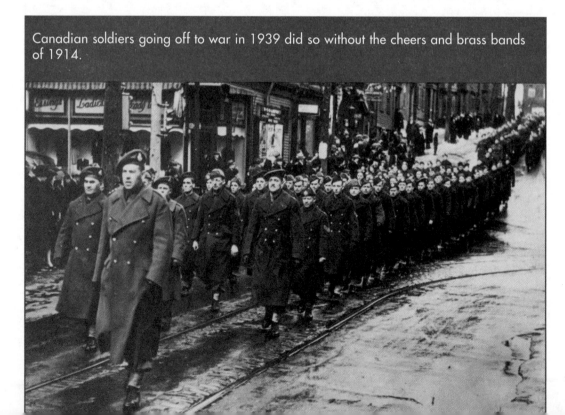

Canadian soldiers going off to war in 1939 did so without the cheers and brass bands of 1914.

in its armed forces and emerged as a major North American supplier of war materials and foodstuffs.

Until the United States entered the war in December 1941, Mackenzie King's government attempted to play the role of mediator between London and an ostensibly neutral Washington. Although King talked of Canada being a "linchpin" in the North Atlantic triangle of states, he had to content himself with a more modest role. The prime minister visited Britain only twice during the war, in 1941 and 1944, and — even though he hosted two Atlantic summit conferences, in August 1943 and September 1944 — King was excluded from the Allies' serious discussions about wartime strategy and postwar planning.

"BROTHERS-IN-ARMS"

The Japanese attack on the U.S. naval base at Pearl Harbor on December 7, 1941, brought Franklin D. Roosevelt and the United States into the war. Once the United States became a belligerent, Canada lost whatever status King had envisioned as a vital link in an Anglo–American alliance. From late 1941 to 1945, the two North American allies fought as "big and little brothers-in-arms," albeit in different theatres of war.[1] Working together for the common defence of North America strengthened economic integration, but it also exposed the clear imbalance of the continental relationship. Yet, by 1945, the Dominion's ties of loyalty to Britain would still run much deeper than those to the United States.

The war in Europe gradually forced a major realignment in the Canada's longstanding relationship with the United States. An early hint of the change came in August 1938, when President Franklin D. Roosevelt pledged that "the people of the United States will not stand idly by if domination of Canadian soil is threatened by any other empire." By the summer of 1940, such fears took on real meaning. Nazi Germany dominated much of continental Europe, and both Canada and the United States awakened to the grim possibility of a threat to North American security. Roosevelt invited King to Ogdensburg, New York, in mid-August to discuss common defence concerns. The result of that momentous meeting was the Ogdensburg Agreement, a simple press release announcing the establishment of the Permanent Joint Board of Defence to monitor "sea, land, and air problems" and the "defence of the north half of the western hemisphere."

From joint defence co-operation to common, planned defence production proved to be a short step. In April 1941, King and Roosevelt finalized another co-operative agreement, the Hyde Park Declaration. By the end of 1940, Canada had faced a looming economic crisis: the British were unable to pay for Canadian-supplied arms and materials, while Canada was short of the American dollars needed to buy machine tools, oil, gas, and other commodities. The United States had just begun to mobilize its army and badly needed arms and military suppliers. Under the Hyde Park arrangement, war purchasing was co-ordinated on a North American basis. This attempt to resolve Canada's wartime manufacturing and exchange problems would prove to be a major step toward the integration of the North American economies.

"TIES THAT BIND": THE WARTIME CONTINENTAL AGREEMENTS

DURING 1940 AND 1941, President Franklin D. Roosevelt and Prime Minister Mackenzie King entered into two international agreements, military and economic, of long-term significance: the Ogdensburg Agreement and the Hyde Park Declaration. Historians differ in their views of these wartime agreements. Why was the Joint Board on Defence made "permanent"? To what extent were King's actions justifiable on practical and military–strategic grounds? How valid is the revisionist argument that the wartime agreements turned Canada into a "protectorate" in the American empire? Read the documents and judge for yourself.

THE OGDENSBURG AGREEMENT, AUGUST 18, 1940

> The Prime Minister and the President have discussed the mutual problems of defence in relation to the safety of Canada and the United States.

In August 1938 at Queen's University in Kingston, President Franklin D. Roosevelt offered his famous pledge to "not stand idly by" if Canada was "threatened by any other empire." As the war clouds gathered in Europe, the two North American nations were drawn closer together.

It has been agreed that a Permanent Joint Board on Defence shall be set up at once by the two countries.

This Permanent Joint Board on Defence shall commence immediate studies relating to sea, land, and air problems including personnel and material.

It will consider in the broad sense the defence of the north half of the Western Hemisphere.

The Permanent Joint Board on Defence will consist of four or five members from each country, most of them from the services. It will meet shortly.

THE HYDE PARK DECLARATION, APRIL 20, 1941

Among other important matters, the President and the Prime Minister discussed measures by which the most prompt and effective utilization might be made of the productive facilities of North America for the purposes both of local and hemisphere defence and of the assistance which in addition to their own programs both Canada and the United States are rendering to Great Britain and the other democracies.

It was agreed as a general principle that in mobilizing the resources of this continent each country should provide the other with the defence articles which it is best able to produce, and, above all, produce quickly, and that production programs should be co-ordinated to this end.

While Canada has expanded its productive capacity manifold since the beginning of the war, there are still numerous defence articles which it must obtain in the United States, and purchases of this character by Canada will be even greater in the coming year than in the past. On the other hand, there is existing and potential capacity in Canada for the speedy production of certain kinds of munitions, strategic materials, aluminum, and ships, which are urgently required by the United States for its own purposes. ... In addition, it is of great importance to the economic and financial relations between the two countries that payment by the United States for these supplies will materially assist Canada in meeting part of the cost of Canadian defence purchases in the United States.

In so far as Canada's defence purchases in the United States consist of component parts to be used in equipment and munitions which Canada is producing for Great Britain, it was also agreed that Great Britain will obtain these parts under the Lease-Lend Act and forward them to Canada for inclusion in the finished articles....

INDUSTRIAL MOBILIZATION

Full-scale industrial mobilization did not begin in Canada until the Department of Munitions and Supply was established in April 1940, under C.D. Howe, a dynamic American-born engineer–businessman and King's former minister of transport. As minister of munitions, Howe proceeded quickly to recruit an impressive team of "dollar-a-year men" to act as business

A recruiting poster for the Canadian Women's Army Corps (CWACs). The entrance of women into the military challenged the male monopoly in the armed forces.

A Victory Bonds poster depicting a patriotic Canadian woman during World War II. "Womanpower" was welcomed in the munitions factories and in the volunteer sales of Victory Bonds.

advisers and commodity controllers. "Howe's Boys" spread out across the country to mobilize, organize, control, restrict, and regulate essential supplies, and to supervise the production of war equipment and arms. True to Howe's freewheeling approach, the department plunged ahead with war production and showed little toleration of waste, confusion, or duplication. Largely because of industrial mobilization, Canada's total production grew by 47 percent from 1940 to 1942 and Canada succeeded in meeting its wartime obligations, including contracts to supply the United States with small arms, strategic materials, and aluminum.

Mobilization for World War II opened up many new employment opportunities for women as well as men. Between September 1939 and mid-1941, military recruitment and war industry virtually ended the unemployment of the Great Depression. In 1941–42, shortages of "manpower" in both the armed forces and industry created opportunities for "womanpower." Increasing numbers of women were hired in plants that manufactured aircraft, guns, ammunition, tanks, and ocean-going ships. Canada's wartime aircraft production of Catalinas, Harvard training planes, Mosquito fighters, and bombers all depended heavily on women's labour. By autumn of 1944, the number of women working full-time in Canada's paid labour force was over 1 million — double what it had been in 1939 — and another 800 000 women worked on farms. Most of the country's 3 million women were also contributing to the war effort through volunteer activities, and by war's end, nearly 50 000 had served in the Canadian armed forces.

Women's war service produced gains that turned out to be temporary. While women entered the workforce in record numbers, they were mainly considered a reserve army of labour. Prevailing public attitudes toward women persisted, and fears were expressed that women in bandanas and overalls, or Khaki uniforms, would lose their femininity. When the war ended, preference for jobs was given to ex-servicemen and women were expected to return to their traditional domestic chores.

THE SOCIAL-SECURITY STATE

A S THE ALLIES INCHED CLOSER TO VICTORY AFTER 1943, public attention in Canada and the United States gradually shifted to postwar concerns. Many Canadians in both English- and French-speaking Canada began to worry that the end of the war would bring an end to full employment and perhaps a return to the Great Depression. In September 1943, a public opinion poll reported that both the Liberal and Conservative parties were trailing the socialist Co-operative Commonwealth Federation (CCF). Alone among the three major political parties, the CCF had emphasized a comprehensive program

Canadian soldiers return home after VE Day, 1945. Happy faces greeted the returnees, but there were also postwar uncertainties in the air.

of postwar social reconstruction. Mackenzie King sensed the growing public impatience with his government and recognized that the solution to the Liberal party's political woes lay in embracing "the great social programs, working classes and the like, which lay at the basis of all else."

The Canadian government, like its counterparts in Britain and the United States, had already taken small steps along these lines. Since the outbreak of war, most Allied governments had launched massive spending programs, assumed a direct role in industrial mobilization, and imposed price and wage controls — all to meet the wartime emergency. In Britain, William Beveridge emerged to champion the social-welfare state, promising war-weary Britons "cradle-to-grave" security when victory was won. Meanwhile, American reformers with the National Resources Planning Board and the Office of Price Administration advocated postwar policies to guarantee national health insurance, expand social security, and extend federal aid to the cities. In Canada, developments were remarkably similar. National unemployment insurance had been introduced, somewhat belatedly, in 1940, and modest programs for veterans' benefits had begun to appear during the war.

The most widely publicized of the wartime proposals for social security was the "Marsh Report" of 1943. Leonard Marsh, a social scientist and research director for a government advisory committee, advocated drastic measures to fend off a possible postwar depression. The Dominion government, he claimed, must commit itself to full employment and to broad "social insurance" plans for sickness, old age, and joblessness. Since large families were responsible for pulling many people below the subsistence level, Marsh proposed the introduction of "family allowances" as an income supplement for all family households. Marsh's proposals aroused the hostility of many wealthy and influential Canadians, so King saw to it that such reforms were buried in the bureaucracy.

THE "DISCOVERY" OF SOCIAL SECURITY

Yet the war years seemed to open minds to new and untried ideas. The wartime Grand Alliance with the Soviet Union had softened, to some extent, virulent anti-communism and allayed public fears of the socialist bogey, in Canada if not the United States. Even the federal Conservative party had been affected. The head of Manitoba's Progressive government, John Bracken, had been chosen the Tories' new national leader in December 1942. As part of the arrangement, the party's official name was changed to the "Progressive Conservative" party. Furthermore, after the Port Hope Conference of 1942, progressive reform ideas were incorporated into the usual Tory platform of conscription and free enterprise.

From mid-1943 onward, Prime Minister King became preoccupied with the twin threat posed by growing labour militancy and the rise of the CCF. A flurry of strikes broke out in 1943, which interrupted wartime production at the Ford automobile plant in Windsor, the steel mills in Sydney and Sault Ste. Marie, and the aircraft plants in Montreal. The government was also watching the activities of the newly formed Canadian Congress of Labour (1940), an umbrella organization of trade unions, which was endorsing the CCF. To alleviate the labour crisis, King turned to C.P. McTague, an industrial relations specialist who had learned much from his involvement with a bitter 1941 Kirkland Lake strike. Acting on McTague's recommendations, the government issued a landmark order-in-council, P.C. 1003, in the fall of 1943. The order, based largely on the U.S. Wagner Act of 1935, formally recognized, for the first time, labour's right to organize, and established machinery to make that right effective.

Meeting the political challenge of the CCF would require different medicine. In July 1943, Ontario's Liberal government had gone down to defeat at the hands of George Drew and the Progressive Conservatives, advocating surprisingly radical Tory reforms. More amazing was the fact that Drew's Conservatives barely edged out the CCF, who had come "from nowhere" to capture 34 seats in the Ontario legislature. In August and September 1943, King's Liberals lost four by-elections, including three to the CCF, and found themselves running behind the CCF in the Gallup poll. Heeding the political winds, King resolved to steal the CCF's thunder. He would counteract CCF socialism with a social-security plan of his own.

MACKENZIE KING'S "NEW SOCIAL ORDER"

In January 1944, King Liberalism was reborn with a new postwar program of reconstruction and social-welfare reforms. The plans for Mackenzie King's "new social order" owed more to the ideas of Ottawa's civil-service mandarins than the social-welfare experiments elsewhere. Most of the postwar program originated with a coterie of young economists recently recruited to government service, a talented group that included W.A. Mackintosh, R.B. Bryce, Louis Rasminsky, and A.F.W. Plumptre. The primary object of postwar domestic policy, King's Liberal program declared, would be "social security and human welfare." The government committed itself to ease

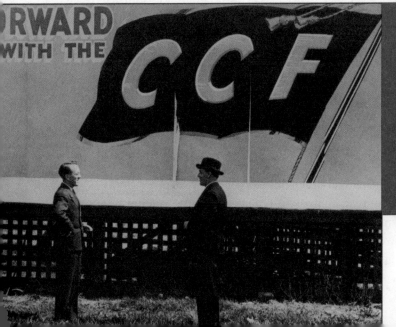

Tommy Douglas (centre), the Co-operative Commonwealth Federation leader in Saskatchewan, inspects a CCF billboard during the 1944 provincial election. Douglas and the CCF swept to power and formed the first democratic socialist government in North America.

the transition from wartime to peace, to guarantee full employment, and to provide a minimum standard of social security for all Canadians.

The actual Liberal program did not quite match the advance billing. King and his cabinet introduced a two-pronged legislative package. The cornerstone of the program was family allowances, a national scheme known popularly as the "baby bonus," scheduled to take effect after the next election, expected in 1945. This program was accompanied by a major reorganization of the federal administration, reflecting the government's postwar legislative priorities. Three new federal departments were established: National Health and Welfare, headed by a new member of the cabinet, Brooke Claxton; Reconstruction, under the supervision of C.D. Howe; and Veterans' Affairs, entrusted to longtime cabinet member Ian Mackenzie. Throughout 1944 and 1945, the government passed a series of measures providing for the baby bonus, Veterans' Land Act (VLA) housing, veterans' rehabilitation, farm product subsidies, and insurance for overseas exports. It all proved to be very popular politically. Campaigning on the slogan "Keep Building A New Social Order," King's Liberals won a clear majority in the June 1945 federal election.

Canada, like Britain and the United States, was well on the way to being transformed into a modern social-security state. The new economic orthodoxy in Ottawa, as in Washington and London, was Keynesianism, a set of theories first proposed by British economist John Maynard Keynes. In hard economic times, the government must be prepared to run deficits and to incur debt for the sake of maintaining "high and stable employment"; in good times like those forecast, it would pile up surpluses and pay off government debt. Politically, the King government and its Liberal successors found increasing social spending much easier than reducing spending levels or raising taxes. Federal initiatives such as family allowances and other social-security measures ran into resistance from the provinces, since they controlled many areas of social spending under the Canadian constitution. Ottawa's proposed social-security program was initially rejected at a 1945 federal–provincial conference on reconstruction and was introduced only after a series of negotiations with the provinces. Together, Canada, Britain, and the United States had met the challenge of global war and were beginning to tackle the problems of postwar reconstruction.

TOWARD A PEACEFUL INTERNATIONAL ORDER

AFTER 1945, Canada underwent a remarkably swift transition from the status of wartime junior partner to that of a sure-footed "middle power." This new middle-power role was based on what Mackenzie King had called in July 1943 the "functional principle," which asserted that Canada laid no claims to being a great power, but had the right to some influence and involvement in areas of policy where the country's interests were involved. Canadian policy-makers sought to shape a postwar order of peace based on "fruitful collaboration" between greater and lesser powers in areas that might reduce the potential for conflict among states.[2] Although wary of Soviet postwar expansion and the swollen power of the United States, King and his external-affairs diplomats saw a new internationalist role for countries like Canada.

ORIGINS OF LIBERAL INTERNATIONALISM

At the beginning of 1947, in a major foreign-policy declaration, Louis St. Laurent, then Canada's secretary of state for external affairs, endorsed a new internationalist role for Canada, broadly acceptable to both English- and French-speaking Canadians. St. Laurent asserted Canada's willingness to accept "international responsibility in keeping with our conception of our role in world affairs." If there was one lesson to be learned from the prewar and wartime experience, St. Laurent said, "it is that security for this country lies in the development of a firm structure of international organization." In this new liberal-internationalist philosophy the United States figured prominently. Fearful that America would return to its isolationism of the 1930s, Canadian policy-makers set out to involve the superpower in international commitments from which it could not easily turn away. For a middle power like Canada, this rather ambitious and perhaps idealistic diplomatic mission would produce its share of disappointments. As a great superpower engaged in a Cold War power struggle with the Soviet Union after 1945, the United States was not about to be led, or much constrained, by Ottawa.

Canada's new approach to foreign policy was first revealed in the movement to found the United Nations. It was formulated not by Prime Minister King but by a new generation of professional diplomats in the Department of External Affairs. This group — headed by Norman Robertson and including Lester B. Pearson, Arnold Heeney, Escott Reid, John Holmes, and Hume Wrong — came to the fore as policy-makers at a time when Canadians seemed to be showing great readiness to join with like-minded states in the search for a permanent peace. To counter European fascist aggression and the rising spectre of Soviet communism, these men saw the need for a worldwide organization to preserve peace. "Nationalism and internationalism," Lester Pearson once commented, were "two sides of the same coin," and "international co-operation for peace" represented "the most important aspect of national policy."[3] To external-affairs

Lester B. Pearson at the founding of the United Nations. After a successful diplomatic career, he became prime minister of Canada.

mandarins, internationalism was the cardinal principle that linked idealism and national self-interest in Canadian foreign policy until 1968, and perhaps afterward.

FORMATION OF THE UNITED NATIONS

In the formative years of the United Nations (U.N.), from 1943 to 1947, Canada earned a fairly secure place as a middle power, although its diplomatic influence remained limited and circumscribed in a postwar world dominated by the Great Powers. Both the American president, Franklin D. Roosevelt, and the British prime minister, Winston Churchill, favoured from the outset a Big Three, or a Big Four, concert system as the only practicable basis for a durable peace. As early as March 1943, Prime Minister King joined with other middle-sized Commonwealth states like Australia and New Zealand in opposing postwar plans that entrusted "our destinies…to the four larger powers." During the critical four years from 1943 to 1947, when the U.N. system took shape, Canadian policy-makers supported a new international order based on a voluntary association of states and the establishment of international organizations.

Canada's attempts to play a functional middle-power role in setting up the U.N. met with limited success. Although Canadian diplomats failed to prevent the domination of the United Nations Relief and Rehabilitation Agency (UNRRA) by the four great powers — the United States, the United Kingdom, the Soviet Union, and China — Canada secured admission to UNRRA in 1945, along with France. In postwar deliberations over the International Monetary Fund (IMF) and other U.N. institutions, Canada's representatives attempted to reduce the power monopoly of the Great Powers and to promote "harmonious" relations among participating countries. At the San Francisco Conference of April 1945, where the Charter of the United Nations was ratified, Mackenzie King and Canada's delegates tried to secure a revision of the Yalta plan for a ruling security council, which gave the right of veto to the five Great Powers. Canada made the case for a general assembly that recognized the variety and strength of the lesser states. When the Canadian proposal was coolly received in Washington and threatened to disrupt the difficult unity attained among the Great Powers, the Canadians relented for the sake of achieving the great object of a general association of states.

PEACEMAKING — ACCORDING TO THE GREAT POWERS

The Great Powers were determined to maintain firm control over the process of peacemaking. In July 1945, the Big Three — Josef Stalin of the Soviet Union, Harry S. Truman, the new president of the United States, and Winston Churchill, who was quickly replaced by the newly elected British prime minister, Clement Attlee — met at Potsdam. They decided, without consulting with other Allied nations, that the peace treaties with Italy and the other belligerent nations would be drawn up by a council of foreign ministers representing the United States, Britain, the Soviet Union, France, and China. Trust had given way to suspicion, and both the United States and the Soviet Union were now caught up in the escalating tensions of the Cold War.

Like many other lesser Allied countries, Canada was invited to participate in a peace conference in the summer of 1946 to review the treaties drafted by the council. Canada's role, King told the Canadian House of Commons in July 1946, would "lie in helping the countries [of Europe] more directly concerned to work out agreed solutions which are fair and will be likely to endure." But for the Canadian delegation, headed by King, the conference proved to be largely an exercise in frustration. Conscious of the need to avoid any action that might increase Cold War tensions between the Soviet Union and the West, the Canadian delegation exerted little influence.

CANADA'S U.N. ROLE: THE PEACEKEEPER

Canada has been called the world's leading "peacekeeper." In the U.N.'s formative years, Canadian policy-makers had expressed their faith in a world peace organization encompassing the United States and founded on the doctrine of collective security. But within a few short years it became clear that the U.N.'s collective security system was not working, as a result of the difficulties in reaching a consensus about taking action in areas where either the Soviet Union or the United States had strategic

Canadian troops in Korea, 1951, fighting under the United Nations flag. Canada was one of the first sixteen countries to send military aid to South Korea in an effort to resist North Korean aggression. Here, troops of the Princess Patricia's Canadian Light Infantry advance through a Korean village.

interests. A system that had been designed to provide global security now seemed calculated to turn small wars into large ones. Confronted with this dilemma, Canada altered its stance. As a middle power strongly supportive of the U.N., it turned to preventing the escalation of small wars into large ones by peacekeeping. The primary aim of Canada as peacekeeper became "preventive diplomacy": preserving the balance of power by intervening to separate localized conflicts and isolate them from the Cold War competition of the Great Powers.

Canada's new middle-power internationalism was perhaps best reflected in the country's participation in U.N. peacekeeping operations. In 1949 Canadians gained their first experience in peacekeeping as members of a U.N. military observer group in Kashmir, supervising a border truce between India and Pakistan. During the U.N. action in the Korean War (1950–54), a Canadian army brigade of 22 000 served under the command of U.S. General Douglas MacArthur, and Canada also supplied destroyer ships and aircraft for the operation. For five years Canadian forces fought in Korea under the U.N. flag, in the thick of some of the heaviest fighting of a gruelling war.

DIPLOMACY OF CONSTRAINT

The Korean War broke out in June 1950 at the height of East–West tensions in the Cold War. In response to Soviet Communist expansion in eastern Europe, the United States had adopted a policy of containment to resist the spread of world communism, which many Americans believed threatened the entire western democratic way of life. A wave of anti-communism swept the United States, stirred up by allegations of communist infiltration made by Wisconsin senator Joseph McCarthy. In this atmosphere, President Truman decided to draw the containment line in the far-off Asian country of Korea.

The actual American intervention in Korea was carried out under the auspices of the United Nations and with the support of Canada and most other member states. In June 1950 Canada supported the U.N. Security Council resolution ordering the North Korean communist forces, who had invaded South Korea with Soviet military support, to withdraw and return the conquered territory. In all, 32 nations, including Canada, sent troops to South Korea to fight under the U.N. flag. The U.N. emergency force was commanded by General MacArthur and most of the troops were American, and the Canadian government of Louis St. Laurent fully supported armed intervention to stop the spread of "communist totalitarian aggression" in Asia. Yet Canadian policy-makers were also consciously pursuing another diplomatic objective: moderating or constraining the exercise of American power to prevent the Americans from getting bogged down in Asia at a time when Europe seemed more threatened by communist expansionism.[4]

THREE AMERICAN VIEWS OF THE KOREAN WAR

DEAN ACHESON ON THE RESPONSE TO COMMUNIST AGGRESSION, 1950

DEAN ACHESON, the American secretary of state, outlined the Truman administration's policy and planning in the Korean crisis to Lester Pearson, then Canada's minister of external affairs, shortly after the outbreak of war in June 1950. Here is how Pearson summarized Acheson's views:

> He emphasized at the beginning that the Korean situation could be understood and intelligently dealt with only as a phase, and not, in the long run, the most important phase, of the general conflict between the free and the communist worlds. Strategically, as they had pointed out more than once, Korea was not an important sector in that conflict, and the decision to meet the challenge represented by the aggression on that sector had been purely political, made by the President as such. When this aggression occurred, the President and his advisers, without delay and without hesitation, agreed that this challenge must be met by the free peoples; that they must call a halt to communist aggressive tactics. He admitted that this decision must have been a

American General Douglas MacArthur, commander of the U.N. forces in Korea, 1951.

"Joltin' Joe" at the microphone, with a Washington aide, 1954. Senator Joseph McCarthy shot into public prominence during the Korean War. Speaking in Wheeling, West Virginia, in 1950, he declared that the United States — "the world's most powerful nation" in 1945 — had "retreated from victory" and fallen into a "position of impotency." The cause of this calamity was "the traitorous actions" of high government officials who had gone "soft" on communism.

surprise to some — including people in Washington. Certainly, if there had been a general aggressive move, they would not have acted so quickly in Korea. But in the circumstances he felt that they were right to act quickly and through the United Nations. We agreed....

...He himself was intensely concerned, as the President was, that the struggle ahead should not be one of the United States vs. the communist world. The American people could be convinced of this if we all acted together on the Korean front as members of the United Nations, and if we worked together to strengthen our defences generally....

Lester B. Pearson, *Mike, vol. 2: 1948–57* (Toronto: University of Toronto Press, 1973), pp. 150–151. Reprinted by permission of the publisher.

HARRY S. TRUMAN ON "LIMITED WAR" IN KOREA, 1951

In a dramatic speech in April 1951, President Harry Truman set out American policy on Korea. He defended "limited war" in Korea, but plainly saw communism as a monolithic global menace:

I want to talk plainly to you tonight about what we are doing in Korea and about our policy in the Far East.

In the simplest terms, what we are doing in Korea is this: We are trying to prevent a third world war.

I think most people in this country recognized that fact last June. And they warmly supported the decision of the government to help the Republic of Korea against the communist aggressors. Now, many persons, even some who applauded our decision to defend Korea, have forgotten the basic reason for our action.

It is right for us to be in Korea. It was right last June. It is right today.

I want to remind you why this is true.

The communists in the Kremlin are engaged in a monstrous conspiracy to stamp out freedom all over the world. If they were to succeed, the United States would be numbered among their principal victims. It must be clear to everyone that the United States cannot — and will not — sit idly by and await foreign conquest. The only question is: When is the best time to meet the threat and how?

The best time to meet the threat is in the beginning. It is easier to put out a fire in the beginning when it is small than after it has become a roaring blaze.

And the best way to meet the threat of aggression is for the peace-loving nations to act together. If they don't act together, they are likely to be picked off, one by one....

I believe that we must try to limit the war to Korea for these vital reasons: to make sure that the precious lives of our fighting men are not wasted; to see that the security of our country and the free world is not needlessly jeopardized; and to prevent a third world war.

President Harry S. Truman, April 11, 1951.

GENERAL DOUGLAS MACARTHUR'S "NO SUBSTITUTE FOR VICTORY" SPEECH, 1951

General Douglas MacArthur was dismissed from U.N. command in Korea for publicly criticizing Truman's decision to "limit" the war. In a haughty and unrepentant 1951 speech to Congress, he explained his "hardline" position:

> [O]nce war is forced upon us, there is no other alternative than to apply every available means to bring it to a swift end. War's very object is victory — not prolonged indecision. In war, indeed, there can be no substitute for victory.
>
> There are some who for varying reasons would appease Red China. They are blind to history's clear lesson. For history teaches with unmistakable emphasis that appeasement but begets new and bloodier war....
>
> ...Of the nations of the world, Korea alone, up to now, is the sole one which has risked its all against communism. The magnificence of the courage and fortitude of the Korean people defies description. They have chosen to risk death rather than slavery. Their last words to me were "Don't scuttle the Pacific."

General Douglas MacArthur, Address to Congress, April 19, 1951.

THE SUEZ MISSION

Canada made a more important contribution to the U.N. mission to resolve the Suez Crisis of October 1956. A brief war between Israel and Egypt, which led to an Anglo–French invasion of Egypt, presented another severe test of international diplomacy. At the United Nations, Canada abstained from supporting a United States motion condemning the French and British military action in Egypt. Instead, Lester Pearson succeeded in winning the support of the U.N. General Assembly members for a United Nations Emergency Force (UNEF), aimed at bringing about a ceasefire and then remaining in the Middle East to patrol the troubled border between Egypt and Israel. A Canadian, Major General E.L.M. Burns, was appointed the first commander of the force, which numbered 6000 and was financed by contributions from U.N. members. UNEF supervised the withdrawal of British and French forces from Egypt and then established posts in the Sinai peninsula to safeguard a precarious peace.

Canada also played a key role in three U.N.-sponsored international commissions for supervision and control, teams drawn from three countries and set up by the Geneva Conference of 1954 to observe the "peace" in Vietnam, Cambodia, and Laos. At the peak of their activity in 1955, 170 Canadians, including 25 professional diplomats, were engaged in these commissions. By the time of their disbandment in 1973, the number had dwindled to 15. In that same year, however, Canada dispatched 290 diplomatic and military personnel to Vietnam to form part of a reconstituted four-party International Commission for Control and

Supervision (ICCS), agreed to under the Paris Peace Accord of 1972. When the Pierre Trudeau government recognized that the ICCS was supervising a Vietnam war rather than a peace, Canadian forces were withdrawn in July 1973.

Canada's peacekeeping activity was enthusiastically supported by Lester Pearson when he became head of the Canadian government. In 1964, some 2122 Canadians were deployed under the U.N. flag in regions including the Congo, Cyprus, Kashmir, and Indochina. By September 1975, the number of Canadians involved in U.N. peacekeeping operations was down to 1547; by late 1983 the figure was 755, engaged in the Middle East, Cyprus, and South Korea (where one Canadian military attaché supervised border violations between North and South Korea).

Canadian peacekeeping force in the Sinai peninsula, 1957. Canada's offer of a peacekeeping force to Egypt was originally rejected because the Egyptians could not distinguish between Canadian and British uniforms and flags.

Canada's record in U.N. peacekeeping has not been unblemished or universally acclaimed. Since 1949, participation in U.N.-sponsored peacekeeping operations has proved expensive, costing Canadian taxpayers several hundred million dollars — over $30 million a year in the 1980s. Defence critics have charged that in accepting most U.N. requests for assistance, Canadian forces have been spread too thin. At least one U.N. appeal — for some additional French-speaking specialists during the 1960–64 Congo operation — had to be turned down for that reason. During the 1956 Suez crisis, the Louis St. Laurent government was strongly criticized in the Canadian press for not taking a more forthright stand, particularly for not rallying to Britain's side in the conflict. In the weeks before the Six Day War of 1967 in the Middle East, the Pearson government made no secret of its pro-Israeli sentiment, effectively abandoning its posture of impartiality. As a direct consequence, when Cairo requested the withdrawal of the UNEF, the Canadians were the first contingent asked to leave. But perhaps the most revealing aspect of Canada's peacekeeping has been the government's clear reluctance to support initiatives in areas like Latin America and eastern Europe, considered by one or the other of the Great Powers as lying within its "sphere of influence."

The contributions made by Canadian soldiers to the U.N. missions were certainly matched by the efforts of Canadian politicians and diplomats in negotiating the establishment of peacekeeping operations, often under emergency conditions. Canada's role in setting up the UNEF was recognized internationally by the award of the Nobel Peace Prize in 1957 to the then minister of external affairs, Lester Pearson. Its part in organizing the Cyprus operation in 1964 narrowly headed off war between two North Atlantic Treaty Organization (NATO) allies, Greece and Turkey. Within the United Nations, Canada persisted throughout the 1960s in pressing for better institutional arrangements for recruiting and financing peacekeeping forces, to which all U.N. members would contribute. Since 1964, Canada has allocated a brigade of troops for U.N. service, and Canadian governments have continued to reaffirm the nation's commitment to peacekeeping. No other nation has done as much as Canada to advance the cause of U.N. peacekeeping. This activity remains, in the words of historian J.L. Granatstein, "an article of faith" for most Canadians.

AMERICA'S U.N. ROLE: DEFENDER OF THE WEST

As the postwar leader of the West, and with extensive global interests, the United States took a decidedly different approach to ensuring a peaceful world order. From early 1943 to 1945, President Roosevelt, Secretary of State Cordell Hull, and Washington policy-makers sought to fashion a United Nations organization that preserved America's freedom of action in the world, yet created a new supranational mechanism for attaining American global objectives. At the Yalta Conference of February 1945, Roosevelt and Winston Churchill managed to secure the support of Josef Stalin and the Soviet Union for the American concept of a United Nations, in return for territorial concessions in the Far East, a free hand in Manchuria, and a broad slice of eastern Poland. The United Nations charter and structure that was approved at the San Francisco conference of 1945 conformed in many ways with the American plans for an international organization. The veto power given to the United States and the other Great Powers; the membership of China on the Security Council; and the membership of the General Assembly, drawn largely from nations favourable to the United States, all testified to the founding of a United Nations compatible with America's national interests in the postwar struggle for power.[5]

By 1945, American policy-makers — in striking contrast to their Canadian counterparts — harboured few illusions about their new creation, the United Nations. President Harry Truman, who succeeded Roosevelt on the eve of the San Francisco conference, reaffirmed the supreme importance Washington attached to building "an organization to help keep the future peace of the world." But many U.S. postwar planners had already come to see the U. N. as an instrument of "power politics, pure and simple," whose prime function would be to marshal the support of smaller states in the interests of American foreign policy. As a U.S. delegate to the San Francisco conference, Senator Arthur Vandenburg, wrote in his diary, the U.N. charter was "anything but a wild-eyed internationalist dream of a world state."

The San Francisco conference produced disturbing signs of a growing rift between the Soviet Union and the West. In the lengthy negotiations over the shape of the United Nations, Russia was ranged against its wartime Allies on a number of prickly issues. The American delegation supported the membership application of pro-western Argentina, although it was a Fascist dictatorship that had openly aided Germany throughout the war. The United States won its point over strong Soviet opposition, and succeeded in barring Poland from immediate membership because its government was friendly to the Soviet Union. The decision to locate the U.N. headquarters in New York City not only symbolized America's acceptance of its global responsibilities; it stirred Soviet suspicions that the new institution would become a tool of the West.

In the early years of the United Nations, the Americans were predominant in the General Assembly and other U.N. bodies. A majority of the U.N.'s 51 original member states were supportive of American postwar leadership and formed an effective bloc. Outnumbered by the United States and its U.N. allies and increasingly suspicious of American motives, the Soviets used their veto in the Security Council — 99 times by 1962 — in defence of Soviet interests. During this period, proposals for an international police force to enforce U.N. decisions, the joint occupation of Berlin, and a system of atomic energy-control and inspection all met with stiff Soviet opposition. "The trouble," as Trygve Lie, the U.N.'s first secretary-general put it in 1948, "lies in the intense conflict over the settlement of the last war...between the two most powerful single nations in the world today — the United States and the Soviet Union."

American influence in the United Nations did not last. It probably reached its height in June 1950, when the U.N. Security Council passed an American-sponsored resolution on the Korean crisis while the Soviet delegate boycotted the proceedings, and 32 U.N. member states sent aid to South Korea. American critics of the U.N. grew in number and strength with the spread of anti-communism in the early 1950s. Charges were levelled by prominent Americans, nourished in part by the fervour of Senator Joseph McCarthy's campaign to eradicate communism in America, that the U.N. had become a "nest" for communists working to utterly destroy American democracy. Beginning in 1955, when U.N. membership expanded to include increasing numbers of newly independent African and Asian states, American dominance in the organization steadily declined. In October 1972, the General Assembly voted overwhelmingly to do what the United States had firmly opposed since 1949: admit the People's Republic of China to U.N. membership. Not only did the China vote signify a loss of American influence at the U.N.; it also contributed greatly to a waning of American public support for the U.N. throughout the 1970s. The

United States began to act, as Richard J. Walton of *The New York Times* once observed, "just as Russia did earlier, undercutting the U.N. in both word and deed."

CANADA AND THE NEW AMERICAN EMPIRE

CANADA'S CHANGED and changing relationship with the United States after 1945 owed more to the shift in world power than to Canadian policies. As World War II drew to a close, America emerged as the world's leading imperial power. It was challenged only by its wartime partner, the Soviet Union. This shift in power to the new "free-world colossus" brought policy changes in Ottawa, London, and other western capitals. The dawning of a new age of nuclear deterrence after Hiroshima caused most nations in the West, including Canada, to look to the United States for security.

With the United States and the Soviet Union locked in a bitter ideological struggle, most Canadians came to accept the need for collaboration and accommodation with the strongest defender of the western world. "I would rather," Mackenzie King confessed in 1945, "have Canada kept within the orbit of the British Commonwealth of Nations than to come within that of the United States." But by the spring of 1946, and in light of the Cold War, King concluded that Canada's postwar security required close North American co-operation. "It might be inevitable," he told cabinet colleagues, "for us to have to submit to [sic] being so few in numbers and no longer able to look to British power for protection."

Clement Attlee, Harry Trumon, and Josef Stalin at the Potsdam Conference, July 1945. In the last major conference of World War II, serious divisions between the Allies were apparent when the British and Americans accused the Soviets of imposing communism on the eastern European states liberated by the Soviet Union.

PERCEPTIONS OF THE COLD WAR

In the early years of the Cold War, Canadian policy-makers — with the possible exception of Escott Reid and a handful of liberal-minded external-affairs officials — seemed to share predominant American perceptions of the Soviet communist threat. "The chief menace now,"

Lester B. Pearson declared in 1948, "is subversive aggressive communism, the servant of power politics." There were, in his words, "no fire-proof houses in the atomic age, or little countries far away…whose fate means nothing to us." For Pearson and most of his external-affairs colleagues, the Cold War was at root the "struggle of free, expanding progressive democracy against tyrannical and reactionary communism." Much like key American foreign policy-makers George F. Kennan and U.S. Secretary of State Dean Acheson, they never doubt-ed that the Soviet Union bore prime responsibility for provoking the Cold War and that the proper response lay in the "containment" of that "Soviet pressure against the free institutions of the western world."

In spite of the public show of western solidarity, Prime Minister King and external-affairs officials were at times uneasy about United States power. It was, according to the prime minister, in the interest of Canada, the Commonwealth, and the U.N. that "the United States should have extensive rights and responsibilities outside [its] own territo-ries." Nevertheless, King was "dubious" about the timing and nature of American actions that might "encourage the Soviet government to make undesirable demands." In August 1974, Escott Reid circulated a Department of External Affairs memorandum suggesting that not all Canadian officials shared the prevailing American view of the Cold War. The Soviet Union alone was not "the source of conflict," Reid wrote, since "both the Soviet Union and the United States are expanding powers" and "a firm, patient, and fair-minded policy" was necessary to avoid provoking *the* Soviets into war.

Canadian Cold War perspectives were coloured, in part, by close wartime defence co-oper-ation between Canada and the United States under the Ogdensburg Agreement of 1940 and the Hyde Park Declaration of 1941. While these agreements had safeguarded Canada's security and economic interests, concerns were raised in the early postwar years about long-term dependen-cy on the Americans. One graphic, though perhaps overstated, expression of that fear was Mackenzie King's May 1946 warning to his cabinet that "the long-range policy of the Americans was to absorb Canada" and "to get this hemisphere as completely one as possible." Provoking a confrontation, however, most felt, might imperil the obvious benefits of association with the United States in a threatening postwar world. Canada had become one of America's staunchest allies, as John Holmes so aptly observed, "aligned as it had never been before — with both com-mon and cross purposes — in search of a congenial world order."

THE COLD WAR AND NATO

The Cold War threat was driven home to Canadians in the years 1945–48. The first shock came in September 1945, when Igor Gouzenko, a Soviet cypher clerk, fled the Soviet embassy in Ottawa with evidence of a widespread Soviet spy ring in Canada. Even after the Gouzenko affair, however, Canadians tended to overlook the fact that the Soviet Union — alone among the Great Powers — was not disarming, was retaining its captured territories, and was

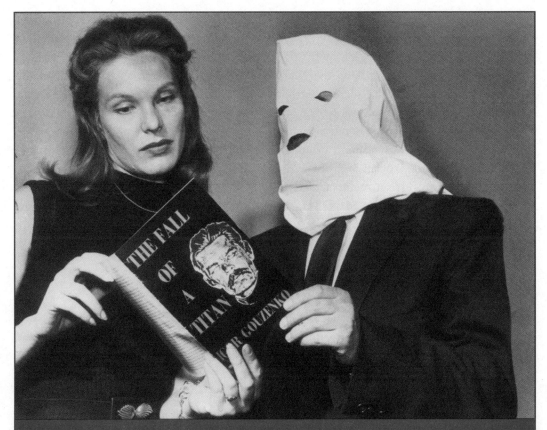

The Igor Gouzenko spy case, 1945. Afraid of a Soviet reprisal, Gouzenko appeared in public wearing a hood to keep his identity secret. His disclosures revealed a large Soviet spy ring, operating in Canada, that was attempting to uncover the secrets of the atomic bomb.

installing friendly governments in the nations of eastern Europe. Most Canadians only really recognized the Cold War threat with the Soviet communist takeover of Czechoslovakia in February 1948 and the Berlin blockade a month later. By late 1950, the Soviet scare had reached such proportions that *Maclean's* could proclaim in bold headlines: "THE REDS ARE READY TO WAGE WAR INSIDE CANADA."

In the face of the escalating Cold War and its threat to a free western Europe, Canada joined with Britain and the United States in founding the North Atlantic Treaty Organization (NATO). Canadian diplomats and politicians were, in fact, among the first to propose the idea of a North Atlantic alliance. They shared St. Laurent's conviction that "totalitarian communist aggression endangers the freedom and peace of every democratic country including Canada." But they also stressed that there was room in the United Nations system for regional associations for collective security, and that these need not be "inconsistent with the ideals of the world organization."

Canada's actual role in making the NATO treaty was largely that of an activist middle power. As participants in the secret three-party talks with the United States and Britain, Canadian diplomats set out the vision of an Atlantic community and urged, unsuccessfully, that France be included in early deliberations as a key European power. In the drafting of the treaty the Canadians succeeded in shaping a multilateral organization linked to U.N. purposes and emphasizing economic, social, and political association as well as military functions. Even though its efforts to restrict membership to the North Atlantic democracies failed, Canada became an important partner in NATO, undertaking a full military commitment to the defence of western Europe. And to offset the close North Atlantic and continental links with Washington, Canadian diplomats began to forge associations through the Commonwealth with India and other states in Asia and Africa.

CANADIAN COLD WAR POLICY: ALTRUISM AND SELF-INTEREST?

While the western powers constructed the North Atlantic alliance, the world was visibly in crisis. In March 1946, Winston Churchill's address at Fulton, Missouri, had given the West a new phrase: the "Iron Curtain." U.S. President Harry Truman had responded to the threat of Soviet communist expansion with the Truman Doctrine of March 1947, pumping massive American military and economic aid into Greece and Turkey. During the Berlin blockade of 1948–49, the Soviet Union's attempt to take control of the entire city (which had been divided into East and West sectors in 1945) was thwarted by a massive Anglo–American airlift.

In the deepening crisis, Canada's response mixed caution with a measure of self-interest. Prime Minister King was shocked and appalled over the 1948 Soviet-sponsored coup in Czechoslovakia, but Canada took no action. Nor would the aging Canadian prime minister, in his final months in office, approve Canadian participation in the Berlin airlift. Instead, Canadian policy-makers pursued economic goals tinged with self-interest. Faced with a critical shortage of Canadian dollars and a worsening financial crisis in the summer of 1947, Ottawa officials sought help through a variety of means, including a sizable U.S. loan, more import restrictions on American-made products, and even economic benefits flowing from Washington's European Recovery Program. The campaign bore fruit when Canada secured a share of offshore procurements under the 1947 Marshall Plan, designed primarily to provide for the postwar rehabilitation of Britain and other European nations. Historian J.L. Granatstein estimated that in the first two years of the plan, Canada gained $1.2 billion (U.S.) through such purchases.[6]

THE TURBULENT 1960s

TOWARD THE END OF THE 1950s, the normally congenial Canadian–American defence relationship entered a period of severe turbulence. In June 1957, the era of Pearsonian diplomacy ended when a new Progressive Conservative government, under John G. Diefenbaker, was elected. In one of its first major acts, the Diefenbaker government in 1958 entered the North American Air Defence (NORAD) system — a common North American arrangement aimed at providing security against the threat of a Soviet bomber attack in the northern hemisphere. But the NORAD agreement left defence issues far from settled. The demands of a revived Cold War, the escalating costs of military hardware, Diefenbaker's conservative nationalist attitude and periodic pressures exerted by the United States on an often reluctant northern neighbour all would contribute to a serious defence débâcle.

A major part of the defence difficulties stemmed from the rocky personal relationship between Prime Minister Diefenbaker and the U.S. president, John F. Kennedy. During Kennedy's visit to Ottawa in 1961, at which the president delivered his famous "Geography has made us neighbours/History has made us friends" address to Parliament, relations deteriorated badly. The private talks were blunt at times, as Kennedy pressed Diefenbaker to join the Organization of American States (OAS) and to increase Canada's foreign aid and NATO contributions. Diefenbaker grew quite incensed when he discovered a Kennedy strategy memo, left inadvertently on a sofa, in which the president was advised to "push" the Canadian prime minister on a series of contentious points. Relations never recovered, as Kennedy began to snub Diefenbaker and the slighted Canadian leader lapsed into a proud but suspicious attitude that smacked of anti-Americanism.

The Kennedys and Diefenbakers together in Ottawa, 1961. A personality clash between the brash, wealthy Ivy-league president and the folksy prime minister spilled over into politics when Kennedy pushed Diefenbaker on defence issues.

CUBA AND THE MISSILE CRISIS

The Cuban missile crisis of October 1962 brought relations between Kennedy and Diefenbaker to the breaking point. Washington viewed Castro's Cuba as a threatening "revolutionary communist regime" and had supported an abortive invasion of Cuba at the Bay of Pigs in April 1961. On the other hand, Ottawa adopted a more flexible and dispassionate position, and maintained normal trade and diplomatic relations with the Castro regime.

Like Britain and other NATO members, Canada was caught by surprise when the Cuban missile crisis occurred in October 1962. President Kennedy sent a special envoy to Ottawa with evidence that the Soviets had secretly installed offensive nuclear weapons in Cuba. Diefenbaker and his defence minister, Douglas Harkness, were briefed on the crisis and informed of the president's plans to place the island of Cuba under a naval quarantine or blockade, just two hours before the president's televised address to the American people. But, during the five critical days when the world teetered on the brink of nuclear annihilation, the prime minister reacted in a curious fashion. At first Diefenbaker called for a United Nations–sponsored mission to Cuba to find out the facts; then he hesitated and delayed putting NORAD forces on alert. Even though the crisis quickly dissolved when Soviet chairman Nikita Khrushchev agreed to withdraw the missiles, the damage had been done. The Americans were angry at the discomforting political delays, and the Canadian public turned decisively against Diefenbaker for his indecision and stubbornness in a time of world crisis.

THE NUCLEAR WARHEADS CONTROVERSY

The Cuban missile crisis made a real impact on Canada and Canadians. Opponents of nuclear weapons claimed that the episode demonstrated the horrible dangers of Cold War confrontation and the need for nuclear disarmament. Nationalists, like political philosopher George Grant, drew some satisfaction from Diefenbaker's assertion of independence at a moment of crisis. The majority of the Canadian public, usually indifferent about defence questions, felt a deep disquiet. And Diefenbaker and his government were forced to clarify their fuzzy position on nuclear weapons for Canada.

The Diefenbaker government's decision to take the American-made Bomarc anti-aircraft missile in September 1958, and its 1959 cancellation of the project to develop the Avro Arrow, an all-Canadian supersonic fighter plane, seemed to indicate that Canada intended to acquire nuclear warheads for its armed forces. Yet Diefenbaker and his minister of external affairs, Howard Green, were very hesitant to accept them, fearing a public outcry if they turned Canada "nuclear" while promoting disarmament at the United Nations. Both the Liberal party, led by Lester Pearson, and the New Democratic Party (NDP), formed in 1961, were on record as opposing the acquisition of nuclear weapons.

"TO THE BRINK": KENNEDY, DIEFENBAKER, AND THE CUBAN MISSILE CRISIS

IN OCTOBER 1962, American U-2 reconnaissance planes photographed Soviet missile sites in Cuba. The Cuban missile crisis developed into the world's most dangerous
Cold War confrontation, bringing the world close to the brink of destruction. After the
imposition of an American naval quarantine of Cuba, a dramatic television address by
President John F. Kennedy, and a hasty exchange of letters between Kennedy and Soviet
Premier Nikita Khrushchev, a settlement was reached: the Soviet Union pledged to
withdraw its missiles from Cuba and, in return, the United States pledged never again
to invade the island of Cuba.

In the immediate aftermath of the Cuban missile crisis, President Kennedy was
hailed as a brilliant and decisive leader of the western world, who had taught the Soviets
a lesson. Since that time questions have been raised about Kennedy's risk-taking in the
crisis. Some harsh American critics claim that the U.S. response embodied a policy of
"brinkmanship," which amounted to playing a "reckless game of nuclear chicken."

American intelligence photos of Soviet missile sites in Cuba. In 1962,
Fidel Castro's Cuban government became convinced that the United States
was planning an invasion, so it asked the Soviet Union for military aid.
The USSR responded by sending nuclear missiles.

President Kennedy and Canada's prime minister John Diefenbaker did not see eye-to-eye on the Cuban missile crisis. Explain how — and why — each leader saw the crisis differently.

PRESIDENT JOHN F. KENNEDY, TELEVISION ADDRESS, 1962

This government, as promised, has maintained the closest surveillance of the Soviet military buildup on the island of Cuba. Within the past week unmistakable evidence has established the fact that a series of offensive missile sites is now in preparation on that imprisoned island. The purpose of these bases can be none other than to provide a nuclear strike capability against the Western Hemisphere....

[T]his secret, swift, and extraordinary buildup of Communist missiles — in an area well known to have a special and historical relationship to the United States and the nations of the Western Hemisphere, in violation of Soviet assurances, and in defiance of American and hemispheric policy — this sudden, clandestine decision to station strategic weapons for the first time outside of Soviet soil — is a deliberately provocative and unjustified change in the *status quo* which cannot be accepted by this country if our courage and our commitments are ever to be trusted again by either friend or foe....

...I call upon Chairman Khrushchev to halt and eliminate this clandestine, reckless, and provocative threat to world peace and to stable relations between our two nations. I call upon him further to abandon this course of world domination and to join in an historic effort to end the perilous arms race and transform the history of man. He has an opportunity now to move the world back from the abyss of destruction — by returning to his government's own words that it had no need to station missiles outside its own territory, and withdrawing these weapons from Cuba — by refraining from any action which will widen or deepen the present crisis — and then by participating in a search for peaceful and permanent solutions.

John F. Kennedy, television address, October 22, 1962.

PRIME MINISTER JOHN DIEFENBAKER, MEMOIRS, 1977

I knew that President Kennedy was still smarting over the 1961 Bay of Pigs fiasco, especially over the charges that he had callously allowed the anti-Castro forces to be sacrificed by failing to provide the umbrella support from the air they had expected. I knew also that the president thought he had something to prove in his personal dealings with Khrushchev after their unpleasant Vienna meeting, where Khrushchev had treated him like a child, referring to him as "the boy." I considered that he was perfectly capable of taking the world to the brink of thermonuclear destruction to prove himself the man for our times, a courageous champion of Western democracy.

> Canada certainly had the right to expect notice longer than two hours, if military measures were to be involved. NORAD had worked out, since 1957–58, agreed secret procedures for consultation to be invoked when a threat to North American security was perceived. It was obvious that Canada was not to be consulted but was expected to accept without question the course to be determined by the President. The partnership in continental defence that my government had worked out with the Eisenhower administration could not long survive the strains imposed upon it by President Kennedy.
>
> John Diefenbaker, *One Canada, vol. 3: The Tumultuous Years, 1962 to 1967* (Scarborough: Macmillan/Signet, 1977), pp. 69–70.

The defence controversy reached a head early in 1963. Pressures from within the Liberal party caused Pearson to begin to modify his opposition to nuclear warheads. Pearson was further influenced by reports brought to the Liberal caucus from NATO command in Europe, claiming that Canada's failure to meet its commitments could endanger the alliance and the nation's place in it. But before he could announce a change in Liberal policy, the retiring supreme commander of NATO, General Lauris Norstad, stated flatly at a press conference in Ottawa that NATO was "counting on Canada to produce some of the tactical atomic strike force." Nine days later, Pearson announced that the Liberal opposition was now pledged to "discharge fully commitments" to accept nuclear warheads. With the Liberal reversal, the defence question became a straight Conservative–Liberal political dogfight. Diefenbaker's cabinet was badly split on the nuclear weapons question; and when the minister of national defence, Douglas Harkness, resigned, Diefenbaker's government fell in the House of Commons. In the ensuing 1963 general election, Pearson's Liberals — with the tacit support of the Kennedy administration — were elected as a minority government, and within months the government had installed the nuclear warheads.

CANADA, THE UNITED STATES, AND THE VIETNAM WAR

The foreign-policy question that dwarfed all others from the mid-1960s to the early 1970s was the United States' intervention in Vietnam. This bloody and futile conflict in Asia not only created tensions between Ottawa and Washington, it also fostered anti-war movements in both countries, and contributed much to the social revolution of the late 1960s.

Canada's involvement in Vietnam actually predated that of the Americans. In 1954, at the request of the Great Powers, the St. Laurent government had sent a team of diplomats and military officers to form with Poland and India an international control commission (ICC) at the end of the France–Indochina war. The ICC had the thankless task of separating the combatants, supervising the truce, and returning war refugees to their homes. Canada was appointed to the ICC as the representative of "the West," and as such was often compelled to uphold American interests in the region. The United States sent military advisers into South Vietnam in the late 1950s and then launched a full-scale military intervention. Canadian policy-makers in the Department of External Affairs were divided over the Indochina problem, and Canada alternated between attempts at mediation and vigorous defences of the American role in resisting communist aggression. Although Canadians in Vietnam and politicians in Ottawa, from Diefenbaker to Trudeau, generally shared the American perception of the communist threat in Vietnam, the nation's ICC obligations compelled Canada to be as impartial as possible. But since Ottawa sent to Washington information gathered by Canadians on the ICC in Vietnam, the whole mediation enterprise was a mockery, according to some critics.

After the Lyndon B. Johnson administration launched a massive escalation of U.S. military involvement in Vietnam in the mid-1960s, growing numbers of Americans and Canadians began to have grave doubts about the wisdom of U.S. policy and the legitimacy of the American presence in South Vietnam. Criticism mounted in the Canadian public and press over

American protesters in the 1960s opposing the Vietnam War in front of the United Nations Plaza.

The Camp David meeting, April 1965. Upon hearing of Lester Pearson's call to halt U.S. air strikes in Vietnam, Lyndon Johnson gave Pearson a "severe talking to" that included a remarkable nose-to-nose harangue. Pearson, always the diplomat, managed to calm Johnson and the two parted in a mood of "geniality."

Johnson's war and Canada's official complicity, especially after the United States began the large-scale bombing of North Vietnam in the spring of 1964. Finally, Pearson broke his usual diplomatic propriety. In an address at Temple University in Philadelphia in April 1965, the prime minister called for a "suspension" of air strikes against North Vietnam in the hope of prompting a resumption of serious peace talks. This statement led to a remarkable private clash between Pearson and Johnson at the president's Camp David retreat, one that was quickly smoothed over by both sides.

Pearson's breach of North American diplomatic harmony would not be repeated. In June 1965, *Canada and the United States: Principles for Partnership*, a report prepared by Livingston Merchant, a senior U.S. diplomat, and Arnold Heeney, a distinguished Canadian civil servant and diplomat, was released. In the conduct of Canada–U.S. relations, the report recommended "quiet diplomacy," a policy of solidarity in public, and the settlement of disagreements in private, between friends. The practice of quiet diplomacy, the report reaffirmed, was "not only neighbourly and convenient to the United States, but is in fact more effective than the alternative of raising a row and being unpleasant in public." From that time forward, most Canadian prime ministers have used quiet diplomacy when dealing with Washington.

THE DANGERS OF COMPLICITY

The Canadian dilemma over Vietnam was graphically illustrated in the last phase of the Vietnam conflict. In January 1973, the United States administration of Richard Nixon asked Canada to serve on a reconstituted international commission for supervision and control in Vietnam. Having urged the Americans to seek a peace settlement and to withdraw from Indochina, Ottawa could hardly refuse to participate in an operation designed to facilitate what Richard Nixon and his secretary of state Henry Kissinger called "peace with honour." The Trudeau government accepted the assignment — conditional on the operation's effectiveness. When the Canadian observers reported the blatant refusal of both the North and South Vietnamese forces to stop fighting, Trudeau mused aloud that the Vietnam peace was war pervading under "the sham of some truce agreement." Shortly after, in July 1973, the government withdrew the Canadian contingent. For Canada in Indochina, the attempt to perform, simultaneously, two virtually incompatible roles — that of impartial international mediator and upholder of United States' interests — had proven futile. It was a sobering episode in Canada's postwar efforts to shape a more peaceful world order.

ACTIVITIES

KEY TERMS AND CONCEPTS

Identify and briefly explain the historical significance of each of the following terms and concepts:

- Total war
- "Linchpin" role
- Social-security state
- Family allowances
- "New social order"
- Middle power
- Liberal internationalism
- U.N. peacekeeping
- Cold War
- Containment
- Igor Gouzenko affair
- "Iron Curtain"
- Kennedy "Push" memorandum (1961)
- Quiet diplomacy
- Complicity in Vietnam

QUESTIONS FOR DISCUSSION

1. The two North American nations were "big
   and little brothers-in-arms" during World War
   II, according to John Herd Thompson and
   Stephen J. Randall in *Canada and the United
   States: Ambivalent Allies* (Montreal and
   Kingston: McGill–Queen's University Press,
   1994). Why do the two historians use this
   metaphor? How valid is their assessment?
2. "The United States and Canada, of all the
   major belligerents in World War II, gained the
   most — and lost the least — from the global
   conflict." Discuss this contention.
3. What led Mackenzie King to embrace the "new
   social order" program in 1944–45? Did King's
   postwar reconstruction policies constitute a
   cohesive, coherent program? To what extent
   were they inspired by New Deal liberalism?

4. Why was the United Nations organization
   formed at the end of World War II? In what
   ways did American and Canadian policy-makers differ in their approach to shaping the
   postwar order?
5. How did American and Canadian policy-makers view the Cold War in its early years? Were
   there any significant differences in their perceptions of the East–West struggle?
6. Why did Canada and the United States
   become embroiled in a series of defence
   crises in the 1960s? What lessons did
   Canadians learn from their "push and shove"
   relations with Washington?

ASSESSING HISTORICAL INTERPRETATIONS

Study the following viewpoints on aspects of postwar Canadian and American foreign policy.
Evaluate and assess the validity of each interpretation, based on your own reading of the evidence.

1. The Shaping of the Postwar World Order

"It can be said of Canadians as of Americans…that
their new international activity was the result more
of responding to a need than of thrusting themselves
forward as world salvationists in accordance with pre-
conceived notions of national mission. The precarious
state of the world after 1945 required the forceful
intervention in the far corners of a benevolent great
power like the United States. It turned out also that
the preservation of order often enough required the
services of middle powers whose principal value was
their very incapacity to threaten or command.
Canada was no longer reluctant to be useful…."

— John W. Holmes, "Canadian External Policies Since
1945," *International Journal* 18 (1963):138. Published by
the Canadian Institute of International Affairs.

"[At the close of World War II] the United States did not wish to repair the prewar world economy, but to construct it anew....

"...American national interests became the foundations of the United States' concept of international welfare. Implicit in America's activity for the United Nations was its belief that it could organize the United Nations with American interests foremost in mind, and that the rest of the world would gladly welcome the world organization as part of an American-led century that would redound to the universal weal...."

— Gabriel Kolko, *The Politics of War* (New York: Random House/Vintage, 1968), pp. 245 and 279.

"Canada entered the Cold War alliance against the Soviet Union not just as a pawn of the United States...but with its own calculations of interest in mind. [Canadian policy-makers]...used...the vague appeal to collective security...as a means not only of deterring aggression but also, somehow, of reining in the wilfulness of Canada's dynamic neighbour."

— Denis Smith, *The Diplomacy of Fear: Canada and the Cold War, 1941–1948* (Toronto: University of Toronto Press, 1988).

2. Canadian and American Roles in the United Nations

"[In the early years] of the cold war and the U.N.'s history, the U.N. did whatever the U.S. decided for, with the exception of a handful of Communist countries and a few neutrals, the U.N. consisted almost entirely of American allies and dependencies who followed Washington's directions almost without question....

"The U.S....seems to be determined to act now just as Russia did earlier, undercutting the U.N. in both word and deed."

— Richard J. Walton, *The New York Times*, May 29, 1972, p. 17.

"In the absence of the consensus on which a strong United Nations authority could rest, the United States has become at times a kind of surrogate United Nations. It is only fair to recognize that it has done so partly out of moral arrogance but to a large extent because we have wanted it to throw its weight around, both its resources and its diplomacy. This asymmetry may not make for a healthy international system, but it is certainly better than one in which the United States again refused to accept the responsibility of power."

— John W. Holmes, *The Shaping of Peace, vol. 1: 1948–1957* (Toronto: University of Toronto Press, 1979), p. 307.

"The Cold War strained Canada's commitment to multilateralism.... A number of factors had changed. For one, the Cold War intensified pressure for bloc solidarity, and in the United Nations vetoes prevented what the superpowers would not accept. In addition, Canada no longer held such a lofty status in the global community. The gradual revival of the European powers pushed Canada ever more firmly into middle power status.... Finally, the emergence of dozens of newly independent states changed the U.N. forever as new members brought new priorities onto the agenda of the General Assembly."

— Tom Keating, *Canada and World Order: The Multilateralist Tradition in Canadian Foreign Policy* (Toronto: McClelland and Stewart, 1993), p.119. Used by permission of the Canadian Publisher, McClelland and Stewart, Toronto.

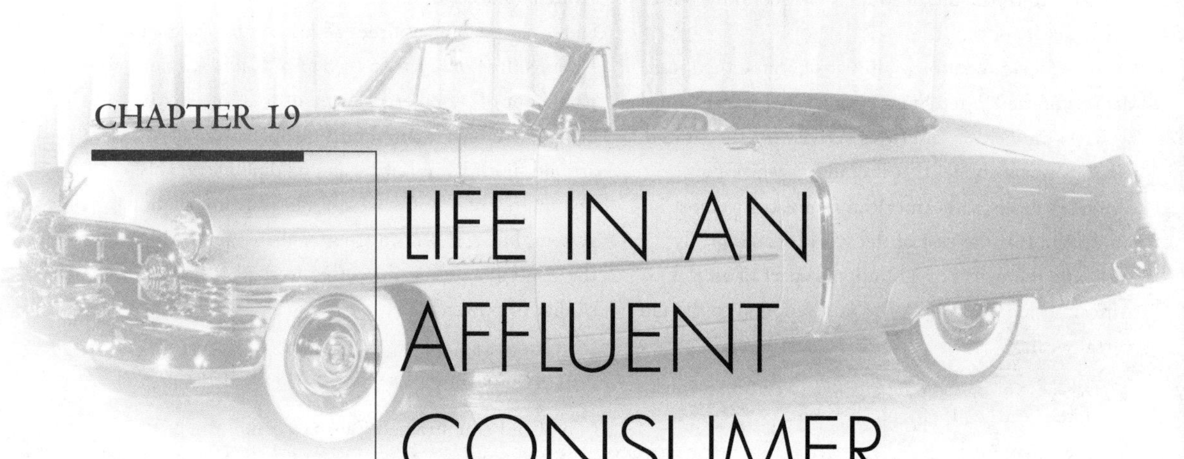

CHAPTER 19

LIFE IN AN AFFLUENT CONSUMER SOCIETY

THE "BOOMING FIFTIES"

THE "GOOD LIFE" AND SUBURBIA

CHALLENGING THE CONSENSUS: SOCIAL
CRITICISM IN THE 1950s

THE IMPACT AND STRAINS OF AFFLUENCE

IN THE DECADES FOLLOWING WORLD WAR II, North American society for the first time experienced the joys and strains of a lasting prosperity. Postwar reconstruction, enhanced by a fresh infusion of consumer spending, banished any threat of a return to depression. After a brief downturn in 1945–46, industrial production in both Canada and the United States soon climbed past its wartime peak levels. In most regions of Canada, the postwar economic boom was astonishing. Veterans and former munitions workers found work in peacetime factories and offices. Supplies of Alberta oil and natural gas, Canadian Shield zinc and copper, Labrador iron ore, and British Columbia coal and lumber found ready markets in the United States as well as industrialized central Canada. With secure employment and decent wages, many Canadians clamoured for the fruits of prosperity: suburban homes, shiny automobiles, furniture, and home appliances that had been beyond their reach or unavailable until now.[1]

Life in postwar Canada, like that in the United States, moved forward amid a new set of Cold War tensions. Yet Canadians and Americans had reason to be content with the remarkable economic growth and affluence of these years. By the 1950s, signs of this economic abundance were visible almost everywhere. Millions of postwar immigrants came to North America to share in the unrivalled opportunities. Cities and suburbs expanded, with new housing developments, urban expressways, and shopping

The suburban dream, 1950–51.

plazas. It was a time that saw the discovery of North American youth, as teenagers took up "rock 'n' roll" and parents fretted about its possible effects. Of all the social changes, none was more important than the spread of television. Not only did TV promote an image of North American prosperity that transcended any cultural or language barriers, it also practically supplanted the school and the family as the transmitter of cultural styles and values.

The advent of affluence and North American consumerism did, however, produce some disquiet. Postwar Canadian prosperity owed much to infusions of billions of dollars of American investment and, as early as 1956, questions were raised about the economic and political consequences of such continental integration. The excesses of economic abundance and materialism also bred disillusionment and even an undercurrent of insistent social criticism. Beneath the veneer of North American affluence, critics pointed out glaring class inequities, instances of commercial manipulation, and signs of youthful rebellion against conformity. All was not completely well in postwar society.

THE "BOOMING FIFTIES"

STATISTICS TELL THE STORY of the postwar economic boom: during the 1950s, Canada's gross national product (GNP) doubled — from $18.4 billion to $36.8 billion — and the American GNP rose 57 percent, reaching $600 billion in 1960. The middle class in both Canada and the United States swelled, and the comfortably-off were transformed from a minority to a majority of the population. In Canada, the average weekly industrial wage — which stood at $45.08 in 1950 — grew almost 75 percent to $73.47 by the decade's end, and little of that increase was attributable to inflation. During the 1950s, Canadians purchased 3.5 million passenger cars, built over 1.1 million new housing units (mostly suburban homes with big lawns and picture windows), and produced more babies (4.3 million) than in any previous decade. In the booming 1950s, as writer Alexander Ross observed, "we learned to live with bigness."[2]

The 1950s boom also extended to Canada's resource hinterlands. Canada produced half the world's newsprint, most destined for U.S. markets, and by 1960 it produced $1.5 billion worth of pulp and paper products each year. With the opening of

Shopping in a Winnipeg department store, 1957 — a favoured leisure-time activity in the affluent consumer society.

new producing oil fields in Alberta after 1947, crude oil production increased five times in volume during the decade. Iron ore production grew dramatically, owing to the development of vast deposits in Labrador and northern Quebec. Canada moved from being a net importer of iron in 1950 to being one of the world's great iron exporters in 1960. Giant mineral producers like the Aluminum Company of Canada and the International Nickel Company experienced sustained growth. Planning for Canada's first atomic-power station began in 1955, and a year later Canada became a leading producer in the highly unstable world market for uranium.[3]

One great exception to the unprecedented growth of the 1950s was agriculture, which until then had been the mainstay of the Canadian economy. The value of agricultural production in Canada in 1960 was $1.7 billion, the same as it had been in 1950, and the number of people employed in farming actually declined. This pattern was repeated in the United States, where farmers left for the cities in droves: America's farm population dropped by nearly 9 million people. A surprising number of people in rural areas were reduced to relative poverty or even to subsistence level, as in the case of Amerindians. The 1950s brought an end to the predominance of the small mixed farm, the ploughhorse, and the hand-stooked wheat in the fields, all familiar sights during the war years. In spite of this, total Canadian farm production increased during the 1950s. Bumper wheat crops recorded early in the decade were over four times larger than those of the first great wheat boom before 1914. Agriculture, like most other industries, was becoming highly mechanized and automated, and the great demand for farm implements increased the postwar boom in manufacturing.

AMERICAN DOLLARS, CANADIAN PROSPERITY

Canada's postwar prosperity depended heavily on the United States. Industrialization increased Canadian demand for foreign capital, entrepreneurship, specialized products, and raw materials not available at home. While the postwar world was eager to obtain Canadian goods and materials, few countries could afford to purchase them amid the difficulties of postwar reconstruction. Canada found itself selling on credit to Britain and other foreign buyers, and paying for needed imports in American dollars. By 1947, Canada faced a severe "dollar crisis."[4] The country's postwar reserve of $1.5 billion in U.S. currency had dropped to only $500 million and was rapidly dwindling. The crisis passed, but only after the federal Department of Finance imposed foreign-exchange controls and banned non-essential imports such as U.S.-produced fresh vegetables.

The United States' postwar reconstruction and its rearmament to meet the Cold War threat combined to channel millions of investment dollars into Canada. In 1948 Congress, as part of the Marshall Plan for European economic recovery, renewed for Canada most of the advantages of continental economic co-operation earlier established under the 1941 Hyde Park agreement. For American strategic planners and industrialists, Canada became the favoured place for capital investment and the safest, closest source of minerals, ranging from iron ore to nickel to uranium, essential to building up U.S. stockpiles in case of a conflict with the Soviet Union.

"PEOPLE OF PLENTY": AMERICAN IDEALS AND REALITY IN THE 1950s

IN THE SUMMER OF 1950, American historian David M. Potter wrote six lectures on the influence of "economic abundance" on the American character. The result was *People of Plenty* (1954), one of the most important and revealing books about America in the 1950s. Potter contended that material abundance — the product of "human ingenuity, human initiative, human adaptability, and human enterprise" — had shaped the American character. Potter saw little evidence of inequality; the word poverty did not even appear in his index. One remarkable passage in Potter's book seemed to capture the pervasive "American consensus" view in the 1950s:

> [I]n every aspect of material plenty America possesses unprecedented riches and…these are widely distributed among one hundred and fifty million American people. If few can cite the figures, everyone knows that we have, per capita, more automobiles, more telephones, more radios, more vacuum cleaners, more electric lights, more bathtubs, more supermarkets and movie palaces and hospitals, than any other nation. Even at mid-century prices we can afford college educations and T-bone steaks for a far higher proportion of our people than receive them anywhere else on the globe.

A similar image of America was promoted by the United States Information Agency, the international propaganda arm of the U.S. government. Idealized versions of American life were important weapons in the Cold War against Soviet communism.

Not every American accepted the popular and idealized image of American society in the 1950s. In *The Affluent Society* (1958), the Canadian-born Harvard University economist John Kenneth Galbraith claimed that poverty persisted in pockets of the United States even in a time of unparalleled prosperity. There was, he argued, a serious "imbalance" in the priority America assigned to "private goods" as compared with "public goods." Too much of America's resources and energies were being spent on opulent private consumption — expensive cars, TVs, and other products; too little on public expenditures to alleviate the "poverty of our schools," the "unloveliness and congestion of our cities," and the potential for "social disorder" associated with economic inequalities. The imbalance should be corrected if all Americans were to share in society's abundance.

GROWING ECONOMIC INTEGRATION

Good economic times brought talk of free trade with the United States. A group of Canadian economists and civil servants, led by John Deutsch, argued that lifting tariffs between Canada and the United States would yield even greater prosperity. While Prime Minister King approached free trade with caution, a number of his senior cabinet members endorsed Deutsch's 1948 plan for Canada–U.S. free trade. Mindful of the lessons of the 1911 reciprocity debate and the growing threat of American domination, King finally scotched the project during his final days in office.

Despite the shelving of free trade, Canadian–American economic integration continued. Tariff barriers gradually began to dissolve when Canada signed the 1949 General Agreement on Tariffs and Trade (GATT), an attempt by the western nations to remove trade barriers blamed for causing the Great Depression. Between 1945 and 1955, U.S. capital in Canada doubled from $4.9 billion to $10.3 billion, while direct investment in plant and equipment tripled.[5] With iron ore deposits almost exhausted in Wisconsin's Mesabi Range, U.S. steel producers looked northward with their capital and engineering know-how. And between 1951 and 1954, American capital financed the Quebec, North Shore and Labrador railway, constructed north from Sept-Îles on the St. Lawrence, through the rugged Precambrian Shield, to the boom town of Schefferville, 576 km away, in the heart of Labrador iron ore country.

JOINT CANADA–U.S. PROJECTS

The most ambitious project of Canada–U.S. co-operation in the early 1950s was the St. Lawrence Seaway. The seaway project had advantages for both Canada and the United States: it would permit large ocean-going vessels to travel the Great Lakes, thus providing a transportation route for expanded international as well as intercontinental trade; it would allow Labrador ore to be shipped to the steel furnaces of the Midwest; and it held out the promise of related hydroelectric power projects. Long the subject of international discussion, the seaway was made a top priority of the Louis St. Laurent government in 1951. Initial American reluctance to

The St. Lawrence Seaway. Ocean-going freighters can travel to the heart of industrial North America.

proceed was overcome when Canada threatened to build it entirely in Canadian territory and Ohio steel interests applied pressure in Washington. A treaty was signed in 1954, and construction of the seaway was completed in 1959. The massive $460 million project was a monument to international co-operation, although it generated much less traffic than its promoters had forecast.

Another grand project, a trans-Canada gas pipeline, was also started in the early 1950s. It was proposed by C.D. Howe to bring Alberta's natural gas straight to the main Canadian market, southern Ontario. No single company was capable of undertaking the project by itself, so Howe helped organize Trans-Canada Pipelines Limited and turned to Texas developers for capital and expertise. The 1956 pipeline project aroused a storm of controversy in Parliament, with both the Conservatives and the CCF favouring an all-Canadian company. However, most Canadians in the 1950s welcomed investment whatever its source, and in the spring of 1956, Howe and the Liberal government rammed the pipeline bill through Parliament, using closure. By October 1958, the 3700 km gas pipeline had been quietly and profitably completed, from Burstall, Saskatchewan, to Montreal.

THE "GOOD LIFE" AND SUBURBIA

THE ECONOMIC BUOYANCY OF THE 1950s was reflected in the public mood and popular trends. It was the age of the North American "baby boom," which started as soon as World War II had ended.[6] With the growth of the suburbs and the new availability of housing, with the new family allowance payments, and with savings accumulated during wartime, young Canadian couples decided to have families — and larger families than the previous generation. In Canada the birth rate reached its peak in 1959, when one out of every five women in their twenties had babies. As increasing numbers of women chose to marry and raise a family, female participation in the workforce declined. While in 1943 women had made up 31.4 percent of the labour force, ten years later the figure was 23.4 percent.

After a decade of economic depression and the years of wartime austerity, Canadians as well as Americans sought a taste of "the good life." People were living in an affluent, consumer society for perhaps the first time since the 1920s, and consumerism injected something new into Canadian life. Fads, sports, and entertainment, ranging from hula hoops to curling to rock 'n' roll, became popular. Teenagers, who had once been regarded as "young adults," emerged during the 1950s as a major social force. Their fads, their affluent lifestyles, and fun-loving innocence seemed to typify the "fabulous fifties."

Of all the agents of the consumer revolution, none was more powerful than television. In the early 1950s, the first television sets spread from the United States into Canada. Several hundred thousand Canadians living within range of American stations already owned sets by the time the Canadian Broadcasting Corporation (CBC) introduced its service in 1952. Before the end of the decade, the new medium had revolutionized North American life more profoundly than any invention since the mass-produced automobile. Family life, eating habits, house designs, conversation, humour, political attitudes — all were influenced by television. Canadian TV watchers showed a strong devotion to "Hockey Night in Canada," which featured the Saturday night games of the Toronto Maple Leafs and the Montreal Canadiens. But American advertising and cheap, imported shows like "I Love Lucy," "The Honeymooners," and "The Howdy Doody Show" dominated the airwaves. Despite the dire predictions of its critics, the "idiot box" did not turn people into passive vegetables or debase mass tastes. In fact, the TV age also witnessed a kind of cultural and educational boom in parts of Canada and the United States.

A family "glued to the set." Living rooms and much of social life were dominated by TV in the 1950s. Television, the ads proclaimed, kept the family together. The scene is a living room in Saskatchewan, 1952.

THE SUBURBAN SOCIETY

The most distinctive urban development in North America at mid-century was the expansion of new residential areas known as suburbs. In the United States, while the population of central cities grew by 11 percent — from 54 to 60 million people — suburbs rose in population by 46 percent — from 41 to 60 million. Between 1950 and 1960, fourteen of America's fifteen largest cities experienced a population decline even as their suburbs underwent a population boom, especially New York City, Chicago, Detroit, and Cleveland. Suburban development did not simply involve a steady continuous outward spreading of urban residential areas, but the rush of millions of North Americans to subdivisions in generally outlying areas.[7]

Between 1946 and 1954, a quarter of a million Canadian families joined the mass movement to the suburbs. Toronto grew fastest of all, even faster than America's leading boom cities of the 1950s, Houston and Los Angeles. In the first half of the decade, Toronto and its surrounding areas grew by at least 50 000 people per year, and the Bell Telephone Company claimed to have installed 160 000 telephones, yet still had a waiting list. Many of the new suburbs were designed to be "planned communities," modelled after America's first such suburb, Levittown, Long Island. In Vancouver's Fraserview, in Winnipeg's Wildwood, and in Toronto's Don Mills, developers laid out houses in self-contained neighbourhoods clustered around schools and shopping plazas. These model communities for the "better-off" middle class promised the ultimate in comfortable living, complete with neat bungalow, picture window, large front lawn, and streets safe for children.

The experience of Toronto in the 1950s was indicative of the process of suburban development in Canada. Between 1941 and 1961, while the population of the City of Toronto proper grew only slightly from 667 000 to 672 000, that of its twelve surrounding municipalities jumped from 243 000 to 946 000. Of that huge increase, 82 percent occurred in the three

Levittown. An aerial view of one of the first American planned suburban housing subdivisions, named after the pioneer developer, William Levitt. A standard Cape Cod house, with a living room, a kitchen, two bedrooms, and an expansion attic, sold for only $7990!

outer municipalities of Etobicoke, North York, and Scarborough. Beyond these townships, in areas stretching out 40 km or more from the city proper, the growth in population was even more striking. By the end of the 1950s, small towns outside Toronto, such as Port Credit, Brampton, Richmond Hill, and Markham, were being transformed into centres of urban population with new subdivisions. It was estimated that at least one person out of every four in the Toronto urban vicinity at the end of the 1950s lived in a residential area not more than five years old, in what was once rural countryside.

Why did young North Americans flock to the suburbs? Some suburbanites may have been resisting city life and unconsciously seeking a sense of community in suburban enclaves like Park Forest, Illinois, or Toronto's Don Mills. Many claimed to be escaping from urban problems, from what one American subdivision ad called "cities too big, too polluted, too crowded, too strident to call home." When asked their reasons for moving, most suburbanites mentioned the joys of home ownership and the "need for more space." For four out of five families who moved to Levittown, Long Island, in the years 1958–60, the principal reason was simply to obtain a house at an affordable price. Often the realities proved much harsher. First-time home-buyers endured muddy roads, faulty fixtures, green lumber, and the tricks of "fly-by-night" builders and contractors.

THE "CHROME BOAT" AND THE SUBURBS

Suburban life was all but impossible without cars and paved roads. Many families looked to the purchase of that first, used car as the beginning of their flight from the older, overcrowded urban districts. Following World War II, the North American automobile industry responded to this new demand: General Motors, Chrysler, Ford, and American Motors offered consumers a new range of "chrome boats," enormous cars with V-8 engines, chrome trim, and gigantic rear fins. As the industry became increasingly dominated by the Big Four automakers, the range of prices narrowed. Between 1945 and 1952, passenger car registrations in Canada doubled, and then doubled again by 1962. The 39 600 km of paved roads had expanded to 112 000 km by 1960. In the United States, the pattern was similar. By 1960, nearly 9 out of 10 American suburban families owned a car (compared with 6 out of 10 urban families), and it was estimated that two-thirds of all employed Americans drove to work each day in an automobile.

Governments — state or provincial, and local as well as federal — built new roads, widened old ones, and constructed highways to accommodate the tremendous increase in automobile traffic. The U.S. Interstate Highway Act was passed in 1956, pouring $100 billion into the construction of a cross-country express highway network. Seven years earlier, Canada had launched its own Trans-Canada Highway, albeit on a much more limited scale. Because of the postwar affluence, many Canadians and Americans now enjoyed paid holidays and summer vacations, which were considered a luxury before the war. Tourism flourished as motor trips to central Ontario "cottage country," the Rockies, the East Coast, or New England's Cape Cod became popular.

"HOME DREAMS": WOMEN IN SUBURBIA, 1945–1960*

IN THE POSTWAR YEARS, residential suburbs sprang up in Canada and the United States and served as "bedroom communities" to the market-oriented, male-dominated world of modern cities. The expanding tracts of new housing subdivisions reflected not only economic and technological trends, but also a gendered landscape. Women and men had long moved in somewhat different worlds; the new suburbs simply reinforced this separation of the sexes. Here women were expected to tend to home and family, while men assumed the role of "breadwinner" and most positions of community leadership.

The rise of suburbia in North America has generally been explained by economic factors such as business expansion, gas and oil discoveries, and the increased use of private automobiles. It has also been linked to the political conservatism, racism, and the "domestication" of women in the 1950s. While postwar suburban development in North America did demonstrate common characteristics, Canadian analysts have identified some marked differences in the suburban experience north of the border.

How did community life in postwar Canada differ? Canada's major cities from Halifax to Montreal and Toronto to Vancouver did not exemplify the stark racial divisions found in American cities and consequently never really lost their attraction for citizens of all classes. Fleeing from urban dangers and decay was not as common in Canada, so Canadian suburbs did not evolve as exclusively white, middle-class housing enclaves. Canadian suburbs, in fact, were composed of not only middle-class WASPs (White Anglo-Saxon Protestants), but also war veterans, industrial workers, rural emigrants, and "new Canadians." Regional variations are also apparent in the rate and ethno-cultural composition of suburban development, distinguishing the experience of Montreal from Toronto and Halifax from

A Domestic Tragedy — "Cake Failure," 1955. The stereotypical American housewife of the 1950s was expected to stay at home and to greet her husband after work with a kiss and the aroma of fresh baked goods.

---

* A capsule summary of Veronica Strong-Boag, "Home Dreams: Women and the Suburban Experiment in Canada, 1945–60," *Canadian Historical Review* 72 (December 1991): 471–504.

Winnipeg, Edmonton, or Vancouver. Facing these differing sets of experiences, Canadian women in suburbia were not mere reflections of American suburbanites.

Betty Friedan's book *The Feminine Mystique* (1963) offered a searing critique of the gendered experience of North American suburbia, a world of limited options that consigned women to subordination, frustration, and ultimately unhappiness. The image projected of suburban women was that of the white, middle-class "housewife" bored with a life of cleaning, floor waxing, shopping, and neighbourhood "coffee klatches." Yet this image may be misleading, for it ignored the fact that many suburban women literally "ruled the roost" and it underestimated the complexity of women's lives.

Many Canadian suburban women firmly rejected the conformist "housewife" stereotype. In 1959, for example, a *Chatelaine* article critical of suburban women prompted an avalanche of 300 letters from enraged women readers, mostly defending women, men, and suburbia itself. Most suburban women saw the new bungalow or storey-and-a-half home in the suburbs as a step up in terms of convenience, comfort, and security, much preferable to crowded "flats" without domestic conveniences. For the independent, self-motivated woman, suburbia had clear advantages: new community associations with home, church, and school; a relatively happy family life; and, often, rewarding relationships with spouses.

Suburban dreams centred on home and family captured the hopes of a generation shaken by world war and economic depression, even though suburbia exemplified the gendered division of labour. Far from being a quiet hell, most suburban women's experiences were neither homogeneous nor uncomplicated. In the 1960s, the daughters of the suburbs — reflecting on their parents' lives — would begin to ask for more.

The word *suburbia* conjured up images of small children and schools, and meeting the new demand for education was one of the biggest challenges posed by suburban migration and the baby boom. After 1947, the number of Canadian children annually reaching school age rapidly doubled. To meet these pressures, ugly utilitarian school buildings were quickly erected, and a new generation of teachers found employment and enhanced bargaining power to secure better salaries. Inside those new schools, however, little changed. In most of Canada — like the United States — the 1950s remained a period of educational conservatism: straight lines, girls' and boys' entrances, seating in rows, and a somewhat old-fashioned curriculum.

CHALLENGING THE CONSENSUS: SOCIAL CRITICISM IN THE 1950s

NOT EVERYONE IN NORTH AMERICA WAS MESMERIZED, or anaesthetized, by the prosperous 1950s. A small but persistent group of social critics emerged to draw attention to imperfections in the North American facade of affluence and conformity. Bureaucratic life, the corporate power structure, crass materialism, mass advertising, planned obsolescence, and the performance of the schools were all subjected to often harsh criticism.

THE "SUBURBAN SADNESS"

The North American suburbs, many critics contended, best illustrated a new social conformity. In *The Organization Man* (1956), William F. Whyte described an emerging group of middle-class, white-collar executives, who accepted "a belief in 'belongingness' as the ultimate need of the individual." Organization men and women, according to Whyte, found their natural habitat in suburbia. The suburban morning coffee klatch, the PTA, and schools full of "nice, clean middle-class kids" perfectly suited those people who sought a sense of community, sociability for its own sake, and conformity to accepted values.

Some observers went further in their criticism. John Sealey and two other sociologists studied *Crestwood Heights*, the Toronto urban community of Forest Hill, and found it an up-scale "suburb" of uniformly nice homes where residents sought to screen out "the unpleasant features of urban existence." The influential Chicago sociologist David Riesman described the "new suburbanite" as "tolerant, even bland," but "parochially civic minded...seldom informed, rarely angry, and only spasmodically partisan." Riesman claimed that suburban life produced a kind of sadness characterized by "an aimlessness, a pervasive low keyed unpleasure" rooted in the fact that people were oriented toward leisure rather than work.[8]

THE "POWER ELITE" CRITIQUE

American society in the Dwight Eisenhower years (1952–60) was under the pervasive influence of the so-called "American consensus." Taking their cue from the new suburbanites, most Americans adhered to "Ike's" moderate brand of Republicanism. Americans settled down to enjoy the fruits of prosperity, and the Eisenhower administration seemed to be a classic case of "the bland leading the bland." College seniors studied "citizenship" and were active in Community Chest charity work. Paying dutiful respect to American social institutions and dressing to conform suggested that most were generally satisfied with life.[9] To a lesser extent, these conservative values were also prevalent in Louis St. Laurent's Canada (1948–57).

One of the few Americans to question the pervasive complacency and self-satisfaction was the radical political sociologist C. Wright Mills (1916–62). Mills attempted to provoke a radical re-examination of aspects of American society such as the structure of power, the political attitudes of the new white-collar class of workers, and the absence of a critical tradition among American social scientists. In his classic work, *The Power Elite* (1956), he unleashed a powerful critique of the American power structure in the 1950s. The mass of "ordinary men and women," Mills wrote, lived in narrowly circumscribed "everyday worlds," unaware that America was dominated by a "power élite," a small circle of "leading men" in the economic, political, and military spheres who controlled "command posts of the major institutional hierarchies" — the

The Canadian magnates of the 1950s. E.P. Taylor (left), a dollar-a-year man during the war, became the major Toronto industrialist investor. K.C. Irving was the Maritime founder of an industrial empire ranging from oil to pulp and paper to broadcasting.

"warlords," the "corporation chieftains," and the "political directorate" — who shared inter-locking associations and came together to form "the power élite of America."[10]

Mills's *Power Elite* sparked much controversy and won one unintended endorsement. In his farewell address of January 1961, none other than President Eisenhower surprised many by issuing a warning against what he called the "military–industrial complex" in America. That statement was cold comfort for C. Wright Mills and his disciples. Dismissed or ignored by the vast majority of Americans in the 1950s, Mills would emerge in the more radical 1960s as something of a cult hero or popular prophet. In Canada, Mills's theories were taken up and refined in John Porter's *The Vertical Mosaic* (1965), a brilliant analysis of the hierarchical structure of class and power in Canadian society.[11]

MASS MANIPULATION AND CONSUMER ADVOCACY

The commercialism and materialism of North American life in the 1950s attracted its share of popular critics. Perhaps foremost among them was the journalist and best-selling author Vance Packard. In *The Hidden Persuaders* (1957), Packard focused on "the new breed of depth men, the motivational researchers" who had come to dominate "Ad Alley" — Madison Avenue — and exert powerful new influences over the lives of ordinary people. Using psychological research techniques, he argued, advertisers were probing the consumer's subconscious mind and charting hidden urges, fears, and wish fulfilments. Through mass-persuasion advertising, they were manipulating people and profoundly influencing what they purchased, believed in, and even voted for. "The use of mass psychoanalysis to guide campaigns of persuasion," according to Packard, had "become the basis of a multimillion-dollar industry."[12]

Consumers and their advocates began in the 1950s to react against such excesses of market manipulation. Another popular American writer, John Keats, published *The Insolent Chariots* (1958), a sensational description of America's "love affair" with the automobile and a devastating critique of Detroit carmakers who produced gigantic power machines designed to wear out in a few short years. Concerns about the "planned obsolescence" of North American products led eventually to the rise of consumer advocacy groups, such as Ralph Nader's Raiders, and sparked the formation of consumer protection associations, in Canada as well as the United States.

TEENAGERS AND THE SCHOOLS

North Americans "discovered" the teenager in the 1950s. In the immediate postwar years, it was fashionable to deplore the conduct of the adolescent generation. A large and alarmingly visible minority of Canadian and American teenagers had adopted what adults called the "Hood Look." By the early 1950s, this style had two essential ingredients for boys: baggy trousers, known as "strides," and a "ducktail" haircut — short on top, long and greased-back on the sides. Girls adopted some of these styles, but many stuck to sweaters, pleated skirts, and white bobby socks. Adolescent ways, language, and clothes were all incomprehensible to adults. Teens danced the "jive" at high school dances and bounced to the beat of pop music, featuring mindless lyrics and catchy tunes. Teen expressions like "bad scene" and "dreamy-lookin' guy" raised the eyebrows of many a parent.

Teenage life in the 1950s. North American high school students in the prosperous postwar years.

ROCK 'N' ROLL: TEENAGE SELF-ABSORPTION OR REBELLION?

"**R**OCK 'N' ROLL" music dates from the early 1950s. It is usually cited as musical evidence that the teenage restlessness that swept North America in the 1960s had its real beginnings in the preceding decade. It was essentially "white" music, but it developed almost entirely from black American musical styles.

Looking back on his high school days in Toronto in the 1950s, Alan Skeoch offered these recollections:

> The man who exerted the greatest musical influence was a former truck driver from the American South who made his first recording in 1956 — in a studio in Nashville, Tennessee. Elvis Presley began a career that would make rock 'n' roll the new image maker of North American culture. It was hypnotic, frenetic, muscle-twitching, heart-pounding music that made you want to dance. "Heartbreak Hotel," "I Want You, I Need You, I Love You," "Don't Be Cruel," "Hound Dog," "All Shook Up," "Jailhouse Rock" all followed in short order. The language of American rock 'n' roll spoke directly to all Canadian teens and drew us tighter into the American cultural milieu.

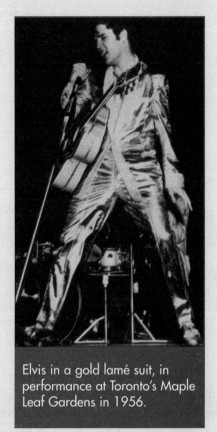

Elvis in a gold lamé suit, in performance at Toronto's Maple Leaf Gardens in 1956.

The following verses, from Elvis Presley's smash hit, "All Shook Up" (1957), are typical of the 1950s rock music style. To what extent did the youth rebellion of the 1960s have its roots in the rock music of the 1950s?

"ALL SHOOK UP" (1957)

Elvis Presley
Written by Otis Blackwell & Elvis Presley.
Copyright: RCA Victor Limited

> Well bless my soul what's wrong with me
> I'm itching like a man in a fuzzy tree
> My friends say I acting wild as a bug

I'm in love...I'm all shook up...
ooh ooh ooh ooh, yea yea yah
ooh ooh ooh ooh, yea, yea...I'm all shook up!

Well my hand is shaking and my knees are weak
I can't seem to stand on my own two feet
Who do you think when you have such luck
I'm in love...I'm all shook up
Well please don't ask me what's on my mind
I'm a little mixed up but I'm feelin' fine
When I met a girl that I love best
My heart break so it scares me to death.

When she touched my hand what a chill I got
Her lips are like a volcano that's hot
I'm proud to say that she's my buttercup
I'm in love...I'm all shook up
My tongue gets tired when I try to speak
My insides shake like a leaf on a tree
There's only one cure for this body of mine
That's to have that girl and a love so fine.

Lyrics of "ALL SHOOK UP" by Otis Blackwell and Elvis Presley. Copyright © 1957 by Shalimar Music Corporation. Copyright Renewed and Assigned to Elvis Presley Music (Administered by R&H Music). International Copyright Secured. Used by Permission. All Rights Reserved.

North American teenagers showed little concern for social issues. Educators complained that they were conservative, smug, apathetic, and altogether unadventurous. They were, as well, extremely conformist: teens lived in fear of being "oddballs." In 1959, a survey by *Maclean's* magazine found that 90 percent of the high school students polled agreed with the statement that "obedience and respect for authority are the most important virtues young people should learn"; and about half the students favoured the West launching a "preventive strike" against the Soviet Union. Some alarmed educators wondered if Canada were headed for some kind of fascist or authoritarian state. "There are no mavericks left," complained one school board psychologist in 1959. "Everybody wants to be like everybody else."

Some social critics saw schools as the source of the complacency among North American youth. Hilda Neatby, a history professor at the University of Saskatchewan, stirred up a minor tempest in Canada. Her book, *So Little for the Mind* (1953), launched a savage attack on "progressive education," which, she charged, neglected the great Western intellectual tradition and discipline in favour of pandering to the "happiness" of the student. Neatby blamed the public education system for producing "graduates" who were "ignorant, lazy, and unaware of the exacting demands of a society from...which they have been carefully insulated."[13] The book aroused a storm of controversy among parents and educators.

THE IMPACT AND STRAINS OF AFFLUENCE

NOT EVERY PART OF CANADA AND THE UNITED STATES conformed with the popular image of the new suburbia or prosperous "fabulous fifties." The postwar boom bypassed some regions, like Cape Breton and America's Appalachia. Crippled by the shift to oil and gas, coal-mining districts on both sides of the border declined. Rural Canadians and Americans saw their lives changed by the spread of electrification, flush toilets, and paved highways. Automobiles and newly paved roads allowed for easier access to urban shopping centres and health services. In rural areas, children were bused long distances to consolidated schools, and far larger numbers of rural students now graduated and found work in the cities.

THE INVISIBLE POOR

Few North Americans in the 1950s gave much thought to the poor. In *The Other America* (1962), Michael Harrington contended that 40–50 million U.S. citizens remained in poverty, almost invisible to the comfortable majority. This "other America," he wrote, consisted of the unskilled and the aged, who lived "in the economic underworld of the world's wealthiest nation."[14] Poverty also persisted in Canada, among Native people, the elderly, and in urban slums or hinterland regions based on marginal industries. Toronto's "Lower Ward," for instance, a bleak, dilapidated slum inhabited by impoverished "old Canadians" and recent immigrants, continued to exist not far from the gentility and comforts of Forest Hill, reputed to be the model upper-class "suburb." In the 1950s, such exceptions to the new affluence were largely overlooked. The social issues that commanded the most attention were by-products of affluence: the demand for decent, affordable housing, new schools, and improved municipal services.

THE COLD WAR AT HOME

The Cold War reached its height in the late 1940s and early 1950s, and its effects were felt by most North Americans. In the United States, Senator Joseph McCarthy of Wisconsin succeeded in whipping up anti-communist hysteria and launched a well-publicized campaign to rid the U.S. State Department and other federal institutions of all known or suspected communists. In response to the wave of anti-communism, President Eisenhower introduced a "government loyalty program" and Congress joined in the hunt by passing the Communist Control Act (1954), which outlawed the Communist party on the grounds that it constituted a "clear, present, and continuing danger." The situation in Canada never reached those proportions. Cold War hysteria did blow northward, and some Canadian politicians like Tory leader George Drew exploited anti-communist sentiment for political ends. But Canada did not ban the Communist party, and an overt, sustained McCarthyite "witch hunt" never materialized.[15] Security screenings, silent purges, and quiet suppression were the favoured tools in Canada's "little Cold War."

JACK KEROUAC, THE BEAT GENERATION, AND ITS IMPACT

In *On the Road*, Jack Kerouac captured the spirit of his own generation, their restlessness and confusions in the years immediately following World War II.

Ann Charters, *Kerouac: A Biography* (New York, 1973)

Jack Kerouac's *On the Road* (1957) was one of the most popular and influential novels of the 1950s. Centring on a number of cross-country automobile trips taken by Kerouac and his friends in the late 1940s, the novel popularized the lifestyle of what was known as the "Beat Generation." The novel's chief characters — Sal Paradise, Dean Moriarty, Carlo Marx, and Old Bull Lee — were supposedly fictional; in real life they were Kerouac, Neal Cassady, Allen Ginsberg, and William Burroughs, a motley collection of writers and free spirits.

Beat writers unabashedly rejected most of the common conventions of the 1950s, notably middle-class conformity and materialism, and showed contempt for the "square" world and the suburban lifestyle. The Beats identified with poets, hoodlums, hoboes, jazz musicians, and poor American blacks — groups, according to the Beats, who were actually the most fortunate Americans: free to take life as it came, free to act on instinct, to appreciate life's finest things, to "dig" everything.

Beat writings like *On the Road* were harshly critical of conformity, technology, and mechanization. Yet Beat writers shared no single political outlook. Poet Allen Ginsberg was perhaps the most radical. In poems like "Howl," he offered a devastating indictment of American society, its anti-communist paranoia and fixation with nuclear weapons. Many like Jack Kerouac might be described as politically alienated or disengaged.

The "Beat style" originated in San Francisco and then spread to other centres throughout North America. It thrived as part of the underground culture in Vancouver, Montreal, and Toronto. The Beats hung around coffee houses, drifted, and favoured either cool jazz or folk music. At Vancouver's The Cellar, Beat poets like San Francisco's Kenneth Patchen frequently performed. A young Montreal poet, Leonard Cohen, got his start in coffee-houses like Dunns in Montreal.

Jack Kerouac's *On the Road* was widely regarded as the "bible" of the Beat Generation. Its author lived a hard life and died at 47, a victim of alcoholism, in 1969.

Beat lingo and habits gradually filtered upward into general use. Such hipster slang as "dig," "bad scene," "cool cat," "groovy," and "something else" could be found a decade later in trendy advertising copy and suburban conversations. Beatniks were the first to renounce the crass materialism and conformity of postwar North American society. Although they were often dismissed as "know-nothing Bohemians," their significance should not be underestimated. The Beat movement was a precursor of the attitudes that would sweep college campuses in the 1960s. Indeed, by the time of Kerouac's death in 1969, they were the firmly established "folk heroes" of the sixties generation.

POSTWAR IMMIGRATION

After World War II, the arrival of a wave of European immigrants again tested the tolerance of Canadian and American society. Few people opposed the admission of those known as "DPs" — "displaced persons" — yet Prime Minister King was careful to pledge that the new 1948 immigration policy would preserve the "fundamental character" of the Canadian population. When the U.S. Congress acted in 1948 to assist Europeans who had been displaced by war, the legislation specifically favoured immigrants of German origin and discriminated against East European Jews. Under the new regulations, 2.5 million immigrants entered Canada between 1946 and 1966, and many millions more landed in the United States.[16]

LEGACY OF THE FIFTIES

In Canada the influx of the postwar immigrants created little fuss. Federal authorities extended full citizenship rights to all Asian Canadians in 1949. Ontario and Saskatchewan introduced human-rights codes aimed at eliminating acts of discrimination against new European immigrants, Jews, blacks, and Native people. Although prejudice could not be eradicated, it was no longer publicly accepted. Toronto, the country's most firmly British and Protestant city in 1939, was transformed by infusions of Italians and Greeks, Ukrainians and Poles. Old prejudices did not die, nor did suspicions about the new immigrants. The availability of jobs and the willingness of the newcomers to work in less desirable occupations, such as farm labour, domestic service, and building construction, helped to dissolve potential conflict. Prosperity went a long way toward promoting tolerance.

The prosperous 1950s brought many trends that carried forward into the 1960s. With the postwar economic boom, growing continental economic integration, and the spread of North American consumer values, new concerns arose about the "Americanization" of Canadian culture and the Canadian economy. The new suburbia, educational expansion, TV, and the "age of rock" were firmly implanted and destined to flourish in the 1960s. For the baby boom generation, the future would bring continued rising standards of living, increased access to mass-produced consumer goods, and even more leisure time to indulge in entertainment. Yet all of this economic abundance would breed, as well, much questioning of the limits and pervasive effects of affluence in a modern consumer society.

ACTIVITIES

KEY TERMS AND CONCEPTS

Identify and explain the historical significance of each of the following terms and concepts:

- Affluence
- American consensus
- St. Lawrence Seaway
- Baby boom
- CBC-TV
- "Home dreams"
- Gender division of labour
- *Crestwood Heights*
- *The Power Elite*
- Planned obsolescence
- "Ducktail" haircut
- Consumer advocacy
- Invisible poor
- Beat Generation
- McCarthyism
- Displaced persons

QUESTIONS FOR DISCUSSION

1. What caused North America to enter a period of economic boom in the 1950s? To what extent did Canada and the United States both benefit from the consequences of war in Europe?
2. How "fabulous" were the 1950s? To what degree were the fruits of prosperity shared by all regions, classes, and ethnic groups?
3. Why are the 1950s in North America considered an age of consensus and conformity?

Support your answer with evidence from the political, social, and cultural spheres.

4. In the early 1950s, the "new suburbia" was hailed as a kind of postwar utopia. Why did it later come under such critical attack?
5. Who were the leading social critics of the postwar corporate and business-dominated society? What criticisms were levelled at the power structure, television, mass advertising, teenage behaviour, and public education?
6. What major strains emerged in the affluent postwar consumer society? Explain the impact of postwar European immigration, uneven economic development, Cold War hysteria, and teenage rebellion.

DRAWING HISTORICAL COMPARISONS

1. Many studies of North American suburbs in the 1950s suggest that suburban life demonstrated a remarkable homogeneity or sameness, both in Canada and in the United States. In what respects was suburban life essentially the same on both sides of the border? Where might an analyst find some marked differences?
2. The popular 1980s film *Back to the Future* raised some fascinating questions about how one era or decade compares with another. Indeed, some leading contemporary

American authorities in the 1980s saw the decade as a kind of "throwback" to the 1950s:

"The new conservatism of the 1980s is really the old conservatism in disguise."

— John Kenneth Galbraith, Harvard University economist (1984).

"Suburban growth goes in fits and starts. It wasn't as big in parts of the 1970s as other times. It's bigger now."

— Kenneth T. Jackson, *Crabgrass Frontier* (1985).

"It's a surprise. You hear a lot less talk about gentrification and investing in run-down areas these days. The news today is that [baby boomers] are behaving like their parents. They're looking for a nice house in the suburbs."

— Landon Y. Jones, *Great Expectations: America and the Baby Boom Generation* (1981).

In what ways were the 1980s much like the 1950s in terms of North American social trends and developments? Identify as many similarities and differences as you can.

CHAPTER 20

THE MODERN WOMEN'S RIGHTS MOVEMENT

THE SECOND WAVE OF FEMINISM

TOWARD EQUALITY AND JUSTICE

THE POLITICS OF THE BODY

GENDER, RACE, AND CLASS

A NEW PHASE OF WOMEN'S ACTIVISM

F OR NORTH AMERICAN WOMEN, the achievement of voting rights seemed to signal the dawn of a "new day" of opportunities. "The bars are down," wrote one optimistic woman in the March 1922 issue of *Maclean's* magazine. "Women today are free as air…to wrest from the workaday world at least some measure of their hopes and aspirations." Yet the realities of the North American women's experience from the 1920s to the 1990s would prove otherwise. The vote, two world wars, government commissions, and even increasing employment opportunities produced only modest changes in the social status of women. After the 1970 report of Canada's Royal Commission on the Status of Women, women made advances, but these gains probably benefited mostly white, urban middle-class women. As Canadian feminist leader Sunera Thobani pointed out in May 1993: "It is only when the concerns of the women who face the harshest levels of discrimination are addressed that the women's movement will remain true to its principles of empowerment and equality of all women."[1]

Native women lead a 1992 march to protest 500 years of white colonization in the Americas.

Active participation in World War I and winning the vote did not produce a real breakthrough for women. Unemployment rose to high levels as men returned from the war, and women were pressured to give up their jobs and accept the prevailing philosophy that "a woman's place is in the home." In the mid-to-late 1920s, the return of prosperity created some new workplace opportunities, although primarily in low-paid, routine clerical work and service jobs such as retail sales and telephone-answering services. The Great Depression of the 1930s benefited some women and disadvantaged others. In some families, only female members could find work; in others, the women were laid off and the jobs given, at even lower pay, to men. Only the outbreak of World War II brought real improvement in conditions, as the armed forces and wartime production created a shortage of labour and women were once again recruited into the workforce.

WOMEN DECLARED "PERSONS"

Women were now voting, but their participation in political life was only just beginning on other fronts. The Liberal and Conservative parties had both formed women's auxiliaries in the 1920s, and women were permitted to stuff envelopes or answer telephones. The "third parties," such as the Co-operative Commonwealth Federation (CCF), were more alert to women's issues; their platforms included measures for protective labour legislation and for birth control, still officially illegal. These parties even recruited women to run in some ridings; the first woman Member of Parliament (MP) in Canada was Agnes Macphail of the Progressive party and later the CCF. She faced discrimination and ridicule at every stage of her election, and during her first session as an MP she was made miserable by the attitude of the male politicians. Only five women were elected to Parliament before 1950; during that same period, 23 women won seats in provincial legislatures from Ontario to British Columbia.

The campaign for the first woman senator was long and arduous. Judge Emily Murphy of Edmonton was proposed by a number of women's organizations as a suitable candidate. Both Arthur Meighen's Conservatives and Mackenzie King's Liberals rejected the request on the grounds that women were not qualified under the terms of the British North America (BNA) Act, 1867. After eight years of denials, Murphy, Nellie McClung, and three other prominent women petitioned the Supreme Court of Canada to rule on the issue. That court in 1928 ruled that the term "qualified persons" in the BNA Act did not include women. This ruling was referred to the highest court of appeal, the Judicial Committee of the Privy Council in England, which reversed the judgment of the Supreme Court of Canada in 1929. The first woman senator, Cairine Wilson, was appointed in 1930, demonstrating that women were now legally recognized as "persons."

Emily Murphy. A police magistrate and judge of the juvenile court in Edmonton, Murphy was the key figure in the "Persons Case" of 1929.

THE SECOND WAVE OF FEMINISM

AS THE PROSPERITY AND COMPLACENCY OF THE "FABULOUS FIFTIES" gave way to the social concerns of the 1960s, a second wave of feminist activism began. In the United States, the Presidential Commission on the Status of Women, established in 1961, served as a catalyst for action. Betty Friedan's *The Feminine Mystique* (1963) described the isolation of the middle-class suburban housewife and inspired changes in attitude in thousands of women in Canada and the United States who realized that their problems were shared by many other women. In Canada, as in most of the western world, women's liberation movements of the 1960s and 1970s grew out of New Left student movements. The Royal Commission on the Status of Women was set up in response to mounting pressure from Canadian women's groups, the example of President John Kennedy's Roundtable on Women, and media support for women's demands.

VOICES OF WOMEN'S LIBERATION IN AMERICA

BETTY FRIEDAN AND *THE FEMININE MYSTIQUE*

OF ALL THE CATALYSTS that sparked the revived feminist movement, none was more influential and evocative than Betty Friedan's 1963 book, *The Feminine Mystique*. A writer from suburban Grandview, New York, Friedan sparked many white, middle-class, professional women to take up the cause. Using the notoriety and royalties from her best-selling book, she spearheaded the founding of the National Organization for Women (NOW) in the fall of 1966.

Present at the creation of NOW were 30 women and two men. By 1967, the organization boasted 1200 members; by 1974, it claimed 48 000 supporters, with 700 chapters in the United States, Canada, and eight other

Leaders of the American women's movement. Congresswoman Bella Abzug (left) and Gloria Steinem at a conference of women's and minorities' rights in July 1972, held in Washington D.C. Dr. Benjamin Spock is in the background. Ms. Steinem is talking to Rev. Jesse Jackson.

countries. In its Bill of Rights for Women, drawn up in 1967, NOW called upon the major political parties to support its feminist goals, including the passing of an Equal Rights Amendment (ERA) and recognition of "the right of women to control their reproductive lives."

The problem lay buried, unspoken for many years in the minds of American women. It was a strange stirring, a sense of dissatisfaction, a yearning that women suffered in the middle of the twentieth century in the United States. Each suburban wife struggled with it alone. As she made the beds, shopped for groceries, matched slip-cover material, ate peanut butter sandwiches with her children, chauffeured Cub Scouts and Brownies, lay beside her husband at night — she was afraid to ask even of herself the silent question — "Is this all?"...

But on an April morning in 1959, I heard a mother of four, having coffee with four other mothers in a suburban development fifteen miles from New York, say in a tone of quiet desperation, "the problem." And the others knew, without words, that she was not talking about a problem with her husband, or her children, or her home. Suddenly they realized they all shared the same problem, the problem that has no name. They began, hesitantly, to talk about it. Later, after they had picked up their children at nursery school and taken them home to nap, two of the women cried, in sheer relief, just to know they were not alone.

Reprinted from *The Feminine Mystique* by Betty Friedan, with the permission of W. W. Norton & Company, Inc. Copyright © 1963, 1973, 1974, 1983 and renewed 1991 by Betty Friedan.

CONSCIOUSNESS RAISING AND SISTERHOOD: THE REDSTOCKINGS MANIFESTO, 1969

The revival of the American women's-rights movement in the late 1960s also involved groups associated with the "radical second centre," composed of younger, college women, largely drawn to feminism through experiences in the peace movement, civil-rights organizations, and the student New Left. Perhaps the most radical feminist groups were the Redstockings and The Feminists, both dedicated to liberating women from "male chauvinist oppression" and building the power of the "sisterhood" through collective action. The practice of feminist "consciousness raising," so central to the radical feminist experience, was pioneered by the Redstockings of New York, and strongly emphasized in their highly publicized 1969 manifesto:

> **V.** We regard our personal experience, and our feelings about that experience, as the basis for an analysis of our common situation. We cannot rely on existing ideologies as they are all products of male supremacist culture. We question every generalization and accept none that are not confirmed by our experience.
>
> Our chief task at present is to develop female class consciousness through sharing experience and publicly exposing the sexist foundation of all our institutions. Consciousness-raising is not "therapy," which implies the existence of individual solutions and falsely assumes that the male–female relationship is purely personal, but the only method by which we can ensure that our program for liberation is based on the concrete realities of our lives.
>
> The first requirement for raising class consciousness is honesty, in private and in public, with ourselves and other women....
>
> **VII.** We call on all our sisters to unite with us in struggle.
>
> We call on all men to give up their male privileges and support women's liberation in the interest of our humanity and their own.
>
> In fighting for our liberation we will always take the side of women against their oppressors. We will not ask what is "revolutionary" or "reformist," only what is good for women.
>
> The time for individual skirmishes has passed. This time we are going all the way.

"Redstockings Manifesto," July 7, 1969.

The social status of women in North America had changed little since the achievement of voting rights. In Canada by 1961, women constituted nearly half the population but were still excluded from the major power centres in business and government. John Porter's *The Vertical Mosaic*

(1965), a massive study of the Canadian social and economic élites of the 1950s, contained not one reference to the status of women. Although the proportion of women — particularly married women — in the labour force had greatly increased, women continued to fill the lower-paid, less prestigious occupations. For example, over 96 percent of the country's office secretaries but only 6.8 percent of the doctors and 2.6 percent of the lawyers were women.

In the 1960s a revived women's movement, known as the second wave, became active. If women were to break out of their socially imposed maternal role or to gain improved status in business, industry, and government, much remained to be done. Women's liberation provided an impetus to examine all aspects of women in society and to revolutionize the thinking of both men and women.

THE BIRTH OF WOMEN'S LIBERATION

The late 1960s in Canada, as in the United States and throughout the western world, saw the emergence of a new women's movement. This modern feminism rejected the limits imposed by women's traditional role and attempted to show the lack of female equality in every aspect of daily life as well as in the political, legal, and economic spheres. One impetus for the movement came from the publication in 1963 of Betty Friedan's *The Feminine Mystique*, which argued that women were trapped by the pervasive belief that the only desirable role for them was that of wife, mother, and housekeeper. Friedan's book played a major part in showing millions of middle-class North American women why they were unfulfilled and unhappy. The reaction stirred by Friedan's book was strengthened by the later writings of other, often more radical, feminists such as Kate Millett, Germaine Greer, and Gloria Steinem.

In Canada the impact of these feminist influences was clearly revealed in a spate of publications, notably *Women Unite! An Anthology of the Women's Movement* (1972). In their writings and media appearances, the women's liberationists held that society's major power relationship was one of domination and oppression of women by men. The existing network of social relationships in the home and workplace, and the functioning of North American society, was critically examined and found wanting.

The women's liberation movement arose among women students and ex-students of the New Left because of their perception that the male students in the movement were discriminating against them. Shortly after the first women's liberation groups were formed in Chicago and New York, a Canadian group met in 1967 at the University of Toronto. Similar groups were organized within a few years at other Canadian universities. In Quebec, a Montreal women's liberation group was founded in 1969, the *Front de libération des femmes du Québec* issued a feminist manifesto in 1970, and the *Centre des femmes* edited the first French-language feminist periodical, *Québecoises deboutte!* (1971–75).

These groups kept their leftist political orientation, their analytical socialist/Marxist approach to issues, and a loose organizational structure without defined leadership roles —

all features of the student left movement. The New Left groups protested the American war in Vietnam and believed in activism to publicize their cause. For example, they attempted to disrupt the 1969 Toronto Miss Winter Bikini Contest by entering a mock contestant and picketing with a mannequin marked off in sections like a side of beef to demonstrate that the contestants were being judged like pieces of flesh. As these groups evolved, they also used American techniques of group consciousness-raising to help improve and increase awareness of discrimination against women in the society at large.

The women's liberation movement was not isolated to Canada. Similar groups were forming elsewhere in the industrialized world, and somewhat earlier in the United States than in Canada. Some of their tactics looked back to the first wave of the women's movement and the tactics it had used in the battle for the right to vote. Women's liberation groups, like the first-wave feminist groups before them, set up services to assist women, particularly services related to women's physical needs and problems.

ORIGINS OF THE ROYAL COMMISSION ON THE STATUS OF WOMEN

At the same time that the women's liberation movement was forming, the existing women's groups were not idle. The major groups — the WCTU, the National Council of Women, the YWCA, and others — had continued to be active during the interwar years in women's causes. In the 1960s, their concerns about women's problems brought together representatives of 30 women's organizations, who formed themselves into the Committee on Equality for Women and called for a royal commission on the status of women. Leaders of the Canadian movement met with members of the American National Organization of Women (NOW) and drew inspiration from the activities and strategies employed by their "sisters" in the United States. Led by Laura Sabia, a prominent Ontario women's leader and president of the Federation of University Women, the delegates to the Committee on Equality for Women represented all major national women's organizations. As well, the peace organization the Voice of Women, whose national president was Kay Macpherson, was involved through its concern for issues relating to motherhood. The response and co-operation was in contrast to similar organizations in the United States, which had rejected taking a public stand on issues of equality.

The Liberal government of Lester B. Pearson ignored the first petition of the Canadian Committee on Equality for Women. But a number of pressures coalesced to persuade the government to set up a commission in 1967. Sabia's rabble-rousing attacks in the media helped, as did pressure from Secretary of State Judy LaMarsh in the cabinet; so too did the fact that women were now voting at the same rate as men and were generally becoming more active in politics — facts that the minority Pearson government could not afford to ignore.

The Royal Commission on the Status of Women in Canada was chaired by Florence Bird, an Ottawa journalist and broadcaster, and included two men and four other women. The commission's mandate was to investigate the current status of Canadian women and to recommend

THE U.S. PRESIDENTIAL COMMISSION ON THE STATUS OF WOMEN

PRODDED BY THE LOBBYING OF AMERICAN WOMEN'S CLUBS and organized labour women, President John F. Kennedy in 1961 set up the President's Commission on the Status of Women. The commission's mandate was to investigate the "prejudice and out-moded customs [that] act as barriers to the full realization of women's basic rights," and to make recommendations in a variety of areas such as employment practices, social security and tax laws, legal treatment of women, and support services needed for working women. The appointment of Eleanor Roosevelt as "chairman" was significant; it assured, as historian Carl Degler once put it, that "the commission would not be feminist in either membership or intent."*

It was the first comprehensive investigation ever undertaken of women's social, economic, and political status in the United States. The commission's report, *American Women*, was published in 1963. While the report confirmed, with statistical evidence, that women — like blacks and minority groups — suffered discrimination and mistreatment, its recommendations were moderate and rather narrowly circumscribed. The expanding role of married women in the labour force was recognized and documented, but the report held to the view that woman's prime social role was as mother and wife. The proposal for an Equal Rights Amendment (ERA) was considered but rejected by the commission on the grounds that existing constitutional guarantees of women's equality were sufficient. Although the commission did lead to the June 1963 enactment of the U.S. Equal Pay Act, guaranteeing women "equal pay for equal work," its real significance lay in the recognition and "profile" it gave to women's concerns.

* Carl N. Degler, *At Odds: Women and the Family in America from the Revolution to the Present* (New York: Oxford University Press, 1980), p. 441.

reforms in areas of federal jurisdiction. Just as the U.S. Presidential Commission on Women had done six years earlier, the Canadian commission played a key role in defining and highlighting the status of women as a legitimate national problem. Starting in the spring of 1968, the royal commission held six months of public hearings in fourteen cities across Canada, including the Far North. The commission received over 460 briefs and many letters. It used the public hearings for media publicity and as a way to educate the general public about women's problems. Perhaps the greatest obstacle to reform was the "silent majority" of Canadian women who were either indifferent to the cause or simply unconcerned about political issues.

The commission's report, released in 1970, contained 167 recommendations on such matters as employment, educational opportunities, and family law. For the first time, national attention was focused on major issues of women's equality, such as equal pay for work of equal value, maternity leave, abortion, discrimination against women under the Indian Act, lack of access to managerial positions, part-time work, and pensions for women. But perhaps the royal commission's chief importance lay in its effect on women's groups. Not only did the report's "social policy" appeal to a broad constituency of women, it also encouraged a network of women's organizations to press for the implementation of the commission's recommendations.

GOVERNMENT ACTION ON THE STATUS OF WOMEN

The Pierre E. Trudeau government endorsed the report's general principles and started to implement some of its proposals. Within three years, new offices and procedures were instituted to deal with women's issues: a portfolio to represent status-of-women issues in the federal cabinet; a co-ordinator of the status of women to monitor the progress of federal ministries in implementing the recommendations; an Office of Equal Opportunities in the Public Service Commission; and an Advisory Council on the Status of Women, composed of up to 30 representatives from national organizations. In addition, the government passed a number of measures to modify various aspects of the Canadian Labour Code, public service superannuation, and citizenship relating to women.

In 1978, a major breakthrough was achieved with the establishment of the Canadian Human Rights Commission. Discrimination on the basis of sex (among other criteria) was expressly prohibited. The Canadian Human Rights Act also contained provisions to ensure "equal pay for work of equal value," specifying that value should be determined with reference to skill, effort, responsibility, and working conditions. Under a new women's program administered by the secretary of state in Ottawa, federal monies were extended for special projects sponsored by community women's groups, such as rape crisis centres, legal research programs, and transition houses for battered women.

The "new woman" of the 1960s immortalized in a statue of Doris K. Elston, supermom and career woman. For many women struggling to be wives and mothers as well as career women, life was full of stresses, since most still bore full responsibilities in the home. Drawing by R. Chast; © 1987. The New Yorker Magazine, Inc.

TOWARD EQUALITY AND JUSTICE

BY THE EARLY 1980s full equality for Canadian women, as for American women, was still beyond reach. Many of the critical issues concerning the economic and social status of women had been identified, but legislative action in Ottawa and the provinces had barely dented the problem. In 1981, full-time female employees earned on average only 62 percent of the wages earned by men; only 5 percent of working women were employed in managerial or administrative positions; and two-thirds of all workers earning only the minimum wage were women. Only 20 percent of the women in the workforce were unionized; and three out of four part-time workers were women — a situation that excluded them from normal employee and company pension benefits. About 70 percent of Canadian widows and women over 70 years of age were reported to live below the poverty line. Studies commissioned by governments and women's groups pointed to an alarming incidence of domestic violence and rapes against women. One estimate suggested that half a million women were physically abused by their husbands or partners.

The established women's organizations continued to address the concerns of working women. Writing in 1979, Doris Anderson, former editor of *Chatelaine* magazine and then president of the Canadian Advisory Council on the Status of Women, identified the prime concerns of moderate feminists: reform of unemployment insurance, maternity benefits, the health needs of women, the problems of increasing violence against women, support systems for parents, the elimination of sex stereotyping, and the worsening child-care situation. Leading American feminist Gloria Steinem, in her book *Outrageous Acts and Everyday Rebellions* (1983), encouraged women to assert their rights and did much to shape the feminist agenda in the 1980s.

THE FIGHT FOR EQUAL PAY

In the 1970s, the women's movement had been fighting for "equal pay for equal work." In the 1980s, inequities in wages and salaries became a major focus, and now the demand was for "equal pay for work of equal value." Aside from the 1978 breakthrough in the federal public service, the campaign met with little success,

The "Marriage Rip-off." A *Chatelaine* magazine cartoon in May 1973 dramatized the plight of a middle-class woman faced with a marriage breakup after sacrificing her career to raise the children.

as most employers claimed that "fair pay schemes" were impractical or disrupted the free labour market. A few "affirmative action" programs were instituted to facilitate the promotion of women into managerial levels, and under pressure from women activists in the Canadian labour movement, unions began to include "equal pay" and other women's issues among their chief contract demands.

Women's groups also began to focus on other strategies for alleviating economic inequities. An embryonic "Wages for Housework" movement, inspired by similar American and European initiatives, sprung up in Canada. Out of concern for the problems faced by working wives and sole-support mothers, drives for day care, better maternity benefits, and changes in the divorce laws were mounted.

THE WOMEN'S LOBBY AND THE NEW CONSTITUTION

The process of formulating a new Canadian constitution from 1979 to 1982 gave rise to a battle for the formal recognition and enshrinement of equal rights for women. To many Canadian feminists, the constitutional conferences held by the prime minister and ten premiers — all men — symbolized the male domination of the political structure. Indeed, no woman, in the words of two Toronto *Globe and Mail* analysts, "was invited to play more than a minor role." Initially women's involvement was limited to a handful of female lawyers and law professors, who had to address the extremely complex legal issues. Acting on behalf of women's organizations, these women prepared detailed legal briefs and lobbied governments for guarantees of equal rights, primarily through presentations to committees.

But the scale and intensity of women's involvement changed dramatically in January 1981, when, under pressure from Liberal cabinet minister Lloyd Axworthy, the Canadian Advisory Council on the Status of Women voted to delay a planned National Women's Constitutional Conference, and its president, Doris Anderson, resigned in angry protest. This situation precipitated the formation of a new coalition of feminist leaders, known as the Ad Hoc Committee on the Constitution, and mobilized women to press ahead with the conference. When the national conference was held in Ottawa a month later, it attracted 1300 women delegates, won massive media attention, and established the women's lobby as a major political force in the constitutional debate.

When the constitutional accord was struck in 1981, Canadian women discovered that earlier promised guarantees of equal rights had been dropped from the Canadian Charter of Rights and Freedoms at the insistence of several provincial premiers. The reaction from women across Canada was swift and furious, described by one women's activist as a "political earthquake." In a manner similar to American ERA campaigners, women's groups, backed by remarkable grassroots support, rallied, held demonstrations, petitioned provincial governments, and kept up pressure on Ottawa. A partial victory was won at the eleventh hour; the provision guaranteeing legal equality, embodied in section 28 of the Charter, was restored:

THE STRUGGLE FOR THE ERA

THE CHIEF LEGISLATIVE GOAL OF AMERICAN FEMINISTS in the 1970s and early 1980s was to add the Equal Rights Amendment (ERA) to the U.S. Constitution. The essential part of the ERA read as follows: "Equality of rights under the law shall not be denied or abridged by the United States or by any State on account of sex." To ERA campaigners across the United States, it came to symbolize the legal capstone for the hard-won rights achieved during the "second wave" of American feminism.

Yet the ERA was hardly a new invention. It had originated in the early 1920s, shortly after the ratification of the Nineteenth Amendment, which gave women the right to vote. A radical feminist, Alice Paul, had first proposed it in an attempt to require American law to recognize and to treat women as individuals, not as members of a sex. But the great majority of suffragists, including Carrie Chapman Catt and Chicago social reformer Jane Addams, had seen it otherwise. To them the ERA had seemed to threaten much of the special protective legislation for women which had been enacted since 1900. So, for the next 50 years, it was opposed by most established American women's leaders on the grounds that it might harm rather than improve women's place in society.

All that changed with the revival of the women's-rights movement in the late 1960s. Under the leadership of Elizabeth B. Koontz, a black women's-rights advocate, the federal Women's Bureau ended its longstanding opposition to the ERA. At Koontz's initiative, the bureau sponsored a 1970 conference that concluded with an endorsement of the proposed amendment. That same year, the federal Department of Labor followed suit. Approved by the two houses of Congress in 1972, it was sent to the state legislatures for the necessary ratification. The ERA was quickly endorsed by two dozen states. Then, after being ratified by 35 of the required 38 states, the ERA campaign stalled completely in the mid-1970s.

The campaign stalled because of a number of factors. The ERA still seemed to threaten some women as well as men. Many conservative-minded women of the so-called "silent majority" were rallied by female opponents of the ERA,

Phyllis Schafly, leader of the anti-ERA movement and a conservative Republican. As a mother of six children and a leading anti-feminist, Schafly campaigned for years, arguing that the ratification of the ERA would deprive women of their rights as wives and mothers.

just as they had been 50 years earlier in opposition to suffrage. The remarks of Senator Sam Ervin from North Carolina, a staunch ERA opponent, probably reflected the views of most hard-core male opponents. "Keep the law responsible where the good Lord put it," declared that self-professed "good ole" southern country lawyer, "on the man to bear the burdens of support and the women to bear the children." It was significant that of all the states in the South only two, Tennessee and Texas, ratified the ERA.

In June 1982, American legislators, with the concurrence of the conservative Republican administration of Ronald Reagan, allowed the ERA to die a political death. Even though some 450 American organizations backed the ERA and opinion polls indicated that over 70 percent of U.S. adults favoured the measure, the campaign fell short in six key states: Illinois, Florida, Oklahoma, North Carolina, Missouri, and Virginia. The pioneer of America's modern women's-rights movement, Betty Friedan, expressed the bitter disappointment felt by countless ERA supporters: "American politicians must have been blinded by the feminine mystique," she declared. "They still thought women voted only as men's wives."

"Notwithstanding anything in this Charter, all the rights and freedoms in it are guaranteed equally to male and female persons." But a second section, 15(1), prohibiting discrimination based on sex, was left subject to "notwithstanding legislation" — it could be overridden by laws passed by either Parliament or the provincial legislatures.

The final constitutional compromise was not greeted with rejoicing. The danger that section 28 would be negotiated away had been averted, and Judy Erola, the federal minister responsible for the status of women, offered some reassurance, claiming that governments would not dare to override the sexual-equality guarantees if women remained vigilant. But Linda Ryan-Nye of Women for Political Action (WPA), speaking for many feminists, saw a different lesson: "Women will never again take equality for granted, or take government's word for what's best for women. We have just begun to fight." The active involvement of women mattered, even if the securing of Section 28 fell short of being an earthquake.[2]

THE POLITICS OF THE BODY

A CENTRAL CONCERN OF THE WOMEN'S MOVEMENT since its revival in the late 1960s was the struggle of women to gain control over their own bodies. Growing violence in Canadian and American cities had a dark underside: domestic violence against women. Battered wives became a major public issue in the North American media largely through the efforts of women's groups committed to exposing the incidence of domestic violence. Laws prohibiting abortion emerged as powerful symbols of state control denying women the right to make decisions affecting their own bodies. On a wide range of fronts, according to historian Ruth Roach Pierson, women "struggled to assert or regain control over [their] bodies" and to "wrest control away from the state, the medical establishment, institutionalized religion, pharmaceutical companies, advertisers, pornographers, institutionalized censorship, the violence of men."[3]

REPRODUCTIVE RIGHTS

For many North American women, "the Pill" opened the door to more sexual freedom. Prior to 1969, women in Canada could not legally obtain information about, or prescriptions for, artificial birth control, since both were outlawed under the Canadian Criminal Code. All that changed in 1969, when Prime Minister Pierre Trudeau's Liberal government acted to legalize the public distribution of birth-control information and the display and sale of contraceptives. Such legislative changes were welcomed by most women, since they decriminalized and made available a wider range of birth-control measures.

"The Pill" brought women a measure of liberation, but it also produced some medical worries. Soon after new birth-control drugs and devices became widely available, health risks and side-effects were identified in leading medical journals. Some brands of the birth-control pill were discovered to cause weight gain, headaches, and worse; and intrauterine devices (IUDs) were linked to painful inflammation, excessive bleeding, and even infertility. Such allegations, whether well-founded or not, raised the suspicions of many women about the ethics of pharmaceutical companies who rushed under-tested products onto the market and showed more concern for profits than for women's health.

Liberalization of Canadian law concerning birth control left the major social issue of abortion unresolved. Abortion was left in the Criminal Code, and only under certain conditions and in exceptional cases could a woman with an unwanted pregnancy obtain a legal therapeutic abortion. Under the revised legislation, the decision was made by a "therapeutic abortion committee" composed of "qualified medical practitioners" appointed by the board of an accredited hospital. In many places in Canada outside major cities, however, the nearest hospital had no recognized committee and therefore did not provide such services.

THE DRIVE FOR ABORTION RIGHTS

One of the earliest protest actions of the women's liberation movement was the spring 1970 Abortion Caravan, which travelled from Vancouver to Ottawa. Organizers of the caravan sought to have abortion decriminalized and proclaimed "the right of all women to have control over their own bodies." In the 1970s, Montreal physician Dr. Henry Morgentaler emerged as the best-known champion of abortion rights for women. A large organization, originally called the Canadian Association for Repeal of the Abortion Law, was formed in 1974 to support Dr. Morgentaler's challenge of the 1969 abortion law.

Dr. Morgentaler was the main catalyst for abortion law reform. Deeply affected by the plight of desperate women, he began performing abortions in his Montreal medical clinic in defiance of existing law. In 1973, Dr. Morgentaler was charged with performing an illegal

A pro-abortion group stages a mock funeral procession in an appeal for free abortions.

abortion and brought to trial. Acquitted by a Quebec jury, the decision was overturned by the Quebec Court of Appeal in 1974, and Morgentaler eventually served a short jail sentence. While he was imprisoned, a number of additional charges of performing illegal abortions were laid against him. Eventually, after another jury acquittal, the Quebec Court of Appeal put an end to the prosecutions. Dr. Morgentaler and his supporters secured a legal victory in 1976 when the Quebec attorney-general declared safe, medical abortions in free-standing clinics legal in the province.

The campaign for legal, free-standing abortion clinics then spread to Toronto and Winnipeg, where Morgentaler opened new clinics. After being charged by the Metropolitan Toronto Police for once again breaking the law, Morgentaler appealed the case to the Supreme Court of Canada. Anti-abortion groups such as the Right to Life organization rallied their supporters with the call to protect "the rights of the unborn child." In late January 1988, the Supreme Court of Canada struck down Canada's abortion law, declaring that it denied women's rights to life, liberty, and security of the person, as guaranteed in the 1982 Charter of Rights and Freedoms.

VIOLENCE AGAINST WOMEN

The prevalence of rape and wife battering was exposed in the 1980s and surfaced as a major concern to women. Domestic violence was shrouded in silence because many abused women felt a sense of shame and, by law, a spouse could not be charged with rape. New halfway houses for female victims of domestic violence gradually sprang up in many cities and towns. Largely because of the media attention generated by feminists, the veil of silence surrounding domestic violence was lifted. Although rape crisis centres had existed in major Canadian cities since 1973, women's groups now staged demonstrations against sexual violence and pressed for changes in the law governing such offences. A 1980 report commissioned by the Canadian Advisory Council on the Status of Women (CACSW) revealed the shocking news that one out of every ten women surveyed claimed to have been battered by a male partner. The growth of violent pornography, chillingly dramatized in the National Film Board documentary *Not a Love Story* (1981), stirred women to join a national lobby group pressing for controls on media pornography degrading to women.

Canadian women march against sexual violence in the streets — and in the home — in the annual "Take Back the Night" walk.

THE MONTREAL MASSACRE: MARC LÉPINE'S 1989 RAMPAGE

ON DECEMBER 6, 1989, Marc Lépine strode into *L'école Polytechnique* at the University of Montreal and shot to death fourteen young engineering students — all women — and then took his own life. Before firing his first volley of shots, Lépine reportedly yelled, "You're women, you're going to be engineers. You're all a bunch of feminists. I hate feminists." The mass murder was doubly shocking because it occurred in the hallowed halls of the university and it represented a brutal act of male violence against women.

The Montreal massacre was initially interpreted in the Canadian and international media as a "senseless slaying" and the act of a crazed "madman." Spokespersons for Canadian women's groups saw the gunning down of fourteen young women differently. As Jane Pepino, a Toronto lawyer and vocal opponent of domestic violence, pointedly asked one day after the shooting: "If we say this man was crazy, does this mean every wife batterer is insane, or anyone who assaults a woman physically or sexually is insane?" Critics of the media coverage also asked why Lépine had chosen women as the targets of his rage. His actions, they pointed out, were likely those of a failed engineering school applicant deeply troubled by the entry of young women into a field once completely dominated by men. The statement left behind by Lépine, though termed a suicide note by *The Globe and Mail*, was more of a "femicide" letter giving vent to his frustrations with women.

December 6 is now a day of solemn remembrance in Canada. In 1991, in response to the lobbying efforts of NAC and other women's groups, the Canadian government designated that date as a National Day of Remembrance and Action on Violence Against Women.

The second-wave feminist movement did succeed in putting the problem of violence against women on the public agenda. In 1983, the Canadian government finally responded by removing the spousal rape exemption from the Criminal Code. A second CACSW study of wife battering in June 1987 indicated that the number of battered women's shelters had tripled since 1982 — from 82 to 264 shelters, spread across Canada. The sexual-assault legislation passed in 1983 included a "rape shield" provision that encouraged women to report rape by providing some legal protection against being victimized in court by lawyers prying into women's personal lives. When the "rape shield" law was struck down by the Supreme Court of Canada in August 1991, then Minister of Justice Kim Campbell responded with a new bill (Bill C-49), enacted in June 1992, to provide women with firmer legal protections in cases of sexual assault.

GENDER, RACE, AND CLASS

IN THE HEADY EARLY DAYS of the rebirth of North American feminism, the movement focused on the "discovery" of female identity. Its leaders were largely white, middle-class, able-bodied, and college-educated. Feminist leaders such as Betty Friedan, Gloria Steinem, and Laura Sabia epitomized the white, mainstream women's movement that appealed to urban, middle-class, career-oriented women seeking to balance careers with heterosexual relationships, marriage, and children. The mainstream movement mounted an effective feminist analysis of modern society and introduced potent words into everyday language, including "sexism," "patriarchy," and "misogyny."[4] Feminist thinkers argued that the so-called "battle of the sexes" was a misnomer. A clear distinction was drawn between "sex," as biologically determined, and "gender," which encompassed all sex differences of social and cultural as well as biological origin. To mainstream feminists, contemporary North American society was a "gendered social order" exemplified by the male-dominated nuclear family, the practice of dressing little girls in pink, and the secretarial pool or "pink ghetto" of the modern business office.

The dominant North American women's movement was slower in addressing the fact that some women were more unequal to men than others. In attempting to reach out to poor, immigrant, and Native women, feminists eventually came to embrace the idea espoused by American women's liberationist Carolyn Egan that "every woman engaged in fighting against her particular oppression is part of the women's movement." Feminist critics of the Canadian movement claimed that its leadership was exclusively white and that oppression was not just a matter of gender, but rather included race, class, and disability. Not until the mid-1980s, however, did the doors of mainstream feminist groups open to members of social groups ranging from the poor, black, Asian, and aboriginal to the elderly and disabled.

The mainstream feminist movement faced stiff challenges in the late 1980s. Under the Progressive Conservative government of Brian Mulroney, REAL (Real Equal and Active for Life) Women emerged to challenge established feminist groups like the National Action Committee (NAC) with an appeal to "family values" and to more conservative women committed to traditional

Mary Richards, the quintessential American career woman, played by TV star Mary Tyler Moore on the popular U.S. sitcom that ran from 1970 to 1977. "Mary" made North American women feel it was "OK" to be single, over 30, and independent.

homemaking practices. Black and Asian women, calling themselves "women of colour," arose within the feminist movement to call attention to "white domination" and the neglect of anti-racism. In 1989, Glenda Simms claimed in *The Womanist* that "attempts at discussing racism within the white women's movement have been incoherent, condescending and patronizing." A prime example of these divisions was the 1992 internal conflict at Nellie's, a Toronto women's shelter, in which prominent Canadian author and social activist June Callwood was forced to resign from the board of directors for resisting changes sought by immigrant, refugee, and minority women.

Canada's largest feminist organization, NAC, attempted in the 1980s and early 1990s to respond to the changing dynamics of contemporary society. Under the controversial leadership of Judy Rebick, a concerted effort was made to be more inclusive, welcoming and embracing immigrant women, visible minorities, and aboriginals. The accession of Sunera Thobani to the presidency of NAC in April 1993 signalled a significant change. Thobani was a "woman of colour" and had emerged as a national leader through her work with the South Asian Women's Action Network. Such efforts to embrace the politics of inclusion did not please all feminists. A critical analysis of NAC written by Margaret Wente of *The Globe and Mail* in February 1995 claimed that the country's biggest lobby group for women was in a state of "sad decline" beset by "identity-based and race-based name-calling" and torn by petty squabbling.[5]

The changing face of Canadian feminism. Sunera Thobani, in Saskatoon on the eve of the 1993 NAC annual meeting, which saw Thobani's election as the group's first visible-minority president.

A NEW PHASE OF WOMEN'S ACTIVISM

A GENERATION AFTER THE REBIRTH OF NORTH AMERICAN FEMINISM, women had gained legal and reproductive rights, pursued higher education, won acceptance in the professions, and over-turned public attitudes about their social role. Although the principles of the women's movement had become mainstream, women in the late 1980s and early 1990s faced a "backlash" and still found themselves entrapped by a powerful ideology of female beauty. During the 1980s, women may have breached the power structure, but eating disorders rose exponentially and cosmetic surgery emerged as the fastest-growing medical specialty. Between 1985 and 1990, U.S. consumer spending doubled, yet pornography superseded both legitimate films and sound recordings in its share of the media entertainment dollar. As Naomi Wolf wrote in her 1990 book *The Beauty Myth*, North American women felt caught in "a violent backlash against feminism" that used "images of female beauty as a political weapon against women's advancement: the beauty myth." Just as women had shed the "feminine mystique of domesticity," Wolf claimed that "the beauty myth took over its lost ground...to carry on its work of social control."[6]

THE ANTI-FEMINIST BACKLASH

In Canada, as in the United States, the 1980s and early 1990s saw a backlash against feminism. Popular magazines like *Time* proclaimed that women's fight for equality had "largely been won," and women were so equal in the United States that Washington lawmakers insisted that women no longer needed an Equal Rights Amendment. Yet beneath the veneer of celebration, the media and popular culture sent out signals that women were "free and equal" yet possibly more miserable than ever before. Some critics of the women's movement like Sylvia Ann Hewlett claimed that women's liberation had actually led to "a lesser life" for many American women struggling to balance career and family.[7]

Throughout the 1980s, TV programs, newspapers, and magazines carried stories that professional women were suffering "burnout" or facing an "infertility epidemic"; single women were grieving from a "man shortage"; and independent women were suffering such loneliness that it represented "a major health problem today." In Republican America, neo-conservative politicians condemned women's liberation, anti-abortion protesters fire-bombed women's clinics, TV evangelists condemned feminists as "whores" and "witches," and talk-show hosts levelled broadsides at

Naomi Wolf, author of *The Beauty Myth* (1990) and leader of the feminist "third wave" movement. Her appeal to inner strength and self-reliance formed the basis for a new form of "power feminism."

"femi-Nazis" in the women's movement. It was, in the words of Susan Faludi, "a powerful counterassault on women's rights, a backlash" and a peculiar attempt to "blame feminism" for all the ills besetting modern women.[8]

A THIRD WAVE

Signs of a North American feminist resurgence began to appear in the early 1990s. A main catalyst for the "third wave" of feminism was the highly publicized testimony of Oklahoma law professor Anita Hill at the October 1991 confirmation hearings of U.S. Supreme Court nominee Clarence Thomas. Ms. Hill's testimony about sexual harrassment may not have upset the nomination, but it certainly touched off a "genderquake" that shook the country and altered the gender balance of power. Over the next two years, the rape trials involving William Kennedy Smith and heavyweight boxer Mike Tyson and the U.S. *Tailhook* convention navy scandal served only to galvanize more women into feminist action.

One of the most influential exponents of the third wave was Naomi Wolf, a Yale-educated feminist writer barely in her thirties. In her second book, *Fire with Fire* (1993), Wolf examined why millions of American women endorsed the goals of feminism while steadfastly resisting the label "feminist." She argued that the Anita Hill hearings, the 1992 election of Bill and Hillary Rodham Clinton to the White House, and a growing solidarity among women had brought about "an open moment." Wolf called upon North American women to abandon what she termed "victim feminism" in favour of a new "power feminism" based upon "a vision of femininity" in which it was "desirable and sexy to wield power." Feminist successes in the "genderquake era," in her view, demonstrated the importance of using money, the electoral process, and the media to fashion a new "flexible feminism" for the 1990s that could "reclaim the majority" of women.

UNRESOLVED ISSUES AND CHALLENGES

As in the United States, the 1990s brought a wave of hope as well as new challenges to the women's movement in Canada. In January 1992, Canadian feminist leaders cheered the decisions, taken by the events' sponsors, to cancel two well-known beauty contests, the Miss Canada pageant and the Miss Toronto contest. Liberal leader Jean Chrétien and a record number of female members of Parliament were elected to office in the October 1993 federal election.

Yet the mounting federal deficits and promises to reduce spending spelled cutbacks in social programs, threatening hard-won gains in services for women. The spread of microtechnology in the North American workplace carried with it an ominous trend, as microcomputers and information systems displaced thousands of office workers who were mainly working women. By the mid-1990s, Canada still lacked a comprehensive national day-care policy, and women's groups regularly claimed that the critical needs of married working women for day care and other family-support programs were still being neglected.

ACTIVITIES

KEY TERMS AND CONCEPTS

Identify and briefly explain the historical signif-icance of each of the following key terms and concepts:

- *The Feminine Mystique* (1963)
- "Women's Lib"
- Sisterhood
- Consciousness-raising groups
- Royal Commission on the Status of Women
- National Action Committee (NAC)
- "Equal pay for work of equal value"
- Equal Rights Amendment (ERA)
- Section 28 of the Canadian Constitution
- "The Pill"
- Dr. Morgentaler's clinic
- "Rape shield" law
- Gendered social order
- Anti-feminist backlash
- "The Beauty Myth"
- Third-wave feminism

QUESTIONS FOR DISCUSSION

1. Why did the women's liberation movement of the late 1960s and 1970s take more militant forms in the United States than in Canada?

2. American social commentator David Reisman, in reviewing the social revolution of the late 1960s in North America, once said that the women's movement was "possibly the most lasting legacy of the...period of protests." Assess the validity of this interpreta-tion from the perspective of the 1990s.

3. Abortion rights for women was the most con-tentious Canadian social issue of the 1970s and early 1980s. Why did Dr. Henry Morgentaler and the reproductive-rights movement tri-umph in the struggle over abortion?

4. American feminist author Susan Faludi described the 1980s as the "backlash decade" in which the media and politicians waged an "undeclared war against American women." Why did North American feminism come under attack? To what extent had women's economic progress led to a "lesser life" for many women?

5. In her 1992 review of the contemporary North American women's movement, Naomi Black contended that "Canadian feminists on occasion accepted American precedents, while insisting on Canadian distinctiveness." Assess the validity of her statement.

ANALYZING THE EVIDENCE

Study each of the following items of historical and statistical evidence relating to the status of women in Canada. For each item of evidence:

1. Identify the problem or issues raised by the data; and

2. Develop a hypothesis (or tentative conclusion, subject to further investigation) based on the evidence.

TABLE 1   LABOUR FORCE PARTICIPATION, EMPLOYMENT AND UNEMPLOYMENT, 1966–82

	PARTICIPATION RATE		WOMEN AS %	UNEMPLOYMENT RATE		WOMAN AS % OF
YEAR	WOMEN	MEN	OF EMPLOYED	WOMEN	MEN	UNEMPLOYED
1966	35.4	79.8	31.3	3.4	3.3	31.8
1967	36.5	79.3	32.1	3.7	3.9	31.4
1968	37.1	78.6	32.7	4.4	4.6	31.8
1969	38.0	78.3	33.2	4.7	4.3	35.1
1970	38.3	77.8	33.6	5.8	5.6	34.7
1971	39.4	77.3	34.2	6.6	6.0	36.8
1972	40.2	77.5	34.5	7.0	5.8	39.1
1973	41.8	78.2	35.1	6.7	4.9	42.6
1974	42.9	78.7	35.6	6.4	4.8	42.6
1975	44.2	78.4	36.3	8.1	6.2	43.2
1976	45.0	77.7	36.9	8.4	6.4	44.2
1977	45.9	77.7	37.3	9.5	7.3	44.1
1978	47.8	77.9	38.3	9.6	7.6	44.8
1979	48.9	78.4	38.3	8.8	6.6	46.1
1980	50.3	78.3	39.7	8.4	6.9	44.8
1981	51.6	78.3	40.7	8.3	7.1	44.7
1982	51.6	76.9	41.2	10.8	11.1	40.6

Sources: For 1966–77, calculated from Statistics Canada, *Historical Labour Force Statistics: Actual Data, Seasonal Factors, Seasonally Adjusted Data* (Cat. no. 71-201) Ottawa, 1978. For 1978, calcuated from Statistics Canada, *Labour Force Annual Averages, 1975–1978* (Cat. no. 71-529) Ottawa, 1979. For 1979-82, calcualted from *The Labour Force* (Cat. no. 71-001), various issues.

Reproduced by authority of the Minister of Industry 1995.

TABLE 2   PORTRAIT OF WOMEN'S POVERTY IN CANADA, 1987

	TOTAL	POOR
Women living alone or with no relatives		
Under age 65	1 008 000	335 000
65 and over	625 000	274 000
Women living in two-spouse families		
Wives under 65, with children under 18	2 981 000	285 000
Wives under 65, no children under 18	2 344 000	164 000
Wives 65 and over	601 000	34 000
Live-in adult daughters and other relatives	1 244 000	77 000
Single women with children under 18		
Never-married mothers	80 000	60 000
Divorced, separated, and widowed mothers	287 000	148 000
Live-in adult daughters and other relatives	73 000	18 000
Other women	759 000	120 000
Total	**10 002 000**	**1 515 000**

Source: National Council of Welfare, *Women and Poverty Revisited* (Summer 1990). Reprinted by permission.

PRINCIPAL POWER IN A SUPERPOWER WORLD, 1968–1988

THE WORLD OF 1968 WAS ENGULFED in social ferment and revolution. In France, a surging student-protest movement filled the streets of Paris and nearly toppled the government of President Charles de Gaulle. In Czechoslovakia, the government in Prague experimented with a more humanized kind of communism, only to be crushed when Moscow sent in the tanks. In the United States, race riots in the streets of Detroit and Washington followed the assassination of civil-rights leader Martin Luther King, Jr., and student demonstrators protested the Vietnam War and brutal police actions during the Democratic party convention in Chicago. Amid all this upheaval, Canada elected a new-style prime minister, Pierre Elliott Trudeau, took some solace in being a more "peaceable kingdom," and exuded an unmistakable air of moral superiority in its prevailing attitude toward the United States. In the ringing words of Canadian rocker Burton Cummings, "I don't need your war machine, I don't need your ghetto scene — American woman, stay away from me."

While the United States was "coming apart at home" over race and Vietnam, Canada embraced Trudeau, an unorthodox leader fond of questioning accepted foreign and domestic policies. Once in power, Trudeau ordered a full-scale review of Canada's post-1945 foreign policies to ensure that its national interests, not Cold War defence priorities, determined the policies' direction. Since the onset of the Cold War, he told a British interviewer, "Canada's foreign policy was largely its policy in NATO, through NATO." Trudeau sought to chart a new course, different from the "helpful fixer" role favoured by the practitioners of Pearsonian diplomacy. In place of the Pearsonian ideal of world peacemaking, he attempted to put Canadian political, economic, and social interests first. Trudeau's conception of foreign policy was not based solely on narrow self-interest, because he sought to transform Canada into a unified mentor state, taking initiatives in its "national interests" to reduce East–West tension and to promote improved North–South relations.[1]

Canada as a principal power: Prime Minister Pierre Trudeau's historic 1973 visit to China.

"HELPFUL FIXER" TO "PRINCIPAL POWER"

Between the late 1960s and the early 1980s, the postwar world order changed dramatically. The pre-eminent United States, which had shaped that postwar order and enforced its effectiveness, underwent severe challenges to its global power and influence. The United States' military setbacks in the Vietnam War, its severe monetary crisis of 1971, and its vulnerability after the Middle East oil shocks of 1973 all highlighted an apparent decline in American military and economic capabilities and a new reluctance to undertake global commitments in defence of the West. With the Soviet Union unable to fill the global power vacuum, a small group of industrial states — notably Japan, West Germany, and France — assumed a more influential role in international affairs, most obviously at western economic summits, the United Nations Security Council, and conferences promoting North-South dialogue.

In the face of America's relative decline and a greater diffusion of power in international affairs, Canada in the Trudeau era was propelled into the new status of a "principal power." Like most principal powers, Canada acted, in the words of political scientists David Dewitt and John Kirton, "autonomously in pursuit of [its] own interests, rather than as [a mediator] among others or [agent] for them."[2] Trudeau's first significant act as prime minister was to proclaim Canada's willingness to recognize the People's Republic of China — the initial step in the sweeping foreign-policy review. In pursuit of his goals, Trudeau relied heavily on Ivan Head, his senior policy adviser, and less on the Department of External Affairs that had guided Canadian foreign policy since its beginnings. The result of his review was a six-pack of booklets known as *A Foreign Policy for Canadians*, issued in 1970, which proposed that Canada refocus its trade and international ties beyond North America toward Europe, Asia, and Latin America. Curiously absent from the papers was any document setting out a position on Canadian–American relations.

Sharing a continent with the United States, Trudeau pointed out on his 1969 visit to Washington, was

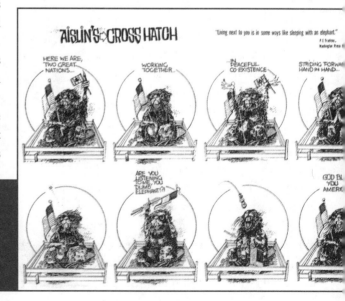

Montreal *Gazette* cartoonist Aislin lampoons Pierre Trudeau's famous "elephant and mouse" speech, delivered in March 1969 at the National Press Club in Washington.

"like sleeping with an elephant." The Vietnam War overshadowed and dominated Canadian–American relations from the late 1960s to the mid-1970s. Since the release of the 1965 report "Principles for Partnership," co-authored by Livingston Merchant and Arnold Heeney, diplomats and politicians seemed to feel that the continental relationship was a subject best left alone. So hostile was the reaction to the recommended policy of "quiet diplomacy" that officials in Washington and Ottawa refrained from publicly preaching what they practised in private, behind diplomatic doors.[3]

From 1968 onward, Canada grew to rival Britain in the Commonwealth, and even France within *la francophonie*, by supporting peaceful decolonization, initiating new programs of development assistance, and winning a sympathetic response from Third World countries. Within the United Nations, the Canadian mission slowly shifted away from its traditional middle-power associates to take on larger responsibilities on the Security Council and to promote improved international aid programs. As a member of the North Atlantic Treaty Alliance (NATO), Trudeau's Canada departed more frequently from the traditional cautious posture of an allied middle power and demonstrated more support for the security and arms-control perspectives of major European powers like West Germany and France. And within North America, Trudeau and his ministers periodically engaged in public diplomacy, conducted continental bargaining on an arm's-length basis, and proposed multilateral approaches to Third World problems and to the global arms race.

CANADA AND THE THIRD WORLD

THE TRUDEAU GOVERNMENT may well have been the first to take up international development as a major foreign-policy priority. But Canada's involvement with colonialism and the struggle for decolonization had a long history. As a member of both the Commonwealth and the United Nations (U.N.), Canada had developed a unique relationship with the emerging postcolonial nations of Asia, Africa, and Latin America. The first contacts with what would soon be called the "Third World" were forged at San Francisco in 1945 with the birth of the United Nations. As a middle power committed to U.N. peacekeeping, Canada was rich enough to be idealistic, free of a colonialist past, and notably without superpower ambitions.

CANADA, THE UNITED STATES, AND COLONIALISM

Membership in the British Commonwealth made Canada's postwar relations with the developing nations different from those of the United States. While America emerged from World War II as the world's greatest imperial power, with a string of bases and colonies throughout the Pacific Ocean, the Caribbean Sea, and Latin America, Canada belonged to an older, more benign imperial federation. In Commonwealth affairs during the 1950s, Louis St. Laurent and Canadian diplomats observed the struggles of nationalist movements for independence and developed an unexpected empathy with leaders of the newer Commonwealth member nations like Jawaharlal Nehru of India. The United States, on the other hand, adopted an official "good neighbour" policy with regard to Latin America and pledged to ensure that the Americas remained free from intervention in "the internal or external affairs of another state."

Growing fears of Soviet communist expansionism in the 1950s and 1960s led to periodic departures from American "good neighbour" policy in Latin America. From 1952 onward, U.S. foreign aid to Latin America was more and more allocated to shoring up the friendly, non-communist régimes in the region. In the ten years following 1952, fully $45 billion of the $50 billion supplied in aid to some 90 countries around the world went for military purposes. The military aid often involved armed intervention to resist the spread of communism, most notably in Guatemala (1954), Cuba (the Bay of Pigs invasion in 1961), and the Dominican Republic (1965).

The changing face of the British Commonwealth. In 1944, the five prime ministers and Mackenzie King represented Great Britain and the "white" dominions. In 1987, the 47 member nations of the Commonwealth included countries representing all areas of the globe and encompassing one-quarter of the world's population.

CANADA AND DECOLONIZATION

Canada remained remarkably detached or aloof from the decolonization movements of the 1950s. Just as Canada had achieved self-government through a process of "constitutional evolution," cabinet minister Paul Martin argued at the United Nations in 1952, so, too, should modern independence movements be gradual and peaceful, involving a step-by-step approach that promoted social progress, constructive collaboration with the "former protector," and an avoidance of "reckless and destructive action" on the part of the colonial peoples. Until about 1959, Canada's policy continued to be "disinterested detachment" in colonial affairs.

By 1960, Ottawa found that the rising tide of anti-colonialism could no longer be resisted. Many of the newly independent states of Africa and Asia were members of the Commonwealth, and in order to maintain good relations with them the traditional, somewhat reactionary, colonial policy had to be modified or abandoned. With the establishment of high commissions in Accra, Ghana (1957), Lagos, Nigeria (1960), and Dar-es-Salaam, Tanzania (1962), and a consulate in Leopoldville, The Congo, the Canadian government received more exposure to African views and African pressures. In addition, the real threat of communist expansion now appeared to be in Asia and Africa rather than in Europe.

The change in Canada's policy on decolonization was made official in 1960 at the U.N. General Assembly. In a session considering the granting of independence to colonial peoples, Canada endorsed a resolution that recognized "the right of all peoples to self-determination" and the obligation of all colonial powers to take immediate steps to "transfer power to their dependent peoples, without conditions or reservations." From that time onward, Canadian governments were actively involved in Africa and Asia in support of the decolonization efforts of black nationalist parties and groups, particularly in Rhodesia (now Zimbabwe) and South Africa. On the issue of apartheid (racial segregation), Prime Minister John Diefenbaker played a leading role in forcing South Africa to withdraw from the Commonwealth in March 1961. A succession of Canadian governments not only spoke out openly in opposition to apartheid but adopted a variety of sanctions against South Africa, ranging from an official sports boycott to oil and air embargoes.

CANADA'S ROLE IN NAMIBIA

In the Trudeau years, the Canadian government's approach to decolonization was best illustrated in Canada's key role on the U.N. Security Council's Namibia Contact Group. The issue was the situation in Namibia, the former German colony of *Sud-West Afrika*, which had been ruled by neighbouring South Africa since World War I. Here, in the late 1970s, the black population was still governed by the white-minority Afrikaner régime at Pretoria and was subject to its policy of apartheid. Aside from South Africa, it was the only remaining large territory in Africa that had not secured independent black-majority rule.

As part of the select Namibian Contact Group, Canada exerted political influence befitting that of a "principal power." In the small task force, the Canadian delegation worked as co-equals with representatives of the major western powers — the United States, Britain, France, and West Germany. For the Canadian contact group team, the hardest test came over the question of Namibian independence. Working under U.N. auspices, Canada joined the other members of the contact group in hammering out a plan for a peaceful transition to majority rule through free, fair, U.N.-supervised elections. Using their two-year, non-permanent position on the U.N. Security Council to full advantage, the Canadian representatives helped to initiate and draft a settlement plan in 1978. Even though the Canadian-backed settlement plan eventually collapsed, Canada had distinguished itself on the contact group as a surprisingly influential "principal power" in the Third World.

CANADA AND DEVELOPMENT ASSISTANCE

As well as supporting peaceful decolonization and U.N. peacekeeping in the Third World, Canada since the mid-1960s gradually emerged as a major participant in foreign aid and development assistance. In World War II, massive amounts of aid had been generated for Britain and its allies. But from 1945 until the mid-1960s, Canadian governments had been less willing to aid the world's poor than to assist the participants in — and victims of — war.

Canada's involvement in postwar economic assistance started small, as part of a big project initiated at the Commonwealth Conference of 1950 in Colombo, Ceylon (now Sri Lanka). The Colombo Plan, first proposed by Australia, outlined a six-year program of development for the less-developed Commonwealth countries in Asia. The Canadian government, after considerable deliberation, decided to put up $25 million for the first year, considerably less than the $300 million committed that year to the NATO Mutual Aid Program in Europe. Throughout the 1950s, Canada's record of development assistance was unimpressive. By 1956–57, Canadian non-military aid totalled just $50 million, composed of $35 million for the Colombo Plan and a variety of smaller contributions for U.N. programs such as technical assistance, refugee aid, and the children's fund (UNICEF).

Hungry people in Ethiopia, waiting for food distributed by the United Nations Children's Fund.

THE "DEVELOPMENT DECADE" PERFORMANCE

Canada's aid performance improved greatly under the Liberal government of Lester Pearson. By 1966–67, total Canadian aid had reached $300 million, of which $40 million went to Colombo Plan countries. External aid had not only expanded but grown more diversified, with allocations for food aid to famine-ravaged India, scholarships, technical assistance, and low-interest, long-term development loans. In addition, Canada was contributing smaller amounts to multilateral programs and agencies, including the Indus water-diversion and development scheme, the World Bank, and the Asian Development Bank. Even though Canadian aid had expanded, the total figure still remained short of the target of 0.7 percent of gross national product (GNP) as recommended in Lester Pearson's 1969 report for the World Bank and endorsed by the U.N.

The arrival of the Trudeau government in 1968 brought a significant upgrading in the Canadian aid effort. The Canadian International Development Agency (CIDA) was set up, and total allocations for aid increased from 15 to 20 percent a year up to 1974–75, even during times of severe budgetary constraint. This increase was more remarkable because it coincided with a drastic drop in the flow of American aid to underdeveloped countries. After 1973, when the aid budget had passed $500 million, however, criticisms were raised in Canada about CIDA and the effectiveness of its programs. Some Canadian critics went so far as to charge that Canada was stepping in to aid countries with whom the United States was severing its aid connections. Other sceptics pointed out that Canadian food aid was still being delivered in the 1970s with big maple leaf flags and the name "CANADA" emblazoned on the sacks of flour.[4]

LA FRANCOPHONIE

One of the most startling changes in the Canadian development-assistance program during the 1970s was the marked increase in aid to *la francophonie* — the French-speaking countries. Between 1960 and 1968, for example, the 21 nations of francophone Africa received only $300 000 annually for technical assistance; by 1973, they had been allocated $80 million, one-fifth of the total CIDA budget. During that time Canada became, next to France and to the *Fonds Européen de Développement,* the single most important donor country in some states of francophone Africa. Aid to *la francophonie* had increased so rapidly that, after 1972, CIDA made efforts to maintain a balance between aid to Commonwealth and francophone Africa.

By providing this aid to the French-speaking areas of the Third World, Trudeau and his government in the 1970s sought, in part, to enhance a "new fibre of unity" in Canada. Before 1968, most of Canada's aid had gone to British Commonwealth nations. For a Canadian government committed to the extension of bilingualism at home, aid to francophone Third

World countries provided a way of promoting that bilingual image abroad. As an external-affairs official explained in 1977, the "French-speaking countries are an essential element of our international relations…because they are the natural outside extension of French Canada's vitality and culture. It is also a very useful area of international co-operation."

Contacts with *la francophonie* were also aimed at pre-empting attempts by France and Quebec to gain an independent status for Quebec in international organizations. At the founding meeting of the Agency for Cultural and Technical Co-operation among French-speaking countries, held in Niger, Quebec — with the aid of France — sought an independent status. But Ottawa succeeded in winning over most of France's former colonies, which received from Canada one-third of the start-up costs for the new agency. Quebec's "diplomatic offensive" among *la francophonie* was resumed in 1976 with the election of René Lévesque's Parti Québécois government. At the 1977 meeting of the agency, in the Ivory Coast, Ottawa again responded to Quebec's assertive nationalism with aid — supplying a Canadian director for the agency, a new special development fund, and a generous increase in Canada's $1 million contribution already pledged to the agency. *La francophonie*, it seemed, benefited enormously from Ottawa's attempts to arrest the domestic forces of Quebec nationalism.

TRUDEAU'S PLEDGES AND ACTUAL PERFORMANCE

Prime Minister Trudeau and his government embraced a philosophy of international development remarkably different from that of the United States and many other advanced industrial nations. In the heady days of the "First Development Decade," as the 1960s were dubbed, Canada — like most other donor nations — had measured development in terms of economic growth, and aid programs were designed to provide foreign exchange, to purchase capital equipment, and to develop the necessary local infrastructure of roads, bridges, and irrigation systems. But economic growth in the Third World countries had left the poorest 40–60 percent of most populations as badly off as ever.

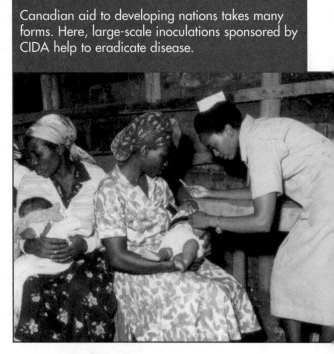

Canadian aid to developing nations takes many forms. Here, large-scale inoculations sponsored by CIDA help to eradicate disease.

In responding to these concerns, Trudeau emphasized the need for "an equitable distribution, worldwide, of resources and opportunities" and proclaimed in 1974 that the role of Western leadership was to promote the "embrace of a global ethic." His vision of development in the 1970s went well beyond promoting economic growth, calling for "net human benefit" as the new standard to replace the GNP.

Canada's performance in the Third World, however, often did not match Trudeau's fine sentiments. While Trudeau expressed sympathy with the call in Third World countries for a "new international economic order," critics claimed that Canada was a party to "new-style colonialism" in Africa and the Caribbean. By encouraging and aiding Canadian multinational corporations and banks to increase their direct foreign investment in independent Africa and Caribbean nations, they pointed out, Canada was making poor African and Caribbean countries dependent on developed-country technology, on primary-product exports, and on Canadian-owned financial institutions. Worsening domestic economic conditions also forced the Trudeau government to cut back on official development assistance (ODA) by the late 1970s.

The 1980s began with Trudeau making a renewed commitment to improving Canadian aid programs and North–South relations. The government decided, upon Trudeau's return to power in 1980, to again attempt the ODA target of 0.7 percent of GNP. This period also witnessed the establishment of two new Canadian international agencies — the Petro-Canada International Assistance Corporation, to aid Third World countries in oil exploration; and the International Centre for Ocean Development to help such countries in their search for food in the oceans. But Prime Minister Trudeau's most visible action to address North–South problems was his leadership role at the economic conference on "International Co-operation and Development" held at Cancun, Mexico, in 1981.

In its approach to Third World development in the early 1980s, Canada took a moderately progressive position compared with that of the United States. Under the Trudeau government from 1980 to 1984, Canada's approach diverged from U.S. President Ronald Reagan's view that American free enterprise provided the only viable model for development. Nor did the Trudeau government's policies reflect the Reagan administration's Cold War perspective on Soviet communist expansion in the socialist or non-aligned nations of Africa and Latin America. Countries with socialist governments, such as Julius Nyerere's Tanzania, continued to receive aid from Canada, as did Castro's Cuba (until its involvement in Angola). Canadian official development assistance continued to Nicaragua after the Sandinista revolution in 1980, running counter to U.S. attempts to topple that country's government. Furthermore, when Ronald Reagan undertook his Caribbean Basin Initiative in late 1981, the Trudeau government's response was cool and suspicious, based on the view that the initiative appeared to be politically motivated, aiding countries friendly to American capital in the region at the expense of others.

PROMOTING THE "NORTH–SOUTH DIALOGUE"

The South, the poor and developing countries including China, has three thousand million people — three-quarters of the world's population, but living on one-fifth of the world's income…. In the poorest countries, one out of every four children dies before the age of five. One fifth or more of all people in the South suffer from hunger and malnutrition.

The Brandt Report, 1980, p. 32.

After his return to power in 1980, Prime Minister Pierre Trudeau redoubled his efforts to force the North–South problem onto the agenda at the summit meetings of the western world's seven principal powers. At the western economic summit held in Ottawa in the summer of 1981, Trudeau used his position as host to single out the North–South problem as a major global concern. In spite of U.S. President Ronald Reagan's firm preference for free-market solutions, the Canadian prime minister made some headway. Under pressure from Canada and European leaders, Reagan agreed to

THE GAP BETWEEN NORTH AND SOUTH

	Developed Nations	Developing Nations
Nations	33%	67%
Population	25%	75%
Income	80%	20%
Industry	91%	9%
Income per capita	$5191	$479
Government health expenditure/capita	$ 208	$ 7
Government education expenditure/capita	$ 293	$ 18
Life expectancy (years)	72	57
Infant mortality (deaths per 1000 births)	19	111
Physicians per 10 000 people	21	3
Daily calories per person	3388	2320
Percent of population with safe water	93%	39%
Adult literacy	98%	55%
Children in school	70%	47%
Teachers per 1000 children	37	15
Working children under 15 (millions)	1	44

Sources: *The Brandt Report*, 1980; *Towards a World Economy That Works*, U.N., 1980; R. Sivard, *World Military & Social Expenditures*, 1978.

participate in a conference on North–South issues and to join, however reluctantly, in a process leading to "global negotiations" on matters of economic redistribution between the rich and the poor countries. Of all the western industrial powers, no country did more than Canada to awaken the United States to the far-reaching demands for economic justice being voiced by the developing nations of the Third World.

The Canadian role in promoting North–South dialogue was readily apparent at the October 1991 conference in Cancun, Mexico, a meeting of 22 leaders from countries in the North and the South. As one of eight northern states invited, as a key force behind U.N. and Commonwealth initiatives on North–South issues, and as a close associate of concerned European states like France, Austria, and Sweden, Canada was well situated to undertake "a bridge-building role" between the United States and Third World representatives.

The Cancun Conference turned out to be a missed opportunity. Prime Minister Trudeau confronted a strange alliance of Third World radicals seeking self-sufficient development and a U.S. administration committed to reducing aid through multilateral institutions. Although Canada and other supporting nations managed to force an open debate on the need for "global negotiations," little of a concrete nature was achieved. In the end, a Canadian proposal to commence such negotiations in a mutually agreeable forum by the end of 1981 was shelved in favour of a more general expression of support for discussions under "mutually agreed procedures."

Under Brian Mulroney's Progressive Conservative government after 1984, an increased emphasis was placed on aid and trade linkages associated with official development assistance. Reacting to business criticisms and a swing in Canadian public opinion, efforts were made to couple foreign-aid expenditure with domestic economic returns. Canadian development-assistance strategy shifted its focus toward bilateral (rather than multilateral) ODA, the use of aid for export promotion purposes, and the encouragement of greater private-sector involvement in Third World development.

The government's decision to postpone the achievement of the 0.7 percent target of GNP to the year

Prime Minister Brian Mulroney (far right) with the leaders of the Group of Seven industrialized nations at the Tokyo Summit in 1987.

2000 suggested that the growth of ODA would be constrained, or possibly less generous. Indeed, in 1985, for the first time the net inflow of capital into Canada from the Third World exceeded by some $300 million the overall outflow of resources to developing countries.

SECURITY IN A NUCLEAR WORLD

SINCE THE DROPPING of the first atomic bomb on Hiroshima in 1945, North America and the world had lived in the shadow of nuclear holocaust. Peace and relative stability in Europe, despite sharp East–West ideological tensions, were maintained by deterrence — an arsenal of nuclear weapons that neither side dared unleash. But every American president had pursued negotiations for the limitation of the nuclear arms race, while maintaining American defence programs deemed essential to the global strategic balance. Although not a member of the "nuclear club," Canada — by virtue of its geographic location between the superpowers and its membership in the North Atlantic Treaty Organization (NATO) and the North American Air Defence Command (NORAD) — had both a stake and a part in the nuclear arms race. In spite of its commitment to peace and nuclear arms control, Ottawa remained a reliable partner in the American nuclear security alliance.

PIROUETTE ON THE WORLD STAGE

During his foreign-policy review in 1969, Prime Minister Trudeau stated that Canada's foreign policy should determine its defence policy, not vice versa. In an effort to help reduce East–West tensions in Europe, the Trudeau government reduced Canada's NATO commitment by cutting the Canadian military contribution in NATO's European theatre by half, beginning to phase out nuclear weaponry, and moving its remaining forces to reserve status. For Trudeau, who had once opposed Pearson's nuclear policy, this signified a modest attempt to send a signal to other nations. It also exemplified the "pirouette" style of Trudeau's foreign policy.

During the Trudeau years (1968–84) Canada's nuclear role was gradually transformed. Between 1970 and 1972, Honest John nuclear missiles were taken from Canada's NATO ground forces in Europe, and CF-104 Starfighters based in Lahr, West Germany, were given only a ground support and reconnaissance role, using conventional weapons. Within NORAD, the Canadian Bomarc missile sites were dismantled in 1971. When the Voodoo interceptor aircraft was replaced in November 1984 by the CF-18 Hornet, conventional rockets replaced nuclear missiles as Canada's air-defence weapon, and the last nuclear weapons had been removed from Canadian forces at home and in Europe.

In spite of the new non-nuclear policy, Canada was still part of the North American defence system and of the global nuclear arms race. As a member of NATO since 1949 and a continental partner in NORAD since 1958, Canada was closely linked with Arctic early warning and coastal anti-submarine operations. It still ranked second only to West Germany in the number (up to 80) of nuclear-weapons related facilities on its soil, consisting mainly of radar and navigation stations. In addition, the Canadian defence industry remained closely integrated with that of the United States and was involved in the development, building, and testing of nuclear parts and components from missile launchers to guidance systems.

CANADA AND NUCLEAR NON-PROLIFERATION

After 1968, Canada also stepped up its attempts to stop the spread or "horizontal proliferation" of nuclear weapons from the Big Five "nuclear club" to other countries. Nuclear proliferation had always posed a quandary for Canadian policy-makers because Canada had been engaged in atomic research since 1942 and was one of the world's largest producers of uranium. The economics of the Canadian uranium-mining and nuclear-reactor industries had required — particularly since the early 1960s — the export of nuclear materials, equipment, and technology.

In May 1974, India shocked the world by detonating a "peaceful" nuclear device. The plutonium fuel came from India-produced uranium, irradiated in a nuclear reactor that had been supplied by Canada under the Colombo Plan in 1956. Although Canada was not alone among the supplier states in helping India "go nuclear," the Canadian press and public reacted with outrage to the detonation, and the Trudeau government was forced to take action. Canada suspended its nuclear co-operation with India and took the lead from 1974 to 1977, as a member of the London "Suppliers' Club," in urging more stringent international safeguards over the export of peaceful nuclear supplies.

During the mid-1970s, Canada's own non-proliferation policies consisted of a series of ad hoc and somewhat inconsistent responses. India's nuclear explosion, a growing concern among supplier states, and the support of the U.S. administration of Jimmy Carter all helped push Canada in the direction of more stringent safeguards. But growing economic competition among nuclear-supplier states, coupled with pressures from Canada's European trading partners, eventually forced a relaxation of Canadian standards. With the "peaceful" nuclear genie out of the bottle, Canadian peaceful nuclear diplomacy was buffeted by the contending pressures of moral self-restraint and economic imperatives.

TRUDEAU AND NUCLEAR POLICY

Pierre Trudeau came into power in 1968 with firm convictions about Canada's role in a nuclear world. Yet, in his first 10 years in office, he exhibited only an episodic interest in global arms control and disarmament. All that changed in May 1978, when — at the urging of external-affairs officials — Trudeau delivered a major address at the United Nations. In an attempt to revive the lagging process of disarmament, he called for "a strategy of suffocation, aimed at depriving the arms race of the oxygen that it needs." By attacking the technological impulse that lies behind the development of strategic nuclear weapons, according to Trudeau, a halt could be brought to the arms race in the laboratory.

NIXON, KISSINGER, AND DÉTENTE

DÉTENTE IS A FRENCH WORD MEANING "a relaxing of tensions, as between nations." In American foreign relations it has been used to describe a time in the late 1960s and early 1970s when a "thaw" set in between the world's superpowers, the United States and the Soviet Union. It was coined by Henry A. Kissinger, President Richard Nixon's national security adviser (1969–73), and later an active secretary of state (1973–77).

President Nixon's inaugural address in January 1969 signalled the beginning of a major American diplomatic revolution. While Nixon came to the presidency with a reputation as a "Cold Warrior," he set out to earn the title of peacemaker by opening "an era of negotiation." Seeking better relations with the Soviet Union and China was politically possible for Nixon because few would ever accuse him of being pro-communist. But perhaps the most important influence on the president was the world view of Henry Kissinger. As an international-relations expert, Dr. Kissinger advocated *realpolitik*, or a policy based on hard, practical power considerations rather than morality or anti-communist ideology. Kissinger's world view appealed to Nixon, who was himself a hard-nosed practical man with little use for sentiments or principles. Within three years of his inauguration, Nixon would reverse his previous ideological stand by staging a dramatic visit offering American friendship to China and by opening the Strategic Arms Limitation Talks (SALT) with the Soviet Union.

In testimony before the Senate Foreign Relations Committee in 1974, Dr. Kissinger set out the essential meaning of détente:

> There can be no peaceful international order without a constructive relationship between the United States and the Soviet Union. There will be no international stability unless both the Soviet Union and the United States conduct themselves with restraint and unless they use their enormous power for the benefit of mankind.
>
> Thus, we must be clear at the outset on what the term "détente" entails. It is the search for a more constructive relationship with the Soviet Union. It is a continuing process, not a final condition. And it has been pursued by successive American leaders though the means have varied as have world conditions.
>
> Some fundamental principles guide this policy:
>
> The United States does not base its policy solely on Moscow's good intentions. We seek, regardless of Soviet intentions, to serve peace through a systematic resistance to pressure and conciliatory responses to moderate behavior.
>
> We must oppose aggressive actions, but we must not seek confrontations lightly.

> We must maintain a strong national defense while recognizing that in the nuclear age the relationship between military strength and politically usable power is the most complex in all history.
>
> Henry Kissinger, U.S. Secretary of State, *Testimony Before the Senate Foreign Relations Committee*, September 19, 1974.

Trudeau's 1978 "strategy of suffocation" speech raised many hopes in Canada and even in parts of the world community. However, except for the appointment of an external-affairs disarmament adviser–ambassador, little was done to promote Trudeau's strategy in places like NATO, the U.N. Disarmament Committee, or NORAD, where such advocacy might have had some effect. Not only did Trudeau and his ministers seem to let the issue drop, they also stopped short of endorsing a comparable proposal advanced by U.S. senators Edward Kennedy and Mark Hatfield calling for "a balanced and verifiable nuclear weapons freeze."

COLD WAR, ENERGY, AND PEACE

A NEW CYCLE OF ARMS-RACE escalation began in the late 1970s. In December 1979, responding to the Soviet Union's replacement of old SS-4 and SS-5 missiles with more accurate, longer-range SS-20s, the NATO ministers decided to proceed with a "two-track strategy" of re-arming western Europe while pressing the Soviet Union to halt the deployment of its new weapons. The planned deployment of a new generation of U.S. land-based Cruise and Pershing II missiles met with staff resistance from Norway, provoked a cool response in the Netherlands, Belgium, and Denmark, and sparked massive anti-nuclear protests in cities throughout Britain and western Europe. Yet in Canada the Progressive Conservative government under Joe Clark endorsed European nuclear deployment without questions, and the Trudeau Liberals, returned to power in 1980, reaffirmed Canada's official support.

REAGAN AND THE NEW COLD WAR

The election of Ronald Reagan in 1980 ushered in a new era of tension in Soviet–American relations. President Reagan's pledge to "make America strong again," his talk of "limited nuclear war" in Europe, and his characterization of the Soviet Union as "an evil empire" caused some commentators to announce the commencement of a new Cold War. Soviet leaders and foreign-policy officials in the Kremlin retaliated with hostile rhetoric and nuclear threats of their own. In 1981, the Soviets under Leonid Brezhnev began their "brink of war" campaign and later referred to President Reagan as a "shameless liar" and Washington officials as "militaristic hotheads."

Beginning in 1980, President Reagan presided over the United States' largest peacetime increase in military spending. His first five-year defence plan cost over $1.4 trillion, with annual U.S. defence budgets of more than $300 billion. Most of the increased defence spending went into the development or modernization of nuclear hardware, including MX or peacekeeper missiles, the Trident fleet, and, most importantly, Pershing II and Cruise missiles. The Strategic Defense Initiative, or "Star Wars" plan, unveiled by Reagan in March 1983 and aimed at developing a defensive space shield, promised to add another $25–$60 billion over the next few years.

THE CANADIAN CONNECTION

Even though Canada had renounced its nuclear role in 1969–70, the new Trudeau government in the early 1980s continued to collaborate with the Reagan administration, NORAD, and the American defence industry. In March 1981, Prime Minister Trudeau renewed the NORAD agreement with little discussion. The agreement was extended for another five years and its name changed from "Air" to "Aerospace" defence agreement, thus threatening to lock Canada into U.S. plans for the militarization of outer space. U.S. warships with a nuclear capability continued to be welcomed at Canadian ports, although they had been banned from New Zealand's harbours since 1973.

A critical view of Prime Minister Pierre Trudeau's non-nuclear policy. What does this cartoon tell you about Canada's ability to speak out against nuclear weapons while remaining protected by American nuclear power?

The most highly publicized aspect of Canada's participation in U.S. nuclear-weapons policy was its involvement in the development, building, and testing of the Cruise missile. Between 1979 and 1982, Litton Systems (Canada) Limited, an American branch plant in Rexdale, Ontario, received $26 million in federal start-up grants and a five-year, interest-free loan of $22 million to develop and produce the navigational guidance system for the Cruise missile. The first Cruise unit was delivered to the U.S. Joint Missile Project in April 1981. Litton supplied 102 guidance systems to the U.S. defence department in 1981–82 and an estimated 305 systems in 1982–83, under contracts worth $80 million. When Litton Canada failed in 1984 to secure the contract for the U.S. advanced "stealth" Cruise missiles, the company's president blamed Canadian "peace protesters" for generating bad publicity in the press.

The U.S. administration's formal request in April 1981 to test the unarmed Cruise missile in Canadian air space touched off a storm of protest and controversy. Although the American defence department originally requested a blanket agreement, the Canadian government insisted on specific test approvals, and a five-year agreement was signed in 1983, over the protests of a vociferous "Refuse the Cruise" movement. Cruise missile testing was justified as an essential part of Canada's commitment to NATO. The first Cruise missile test took place in March 1984 at the Primrose Lake test range near Cold Lake, Alberta. Three more were held before the end of 1985, and Cruise testing during 1986 included a space-defence-related experiment. Critics of the program contended that Cruise missile testing not only contradicted Trudeau's 1978 strategy of suffocation, but also violated Canada's earlier practice of nuclear restraint.

ENERGY: TWEAKING THE EAGLE'S BEAK

With the return of Trudeau in 1980 and the election of Ronald Reagan, Canadian relations with Washington went into a cold chill.[5] The National Energy Program (NEP), announced in the Liberal government's October 1980 budget, cast a pall over border relations. In response to sharply rising world oil prices, Ottawa attempted to ensure a security of supply, to control prices, and to readjust the distribution of oil and gas income. The federal government set a "blended oil pricing régime" to keep domestic prices below international levels. The NEP also included export controls, production taxes, and a petroleum incentives program to encourage exploration and development by Canadian-owned oil and gas firms. Its goal was to promote "Canadianization" of the largely American-owned industry with a target of 50 percent domestic ownership by 1990.

The NEP drew intense fire from the American multinational oil companies, the oil-producing province of Alberta, and the Reagan administration. Reagan officials and supporters saw the NEP as an attack on their free-market values and reacted with horror. In March 1981, U.S. Secretary of State Alexander Haig sent a stern protest note to Ottawa, implying that Washington was considering retaliation against Canadian investments in the United States. Paul Robinson, the tough-talking U.S. ambassador to Canada, resorted to some "finger-twisting," but cooler heads prevailed.

Although the NEP crisis subsided, deep differences remained in Trudeau–Reagan relations. Reagan and his administration viewed Trudeau's Canada as a First World nation that had adopted the mentality and policies of the Third World. Through recession and falling prices and into the great oil glut of 1984, the Trudeau government held firm with the NEP. American oil rigs were pulled out of Alberta and back to the United States, but the "Canadianization" of the oil industry remained surprisingly popular in Canada as Petro-Canada, the crown oil company, expanded into retail gas operations. Not until Brian Mulroney's Progressive Conservatives took power in 1984 would the NEP be dismantled, much to the delight of the Reagan administration.

THE TRUDEAU PEACE INITIATIVE

In the final months of his prime ministership, Pierre Trudeau embarked on a "peace initiative" with the ambitious aims of reducing East–West tensions and reversing the arms race. Beginning in the summer of 1981, Trudeau's public speeches and private utterances reflected a growing concern over heightened tensions in East–West relations and the Reagan administration's emphasis on rearmament and confrontation with the Soviet Union. In a speech in Indiana in May 1982, he warned of the growing rift between the two superpowers and suggested that Canada was edging toward "equidistance." At the United Nations in June 1982, Trudeau irritated American defence officials by warning of the dangers of space wars and urging an early agreement to prohibit the militarization of outer space. During the G-7 Summit conference in Williamsburg in May 1983, the Canadian prime minister intervened sharply to insist that a pledge to "devote our full political resources to reducing the threat of war" be inserted into an otherwise hardline final communiqué. So incensed was British Prime Minister Margaret Thatcher that she classified Trudeau in her memoirs as a "Liberal leftist" inclined to be soft on communism.

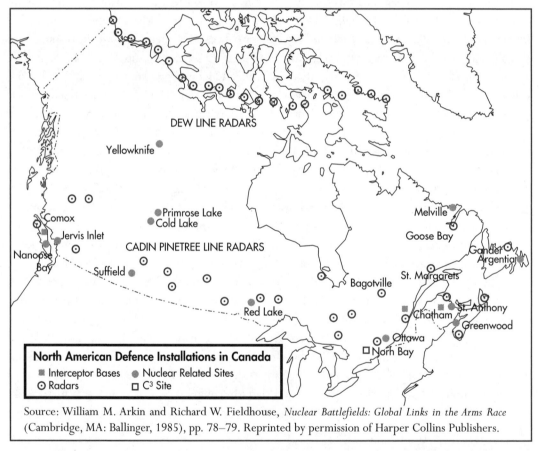

Source: William M. Arkin and Richard W. Fieldhouse, *Nuclear Battlefields: Global Links in the Arms Race* (Cambridge, MA: Ballinger, 1985), pp. 78–79. Reprinted by permission of Harper Collins Publishers.

A North American defence installation in Canada, 1985. A controversial 1985 book written by William Arkin and Richard Fieldhouse entitled *Nuclear Battlefields* provided a detailed analysis of the North American and global nuclear infrastructure. At the time, Canada was second only to West Germany as a host of nuclear-related facilities. It had nearly 80 installations, including 21 DEW line stations and 24 CADIN Pinetree stations closer to the U.S.–Canada border.

With global arms talks at Geneva breaking down, the Reagan administration pressing ahead on a new "Star Wars" research program, and Cold War rhetoric at its height over the Soviet downing of a Korean jetliner, Trudeau decided in September 1983 that the time had come to act. His peace strategy took a dual approach: a general appeal for a renewal of meaningful East–West dialogue, and a series of specific arms-control proposals. Its primary purpose was to get a credible foot in the door of the White House and the Kremlin and to encourage, through face-to-face encounters, a toning down of the escalating "megaphone diplomacy" between Washington and Moscow. To that end, Trudeau embarked on three months of diplomatic consultations that began with a long letter to President Reagan, then took him to the NATO, Japanese, Chinese and eastern European capitals, and ended with visits to Washington and the Kremlin.

While the peace venture won a favourable public response in Canada, Trudeau's unilateral intervention into the arms-control debate received a mixed reception in foreign capitals. It was also greeted with considerable puzzlement by the Reagan White House. In spite of its short duration, the Trudeau peace initiative did help to change the "trend line" in East–West relations from a collision course to a more productive dialogue. While his specific proposals for a five-power forum on arms control, a ban on high-altitude anti-satellite (AST) systems, and a verification code for new weapons systems received polite rejections in Washington and Moscow, Reagan and British Prime Minister Margaret Thatcher did begin to moderate their hostility to the Soviets. The Trudeau initiative, however, died a quick death when the prime minister retired in February 1984 after a "walk in the snow." Whether genuinely farsighted or naive and ill-conceived, the peace mission demonstrated that Trudeau mattered and cut quite a figure in world affairs.[6]

MULRONEY'S FOREIGN AND DEFENCE POLICY: A CHANGE IN POSTURE

Brian Mulroney came to power in Ottawa in 1984 with few foreign-policy convictions beyond the need for a closer relationship with Washington. Canada's new prime minister, as his biographers noted, saw Canada in "a firm lockstep with the United States" and shared, to some extent, "the Yalta theory of spheres of influence as it applies to Canada." In October 1983, while opposition leader, Mulroney had responded to the U.S. invasion of Grenada by giving the Americans, as western allies, "the benefit of the doubt." As prime minister, he went further in his support of American foreign and defence policies.

In early 1985, Mulroney responded warmly to Reagan's invitation to join the Strategic Defence Initiative (SDI) research program. In stark contrast to Trudeau's position, he indicated that Canada would "shoulder its fair share of the load." But the government's eventual response amounted to a compromise. After much public debate, the cabinet in September 1985 declined formal government-to-government involvement in Star Wars research. On the other hand, the

Mulroney government left the door open for Canadian participation by private companies and continued to endorse SDI as a "prudent" response to the Soviet ABM program. Furthermore, following the Star Wars decision, Ottawa continued to voice support for SDI in NATO and other international arenas.

In the area of North American defence, Mulroney's government did move to modernize and strengthen the NORAD system. In March 1985, Ottawa and the Reagan administration announced a $7 billion overhaul of North America's air defences, including the installation of a new North Warning System to replace the 30-year-old DEW (Distant Early Warning) Line. The agreement provided for the establishment of a modernized warning system against Soviet air attack around the entire perimeter of continental North America, capable of detecting all forms of Soviet bombers and transpolar cruise missiles. While the agreement had been negotiated largely by the previous Liberal government, Deputy Prime Minister Erik Nielsen hailed the deal as "an important step forward in ensuring that Canada can carry out the responsibilities we share with the United States for the defence of North America." Opposition critics did not share that enthusiasm, claiming that the agreement would "link" Canada in the future to the American SDI space-weapons system.

RHETORIC AND PERFORMANCE

The Mulroney government promised to rebuild the Canadian forces and restore Canada's commitment to western security. Between 1984 and 1985, Defence Minister Robert Coates pledged to strengthen Canadian military capabilities and announced a program to convert the armed forces back to multiservice uniforms. Spending on defence, however, was less than expected because of the government's stated objective of reducing the size of the federal deficit and to do so without severely curtailing social expenditures. Throughout 1986, the Mulroney government undertook a major defence-policy review and promised a white paper on the future direction of the armed forces.

Although Canada's overall defence strategy remained oriented toward enhancing national and western security, northern sovereignty surfaced as a major public issue and forced its way onto the defence agenda. In response to public concern raised by the 1985 voyage of the U.S. Coast Guard ship *Polar Sea* through the disputed Northwest Passage and a similar 1986 submarine incident, defence policy-makers shifted their attention to the question of Canada's arctic sovereignty. The government first announced plans for the construction of a Canadian arctic icebreaker, partially funded by the Department of National Defence. Then, in the spring of 1987, Defence Minister Perrin Beatty unveiled the long-awaited white paper on defence, which emphasized upgrading the armed forces and proposed major expenditures on the acquisition of nuclear-powered submarines for arctic patrol duty. The defence policy was poorly received and the nuclear submarines were never acquired because of defence budget cuts.

THE SUPERPOWER THAW

In the late 1980s, superpower relations underwent a major thaw. After six years of acrimonious arms talks and a series of major concessions by Soviet leader Mikhail Gorbachev, a major U.S.–Soviet arms deal was tentatively reached in September 1987. Under the terms of the historic treaty, signed on December 8, 1987, at a White House Summit meeting, Reagan and Gorbachev agreed to eliminate some 3800 intermediate range nuclear (INF) warheads from their countries' arsenals. Although the INF treaty covered only 4–6 percent of the world's nuclear stockpile, it signified the first time the superpowers had agreed to eliminate an entire class of nuclear weapons. Most Canadian and American commentators hailed the INF treaty as the end of the "second Cold War," and Prime Minister Mulroney praised President Reagan for his actions.

Under the first Mulroney government, Canadian foreign and defence policies tilted more in the direction of strengthening the North Atlantic alliance.[7] Although the Progressive Conservative government renounced Trudeau's "solo efforts" at arms control in 1984, it continued to promote "progress on arms limitation" at the United Nations and showed little inclination to substantially alter the longstanding policy of limiting Canada's nuclear role. The changes that were initiated — the "good neighbour" approach to Washington, the modernization of the NORAD system, and the aborted 1987 nuclear submarine plans — sprang more from the Conservative faith in a strong defence establishment and closer continental ties than from an altered perception of the world. The rapidity with which the Cold War dissolved would catch the Mulroney government almost by surprise.

ACTIVITIES

KEY TERMS AND CONCEPTS

Identify and briefly explain the historical significance of each of the following terms and concepts:

- Principal power
- Decolonization
- Apartheid
- Namibia Contact Group
- Colombo Plan
- Canadian International Development Agency (CIDA)
- *La francophonie*
- First development decade

- New International Economic Order (NIEO)
- North–South dialogue
- Trudeau pirouette
- "Nuclear club"
- Indian Shock of 1974
- National Energy Program (NEP)
- New Cold War
- Strategic Defence Initiative (SDI)
- Trudeau peace initiative
- North Warning System
- INF Treaty (1987)

QUESTIONS FOR DISCUSSION

1. Canadian political scientists David Dewitt and John Kirton have contended that Canada in the years after 1968 emerged as a "principal power." How valid is that interpretation?

2. Was there a common North American attitude toward European colonialism and decolonization movements in the years after 1945? To what extent were Canadian and American responses to decolonization influenced by the circumstances of each country's origins?

3. Why might Canadian foreign-aid programs until the mid-1960s be judged as little better than modest? Were American aid programs any better?

4. To what extent did Canadian foreign-aid programs during the Trudeau years live up to their early promise?

5. Since 1968, Canadian and American governments have responded quite differently to the nuclear threat, détente, and the energy crisis. What might explain those differences in attitude and policy?

6. In the years after 1984, Prime Minister Brian Mulroney and President Ronald Reagan worked to rekindle and restore the "special relationship" between the two North American nations. To what extent did Mulroney's approach to Washington jeopardize — or possibly undermine — Canada's autonomous status as a principal power?

ANALYZING HISTORICAL INTERPRETATIONS

Study each of the following statements about and interpretations of Canada's role in the world from 1968 to 1984. Assess the validity of each viewpoint on the basis of your reading of the evidence.

"Canada [has become] a foremost power — foremost in the sense of being a most notable or prominent nation in a world where the substance, and hence the distribution, of power has undergone a swift and radical change."

— James Eayrs, *International Perspectives* (May–June 1975).

"Canadian policies in recent years have been determined more by what has happened in Washington or Houston, Brussels or Tegucigalpa, than by what has been decided or sought in Ottawa.... I am not hereby proclaiming, as do our archaic Marxists, that Canada is a bound victim of American imperialism. We have considerably more room for manoeuvre than most middle powers, but even superpowers have a limited range of choice in these intervulnerable times."

— John W. Holmes, "Most Safely in the Middle," *International Journal* 39 (Spring 1984): 372. Published by the Canadian Institute of International Affairs.

"[A]fter sixteen years in power, [Pierre] Trudeau really did not seem to understand how great-power relations worked. He simply could not understand that the United States and the USSR did not want the smaller states interfering in...their affairs. Nor did he appear to realize that Canada, a small power without much clout, had little influence on the course of events....

...Trudeau won and kept the respect and affection of Third World leaders.... Even those who detested the man had to recognize that he cut a figure in world affairs.... Trudeau mattered and so, therefore, did Canada and Canadians."

— Norman Hillmer and J.L. Granatstein, *Empire to Umpire: Canada and the World to the 1990s* (Toronto: Copp Clark Longman, 1994), pp. 310 and 311. Reprinted with permission of Copp Clark and the authors.

DEBATE AND DISCUSS

Support or refute each of the following contentious statements pertaining to Canadian foreign relations in the Trudeau era. Base your argument on concrete historical evidence.

1. North–South Relations

"Canadian policies on New International Economic Order (NIEO) issues …continued to be primarily motivated by narrowly defined Canadian economic interests…."

— Cranford Pratt, *Internationalism Under Strain* (Toronto: University of Toronto Press, 1989), p. 36.

2. Canadian–American Relations

"Trudeau… 'enjoyed tweaking the eagle's beak'; he…also learned how difficult it was for Canada to move beyond range of the eagle's talons."

— John Herd Thompson and Stephen J. Randall, *Canada and the United States: Ambivalent Allies* (Montreal & Kingston: McGill–Queen's University Press, 1994), p. 273.

CHAPTER 22

ONE CONTINENT, TWO NATIONS, MANY IDENTITIES, 1960–1984

CULTURE, REGION, AND ETHNICITY

THE CHANGING FACE OF QUEBEC

THE CHALLENGE OF QUEBEC NATIONALISM

IMMIGRATION, INTEGRATION, AND ETHNICITY

C ANADA'S BESTSELLING NOVEL OF 1973 was Richard Rohmer's surprising thriller, *Ultimatum*. In this book, a Canadian government refuses American demands to surrender vast quantities of natural gas. After heroic resistance, Canada is militarily occupied and annexed to the United States. The astonishing aspect of *Ultimatum's* success was not the novel's preposterous plot or its stereotyped characters, but rather the fact that a Canadian writer had cracked into the American-dominated Canadian mass-paperback market. In that year, 60 percent of all books sold in Canada were American authored and published and the bestseller dramatized a fictional takeover of the country.[1] By the mid-1970s, Canada was regarded by American publishers, authors, and movie-makers as the "added 10 percent" of the North American market and, in the words of one *Time* magazine executive, "the candy store" for producers of American mass culture.

Visitors crossing Canada and the United States by automobile during the 1970s and early 1980s could not help but notice the sameness of North American mass culture. Driving along major highways that looked alike, they could stop to eat in almost any town at a McDonald's restaurant or a Kentucky Fried Chicken franchise, spot street-corner boxes for *USA Today*, and get caught in traffic jams outside suburban branches of Toys 'R Us or Pizza Hut pizza parlours. From Nova Scotia to British Columbia, or Michigan to Texas, a tourist could spend a night at a Holiday Inn or a Best Western hotel and recognize the icemaker, the luggage rack, the TV set, the cellophane wrapping on the drinking glass or the paper festoon on the toilet seat. In short, with the notable exception of French-speaking Quebec, crossing provincial or state boundaries was to encounter "an almost imperceptible interruption." In Canada, critics of the trend to North American cultural integration called the phenomenon "Americanization." But, as Canadian literary critic Northrop Frye pointed out, "the growth of an anonymous, mass-produced, mindless sub-culture" had an effect on "genuine American culture" that was "quite as lethal as its effect everywhere else."[2]

Beneath this veneer of North American uniformity, however, cultural, regional, and ethnic differences have persisted in both Canada and the United States. Commonly accepted conceptions of national identity have been increasingly challenged since 1960 by the rising aspirations of *Québécois*, American blacks, and other minorities, and by large-scale immigration, first from Europe and then from the Third World. In both nations, these "identities" — whether in the form of the *Québécois'* assertion of nationalism, the black Americans' sense of social injustice, or recent Canadian immigrants' pride in ethnicity — have changed both laws and attitudes. Despite signs of a growing North American cultural integration, these distinctions of race, region, and ethnic origin have continued to shape the lives of most Canadians and, perhaps to a lesser extent, most Americans.

From 1960 to the 1980s, Canada did not develop a sense of national identity as cohesive as that of the United States. Rather, it emerged as a modern pluralistic society of two founding European races, two official languages, and a multiplicity of cultures. English Canada was characterized primarily by the persistence of local and regional allegiances and a general weakness of nationalizing forces. There were more dividers than unifiers. Provincial loyalties and regional cultures were so strong by the late 1970s that historian David J. Bercuson pronounced Canada "a country of regions," and prominent Canadian political scientists theorized about the "small worlds" inhabited by Canada's provincial premiers. As Robert Fulford, editor of *Saturday Night* magazine, put it in late 1977:

> Canadians have never acquired the quasi-religious nationalism that marks the Americans (or the French or the Germans) — our nationalism is expressed in a modest and tentative style, without accompanying coercion. We have no belief in a "Canadian way" as being better than some other way. We have nothing we want to impose on immigrants in the sense of a national ideology.

Not for Canadians the American national motto, *E Pluribus Unum,* "Out of the many, one."

Unlike the United States, Canada officially recognized the need to preserve cultural diversity. In establishing the Royal Commission on Bilingualism and Biculturalism in 1963, Lester Pearson's government proclaimed Canada's "cultural duality" and its need for a national unity that respected the traditions and rights of the "two founding peoples." Later, in the commission's report published in 1969, the multicultural character of Canadian society was formally, if somewhat cautiously, recognized:

> The presence of the *other* cultural groups in Canada is something for which all Canadians should be thankful. Their members must always enjoy the right — a basic human one — to safeguard their languages and cultures.... In our opinion, these [cultural] values are far more than ethnic differences; we consider them an integral part of the national wealth.

From public recognition to official sanction was a short step. In October 1971, Prime Minister Pierre Trudeau made ethnic pluralism state policy, offering support for

Prime Minister Pierre Trudeau presenting President Gerald Ford with *Between Friends,* a book commemorating the close ties between Canada and the United States, on the occasion of the American Bicentennial, 1976.

"multiculturalism within a bilingual framework." Yet in both French-speaking Quebec and parts of English Canada, this endorsement of a Canadian national identity based on respect for cultural differences met with much dissent.

CULTURE, REGION, AND ETHNICITY

WHEN CANADA CELEBRATED ITS CENTENNIAL IN 1967, the visions of the nation-builders had not come to pass. Seasoned Canadian observers, peering through that celebratory nationalism, saw in modern Canada "one nation, eminently divisible." Addressing Canada's perennial problem, its lack of national unity and identity, historian Ramsay Cook urged Canadians to concentrate on unravelling the country's "regional, ethnic, and class identities" rather than seeking to find some common yet elusive national identity: "It might just be that it is in these limited identities that 'Canadianism' is found." Two years later, J.M.S. Careless went further: "The distinctive nature of much of the Canadian experience," he asserted, "has produced a continent-wide entity identifiable in its very pluralism, constraints, and compromises."[3] Entering its second century, Canada had become a curious collection of regional, cultural, and ethnic communities. Each part viewed the whole from a different perspective, unified by some invisible bond of Canadianism, and accepting of the country's limitations as well as its shared benefits.

LA SURVIVANCE AND THE RISE OF QUEBEC NATIONALISM

Nowhere was the commitment to cultural survival stronger than among the French-speaking populace of Quebec. In spite of the constant threat of assimilation by the English-speaking majority on the continent, they had managed to maintain their language and culture over the two centuries since the conquest of 1760. Throughout that struggle for *la survivance*, a succession of Lower Canadian and Quebec provincial governments, supported by the Roman Catholic church, had concentrated their energies on preserving traditional French-Canadian values rooted in a rural, agrarian, and Catholic way of life.

The traditional attachment of French Canadians to rural, agrarian ways was, however, becoming little more than a myth. Between 1941 and 1961, the proportion of the Quebec population living in cities and towns rose from 67 to 75 percent, and only one in five Quebeckers was engaged in agriculture. The twin forces of industrialism and urbanism were inexorably changing the face of Quebec. Families were becoming smaller as Quebec went from having the highest birth rate in Canada to the lowest. Labour unions replaced the church in the people's loyalties. Values were in a state of flux. The *Québécois* saw that most of the industrial growth was financed by English-Canadian and American investment. The result was inevitable: English-speakers controlled, and the French-speaking *Québécois* were controlled. Such conditions gave rise to a unique brand of defensive nationalism known as *duplessisme*.

Premier Maurice Duplessis, *Le Chef*, addressing a rural Quebec gathering in September 1951.

Maurice Duplessis, as both premier and attorney-general, asserted Quebec's provincial autonomy. In 1948 his government adopted the *fleur-de-lis* as the province's official flag, symbolizing that Quebec was a homeland distinct from the rest of North America. In his defence of provincial autonomy, *le chef* (as Duplessis was called) turned down lucrative tax arrangements with Ottawa, refused federal funds for road paving, and prevented Quebec's universities from accepting federal grants. His ideology of conservative *nationalisme* found clear expression, in 1956, in the Tremblay Commission report inquiring into Quebec's constitutional position. "The consolidation and expansion of agriculture," the commission reported, was "the first article of a program of social restoration and stabilization," since French Canadians "owe their national survival to agriculture and rural modes of organization and life."

Confronted with the onslaught of economic and social "modernization," Duplessis strongly defended conservative nationalism and laissez faire economic policies. As Union Nationale premier from 1944 to his death in 1959, he acknowledged the power of the Roman Catholic church and bound the people to him with a potent mixture of paternalism, personal largesse, and corrupt, anti-democratic practices. He encouraged outside investment by hindering union organization and promising to keep wages low. His was an invitation to exploit both Quebec's natural resources and its labour force. At a time when French-speaking Quebec workers endured low wages, abysmal working conditions, and union-busting, Duplessis posed as the protector of Quebec against the multiple "evils" of communism, materialism, atheism, and trade unionism.

PRELUDE TO QUEBEC'S QUIET REVOLUTION

The foundations of Duplessis's power and *nationalisme* underwent a slow erosion as the 1950s wore on. An early sign of coming change was the asbestos strike of 1949, which Duplessis crushed with his provincial police. Even though Duplessis had the support of most *nationaliste* and English-speaking Quebec leaders, his régime was challenged by a Roman Catholic trade union, the influential Montreal newspaper *Le Devoir*, and some leading Catholic clergymen like Archbishop Charbonneau of Montreal. His iron grip on the forces of change was again challenged at the violent 1956 Murdochville strike. The shift in attitudes within French Canada reflected Quebec's transition to an urban industrial society. Not only was there a massive migration of *Québécois* to the cities, but the spread of radio and television further eroded the traditional agrarian values in smaller communities.

A growing number of Quebec critics responded to these social changes. The small but influential journal, *Cité Libre*, was launched in 1950 by Pierre Elliott Trudeau, then a wealthy young law professor and intellectual, and Gérard Pelletier, a reform-minded journalist once active in the Roman Catholic youth movement. *Cité Libre* expressed a left-liberal defence of democratic freedoms and was critical of the Duplessis régime and traditional French-Canadian élites. In a book he edited on the asbestos strike, *La Grève de l'amiante* (1956), Trudeau levelled a devastating indictment of the paternalistic and authoritarian régime of Duplessis. A new nationalism was expressed in *Le Devoir*; its editor, Andre Laurendeau, had long been advocating provincial autonomy for Quebec. He criticized the premier as a figurehead ruler acting at the behest of British and Anglo-American economic interests. *Le Devoir* became a leading advocate of an interventionist provincial government, one that would improve the economic power and status of French Canadians. Opposition to Duplessis also came from a Montreal civic reform movement led by mayor Jean Drapeau as well as from broadcast journalist René Lévesque, host of CBC-TV's popular news and current-affairs program *Point de mire*.

Even within the Roman Catholic church, there were stirrings for reform. Beginning in 1949, a few priests, including Archbishop Charbonneau, disturbed by the poverty and discontent of French-Canadian workers, attempted to identify the church with the economic as well as spiritual needs of its parishioners. The church, which had organized and supervised Quebec's Catholic trade unions, gradually began in the 1950s permitting laymen to assume union leadership. In 1959, a series of letters written by a Marist order priest and published in *Le Devoir* caused a major stir. The letters were later published in a bestselling book, *The Impertinence of Brother Anonymous* (1960). For Duplessis and his Union Nationale régime, these cracks in the traditional alliance between church and state were ominous signs that change was in the air.

THE RISE OF PROVINCIALISM

Quebec was not the only province asserting its autonomy. Provincialism could be traced back to the beginning of the Canadian social-security system in the early postwar years. After 1945, a succession of federal governments expanded state intervention and spending in social-service fields such as transportation, education, health, and social welfare. Since most of these new responsibilities fell within provincial jurisdiction, economic and, to some extent, political power slowly shifted from Ottawa to the provinces. By the late 1950s, the trend toward provincialism was so pronounced that Quebec, Ontario, and other provinces were publicly criticizing tax-sharing arrangements and demanding more money from Ottawa. A succession of strong provincial leaders such as John Robarts in Ontario, Jean Lesage in Quebec, and Joey Smallwood in Newfoundland sought to change the cost-sharing arrangements between Ottawa and the provinces. A major dispute between Ottawa and the British Columbia government of Premier W.A.C. Bennett in 1961 almost scuttled a treaty with the United States providing for the development of power on the Columbia River, and that province's estrangement from Ottawa became so severe by 1964 that there was talk of B.C. separatism.

The Roman Coliseum: the Federal–Provincial Conference of 1960 is depicted by Kuch of the *Winnipeg Free Press* as a contest pitting Prime Minister John Diefenbaker and his finance minister against some ferocious provincial lions.

THE ALBERTA–OTTAWA TUG OF WAR

In both the West and Atlantic Canada, deep-seated economic, social, and political grievances resulted in growing friction in federal–provincial relations. Attempts by Pierre Trudeau's Liberal governments (1968–79 and 1980–84) to stem the tide of provincialism and to reassert federal authority in the areas of official bilingualism, oil pricing and energy policy, and constitutional reform all met stiff resistance in the West. Premiers of these booming, staple economies, strongly supported by a new entrepreneurial class, interpreted most of the policies as examples of "centralization" aimed at perpetuating central Canadian economic and political domination over the prairie West. Led by Alberta Premier Peter Lougheed, they began to demand political influence in Canadian federation commensurate with their new-found economic power.

Western regionalism was scarcely a new phenomenon. But added to the traditional grievances of the protective tariff, the CPR, the eastern-controlled banks and grain-handling facilities were a whole set of new grievances. Federal bilingualism programs, associated with the Official Languages Act of 1969, were widely seen as an attempt by the Trudeau Liberals to "shove French down the throats" of westerners. The Liberal dominance in Ottawa, under a French-Canadian prime minister and almost completely lacking support west of Ontario after 1972, bred not only feelings of alienation from national politics but also "Trudeauphobia."[4]

Much of the resurgence of western provincialism in the 1970s stemmed from a strong aversion to federal oil-pricing and energy policies, which were seen as a threat to provincial control over resources. In response to the 1973–74 OPEC (Organization of Petroleum Exporting Countries) oil crisis and the subsequent quadrupling of world oil prices, Trudeau angered Albertans by adopting new energy policies that maintained domestic oil prices below world levels and by imposing a tax on energy exports to the United States. These federal policies, aimed at stabilizing energy costs for industry, favoured the oil-consuming provinces of central Canada at the expense of the oil-producing provinces. Ottawa–Alberta relations reached a new low in 1980 when the Trudeau government introduced its National Energy Program (NEP), designed to "Canadianize" the oil industry and assure future energy self-suffi-

A satirical look at Anne Murray, the Nova Scotia–born popular singer, lampooning her Bluenose origins. Bob Chambers' cartoon in the Halifax *Chronicle-Herald* (May 15, 1972) provoked a storm of controversy and an avalanche of protest letters.

ciency. Premier Lougheed and most western Canadians denounced the NEP, seeing it as an unwarranted intrusion into the oil industry and a dire threat to western oil exploration and discovery.

WESTERN SEPARATISM

In the February 1980 federal election, Trudeau's Liberals, after only nine months out of office, defeated Alberta-born Joe Clark and the Progressive Conservatives. In capturing this majority government, however, Trudeau managed to win only two seats west of Ontario. Results flashed across TV screens even as westerners were still casting their votes captured their sense of powerlessness and inflamed their alienation. A vitriolic letter to *The Edmonton Journal,* written by Elmer Knutsen, a 66-year-old Conservative dissident and wealthy tractor-parts dealer, which labelled the 1980 election "the second battle of the Plains of Abraham" and ended with an emotional appeal for western separation, generated 3000 enthusiastic replies. In a series of opinion surveys among western Canadians, a strong majority consistently expressed general dissatisfaction with "national politics," while support for western independence rose dramatically, especially in Alberta.

The radical western separatist movement of the early 1980s was short-lived as a major force. From its inception, the movement remained divided organizationally, divided in its loyalties, and confused in its objectives. In February 1982, a Western Canada Concept party candidate won an Alberta by-election in the rural Olds-Didsbury riding. However, little could be built on that breakthrough. The party's platform was a confused amalgam of the American right wing, populism, and conservatism. It called for flat tax rates, capital punishment, the right to bear arms, and an end to metrication, the NEP, and bilingual packaging. However, after the adoption of the new federal constitution, most westerners turned away from "fed bashing" to focus more on economic conditions associated with the severe recession of 1981–82, and its consequences in western Canada.[5]

ATLANTIC CANADA'S RESPONSE TO CRISIS

Although the Atlantic provinces and the West shared a general antipathy toward federal policies, the concerns and demands emanating from Atlantic Canada were markedly different. Amid the atmosphere of national crisis hanging over the Canadian state, provincial Maritime leaders responded in a somewhat paradoxical fashion, stressing their "Maritime-ness" as well as their commitment to "larger Canadianism." Threats to Canada's survival posed by Quebec independence and signs of western alienation seemed to awaken many Maritime leaders to the economic vulnerability of a "dependent" region like Atlantic Canada. By the mid-1970s, the evidence of that vulnerability was clear. In spite of massive intervention by governments to alleviate regional disparities, all four Atlantic provinces lagged behind economically and remained dependent on Ottawa transfer payments for between one-third and one-half of their net provincial incomes. Clearly, any break-up of the country would leave the Atlantic provinces in deep trouble.

Nevertheless, the regional concerns of Atlantic Canada were far from monolithic. By the 1970s, strong regional identities did not fit neatly into provincial boundaries, but rather crossed those political lines and existed within them, especially in the case of Cape Breton and Labrador. Regional concerns and demands in the Atlantic provinces, unlike those in Quebec and the prairie West, were mostly expressed by premiers and economic-development agencies rather than by political movements. While such concerns and demands were primarily economic, they varied from province to province. For New Brunswick and Prince Edward Island, the critical issues were the health of the agricultural economy and control over natural resources; for Newfoundland and Nova Scotia, the main issue was the right to a full share in the development of offshore energy resources.

THE COMING OF THE "NEW CANADIANS"

A new challenge was that of Canada's growing ethnic diversity. Whereas Canada was once essentially a bicultural society, British and French, it was now being transformed into a multicultural one. After the end of World War II, substantial immigration to Canada had resumed; by 1961, some 2 million postwar immigrants had arrived. The largest group of new arrivals from 1945 to the 1960s were British in origin; but the "new Canadians" from Italy, Germany, the Netherlands, Poland, and other parts of Europe made up two-thirds of the total immigration.[6]

Although a sizable number of these immigrants gravitated to Montreal and Vancouver, Toronto was transformed into the new "immigrant metropolis" of Canada. By 1961, almost 42 percent of the residents of the city proper, and fully one-third of those in the greater metropolitan area, were born outside Canada. Some 29 percent of the population of Metropolitan Toronto had immigrated between 1946 and 1961. Demographic changes were bringing a host of other changes. By the 1980s, more than half of Metro's populace would claim as their mother tongue a language other than English or French. Politics was taking on more of an ethnic complexion. The rise of sizable new ethnic communities of Italians, Greeks, and central Europeans gradually revolutionized "Toronto the Good," formerly "derided by the rest of Canada for its smugness, its snobbery, and its sterility."

Much of this change in Canada's ethnic composition was the result of postwar immigration liberalization. The tone of postwar immigration policy was set by Prime Minister Mackenzie King, when in May 1947 he advocated fostering the economic growth of Canada through the encouragement of immigration up to the "absorptive capacity" of the country. Annual immigration rates rose steadily to more than a quarter of a million. Britain, the United States, and France (after 1949) were the "preferred nations," but the policy was liberalized to allow southern Europeans to settle in urban areas, and Asians were now allowed to sponsor family members.

In the postwar period, the chain migration of family and kinship relations emerged as a major phenomenon in Canada and the United States. It was an important factor in Italian immigration, which ranked second only to that of the British from 1945 to 1961 and actually surpassed the British in the 1958–61 period. The migration of people to the cities raised fears, often unfounded, that sponsored immigrants might impose an intolerable burden on their sponsoring families. In Toronto and Montreal, as well as Chicago and New York, critics of postwar immigration readily, and unfairly in many cases, associated the growth of ethnic neighbourhoods with increasing urban "social problems."

The arrival of Hungarian refugees, 1956. Most Hungarians entered Canada in the years following the abortive revolution of October 1956.

SEEKING "THE AMERICAN DREAM": POSTWAR WAVES OF IMMIGRATION

IN THE TWO DECADES FOLLOWING WORLD WAR II, millions of immigrants entered the United States as much to fill the needs of the labour market as in pursuit of the fabled "American Dream." From 1940 to 1970, 16 million white Southerners were displaced from their farms by the mechanization of southern agriculture. Most of them migrated to the cities in search of work; these southern whites were joined by 4 million blacks who left rural communities for factory work in the northern industrial cities. With so many Southerners migrating northward, a serious shortage of agricultural labour emerged, especially in Texas and the Southwest.

THE INFLUX OF *BRACEROS*

In 1942, the United States and Mexico signed the first of a series of agreements to allow the "temporary entry" of Mexican nationals into America. The Mexican government screened the prospective farm labourers, and U.S. authorities placed them on farms or in related enterprises. Over the years, almost 5 million *braceros*, as the contract labourers were called, came to the United States, mainly to California. The Mexicans worked for grape growers and earned 30–50¢ an hour for their labour, rarely taking in more than $500 a year. Labour costs were kept low through the use of illegal Mexican immigrants. Rural Mexicans were so poor that after the 1940s, some 5 million drifted across the border to work in the United States, mostly for giant agribusinesses. Later, these Mexican Americans, known as *Chicanos*, gradually migrated to cities in California, Texas, and even the Midwest.

THE ENTRY OF PUERTO RICANS

On the East Coast, migrants from the South, Puerto Ricans, and displaced Europeans filled the need for unskilled labour in the cities. Of these groups, the Puerto Ricans attracted the most attention because of their great numbers, skin colour, and their tendency to settle in New York City — nearly 1 million came from 1945 to the 1970s. While the Puerto Ricans were recognized as American citizens, they were mostly poor, spoke little English, and worked in the city's restaurants, hotels, and hospitals, or in ramshackle old factories. Like many immigrant groups in New York, they became the object of discrimination.

THE ADMISSION OF "DISPLACED PERSONS"

After the war, the United States opened its doors to European immigrants. Most Americans looked favourably on immigrants who came as "survivors of war," but

Congress moved slowly — and cautiously — before lifting its quota limits for the displaced Europeans. When Congress finally did act, in 1948, the legislation favoured the admission of people of German origin, while discriminating against one of the war's most victimized groups — East European Jews. Most of the resistance to eastern Europeans came from those who saw all immigrants from the Soviet-bloc countries as "communists." In 1950, after the newly created state of Israel opened its doors to that group, Congress rescinded most of the discriminatory provisions. As a result of the two Displaced Persons Acts, about 400 000 Europeans — mostly Germans, residents of the Baltic states, Poles, and Jews — sought refuge in America.

ACCEPTING COMMUNIST "VICTIMS"

Exemptions from America's selective immigration system were made throughout the Cold War years after 1950 for people believed to be the victims of "communist tyranny." Following the Hungarian Revolution of 1956, the United States — like Canada — accepted political refugees and admitted 40 000 Hungarians, many of whom settled in Hungarian ethnic communities in New Jersey, Cleveland, and New York City. The largest group of political refugees, totalling about 750 000 by the mid-1970s, came from Cuba after Fidel Castro's revolution in 1959. Over the next 15 years, an estimated 5 percent of Cuba's population, mostly from the business and managerial élite and the wealthy landowning class, came to the United States. Many Cuban exiles settled in and around Miami, Florida; others migrated to New York City and vicinity. By 1975, Cubans constituted a majority of Miami's population and were dominant in certain businesses, notably the real estate industry.

Canadian postwar immigration included some 300 000 refugees displaced by political disruptions in their homelands. Many of these newcomers were Europeans from urban centres who were generally well-educated professionals or skilled in the trades. The best-known group of postwar refugees were Hungarians who fled from communist rule after the Hungarian Revolution of 1956, but this stream of peoples also included large numbers of Jews, Ukrainians, Poles, Lithuanians, Estonians, and Latvians. Jewish refugees who came after the war were mainly from Poland, although later groups who fled religious restrictions were from Hungary, Egypt, and North Africa. As a result of this migration, by 1960 both Toronto and Montreal had sizable Jewish communities.

Postwar immigration accentuated differences between Canada's regions. The majority of "new Canadians" who entered from 1945 to 1960 were Europeans who settled in Toronto and other Canadian cities. Residents of non-British and non-French ethnic origins made up 47 percent of the population of the Prairie provinces, 34 percent of that of British Columbia, and 29 percent of Ontario. Yet the Maritime provinces and Newfoundland remained predominantly British, and Quebec, with the exception of Montreal, largely French. The growing visibility of Native Canadians formed another significant aspect of this changing cultural pattern of Canada. By the time of the 1991 census, more than 1 million Canadians claimed Native ancestry, and it was abundantly clear that the old days of a bicultural nation were long gone.

THE CHANGING FACE OF QUEBEC

JUST AS QUEBEC had been transformed before 1960 by industrialization and urbanization, so too would the province be redefined after 1960 by its politics. As Quebec entered the 1960s, it embarked on a period of economic and social change known as the "Quiet Revolution." *La revolution tranquille*, which reached its peak in the years 1960–66, became a catchword to summarize the political awakening and modernization of Quebec. Yet, compared with the American social revolution and civil-rights movement of the 1960s, Quebec's Quiet Revolution was short of being revolutionary. Under the Liberal government of Jean Lesage, the economic role of the Quebec state was expanded, but government activities remained quite limited and in some areas hardly changed from the Duplessis years. If a new and modern Quebec did emerge out of the ashes of *duplessisme*, it was a society that — except for language — looked and behaved much like any other political entity in North America. In common with American liberal reformers and civil-rights activists, Quebec's "Quiet Revolutionaries" denounced their political predecessors and appropriated all that was "new" and "dynamic" on the provincial scene.

"MAÎTRES CHEZ NOUS"

With the campaign slogan of *C'est le temps pour change*, the Lesage Liberal government took up the spirit and sentiment of Quebec nationalism. Religion, language, and the French-Canadian family, the traditional pillars of *la survivance*, would now be safeguarded by the state instead of the church. The historic threat of domination by Anglo-Canadian and American economic interests would be combated by expanding the role of the Quebec government in the economy. Quebec was still "not a province like the others," but henceforth the state would speak for the French-Canadian "nation" — clearly a harbinger of the future "distinct society" debate. One of the chief architects of the Liberal reform program, René Lévesque, described the new role of the state: "It must be more than a participant in the economic development and emancipation of Quebec; it must be a creative agent.... It is alone, through our state, we can become *maîtres chez nous,* masters in our own house."

The triumph of the Lesage Liberals marked the ascendancy of a new French urban middle class. This class, which emerged in the last years of the Duplessis régime, was composed of a new generation of educated *Québécois* who in increasing numbers were turning away from the traditional French-Canadian professions: law, medicine, journalism, and the church. Instead, they turned to business, engineering, and the social sciences, often furthering their education at American or British graduate schools. Infused with new confidence and politically aware, they sought to transform Quebec into a more efficient, technological society, managed and directed by French Canadians. The goal of this new breed of francophone nationalists was *ratra-page* — catching up — to social and economic development elsewhere in North America.[7]

In its first two years, the Lesage government concentrated on consolidating its power, cleaning up corruption in the Quebec administration, and preparing the ground for educational reform. In 1962, a major economic initiative was undertaken: completion of the Hydro-Québec system (founded in 1944) by nationalizing the giant Shawinigan Power Company and 10 other private hydro-electric utilities. The author of the policy — and of the campaign slogan of *"Maîtres chez nous"* — was Lesage's minister of natural resources, René Lévesque. The main intention was to ensure government control of a vital resource — power — but nationalization also created a large state-owned enterprise that provided new opportunities for French-Canadian managers and technocrats. In the 1962 Quebec election, called by Lesage to secure a mandate for this nationalization, the Liberals swept back into power. Soon the remaining private hydro-electric companies were nationalized with $300 million in funds obtained on the American market.

THE QUEBEC BUREAUCRATIC STATE

The new Hydro-Québec was only the most dramatic of the Liberal government's reforms. In 1962 a provincially run finance corporation, the *Société generale de financement* (SGF), was established; it attempted, with mixed success, to strengthen the small sector of marginal, often family-run, French-Canadian industrial and commercial enterprises. Two years later, *Sidérurgie Québécoise* (SIDBEC) was set up to stimulate iron and steel development. A new Ministry of Education, established in 1964, instituted permanent changes in the provincial curriculum. The Quebec educational system, public and private, which had long been run and administered by Roman Catholic and Protestant religious authorities, was placed under state control and reorganized, although a Superior Council, composed of Catholic and Protestant committees, was retained to ensure the "confessional" character of the schools. In addition, the government laid the ground work for a new, secular system of postsecondary applied arts and technology colleges known as CEGEPs.

The new programs of the Lesage government greatly expanded the Quebec governmental structure. From 1960 to 1966, six new ministries, eight public enterprises, and nine other agencies were created, and the Quebec civil service (excluding public enterprises) grew from 29 300 to 41 800 employees. Yet the actual pattern of governmental expenditures was quite illuminating. While the size of the annual provincial budget skyrocketed, reaching $2 billion in 1966, the trend of spending — away from transportation and natural resources and into human and social services — was surprisingly consistent with the Duplessis budgets of the 1950s. And when compared with the scale and scope of government involvement in economic life elsewhere in Canada or the United States, the Quiet Revolution seemed a good deal less original or innovative than its advance billing.[8]

THE AMERICAN CIVIL-RIGHTS MOVEMENT

A T THE TIME THAT THE "QUEBEC REVOLUTION" emerged in Canada, the civil-rights movement to end racial segregation and discrimination erupted in the American South. Its inspirational driving force was Rev. Martin Luther King, Jr., who, after leading the Montgomery, Alabama, bus boycott, organized the Southern Christian Leadership Conference (SCLC) and rose quickly to national prominence as an impassioned fighter for civil rights.

The American civil-rights movement drew its impetus from a new generation of educated blacks and was enthusiastically supported by young liberal whites, who were mostly from the North and working through the Democratic party or the student movement. Their principal strategy was non-violent civil disobedience — sit-ins, "freedom rides" on buses, and mass peaceful demonstrations that defied the segregation of southern lunch counters, bus stations, hotels, washrooms, and other public facilities.

One of the most highly publicized civil-rights actions provoked brutality by white southerners. In May 1963, when Reverend King and southern college students launched massive demonstrations against segregation in Birmingham, Alabama, the local police responded with fire hoses, German shepherd dogs, and arrests of peaceful protesters.

Rev. Martin Luther King, Jr.'s "I Have a Dream" speech was the first television program carried by satellite around the world.

Not all blacks subscribed to King's strategy of love, brotherhood, and non-violent resistance. Beginning in the late 1950s, a small, yet growing number of impatient blacks dismissed King's tactics as naive and concluded that bringing an end to racial injustice required more than non-violent resistance. Most prominent among the groups of that persuasion were the Malcolm X–led Black Muslims and the more militant Black Panthers.

MARTIN LUTHER KING: "I HAVE A DREAM" — AUGUST 18, 1963

The symbolic high point of the American civil-rights movement came in the summer of 1963, the one-hundredth anniversary of the U.S. Emancipation Proclamation, when over 250 000 blacks and whites joined in a peaceful march on Washington, D.C. On the steps of the Lincoln Memorial, Reverend King delivered his most passionate and moving statement of the aims and hopes of the non-violent civil-rights movement.

Five score years ago, a great American, in whose symbolic shadow we stand, signed the Emancipation Proclamation. This momentous decree came as a great beacon light of hope to millions of Negro slaves who have been seared in the flames of withering injustice. It came as a joyous daybreak to end the long night of captivity....

But one hundred years later, we must face the tragic fact that the Negro is still not free. One hundred years later, the life of the Negro is still sadly crippled by the manacles of segregation and the chains of discrimination. One hundred years later, the Negro lives on a lonely island of poverty in the midst of a vast ocean of material prosperity. One hundred years later, the Negro is still languished in the corners of American society and finds himself an exile in his own land. So we have come here today to dramatize an appalling condition....

I say to you today, my friends, that in spite of the difficulties and frustrations of the moment I still have a dream. It is a dream deeply rooted in the American dream.

I have a dream that one day this nation will rise up and live out the true meaning of its creed: "We hold these truths to be self-evident; that all men are created equal."

I have a dream that one day on the red hills of Georgia the sons of former slaves and the sons of former slaveholders will be able to sit down together at the table of brotherhood.

I have a dream that one day even the state of Mississippi, a desert state sweltering with the heat of injustice and oppression, will be transformed into an oasis of freedom and justice.

I have a dream that my four little children will one day live in a nation where they will not be judged by the color of their skin but by the content of their character.

I have a dream today....

This is our hope. This is the faith with which I return to the South. With this faith we will be able to hew out of the mountain of despair a stone of hope. With this faith we will be able to transform the jangling discords of our nation into a beautiful symphony of brotherhood. With this faith we will be able to work together, to pray together, to struggle together, to go to jail together, to stand up for freedom together, knowing that we will be free one day.*

A Civil Rights Act was passed in 1964, following the assassination of President John Kennedy and in response to forceful prodding by his successor, Lyndon B. Johnson. Gradually, over the next ten years the system of racial segregation, overt discrimination, and street justice crumbled in the South, and blacks gained at least a form of legal equality. Tragically, King never saw his "dream" realized, even partially: he was gunned down in 1968 in a Memphis, Tennessee, motel, where he had gone to support striking city workers.

*Reprinted by arrangement with The Heirs to the Estate of Martin Luther King, Jr., c/o Joan Daves Agency as agent for the proprietor. Copyright 1963 by Martin Luther King, Jr., copyright renewed 1991 by Coretta Scott King.

THE CHALLENGE OF QUEBEC NATIONALISM

THE LESAGE ADMINISTRATION did approach Ottawa with a different agenda from that of its predecessors. Expansion of the Quebec state required massive expenditures, which imposed a severe strain on the financial resources then available to the province. The Quebec government discovered that the purposes and goals of some of its new programs conflicted with federal programs or caused jurisdictional disputes with Ottawa. Conscious of the growing aspirations of Quebeckers for *l'epanouissement* (the flowering of a "distinct people") and committed to a program of modernization, the Quebec government became more assertive in federal–provincial relations. The concentration of power and fiscal resources in Ottawa had to be confronted head on, and Quebec's "particular status" within Confederation had to be formally recognized.

Quebec–Ottawa relations during the Quiet Revolution were tense. In keeping with the aspirations of the "new Quebec," Premier Lesage sought "more money, more power, and more status." At a series of federal–provincial conferences from October 1960 onward, Lesage advanced Quebec's claim to "special status" based on the French-Canadian view that Canada was a country not of ten provinces but of *deux nations* (two nations). Asserting the right to be *maîtres chez nous* (masters in our own house), Quebec demanded that the federal government withdraw from national spending programs but provide adequate finances to allow the provinces to manage their own programs. The arrangement, known as "opting out," was to be applied to a whole range of programs in health, education, and social security. At a time when Lesage was hard-pressed to finance his social and economic programs, "opting out" provided for a shift of responsibilities and fiscal resources from Ottawa to Quebec.

Like most of English-speaking Canada, governments in Ottawa wrestled with a perplexing problem: what does Quebec want? Before the Diefenbaker government could come to grips with the new Quebec, it was defeated in the general election of April 1963. Lester B. Pearson's new Liberal

Premier Jean Lesage with Prime Minister Lester Pearson at the federal–provincial conference in Quebec City, 1964, where Lesage argued the case for Quebec's "particular status" and secured the right to opt out of the national pension plan.

minority government, heavily dependent on political support from Quebec and Ontario, could not afford to ignore or dismiss the concerns of French Canada. While Pearson defended Ottawa's powers under the BNA Act, he adopted a form of "co-operative federalism" and attempted to conciliate Quebec and other provinces seeking fuller constitutional powers. In 1964, Quebec was allowed to opt out of the national contributory pension plan and administer its own Quebec Pension Plan. Before long, it had established its own system of student loans, youth allowances, and hospital/medical insurance, using an increased share of income and corporate tax revenues from Ottawa.

The Pearson Liberals moved on other fronts as well to meet the new aspirations of Quebec and French Canada. Canada's commonly accepted flag, the "Red Ensign," a British symbol that many French Canadians found objectionable, was replaced in February 1965, after months of stormy debate, by the Maple Leaf flag. Another important move by Ottawa was the July 1963 decision to create the Royal Commission on Bilingualism and Biculturalism. In instructing the co-chairs, Andre Laurendeau and Davidson Dunton, to advise on how the Canadian federal system could accommodate "an equal partnership between two founding races," Ottawa recognized that Quebec's problems in the 1960s were Canada's problems and that common solutions must be found if the country were to survive its crisis of unity.

THE UNDERCURRENT OF SOCIAL TURMOIL

Not every Quebecker was satisfied with the pace or direction of social and political change. A thriving separatist movement emerged in Quebec, composed of radical intellectuals, nationalistic journalists, and disenchanted youth. For many Quebec separatists, the social and economic conditions facing the mass of French-speaking *Québécois* were a powerful inducement to radicalism. By the 1960s, they saw themselves facing an increased threat of English-Canadian assimilation. French Canadians, according to Marcel Chaput in *Pourquoi je suis separatiste* (1961), were "an eternal minority, in eternal retreat in an immense country which doesn't belong to it," and must choose, through independence, to become "a living and progressive majority, in a country which is smaller but all its own."

The problem of French Canada's minority position in Canada was compounded by the status of French-speaking Canadians within Quebec itself. Although English-speaking Quebeckers made up only 13 percent of the population, they controlled — together with British and American interests — all the important sectors of the economy: banking and finance, manufacturing, and the resource industries. In Quebec manufacturing industries, French-speaking Quebeckers formed the bulk of the lowest-paid wage earners, and in 1961 French-speaking workers earned an average income 60–65 percent less than that of their English-speaking counterparts. English was the required working language in industry, so increasingly immigrants wanted to have their children attend English schools. Unemployment was highest among French-speaking Quebeckers. French-speakers entering business faced various forms of discrimination. The charges levelled by radical separatists in the 1960s — that French-speaking Quebeckers had been colonized by English-speaking capitalists and relegated to economic servitude in the industrial sector — were not without foundation. The smouldering lower-class resentment was portrayed in writings such as Pierre Vallières' personal autobiography, which claimed that the *Québécois* were the "*nègres blancs d'Amérique*/ white niggers of America."

THE STRUGGLE FOR QUEBEC INDEPENDENCE

The mounting frustrations and discontents burst forth in the early 1960s in the formation of *indépendantiste* groups and parties. The largest, the *Rassemblement pour l'independance nationale*

(RIN), formed in September 1960 by Marcel Chaput and Pierre Bourgault, rallied significant numbers of mainly middle-class francophone students and young professionals to the cause of independence. After a 1962 split within the RIN over the prominence given to socialism in its program, Chaput and his moderate followers organized their own separatist party, the *Parti republicain du Québec*. Another group of more conservative separatists associated with Quebec's Social Credit faction, the *Créditistes*, joined with Gilles Grégoire in 1966 to form the *Rassemblement national* (RN). The tempo of separatist activities increased after Bourgault became president of the RIN in May 1964. RIN supporters mounted demonstrations in the spring and fall of 1964 during a Quebec City federal–provincial conference and a Royal visit by Queen Elizabeth. Yet the Quebec independence movement was badly splintered. Not until 1967 and 1968, after René Lévesque had bolted the Liberals to form the *Mouvement souveraineté* association (MSA) and then merged with the RIN to create the *Parti Québécois* (PQ), did a coalition of democratic *indépendantiste* forces emerge to challenge for political power in Quebec.

The state visit of Charles de Gaulle, president of France, in August 1967. His cry, *"Vive le Québec libre,"* at the Montreal City Hall helped stir the desire for Quebec independence.

THE FLQ AND RADICAL SEPARATISM

Small bands of *Québécois* were not prepared to wait for democratic change. The *Front de libération du Québec* (FLQ) was a violent fringe of the separatist movement founded in 1960 by George Shoeters among francophone students at the *Université de Montreal*. Violence did not erupt, however, until after the two leading separatist parties, the RIN and the RN, were defeated in the 1962 Quebec provincial election. In March 1963, the FLQ adopted a strategy of violent "retaliation" and a month later initiated a campaign of terrorism, exploding bombs outside a Montreal army recruiting centre, bombing "Royal Mail" boxes in Montreal's rich English suburb of Westmount, and raiding military facilities to obtain arms, ammunition, and explosives.

Following the arrest of 18 FLQ sympathizers in June 1963 for various acts of violence, the radical faction went "underground." The FLQ then developed a loose organization of "revolutionary cells" patterned after Fidel Castro's Cuban model of guerrilla warfare. In a series of hit-and-run operations from 1965 to 1969, FLQ members robbed banks, raided armouries, bombed Quebec companies engaged in strikes with francophone workers, and set off bombs at the Montreal Stock Exchange. Through hunger strikes and the distribution of FLQ handbills, the group attempted to attract attention and voice the concerns of Quebec workers "exploited" by Anglo-Canadian "bosses." In spite of vigorous and occasionally surreptitious investigations by the RCMP and the Quebec Provincial Police, the small group of FLQers refused to be stamped out of existence.

The climax came in October 1970, when the Chenier and Liberation "cells" captured world attention by kidnapping a British diplomat, James Cross, and the provincial labour minister, Pierre Laporte. Most *Québécois* as well as English Canadians were horrified at these acts of terrorism. Prime Minister Pierre Trudeau quickly seized the initiative by sending in the army and imposing the War Measures Act, which authorized the arrest of over 400 suspected FLQ sympathizers. Laporte was found in the trunk of a car, strangled with his crucifix. In return for the kidnappers' safe passage to Cuba, Cross was released after 66 days of captivity. The strategy worked: Quebec's tiny yet potentially dangerous terrorist group was virtually eradicated.

THE PQ: HEIRS TO THE QUIET REVOLUTION

René Lévesque completely divorced his movement from what had transpired during the October crisis. If independence was to be achieved it would be by the ballot box, not the bomb. Six years later, a new and more assertive stage in Quebec's transformation was reached with the election of Lévesque and the *Parti Québécois*. Although it had existed since 1968 and grown steadily in popular support, the 1976 triumph came as a jolt for Quebec federalists and most English-speaking Canadians. In winning 71 of 110 seats in the Quebec National Assembly and 41 percent of the popular vote, the PQ dealt the Robert Bourassa's Liberal government a staggering upset. Outside Quebec, the reaction in the press was one of shock. A sense of crisis swept English Canada. In July 1977, Prime Minister Trudeau launched a task force on Canadian unity, chaired by Jean-Luc Pepin and John Robarts. Fears of separatism arose in spite of the fact that the PQ had not campaigned for outright separation and that the election verdict really signified a vote against a discredited government. Indeed, Lévesque and the PQ rode to victory with promises of a return to "good government" and a provincial referendum on "sovereignty-association" within their first term of office.

The *Parti Québécois* did not represent a new development in Quebec politics. In its nationalist and reformist impulses, the party represented a continuation of the social movement born with the so-called Quiet Revolution of the 1960s. All of the main leaders of the PQ — Lévesque, Jacques Parizeau, and Claude Morin — were modern French-speaking Quebeckers who had emerged during the Lesage years. The prime goals of the PQ were not significantly different from those pursued by the Lesage government, though the means of achieving them were clarified. Like Lesage's Liberal government, the *péquistes* were dominated by technocratic moderates, but under pressure from *indépendantiste* supporters who wanted to go farther, faster.

THE PQ IN POWER

While concerned Canadians debated the unthinkable, Lévesque and his *péquiste* government moved cautiously along the road to "sovereignty-association." The PQ government of the first three years was marked more by continuity than by dramatic change. After an initial flurry of symbolic changes such as changing Quebec's official motto from *"La Belle Province"* to *"Je me souviens"* (I remember), the PQ concentrated on a gradual step-by-step approach to independence, known as *étapisme*. The *péquistes* minimized fears of the costs of "separatism" by linking sovereignty to close economic association with the rest of Canada. Lévesque moved quickly to assure the Montreal and New York business communities of his government's commitment to fiscal responsibility.

The major policy initiative, Bill 101, the Charter of the French Language, was passed in the summer of 1977. It was a response to both popular concerns and strong pressures within Quebec's French-speaking community. By the mid-1970s, many *Québécois* feared that the French language was disappearing as a result of Quebec's low birth rate and the fact that most immigrants took up English as their preferred working language. Bill 101 required that French be the *only* language used on public signs and in most forms of commercial advertising. In addition, it limited access to English-language schools, in effect denying most immigrant children the right to an education in English. These provisions raised the ire of most English-speaking Canadians, particularly Quebec's vocal anglophone community, centred in Montreal.

The Parti Québécois triumph, November 15, 1976. René Lévesque addresses his cheering supporters in Montreal. The PQ victory in that provincial election signalled the onset of a new "Quebec crisis" in English-speaking Canada and caused alarm even in the United States.

THE QUEBEC REFERENDUM OF 1980

The great test came in the May 1980 referendum on sovereignty-association. Throughout 1979 and into 1980, the Trudeau government said that Quebec's aspiration would be met through constitutional reform. However, the report of the Pepin–Robarts task force, *A Future Together* (1979), and Trudeau's proposal of "renewed federalism" failed to produce a federal–provincial consensus. The PQ government determined that its best chance of obtaining a positive vote was to word the referendum "question" as broadly as possible. Instead of asking Quebeckers to vote for or against independence, the referendum only asked whether the people wished to give their provincial government "the mandate to negotiate" sovereignty-association with Ottawa on the basis of "an equality of nations." The federalist "Non" side was led by Prime Minister Trudeau, federal Justice Minister Jean Chrétien, and former *Le Devoir* editor, and now Quebec Liberal opposition leader, Claude Ryan.

In spite of its spirited campaign, the PQ-led "Oui" side suffered a major setback when cabinet minister Lise Payette unwisely slurred women supporting the "Non" forces. As a result, 12 000 enraged women rallied at the Montreal Forum against the *péquiste* option. Trudeau may have turned the tide in a late, but dramatic, intervention by promising that a "Non" vote was a vote for "a made-in-Canada Constitution." With 59.5 percent of the vote, the "Non" side claimed a clear victory. Lévesque counselled his shattered supporters: "Let us accept [defeat], but not let go, never lose sight of such legitimate, universal objectives as equality. It will come." By winning an increased majority in the next provincial election in April 1981, the PQ proved that independence may have been addressed but had scarcely been resolved.[9]

IMMIGRATION, INTEGRATION, AND ETHNICITY

IN EARLY OCTOBER 1971, Prime Minister Trudeau rose in Parliament to make his first — and only — major statement on Canada's official policy of multiculturalism. Responding to the recommendations of the Royal Commission on Bilingualism and Biculturalism (1969), he proclaimed "a policy of multiculturalism within a bilingual framework." The new policy officially recognized ethnic groups' "collective will to exist," but the prime minister emphasized that the preservation of ethnic identity was a *voluntary* matter, "the conscious support of individual freedom of choice." The government also pledged to provide support to all Canadian cultural groups to "help to break down discriminatory attitudes and cultural jealousies" and to assist immigrants to acquire facility in one of Canada's official languages.

Leaders of Canada's ethnic groups hailed the statement as formal recognition that Canada was a "cultural mosaic" distinct from the American "melting pot." Yet the rhetoric of *policy* in the 1970s did not necessarily correspond with social *reality* in Canada or the United States. One of the chief architects of Canada's policy of multiculturalism, sociologist Jean Burnet, conceded in a 1973 paper that such a policy, properly interpreted, was "something very North American: voluntary marginal differentiation among peoples who are equal participants in the society." At about the same time American popular studies like Michael Novak's *The Rise of the Unmeltable Ethnics* (1971) and bestsellers such as Alex Haley's *Roots* seemed to testify that the melting pot did not melt, that ethnic consciousness existed and would in all probability continue to thrive in the United States.

THE EMERGENCE OF MULTICULTURALISM

Multiculturalism grew mainly out of a quest for identity and acceptance among Canada's upwardly mobile "white ethnics" — second- and third-generation central and eastern Europeans. It also developed in reaction to the terms of reference of the Royal Commission on Bilingualism and Biculturalism, which endorsed a bicultural Canada and merely noted the "contribution" made by "other ethnic groups" to national life. In the eyes of many non-British, non-French groups, this categorized them as second-class citizens, and a host of these groups, particularly Ukrainians in western Canada, opposed the concept of a bicultural Canada. A partial resolution of the dilemma came in 1971 with Trudeau's assertion that Canada was a *multicultural* country with two official languages, English and French. Further confirmation of this view came shortly after, when the federal opposition leaders expressed basic agreement with the policy, and four provinces with large numbers of "other ethnics" — Ontario, Manitoba, Saskatchewan, and Alberta — initiated their own multicultural policies and programs.

With the founding of the Ministry of Multiculturalism in 1972 by Prime Minister Pierre Trudeau, various ethnic and cultural groups across the nation began to receive federal funding.

CHANGING PATTERNS OF IMMIGRATION

The government's multiculturalism policy was no doubt a response to important changes in the pattern of immigration. Prodded by economically buoyant times and public criticism of inequities in the immigration laws, governments in Canada and the United States took steps to reduce, if not eliminate, the old ethnic and racial biases. In Canada, immigration regulations were altered in 1962 to end the former preferences for immigrants from certain geographic areas, while south of the border, the U.S. Immigration and Nationality Act of 1965 removed racial discrimination based on a "national origins quota system." The biggest change in Canadian policy, however, came in the new 1967 regulations: discrimination on the basis of race or national origin was explicitly eliminated, and immigrants were selected on the basis of accumulated "points" for education, occupation, and language.[10] In Canada as in the United States, the basic corner-stones of immigration policy after 1967 became family reunification, the need for skilled and professional persons, labour-market requirements, and special humanitarian provisions for the acceptance of refugees.

After 1967, large numbers of people came from the Third World countries of Asia, Africa, the West Indies, and South America: most had professional, technical, or managerial backgrounds. Whereas not one Jamaican had been admitted to Canada in the 1950s, over 54 000 arrived in the eight years from 1968 to 1976. Although fewer than 10 000 persons had come from Hong Kong between 1946 and 1962, almost 80 000 entered between 1968 and 1976. In 1980, official figures showed that fully 50 percent of new immigrants came from Asia (71 602), 29 percent from Europe (41 128), 7 percent from the USA (9926), and 12 percent from the Caribbean (7361), South America (5433), and Africa (4300). While economic conditions, including high levels of unemployment, worked to reduce the flow of immigrants in the late 1970s and early 1980s, the pattern had been set. Canada had become a truly multiethnic society, with about 150 ethnic groups and more than 2 million immigrants who had arrived since 1971.

RESPONSES TO REFUGEES AND "VISIBLE MINORITIES"

The wave of immigrants was swelled by successive migrations of refugees admitted on human-itarian grounds. Occasionally their numbers tested the limits of Canada's ethnic tolerance. After the Soviet Union invaded Czechoslovakia in 1968, the doors were opened to 12 000 Czechs fleeing their homeland. Canada accepted 240 Tibetans displaced by Chinese invasion in 1971, 7000 South Asians expelled from Uganda in 1972, and several thousand Chileans escaping a repressive military rule in 1973–74. Two sizable waves of Indochinese refugees came to Canada in the late 1970s: Vietnamese fleeing south Vietnam after the fall of Saigon in 1975, and 60 000 of the hundreds of thousands of "boat people" driven from Vietnam, Laos, and Kampuchea in 1978–82. Not all recent immigrants, however, came by legal means. An estimated 100 000 to 160 000 persons who entered as "visitors" stayed on in Canada without official landed-immigrant status and lived in what a *Toronto Star* reporter in 1976 called "the invisible community of illegal immigrants."

The increasing numbers of non-white "visible minorities" did not go unnoticed. In the post-war period Canada had admitted an estimated 5 million immigrants, or roughly half as many as the United States, although Canada had only one-tenth the population of the United States. By the late 1970s, visible minorities were more visible in Canada than in the United States, par-ticularly in the large metropolitan areas of Toronto, Montreal, and Vancouver. These new addi-tions to Canadian society were not always welcomed. In the late 1970s, when thousands of new immigrants were struggling for acceptance, the "image" of racial harmony in Canadian cities was shattered by a rash of physical assaults on South Asians and other "visible minorities" in Toronto and Calgary and by periodic attacks on the property of Sikh families in Vancouver.

THE RISE OF AMERICA'S "UNMELTABLE ETHNICS"

IN THE 1970s, America experienced an ethnic revival, mainly driven by the rising ethnic consciousness of white European-Americans. To some extent it was a backlash among "white ethnics" against the reforms won by black Americans. Many Euro-Americans had resisted black demands for access to "their" neighbourhoods, schools, and jobs, and resented being asked to compensate blacks for a history of oppression in which these whites had had little part. By the 1970s, "white ethnicity" was being redis-covered by government agencies, private foundations, and universities, both as a prob-lem and as a political force to be reckoned with.

Michael Novak's *The Rise of the Unmeltable Ethnics* (1971) served as a kind of mani-festo of the white ethnic movement in the United States and may have had some resid-ual influence in Canada among second- and third-generation Euro-Canadians. Novak, a Slovak American, viewed the persistence of ethnicity as a vital and creative force in modern America. He and many other Euro-Americans saw "white ethnics" confronted by a power structure dominated by the Anglo-Americans.

> [M]illions of Americans, who for a long time tried desperately even if unconsciously to become "Americanized," are delighted to discover that they no longer have to pay that price; are grateful that they were born among the people destiny placed them in; are pleased to discover the possibilities and the limits inherent in being who they are; and are openly happy about what heretofore they had disguised in silence. There is a creativity and new release, there is liberation, and there is hope.
>
> America is becoming America.

Critics of the new ethnicity movement in the 1970s dismissed it as a pipe dream concocted by "romantic" Euro-American intellectuals and journalists. White ethnicity never really materialized as an autonomous force in American politics. The conserva-tive attitudes held by most traditional-minded Euro-Americans on key social issues like abortion, sexual relations, drugs, and race prevented a fusion of interests with the working class and blacks. In the presidential elections of 1972, 1980, and 1984, Republican positions on these issues split off large segments of the white ethnic vote, which had remained loyal to the Democratic party since the New Deal in the 1930s.

The new ethnicity, however, was one of the major social phenomena of the 1970s in America as in Canada. Novak's *The Rise of the Unmeltable Ethnics* asserted that it was, in the 1970s idiom, "OK to be ethnic." Just as the "black pride" movement had affirmed black identity, buttons and bumper stickers soon proclaimed "Kiss Me, I'm Finnish," "Ukrainian is Beautiful," and "Slovak Power." More than a few Canadian analysts saw close connec-tions between America's ethnic revival and the rise of multiculturalism in Canada.

THE IMPACT OF MULTICULTURALISM

Canada's official policy of multiculturalism did not meet with universal acceptance in either English Canada or French Canada. The Trudeau government appointed, in 1972, a federal cabinet minister for multiculturalism, set up the Canadian Consultative Council on Multiculturalism, and increased funding for ethnic studies, immigrant aid, and employment training in a time of fiscal restraint. But a 1976 survey on multiculturalism and ethnic attitudes revealed that only 27.5 percent of the respondents had ever heard of the government's policy. Ten years after the policy's inception, one Canadian ethnic historian expressed fears that the nation's ethnic groups and those who studied them had come "to rely too much on the state" and, accustomed to lavish government spending, might prove "incapable of sustaining themselves in the harsher world of assimilationist, or at least homogenizing, public institutions and meaner times upon us now."

In the early 1980s, tough questions were raised about the ethnic tolerance of the Canadian public and the effect of the multiculturalism policy. The 1976 attitude survey had shown that over 80 percent of the respondents looked favourably upon "folk festivals" aimed at perpetuating old ethnic traditions, but less than one-third accepted the need for heritage language classes in schools or government support of "foreign-language" broadcasting. The majority of the Anglo-Celtic respondents felt that "ethnics" should speak English and conform in public, while communicating in native languages and wearing "traditional clothes" at home or on special holidays. For most *Québécois*, the multiculturalism policy remained an anathema, perceived by many as another means of Anglophone assimilation which could only lead to the "neutralizing" of special claims for the French language and founding culture. A vocal minority of English Canadians objected to multiculturalism as divisive, as an attempt by the Liberal party to "buy the ethnic vote," or as pandering to "ethnics" who should conform or "go through what we went through" to get established in Canada.

Even thoughtful, liberal social scientists and Euro-ethnic group leaders criticized the policy for emphasizing the preservation of "cultural identities" while ignoring or perpetuating the inequalities of income and economic status among groups within the "vertical ethnic mosaic." If a policy aimed at

The arrival of boatloads of Sri Lankan Tamils in 1986 and Indian Sikhs in 1987 claiming refugee status caused a major controversy over Canada's refugee policy. These Sikh refugees are boarding buses after arriving on the Nova Scotia coast.

supporting the folk traditions and associational life of the white European ethnics had once effectively assisted social adjustment in the 1950s and 1960s, critics pointed out that the "new immigration," composed mostly of non-white Asians and West Indians, demanded a completely different strategy of integration. One ethnic-studies expert predicted in 1984 that the movement to "mainstream multiculturalism" might become "an instrument for Canadianization rather than a defence of cultural diversity."

ETHNICITY IN A TECHNOLOGICAL WONDERLAND

Canadian society by the mid-1980s was — to use the well-worn metaphor — neither a "mosaic" nor an American-style "melting pot," but something in between. The Canadian vision of cultural duality based upon a French–English partnership remained a far cry from the "One nation under God" ideology of modern America. Compared with the United States, Canada had a higher proportion of foreign-born, particularly non-white, immigrants in its total population and still seemed to exhibit less nativism and greater acceptance of ethnic pluralism. Some modern critics of multiculturalism questioned whether pluralism, by recognizing everyone's differences, threatened to leave Canadians with nothing in common. Multiculturalism, according to political scientist Gad Horowitz, amounted to "the masochistic celebration of nothingness."[11]

Yet Canada was far from being a genuine "cultural mosaic" in the early 1980s. Aside from perhaps *Québécois* culture, the mass media, microtechnology, public schooling, intermarriage, and the language of the workplace were assimilationist forces at work on both sides of the border. University of Toronto sociologist Wsevolod Isajiw aptly described the situation in both Canada and the United States as akin to living in a "technological wonderland" where "ethnic traits do not form a way of life and do not function as a whole anymore."[12] For many Canadians in the 1980s, both English-speaking and French-speaking, ethnic identities provided at least some defence against the homogeneity of mass technological society.

ACTIVITIES

KEY TERMS AND CONCEPTS

Identify and briefly explain the historical significance of each of the following terms and concepts:

- Mass culture
- Pluralistic society
- Cultural duality
- "Limited identities"
- Provincialism
- "New Canadians"
- *Chicanos*

- Duplessis's *nationalisme*
- Quiet Revolution
- Particular status
- Non-violent resistance
- *Ratrapage*
- Opting out
- FLQ terrorism
- *Deux nations*/Two nations theory
- "Melting pot" and "mosaic"

- Points system
- "Visible minorities"
- "Unmeltable ethnics"

QUESTIONS FOR DISCUSSION

1. During the 1950s, French-speaking Quebeckers experienced many economic and social inequities in a province ruled by Maurice Duplessis's *Union Nationale* and dominated increasingly by Anglo-American enterprise. Was the position and experience of francophone Quebeckers comparable with that of blacks in the American South? Are such comparisons misleading?

2. Was the assertion of Quebec nationalism in the 1960s a "Quiet Revolution" or a "Noisy Evolution" that merely brought the province into line with the rest of North America? Was it a new phenomenon or a variation on a longstanding tradition in French Canada?

3. What were the connections, if any, between the emergence of modern Quebec nationalism in the 1960s and the eruption of the U.S. civil-rights movement among blacks?

4. In 1971, Canada adopted an official policy of multiculturalism, while the United States was experiencing the beginnings of its own "ethnic revival." How did Canada's state policy of multiculturalism affect the country? Have Canadian ethnic minorities been more, or less, successful than their American counterparts in preserving their cultural identities?

5. The popular image of America as a "melting pot" and Canada as a multicultural "mosaic" are well known. Did the theories reflect social reality in Canada and the United States in the 1970s? Do they today?

6. Many observers of North American society in the 1970s and 1980s pointed to a trend toward homogeneity and conformity in areas of mass tastes and technological culture. Will the "new ethnicity" survive this onslaught of technological culture?

INTERPRETATION OF EVIDENCE

Following are statistics and documentary evidence pertaining to the ethnic composition of Canada and the United States around 1980.

1. Study the evidence carefully, noting the differences in data bases.
2. Develop *five* provable *hypotheses* (tentative judgments) based on your analysis of the evidence.

DEBATE AND DISCUSS

Assess the following statements on ethnicity and society in Canada and the United States. *Support* or *refute* the point of view in a reasoned argument based on historical evidence.

1. "Drawing the distinction between 'a Canadian mosaic' and 'an American melting pot'...oversimplifies both the American and the Canadian experiences."

   — Howard Palmer, *International Journal* (1979).

2. "When a country like Canada enshrines pluralism through policies such as multiculturalism and bilingualism and the guaranteeing of individual rights — the outcome is coexistence — no more, no less.... Pluralism ceases to have a cause. The result: mosaic madness."

   — Reginald Bibby, *Mosaic Madness: The Poverty and Potential of Life in Canada* (Toronto: Stoddart, 1990), pp. 103–104.

TOWARD THE NEW MILLENNIUM: THE 1990s AND BEYOND

I N 1989, THE OLD COLD WAR ORDER and alliances began to collapse with astonishing speed. Soviet leader Mikhail Gorbachev announced that the Soviet Union recognized the right of every country "to choose the paths and forms of its development." The Berlin Wall, symbol of the Cold War, crumbled. In August 1991, a failed coup attempt against Gorbachev failed but brought cataclysmic change in its wake. Gorbachev dissolved the Soviet Communist party, and a newly elected president of Russia, Boris Yeltsin, trading on the popularity he gained in resisting the coup, took power in the Kremlin. By December 1991, the Soviet Union had disintegrated and was replaced by a fragile Commonwealth of Independent States. Mighty forces, such as nationalism and ancient ethnic tensions, that had long been suppressed were now set loose in eastern Europe, Asia, and elsewhere. The collapse of the Soviet system, in the words of writer John Ralston Saul, "loosed its multitude of nationalisms in a dangerous and unpredictable way."[1]

As Canada and the United States entered the 1990s, the world took on a new and unfamiliar shape. The end of the Cold War, the collapse of Soviet communism, and the emergence of what U.S. President George Bush termed "the new world order" were profound events that transformed the politics of both nations. Peoples and governments oriented to resisting communism through alliance and heavy defence spending were compelled to reformulate their relations. With the old enemy having disappeared, Canada, the United States, and other members of the North Atlantic alliance found themselves grappling with new uncertainties ranging from globalization to nationalistic hostilities in eastern Europe.[2]

Canadians on patrol near Visoko, Bosnia-Herzegovina, 1992. Canadian peacekeeping forces supervise an uneasy truce between Serbs, Croats, and Muslims.

A CRITICAL JUNCTURE

M oving toward the twenty-first century, Canada arrived at a critical juncture in its history as a North American, as well as a global, nation. Canadians wrestled with their fundamental problems of identity and community, new "faultlines" appeared in the traditional political system, and a succession of leaders struggled for a vision capable of inspiring unity and commitment.[3] Quebec's historic search for national recognition continued with the added support of the *Bloc Québécois*, elected as the official opposition in Ottawa in the 1993 federal election. Despite many attempts, from the Citizen's Forum on Canada's Future to the Meech Lake and Charlottetown accords, Canada seemed no closer to reaching a constitutional consensus on Quebec's place in a renewed federation.

Many other vexing political and social issues further divided Canadians. On political issues such as accountability and patronage, economic ones such as the deficit and the goods and services tax (GST), social concerns such as multiculturalism and urban crime, or ethical dilemmas such as abortion and euthanasia, Canadians could find little agreement. Just as definition was sought within the domestic realm, so too were Canadians searching for a new international role. With the end of the Cold War and the establishment of "the new world order," Canadians were struggling to find that new role in places such as the Persian Gulf, Bosnia, Somalia, Haiti, and Rwanda.

Much of Canadian development in this period was strongly affected by influences, pressures, and innovations from the "other side" of the 49th parallel. After suffering a loss of global economic status and military prowess in the late 1970s, symbolized by the Iranian hostage affair, the United States responded with a renewed stridency. Under President Ronald Reagan (1981–88), Americans turned to free-market capitalism at home and assertionism abroad. Canada joined in "drawing a line in the sand" in the Persian Gulf, and followed the American lead in other "hot spots" as disparate as Somalia and Haiti. Domestically, Canada remained dwarfed by a gigantic neighbour with ten times its population, which now absorbed over three-quarters of Canadian exports. Most of the Canadian populace was strung out in a narrow band along the 8000 km continental border, living within 150 km of the United States. The historic Free Trade Agreement (FTA) was reached in 1988 and expanded under the North American Free Trade Agreement (NAFTA) to include Mexico in 1993. North American mass cultural influences continued to expand as a new generation of Canadians

Talking heads: two Canadians protesting the Reagan–Mulroney summit of April 1987 in Ottawa perform an impromptu show satirizing the "special relationship" between Canada and the United States.

grew up in a world dominated by American culture.[4] That continental, if not global, trend promised to increase with the influence of trade alignments, the 500-station satellite network, and "the information highway."

THE NEW WORLD ORDER

As both Canada and the United States approached the twenty-first century, the global situation was not only radically altered but also unpredictable. The Soviet Union, the "Iron Curtain" dividing Europe, and even the nuclear arms race were no more. Not only was the Soviet empire gone, so too were East and West Germany. In November 1989, the Berlin Wall came crashing down and the two Germanys were formally reunited the following year. In April 1994, multiracial democracy came to South Africa, the former bastion of white supremacist rule. After decades of conflict, the Middle East was moving haltingly toward peace through the Camp David Accord (1978) and treaties signed between Israel and the Palestine Liberation Organization (PLO) (1993) and Israel and Jordan (1994). As part of United Nations operations in Bosnia, Somalia, and Haiti, both North American nations experienced the change from the more passive peace-keeping to the more assertive peacemaking role.

If the new international order had an initiator, it was Mikhail Gorbachev, Soviet president from 1985 until his fall from power in 1991. Under Gorbachev, the forces of change in the Soviet system were unleashed. An independent trade union, Solidarity, was allowed in Poland, and free elections were also permitted there; the Berlin Wall was dis-

Jubilant young Berliners smash the historic wall separating East and West Berlin, November 1989. A powerful symbol of the Cold War comes tumbling down, signifying the onset of a "new world order."

mantled, and the two Germanys were reunited; the Warsaw Pact disappeared, and communism was abandoned as various communist parties voted themselves out of existence; and the republics of the Soviet Union became autonomous nations. Two key processes underlay all these momentous changes — *perestroika* and *glasnost*. The former referred to Gorbachev's desire to "restructure" the Soviet economy along the lines of a Western-style free market, while the latter meant "openness" and pointed to the fact that, if the economy was to be radically altered, then politics and society must change as well. Soviets would be allowed many previously unheard of freedoms, including the right to criticize their government and its leaders. As a result, more than a dozen republics within the former Soviet Union claimed independence.

The impact of the changes within the former Soviet Union were felt worldwide. Clearly, Canada and the United States could not remain immune. Relations between the United States and Russia as well as between Canada and Russia were far more cordial than they were during the 1970s era of détente. Separate summits were held between the leaders of the three countries and produced closer relations in a wide range of areas. Everyone from hockey players to ballerinas travelled freely. A number of arms-limitation agreements were signed. Movement, exchange, and trade increased.

Both Canada and the United States had to seriously adjust their defence posture in light of changing realities. Cuts were made in defence budgets and staffs. Canada, responding to both military and economic imperatives, closed NATO bases in Europe as well as military bases in Canada. A defence white paper in late 1994 proposed further cuts: of military personnel from 66 700 to 60 000; of the civilian workforce from 25 000 to 20 000; and of reserve troops from 29 000 to 20 000. However, the massive changes in Russia in the latter part of the 1980s and early 1990s were not the only international events that caused a paradigm shift for Canada and the United States.

The Golden Arches in Moscow. The opening of the first McDonald's restaurant in Moscow in January 1990 drew record crowds.

"A LINE IN THE SAND"

In late August 1990, Iraqi leader Saddam Hussein ordered his troops to invade neighbouring Kuwait in an attempt to annex it, thereby benefiting from its rich oil reserves. Cat-and-mouse negotiations continued for the next four-and-a-half months as the United Nations attempted to get Iraq to comply with demands for a withdrawal from Kuwait. The negotiations proved to be fruitless. Then, on January 15, 1991, remembering the fateful lesson of World War II appeasement, U.S. President George Bush ordered the transformation of Operation Desert Shield into Desert Storm. He was drawing "a line in the sand." The Persian Gulf War proved to be a techno-war that included Scud, Tomahawk, and Patriot missiles, as well as an entirely new military jargon that confused rather than clarified. The daily briefings, whether provided by press secretary Dick Cheney or Chairman of the Joint Chiefs of Staff Colin Powell, obfuscated far more than they illuminated. A major concern was that Iraqi missiles falling on Israel would bring that country into the conflict, thereby shattering the fragile U.N.-sponsored coalition. However, that did not come about, as Iraq suffered massive and relentless bombings. The international coalition, including Canada and even more prominently the United States, announced Iraq's defeat on February 27, 1991, less than a month and half after the night sky of Baghdad had first been lit up by coalition missiles.

The Persian Gulf War was a significant event for both Canada and the United States. Despite claims that the war was fought at the behest of the international oil multinationals, solid majorities in both nations supported their respective countries' involvement. NDP leader Audrey McLaughlin could rouse little support for her principled opposition to Canadian participation. In the West, Hussein was seen as the personification of evil; somebody who had to be stopped. The war made a hero out of U.N. Commander Norman Schwarzkopf, and Canadian Prime Minister Brian Mulroney was recognized as a "world leader" in popular sets of "Desert Storm" trading cards.

After the Persian Gulf ceasefire, Canadians and Americans both participated in various U.N. operations to maintain the peace as well as to enforce compliance and inspection of suspected Iraqi nuclear installations. Both nations were involved in humanitarian efforts to assist displaced Kurdish rebels in northern Iraq who contested Hussein's hold on power. Both assisted in rebuilding the shattered economy of Kuwait by putting out over 550 oil-well fires that blazed across the desert. The Persian Gulf War taught the entire world community that as costly as winning the war had been, maintaining the peace would prove to be even more difficult. In many ways, the vexing problems of the entire Middle East region appeared to make it the prime trouble spot in this new world order.

PEACEKEEPING TO PEACEMAKING

The real "powder keg" of Europe was Yugoslavia, a nation cobbled together out of a volatile mixture of cultures, religions, and nationalities at the Versailles Peace Conference of 1919. The bonds that held together the inherently unstable federation of six republics and two provinces disappeared in 1980, when Marshall Tito's 35-year reign as the country's strongman ended with his death. The old rivalries among Serbs, Croatians, and Muslims began to reassert themselves, until the summer of 1991 witnessed internecine violence as breakaway republics demanded independence. A number of them — Bosnia, Serbia, Croatia, and Slovenia — were recognized, but the cost was tremendous. As the civil war continued into the mid-1990s, more than 100 000 people were killed and more than 2 million became refugees. The practice of "ethnic cleansing" — the systematic torture, rape, and murder of the Muslim population by

Serbian soldiers, raised fears of a repeat of the horror of the Holocaust of World War II. Yugoslavia was no more, but what had replaced it was tremendous suffering, instability, and destruction. Sarajevo, the former capital, as it had in 1914, once again sounded an alarm that had to be answered by the international community.

The United Nations, adopting a more active and assertive role, responded by despatching a 14 000-member peacekeeping force. Led by Canadian Major-General Lewis Mackenzie, it attempted to enforce over 500 "ceasefires" and "no-fly zones," all of which were broken by both sides with casual disregard. Realizing that he was engaged in a qualitatively different operation, Mackenzie, showing "grace under pressure," was loudly applauded by the international community for his common sense, modesty, and courage. Opening the Sarajevo airport against heavy bombardment in order to allow much-needed supplies to reach the people won Mackenzie and the U.N. troops considerable international praise. Clearly, there was no real peace to keep, so Mackenzie saw that peacemaking was more his mandate. Despite the intervention of scores of international diplomats, from U.N. Secretary-General Boutros Boutros-Ghali to NATO Secretary-General Manfred Woerner, peace in Bosnia remained highly elusive. Bosnia signalled a changing role for the United Nations as well as a realization that old-style diplomacy could not resolve a quagmire of religious and ethnic conflict.

Major-General Lewis MacKenzie, chief of staff of the U.N. force in the former Yugoslavia, 1992.

TWO STEPS FORWARD, ONE STEP BACK

That same kind of dispute — in this case in the Middle East — was giving way to progress, albeit a progress that was halting and inconsistent. On the one hand, historic advances had been made. The U.S.-brokered Camp David Accord of 1978 saw Israel embrace the concept of "land for peace" for the first time. Israeli Prime Minister Menachem Begin returned most of the Sinai Peninsula, captured in the 1967 Six Day War, to Egyptian President Anwar Sadat. Fifteen years later, in 1993, Israel and the Palestine Liberation Organization (PLO) signed a historic peace accord. The next year saw Jordan and Israel do the same thing, thereby ending 46 years of hostility. Yet there were many bumps along the road to peace: Sadat's assassination, the Palestinian *Intifada* (uprising), massacres at Shabra, Shatila, Temple Mount, and Hebron, and the continuing terrorism of the Islamic fundamentalist Hamas and Lebanon-based Hezbollah. However, as the world approached the new millennium, the prospects of lasting peace in the Middle East rarely appeared better.

Canada and the United States came to share remarkably similar policies on the evolving new world order. They applauded the establishment of multiracial democracy in South Africa. With their sizable Irish populations, the two North American nations applauded the tenuous arrival of peace in Northern Ireland. In December 1992, both the United States and Canada participated in the U.N. operation to bring relief to Somalia, an African nation torn apart by war and famine. For Canadians, that operation ended with a trial, public censure, and a suicide over a teenaged Somalian who had been tortured and killed while in Canadian custody. The unit stationed in northern Somalia found its reputation sullied, as cases of murder, torture, racist slurs, and obscene initiation rituals surfaced. The Canadians left Somalia, but a string of court martials and media revelations demonstrated that peacekeeping could have a darker side.

The two North American nations were attempting to find their rightful place in a world that had left the Cold War behind. In that world, it was far more difficult to determine who one's enemies were or where the next "hot spot" would be. The "terms of engagement" had been irrevocably altered. Internationally, both North American nations began looking to the Pacific Rim far more than they ever had as both Canadian Prime Minister Jean Chrétien (elected in October 1993) and U.S. President Bill Clinton eagerly sought to forge closer ties with China, home to almost one-quarter of the world's population.

CONTINENTALISM AND FREE TRADE

THE ECONOMIC WORLD OF THE 1980s was marked by growing international competitiveness and rising protectionism. Canadian efforts to diversify trade met with disappointing results, as both Japan and the European Common Market (later the EC — European Community) manoeuvred to keep foreign goods out of their markets. Trudeau had advocated a "third option," but it would only be toward the end of the century that both Canada and the United States were able to make substantial

The Shamrock Summit, March 1985. Prime Minister Brian Mulroney and President Ronald Reagan renewed the "special relationship" between the two nations. At the summit, Reagan broached the subject of negotiating a "North American free trade area."

inroads into the Asian market, most notably China. As long as Canadian goods could be sold in the United States, such Japanese and EC policies could be tolerated. But the situation changed when the Americans became alarmed over the flight of U.S. capital to the low-wage economies of Korea, Taiwan, and Singapore and the increasing domination of the Japanese manufacturers over large segments of the automobile, appliance, and electronic markets. The huge American trade deficit each year revealed the extent of the damage and eventually sparked a rise in protectionist sentiment in Washington. In spite of President Reagan's professed belief in a freer trading world, Congress came to be dominated by a protectionist mood.

MULRONEY'S FREE-TRADE GAMBLE

The Progressive Conservative majority government of Brian Mulroney, elected in September 1984, was committed to restoring Canada's "market-driven economy" and to improving relations with the United States. As Mulroney announced very early in his tenure, "Canada is open for business." Toward the end of his first year in office, he decided to take the "free-trade gamble." A number of powerful influences and inducements had come into play. A spate of protectionist bills were being introduced in the U.S. Congress, and the American ambassador to Canada, Paul Robinson, warned Canadian business leaders that the results could be damaging to trading partners like Canada.

In January 1985 James Kelleher, then minister of trade, announced that the government was considering the possibilities for a new Canada–U.S. trade deal, and three months later at the Quebec "Shamrock Summit" President Reagan made the case in direct talks with Prime Minister Mulroney. The Report of the Royal Commission on the Economy, headed by Donald MacDonald and published in September 1985, called for Canada to take such "a leap of faith," and this only solidified the government's position. On September 26, 1985, two weeks after turning down direct government-to-government involvement in Reagan's Star Wars research program, Mulroney announced Canada's intention to pursue "a new trade agreement" in negotiations with Washington.

THE FREE-TRADE DEBATE

The launching of the Mulroney–Reagan free-trade negotiations touched off the first nationwide trade debate since the decisive 1911 election campaign over reciprocity. Mulroney and the free-trade supporters claimed that the creation of "a Canadian–American free-trade area" would provide freer access to a North American market of over 250 million consumers and would safeguard Canada against protectionist measures imposed by the U.S. Congress. Advocates of free trade argued that secure access to the American market was essential, since close to 80 percent of Canada's exports went to the United States and over 2 million jobs in Canada were dependent upon that trade. From the outset of negotiations, Mulroney attempted to assure Canadians that "political sovereignty, our system of social programs, our commitment to fight regional disparities, our unique cultural identity, our special linguistic character" were "not at issue."

THE AMERICANIZATION OF CANADIAN SPORTS

PROFESSIONAL SPORTS, a staple of Canadian popular culture in the 1990s, demonstrated an inexorable trend toward continentalism. The "big three" sports — baseball, hockey and football — were organized along continental lines and appealed to TV "couch potatoes" and live spectators on both sides of the border. Sports also generated spinoff industries with a continental orientation, such as the $11 billion sports-merchandise and $2.5 billion sports-trading-card industries (1993 figures). Just as National Hockey League (NHL) hockey was losing its claim as Canada's favourite sports pastime, so too baseball was no longer seen as "America's game," and the venerable Canadian Football League struggled for survival.

The Toronto Blue Jays hit the big time in October 1992 by winning major-league baseball's first "foreign" World Series. People ignored the fact that there was not one Canadian player on the Blue Jays' roster. They were still "Canada's team." In a time of intense national uncertainty, they united much of the country behind them. More than the CBC, the CPR, the flag, or any other traditional "unifier," the Blue Jays were something all Canadians could rally behind. It was almost a repeat of what had transpired 20 years earlier, when Paul Henderson's dramatic goal in the last minute of the final game gave Team Canada a victory over the Soviet Union in the 1972 "hockey summit" series. The parading of the Canadian flag upside down prior to the start of the first 1992 game in Atlanta, Georgia, and the various renditions of the national anthem became the focus of considerable international attention. That the Blue Jays were able to repeat as World Series champions in 1993 only reinforced the allure of major-league sports, especially among Canadian youth.

The Montreal Canadiens' all-time goaltending great Ken Dryden described hockey as Canada's "home game," but it was also taking on a more continental complexion. Expansion of the National Hockey League, occurring at various times after 1967, had reached such places as San Jose, Buffalo, New Jersey, St. Louis, and Washington. By the mid-1990s, even American

At pregame ceremonies during the 1992 World Series in Atlanta, a Marine Color Guard mistakenly flew the Canadian flag upside down.

"Sun Belt" cities such as Orlando, Anaheim, and Dallas embraced hockey as passionately as any Canadian city. Whereas in the 1960s only a handful of NHL players were American-born, by the 1990s NHL rosters were comprised of almost one-quarter American-born players as well as scores of Europeans. In August 1988, the icon of hockey, Wayne Gretzky, was traded in a blockbuster deal from the Edmonton Oilers to the Los Angeles Kings; in 1992, a "non-hockey man," American Gary Bettman, became the commissioner of the NHL; and two years later the NHL signed a lucrative $200 million television deal with the American Fox Network. Hockey, once the preserve of Canadians, was by the mid-1990s a continental, if not global, sport — and business.

The truly unique Canadian Football League (CFL) was by the mid-1990s attempting to transform itself into a North American league. What had been a thriving nine-team league in the 1960s was losing a succession of owners and even franchises to bankruptcy. Canada's second-largest metropolis, Montreal, had been without a team since the 1980s, and the original franchises in Hamilton, Calgary, and Ottawa were on shaky ground. In Toronto, the CFL Argonauts faced stiff competition from the Blue Jays, the Toronto Maple Leafs, and the brand-new National Basketball Association (NBA) Raptors for a share of the fans' sports dollars. By the 1995 season, almost half the teams of the *Canadian* Football League were located in American cities. The expansion that occurred took place only in American locales. The once sacrosanct quota of 20 Canadians per team was reduced for Canadian-based teams and eliminated for American-based teams.

Perhaps the last gasp for the old-style CFL occurred in November 1994, when the Grey Cup, emblematic of league supremacy, was won by the British Columbia Lions over an all-American team from Baltimore on a last-play field goal by Vancouver-born Lou Passaglia. The "C" in the league's name now appeared to stand more for "Continental" than "Canadian."

Not every observer shared the prevailing attitude of pessimism concerning Canadian football. The CFL, sociologist Robert Stebbins wrote recently, remains "a master-symbol of Canadian popular culture."* It represents a unique blend of English rugby and American football and inspires a "characteristically Canadian" and "whimsically ambivalent" fan response. "Canadian football," he contended, "will survive — whether we like it or not and despite the mass media."

* See Robert A. Stebbins, "Ambivalence at the Fifty-five-Yard Line: Transformation and Resistance in Canadian Football," in David H. Flaherty and Frank E. Manning, eds., *The Beaver Bites Back? American Popular Culture in Canada* (Montreal and Kingston: McGill–Queen's University Press, 1993), pp. 163–174.

Opposition to the Mulroney–Reagan free-trade initiative was not long in forming. From late 1985 onward, a revived economic nationalist movement arose that voiced the concerns of a cross-section of interests. The anti–free-trade coalition embraced the 7000-member Council of Canadians, labour organizations like the Canadian Auto Workers and the Canadian Labour Congress, farm commodity producers, most cultural groups, and even some industry trade associations threatened by tariff cuts. Most of the opposition groups saw the free-trade initiative as either a serious miscalculation that would jeopardize Canada's trade position, or worse — an unabashed "sellout" of Canadian economic, cultural, and perhaps political sovereignty.

While the Mulroney government enjoyed the strong support of most provincial premiers and a business–finance alliance, the opposition won to its cause the federal Liberals and NDP and the Ontario government of David Peterson and the Prince Edward Island government of Joseph Ghiz. At the Halifax first ministers' conference in late November 1985, Mulroney promised full provincial participation in the free-trade negotiations, but this later amounted to regular "consultations" rather than a direct provincial role.

THE FREE-TRADE AGREEMENT

The free-trade negotiations proved to be anything but smooth sailing. The two sides entered the talks with differing aims and agendas, not to mention bargaining positions at variance on many issues. Canada's chief negotiator was Simon Riesman, while his American counterpart was Peter Murphy. From the outset, Murphy insisted that the agreement must extend from tariff and non-tariff barrier reductions to areas such as Canadian investment restrictions, social programs viewed as "unfair subsidies," and the Auto Pact of 1965. The Canadian strategy focused on countering the U.S. protectionist threat to Canada's trade interests and sought to gain secure and enhanced access to the U.S. market and to insulate Canadian trade from American countervailing duties, anti-dumping measures, and safeguard actions. There were continual demands for "a level playing field" as well as protracted discussions as to exactly what constituted a "subsidy."

After months of off-and-on bargaining and an eleventh-hour Canadian walkout, a historic free-trade deal was reached shortly before the October 1987 deadline imposed by the U.S. Congress. In announcing the release of the official 218-page text in December 1987, Mulroney hailed the agreement as "a major step forward for Canada," which established "clear and mutually advantageous rules" to govern Canada–U.S. trade. While termed a free-trade agreement, the deal was in fact both more and less than that. It did not provide for a customs union or eliminate all non-tariff barriers, but it extended beyond trade into areas of investment, export subsidies, and energy policy. Under the deal, Canada gained a new dispute-resolving tribunal and an agreement to phase out all bilateral tariffs within 10 years, starting in 1989. Among the trade-offs, however, were concessions that established a continental (or free) energy market; eased restrictions on American investment and acquisitions; opened the Canadian market to U.S. farm imports such as grain products, poultry, and eggs; altered the terms of the Canada–U.S. automobile trade; and permitted greater access of U.S. wines to the domestic market after a seven-year transition period.

"A PARTING OF THE WAYS"

With the publication of the free-trade text at the end of 1987, Canada stood anew at what *The Globe and Mail* called "a parting of the ways." Mulroney's Progressive Conservative government was urging Canadians to endorse free trade and thereby express their faith in Canada's new competitiveness. In the popular press, comparisons were being drawn between Wilfrid Laurier's ill-fated 1911 campaign for reciprocity and the current Mulroney free-trade initiative. In a historical irony, the political parties had reversed their respective positions on the issue of free trade. Historians in Canada, however, saw other parallels between the contemporary free-trade debate and the continental-union controversy of the 1880s, precisely 100 years before.

The raging public debate over free trade produced a familiar polarization between free traders and economic nationalists, between Mulroney Conservatives and Liberal–social democrats, between corporate business interests and the organized labour movement. Echoing the arguments of Mulroney and the free-trade alliance, *The Globe and Mail* claimed that the free-trade agreement was "a significant achievement in liberalizing economic ties" and represented a "net gain on balance" for Canada. Liberal opposition leader John Turner condemned the document as "the most massive betrayal in history…(and) the first step toward our becoming the 51st state of the American union." Like Turner, NDP leader Ed Broadbent rejected the deal and promised to "tear it up" if elected in the next federal election.

Yet the free-trade debate also brought into sharper relief the very nature of the Canadian community in the late 1980s. For most Canadians, the nation's perpetual "identity crisis" seemed to have subsided. Many Canadians now accepted Richard Gwyn's dictum that they were "no longer 'not-Americans'" but "a quite distinct kind of North American." Regionalism not only persisted, but appeared as powerful as ever. British Columbians, Prairie

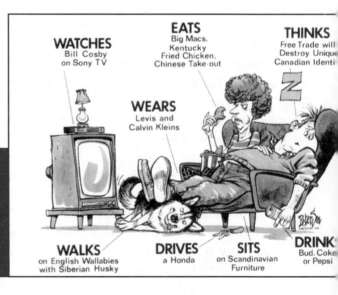

EATS
Big Macs.
Kentucky
Fried Chicken.
Chinese Take-out

WATCHES
Bill Cosby
on Sony TV

THINKS
Free Trade will
Destroy Unique
Canadian Identi

WEARS
Levis and
Calvin Kleins

WALKS
on English Wallabies
with Siberian Husky

DRIVES
a Honda

SITS
on Scandinavian
Furniture

DRINK
Bud, Coke
or Pepsi

Mr. and Mrs. Average Canadian. A critical commentary on the state of Canadian identity in the 1980s' world of North American mass culture. How exaggerated is the image conveyed by the 1987 cartoon?

westerners, and to a lesser extent Maritimers generally welcomed more North–South commercial links because these links would free them from central Canadian economic dominance and possibly from Toronto's perceived monopoly on the nation's wealth. Most Ontarians and their provincial government did not understand the regional mentality that made oil workers, farmers, and fishers place regional economic interests ahead of their allegiance to national institutions, values, or symbols. Canadians also emerged with a clearer sense of the essential ingredients of their distinctive society in North America. Significantly, both sides in the free-trade debate shared a rough consensus on the importance of protecting Canada's health-care and social-security system, cultural institutions, monetary system, and regional-development programs.

FTA TO NAFTA

The 1988 election returned Brian Mulroney and the Progressive Conservatives to power with a second consecutive majority government. Just as the 1911 election had been fought largely over reciprocity, the 1988 election hinged on free trade. The Free Trade Agreement (FTA) came into effect on January 1, 1989, and just as there had been strong debate prior to the signing of the agreement and throughout one of the most spirited election campaigns, no consensus emerged on the merits of the deal afterward. Critics pointed to the loss of about half a million Canadian manufacturing jobs. Supporters blamed those losses on the deep recession that coincided with the introduction of free trade. Nationalists expressed concern over Canadian social programs, such as medicare, as well as access to Canadian natural resources, such as water and oil.

The FTA led eventually to an expanded trade pact that included Mexico. After 14 months of intense, closed-door negotiations, the North American Free Trade Agreement (NAFTA) was signed at the Watergate Hotel in Washington on August 12, 1992. Canada's Michael Wilson, the United States' Carla Hills, and Mexico's Jaime Serra Puche created the world's largest trading bloc of 360 million people and a market worth almost $7 trillion, about one-third of the world's total. The agreement, which went into effect on January 1, 1994, eliminated tariffs and quotas on some goods and services and called for a phased-out reduction over the next 10 years of others. In concluding the accord, the nations had established an important precedent for trade and economic co-operation between the industrialized countries of the North and the developing countries of the South. Furthermore, FTA and NAFTA had radically altered the economic realities for the United States, and even more so for Canada, in the 1990s and beyond.

THE CONSTITUTIONAL IMPASSE

A RESURGENCE OF QUEBEC NATIONALISM AND PROVINCIALISM in the late 1980s imposed new strains on Canadian federalism and existing constitutional arrangements. The 1982 "National Deal" reached between the Pierre Trudeau government and nine provinces gave Canada a new patriated constitution with an entrenched Charter of Rights and Freedoms, but it left the Quebec question unresolved. When the deal was struck in November 1981, Quebec Premier René Lévesque was not present, and he responded angrily that Quebec had been treated in "the Canadian way," meaning that it had been isolated from the provinces of English-speaking Canada. On patriation day, April 17, 1982, while most English Canadians either quietly celebrated or heaved a sigh of relief, Quebec's *fleur de lis* flags were lowered to half mast and Lévesque led a PQ march of protest through the streets of Montreal. A new constitution had been achieved; the political reconciliation of Quebec remained far from complete.

THE MEECH LAKE ACCORD

The election of Brian Mulroney's Progressive Conservative government in September 1984, however, signalled the beginning of a rare period of federal–provincial accommodation and "national reconciliation," as well as the start of the "Quebec round" of constitutional negotiations. With the return to power of the Quebec Liberals under Robert Bourassa in 1985, constitutional talks were resumed in an attempt to reach an agreement acceptable to Quebec. Amid an atmosphere of federal–provincial harmony, the eleven first ministers reached a consensus in late April 1987 on the Meech Lake Accord; a month later the deal was reaffirmed in what came

A rare show of federal–provincial harmony in May 1987. Premiers Robert Bourassa (Quebec), David Peterson (Ontario), John Buchanan (Nova Scotia), and William Vander Zalm (British Columbia) join in applauding Prime Minister Brian Mulroney for negotiating the Meech Lake Accord.

to be known as the Langevin Accord (named after the building housing the prime minister's office). A major stipulation was that there was a three-year "window" from the date the agreement was signed, June 23, 1987, during which the ratification of all ten provincial governments as well as the federal government had to be obtained.

The Meech Lake Accord was hailed by many as a triumph for Mulroney's strategy of compromise and conciliation. The first ministers agreed to a series of constitutional amendments, most of which met conditions laid down by Bourassa's Quebec government. The proposed accord would (1) recognize Quebec as a "distinct society"; (2) establish immigration as a concurrent (federal and provincial) field of jurisdiction; (3) provide for reasonable federal compensation to provinces that elected not to participate in national shared-cost programs; (4) tighten the constitutional amending formula by requiring unanimous provincial consent for changes to certain national institutions; and (5) allow the provinces to supply nomination lists from which members of the Supreme Court and Senate would be selected. This Meech Lake Accord drew the official, though unsettled, support of both the federal Liberals and the NDP.

Many critics of the 1987 accord quickly emerged, mostly outside of Parliament. Two of the most vocal, Robert Fulford of *Saturday Night* magazine and Pierre Trudeau, condemned the deal as a massive transfer of federal authority to the provinces, a move tantamount to "the surrender of Canada." Acceptance of the changes, Trudeau warned, would "render the Canadian state totally impotent" and "destine it…to eventually be governed by eunuchs." Such dissent did not stop the premiers from passing provincial resolutions aimed at bringing Quebec back into "the Canadian constitutional family."

DEATH OF THE ACCORD

Optimistic hopes for constitutional peace were crushed on June 23, 1990, when time ran out for ratifying the Meech Lake Accord. Newfoundland Premier Clyde Wells had submitted the accord to the legislature of his home province and allowed it to go down to defeat. In the Manitoba legislature, Native member of the legislative assembly Elijah Harper had effectively blocked passage by refusing his consent to bring the accord to a vote. What remained was anger, recrimination, and division. Opponents claimed that the accord failed to address the needs of a variety of groups, such as the Native peoples and women. Others, such as newly elected Manitoba Premier Gary Filmon, pointed an accusing finger at Quebec Premier Bourassa's invoking of the "notwithstanding" clause in order to maintain Quebec's desired sign-law legislation.

The Meech Lake Accord became a lightning rod for a wide range of rising popular discontents. It was identified in the public mind with a cluster of other controversial issues — Brian Mulroney's lavish personal style, the rising deficit, the goods and services tax (GST), and a variety of Tory government scandals.[5] The growing antipathy toward Mulroney and most other politicians made ratification extremely difficult. Leading political commentators and pollsters noted the public frustration with incessant constitutional wrangling and urged Mulroney to declare a cooling-off period.

MORDECAI RICHLER: CONTINENTAL GADFLY AND *AGENT PROVOCATEUR*

IN LATE 1991, one of Canada's most celebrated writers, Mordecai Richler, entered the debate over Quebec's future with a *New Yorker* magazine article that provoked an outpouring of passions. The lengthy essay, published on September 23, 1991, depicted modern Quebec as a society beset by "tribal racism" in the guise of French-speaking Quebec nationalism. With a satirical eye, Richler — a Montrealer himself — dissected aspects of Quebec society that exemplified *Québécois* tribalism and a streak of anti-Semitism running through modern Quebec history. That Richler chose a leading American magazine as the initial vehicle for his contentious views was noteworthy. He set out to provoke, and did so in an American publication, airing "conflicts" that had previously been kept inside Canada.

The controversial *New Yorker* article was the first installment of a larger project, Richler's 1992 book, *Oh Canada! Oh Quebec! Requiem for a Divided Country*. In it, he described the Quebec sovereignty movement's campaign for a referendum as "the western world's goofiest and most unnecessary political crisis." Ridiculing the so-called "self-appointed vigilantes" who presided over Quebec's Bill 178 exterior-sign law and other "absurd and draconian language laws," Richler dramatized the plight of Anglo-Quebeckers like himself. He cited numerous examples of anti-Semitism in Quebec, often perpetrated by icons of Quebec nationalism like Abbé Lionel Groulx, founder of the influential *L'Action nationale* in the 1930s and still regarded as the patron saint of the *indépendantistes*. In launching his critique, Richler undercut Quebec nationalists' plea for acceptance of Quebec as a distinct society. His depiction of that nationalism as restrictive, paranoid, and anti-Semitic left no middle ground and became a lightning rod for constitutional debate.

A few excerpts from *Oh Canada! Oh Quebec!* demonstrate Richler's acerbic style and trenchant commentary:

"I was brought up in a Quebec that was reactionary, church-ridden, and notoriously corrupt — a stagnant backwater — its *chef* for most of that time, Premier Maurice Duplessis, a political thug — even its intellectuals sickeningly anti-Semitic for the most part."

"Sometimes it appears to me that Canada, even an intact Canada, is not so much a country as a continental suburb, where Little Leaguers govern ineffectually, desperate for American approval."

"[F]ollowing an initial decade of economic sorrows, I have no doubt that a combination of Francophone ingenuity and imagination could make Quebec a viable little country. Its citizens would find it a decent place to live, *provided they were French-speaking*. But, without the rest of Canada acting as an increasingly bilingual buffer, it would become even more isolated from the North American mainstream, its standard of living diminished. Eventually, I suspect, it would revert to being a folkloric society. A place that people came from. Ireland without that country's genius."

From *Oh Canada! Oh Quebec!* by Mordecai Richler. Copyright © Mordecai Richler Productions Inc., 1992. Reprinted by permission of the author and Penguin Books Canada Limited.

THE CHARLOTTETOWN ACCORD VERDICT

The respite from constitutional talks did not last long. Mulroney and his government examined the Meech Lake experience and concluded that the process of constitution-making, not the substance of the accord, was to blame for its failure. Top advisers and pollsters like Allan Gregg and Michael Adams claimed that the Canadian public perceived the Meech Lake Accord as a deal "cooked up by backroom politicians," behind closed doors and without proper public consultation. The result of this review was a new round of negotiations on a broader range of issues, from the economic union to First Nations' rights to the Quebec question.

The 1992 "Canada Round" of consultations, led by Mulroney's Minister of Constitutional Affairs Joe Clark, was a broad and inclusive process. It began with an extensive series of citizens' forums, constituent assemblies, and investigations to formulate a new set of constitutional proposals, and it ended with top-level negotiations over a redesigned accord, including a modified version of the Meech Lake proposal. The result of this massive national pulse-taking was the August 1992 Charlottetown Accord.

CONSTITUTIONAL FATIGUE

The Charlottetown Accord was finally put to the people in a national referendum in October 1992. But, in surprising and decisive fashion, six provinces and one territory rejected the appeals of the well-financed "yes" campaign and virtually every prominent Canadian politician. CBC national news anchor Peter Mansbridge opened his coverage of the results with the statement, "The accord is DOA — dead on arrival." Opposition from Reform party leader Preston Manning, Pierre Trudeau,

Charges of excess: a smiling Prime Minister Brian Mulroney brushes past Parliament Hill anti-corruption protester Glen Kealey outside the National Press Building in 1989.

leading scholars, and women's groups struck a responsive chord with a disillusioned public. With a voter turnout of 72 percent, the accord was rejected by 55 percent of the voters.

A new Liberal government, headed by Prime Minister Jean Chrétien, came to power in October 1993 determined to focus on economic renewal and to lay the constitution to rest. Confronted with widespread "constitutional fatigue" as well as the separatist official opposition Bloc Québécois, led by Lucien Bouchard, Chrétien's government shied away from any further constitutional initiatives. Matters were further muddied with the September 1994 election in Quebec of a Parti Québécois government under Jacques Parizeau. The PQ government's announced intention to hold a 1995 Quebec referendum on "sovereignty-association" set the stage for another intense public debate much like that in the 1980 referendum, 15 years earlier.

Bloc Québécois leader Lucien Bouchard and Quebec Premier Jacques Parizeau campaign together for Quebec sovereignty.

POSTMODERN SOCIETIES

BY THE MID-1990s, Canada and the United States were being described as postmodern nations. Since 1960, North American society had seen the rise of a succession of social movements committed to civil rights, gender equity, ethnic and linguistic equality, and Native sovereignty. Students from the baby boom generation in Canada, the United States, and Europe had pushed successfully for reforms in government services, the schools, and universities. Gradually the movement for empowerment came to touch the lives of most North Americans, as women, aboriginal peoples, visible minorities, the poor, and even the aggrieved middle class mobilized to claim what they considered their human rights. Whether the two North American nations could accommodate the variety and diversity of interests and manage to move forward as coherent and self-sustaining societies was the central question of this postmodern age.

THE FIRST BORDERLESS STATE

In November 1994, national columnist Richard Gwyn delivered an address at Brock University in St. Catharines, Ontario, in which he claimed that Canada was on the verge of becoming one of the world's first postmodern, borderless nations. He gazed into the future and forecast that Canada would *either* dissolve as an independent North American nation or reinvent itself as perhaps "the world's first postmodern nation" by demonstrating the viability of a borderless state. No other modern country, he contended, was officially multicultural, guaranteed gender equality in its constitution, delegated so much power to its provinces or states, and had undergone such a demographic change through immigration. Canada would become a true postmodern society if it succeeded in finding "a way to contain all our disparate parts within a whole larger than their sum."[6]

Canada in the 1990s was barely recognizable. The 1991 census revealed some significant changes in its demographic, social, and economic composition. Far more women were employed than ever before. The number of self-employed people, especially women, continued to grow. Jobs in the manufacturing sector declined, so that seven out of ten workers earned their livelihood in the service sector. One out of three Canadian homes had a personal computer. The traditional pattern of work was changing as thousands more were working out of their homes. There was a sharp rise in the number of single-parent families, 60 percent of whom were headed by women. The number of single-parent families continued to grow faster than the number of husband–wife families. One in three Canadians reported a background other than that of the two founding European groups. For the first time, a majority of Canadians had as their mother tongue something other than French or English. Perhaps most startlingly, more than 1 million Canadians, out of some 27.3 million citizens, claimed Native ancestry.

The forces of globalization — the transnational movement of people, goods, and services — did not respect national borders. Canada and the United States were profoundly influenced by the international movement of products, capital, production facilities, know-how, technology, and consumer tastes. Regional trading blocs like NAFTA and the European Union simply quickened the gradual erosion of the nation-state as an instrument of policy. A Canadian sense of identity once associated with national institutions such as the Canadian Broadcasting Corporation, Canadian National Railways, Air Canada, and Petro-Canada was slowly waning. In its place, Canadians took some solace in a Canadian "social safety net" reflecting "civility and compromise" rather than, as in the United States, the "free-market values" of competitiveness and individual responsibility.[7]

IMPLOSION OF THE NATION-STATE

A major external force affecting the nation-state was the "information revolution." The late Canadian media expert Marshall McLuhan once described the phenomenon as the "global village"; by the 1990s, it was called the "wired world." In this electronic world, the "information highway" linked "virtual communities" in which computer users in rural and small-town Ontario could be linked, by Internet, E-mail, Fax, and laptop computer, to contacts in San Francisco, New York, London, or Tokyo. The prospect of a 500-channel TV universe simply reinforced the trend. In 1994, CBC-TV accounted for only 13 percent of viewing time in English-speaking Canada, down from 21 percent a decade earlier. Such developments prompted critics like French social analyst Elihu Katz to warn of the loss of "the public space," the common shared experience of living in local and national communities.

Internal forces in Canada also threatened the viability of the nation-state. The unpredictable and perhaps waning support for Quebec sovereignty in the mid-1990s suggested that the *Québécois* were becoming more global and North American in outlook. It was also possible that Quebec had already achieved recognition as a "distinct nation" within the loose Canadian federation and therefore no longer felt the compelling need for complete sovereignty. Native peoples were also moving along the same path, forming First Nations governments, negotiating their own legal, educational, and policing systems, and even reviving Native languages. In effect, Quebeckers, Native peoples, and other groups were rewriting the terms of their contract with the Canadian state to suit their own needs and circumstances.

PRIVATIZED WORLDS

Social critics in the United States and Canada pointed with alarm to the prevailing trend toward "cocooning" and creating "privatized worlds." In his book *The Revolt of the Elites*, the American critic Christopher Lasch expressed concern about those Americans who have, in his words, "ceased to think of themselves as Americans in any important sense."[8] The affluent upper classes, Lasch argued, had turned their back upon America's crumbling cities and rejected the traditional values of Middle America to retreat into private education, private medicine, and private security within walled estate homes. In the process, he contended, they had withdrawn from America into "an international culture of work and leisure, business and entertainment." Some commentators, like Richard Gwyn, saw evidence of this phenomenon north of the border.

FIRST NATIONS' RIGHTS

From quiet rumblings in the 1980s to loud outbursts in the 1990s, bitter controversies arose as Canada attempted to deal with its First Nations. By the 1990s, the resurgence of a Native sovereignty movement and the stance taken by white governments led to a number of confrontations.[9] The summer of 1990 witnessed the disturbing sight of the Canadian military confronting Mohawks at Kahnawake, near Oka, Quebec. What originally had begun as a dispute over the expansion of a golf course rapidly became the symbol of all the economic, social, political, and legal grievances of the Native peoples. The standoff between the Canadian army and the Mohawk Warriors raised many troubling questions. Concepts such as Native self-government, Native land claims, and a separate legal system for the Native peoples were raised, and the armed standoff attracted media attention across North America.

Late in 1994, Quebec officials announced that they were bowing to intense Native pressure and suspending the mammoth James Bay hydro project in Quebec. The $12.7 billion plan

The standoff at Oka, summer 1990.

to dam five rivers and flood an area almost equal to the size of Prince Edward Island would have been an economic boon to Quebec, expanding hydro-electric power production, creating 62 000 jobs, and enabling Quebec to export vast quantities of power to energy-needy New York state. However, the cultural and environmental concerns of the 10 500 Cree and 7000 Inuit, whose ancestors had lived, hunted, and fished in the area for 5000 years, eventually resulted in the cancellation of the project. Environmental assessments, the violation of ancestral lands, and the destruction of many species of fish determined that while the Great Whale Project may have marked "progress" in a strictly economic sense, in a larger sense, it spelled something very different.

POVERTY, CIGARETTES, AND INJUSTICE

The appalling conditions for the thousands of Canadian Native peoples who lived on reservations became an international issue in January 1993. A home-made video of six children attempting to commit suicide in the Innu community of Davis Inlet on the Labrador coast received world-wide condemnation. Mirroring the alcoholism, physical abuse, clash of values, and despair on many reservations, Davis Inlet became the symbol for Native demands for improved living conditions. A different issue — cigarette smuggling — emerged on the Akwesasne Nation, which straddles the borders dividing Ontario, Quebec, and New York state. A heavy tax on Canadian cigarettes and a desire to demonstrate their own sovereignty led some Mohawks to begin a huge illegal operation. The Indian Act allowed the Mohawks not to pay taxes for cigarettes on their reserve. As a result, an estimated $800 million worth of cigarettes was smuggled annually back into Canada. Rather than charging the common price of about $45 per carton, Mohawks sold the cigarettes for under $20 on the reserve, which was perfectly legal. The problem arose when thousands of cartons began appearing off the reserve. For the Native traders, the cigarette trade was critical as a source of income to support themselves and improve their living conditions, and any interference posed a threat to Native sovereignty.

The case of Donald Marshall, a Nova Scotia Micmac who spent more than 11 years in prison for a crime he did not commit, raised questions about the fairness of Canada's legal system to Native peoples. His case was as straightforward as it was tragic. In subsequent investigations, it was revealed that the Halifax police and the Nova Scotia judicial system had been racist in selecting Marshall as a scapegoat. Because he was at the wrong place at the wrong time and, more significantly, because he was a Native person, Marshall had been denied the fundamental legal right of the presumption of innocence. Evidence had been suppressed, witnesses were coerced, and incorrect procedures were used, all of which resulted in a gross miscarriage of justice. Native people appeared to be the victims, rather than the benefactors, of the Canadian legal system. Two other legal cases, involving the 1971 murder of Manitoba Cree teenager Helen Betty Osborne and the 1980 killing of Native activist J.J. Harper by Winnipeg police, added credence to these allegations of injustice.

VIOLENCE AND CRIME

The Canadian "peaceable kingdom" became less so in the 1990s. The consciousness of all Canadians about the issue of violence against women took a quantum leap forward on December 6, 1989. On that day, Marc Lépine, a deeply disturbed anti-feminist, entered Montreal's École Polytechnique and randomly shot and killed fourteen women. That "Montreal Massacre" led to major investigations and policy initiatives in the area of violence, violence against women, and gun control. A $10 million study produced a document entitled "Changing the Landscape: Ending Violence — Achieving Equality," which had as its central recommendation the conceptual strategy of "zero tolerance."

Violence itself remained a compelling concern for Canadians throughout the 1990s. "Zero tolerance" was adopted as policy by Toronto-area school boards. Far greater attention, advertising, and money were directed against spousal abuse. In late 1994, federal Minister of Justice Allan Rock, under considerable pressure, introduced legislation to stiffen punishments for individuals convicted of committing a crime while using a gun. In addition, despite considerable organized opposition from the gun lobby, he also introduced a national firearms registry.

RIGHT TO LIFE — AND TO DEATH

The old and the new confronted Canadians in another debate, a debate about life itself. Increasing medical sophistication, whether through drugs or surgery, was prolonging the lives of Canadians. Average life expectancy had risen dramatically. However, serious ethical, medical, and economic questions were being raised as a result. Three celebrated cases forced Canadians to attempt to grapple with some fundamental issues. The cases were those of Nancy B, a 24-year-old Quebec City woman suffering from the incurable Guillain–Barre syndrome; Sue Rodriguez, a British Columbia woman dying of Lou Gehrig's disease; and Robert Latimer, a Battleford, Saskatchewan, farmer found guilty of putting his daughter to death to spare her the chronic and crippling pain of cerebral palsy.

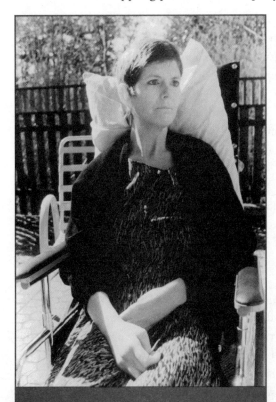

Sue Rodriguez, afflicted with incurable ALS, took her case for the right to die to the Supreme Court of Canada in 1994 and lost in a historic 5–4 ruling. Unable to eat or take care of herself, she committed suicide at her home in Saanich, B.C.

Neil Bissoondath's book, *Selling Illusions* (1994), provoked a serious re-examination of multiculturalism policy.

MULTICULTURALISM AND SOCIAL DIVISIONS

The official Canadian policy of multiculturalism was another "sacred cow" that came under critical attack in the 1990s. National bestsellers like William Gairdner's *The Trouble with Canada* (1990) and Reginald Bibby's *Mosaic Madness* (1990) identified multiculturalism or the promotion and protection of ethnic identities as a major source of social divisiveness in English-speaking Canada.[10] According to the critics, multiculturalism was intended to bring people together by promoting greater tolerance of, and sensitivity toward, the "new Canadians." It had, by the 1990s, produced a more diverse and fragmented society of hyphenated Canadians who saw themselves as Ukrainian-Canadians, Italian-Canadians, or Somali-Canadians and who lacked a strong sense of Canadian nationality.

The most influential critique of Canadian multiculturalism came from Neil Bissoondath, a celebrated Canadian novelist who had emigrated to Canada from Trinidad in 1973. In his personal narrative, *Selling Illusions: The Cult of Multiculturalism in Canada* (1994), he bore testimony to his stubborn refusal over two decades to accept the role of "ethnic" and his determination to avoid the "burden of hyphenation" — a burden that would label him "an East Indian–Trinidadian–Canadian living in Quebec." Bissoondath argued that the policy of multiculturalism, whatever its intentions, was "a gentle and insidious form of cultural apartheid" that had "done little more than lead an already divided land down the path to further social divisiveness."[11]

GAZING INTO THE FUTURE

If loyalty to the traditional Canadian nation-state is declining, then Canada faces new challenges as it enters the new millennium. Multiculturalism, Quebec nationalism, and stubborn regional identities all testify to the persistence of social divisiveness. Canada, like the United States, is being transformed more by multinationalism than by immigration and the legacy of multicultural policies. Signs did exist that a growing number of English Canadians were engaged in a movement of popular resistance against state-enforced "diversity," high personal taxes, and policies based on notions of "political correctness." To a significant degree, the rise of Preston Manning's Reform party and a spate of conservative reform groups exemplified this trend. Even Prime Minister Chrétien and his Liberal party, once defenders of the Canadian social-security state, were tilting by the mid-1990s toward a redefinition of the role of the state and proclaiming their commitment to a "smaller, smarter government."

On the eve of the twenty-first century, looking to the past in order to comprehend the future, Canada has undergone an interesting transformation. It has evolved through three distinct phases: national, continental, and global. In the latest phase of globalism, Canadians and Americans interact not just as continental partners, but as peoples with multinational interests. Global involvement occurs through United Nations peacekeeping ventures, humanitarian assistance to the world's refugees, and military interventions in places like Bosnia, Haiti, and Rwanda. Canadian and American membership in the G-7, negotiations in the GATT discussions, participation in NAFTA, international trade missions to the Pacific Rim — all clearly demonstrate that economics on the eve of the next century must be considered in a larger global context. Yet ample evidence remains of resurgent ethnic nationalism and cultural fragmentation running counter to the powerful forces of globalization.

Narrow national — or continental — thinking is being challenged by global trends and transformations. Globalism is intensified by what social critic Neil Postman termed "technopoly," the preponderant influence of technology over social institutions and national life.[12] North American society is being remade by computer technology and the "information revolution," whether through the 500-station TV universe or the pervasive impact of the Internet. Social problems, be they AIDS or overpopulation, as well as environmental issues such as global warming and the destruction of the rain forest, if they have any hope of resolution, seem to cry out for worldwide initiatives. The outlook of Canadians and Americans is being irrevocably altered as the two societies proceed toward the new millennium.

Tax protest, 1995. Canada's middle class rose up in protest in the weeks preceding Liberal Finance Minister Paul Martin's March 1995 federal budget. The protest focused on the heavy tax burden borne by ordinary Canadians and demanded more accountability from politicians.

ACTIVITIES

KEY TERMS AND CONCEPTS

Identify and explain the historical significance of each of the following terms and concepts:

- "New world order"
- *Perestroika* and *glasnost*
- Peacemaking
- Desert Storm
- "Ethnic cleansing"
- Continentalism
- FTA and NAFTA
- Patriation
- Meech Lake Accord
- "Constitutional fatigue"
- Postmodern state
- Globalization
- Social safety net
- Information Highway
- Zero tolerance
- Technopoly

QUESTIONS FOR DISCUSSION

1. In the years after 1989, the Soviet Union disintegrated and the Cold War came to an end. What impact did these dramatic changes have on Canada, the United States, and continental relations?

2. Canada joined the United States and the coalition forces in the 1991 intervention in the Persian Gulf War. Was the Canadian involvement in the war against Saddam Hussein consistent with, or a departure from, the traditional postwar policy of liberal internationalism?

3. A *Globe and Mail* editorial in December 1984 prophesied that North American free trade would bring Canada to "a parting of the ways." How accurate was the comment? What were the options — and, in each case — the possible consequences?

4. Why did the Meech Lake Accord fail to gain ratification in June 1990? To what extent was the rejection of the accord a repudiation of the deal-makers?

5. What caused Prime Minister Jean Chrétien to set aside constitutional renewal upon his election to office in October 1993? Explain the legacy of the failed Charlottetown Accord.

6. Canada and, to a lesser extent, the United States were being described in the 1990s as postmodern, borderless states. How accurate was that description?

7. What did the public controversies over Native sovereignty, urban crime, gun control, and the right to die reveal about North American society in the 1990s? Why were moral and ethical values so much in conflict?

8. In the "wired world" of the 1990s, technology was viewed by many North Americans as a panacea, if not a god. To what extent did Internet, E-mail, and the 500-channel universe carry an ambivalent legacy? What was the impact of "technopoly" on national societies and local communities?

DEBATE THE FUTURE

Each of the following statements offers a comment on the future of Canada in North America and the world. Support or refute each statement on the basis of evidence presented in this book.

"The One Canada that John Diefenbaker once proudly proclaimed is anachronistic as we approach the millennium. We are destined to become a global nation, or a microcosm of the whole world....Within this Canada, multiple loyalties and multiple identities will become as distinctively Canadian as once were our airwaves, our crown corporations, and the Canadian Football League."

— Richard Gwyn, D.G. Wilmot Lecture, Brock University, November 23, 1994.

"In the aftermath of the Charlottetown debacle, Canada lay politically prostrate, exhausted and drained by the ordeal. Solutions deemed workable had been turned to dust....Having repudiated its political establishment at the polls, the country seemed to be casting itself adrift from those institutions and faiths that had anchored its past.... Canadians were...sleepwalking toward extinction."

— Lansing Lamont, *Breakup: The Coming End of Canada and the Stakes for America* (New York: W.W. Norton, 1994), p.144.

"The fading away of the Cold War has brought an era of ideological conflict to an end. But it has not, as forecast, brought an end to history.... Ethnic and racial conflict...will now replace the conflict of ideologies as the explosive issue of our times."

— Arthur Schlesinger, Jr., *The Disuniting of America: Reflections on A Multicultural Society* (New York: W.W. Norton, 1993), pp. 9 and 10.

PHOTO AND ILLUSTRATION CREDITS

Note: NAC refers to National Archives of Canada.

page viii Courtesy of the Library of Congress; **page 2** UPI/Bettmann; **page 5** NAC/C-078568; **page 6** Photo by the Denver Public Library, Western History Department; **page 11** © Dave More; **page 12** McDonald's Restaurants of Canada Ltd.; **page 14** Canapress; **page 20** Courtesy of Manitoba Culture, Heritage and Citizenship, Historic Resources Branch; **page 24** NAC(detail)/C-113067; **page 33** John Carter Brown Library at Brown University; **page 40** National Archives (NA208-LV-251-7); **page 45** History Collection, Nova Scotia Museum; **page 46** Courtesy of the Royal Ontario Museum, Toronto, Ontario; **page 48** München, Bayer. Staatsbibliothek, Einblattdruck V, 2; **page 51** NAC/C-005136; **page 54** National Maritime Museum, London; **page 57** Courtesy of the Royal Ontario Museum, Toronto, Ontario; **page 59** NAC/C-43934; **page 64** Metropolitan Toronto Reference Library; **page 67** Edward Sheriff Curtis Collection/NAC/C-020848; **page 71** Courtesy of the Library of Congress; **page 72** Metropolitan Toronto Reference Library/T-15708; **page 76** NAC/C-029486; **page 79** NAC/C-113049; **page 82** Musée des Augustines de l'Hôtel-Dieu de Québec; **page 83** The Bettmann Archive; **page 88** (left) NAC/C-34199; **page 88** (right) Archives des Augustines de l'Hopital Général de Québec; **page 94** (top) Metropolitan Toronto Reference Library, T-15508; **page 94** (bottom) NAC/C-002421; **page 100** NAC/C-1168; **page 102** Charles William Jeffreys (Canadian 1869–1951), "The Founding of Halifax," 1749, Art Gallery of Ontario, Toronto; **page 110** NAC(detail)/C-14913; **page 117** Museum of the City of New York, C&I, #58.300.17; **page 119** Unknown artist. "Ex-voto of Madame Riverin and her children," 1703. Musée de Sainte-Anne-de-Beaupré, Québec; **page 120** (bottom) Courtesy of the Library of Congress; **page 123** Courtesy, Peabody Essex Museum, Salem, Massachusetts; **page 128** Metropolitan Toronto Reference Library, T-10645; **page 136** NAC/C-8983; **page 141** Courtesy of the Royal Ontario Museum, Toronto, Ontario; **page 142** National Archives of Quebec; **page 143** "Marie de l'Incarnation," attributed to Hugues Pommier, oil on canvas, circa 1672, collection des Ursulines de Québec; **page 144** NAC/C-360; **page 149** Metropolitan Toronto Reference Library, T-15450; **page 150** NAC/C-6150; **page 154** National Archives (NA22-148-GW-622); **page 159** Picture provided courtesy of Molson Breweries; **page 163** Courtesy of the Library of Congress/LC-USZ62-35522; **page 168** (top) National Archives (NA9-111-SC-92639); **page 168** (bottom) National Portrait Gallery, Smithsonian Institution; **page 169** National Archives (NA31-66-G-150-25); **page 170** Courtesy of the Library of Congress; **page 172** (top) National Archives (NA60-148-GW-436); **page 174** Courtesy of the Library of Congress; **page 180** NAC/C-000017; **page 184** NAC/C-93963; **page 186** NAC/C-2001; **page 189** British Columbia Archives and Records Service/No. 3909; **page 191** NAC/C-003904; **page 192** (left) NAC/C-007043; **page 192** (right) Archives of Ontario, [miniature], Langton Family Papers, F1077; **page 194** NAC/C-001669; **page 197** State Historical Society of Wisconsin, WHi(X3)46720; **page 200** National Archives (111-SC-96969); **page 204** National Archives (21-148-CCD-35); **page 210** NAC/C-16404; **page 213** (top) NAC/C-000276; **page 213** (bottom) Courtesy of the Library of Congress; **page 220** NAC/C-010717; **page 221** Courtesy of the Royal Ontario Museum, Toronto, Ontario; **page 225** NAC/C-000393; **page 226** George Theodore Berthon (Canadian, 1806–1892), "The Three Robinson Sisters," 1846, Art Gallery of Ontario, Toronto. On loan from the Estate of Mrs. J. B. Robinson, Toronto; **page 228** Metropolitan Toronto Reference Library, T-15000; **page 232** NAC/C-5435; **page 234** National Portrait Gallery, Smithsonian Institution; **page 238** (top) NAC/C-11923; **page 238** (bottom) NAC/C-11206; **page 240** NAC/C-17937; **page 242** (top) NAC/C-7964; **page 242** (bottom) NAC/C-5434; **page 243** Metropolitan Toronto Reference Library; **page 245** NAC/C-11228; **page 247** Metropolitan Toronto Reference Library, T-15591; **page 252** Courtesy of the Library of Congress; **page 255** NAC/C-000733; **page 257** W. J. Topley/

NAC/C-3207; **page 261** Courtesy of the Library of Congress; **page 263** Courtesy of the Library of Congress; **page 271** NAC/C-18737; **page 276** Stamp reproduced courtesy of Canada Post Corporation; **page 279** NAC/C-016588; **page 282** (left) NAC/PA-25477; **page 282** (right) National Archives (111-B-4211); **page 284** NAC/C-95148; **page 291** NAC/C-78560; **page 292** Courtesy of the Royal Ontario Museum, Toronto, Ontario; **page 293** NAC/C-2775; **page 298** NAC/C-078979; **page 300** NAC/C-78864; **page 303** (right)NAC/C-3844; **page 306** Massey Ferguson Archives, Ontario Agricultural Museum; **page 310** NAC/C-058597; **page 314** Courtesy of the Library of Congress; **page 316** Metropolitan Toronto Reference Library, *Grip*, Vol. 6, No. 14, February 26, 1876; **page 317** National Portrait Gallery, Smithsonian Institution; **page 318** Photo by the Denver Public Library, Western History Department; **page 322** Courtesy of the Library of Congress; **page 324** (left) National Portrait Gallery, Smithsonian Institution; **page 324** (centre) National Portrait Gallery, Smithsonian Institution; **page 324** (right) The Bettmann Archive; **page 326** Metropolitan Toronto Reference Library, T-10914; **page 328** NAC/C-085579; **page 339** Courtesy of the Library of Congress; **page 346** Glenbow Archives, Calgary, NA-2676-6; **page 348** Courtesy of the Library of Congress; **page 349** NAC/C-068842; **page 351** (left) NAC/C-030620; **page 351** (top) NAC/C-089536; **page 351** (bottom) NAC/C-089542; **page 352** Glenbow Archives, Calgary, NA-863-4; **page 353** Victor Kangas Collection/NAC/PA-127086; **page 357** Courtesy of the Beaton Institute, University College of Cape Breton; **page 359** George F. Ridsdale Collection/NAC/PA-122688; **page 361** British Columbia Archives and Records Service, #75600; **page 364** Provincial Archives of Manitoba, N12295, Winnipeg Strike 4; **page 366** Museum of the City of New York, Photo by Jacob A. Riis, #167; **page 368** NAC/PA-87848; **page 372** City of Toronto Archives, SC244-727; **page 374** NAC/C-001867; **page 380** Courtesy of the Library of Congress; **page 382** NAC/C-20442; **page 385** NAC/C-4729; **page 387** Department of National Defence/NAC/PA-000832; **page 388** Photography Collection, Harry Ransom Humanities Research Center, The University of Texas at Austin; **page 390** NAC/C-57365; **page 393** National Portrait Gallery, Smithsonian Institution, Transfer from the National Museum of American Art, Gift of an anonymous donor through Mrs. Elizabeth Rogerson, 1926; **page 402** Glenbow Archives, Calgary, NA-2440-3; **page 408** (top) Provincial Archives of Manitoba, N7968; **page 408** (bottom) The United Church of Canada/Victoria University Archives; **page 409** City of Toronto Archives, RG8-32-324; **page 412** (top) Museum of the City of New York, Photo by Jacob A. Riis, #101; **page 412** (bottom) Museum of the City of New York, Photo by Jacob A. Riis, #97; **page 414** Archives of Ontario, Accession No. 6520 S 13461; **page 415** National Portrait Gallery, Smithsonian Institution, Gallery purchase and Gift of Mrs. Nancy Pierce York & Mrs. Grace Pierce Forbes; **page 417** NAC/C-9480; **page 419** Flora MacDonald Denison Papers, Thomas Fisher Rare Book Library, University of Toronto; **page 420** From the Thunder Bay Finnish Canadian Historical Society Collection (MG8) at the Chancellor Paterson Library Archives, Lakehead University; **page 422** Archives of Ontario, Records of the Department of Health, RG10-30-A-2-3-.03; **page 432** NAC/PA-24468; **page 434** NAC/C-56796; **page 437** Photo courtesy of Ford of Canada; **page 438** Metropolitan Toronto Reference Library, T-13569; **page 440** NAC/PA-17203; **page 444** NAC/C-29350; **page 445** NAC/PA-22784; **page 448** Provincial Archives of Manitoba, N12296; **page 450** Provincial Archives of Manitoba, N5034, Agriculture-Machinery 160; **page 453** Lawren S. Harris (Canadian 1885–1970), "Glace Bay," c. 1925, Private Collection. Courtesy Art Gallery of Ontario; **page 455** Courtesy of Acadia University Archives; **page 456** Provincial Archives of Manitoba, Flin Flon Strike 16; **page 458** National Archives (NA306-NT-177.476); **page 460** Glenbow Archives, Calgary, ND3-6742; **page 462** CNE Archives, Poster Collection, Transportation and Communications Year, 1939; **page 464** Glenbow Archives, Calgary, NA-700-6; **page 466** Courtesy of the Library of Congress; **page 468** Saskatchewan Archives Board, Ref. No. R-B171-3; **page 470** (both) Courtesy of the Library of Congress; **page 474** City of Toronto Archives, The Globe and Mail Collection, SC 266-23267; **page 476** (left) UPI/Bettmann; **page 476** (right) NAC/C-19526; **page 477** NAC/C-029298;

page 482 N.A.S.A.; **page 488** Department of National Defence/NAC/PA-122737; **page 489** NAC/C-1700; **page 490** Provincial Archives of New Brunswick; **page 492** NAC/C-85031; **page 494** (left) Provincial Archives of Manitoba, Canadian Army Photo Collection 162, N10857; **page 494** (right) NAC/C-5787; **page 495** NAC/C-3226; **page 497** Saskatchewan Archives Board; **page 499** United Nations photo; **page 501** Bill Olson/NAC/PA-115564; **page 503** (left) National Archives, 111-SC-180014; **page 503** (right) UPI/Bettmann; **page 506** Department of National Defence/NAC/PA-122737; **page 509** The Bettmann Archive; **page 511** Montreal Star/NAC/PA-129625; **page 513** John Fitzgerald Kennedy Library; **page 515** Keystone Press Agency; **page 518** (top) UPI/Bettmann; **page 518** (bottom) Reprinted with permission — The Toronto Star Syndicate; **page 522** Used with permission, GM Media Archives, © 1978 General Motors Corp.; **page 523** Courtesy of Canada Mortgage and Housing Corp.; **page 524** NAC/PA-111537; **page 527** Chris Lund/NAC/PA-142854; **page 529** Harrington/ NAC/PA-111390; **page 530** UPI/Bettmann; **page 532** © The Curtis Publishing Group; **page 535** (left) NAC/C-028739; **page 535** (right) Provincial Archives of New Brunswick; **page 536** World Wide Photo/Canapress; **page 537** NAC/C-035680; **page 540** Canapress; **page 544** Glenbow Archives, Calgary, Calgary Herald Collection; **page 545** *The Globe and Mail*, Toronto; **page 546** NAC/PA-138847; **page 547** UPI/Bettmann; **page 553** Reprinted by permission of Gerry Sevier; **page 555** UPI/Bettmann; **page 558** John Sharp/ Canada Wide Feature Service Ltd.; **page 559** Glenbow Archives, Calgary, Calgary Herald Collection; **page 561** (top) Canapress; **page 561** (bottom) Todd Korol/ Canapress; **page 562** Canada Wide Feature Service Ltd.; **page 566** Photo courtesy of UNICEF/Edith Simmons; **page 567** NAC/PA-136978; **page 568** Aislin/*The Montreal Star*; **page 570** (top) NAC/C-13193; **page 570** (bottom) Canapress; **page 572** Photo courtesy of UNICEF/Edith Simmons; **page 574** CIDA Photo/Doug Curran; **page 577** Itsuo Inouye/Canapress; **page 582** Reprinted with permission — The Toronto Star Syndicate; **page 590** NAC/PA-125700; **page 592** Canapress; **page 594** NAC/C-019522; **page 596** Peter Kuch, *Winnipeg Free Press*; **page 597** Bob Chambers, *The Halifax Chronicle-Herald*. Reprinted by permission of the cartoonist; **page 599** NAC/PA-125700; **page 604** UPI/Bettmann; **page 606** NAC/PA-113500; **page 608** NAC/C-047572; **page 610** Canapress; **page 612** Canapress; **page 615** Belle Hatfield/Canapress; **page 618** Tourism Nova Scotia; **page 619** Tom Hanson/Canapress; **page 620** Fred Chartrand/Canapress; **page 621** Rudi Blaha/Canapress; **page 622** Courtesy of McDonald's Restaurants of Canada Ltd.; **page 624** Morten Hvaal/Canapress; **page 625** Ryan Remiorz/Canapress; **page 627** Hans Deryk/Canapress; **page 630** Courtesy of Roy Peterson/*Vancouver Sun*; **page 632** Charles Mitchell/Canapress; **page 635** John Hryniuk Photography; **page 636** Robert Galbraith/Canapress; **page 639** Shaney Komulainen/Canapress; **page 641** (left) Canapress; **page 641** (right) Canapress; **page 643** © Todd Korol

ADDITIONAL TEXT CREDITS

Readers wishing additional information on data provided through the cooperation of Statistics Canada may obtain copies of related publications by mail from Publications Sales, Statistics Canada, Ottawa, Ontario, K1A 0T6, or by calling (613) 951-7277 or toll-free 800-267-6677. Readers may also facsimile their order by dialing (613) 951-1584.

COVER CREDITS

Front (left) Photo courtesy of Glenbow Archives, Calgary, Alberta, #NA 2440-3
Back (left) Library of Congress; (left inset) NAC/C-16551; (right inset) NAC/C-11033

INDEX